Programming Abstractions in C

A Second Course in Computer Science

ERIC ROBERTS
Stanford University

 **ADDISON-WESLEY**

Addison-Wesley is an imprint
of Addison Wesley Longman, Inc.

Reading, Massachusetts • Harlow, England • Menlo Park, California
Berkeley, California • Don Mills, Ontario • Sydney • Bonn • Amsterdam
Tokyo • Mexico City

Sponsoring Editor: Susan Hartman
Production Editor: Amy Willcutt
Editorial Assistant: Julie Dunn
Developmental Editor: Lauren Rusk
Cover Designer: Diana Coe

Library of Congress Cataloging-in-Publication Data

Roberts, Eric S.
    Programming abstractions in C : a second course in computer
science / Eric Roberts.
        p.   cm.
    Includes index.
    ISBN 0-201-54541-1
    1. C (Computer program language) 2. Abstract data types (Computer
science) I. Title.
QA76.73.C15R625   1998
005.7'3—dc21
                                     97-15248
                                       CIP
                                       AC

Reproduced by Addison-Wesley from camera-ready copy supplied by the author.

Cover photograph of the interior of the George Peabody Library © Greg Pease/
Tony Stone Images.

Access the latest information about Addison-Wesley titles from our World Wide
Web site http://www.awl.com/cseng

2 3 4 5 6 7 8 9 10-MA-0100999897

In loving memory of Rae Pober (1900–1997) for all
the joy she brought, not only to my grandmother,
but to everyone whose life she touched.

To the Student

Each year, the world of computing gets more and more exciting. Computing hardware is smaller, faster, and cheaper than ever before. The shelves of your local computer store are lined with all sorts of application programs that would have been unimaginable a decade ago. Technological innovations like the Internet and the World Wide Web are revolutionizing the way people find information, transact business, and communicate with one another. And through it all, the opportunities available to people who understand computing technology seem to grow without bounds.

The study of computer science often works in a similar way. With each new concept you learn, programming becomes increasingly exciting. You can be more creative, solve harder problems, and develop more sophisticated programs and tools. If you are reading this book, you probably have completed an introductory computer science course and understand a little about the sense of empowerment that programming conveys. But you have only scratched the surface.

Most introductory courses focus on the mechanics of programming. You learn about the syntax of a particular language and how to write simple programs in that language. The purpose of this book is to expand your horizons by introducing you to the more intellectually challenging aspects of the programming process. Programming is not about memorizing rules or writing the code for simple processes you already understand. Programming is about solving hard problems. Solving hard problems requires a lot of thought and, in most cases, a great deal of work.

You can, however, simplify the process by taking advantage of the strategies and methodologies presented in this book. Many of the concepts you will learn as you study the different parts of this text—from broad strategies like recursion to specific techniques like hashing—will enable you to solve problems that now seem completely beyond your reach. Learning those concepts will certainly be challenging. It may at times be frustrating. If you rise to the challenge and work past the frustrations, your reward at the end will be a deeper understanding of the power of computing that will create still more opportunities on the path ahead.

I wish you a pleasant journey along that road.

Eric Roberts
Department of Computer Science
Stanford University
June 1997

To the Instructor

This text is intended for use in the second programming course in a typical college or university curriculum. It covers the material in the standard CS2 course, as defined by the ACM *Curriculum '78* report and includes most of the knowledge units in the "Algorithms and Data Structures" subject area of *Computing Curriculum 1991*.

Programming Abstractions in C provides students with solid methodological skills that are consistent with the principles of modern software engineering. It builds on the foundation provided by my 1995 textbook, *The Art and Science of C*, and focuses on abstraction and interface design as central themes. Both texts use a common set of libraries that make coding in C far less complex and consequently much more accessible to the novice. These libraries have proven extremely successful with students, not only at Stanford, but at many other institutions as well. That success, however, depends on having the faculty or staff at each local institution provide libraries for the platforms the students use. The code for the libraries is available by FTP from Addison-Wesley at the following URL:

```
ftp://aw.com/aw.computer.science/Roberts.CS1.C
```

Even though I conceived of the two books as a sequence, you can easily use *Programming Abstractions in C* on its own. Part One of this book includes all the background information students might need from *The Art and Science of C*—certainly enough to understand both the examples and the overall approach taken in the rest of the book. Because the presentation in Part One is fast-paced, students should already be familiar with fundamental programming concepts at the level of an introductory course. They do not, however, need any prior exposure to C, which is covered in the first few chapters. Students who have studied *The Art and Science of C* can simply skip Part One altogether.

With the background provided by Part One, students are ready to move to new material. Part Two focuses on recursion, with an extensive set of examples that spans four chapters. In my experience, the optimal place to introduce recursion is at the beginning of the second programming course, largely for tactical reasons. Many students find recursion a difficult concept—one that requires considerable time to master. If they confront recursion at the beginning of a term, students have more time to come to grips with the concept. The placement of recursion early in this text allows you to include recursion on homework assignments and exams throughout the term. Students who do poorly on recursive problems at midterm time will be alerted to this gap in their understanding early enough to take corrective action.

If you are pressed for time in your treatment of recursion, you can omit Section 6.1 of Part Two without disturbing the flow of the presentation. Although the minimax algorithm may be too complicated for some students, it demonstrates the enormous power of recursion to solve difficult problems with a small amount of code. Similarly, the sections in Chapter 7 that cover the theoretical foundations of big-O notation and mathematical induction are not essential to the rest of the text.

Part Three has a twofold purpose. On the one hand, it introduces the principal nonrecursive types one expects to see in a data structures course, including stacks, queues, and symbol tables. On the other, this part of the text provides students with the tools they need to understand data abstraction in the context of interface-based programming. The concept that unifies the chapters in this part is the *abstract data type* or *ADT,* which is defined by its behavior rather than its representation.

One of the important features of this book is that it uses the incomplete type facility of ANSI C to define ADTs whose internal representation is completely inaccessible to the client. Because this programming style enforces the abstraction barrier, students develop the programming habits they need to write well-structured, modular code. I have also taken the position that the interfaces presented in the text should be useful tools in their own right. In most cases, students will be able to incorporate these interfaces and implementations directly into their own code.

The last chapter in Part Three, Chapter 11, introduces several important concepts, including function pointers, mapping functions, and iterators. Iterators are a relatively new addition to the Stanford course, but an extremely successful one. In our experience, the extra work required to build the iterator abstraction is more than offset by the reduction in complexity of client code.

Parts Three and Four both focus on abstract data types. To a certain extent, the division between these parts is artificial. The difference is that the ADTs in Part Four are implemented recursively while those in Part Three are not. The advantage of this organization is that Part Four plays a unifying role, drawing together the topics of recursion and ADTs in the two preceding parts.

Although the material on expression trees in Chapter 14 may be omitted without losing continuity, I have found it valuable to include this material as early as possible in the curriculum, because doing so reduces the level of mystery surrounding the operation of the C compiler and therefore helps students feel more in control about programming.

Chapter 17 does not really belong to the main body of the text but instead pushes the limits of the material toward the next set of topics that the students are likely to encounter. This final chapter focuses on object-oriented programming, using Java to illustrate the major concepts. Although some institutions have already begun to use Java in the introductory sequence, we believe that it is still makes sense to introduce the procedural approach first and move on to object-oriented programming thereafter for the following reasons:

1. Java environments are changing too rapidly to offer a stable base for teaching.
2. Students need to understand the procedural programming paradigm.
3. If you emphasize data abstraction and interfaces in the introductory courses, students are well prepared for the transition to object-oriented programming.

Our experience at Stanford convinces us that this strategy works remarkably well and allows students to adopt the object-oriented paradigm with relative ease.

Acknowledgments

Writing a textbook is never the work of a single individual. In putting this book together, I have been extremely fortunate to have the help of many talented and dedicated people. I particularly want to thank the following colleagues at Stanford, who have contributed to this project in so many different ways:

- The lecturers who have taught from draft versions of this text over the last few years, including Jerry Cain, Maggie Johnson, Bob Plummer, Mehran Sahami, and Julie Zelenski
- My teaching assistants, Stacey Doerr and Brian O'Connor, who helped refine the assignments for the course, many of which appear as exercises
- The entire team of undergraduate section leaders, who had to explain to students all the concepts that I left out of the earlier drafts
- Steve Freund and the members of the Thetis development team, who have provided a wonderful computing environment for student use
- The staff of the Education Division, most notably Claire Stager and Eddie Wallace, for keeping everything running smoothly
- The participants in my seminar on teaching introductory computer science
- The Stanford students who have taken our courses and showed us the amazing things they can accomplish

I appreciate the contributions provided by Addison-Welsey reviewers, whose comments definitely improved the structure and quality of the book:

- Phillip Barry, *University of Minnesota*
- Martin Cohn, *Brandeis University*
- Dan Ellard, *Harvard University*
- Gopal Gupta, *New Mexico*
- Phillip W. Hutto, *Emory University*
- Randall Pruim, *Boston University*
- Zhong Shao, *Yale University*

I also received extremely useful suggestions from Joe Buhler at Reed College, Pavel Curtis at PlaceWare, Inc., and Jim Mayfield at the University of Maryland, Baltimore County. Much of the work on the book took place while I was on sabbatical at Reed, and I am grateful to Joe and his colleagues in the Mathematics Department for providing such a wonderful place to work.

I want to express my gratitude to my editor, Susan Hartman, and the entire staff at Addison-Wesley—Cynthia Benn, Lynne Doran Cote, Jackie Davies, Julie Dunn, Peter Gordon, Amy Willcutt, Bob Woodbury, and Tom Ziolkowski—for their support on this book as well as its predecessor.

Most of all, I want to thank my partner Lauren Rusk, who has again worked her magic as my developmental editor. Lauren's expertise adds considerable clarity and polish to the text. Without her, nothing would ever come out nearly as well.

Contents

3   Libraries and Interfaces   107

Programming Abstractions in C

A Second Course in Computer Science

Preliminaries

Overview

Part One covers the basics of programming in ANSI C and the concept of interface-based design. If you are just starting to work with C after learning to program in some other language, the material in these chapters will give you the background you need to understand the programs in the rest of the book. If you have already programmed in C, much of this material will be review. Even so, it is worth reading through these chapters—particularly Chapter 3—to get a sense of how this text uses libraries and interfaces.

CHAPTER 1

An Overview of ANSI C

Out of these various experiments come programs. This is our experience: programs do not come out of the minds of one person or two people such as ourselves, but out of day-to-day work.

—— Stokely Carmichael and Charles V. Hamilton, *Black Power*, 1967

Objectives

- To recognize the components of a typical C program.

- To understand the predefined data types in C and how they can be used to store information in a program.

- To become familiar with the facilities in the simplified and standard input/output (I/O) libraries for reading input data and displaying results.

- To understand the structure of expressions in C and how to use the common operators to express calculations.

- To recognize the statement forms `if`, `switch`, `while`, and `for` and be able to use them in simple programs.

- To appreciate the importance of decomposing a program into individual functions and understand how those functions operate.

- To be able to write simple programs that integrate the various control facilities presented in this chapter.

In Lewis Carroll's *Alice's Adventures in Wonderland,* the King asks the White Rabbit to "begin at the beginning and go on till you come to the end: then stop." Good advice, but only if you're starting from the beginning. This book is designed for a second course in computer science and therefore assumes that you have already begun your study of programming. At the same time, because first courses vary considerably in what they cover, it is difficult to rely on any specific material. Some of you, for example, will already have experience programming in C. Many of you, however, are coming from a first course taught in Pascal or some other language.

Because of this wide disparity in background, the best approach is to adopt the King's advice and begin at the beginning. The first three chapters in this text therefore move quickly through the material I consider to be essential background for the later chapters. If you've used my earlier textbook, *The Art and Science of C,* you can skip these chapters entirely and start with Chapter 4. If you've had experience with C in some other context, you should skim through Chapters 1 and 2 to get a sense of the overall approach and then continue with the discussion of interfaces in Chapter 3. If you know something about programming but are unfamiliar with C, you can start your study here and read through all three chapters to bring yourself up to speed on the fundamentals of C programming.

1.1 What is C?

In the early days of computing, programs were written in **machine language,** which consists of the primitive instructions that can be executed directly by the machine. Machine-language programs are difficult to understand, mostly because the structure of machine language reflects the design of the hardware rather than the needs of programmers. In the mid-1950s, a group of programmers under the direction of John Backus at IBM had an idea that profoundly changed the nature of computing. Would it be possible, they wondered, to write programs that resembled the mathematical formulas they were trying to compute and have the computer itself translate those formulas into machine language? In 1955, this team produced the initial version of Fortran (whose name is an abbreviation of *formula translation*), which was the first example of a **higher-level programming language.**

Since that time, many new programming languages have been invented. Of these, one of the most successful is a language called *C,* which was designed at Bell Laboratories by Dennis Ritchie in 1972 and then later revised and standardized by the American National Standards Institute (ANSI) in 1989. In the 25 years since its invention, C has become one of the most widely used languages in the world. One indicator of its success is that many emerging languages today are based on C, including C++ and Java.

When you write a program in C, your first step is to create a file that contains the text of the program, which is called a **source file.** Before you can run your program, you need to translate the source file into an executable form. The first step in that process is to invoke a program called a **compiler,** which translates the source file into an **object file** containing the corresponding machine-language instructions.

This object file is then combined with other object files to produce an **executable file** that can be run on the system. The other object files typically include predefined object files, called **libraries,** that contain the machine-language instructions for various operations commonly required by programs. The process of combining all the individual object files into an executable file is called **linking.** The process is illustrated by the diagram shown in Figure 1-1.

Unfortunately, the specific details of the compilation process vary considerably from one machine to another. There is no way that a general textbook like this can tell you exactly what commands you should use to run a program on your system. Because those commands are different for each system, you need to consult the documentation that comes with the C compiler you are using on that machine. The good news, however, is that the C programs themselves will look the same. One of the principal advantages of programming in a higher-level language like C is that doing so often allows you to ignore the particular characteristics of the hardware and create programs that will run on many different machines.

■■■ 1.2 The structure of a C program

The best way to get a feeling for the C programming language is to look at a sample program such as the one shown in Figure 1-2. This program generates a table

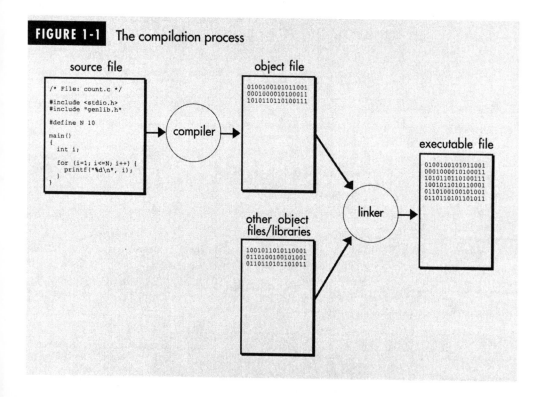

FIGURE 1-1   The compilation process

comparing the values of N^2 and 2^N for various values of N—a comparison that will prove to be important in Chapter 7. The output of the program looks like this:

```
         |   2 |    N
    N    |   N |    2
    -----+-----+------
     0 |   0 |    1
     1 |   1 |    2
     2 |   4 |    4
     3 |   9 |    8
     4 |  16 |   16
     5 |  25 |   32
     6 |  36 |   64
     7 |  49 |  128
     8 |  64 |  256
     9 |  81 |  512
    10 | 100 | 1024
    11 | 121 | 2048
    12 | 144 | 4096
```

FIGURE 1-2   Sample program `powertab.c`

```
/*
 * File: powertab.c
 * -----------------
 * This program generates a table comparing values
 * of the functions n^2 and 2^n.
 */

#include <stdio.h>
#include "genlib.h"

/*
 * Constants
 * ---------
 * LowerLimit -- Starting value for the table
 * UpperLimit -- Final value for the table
 */

#define LowerLimit  0
#define UpperLimit 12

/* Private function prototypes */

static int RaiseIntToPower(int n, int k);
```

program comment

library inclusions

section comment

constant definitions

function prototype

```
/* Main program */

main()
{
    int n;

    printf("     |  2 |    N\n");
    printf(" N | N |    2\n");
    printf("----+-----+------\n");
    for (n = LowerLimit; n <= UpperLimit; n++) {
        printf(" %2d | %3d | %4d\n", n,
                RaiseIntToPower(n, 2),
                RaiseIntToPower(2, n));
    }
}

/*
 * Function: RaiseIntToPower
 * Usage: p = RaiseIntToPower(n, k);
 * ---------------------------------
 * This function returns n to the kth power.
 */

static int RaiseIntToPower(int n, int k)
{
    int i, result;

    result = 1;
    for (i = 0; i < k; i++) {
        result *= n;
    }
    return (result);
}
```

main program

function comment

local variable declarations

body of function

function definition

As the annotations in Figure 1-2 indicate, the `powertab.c` program is divided into several components, which are discussed in the next few sections.

Comments

Much of the text in Figure 1-2 consists of English-language comments. A **comment** is text that is ignored by the compiler but which nonetheless conveys information to other programmers. In C, a comment consists of text enclosed between the markers `/*` and `*/` and may continue over several lines. The `powertab.c` program includes a comment at the beginning that describes the operation of the program as a whole, one before the definition of the `RaiseIntToPower` function that describes what it does, and a couple of one-line comments that act very much like section headings in English text.

Library inclusions

The lines

```
#include <stdio.h>
#include "genlib.h"
```

which follow the program comment indicate that the compiler should read in definitions from two **header files: stdio.h** and **genlib.h**. Each of these header files indicates that the program uses facilities from a **library,** which is a collection of prewritten tools that perform a set of useful operations. The different punctuation in the two **#include** lines reflects the fact that the libraries come from different sources. The angle brackets are used to specify a system library, such as the standard input/output library (**stdio**) that is supplied along with ANSI C. The quotation marks are used for private libraries, including the general library (**genlib**), which was designed for use with the programs in this text and *The Art and Science of C*. Every program in this book will include at least these two libraries; most will require other libraries as well and must contain an **#include** line for each one.

Program-level definitions

After the **#include** lines for the libraries, most programs include definitions that apply to the program as a whole. In the **powertab.c** program, these definitions are represented by the following lines

```
#define LowerLimit  0
#define UpperLimit 12
```

which introduce two constants named **LowerLimit** and **UpperLimit**.

The **#define** specification is typically used to assign a symbolic name to a constant. Such a definition has the form

```
#define name value
```

and defines the symbol *name* as equivalent to *value*. Whenever that name appears anywhere in the program after **#define** is introduced, the specified value is substituted in its place. For example, after encountering the line

```
#define Pi 3.14159265
```

any subsequent occurrence of the name **Pi** is replaced by **3.14159265**.

Giving symbolic names to constants has two important advantages in terms of programming style. First, the names often give readers of the program a better sense of what the constant value means. Second, centralizing such definitions at the top of the file makes it easier to change the value associated with a name. For example, all you need to do to change the limits used for the table in the **powertab.c** program is change the values of the constants.

In addition to constants, programs often define new data types in this section of the source file, as you will see in Chapter 2.

Function prototypes

Computation in a C program is carried out in the context of functions. A **function** is a unit of code that (1) performs a specific operation and (2) is identified by name. The `powertab.c` program contains two functions—`main` and `RaiseIntToPower`—which are described in more detail in the next two sections. The line

```
static int RaiseIntToPower(int n, int k);
```

is an example of a **function prototype,** a declaration that tells the compiler the information it needs to know about a function to generate the proper code when that function is invoked. This prototype, for example, indicates that the function `RaiseIntToPower` takes two integers as arguments and returns an integer as its result. The keyword `static` indicates that the function is private to this source file and therefore cannot be confused with a similarly named function in some other source file.

To remain compatible with earlier versions of C, ANSI C allows you to omit function prototypes in certain cases. Even so, it is good programming practice to include a prototype for each function you define. Doing so makes it easier for the compiler to check whether calls to those functions are compatible with the corresponding prototypes and can therefore aid in the process of finding errors in your code.

The main program

Every C program must contain a function with the name `main`. This function specifies the starting point for the computation and is called when the program starts up. When `main` has finished its work and returns, execution of the program ends.

In the `powertab.c` example, the first line of `main` is the variable declaration

```
int n;
```

which introduces a new variable named n capable of holding values of type `int`, the standard type used to represent integers. The syntax of variable declarations is discussed in more detail in the section on "Variables, values, and types" later in this chapter. For now, all you need to know is that this declaration creates space for an integer variable that you can then use in the body of the function `main`.

The first three statements in `main` are calls to the function `printf`, which is used to display output on the screen and appears in almost every program in this book. A few useful notes about `printf` are included in the section on "Simple input and output" later in this chapter, but its features are not explored in detail until Chapter 3. Even so, you need to have an informal sense of how `printf` works to understand any programming example that communicates results to the user. In its simplest form, `printf` takes a string enclosed in double quotes and displays that string on the console. When you use `printf`, you must indicate explicitly that you want to move on to the next line by including the special character called **newline,** which is indicated in the string by the two-character sequence \n. Thus, the first three lines in main display the header for the table.

The rest of the function main in the **powertab.c** program consists of the following code, which is responsible for displaying the table itself:

```
for (n = LowerLimit; n <= UpperLimit; n++) {
    printf(" %2d | %3d | %4d\n", n,
            RaiseIntToPower(n, 2),
            RaiseIntToPower(2, n));
}
```

This code is an example of a **for loop,** which is used to specify repetition. In this case, the **for** statement indicates that the **body** of the loop, which consists of the statement

```
printf(" %2d | %3d | %4d\n", n,
        RaiseIntToPower(n, 2),
        RaiseIntToPower(2, n));
```

should be repeated for each of the values of n from **LowerLimit** to **UpperLimit.** A section on the detailed structure of the **for** loop appears later in the chapter, but the example shown here represents a common idiomatic pattern that you can use to count between any specified limits.

The body of the loop is a call to **printf** that illustrates an important new feature: the ability to include values as part of the output display. The string passed to **printf** includes three **format codes,** beginning with a percent sign (%) and extending up to a letter that indicates what type of value is involved. In this case, the letter **d** indicates that the values are decimal integers. Whenever **printf** encounters a format code in the output, it replaces the format code with the value passed as the next argument to the **printf** function. The type and displayed appearance of that value are controlled by the format code. For example, the specification **%2d** indicates that **printf** should display the value as an integer in a field that is two characters wide. The value being displayed is that of the next argument in the **printf** call, which is the integer n. The next format code is **%3d,** which indicates a three-character decimal number whose value is taken from the argument expression **RaiseIntToPower(n, 2).** Obtaining the value of that expression requires making a call on the **RaiseIntToPower** function, which is discussed in the following section. The value that **RaiseIntToPower** returns is displayed as part of the **printf** output. So is the result of the call to **RaiseIntToPower(2, n),** which supplies the value for the third column in the table.

Function definitions

Because large programs are difficult to understand in their entirety, most programs are broken down into several smaller functions, each of which is easier to understand. In the **powertab.c** program, the function **RaiseIntToPower** is responsible for raising an integer to a power—an operation that is not built into C and must therefore be defined explicitly.

Like the function `main`, `RaiseIntToPower` begins by declaring its variables, which in this case are the integer variables `i` and `result`. The first line in the body of `RaiseIntToPower` is

```
result = 1;
```

This statement is a simple example of an **assignment statement,** which sets the variable on the left of the equal sign to the value of the expression on the right. In this case, the statement sets the variable `result` to the constant 1. The next statement in the function is a `for` loop that executes its body `k` times. The repeated code consists of the line

```
result *= n;
```

which is a C shorthand for the English sentence "Multiply `result` by `n`." Because the function initializes the value of `result` to 1 and then multiplies `result` by `n` a total of `k` times, the variable `result` ends up with the value n^k.

The last statement in `RaiseIntToPower` is

```
return (result);
```

which indicates that the function should return `result` as the value of the function.

▇ 1.3 Variables, values, and types

One of the fundamental characteristics of programs is that they manipulate data. To do so, programs must be able to store data as part of their operation. Moreover, programs today work with many different kinds of data, including numbers and text, along with many more sophisticated data structures, such as those introduced in Part Three of this book. Learning how to store data of various types is an important part of mastering the basics of any language, including C.

Variables

Data values in a program are usually stored in variables. In C, if you want to use a variable to hold some information, you must **declare** that variable before you use it. Declaring a variable establishes the following properties:

- *Name.* Every variable has a name, which is formed according to the rules described in the section entitled "Naming conventions" later in this chapter. You use the name in the program to refer to the variable and the value it contains.
- *Type.* Each variable in a C program is constrained to hold values of a particular data type. C includes several predefined types and also allows you to define new types of your own, as discussed in Chapter 2.
- *Lifetime.* Depending on how they are declared, some variables persist throughout the entire program, while others are created and destroyed dynamically as the program moves through various levels of function call.

- *Scope.* The declaration of a variable also controls what parts of the program have access to the variable, which is called its **scope.**

The standard syntax for declaring a variable is

type namelist;

where *type* indicates the data type and *namelist* is a list of variable names separated by commas. For example, the function `RaiseIntToPower` in the `powertab.c` program contains the line

```
int i, result;
```

which declares the variables `i` and `result` to be of type `int`.

In C, the initial contents of a variable are undefined. If you want a variable to have a particular initial value, you need to initialize it explicitly. One approach is to use an assignment statement in the body of the function to assign a value to each variable before you use it. You can, however, include initial values directly in a declaration by writing an equal sign and a value after a variable name. Thus, the declaration

```
int result = 0;
```

is shorthand for the following code, in which the declaration and assignment are separate:

```
int result;

result = 0;
```

An initial value specified as part of a declaration is called an **initializer.**

Naming conventions

The names used for variables, functions, types, constants, and so forth are collectively known as **identifiers.** In C, the rules for identifier formation are as follows:

1. The name must start with a letter or the underscore character (_).
2. All other characters in the name must be letters, digits, or the underscore. No spaces or other special characters are permitted in names.
3. The name must not be one of the following keywords:

auto	double	int	struct
break	else	long	switch
case	enum	register	typedef
char	extern	return	union
const	float	short	unsigned
continue	for	signed	void
default	goto	sizeof	volatile
do	if	static	while

Uppercase and lowercase letters appearing in an identifier are considered to be different. Thus, the name `ABC` is not the same as the name `abc`. Identifiers can be of any length, but C compilers are not required to consider any more than the first 31 characters in determining whether two names are identical. Implementations may impose additional restrictions on identifiers that are shared between modules.

You can improve your programming style by adopting conventions for identifiers that help readers identify their function. In this text, names of variables and data types begin with a lowercase letter, such as `n1`, `total`, or `string`. By contrast, function and constant names, such as `RaiseIntToPower` or `LowerLimit`, usually begin with an uppercase letter. Moreover, whenever a name consists of several English words run together, the first letter in each word after the first is capitalized to make the name easier to read.

Local and global variables

Most variables are declared at the beginning of a function. Such variables are called **local variables.** The scope of a local variable is the function in which it appears, which means that other functions have no direct access to it. The lifetime of a local variable is the time during which that function is active. When the function is called, space for each local variable is allocated for the duration of that function call. When the function returns, all its local variables disappear.

If a variable declaration appears outside any function definition, that declaration introduces a **global variable.** The scope of a global variable is the remainder of the file in which it is declared. Its lifetime continues throughout the entire execution of a program. Global variables are therefore able to store values that persist across function calls. Although they have important applications, global variables can easily be overused. Because global variables can be manipulated by many different functions, it is harder to keep those functions from interfering with each other. Because of these dangers, global variables are used infrequently in this text.

The concept of a data type

One of the reasons C requires all variables to be declared is that doing so constrains their contents to values of a particular data type. From a formal perspective, a data type is defined by two properties: a *domain,* which is the set of values that belong to that type, and a *set of operations,* which defines the behavior of that type. For example, the domain of the type `int` includes all integers (. . . –2, –1, 0, 1, 2 . . .) up to the limits established by the hardware of the machine. The set of operations applicable to values of type `int` includes, for example, the standard arithmetic operations like addition and multiplication. Other types have a different domain and set of operations.

As you will learn in Chapter 2, much of the power of higher-level languages like C comes from the fact that you can define new data types from existing ones. To get that process started, ANSI C includes several fundamental types that are defined as part of the language. These types, which act as the building blocks for C's type system as a whole, are called **atomic types.** These predefined types are grouped into four categories—integer, floating-point, text, and Boolean—which are discussed in the sections that follow.[1]

Integer types

Although the concept of an integer seems like a simple one, ANSI C actually includes several different data types for representing integer values. In most cases, all you need to know is the type `int`, which corresponds to the standard representation of an integer on the computer system you are using. In certain cases, however, you need to be more careful. Like all data, values of type `int` are stored internally in storage units that have a limited capacity. Those values therefore have a maximum size, which limits the range of integers you can use. To get around this problem, C defines three integer types—`short`, `int`, and `long`—distinguished from one another by the size of their domains.

Unfortunately, the language definition for ANSI C does not specify an exact range for these three types. As a result, the range for the different integer types depends on the machine and the C compiler you're using. On many personal computers, the maximum value of type `int` is 32,767, which is rather small by computational standards. If you wanted, for example, to perform a calculation involving the number of seconds in a year, you could not use type `int` on those machines, because that value (31,536,000) is considerably larger than the largest available value of type `int`. The only properties you can rely on are the following:

- The internal size of an integer cannot decrease as you move from `short` to `int` to `long`. A compiler designer for C could, for example, decide to make `short` and `int` the same size but could not make `int` smaller than `short`. Another way to think about this rule is that ANSI guarantees that the type `long` includes all values of type `int`, which in turn must include all values of type `short`.
- The maximum value of type `int` must be at least 32,767 (2^{15}–1).
- The maximum value of type `long` must be at least 2,147,483,647 (2^{31}–1).

Because the only guarantee that C makes about values of type `int` is that they can be at least as large as 32,767, you should use type `int` only if you are certain that the value of a variable or expression can never exceed that limit. If a value might conceivably be larger than 32,767, it is best to use the data type `long`, which indicates to the compiler that a larger integer domain is required. While ANSI C specifies that variables of type `long` must be able to hold values at least as large as 2,147,483,647, some compilers may allow even larger values.

---

[1] Two of the types introduced in these sections—`string` and `bool`—are not actually part of the C language but are instead defined in the `genlib` library that is included in every program in this text. From your perspective, it doesn't matter whether a type is defined in the language or as part of a library. In either case, the type becomes part of your repertoire of data types. Because the types `string` and `bool` are very useful in developing your conceptual understanding, you should think of them as if they were an integral part of C.

The designers of ANSI C could have chosen to define the allowable range of type int more precisely. For example, they could have declared—as the designers of Java did—that the maximum value of type int would be $2^{31}-1$ on every machine. Had they done so, it would be easier to move a program from one system to another and have it behave in the same way. The ability to move a program between different machines is called **portability,** which is an important consideration in the design of a programming language.

In C, each of the integer types int, long, and short may be preceded by the keyword unsigned. Adding unsigned creates a new data type in which only nonnegative values are allowed. Because unsigned variables do not need to represent negative values, declaring a variable to be one of the unsigned types allows it to hold twice as many positive values. For example, if the maximum value of type int is 32,767, the maximum value of type unsigned int will be 65,535. C allows the type unsigned int to be abbreviated to unsigned, and most programmers who use this type tend to follow this practice. For the most part, you will not need to use unsigned types unless you are writing programs that require you to maintain extremely tight control over the internal representation used by the machine.

An integer constant is ordinarily written as a string of digits representing a number in base 10. If the number begins with the digit 0, however, the compiler interprets the value as an octal (base 8) integer. Thus, the constant 040 is taken to be in octal and represents the decimal number 32. If you prefix a numeric constant with the characters 0x, the compiler interprets that number as hexadecimal (base 16). Thus, the constant 0xFF is equivalent to the decimal constant 255. You can explicitly indicate that an integer constant is of type long by adding the letter L at the end of the digit string. Thus, the constant 0L is equal to 0, but the value is explicitly of type long. Similarly, if you use the letter U as a suffix, the constant is taken to be unsigned.

Floating-point types

Numbers that include a decimal fraction are called **floating-point numbers**, which are used to approximate real numbers in mathematics. As with integers, C defines three different floating-point types: float, double, and long double. Although ANSI C does not specify the exact representation of these types, the way to think about the difference is that types that appear later in the list allow numbers to be represented with greater precision but require more memory space. Unless you are doing exacting scientific calculation, the differences between these types will not matter a great deal. In keeping with a common convention among C programmers, this text uses the type double as its standard floating-point type.

Floating-point constants in C are written with a decimal point. Thus, if 2.0 appears in a program, the number is represented internally as a floating-point value; if the programmer had written 2, this value would be an integer. Floating-point values can also be written in a special programmer's style of scientific notation, in which the value is represented as a floating-point number multiplied by a integral power of 10. To write a number using this style, you write a floating-point number in standard notation, followed immediately by the letter E and an integer exponent, optionally preceded by a + or – sign. For example, the speed of light in meters per second can be written in C as

```
2.9979E+8
```

where the **E** stands for the words *times 10 to the power.*

Text types

In the early days, computers were designed to work only with numeric data and were sometimes called *number crunchers* as a result. Modern computers, however, work less with numeric data than they do with text data, that is, any information composed of individual characters that appear on the keyboard and the screen. The ability of modern computers to process text data has led to the development of word processing systems, on-line reference libraries, electronic mail, and a wide variety of other useful applications.

The most primitive elements of text data are individual characters, which are represented in C using the predefined data type **char**. The domain of type **char** is the set of symbols that can be displayed on the screen or typed on the keyboard: the letters, digits, punctuation marks, spacebar, Return key, and so forth. Internally, these values are represented inside the computer by assigning each character a numeric code. In most implementations of C, the coding system used to represent characters is called **ASCII,** which stands for the *American Standard Code for Information Interchange.* The numeric values of the characters in the ASCII set are shown in Table 1-1.

TABLE 1-1 ASCII codes

	0	1	2	3	4	5	6	7	8	9
0	\000	\001	\002	\003	\004	\005	\006	\a	\b	\t
10	\n	\v	\f	\r	\016	\017	\020	\021	\022	\023
20	\024	\025	\026	\027	\030	\031	\032	\033	\034	\035
30	\036	\037	space	!	"	#	$	%	&	'
40	(	)	*	+	,	–	.	/	0	1
50	2	3	4	5	6	7	8	9	:	;
60	<	=	>	?	@	A	B	C	D	E
70	F	G	H	I	J	K	L	M	N	O
80	P	Q	R	S	T	U	V	W	X	Y
90	Z	[	\	]	^	_	`	a	b	c
100	d	e	f	g	h	i	j	k	l	m
110	n	o	p	q	r	s	t	u	v	w
120	x	y	z	{			}	~	\177		

Although it is important to know that characters are represented internally using a numeric code, it is not generally useful to know what numeric value corresponds to a particular character. When you type the letter *A*, the hardware logic built into the keyboard automatically translates that character into the ASCII code 65, which is then sent to the computer. Similarly, when the computer sends the ASCII code 65 to the screen, the letter *A* appears.

You can write a character constant in C by enclosing the character in single quotes. Thus, the constant `'A'` represents the internal code of the uppercase letter *A*. In addition to the standard characters, C allows you to write special characters in a two-character form beginning with a backward slash (\). These two-character combinations are called **escape sequences.** A list of the legal escape sequences in C appears in Table 1-2.

Characters are most useful when they are collected together into sequential units. In programming, a sequence of characters is called a **string.** Strings make it possible to display informational messages on the screen. You have already seen examples of strings in the sample programs `powertab.c`. It is important, however, to recognize that strings are data and that they can be manipulated and stored in much the same way that numbers can.

Although the designers of C provided several operations that work with strings in the libraries associated with the language, they did not define an explicit `string` type. This omission poses a problem for the student programmer. To make up for this deficiency, however, the type `string` is defined in the `genlib` library. The details of type `string` are not important at this point; strings are considered in more detail in Chapter 3. In this chapter, strings are treated as if they were atomic values and used exclusively to specify text that is displayed directly on the display screen.

TABLE 1-2 Escape sequences

`'\a'`	The alert character (the terminal beeps)
`'\b'`	Backspace
`'\f'`	Formfeed (starts a new page)
`'\n'`	Newline
`'\r'`	Return (returns to the beginning of the line without advancing)
`'\t'`	Tab
`'\v'`	Vertical tab
`'\\'`	The character \ itself
`'\''`	The character ' (the backslash is required only in single characters)
`'\"'`	The character " (the backslash is required only in strings)
`'\ddd'`	The character whose ASCII code is the octal (base 8) number *ddd*
`'\xdd'`	The character whose ASCII code is the hex (base 16) number *dd*
`'\0'`	The null character (with zero as its character code)

You write string constants in C by enclosing the characters contained within the string in double quotes. C supports the same escape sequences for strings as for characters. If two or more string constants appear consecutively in a program, the compiler concatenates them together. The most important implication of this rule is that you can break a long string over several lines so that it doesn't end up running past the right margin of your program.

Boolean type

In the programs you write, it is often necessary to test a particular condition that affects the subsequent behavior of your code. Typically, that condition is specified using an expression whose value is either true or false. This data type—for which the only legal values are true and false—is called **Boolean data,** after the mathematician George Boole, who developed an algebraic approach for working with such values.

Most modern programming languages define a special Boolean type whose domain consists of the values `TRUE` and `FALSE`. C does not define such a type—a deficiency that makes understanding the nature of logical decisions much more difficult for new programmers. To correct this shortcoming, the `genlib` library defines a special type called `bool`. It also defines the constant names `TRUE` and `FALSE`, both of which must be written entirely in upper case. You can declare variables of type `bool` and manipulate them in the same way as other data objects.

Simple input and output

Before you can write programs that interact with the user, you need to have some way of accepting input data from the user and displaying results on the screen. In C, none of this functionality is provided directly within the language. Instead, all input and output operations—which are often referred to collectively as **I/O operations**—are performed by calling functions provided as part of a library.

Unfortunately, the standard library functions for reading input data from the user, which are described in Chapter 3, are quite complicated in their operation and provide more power than you need at this point. For most of the programs in this text, it is more convenient to use functions defined in a simplified I/O library that I designed to make it easier for beginning students to learn the important concepts of programming without getting bogged down in extraneous details. To use this library, you need to add the following line to the library-inclusion section at the beginning of your program:

```
#include "simpio.h"
```

The `simpio` library defines the functions `GetInteger`, `GetLong`, `GetReal`, and `GetLine`, which wait for the user to enter a line at the keyboard and then return a value of type `int`, `long`, `double`, and `string`, respectively. To let the user know what value is expected, it is conventional to display a message to the user, which is called a **prompt,** before calling the input function. Thus, if you need to request a value from the user for the integer variable `n`, you would typically use a pair of statements like this:

```
printf("Enter an integer: ");
n = GetInteger();
```

Output operations in this book use the ANSI function `printf`, which is part of the standard I/O library. The first argument to the `printf` function is a string, which is called the **control string**. The operation of `printf` is to go through the control string one character at a time, displaying those characters on the screen. Whenever `printf` encounters a percent sign (`%`) in the string, however, it interprets that character as the beginning of a **format code** which extends from the percent sign to a letter indicating how the next argument value should be displayed. Several of the most common format codes are shown in Table 1-3.

TABLE 1-3 Common format codes for `printf`

`%d`
`%hd`
`%ld`
	These formats display the value as a decimal number and are used with values of type `int`, `short`, and `long`, respectively. The `%` in the format code can be followed by a number representing the minimum field width. If the number is too short to fill the entire field, extra space is added at the left so that all numbers in that column will line up on the right.

`%f`	This format is used with values of type `float` or `double` and displays them as a number containing a decimal point. The `%f` format code may include a field width as in the `%d` format and may also include an indication of the desired precision, which is separated from the field width by a decimal point. In `%f` format, the precision indicates how many digits should be displayed to the right of the decimal point. Thus, if you use the format `%7.3f`, a number will be displayed in a seven-character field with three digits after the decimal point.
`%g`	This format is used with values of type `float` or `double` and is similar to the `%f` format as long as the number fits in a small space. Numbers whose magnitude is either very large or very small, such as 6300000.0 or .0000007, can be represented more compactly by displaying them in scientific notation, in which case they appear as 6.3e+6 or 7.0e–7. The `%g` format code may include a field width and precision as in the `%f` format, although the precision in `%g` format specifies the number of significant digits instead of the number of digits to the right of the decimal point.
`%c`	This format is used with values of type `char` and displays a single character.
`%s`	This format displays a string on the screen, character by character, and is used with arguments of type `string`. Percent signs appearing within the displayed string have no special effect. The format `%s` allows a field width and a precision like the numeric formats. For strings, the field width is usually preceded by a negative sign, which means that the field is aligned on the left side of the field rather than the right. The precision in the `%s` format specifies the maximum number of characters to be displayed.
`%%`	The `%%` specification is not really a format code but instead provides a way to display a single percent sign as part of the output.

As an example of the use of the simple I/O facilities, the following main program reads in three floating-point values and displays their average:

```
main()
{
    double n1, n2, n3, average;

    printf("This program averages three numbers.\n");
    printf("1st number: ");
    n1 = GetReal();
    printf("2nd number: ");
    n2 = GetReal();
    printf("3nd number: ");
    n3 = GetReal();
    average = (n1 + n2 + n3) / 3;
    printf("The average is %g\n", average);
}
```

▓▓▓ 1.4 Expressions

Whenever you want a program to perform calculations, you need to write an expression that specifies the necessary operations in a form similar to that used for expressions in mathematics. For example, suppose that you wanted to solve the quadratic equation

$$ax^2 + bx + c = 0$$

As you know from high-school mathematics, this equation has two solutions given by the formula

$$x = \frac{-b \pm \sqrt{b^2 - 4ac}}{2a}$$

The first solution is obtained by using + in place of the ± symbol; the second is obtained by using – instead. In C, you could compute the first of these solutions by writing the following expression:

```
(-b + sqrt(b * b - 4 * a * c)) / (2 * a)
```

There are a few differences in form—multiplication is represented explicitly by a `*`, division is represented by a `/`, and the square root function is spelled out—but the expression nonetheless captures the intent of its mathematical counterpart in a way that is quite readable, particularly if you've written programs in any modern programming language.

In C, an expression is composed of terms and operators. A term, such as the variables **a**, **b**, and **c** or the constants 2 and 4 in the preceding expression, represents a single data value and must be either a constant, a variable, or a function call. An operator is a character (or sometimes a short sequence of characters) that indicates a computational operation. The complete list of operators available in C is shown in

Table 1-4. The table includes familiar arithmetic operators like + and − along with several others that pertain only to types that are introduced in later chapters.

Precedence and associativity

The point of listing all the operators in a single table is to establish how they relate to one another in terms of **precedence,** which is a measure of how tightly an operator binds to its operands in the absence of parentheses. If two operators compete for the same operand, the one that appears higher in the precedence table is applied first. Thus, in the expression

```
(-b + sqrt(b * b - 4 * a * c)) / (2 * a)
```

the multiplications (**b * b** and **4 * a * c**) are performed before the subtraction because * has a higher precedence than −. It is, however, important to note that the − operator occurs in two forms. When it is written between two operands, it is a **binary operator** representing subtraction. When it is written in front of a single operand, as in **−b**, it is a **unary operator** representing negation. The precedences of the unary and binary versions of an operator are different and are listed separately in the precedence table.

If two operators have the same precedence, they are applied in the order specified by their **associativity,** which indicates whether that operator groups to the left or to the right. Most operators in C are **left-associative,** which means that the leftmost operator is evaluated first. A few operators—primarily the assignment operator, which is discussed in more detail later in this chapter—are **right-associative,** which means that they are evaluated from right to left. The associativity for each operator appears in Table 1-4.

TABLE 1-4 Complete precedence table for C operators

Operator	Associativity	
() [] −> .	left	*highest precedence*
unary operators: − ++ −− ! & * ~ *(type)* `sizeof`	right	
* / %	left	
+ −	left	
<< >>	left	
< <= > >=	left	
== !=	left	
&	left	
^	left	
		left	
&&	left	
||	left	
?:	right	
= *op=*	right	*lowest precedence*
,	left	

The quadratic formula illustrates the importance of paying attention to associativity rules. Consider what would happen if you wrote the expression without the parentheses around `2 * a`, as follows:

`(-b + sqrt(b * b - 4 * a * c)) / 2 * a`   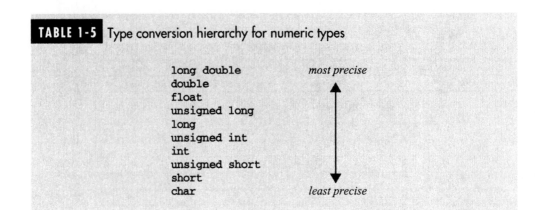   Should be `(2 * a)`

Without the parentheses, the division operator would be performed first because `/` and `*` have the same precedence and associate to the left.

Mixing types in an expression

In C, you can write an expression that includes values of different numeric types. If C encounters an operator whose operands are of different numeric types, the compiler automatically converts the operands to a common type by determining which of the two operand types appears closest to the top in Table 1-5. The result of applying the operation is always that of the arguments after any conversions are applied. This convention ensures that the result of the computation is as precise as possible.

As an example, suppose that `n` is declared as an `int`, and `x` is declared as a `double`. The expression

`n + 1`

is evaluated using integer arithmetic and produces a result of type `int`. The expression

`x + 1`

however, is evaluated by converting the integer 1 to the floating-point value 1.0 and adding the results together using double-precision floating-point arithmetic, which results in a value of type `double`.

TABLE 1-5 Type conversion hierarchy for numeric types

```
long double         most precise
double
float
unsigned long         ↑
long
unsigned int
int
unsigned short        ↓
short
char                least precise
```

Integer division and the remainder operator

The fact that applying an operator to two integer operands generates an integer result leads to an interesting situation with respect to the division operator. If you write an expression like

```
9 / 4
```

C's rules specify that the result of this operation must be an integer, because both operands are of type `int`. When C evaluates this expression, it divides 9 by 4 and discards any remainder. Thus, the value of this expression in C is 2, not 2.25.

If you want to compute the mathematically correct result of 9 divided by 4, at least one of the operands must be a floating-point number. For example, the three expressions

```
9.0 / 4
9 / 4.0
9.0 / 4.0
```

each produce the floating-point value 2.25. The decimal fraction is thrown away only if both operands are of type `int`. The operation of discarding a decimal fraction is called **truncation**.

C includes an additional arithmetic operator, indicated by a percent sign (%), that computes a remainder. The % operator returns the remainder when the first operand is divided by the second, and requires that both operands be of one of the integer types. For example, the value of

```
9 % 4
```

is 1, since 4 goes into 9 twice, with 1 left over. The following are some other examples of the % operator:

```
0 % 4   =   0           19 % 4   =   3
1 % 4   =   1           20 % 4   =   0
4 % 4   =   0         2001 % 4   =   1
```

The / and % operators turn out to be extremely useful in a wide variety of programming applications. The % operator, for example, is often used to test whether one number is divisible by another. For example, to determine whether an integer n is divisible by 3, you just check whether the result of the expression n % 3 is 0.

It is, however, important to use caution if either or both of the operands to / and % might be negative, because the results may differ from machine to machine. On most machines, division truncates its result toward 0, but this behavior is not actually guaranteed by the ANSI standard. In general, it is good programming practice to avoid using these operators with negative values.

Type casts

In C, you can specify explicit conversion by using what is called a **type cast,** a unary operator that consists of the desired type in parentheses followed by the value you wish to convert. For example, if `num` and `den` were declared as integers, you could compute the floating-point quotient by writing

```
quotient = (double) num / den;
```

The type cast has a high precedence and therefore binds more tightly than the `/` operator. Thus, the first step in evaluating the expression is to convert `num` to a `double`, after which the division is performed using floating-point arithmetic as described in the section on "Mixing types in an expression" earlier in this chapter.

As long as the conversion moves upward in the hierarchy shown in Table 1-5, the conversion causes no loss of information. If, however, you convert a value of a more precise type to a less precise one, some information may be lost. For example, if you use a type cast to convert a value of type `double` to type `int`, any decimal fraction is simply dropped. Thus, the value of the expression

```
(int) 1.9999
```

is the integer 1.

The assignment operator

In C, assignment of values to variables is built into the expression structure. The `=` operator takes two operands, just like `+` or `*`. The left operand must indicate a value that can change, which is typically a variable name. When the assignment operator is executed, the expression on the right-hand side is evaluated, and the resulting value is then stored in the variable that appears on the left-hand side. Thus, if you evaluate an expression like

```
result = 1
```

the effect is that the value 1 is assigned to the variable `result`. In most cases, assignment expressions of this sort appear in the context of simple statements, which are formed by adding a semicolon after the expression, as in the line

```
result = 1;
```

that appears in the `powertab.c` program. Such statements are usually called **assignment statements,** although they in fact have no special status in the language definition.

The assignment operator converts the type of the value on the right-hand side so that it matches the declared type of the variable. Thus, if the variable `total` is declared to be of type `double`, and you write the assignment statement

```
total = 0;
```

the integer 0 is converted into a `double` as part of making the assignment. If `n` is declared to be of type `int`, the assignment

```
n = 3.14159265;
```

has the effect of setting **n** to 3, because the value is truncated to fit in the integer variable.

Even though assignment operators usually occur in the context of simple statements, they can also be incorporated into larger expressions, in which case the result of applying the assignment operator is simply the value assigned. For example, the expression

```
z = (x = 6) + (y = 7)
```

has the effect of setting **x** to 6, **y** to 7, and **z** to 13. The parentheses are required in this example because the = operator has a lower precedence than +. Assignments that are written as part of larger expressions are called **embedded assignments.**

Although there are some contexts in which embedded assignments are extremely convenient, they often make programs more difficult to read because the assignment is easily overlooked in the middle of a complex expression. For this reason, this text limits the use of embedded assignments to a few special circumstances in which they seem to make the most sense. Of these, the most important is when you want to set several variables to the same value. C's definition of assignment as an operator makes it possible, instead of writing separate assignment statements, to write a single statement like

```
n1 = n2 = n3 = 0;
```

which has the effect of setting all three variables to 0. This statement works because C evaluates assignment operators from right to left. The entire statement is therefore equivalent to

```
n1 = (n2 = (n3 = 0));
```

The expression **n3 = 0** is evaluated, which sets **n3** to 0 and then passes 0 along as the value of the assignment expression. That value is assigned to **n2**, and the result is then assigned to **n1**. Statements of this sort are called **multiple assignments.**

As a programming convenience, C allows you to combine assignment with a binary operator to produce a form called a **shorthand assignment.** For any binary operator *op*, the statement

variable op= expression;

is equivalent to

variable = variable op (expression);

where the parentheses are required only if the expression contains an operator whose precedence is lower than that of *op*. Thus, the statement

```
balance += deposit;
```

is a shorthand for

```
balance = balance + deposit;
```

which adds **deposit** to **balance**.

Because this same shorthand applies to any binary operator in C, you can subtract the value of **surcharge** from **balance** by writing

```
balance -= surcharge;
```

Similarly, you can divide the value of **x** by 10 using

```
x /= 10;
```

or double the value of **salary** by using

```
salary *= 2;
```

Increment and decrement operators

Beyond the shorthand assignment operators, C offers a further level of abbreviation for two particularly common programming operations—adding or subtracting 1 from a variable. Adding 1 to a variable is called **incrementing** it; subtracting 1 is called **decrementing** it. To indicate these operations in an extremely compact form, C uses the operators ++ and --. For example, the statement

```
x++;
```

in C has the same ultimate effect as

```
x += 1;
```

which is itself short for

```
x = x + 1;
```

As it happens, the ++ and -- operators are more intricate than the previous example would suggest. To begin with, each of these operators can be written in two ways. The operator can come after the operand to which it applies, as in

```
x++
```

or before the operand, as in

```
++x
```

The first form, in which the operator follows the operand, is called the **postfix** form, the second, the **prefix** form.

If all you do is execute the ++ operator in isolation—as you do in the context of a separate statement or a typical **for** loop like those in the **powertab.c** example—the prefix and postfix operators have precisely the same effect. You notice the difference only if you use these operators as part of a larger expression. Then, like all operators, the ++ operator returns a value, but the value depends on where the operator is written relative to the operand. The two cases are as follows:

x++ Calculates the value of **x** first, and then increments it. The value returned to the surrounding expression is the original value *before* the increment operation is performed.

++x Increments the value of **x** first, and then uses the new value as the value of the ++ operation as a whole.

The -- operator behaves similarly, except that the value is decremented rather than incremented.

For example, if you were to execute the following program:

```
main()
{
    int x, y;

    x = 5;
    y = ++x;
    printf("x = %d, y = %d\n", x, y);
}
```

the output would look like this:

```
x = 6, y = 6
```

If, on the other hand, the program had been written as

```
main()
{
    int x, y;

    x = 5;
    y = x++;
    printf("x = %d, y = %d\n", x, y);
}
```

the final result would be

```
x = 6, y = 5
```

The statement

```
y = x++;
```

increments **x** so that it has the value 6, but the value assigned to **y** is the value prior to the increment operation, which is 5.

You may wonder why anyone would use such an arcane feature. The ++ and -- operators are certainly not essential. Moreover, there are not many circumstances in which programs that embed these operators in larger expressions are demonstrably better than those that use a simpler approach. Even so, ++ and -- are firmly entrenched in the historical tradition shared by C programmers. They are idioms, and programmers use them frequently. Because these operators are so common, you need to understand them so that you can make sense of existing code.

Boolean operators

C defines three classes of operators that manipulate Boolean data: the relational operators, the logical operators, and the **?** **:** operator. The **relational operators** are used to compare two values. C defines six relational operators, as follows:

==	Equal
!=	Not equal
>	Greater than
<	Less than
>=	Greater than or equal to
<=	Less than or equal to

When you write programs that test for equality, be careful to use the == operator, which is composed of two equal signs. A single equal sign is the assignment operator. Since the double equal sign violates conventional mathematical usage, replacing it with a single equal sign is a particularly common mistake. This mistake can also be very difficult to track down because the C compiler does not usually catch it as an error. A single equal sign usually turns the expression into an embedded assignment, which is perfectly legal in C; it just isn't at all what you want.

The relational operators can only be used to compare atomic data values like integers, floating-point numbers, Boolean values, and characters. Strings, on the other hand, are not atomic because they are composed of individual characters and therefore cannot be compared using the relational operators. A function that compares string values will be introduced in Chapter 3.

In addition to the relational operators, C defines three **logical operators** that take Boolean operands and combine them to form other Boolean values:

!	Logical *not* (TRUE if the following operand is FALSE)
&&	Logical *and* (TRUE if both operands are TRUE)
||	Logical *or* (TRUE if either or both operands are TRUE)

These operators are listed in decreasing order of precedence.

Although the operators &&, | |, and ! closely resemble the English words *and, or,* and *not,* it is important to remember that English can be somewhat imprecise when it comes to logic. To avoid that imprecision, it is often helpful to think of these operators in a more formal, mathematical way. Logicians define these operators using **truth tables,** which show how the value of a Boolean expression changes as the values of its operands change. The following truth table illustrates the result for each of the logical operators, given all possible values of the variables p and q:

p	q	p && q	p || q	!p
FALSE	FALSE	FALSE	FALSE	TRUE
FALSE	TRUE	FALSE	TRUE	TRUE
TRUE	FALSE	FALSE	TRUE	FALSE
TRUE	TRUE	TRUE	TRUE	FALSE

C interprets the && and || operators in a way that differs from the interpretation used in many other programming languages such as Pascal. Whenever a C program evaluates an expression of the form

exp_1 **&&** exp_2

or

exp_1 **||** exp_2

the individual subexpressions are always evaluated from left to right, and evaluation ends as soon as the answer can be determined. For example, if exp_1 is **FALSE** in the expression involving &&, there is no need to evaluate exp_2 since the final answer will always be **FALSE**. Similarly, in the example using ||, there is no need to evaluate the second operand if the first operand is **TRUE**. This style of evaluation, which stops as soon as the answer is known, is called **short-circuit evaluation.**

The C programming language provides another Boolean operator that can be extremely useful in certain situations: the ?: operator. (This operator is referred to as *question-mark colon*, even though the two characters do not appear adjacent to each other in the code.) Unlike any other operator in C, ?: is written in two parts and requires three operands. The general form of the operation is

(*condition*) ? exp_1 : exp_2

The parentheses around the condition are not technically required, but C programmers often include them to emphasize the boundaries of the conditional test.

When a C program encounters the ?: operator, it first evaluates the condition. If the condition turns out to be **TRUE**, exp_1 is evaluated and used as the value of the entire expression; if the condition is **FALSE**, the value is the result of evaluating exp_2. For example, you can use the ?: operator to assign to **max** either the value of **x** or the value of **y**, whichever is greater, as follows:

```
max = (x > y) ? x : y;
```

1.5 Statements

Programs in C are composed of functions, which are made up in turn of statements. As in most languages, statements in C fall into one of two principal classifications: **simple statements,** which perform some action, and **control statements,** which affect the way in which other statements are executed. The sections that follow review the principal statement forms available in C and give you the fundamental tools you need to write your own programs.

Simple statements

The most common statement in C is the **simple statement,** which consists of an expression followed by a semicolon:

> *expression*;

In most cases, the expression is a function call, an assignment, or a variable followed by the increment or decrement operator.

Blocks

As C is defined, control statements typically apply to a single statement. When you are writing a program, you often want the effect of a particular control statement to apply to a whole group of statements. To indicate that a sequence of statements is part of a coherent unit, you can assemble those statements into a **block,** which is a collection of statements enclosed in curly braces, as follows:

```
{
    statement₁
    statement₂
      . . .
    statementₙ
}
```

When the C compiler encounters a block, it treats the entire block as a single statement. Thus, whenever the notation *statement* appears in a pattern for one of the control forms, you can substitute for it either a single statement or a block. To emphasize that they are statements as far as the compiler is concerned, blocks are sometimes referred to as **compound statements.** In C, the statements in any block may be preceded by declarations of variables. In this text, variable declarations are introduced only in the block that defines the body of a function.

The statements in the interior of a block are usually indented relative to the enclosing context. The compiler ignores the indentation, but the visual effect is extremely helpful to the human reader, because it makes the structure of the program jump out at you from the format of the page. Empirical research has shown that indenting three or four spaces at each new level makes the program structure easiest to see; the programs in this text use four spaces for each new level. Indentation is critical to good programming, so you should strive to develop a consistent indentation style in your programs.

The only aspect of blocks that tends to cause any confusion for new students is the role of the semicolon. In C, the semicolon is part of the syntax of a simple statement; it acts as a statement *terminator* rather than as a statement *separator*. While this rule is perfectly consistent, it can cause trouble for people who have previously been exposed to the language Pascal, which uses a different rule. In practical terms, the differences are:

1. In C, there is always a semicolon at the end of the last simple statement in a block. In Pascal, the semicolon is usually not present although most compilers allow it as an option.
2. In C, there is never a semicolon after the closing brace of a statement block. In Pascal, a semicolon may or may not follow the **END** keyword, depending on the context.

The convention for using semicolons in C has advantages for program maintenance and should not cause any problem once you are used to it.

The `if` statement

In writing a program, you will often want to check whether some condition applies and use the result of that check to control the subsequent execution of the program. This type of program control is called **conditional execution.** The easiest way to express conditional execution in C is by using the `if` statement, which comes in two forms:

```
if (condition)  statement
if (condition)  statement else statement
```

You use the first form of the `if` statement when your solution strategy calls for a set of statements to be executed only if a particular Boolean condition is **TRUE**. If the condition is **FALSE**, the statements that form the body of the `if` statement are simply skipped. You use the second form of the `if` statement for situations in which the program must choose between two independent sets of actions based on the result of a test. This statement form is illustrated by the following program, which reads in a number and classifies it as either even or odd.

```
main()
{
    int n;

    printf("This program labels a number as even or odd.\n");
    printf("Enter a number: ");
    n = GetInteger();
    if (n % 2 == 0) {
        printf("That number is even.\n");
    } else {
        printf("That number is odd.\n");
    }
}
```

As with any control statement, the statements controlled by the `if` statement can be either a single statement or a block. Even if the body of a control form is a single statement, you are free to enclose it in a block if you decide that doing so improves the readability of your code. The programs in this book enclose the body of every control statement in a block unless the entire statement—both the control form and its body—is so short that it fits on a single line.

The `switch` statement

The `if` statement is ideal for those applications in which the program logic calls for a two-way decision point: some condition is either **TRUE** or **FALSE**, and the program acts accordingly. Some applications, however, call for more complicated decision structures involving several mutually exclusive cases: in one case, the program should do x; in another case, it should do y; in a third, it should do z; and so forth. In many applications, the most appropriate statement to use for such situations is the `switch` statement, which has the following syntactic form:

```
switch (e) {
  case c₁:
    statements
    break;
  case c₂:
    statements
    break;
  more case clauses
  default:
    statements
    break;
}
```

The expression e is called the **control expression.** When the program executes a `switch` statement, it evaluates the control expression and compares it against the values c_1, c_2, and so forth, each of which must be a constant. If one of the constants matches the value of the control expression, the statements in the associated `case` clause are executed. When the program reaches the `break` statement at the end of the clause, the operations specified by that clause are complete, and the program continues with the statement that follows the entire `switch` statement.

The `default` clause is used to specify what action occurs if none of the constants match the value of the control expression. The `default` clause, however, is optional. If none of the cases match and there is no `default` clause, the program simply continues on with the next statement after the `switch` statement without taking any action at all. To avoid the possibility that the program might ignore an unexpected case, it is good programming practice to include a `default` clause in every `switch` statement unless you are certain you have enumerated all the possibilities, even if the `default` clause is simply

```
default:
  Error("Unexpected case value");
```

The **Error** function is part of the **genlib** library and provides a uniform way of responding to errors. This function has the same argument structure as **printf**, which means that the error message may include format codes that are replaced with values taken from the argument list. The major difference is that the **Error** function does not return; after the error message is displayed, the program terminates.

The code pattern I've used to illustrate the syntax of the **switch** statement deliberately suggests that **break** statements are required at the end of each clause. In fact, C is defined so that if the **break** statement is missing, the program starts executing statements from the next clause after it finishes the selected one. While this design can be useful in some cases, it causes many more problems than it solves. To reinforce the importance of remembering to exit at the end of each **case** clause, the programs in this text always include a **break** or **return** statement in each such clause.

The one exception to this rule is that multiple **case** lines specifying different constants can appear together, one after another, before the same statement group. For example, a **switch** statement might include the following code:

```
case 1:
case 2:
    statements
    break;
```

which indicates that the specified statements should be executed if the **select** expression is either 1 or 2. The C compiler treats this construction as two **case** clauses, the first of which is empty. Because the empty clause contains no **break** statement, a program that selects the first path simply continues on with the second clause. From a conceptual point of view, however, you are better off if you think of this construction as a single **case** clause representing two possibilities.

The operation of the **switch** statement is illustrated by the following function, which computes the number of days for a given month and year:

```
int MonthDays(int month, int year)
{
    switch (month) {
      case September:
      case April:
      case June:
      case November:
        return (30);
      case February:
        return ((IsLeapYear(year)) ? 29 : 28);
      default:
        return (31);
    }
}
```

The code assumes that there is a function **IsLeapYear(year)** which tests whether **year** is a leap year and that the names of the months have been defined using constants, as follows:

```
#define January     1
#define February    2
#define March       3
#define April       4
#define May         5
#define June        6
#define July        7
#define August      8
#define September   9
#define October    10
#define November   11
#define December   12
```

The constants in a `switch` statement must be of integer type or a type that behaves like an integer. (The actual restriction is that the type must be a *scalar type,* which is defined in Chapter 2.) In particular, characters are often used as `case` constants, as illustrated by the following function, which tests to see if its argument is a vowel:

```
bool IsVowel(char ch)
{
    switch (ch) {
      case 'A': case 'E': case 'I': case 'O': case 'U':
      case 'a': case 'e': case 'i': case 'o': case 'u':
        return (TRUE);
      default:
        return (FALSE);
    }
}
```

The `while` statement

In addition to the conditional statements `if` and `switch`, C includes several control statements that allow you to execute some part of the program multiple times to form a loop. Such control statements are called **iterative statements.** The simplest iterative construct in C is the `while` statement, which executes a statement repeatedly until a conditional expression becomes `FALSE`. The general form for the `while` statement looks like this:

```
while (conditional-expression) {
    statements
}
```

When a program encounters a `while` statement, it first evaluates the conditional expression to see whether it is `TRUE` or `FALSE`. If it is `FALSE`, the loop **terminates** and the program continues with the next statement after the entire loop. If the condition is `TRUE`, the entire body is executed, after which the program goes back to the beginning of the loop to check the condition again. A single pass through the statements in the body constitutes a **cycle** of the loop.

There are two important principles about the operation of a `while` loop:

1. The conditional test is performed before every cycle of the loop, including the first. If the test is **FALSE** initially, the body of the loop is not executed at all.
2. The conditional test is performed only at the *beginning* of a loop cycle. If that condition happens to become **FALSE** at some point during the loop, the program doesn't notice that fact until a complete cycle has been executed. At that point, the program evaluates the test condition again. If it is still **FALSE**, the loop terminates.

The operation of the `while` loop is illustrated by the following function, which computes the sum of the digits in an integer:

```
int DigitSum(int n)
{
    int sum;

    sum = 0;
    while (n > 0) {
        sum += n % 10;
        n /= 10;
    }
    return (sum);
}
```

The function depends on the following observations:

- The expression `n % 10` always returns the last digit in a positive integer `n`.
- The expression `n / 10` returns a number without its final digit.

The `while` loop is designed for situations in which there is some test condition that can be applied at the beginning of a repeated operation, before any of the statements in the body of the loop are executed. If the problem you are trying to solve fits this structure, the `while` loop is the perfect tool. Unfortunately, many programming problems do not fit easily into the standard `while` loop structure. Instead of allowing a convenient test at the beginning of the operation, some problems are structured in such a way that the test you want to write to determine whether the loop is complete falls most naturally somewhere in the middle of the loop.

The most common example of such loops are those that read in data from the user until some special value, or **sentinel,** is entered to signal the end of the input. When expressed in English, the structure of the sentinel-based loop consists of repeating the following steps:

1. Read in a value.
2. If the value is equal to the sentinel, exit from the loop.
3. Perform whatever processing is required for that value.

Unfortunately, there is no test you can perform at the beginning of the loop to determine whether the loop is finished. The termination condition for the loop is reached when the input value is equal to the sentinel; in order to check this condition, the program must first read in some value. If the program has not yet read in a value, the termination condition doesn't make sense. Before the program can make any meaningful test, it must have executed the part of the loop that reads in the input value. When a loop contains some operations that must be performed before testing for completion, you have a situation that programmers call the **loop-and-a-half problem.**

One way to solve the loop-and-a-half problem in C is to use the **break** statement, which, in addition to its use in the **switch** statement, has the effect of immediately terminating the innermost enclosing loop. By using **break**, it is possible to code the loop structure for the sentinel problem in a form that follows the natural structure of the problem:

```
while (TRUE) {
    Prompt user and read in a value.
    if (value == sentinel) break;
    Process the data value.
}
```

Note that the

```
while (TRUE)
```

line itself seems to introduce an infinite loop because the value of the constant **TRUE** can never become **FALSE**. The only way this program can exit from the loop is by executing the **break** statement inside it. The loop-and-a-half strategy is illustrated by the **addlist.c** program in Figure 1-3, which computes the sum of a list of integers terminated by the sentinel value 0.

There are other strategies for solving the loop-and-a-half problem, most of which involve copying part of the code outside the loop. However, empirical studies have demonstrated that students are more likely to write correct programs if they use a **break** statement to exit from the middle of the loop than if they are forced to use some other strategy. This evidence and my own experience have convinced me that using the **break** statement inside a **while** loop is the best solution to the loop-and-a-half problem.

The `for` statement

One of the most important control statements in C is the **for** statement, which is used in situations in which you want to repeat an operation a particular number of times. The general form is

```
for (init; test; step) {
    statements
}
```

FIGURE 1-3	Program to add a list of integers

```
/*
 * File: addlist.c
 * ---------------
 * This program adds a list of numbers.  The end of the
 * input is indicated by entering a sentinel value, which
 * is defined by setting the value of the constant Sentinel.
 */

#include <stdio.h>
#include "genlib.h"
#include "simpio.h"

/*
 * Constants
 * ---------
 * Sentinel -- Value that terminates the input list
 */

#define Sentinel 0

/* Main program */

main()
{
    int value, total;

    printf("This program adds a list of numbers.\n");
    printf("Use %d to signal the end of list.\n", Sentinel);
    total = 0;
    while (TRUE) {
        printf(" ? ");
        value = GetInteger();
        if (value == Sentinel) break;
        total += value;
    }
    printf("The total is %d\n", total);
}
```

which is equivalent to the `while` statement

```
init;
while (test) {
    statements
    step;
}
```

The operation of the `for` loop is determined by the three italicized expressions on the `for` control line: *init*, *test*, and *step*. The *init* expression indicates how the `for` loop should be initialized and usually sets the initial value of the index variable. For example, if you write

```
for (i = 0; . . .
```

the loop will begin by setting the index variable i to 0. If the loop begins

```
for (i = -7; . . .
```

the variable i will start as −7, and so on.

The *test* expression is a conditional test written exactly like the test in a `while` statement. As long as the test expression is TRUE, the loop continues. Thus, the loop

```
for (i = 0; i < n; i++)
```

begins with i equal to 0 and continues as long as i is less than n, which turns out to represent a total of n cycles, with i taking on the values 0, 1, 2, and so forth, up to the final value n−1. The loop

```
for (i = 1; i <= n; i++)
```

begins with i equal to 1 and continues as long as i is less than or equal to n. This loop also runs for n cycles, with i taking on the values 1, 2, and so forth, up to n.

The *step* expression indicates how the value of the index variable changes from cycle to cycle. The most common form of step specification is to increment the index variable using the ++ operator, but this is not the only possibility. For example, one can count backward by using the -- operator, or count by twos by using += 2 instead of ++.

As an illustration of counting in the reverse direction, the program

```
main()
{
    int t;

    for (t = 10; t >= 0; t--) {
        printf("%2d\n", t);
    }
    printf("Liftoff!\n");
}
```

generates the following sample run:

```
10
 9
 8
 7
 6
 5
 4
 3
 2
 1
 0
Liftoff!
```

The expressions *init*, *test*, and *step* in a `for` statement are each optional, but the semicolons must appear. If *init* is missing, no initialization is performed. If *test* is missing, it is assumed to be TRUE. If *step* is missing, no action occurs between loop cycles.

■ 1.6 Functions

A **function** consists of a set of statements that have been collected together and given a name. The act of using the name to invoke the associated statements is known as **calling** that function. To indicate a function call in C, you write the name of the function, followed by a list of expressions enclosed in parentheses. These expressions, called **arguments,** allow the calling program to pass information to the function. For example, in the `powertab.c` program at the beginning of this chapter, the function `RaiseIntToPower` took two integer arguments, n and k, which are the values it needs to know in order to compute n^k. If a function requires no information from its caller, it need not have any arguments, but an empty set of parentheses must still appear in the function call.

Once called, the function takes the data supplied as arguments, does its work, and then returns to the program step from which the call was made. Remembering what the calling program was doing and being able to get back precisely to that point is one of the defining characteristics of the function-calling mechanism. The operation of going back to the calling program is called **returning** from the function.

Returning results from functions

As they return, functions can send results back to the calling program. Thus, when the `RaiseIntToPower` function returns with the statement

```
return (result);
```

the value of the local variable `result` is passed back to the main program as the value of the function. This operation is called **returning a value.**

Functions can return values of any type. The following function, for example, returns a value of type `bool`, which can then be used in conditional expressions:

```
bool IsLeapYear(int year)
{
    return ( ((year % 4 == 0) && (year % 100 != 0))
            || (year % 400 == 0) );
}
```

Functions that return Boolean results play an important role in programming and are called **predicate functions.**

Functions, however, do not need to return a value at all. A function that does not return a value and is instead executed for its effect is called a **procedure.**

Procedures are indicated in the definition of a function by using the reserved word void as the result type.

The return statement in C has two forms. For procedures, you write the statement as

```
return;
```

For functions that return a value, the return keyword is followed by an expression, as follows:

```
return expression;
```

By tradition, many C programmers enclose the expression in parentheses, although there is no formal requirement to do so.

Executing either form of the return statement causes the current function to return immediately to its caller, passing back the value of the expression, if any, to its caller as the value of the function.

Function definitions and prototypes

A function definition has the following syntactic form:

```
result-type name (parameter-list)
{
    body of function
}
```

In this example, *result-type* is the type of value returned by the function, *name* is the function name, and *parameter-list* is a list of declarations separated by commas, giving the type and name of each parameter to the function. **Parameters** are placeholders for the arguments supplied in the function call and act like local variables except for the fact that they are given initial values by the calling program. If a function takes no parameters, the entire parameter list in the function header line is replaced with the keyword void. The body of the function is a block and typically contains declarations for the local variables required by the function.

Before you use a function in a C program, it is good practice to declare it by specifying its prototype. A prototype has exactly the same form as a function definition, except that the entire body is replaced by a semicolon. The names of the parameter variables are optional in a prototype, but supplying them usually helps the reader.

The mechanics of the function-calling process

When you call a function in a program, the following steps occur:

1. The calling program computes values for each argument. Because the arguments are expressions, this computation can involve operators and other

functions, all of which are evaluated before execution of the new function actually begins.

2. The system creates new space for all the local variables required by the new function, including the parameter variables. These variables are usually allocated together in a block, which is called a **stack frame.**

3. The value of each argument is copied into the corresponding parameter variable. If there is more than one argument, the arguments are copied into the parameters in order; the first argument is copied into the first parameter, and so forth. If necessary, type conversions are performed between the argument values and the parameter variables, as in an assignment statement. For example, if you pass a value of type `int` to a function that expects a parameter of type `double`, the integer is converted into the equivalent floating-point value before it is copied into the parameter variable.

4. The statements in the function body are executed until a `return` statement is encountered or there are no more statements to execute.

5. The value of the `return` expression, if any, is evaluated and returned as the value of the function. If the value being returned does not precisely match the result type declared for the function, a type conversion is performed. Thus, if a `return` statement specifies a floating-point value in a function defined to return an `int`, the result is truncated to an integer.

6. The stack frame created for this function call is discarded. In the process, all local variables disappear.

7. The calling program continues, with the returned value substituted in place of the call.

Stepwise refinement

Procedures and functions enable you to divide a large programming problem into smaller pieces that are individually easy to understand. The process of dividing a problem into manageable pieces, called **decomposition,** is a fundamental programming strategy. Finding the right decomposition, however, turns out to be a difficult task that requires considerable practice. If you choose the individual pieces well, each one will have conceptual integrity as a unit and make the program as a whole much simpler to understand. But if you choose unwisely, the decomposition can get in your way. There are no hard-and-fast rules for selecting a particular decomposition; you will learn how to apply this process through experience.

When you are faced with the task of writing a program, the best strategy is usually to start with the main program. At this level, you think about the problem as a whole and then try to identify the major pieces of the entire task. Once you figure out what the big pieces of the program are, you can define them as independent functions. Since some of these functions may themselves be complicated, it is often appropriate to decompose them into still smaller ones. You can continue this process until every piece of the problem is simple enough to be solved on its own. This process is called **top-down design,** or **stepwise refinement.**

■ Summary

This chapter is itself a summary, which makes it hard to condense it to a few central points. Its purpose was to introduce you to the ANSI C programming language and give you a crash course in how to write simple programs in that language. This chapter concentrated on the low-level structure of the language, proceeding in turn through the topics of expressions, statements, and functions. The facilities that ANSI C offers for defining new data structures are detailed in Chapter 2.

Important points in this chapter include:

- In the 25 years of its existence, the C programming language has become one of the most widely used languages in the world.
- A typical C program consists of comments, library inclusions, program-level definitions, function prototypes, a function named `main` that is called when the program is started, and a set of auxiliary function definitions that work together with the main program to accomplish the required task.
- Variables in a C program must be declared before they are used. Most variables in C are *local variables,* which are declared at the beginning of a function and can only be used inside the body of that function.
- A *data type* is defined by a domain of values and a set of operations. C includes several predefined types that allow programs to store data of several different types, such as integers, floating-point numbers, and characters. In addition to these built-in types, the `genlib` library defines the types `bool` and `string`, which are treated in this book as if they were an integral part of the language.
- The easiest way to read input data from the user is to call functions in the simplified I/O library (`simpio`), which defines such functions as `GetInteger`, `GetReal`, and `GetLine`. To display output on the computer screen, the usual approach is to call the `printf` function from the standard I/O library. The `printf` function defines a collection of format codes that allow you to substitute values into the output text. The most common format codes are listed in Table 1-3.
- Expressions in C are written in a form similar to that in most programming languages, with individual terms connected by operators. A complete list of the operators available in C appears in Table 1-4, which also indicates the relative precedence of each operator.
- Statements in C fall into two classes: simple statements and control statements. A simple statement consists of an expression—typically an assignment or a function call—followed by a semicolon. The control statements described in this chapter are the `if`, `switch`, `while`, and `for` statements. The first two are used to express conditional execution, while the last two are used to specify repetition.
- C programs are typically subdivided into several functions. Each function consists of a sequence of statements that can be invoked by writing the name of the function, followed by a list of arguments enclosed in parentheses.

These arguments are copied into the corresponding parameter variables inside the function. The function can return a result to the caller by using the `return` statement.

REVIEW QUESTIONS

1. What is the difference between a source file and an object file?

2. What characters are used to mark comments in a C program?

3. In an `#include` line, the name of the library header file can be enclosed in either angle brackets or double quotation marks. What is the difference between the two forms of punctuation?

4. How would you define a constant called `CentimetersPerInch` with the value 2.54?

5. What is the name of the function that must be defined in every C program?

6. What is the purpose of the special character `\n` that appears at the end of most strings passed to `printf`?

7. What four properties are established when you declare a variable?

8. Indicate which of the following are legal variable names in C:

   a. `x`
   b. `formula1`
   c. `average_rainfall`
   d. `%correct`
   e. `short`
   f. `tiny`
   g. `total output`
   h. `aReasonablyLongVariableName`
   i. `12MonthTotal`
   j. `marginal-cost`
   k. `b4hand`
   l. `_stk_depth`

9. What are the two attributes that define a data type?

10. What is the difference between the types `short`, `int`, and `long`?

11. What does ASCII stand for?

12. List all possible values of type `bool`.

13. What statements would you include in a program to read a value from the user and store it in the variable `x`, which is declared as a `double`?

14. Suppose that a function contains the following declarations:

```
int i;
long l;
float f;
double d;
char c;
string s;
```

Write a series of `printf` calls that display the values of each of these variables on the screen.

15. Indicate the values and types of the following expressions:

    a. 2 + 3   d. 3 * 6.0

    b. 19 / 5   e. 19 % 5

    c. 19.0 / 5   f. 2 % 7

16. What is the difference between the unary minus operator and the binary subtraction operator?

17. What does the term *truncation* mean?

18. By applying the appropriate precedence rules, calculate the result of each of the following expressions:

    a. 6 + 5 / 4 - 3
    b. 2 + 2 * (2 * 2 - 2) % 2 / 2
    c. 10 + 9 * ((8 + 7) % 6) + 5 * 4 % 3 * 2 + 1
    d. 1 + 2 + (3 + 4) * ((5 * 6 % 7 * 8) - 9) - 10

19. How do you specify a shorthand assignment operation?

20. What is the difference between the expressions ++x and x++?

21. What does the term *short-circuit evaluation* mean?

22. Write out the general syntactic form for each of the following control statements: `if, switch, while, for`.

23. Describe in English the general operation of the `switch` statement.

24. What is a sentinel?

25. What `for` loop control line would you use in each of the following situations?

    a. Counting from 1 to 100
    b. Counting by sevens starting at 0 until the number is three digits long
    c. Counting backward by twos from 100 to 0

26. What is a function prototype?

27. In your own words, describe what happens when you call a function in C.

28. What is meant by the term *stepwise refinement?*

PROGRAMMING EXERCISES

1. Write a program that reads in a temperature in degrees Celsius and displays the corresponding temperature in degrees Fahrenheit. The conversion formula is

$$F = \frac{9}{5}C + 32$$

2. Write a program that converts a distance in meters to the corresponding English distance in feet and inches. The conversion factors you need are

1 inch = 0.0254 meters
1 foot = 12 inches

3. According to legend, the German mathematician Karl Friedrich Gauss (1777–1855) began to show his mathematical talent at a very early age. When he was in elementary school, Gauss was asked by his teacher to compute the sum of the numbers between 1 and 100. Gauss is said to have given the answer instantly: 5050. Write a program that computes the answer to the question Gauss's teacher posed.

4. Write a program that reads in a positive integer N and then calculates and displays the sum of the first N odd integers. For example, if N is 4, your program should display the value 16, which is $1 + 3 + 5 + 7$.

5. Write a program that reads in a list of integers from the user until the user enters the value 0 as a sentinel. When the sentinel appears, your program should display the largest value in the list, as illustrated in the following sample run:

```
This program finds the largest integer in a list.
Enter 0 to signal the end of the list.
 ? 17↵
 ? 42↵
 ? 11↵
 ? 19↵
 ? 35↵
 ? 0↵
The largest value is 42
```

6. Using the `DigitSum` function from the section entitled "The `while` statement" as a model, write a program that reads in an integer and then displays the number that has the same digits in the reverse order, as illustrated by this sample run:

```
This program reverses the digits in an integer.
Enter a positive integer: 123456789↵
The reversed number is 987654321
```

To make sure your program can handle integers as large as the one shown in the example, use the type `long` instead of `int` in your program.

7. Greek mathematicians took a special interest in numbers that are equal to the sum of their proper divisors (a proper divisor of N is any divisor less than N itself). They called such numbers **perfect numbers.** For example, 6 is a perfect number because it is the sum of 1, 2, and 3, which are the integers less than 6 that divide evenly into 6. Similarly, 28 is a perfect number because it is the sum of 1, 2, 4, 7, and 14.

   Write a predicate function `IsPerfect` that takes an integer `n` and returns **TRUE** if `n` is perfect, and **FALSE** otherwise. Test your implementation by writing a main program that uses the `IsPerfect` function to check for perfect numbers in the range 1 to 9999 by testing each number in turn. When a perfect number is found, your program should display it on the screen. The first two lines of output should be 6 and 28. Your program should find two other perfect numbers in the range as well.

8. Every positive integer greater than 1 can be expressed as a product of prime numbers. This factorization is unique and is called the **prime factorization.** For example, the number 60 can be decomposed into the factors $2 \times 2 \times 3 \times 5$, each of which is prime. Note that the same prime can appear more than once in the factorization.

   Write a program to display the prime factorization of a number N, as illustrated by the following sample run:

```
Enter number to be factored: 60↵
2 * 2 * 3 * 5
```

9. When a floating-point number is converted to an integer in C, the value is truncated by throwing away any fraction. Thus, when 4.99999 is converted to an integer, the result is 4. In many cases, it would be useful to have the option of *rounding* a floating-point value to the nearest integer. For a positive floating-point number `x`, the rounding operation can be achieved by adding 0.5 to `x` and then truncating the result to an integer. If the decimal fraction of `x` is less than .5, the truncated value will be the integer less than `x`; if the fraction is .5 or more, the truncated value will be the next larger integer. Because truncation always moves toward zero, negative numbers must be rounded by subtracting 0.5 and truncating instead of by adding 0.5.

   Write a function `Round(x)` that rounds a floating-point number `x` to the nearest integer. Demonstrate that your function works by designing a suitable main program to test it.

10. The German mathematician Leibniz (1646–1716) discovered the rather remarkable fact that the mathematical constant π can be computed using the following mathematical relationship:

$$\frac{\pi}{4} \cong 1 - \frac{1}{3} + \frac{1}{5} - \frac{1}{7} + \frac{1}{9} - \frac{1}{11} + \cdots$$

The formula to the right of the equal sign represents an infinite series; each fraction represents a term in that series. If you start with 1, subtract one-third, add one-fifth, and so on, for each of the odd integers, you get a number that gets closer and closer to the value of π/4 as you go along.

Write a program that calculates an approximation of π consisting of the first 10,000 terms in Leibniz's series.

11. You can also approximate π by approximating the area bounded by a circular arc. Consider the following quarter circle:

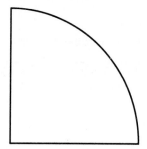

which has a radius *r* equal to two inches. From the formula for the area of a circle, you can easily determine that the area of the quarter circle should be π square inches. You can also approximate the area computationally by adding up the areas of a series of rectangles, where each rectangle has a fixed width and the height is chosen so that the circle passes through the midpoint of the top of the rectangle. For example, if you divide the area into 10 rectangles from left to right, you get the following diagram:

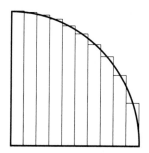

The sum of the areas of the rectangles approximates the area of the quarter circle. The more rectangles there are, the closer the approximation.

For each rectangle, the width w is a constant derived by dividing the radius by the number of rectangles. The height h, on the other hand, varies depending on the position of the rectangle. If the midpoint of the rectangle in the horizontal direction is given by x, the height of the rectangle can be computed using the distance formula

$$h = \sqrt{r^2 - x^2}$$

The area of each rectangle is then simply $h \times w$.

Write a program to compute the area of the quarter circle by dividing it into 100 rectangles.

12. When you write a check, the dollar amount appears twice: once as a number and once as English text. For example, if you write a check for $1729, you need to translate that number to the English text "one thousand seven hundred twenty-nine." Your task in this problem is to write a program that reads in integers from the user and writes out the equivalent value in figures on the next line, stopping when the user enters any negative number. For example, the following is a sample run of this program:

```
Enter numbers in their decimal form.
To stop, enter a negative value.
Number: 0.
zero
Number: 1.
one
Number: 11.
eleven
Number: 42.
forty-two
Number: 1729.
one thousand seven hundred twenty-nine
Number: 2001.
two thousand one
Number: 12345.
twelve thousand three hundred forty-five
Number: 13000.
thirteen thousand
Number: -1.
```

The key idea in this exercise is decomposition. The problem is not nearly as hard as it looks if you break it down into separate procedures that accomplish parts of the task. Many of these procedures will have a form that looks something like this:

```
static void PrintOneDigit(int d)
{
    switch (d) {
      case 0: printf("zero"); break;
      case 1: printf("one"); break;
      case 2: printf("two"); break;
      case 3: printf("three"); break;
      case 4: printf("four"); break;
      case 5: printf("five"); break;
      case 6: printf("six"); break;
      case 7: printf("seven"); break;
      case 8: printf("eight"); break;
      case 9: printf("nine"); break;
      default: Error("Illegal call to PrintOneDigit");
    }
}
```

In writing your program, you should keep the following points in mind:

- You don't need to perform any string manipulation. All you have to do is display the value on the screen, which means that `printf` is all you need.
- Your program need work only with values up to 999,999, although it should give the user some kind of error message if a number is outside of its range.
- It is perfectly acceptable for all the letters in the output to be lowercase. The problem is much harder if you try to capitalize the first word.
- You should remain on the lookout for functions that you can reuse. For example, printing the number of thousands is pretty much the same as printing out the last three digits, and you should be able to use the same procedure more than once.
- Several special cases arise in this problem. For example, the number 11 must be treated differently than 21 or 31, because *eleven* doesn't fit the pattern established by *twenty-one* and *thirty-one*.

CHAPTER 2

Data Types in C

It is a capital mistake to theorise before one has data. Insensibly one
begins to twist facts to suit theories, instead of theories to suit facts.

— Sherlock Holmes, in Sir Arthur Conan Doyle's *A Scandal in Bohemia,* 1892

Objectives

- To appreciate the fact that data values have hierarchical relationships that can be reflected in the data structure of a program.

- To be able to define new atomic types by enumerating the elements of their domain.

- To recognize that data values stored within a program are located at some address in memory, which means that the address can be used as a pointer to the original data.

- To be able to use the three fundamental structures: pointers, arrays, and records.

- To understand the relationship between pointers and arrays in C.

- To be able to use dynamic allocation to create storage for array and record values.

Chapter 1 of this text is a capsule summary of the features of ANSI C necessary to code the algorithmic structure of a program. The algorithmic structure, however, represents only part of the story. It is equally important to consider the structure of the data.

Like control statements and function calls—each of which can be nested hierarchically to represent increasingly complex algorithmic structures—data types in a language also form a hierarchy. The base of the hierarchy is composed of the atomic types that were introduced in Chapter 1, coupled with a new class of atomic types called *enumeration types* that are introduced in the following section. Starting from this base, you can extend the hierarchy using the following mechanisms for creating new types from existing ones:

- *Pointers.* A **pointer** is simply the internal machine address of a value inside the computer's memory. C allows you to work directly with pointers as data and makes them part of the type hierarchy, which means that you can define new types whose domains consist of pointers to values of some existing type.
- *Arrays.* An **array** is an ordered collection of data values, each of which has the same type.
- *Records.* A **record** is a collection of data values that represents some logically coherent whole. The individual components are identified by name rather than by order and may be of different types.

Each of these types is described in detail in a separate section later in this chapter. For now, the main point is that you can combine these mechanisms to generate new types at whatever level of complexity the program requires. You can, for example, create new types that are pointers to records containing arrays or any other nested structure you choose. The hierarchy of types in a program defines its **data structure.**

2.1 Enumeration types

Before moving on to the question of how to create new types from existing ones, it is important to complete the set of atomic types that form the base of the type hierarchy. The most common atomic types are the various built-in types described in Chapter 1: integers, floating-point numbers, characters, and so on. Like many languages, however, C makes it possible to define new atomic types by listing the elements that constitute their domains. Such types are called **enumeration types.**

In this text, new enumeration types are defined using the following syntactic form:

```
typedef enum { element-list } name;
```

where *element-list* is a list of identifiers, which are called **enumeration constants,** and *name* is the name of the new type. For example, the following enumeration type defines the four principal compass directions:

```
typedef enum { North, East, South, West } directionT;
```

Similarly, the following definition introduces the type `colorT`, which consists of the six primary and secondary colors available on a standard color monitor:

```
typedef enum {
    Red, Green, Blue, Yellow, Cyan, Magenta
} colorT;
```

Once you have defined an enumeration type, you can declare variables of that type just as you do with any of the built-in types. For example, the declaration

```
directionT dir;
```

declares the variable `dir` to be of type `directionT`, which means that it can take on any of the values `North`, `East`, `South`, or `West`.

Internal representation of enumeration types

The values of an enumeration type are stored internally as integers. When the compiler encounters a new enumeration type, it ordinarily assigns consecutive integers to the enumeration constants, starting with the integer 0. Thus, in the `directionT` example, the constants have the following values: `North` = 0, `East` = 1, `South` = 2, and `West` = 3. You can, however, control the encoding used for enumeration types by writing an equal sign and an integer constant after any of the element names. For example, after the definition

```
typedef enum {
    Penny = 1,
    Nickel = 5,
    Dime = 10,
    Quarter = 25,
    HalfDollar = 50
} coinT;
```

each of the enumeration constants `Penny`, `Nickel`, `Dime`, `Quarter`, and `HalfDollar` is represented internally as its corresponding monetary value. If the value of any enumeration constant is not specified, the compiler simply adds one to the value of the previous constant. Thus, in the definition,

```
typedef enum {
    January = 1, February, March, April, May, June,
    July, August, September, October, November, December
} monthT;
```

the constant `January` is represented internally as 1, `February` as 2, and so on.

Defining an enumeration type is in many ways similar to using `#define` to introduce named constants. In the `monthT` example, you could achieve the same effect by making the following definitions:

```
#define January      1
#define February     2
#define March        3
#define April        4
#define May          5
#define June         6
#define July         7
#define August       8
#define September    9
#define October     10
#define November    11
#define December    12
```

Inside the machine, the two strategies produce exactly the same result: every element of the enumeration type is represented by an integer code. From the programmer's point of view, however, defining separate enumeration types has these advantages:

- The programmer does not need to specify the internal codes explicitly.
- The fact that there is a separate type name often makes the program easier to read because declarations can use a meaningful type name instead of the general-purpose designation int.
- On many systems, programs that use enumeration types are easier to debug because the compiler makes the names of the enumeration constants available to the debugger. Thus, if you ask it about a value of type monthT, a well-designed debugger would be able to display the value January instead of the integer constant 1.

Scalar types

In C, enumeration types, characters, and the various representations of integers form a more general type class called **scalar types.** When a value of a scalar type is used in a C expression, the compiler automatically converts it to the integer used to represent that value. The effect of this rule is that the operations you can perform on values of any scalar type are the same as those for integers.

As an example, suppose that you want to write a function RightFrom(dir) that takes a directionT and returns the direction you would be facing if you turned 90 degrees from that starting position. Thus, RightFrom(North) should return East. Because the directions appear in order as you move right around the compass points, turning right corresponds arithmetically to adding one to the underlying value, except for RightFrom(West), which has to generate 0 instead of 4 as the underlying value. As is often the case with enumerated types that represent a value which is logically cyclical, you can use the % operator to write a one-line implementation of RightFrom, as follows:

```
directionT RightFrom(directionT dir)
{
    return ((dir + 1) % 4);
}
```

You can use scalar types in any context in which an integer might appear. For example, a variable of an enumeration type can be used as the control expression in a `switch` statement, so that you can define a function `DirectionName(dir)`, which returns the name of a direction as a string, like this:

```
string DirectionName(directionT dir)
{
    switch (dir) {
      case North: return ("North");
      case East:  return ("East");
      case South: return ("South");
      case West:  return ("West");
      default:    Error("Illegal direction value");
    }
}
```

You can also use scalar types as index variables in `for` loops. For example, you can cycle through each of the four directions using the following loop control line:

```
for (dir = North; dir <= West; dir++)
```

Understanding `typedef`

The standard form used in this text to define a new enumeration type begins with the keyword `typedef`, which is used in ANSI C to introduce new type names. Unfortunately, the syntax of `typedef` can sometimes be confusing, particularly if you have programmed in other languages in which type definitions resemble other definitions. C's syntax for `typedef` has an underlying logic to it, but that logic is difficult to see unless you think of it in the right way.

The best way to think about the syntax of `typedef` is reflected in the following general form:

> `typedef` *declaration*`;`

In this form, *declaration* is simply a variable declaration, just like the ones you write at the beginning of a function. If you were to write *declaration* without the `typedef` keyword, it would declare some collection of variables. If you include the `typedef` keyword, those same names are defined as the corresponding types.

To illustrate this idea, consider the following `typedef` statement:

> `typedef int partNumberT, serialNumberT;`

Had you omitted the `typedef` keyword, the declaration would have introduced two variables of type `int`. Because of the `typedef` keyword, however, this definition instead introduces two new type names, `partNumberT` and `serialNumberT`, each of which is identical to the built-in type `int`. No matter how complicated type definitions become, this strategy for interpreting a `typedef` line will always let you determine exactly what types it defines.

Even a simple type definition like the one that declares `partNumberT` and `serialNumberT` can be useful in a program. For one thing, the new type names provide more information to the reader about what that type represents. The declaration

```
int pn;
```

for example, is considerably less informative than

```
partNumberT pn;
```

even though the two are equivalent from the compiler's point of view. Another advantage of giving names to simple types is that doing so enhances the portability of your code. If your C compiler uses small integers, the type `int` is probably insufficient to represent a complete part or serial number. If you've used a type definition to introduce new type names, you can change the underlying representation for these types simply by editing the `typedef` line, as follows:

```
typedef long partNumberT, serialNumberT;
```

In fact, if you are concerned about portability, it would probably be better to use this definition from the beginning so that your program will run unchanged on a wider range of machines.

2.2 Data and memory

Before you can understand C's type system in any detail, you need to know how information is stored inside a computer. Every modern computer contains some amount of high-speed internal memory that is its principal repository for information. In a typical machine, that memory is built out of a special integrated-circuit chip called a **RAM,** which stands for *random-access memory*. Random-access memory allows the program to use the contents of any memory cell at any time. The technical details of how the RAM chip operates are not important to most programmers. What is important is how the memory is organized.

Bits, bytes, and words

At the most primitive level, all data values inside the computer are stored in the form of fundamental units of information called *bits*. A **bit** is a unit of memory that has only two possible states. If you think of the circuitry inside the machine as if it were a tiny light switch, you might label those states as *on* and *off*. Historically, the word *bit* is a contraction of *binary digit*, and it is therefore more common to label those states using the symbols 0 and 1, which are the two digits used in the binary number system on which computer arithmetic is based.

Since a single bit holds so little information, the bits themselves do not provide a particularly convenient mechanism for storing data. To make it easier to store such traditional types of information as numbers or characters, individual bits are collected together into larger units that are then treated as integral units of storage. The smallest such combined unit is called a **byte** and is large enough to hold a value of type `char`, which typically requires eight individual bits. On most machines, bytes are assembled into larger structures called **words,** where a word is usually defined to be the size required to hold a value of type `int`. Some machines use two-byte words (16 bits), some use four-byte words (32 bits), and some use less conventional sizes.

Memory addresses

Within the memory system, every byte is identified by a numeric **address.** Typically, the first byte in the computer is numbered 0, the second is numbered 1, and so on, up to the number of bytes in the machine. For example, if your computer has four megabytes of memory (which actually means 4×2^{20} or 4,194,304 bytes), the addresses of the memory cells would look like this:

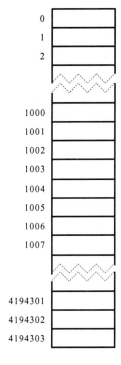

Each byte of memory is large enough to hold one character. For example, if you were to declare the character variable `ch`, the compiler would reserve one byte of storage for that variable as part of the current function frame. Suppose that this byte happened to be at address 1000. If the program then executed the statement

```
ch = 'A';
```

the internal representation of the character `'A'` would be stored in location 1000. Since the ASCII code for `'A'` is 65, the resulting memory configuration would look like this:

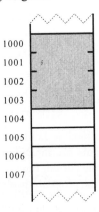

In most programming applications, you will have no way of predicting the actual address at which a particular variable is stored. In the preceding diagram, the variable `ch` is assigned to address 1000, but this choice is entirely arbitrary. Whenever your program makes a function call, the variables within the function are assigned to memory locations, but you have no way of predicting the addresses of those variables in advance. Even so, you may find it useful to draw pictures of memory and label the individual locations with addresses beginning at a particular starting point. These addresses—even though you choose them yourself—can help you to visualize what is happening inside the memory of the computer as your program runs.

Values that are larger than a single character are stored in consecutive bytes of memory. For example, if an integer takes up four bytes on your computer, that integer requires four consecutive bytes of memory and might therefore be stored in the shaded area in the following diagram:

Data values requiring multiple bytes are identified by the address of the first byte, so the integer represented by the shaded area is the word stored at address 1000.

When you write a C program, you can determine how much memory will be assigned to a particular variable by using the `sizeof` operator. The `sizeof` operator takes a single operand, which must be a type name enclosed in parentheses or an expression. If the operand is a type, the `sizeof` operator returns the number of bytes required to store a value of that type; if the operand is an expression, `sizeof` returns the number of bytes required to store the value of that expression. For example, the expression

```
sizeof(int)
```

returns the number of bytes required to store a value of type `int`. The expression

```
sizeof x
```

returns the number of bytes required to store the variable **x**.

2.3 Pointers

One of the principles behind the design of C was that programmers should have as much access as possible to the facilities provided by the hardware itself. For this reason, C makes the fact that memory locations have addresses visible to the programmer. A data item whose value is an address in memory is called a **pointer.** In many high-level programming languages, pointers are used sparingly because those languages provide other mechanisms that eliminate much of the need for pointers; the Java programming language, for example, hides pointers from the programmer altogether. In C, pointers are pervasive, and it is impossible to understand C programs without knowing how pointers work.

In C, pointers serve several purposes, of which the following are the most important:

- *Pointers allow you to refer to a large data structure in a compact way.* Data structures in a program can become arbitrarily large. No matter how large they grow, however, the data structures still reside somewhere in the computer's memory and therefore have an address. Pointers allow you to use the address as a shorthand for the complete value. Because a memory address typically fits in four bytes of memory, this strategy offers considerable space savings when the data structures themselves are large.
- *Pointers facilitate sharing data between different parts of a program.* If you pass the address of some data value from one function to another, both functions have access to the same data. This application of pointers is explained in the section on "Passing parameters by reference" later in this chapter.
- *Pointers make it possible to reserve new memory during program execution.* Up to now, the only memory you could use in your programs was the memory assigned to variables that you have declared explicitly. In many applications, it is convenient to acquire new memory as the program runs and to refer to that memory using pointers. This strategy is discussed in the section on "Dynamic allocation" later in this chapter.
- *Pointers can be used to record relationships among data items.* In advanced programming applications, pointers are used extensively to model connections between individual data values. For example, programmers often

indicate that one data item follows another in a conceptual sequence by including a pointer to the second item in the internal representation of the first. This application of pointers is introduced in Chapter 9.

Using addresses as data values

In C, any expression that refers to an internal memory location capable of storing data is called an **lvalue** (pronounced "ell-value"). The *l* at the beginning of *lvalue* comes from the observation that lvalues can appear on the left side of an assignment statement in C. For example, simple variables are lvalues because you can write a statement like

```
x = 1.0;
```

Many values in C, however, are not lvalues. For example, constants are not lvalues, because a constant cannot be changed. Similarly, although the result of an arithmetic expression is a value, it is not an lvalue, because you cannot assign a value to the result of an arithmetic expression.

The following properties apply to lvalues in C:

- Every lvalue is stored somewhere in memory and therefore has an address.
- Once it has been declared, the address of an lvalue never changes, even though the contents of the lvalue may change.
- Depending on their data type, different lvalues require different amounts of memory.
- The address of an lvalue is a pointer value, which can be stored in memory and manipulated as data.

Declaring pointer variables

As with all other variables in C, you must declare pointer variables before you use them. To declare a variable as a pointer, you precede its name with an asterisk (*) in a standard declaration. For example, the line

```
int *p;
```

declares the variable **p** to be of the conceptual type pointer-to-`int`. Similarly, the line

```
char *cptr;
```

declares the variable `cptr` to be of type pointer-to-`char`. These two types—pointer-to-`int` and pointer-to-`char`—are distinct in C, even though each of them is represented internally as an address. To use the value at that address, the compiler needs to know how to interpret it and therefore requires that its type be specified explicitly. The type of the value to which a pointer points is called the **base type** of that pointer. Thus, the type pointer-to-`int` has `int` as its base type.

It is important to note that the asterisk used to indicate that a variable is a pointer belongs syntactically with the variable name and not with the base type. If you use the same declaration to declare two pointers of the same type, you need to mark each of the variables with an asterisk, as in

```
int *p1, *p2;
```

The declaration

```
int *p1, p2;
```

declares `p1` as a pointer to an integer, but declares `p2` as an integer variable.

The fundamental pointer operations

C defines two operators that allow you to move back and forth between values and pointers to those values:

&	Address-of
*	Value-pointed-to

The `&` operator takes an lvalue as its operand and returns the memory address in which that lvalue is stored. The `*` operator takes a value of any pointer type and returns the lvalue to which it points. This operation is called **dereferencing** the pointer. The `*` operation produces an lvalue, which means that you can assign a value to a dereferenced pointer.

The easiest way to illustrate these operators is by example. Consider the declarations

```
int x, y;
int *p1, *p2;
```

These declarations allocate memory for four words, two of type `int` and two of type pointer-to-`int`. For concreteness, let's suppose that these values are stored in the machine addresses indicated by the following diagram:

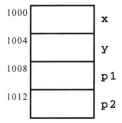

You can assign values to **x** and **y** using assignment statements, just as you always have. For example, executing the assignment statements

```
x = -42;
y = 163;
```

results in the following memory state:

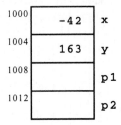

To initialize the pointer variables **p1** and **p2**, you need to assign values that represent the addresses of some integer objects. In C, the operator that produces addresses is the **&** operator, which you can use to assign the addresses of **x** and **y** to **p1** and **p2**, respectively:

```
p1 = &x;
p2 = &y;
```

These assignments leave memory in the following state:

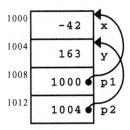

The arrows in the diagram are used to emphasize the fact that the values of the variables **p1** and **p2** point to the cells indicated by the heads of the arrows. Drawing arrows makes it much easier to understand how pointers work, but it is important to remember that pointers are simply numeric addresses and that there are no arrows inside the machine.

To move from a pointer to the value it points to, you use the * operator. For example, the expression

```
*p1
```

indicates the value in the memory location to which **p1** points. Moreover, since **p1** is declared as a pointer to an integer, the compiler knows that the expression ***p1** must refer to an integer. Thus, given the configuration of memory illustrated in the diagram, ***p1** turns out to be another name for the variable **x**.

Like the simple variable name **x**, the expression ***p1** is an lvalue, and you can assign new values to it. Executing the assignment statement

```
*p1 = 17;
```

changes the value in the variable **x** because that is where **p1** points. After you make this assignment, the memory configuration is

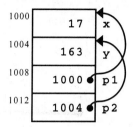

You can see that the value of **p1** itself is unaffected by this assignment. It continues to hold the value 1000 and therefore still points to the variable **x**.

It is also possible to assign new values to the pointer variables themselves. For instance, the statement

```
p1 = p2;
```

instructs the computer to take the value contained in the variable **p2** and copy it into the variable **p1**. The value contained in **p2** is the pointer value 1004. If you copy this value into **p1**, both **p1** and **p2** point to the variable **y**, as the following diagram shows:

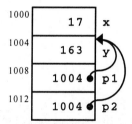

In terms of the operations that occur inside the machine, copying a pointer is exactly the same as copying an integer. The value of the pointer is simply copied unchanged to the destination. From a conceptual perspective, the diagram shows that the effect of copying a pointer is to replace the destination pointer with a new arrow that points to the same location as the old one. Thus, the effect of the assignment

```
p1 = p2;
```

is to change the arrow leading from **p1** so that it points to the same memory address as the arrow originating at **p2**.

It is important to be able to distinguish the assignment of a pointer from that of a value. **Pointer assignment,** such as

```
p1 = p2;
```

makes **p1** and **p2** point to the same location. **Value assignment,** which is represented by the statement

```
*p1 = *p2;
```

copies the values from the memory location addressed by `p2` into the location addressed by `p1`.

The special pointer NULL

In many pointer applications, it is useful to be able to store in a pointer variable a special value indicating that the variable does not in fact point to any valid data, at least for the present. C defines a special constant called `NULL` for this purpose.[1] The constant `NULL` can be assigned to any pointer variable and is represented internally as the address value 0.

If a pointer variable has the value `NULL`, it is important not to dereference that variable with the `*` operator. The intent of the `NULL` value is to indicate that the pointer does not point to valid data, so the idea of trying to find the data associated with a `NULL` pointer does not really make sense. Unfortunately, most compilers do not produce programs that explicitly check for this error. If you dereference `NULL`, most computers will interpret the 0 value as an address and return whatever data value is stored at address 0. If you happen to change that value by performing value assignment through a `NULL` pointer, the program can easily crash, giving no hint of the cause. The same problems can arise if you use pointer variables whose values have not yet been initialized.

The uses of the `NULL` pointer will be introduced in this text as they become relevant to a particular application. For now, the important thing to remember is that this constant exists.

Passing parameters by reference

To get a sense of how pointer variables are used in practice, it is helpful to look at one of the most common applications of pointers in C—the technique of passing pointers to a function to allow that function to manipulate data in its caller. In C, whenever you pass a simple variable from one function to another, the function gets a copy of the calling value. Assigning a new value to the parameter as part of the function changes the local copy but has no effect on the calling argument. For example, if you try to implement a function that initializes a variable to zero using the code

```
void SetToZero(int var)
{
    var = 0;
}
```

This function has no effect.

---

[1] The constant **NULL** is actually defined in the `stdlib.h` header file, which is automatically included whenever a program includes the `stdio.h` header file. Because all programs in this book include `stdio.h`, you can proceed as if **NULL** were a built-in constant in C.

the function has no effect whatever. If you call

```
SetToZero(x);
```

the parameter **var** is initialized to a copy of whatever value is stored in **x**. The assignment statement

```
var = 0;
```

inside the function sets the local copy to 0 but leaves **x** unchanged in the calling program.

One approach to fixing this problem is to pass the function a pointer to a variable instead of the variable itself. Although adopting this strategy changes the structure of the function, making this change is necessary for the function to work at all. The new coding is

```
void SetToZero(int *ip)
{
    *ip = 0;
}
```

To use this function, the caller must supply a pointer to an integer variable. To set **x** to 0, for example, you would need to make the following call:

```
SetToZero(&x);
```

Leaving out the **&** would be an error because **x** does not have the required type; **SetToZero** requires a pointer to an integer and not the integer itself.

The use of pointers as parameters makes it possible for functions to change values in the frame of their caller. In C, you must explicitly indicate your intention to allow such changes by declaring a parameter as a pointer type and then passing an address as the corresponding argument. This mechanism is referred to as **call by reference.**

In C, one of the common uses of call by reference occurs when a function needs to return more than one value to the calling program. A single result can easily be returned as the value of the function itself. If you need to return more than one result from a function, the return value is no longer appropriate. The standard approach to solving the problem is to turn that function into a procedure and pass values back and forth through the argument list.

As an example, suppose that you wanted to write a program to solve the quadratic equation

$$ax^2 + bx + c = 0$$

but that—because of your desire to practice good programming style—you were committed to dividing the work of the program into three phases as represented by the boxes in the following flowchart:

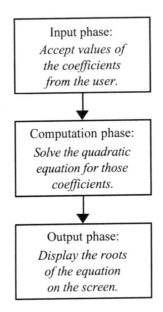

Decomposing this problem into separate functions that are responsible for each of these phases is somewhat tricky because several values must be passed from each phase to the next. Because there are three coefficients, you would like the input phase to return three values. Similarly, the computation phase must return two values, because a quadratic equation has two solutions.

Figure 2-1 shows how call by reference makes it possible to decompose the quadratic equation problem in this way. At each level, parameters that act as input to each function are passed in the conventional way; parameters that represent output from the function are declared as pointers and passed by reference.

■ 2.4 Arrays

An **array** is a collection of individual data values with two distinguishing characteristics:

1. *An array is ordered.* You must be able to count off the individual components of an array in order: here is the first, here is the second, and so on.
2. *An array is homogeneous.* Every value stored in an array must be of the same type. Thus, you can define an array of integers or an array of floating-point numbers but not an array in which the two types are mixed.

From an intuitive point of view, it is best to think of an array as a sequence of boxes, one box for each data value in the array. Each of the values in an array is called an **element.** For example, the following diagram represents an array with five elements:

FIGURE 2-1 Implementation of `quadeq.c` that illustrates call by reference

```c
/*
 * File: quadeq.c
 * --------------
 * This program finds roots of the quadratic equation
 *
 *          2
 *      a x    + b x  +  c = 0
 */

#include <stdio.h>
#include <math.h>
#include "genlib.h"
#include "simpio.h"

/* Private function prototypes */

static void GetCoefficients(double *pa, double *pb, double *pc);
static void SolveQuadratic(double a, double b, double c,
                           double *px1, double *px2);
static void DisplayRoots(double x1, double x2);

/* Main program */

main()
{
    double a, b, c, x1, x2;

    GetCoefficients(&a, &b, &c);
    SolveQuadratic(a, b, c, &x1, &x2);
    DisplayRoots(x1, x2);
}


/*
 * Function: GetCoefficients
 * Usage: GetCoefficients(&a, &b, &c);
 * -----------------------------------
 * This function is responsible for reading in the coefficients
 * of a quadratic equation.  The values of the coefficients are
 * passed back to the main program in the variables a, b, and c,
 * which are passed by reference.
 */

static void GetCoefficients(double *pa, double *pb, double *pc)
{
    printf("Enter coefficients for the quadratic equation:\n");
    printf("a: ");
    *pa = GetReal();
    printf("b: ");
    *pb = GetReal();
    printf("c: ");
    *pc = GetReal();
}
```

```
/*
 * Function: SolveQuadratic
 * Usage: SolveQuadratic(a, b, c, &x1, &x2);
 * -------------------------------------------
 * This function solves a quadratic equation.  The coefficients
 * are supplied as the arguments a, b, and c, and the roots are
 * returned in x1 and x2, which are passed by reference.
 */

static void SolveQuadratic(double a, double b, double c,
                           double *px1, double *px2)
{
    double disc, sqrtDisc;

    if (a == 0) Error("The coefficient a must be nonzero");
    disc = b * b - 4 * a * c;
    if (disc < 0) Error("The solutions are complex numbers");
    sqrtDisc = sqrt(disc);
    *px1 = (-b + sqrtDisc) / (2 * a);
    *px2 = (-b - sqrtDisc) / (2 * a);
}

/*
 * Function: DisplayRoots
 * Usage: DisplayRoots(x1, x2);
 * ----------------------------
 * This function displays the values x1 and x2, which are
 * the roots of a quadratic equation.
 */

static void DisplayRoots(double x1, double x2)
{
    if (x1 == x2) {
        printf("There is a double root at %g\n", x1);
    } else {
        printf("The roots are %g and %g\n", x1, x2);
    }
}
```

In C, each array has two fundamental properties:

- The **element type,** which is the type of value that can be stored in the elements of the array
- The **array size,** which is the number of elements the array contains

Whenever you create a new array in your program, you must specify both the element type and the array size.

Array declaration

Like any other variable in C, an array must be declared before it is used. The general form for an array declaration is

type name [*size*] ;

where *type* is the type of each element in the array, *name* is the name of the array variable, and *size* is a constant indicating the number of elements allocated to the array. For example, the declaration

```
int intArray[10];
```

declares an array named `intArray` with 10 elements, each of which is of type `int`. In most cases, however, you should specify the size as a symbolic constant rather than an explicit integer so that the array size is easier to change. Thus, a more conventional declaration would look like this:

```
#define NElements 10

int intArray[NElements];
```

You can represent this declaration pictorially by drawing a row of 10 boxes and giving the entire collection the name `intArray`:

`intArray`

Each element in the array is identified by a numeric value called its **index.** In C, the index numbers for an array always begin with 0 and run up to the array size minus one. Thus, in an array with 10 elements, the index numbers are 0, 1, 2, 3, 4, 5, 6, 7, 8, and 9, as the preceding diagram shows.

As is the case with any variable, you use the name of an array to indicate to other readers of the program what sort of value is being stored. For example, suppose that you wanted to define an array that was capable of holding the scores for a sporting event, such as gymnastics or figure skating, in which scores are assigned by a panel of judges. Each judge rates the performance on a scale from 0 to 10, with 10 being the highest score. Because a score may include a decimal fraction, as in 9.9, each element of the array must be of some floating-point type, such as `double`. Thus the declaration

```
#define NJudges 5

double scores[NJudges];
```

declares an array named `scores` with five elements, as shown in the following diagram:

Array selection

To refer to a specific element within an array, you specify both the array name and the index corresponding to the position of that element within the array. The process of identifying a particular element within an array is called **selection,** and is indicated in C by writing the name of the array and following it with the index written in square brackets. The result is a **selection expression,** which has the following form:

  array [*index*]

Within a program, a selection expression acts just like a simple variable. You can use it in an expression, and, in particular, you can assign a value to it. Thus, if the first judge (judge #0, since C counts array elements beginning at zero) awarded the contestant a score of 9.2, you could store that score in the array by writing the assignment statement

  scores[0] = 9.2;

The effect of this assignment can be diagrammed as follows:

You could then go ahead and assign scores for each of the other four judges using, for example, the statements

  scores[1] = 9.9;
  scores[2] = 9.7;
  scores[3] = 9.0;
  scores[4] = 9.5;

Executing these statements results in the following picture:

scores

9.2	9.9	9.7	9.0	9.5
0	1	2	3	4

In working with arrays, it is essential to understand the distinction between the *index* of an array element and the *value* of that element. For instance, the first box in the array has index 0, and its value is 9.2. It is also important to remember that you can change the values in an array but never the index numbers.

The real power of array selection comes from the fact that the index value need not be constant, but can be any expression that evaluates to an integer or any other scalar type. In many cases, the selection expression is the index variable of a `for` loop, which makes it easy to perform an operation on each element of the array in turn.   For example, you can set each element in the `scores` array to 0.0 with the following statement:

```
for (i = 0; i < NJudges; i++) {
    scores[i] = 0.0;
}
```

Effective and allocated sizes

At the time you write a program, you often will not know exactly how many elements an array will contain. The number of array elements usually depends on the user's data. Some users may require large amounts of array storage, while others need less. Unfortunately, you can't simply declare an array as

```
int dataValues[n];
```

Array bounds must be constant.

where `n` is a variable whose value changes in response to the needs of the application. C requires that arrays be declared with a constant size.

The usual strategy for solving this problem is to declare an array that is larger than you need and use only part of it. Thus, instead of declaring the array based on the *actual* number of elements—which you often do not know in advance—you define a constant indicating the *maximum* number of elements and use that constant in the declaration of the array. On any given use of the program, the actual number of elements is always less than or equal to this bound. When you use this strategy, you need to maintain a separate integer variable that keeps track of the number of values that are actually in use. The size of the array specified in the declaration is called the **allocated size;** the number of elements actively in use is called the **effective size.**

As an example, suppose that you wanted to change the declaration of the array `scores` introduced in the preceding section so that the program would work with any reasonable number of judges. Since you can't imagine that the number of judges at a sports event would ever be larger than 100, you might declare the array like this:

```
#define MaxJudges 100

int scores[MaxJudges];
```

To keep track of the effective size, you would need to declare an additional variable, as follows:

```
int nJudges;
```

Passing arrays as parameters

Functions in C can take entire arrays as parameters. When they do, it is common—particularly if the allocated and effective sizes might be different—to omit the maximum bound in the parameter declaration and use empty brackets instead. For example, the following function takes an array of type **double** and an integer indicating the effective size of the array and returns the **mean,** or arithmetic average, of the elements in the array:

```
double Mean(double array[], int n)
{
    int i;
    double total;

    total = 0;
    for (i = 0; i < n; i++) {
        total += array[i];
    }
    return (total / n);
}
```

When a function takes an array argument, the value of that argument is not copied in the way that simple variables are. Instead, the function always gets a pointer to the array, which means that the storage used for the parameter array is shared with that of the actual argument. Changing the value of an element of the parameter array therefore changes the value of the corresponding element in the argument array. A useful way to think about this behavior is that arrays are automatically passed by reference.

The use of arrays as parameters is illustrated by the **gymjudge.c** program shown in Figure 2-2, which asks the user to enter the score for each judge and then displays the average score. Note that the **ReadAllScores** function depends on the fact that arrays are passed by reference. The whole point of the function is to fill up the elements in the array **scores.** If **ReadAllScores** were unable to make changes to the elements of the calling array, you would be forced to seek a different implementation strategy.

Initialization of arrays

Array variables can be given initial values at the time they are declared. In this case, the equal sign specifying the initial value is followed by a list of initializers enclosed in curly braces. For example, the declaration

```
int digits[10] = { 0, 1, 2, 3, 4, 5, 6, 7, 8, 9 };
```

declares an array called **digits** in which each of the 10 elements is initialized to its own index number. When initializers are provided for an array, it is legal to omit the array size from the declaration. Thus, you could also write the declaration of **digits** like this:

```
int digits[] = { 0, 1, 2, 3, 4, 5, 6, 7, 8, 9 };
```

FIGURE 2-2   Program to average a set of scores

```c
/*
 * File: gymjudge.c
 * ----------------
 * This program averages a set of gymnastic scores.
 */

#include <stdio.h>
#include "genlib.h"
#include "simpio.h"

/* Constants */

#define MaxJudges 100
#define MinScore    0.0
#define MaxScore   10.0

/* Private function prototypes */

static void ReadAllScores(double scores[], int nJudges);
static double GetScore(int judge);
static double Mean(double array[], int n);

/* Main program */

main()
{
    double scores[MaxJudges];
    int nJudges;

    printf("Enter number of judges: ");
    nJudges = GetInteger();
    if (nJudges > MaxJudges) Error("Too many judges");
    ReadAllScores(scores, nJudges);
    printf("The average score is %.2f\n", Mean(scores, nJudges));
}

/*
 * Function: ReadAllScores
 * Usage: ReadAllScores(scores, nJudges);
 * --------------------------------------
 * This function reads in scores for each of the judges.  The
 * array scores must be declared by the caller and must have
 * an allocated size that is at least as large as nJudges.
 */

static void ReadAllScores(double scores[], int nJudges)
{
    int i;

    for (i = 0; i < nJudges; i++) {
        scores[i] = GetScore(i);
    }
}
```

```
/*
 * Function: GetScore
 * Usage: score = GetScore(judge);
 * -----------------------------
 * This function reads in the score for the specified judge.
 * The implementation makes sure that the score is in the
 * legal range before returning.
 */

static double GetScore(int judge)
{
    double score;

    while (TRUE) {
        printf("Score for judge #%d: ", judge);
        score = GetReal();
        if (score >= MinScore && score <= MaxScore) break;
        printf("That score is out of range.  Try again.\n");
    }
    return (score);
}

/*
 * Function: Mean
 * Usage: mean = Mean(array, n);
 * -----------------------------
 * This function returns the statistical mean (average) of a
 * distribution stored in array, which has effective size n.
 */

static double Mean(double array[], int n)
{
    int i;
    double total;

    total = 0;
    for (i = 0; i < n; i++) {
        total += array[i];
    }
    return (total / n);
}
```

When the compiler encounters an array declaration that includes initializers but no size specification, it counts the number of initializers and reserves exactly that many elements for the array. In the `digits` example, there is little advantage in leaving out the array bound. You know that there are 10 digits and that new digits are not going to be added to this list. For arrays whose initial values may need to change over the life cycle of the program, having the compiler compute the array size from the initializers is useful for program maintenance because it frees the programmer from having to maintain the element count as the program evolves.

For example, imagine you're writing a program that requires an array containing the names of all U.S. cities with populations of over 1,000,000. Taking data from the 1990 census, you could declare and initialize `bigCities` as a static global array using the following declaration:

```
static string bigCities[] = {
    "New York",
    "Los Angeles",
    "Chicago",
    "Houston",
    "Philadelphia",
    "San Diego",
    "Detroit",
    "Dallas",
};
```

When the figures are in from the 2000 census, it is likely that Phoenix and San Antonio will have joined this list. If they have, you can then simply add their names to the initializer list. The compiler will expand the array size to accommodate the new values. Note that the last initializer for the `bigCities` array is followed by a comma. This comma is optional, but it is good programming practice to include it. Doing so allows you to add new cities without having to change the existing entries in the initializer list.

If you write a program that uses the `bigCities` array, you will probably need to know how many cities the list contains. The compiler has this number because it counted the initializers. The question is how to make that information available to the program. In C, there is a standard idiom for determining the number of elements in an array whose size is established by static initialization. Given any array **a**, the number of elements in **a** can be computed using the expression

```
sizeof a / sizeof a[0]
```

Described in English, this expression takes the size of the entire array and divides it by the size of the initial element in the array. Because all elements of an array are the same size, the result is the number of elements in the array, regardless of the element type. Thus you could initialize a variable `nBigCities` to hold the number of cities in the `bigCities` array by writing

```
static int nBigCities = sizeof bigCities / sizeof bigCities[0];
```

Multidimensional arrays

In C, the elements of an array can be of any type. In particular, the elements of an array can themselves be arrays. Arrays of arrays are called **multidimensional arrays.** The most common form is the two-dimensional array, which is most often used to represent data in which the individual entries form a rectangular structure marked off into rows and columns. This type of two-dimensional structure is called a **matrix.** Arrays of three or more dimensions are also legal in C but occur much less frequently.

The following declaration, for example, introduces a 3 × 3 matrix, each of whose elements is of type **double**:

```
double mat[3][3];
```

Conceptually, the storage for **mat** forms a two-dimensional structure in which the individual elements are laid out like this:

mat[0][0]	mat[0][1]	mat[0][2]
mat[1][0]	mat[1][1]	mat[1][2]
mat[2][0]	mat[2][1]	mat[2][2]

Internally, C represents the variable **mat** as an array of three elements, each of which is an array of three floating-point values. The memory allocated to **m** consists of nine cells arranged in the following form:

In the two-dimensional diagram, the first index is assumed to indicate the row number. This choice, however, is arbitrary because the two-dimensional geometry of the matrix is entirely conceptual; in memory, these values form a one-dimensional list. If you want the first index to indicate the column and the second to indicate the row, you do not need to change the declaration, only the way in which you select the elements. In terms of the internal arrangement, however, it is always true that the first index value varies least rapidly. Thus all the elements of **mat[0]** appear in memory before any elements of **mat[1]**.

Multidimensional arrays are passed between functions just as single-dimensional arrays are. The parameter declaration in the function header looks like the original declaration of the variable and includes the index information. C requires that you specify the size of each index in a parameter array, except for the first. However, because leaving out the first index bound makes the declaration unsymmetrical, it is common to include the array bounds for each index in the declaration of a multidimensional array parameter.

You can use static initialization with multidimensional arrays just as with single-dimensional arrays. To emphasize the overall structure, the values used to initialize each internal array are usually enclosed in an additional set of curly braces. For example, the declaration

```
static double identityMatrix[3][3] = {
    { 1.0, 0.0, 0.0 },
    { 0.0, 1.0, 0.0 },
    { 0.0, 0.0, 1.0 }
};
```

declares a 3×3 matrix of floating-point numbers and initializes it to contain the following values:

1.0	0.0	0.0
0.0	1.0	0.0
0.0	0.0	1.0

This particular matrix comes up frequently in mathematical applications and is called the **identity matrix.**

As in the case of parameters, the declaration of a statically initialized multidimensional array must specify all index bounds except possibly the first, which can be determined by counting the initializers. As was true with parameters, however, it is usually best to specify all the index bounds explicitly when you declare a multidimensional array.

◼ 2.5 Pointers and arrays

In C, arrays and pointers are defined in such a way that a complete understanding of either topic requires that you understand the other. Arrays, for example, are implemented internally as pointers. The operations on pointers only make sense if you consider them in relation to an array. Thus, in order to give you the full picture of how arrays and pointers work, it is important to consider the two concepts together.

To get a sense of the relationship, consider the simple array declaration

```
double list[3];
```

which reserves enough space for three values of type **double**. Assuming that a **double** is eight bytes long, the memory diagram for the array would look like this:

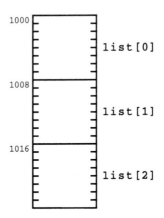

Because each of the elements in the array is an lvalue, it has an address that can be derived using the **&** operator. For example, the expression

&list[1]

has the pointer value 1008 because the element **list[1]** is stored at that address. Moreover, the index value need not be constant. The selection expression

list[i]

is an lvalue, and it is therefore legal to write

&list[i]

which indicates the address of the ith element in **list**.

Because the address of the ith element in **list** depends on the value of the variable **i**, the C compiler cannot compute this address when compiling the program. To determine the address, the compiler generates instructions that take the base address of the array and then add the value of **i** multiplied by the size of each array element in bytes. Thus, the numeric calculation necessary to find the address of **list[i]** is given by the formula

$$1000 + i \times 8$$

If **i** is 2, for example, the result of the address calculation is 1016, which matches the address shown in the diagram for **list[2]**. Because the process of calculating the address of an array element is entirely automatic, you don't have to worry about the details when writing your programs.

Pointer arithmetic

In C, you can apply the operators **+** and **–** to pointers. The results are similar to the familiar arithmetic operations in certain respects but different in others. The process of applying addition and subtraction to pointer values is called **pointer arithmetic.**

Pointer arithmetic is defined by a simple rule. If **p** is a pointer to the initial element in an array **arr**, and **k** is an integer, the following identity always holds:

p + k   *is defined to be*   **&arr[k]**

In other words, if you add an integer **k** to a pointer value, the result is the address of the array element at index **k** for an array beginning at the original pointer address.

To illustrate how this rule applies, let's suppose that a function contains the following declarations:

```
double list[3];
double *p;
```

Each of these variables is given space in the frame for this function. For the array variable **list**, the compiler allocates space for the three elements in the array, each of which is large enough to hold a **double**. For **p**, the compiler allocates enough space for a pointer, which will be used to hold the address of some lvalue of type **double**. If the frame begins at location 1000, the memory allocation looks like this:

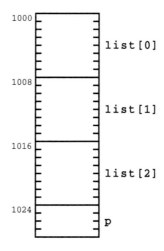

Since no values have been assigned to any of these variables, their initial contents are undefined. Suppose that you use the following assignment statements to store values in each of the array elements:

```
list[0] = 1.0;
list[1] = 1.1;
list[2] = 1.2;
```

and initialize the pointer variable **p** to the beginning of the array by executing the assignment statement

```
p = &list[0];
```

After these assignments, the memory cells hold the following values:

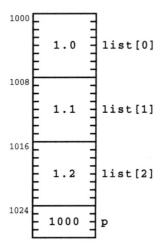

In this diagram, **p** now points to the initial address in the array **list**. If you add an integer **k** to the pointer **p**, the result is the address corresponding to the array element at index position **k**. For example, if a program contained the expression

    p + 2

the result of evaluating this expression would be a new pointer value that references **list[2]**. Thus, in the preceding diagram, in which **p** points to address 1000, **p + 2** points to the address of the element that appears two elements later in the array, which is at address 1016. It's important to note that pointer addition is not equivalent to traditional addition because the arithmetic must take into account the size of the base type. In this example, for each unit that is added to a pointer value, the internal numeric value must be increased by eight to take account of the fact that a **double** requires eight bytes.

The C compiler interprets subtraction of an integer from a pointer in a similar way. The expression

    p - k

in which **p** is a pointer and **k** is an integer, computes the address of an array element located **k** elements before the address currently indicated by **p**. Thus, if you had set **p** to the address of **list[1]** using

    p = &list[1];

the addresses corresponding to **p − 1** and **p + 1** would be the addresses of **list[0]** and **list[2]**, respectively.

The arithmetic operations *****, **/**, and **%** make no sense for pointers and cannot be used with pointer operands. Moreover, the uses of **+** and **−** with pointers are limited.

In C, you can add or subtract an integer from a pointer, but you cannot, for example, add two pointers together. The only other arithmetic operation defined for pointers is subtracting one pointer from another. The expression

```
p1 - p2
```

where both `p1` and `p2` are pointers, is defined to return the number of array elements between the current values of `p2` and `p1`. For example, if `p1` points at `list[2]` and `p2` points at `list[0]`, the expression

```
p1 - p2
```

has the value 2, since there are two elements between the current pointer values.

Incrementing and decrementing pointers

The definition of pointer arithmetic makes it possible to explain one of the most common idiomatic constructions in C, which is the expression

```
*p++
```

In this expression, the `*` operator and the `++` operator compete for the operand `p`. Because unary operators in C are evaluated in right-to-left order, the `++` takes precedence over the `*`, so the compiler interprets this expression as if it had been written like this:

```
* (p++)
```

As you learned in Chapter 1, the postfix `++` operator increments the value of `p` and then returns the value that `p` had prior to the increment operation. Since `p` is a pointer, you need to define the increment operation in terms of pointer arithmetic. Thus, in evaluating `p+1`, you know that the resulting value should point to the next element in the array. If `p` originally pointed to `arr[0]`, for example, the increment operation would cause it to point to `arr[1]`. Thus, the expression

```
*p++
```

has the following meaning in English:

> Dereference the pointer `p` and return as an lvalue the object to which it currently points. As a side effect, increment the value of `p` so that, if the original lvalue was an element in an array, the new value of `p` points to the next element in that array.

To see why this operator might be useful, it is necessary to consider in more detail how pointers and arrays relate to each other.

The relationship between pointers and arrays

Among the unusual characteristics of C, one of the most interesting is that the name of an array is treated as being synonymous with a pointer to the initial element in that array. This concept is most easily illustrated by example.

The declaration

```
int intList[5];
```

allocates space for an array of five integers, which is assigned storage somewhere inside the computer's memory, as illustrated in the following diagram:

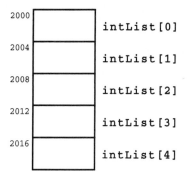

The name `intList` represents an array but can also be used directly as a pointer value. When it is used as a pointer, `intList` is defined to be the address of the initial element in the array. For any array `arr`, the following identity always holds in C:

> `arr`   *is defined to be identical to*   `&arr[0]`

Given any array name, you can assign its address directly to any pointer variable.

The most common example of this equivalence occurs when an array is passed from one function to another. For example, suppose that you make the function call

```
sum = SumIntegerArray(intList, 5);
```

where the definition of `SumIntegerArray` is

```
int SumIntegerArray(int array[], int n)
{
    int i, sum;

    sum = 0;
    for (i = 0; i < n; i++) {
        sum += array[i];
    }
    return (sum);
}
```

The `SumIntegerArray` function would work exactly the same way if the prototype had been written as

```
int SumIntegerArray(int *array, int n)
```

In this case, the first argument is declared as a pointer, but the effect is the same as in the preceding implementation, which declared this parameter as an array. The address of the first element in `intList` is copied into the formal parameter `array` and manipulated using pointer arithmetic. Inside the machine, the declarations are equivalent and the same operations can be applied in either case.

As a general rule, you should declare parameters in the way that reflects their use. If you intend to use a parameter as an array and select elements from it, you should declare that parameter as an array. If you intend to use the parameter as a pointer and dereference it, you should declare it as a pointer. For example, a pointer-based implementation of `SumIntegerArray` that is consistent in its declaration and use of its argument might look like this:

```
int SumIntegerArray(int *ip, int n)
{
    int i, sum;

    sum = 0;
    for (i = 0; i < n; i++) {
        sum += *ip++;
    }
    return (sum);
}
```

The crucial difference between arrays and pointers in C comes into play when variables are originally declared, not when those values are passed as parameters. The fundamental distinction between the declaration

```
int array[5];
```

and the declaration

```
int *p;
```

is one of memory allocation. The first declaration reserves five consecutive words of memory capable of holding the array elements. The second declaration reserves only a single word, which is large enough to hold a machine address. The implication of this difference is extremely important to you as a programmer. If you declare an array, you have storage to work with; if you declare a pointer variable, that variable is not associated with any storage until you initialize it.

Given your current level of understanding, the only way to use a pointer as an array is to initialize the pointer by assigning the base address of the array to the pointer variable. If, after making the preceding declarations, you were to write

```
p = array;
```

the pointer variable `p` would then point to the same address used for `array`, and you could use the two names interchangeably.

The technique of setting a pointer to the address of an existing array is rather limited. After all, if you already have an array name, you might as well use it. Assigning that name to a pointer does not really do you any good. The real advantage of using a pointer as an array comes from the fact that you can initialize that pointer to new memory that has not previously been allocated, which allows you to create new arrays as the program runs. This important programming technique is described in the section on "Dynamic allocation" later in this chapter.

◼ 2.6 Records

To understand the idea of a record, imagine for a moment that you are in charge of the payroll system for a small company. You need to keep track of various pieces of information about each employee. For example, in order to print a paycheck, you need to know the employee's name, job title, Social Security number, salary, withholding status, and perhaps some additional data as well. These pieces of information, taken together, form the employee's data record.

What do employee records look like? It is often easiest to think of records as entries in a table. For example, consider the case of the small firm of Scrooge and Marley, portrayed in Charles Dickens's *A Christmas Carol*, as it might appear in this day of Social Security numbers and withholding allowances. The employee roster contains two records, which might have the following values:

Name	*Job title*	*Soc. Sec. #*	*Salary*	*# With.*
`Ebenezer Scrooge`	`Partner`	`271-82-8183`	`250.00`	`1`
`Bob Cratchit`	`Clerk`	`314-15-9265`	`15.00`	`7`

Each record is broken up into individual components that provide a specific piece of information about the employee. Each of these components is usually called a **field,** although the term **member** is also used, particularly in the context of C programming. For example, given an employee record, you can talk about the name field or the salary field. Each of the fields is associated with a type, which may be different for different fields. The name and title field are strings, the salary field might well be represented as a floating-point number, and the number of withholding exemptions is presumably an integer. The Social Security number could be represented as either an integer or a string; because Social Security numbers are too big to fit within the limits imposed on integers by many systems, they are represented here as strings.

Even though a record is made up of individual fields, it must have meaning as a coherent whole. In the example of the employee roster, the fields in the first line of the table represent a logically consistent set of data referring to Ebenezer Scrooge; those in the second line refer to Bob Cratchit. The conceptual integrity of each record suggests that the data for that employee should be collected into a compound data structure. Moreover, since the individual fields making up that structure are of different types, arrays are not suited to the task. In cases such as this, you need to define the set of data for each employee as a record.

Defining a new structure type

Creating new records in C is conceptually a two-step process.

1. *Define a new structure type.* Before you declare any variables, you must first define a new structure type. The type definition specifies what fields make up the record, what the names of those fields are, and what type of information each field contains. This structure type defines a model for all objects that have the new type but does not by itself reserve any storage.
2. *Declare variables of the new type.* Once you have defined the new type, you can then declare variables of that type so that you can store actual data values.

Although it is not strictly necessary, this text uses the **typedef** facility to ensure that every new structure type has a simple type name. The general form for defining a new structure type looks like this:

```
typedef struct {
    field-declarations
} name;
```

where *field-declarations* are standard variable declarations used to define the fields of the structure and *name* indicates the name of the newly defined type. For example, the following code defines a new structure type called **employeeRecordT** to represent employee records:

```
typedef struct {
    string name;
    string title;
    string ssnum;
    double salary;
    int withholding;
} employeeRecordT;
```

This definition provides a template for all objects that have the new type **employeeRecordT**. Each such object will have five fields, starting with a **name** field, which is a **string**, and continuing through a **withholding** field, which is an **int**.

Declaring structure variables

Now that you have defined a new type, the next step is to declare variables of that type. For example, given the type **employeeRecordT**, you can declare **empRec** to be a variable of that type by writing

```
employeeRecordT empRec;
```

If you want to illustrate this variable using a box diagram, you can choose to represent it in either of two ways. If you take a very general view of the situation—which corresponds conceptually to looking at the diagram from a considerable distance—what you see is just a box named **empRec**:

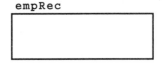

If, on the other hand, you step close enough to see the details, you discover that the box labeled `empRec` is composed internally of five individual boxes:

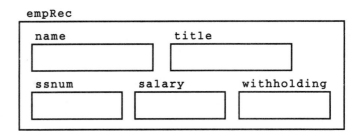

Record selection

Once you have declared the variable `empRec` by writing

```
employeeRecordT empRec;
```

you can refer to the record as a whole simply by using its name. To refer to a specific field within a record, you write the name of the complete record, followed by a period, followed by the name of the field. Thus, to refer to the job title of the employee stored in `empRec`, you need to write

```
empRec.title
```

When used in this context, the period is invariably called a *dot,* so that you would read this expression aloud as "`empRec` dot `title`." Selecting a field using the dot operator is called **record selection.**

Initializing records

As with any other type of variable, you can initialize the contents of a record variable by assigning values to its components. The dot operator returns an lvalue, which means that you can assign values to a record selection expression. For example, if you were to execute the statements

```
empRec.name = "Ebenezer Scrooge";
empRec.title = "Partner";
empRec.ssnum = "271-82-8183";
empRec.salary = 250.00;
empRec.withholding = 1;
```

you would create the employee record for Ebenezer Scrooge used in the earlier examples.

You can also initialize its contents at the time the record is declared, using much the same syntax as you use to initialize the elements of an array. Initializers for a record are specified in the order in which they appear in the structure definition. Thus, you could declare and initialize a static global record named **manager** that contains the data for Mr. Scrooge, as follows:

```
static employeeRecordT manager = {
    "Ebenezer Scrooge", "Partner", "271-82-8183", 250.00, 1
};
```

Pointers to records

Although small records are sometimes used directly in C, variables that hold structured data in C are usually declared to be pointers to records rather than the records themselves. A pointer to a record is usually smaller and more easily manipulated than the record itself. More importantly, if you pass a pointer to a record to a procedure, that procedure can change the contents of the record. If you try to pass the record itself, the record will be copied (just as an integer is copied), and you will then be unable to make any permanent changes. Passing a pointer to a record allows functions to manipulate the fields of that record.

Suppose, for example, that you want to declare a variable that points to employee records. The syntax for such a declaration is the same as that for any other pointer. The line

```
employeeRecordT *empPtr;
```

declares the variable **empPtr** as a pointer to an object of type **employeeRecordT**. When you make this declaration, space is reserved only for the pointer itself. Before using **empPtr**, you still need to provide the actual storage for the fields in the complete record. The best approach is to allocate space for a new record as described in the next section, on "Dynamic allocation." For the moment, let's assume that the earlier declaration

```
employeeRecordT empRec;
```

is still around, which means that you can make **empPtr** point to the **empRec** record by writing

```
empPtr = &empRec;
```

The conceptual picture of memory now looks like this:

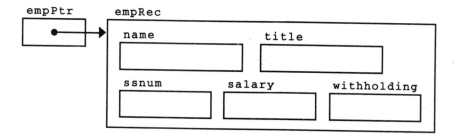

Starting from `empPtr`, how can you refer to an individual field in the underlying record? In seeking an answer to this question, it is easy to be misled by your intuition. It is *not* appropriate to write, for example,

`*empPtr.salary` The order of operations is incorrect.

Contrary to what you might have expected, this statement does not select the salary component of the object to which `empPtr` points, because the precedence of the operators in the expression does not support that interpretation. The selection operator takes precedence over dereferencing, so the expression has the meaningless interpretation

`* (empPtr.salary)`

rather than the intended

`(*empPtr) .salary`

The latter form has the desired effect but is much too cumbersome for everyday use. Pointers to structures are used all the time. Forcing programmers to include parentheses in every selection would make records much less convenient. For this reason, C defines the operator `->`, which combines the operations of dereference and selection into a single operator. Thus, the conventional way to refer to the salary in the record to which `empPtr` points is to write

`empPtr->salary`

■ 2.7 Dynamic allocation

Up to this point in the text, you have seen two mechanisms for assigning memory to variables. When you declare a global variable, the compiler allocates memory space for that variable which persists throughout the entire program. This style of allocation is called **static allocation** because the variables are assigned to fixed locations in memory. When you declare a local variable inside a function, the space for that variable is allocated on the system stack. Calling the function assigns memory to the variable; that memory is freed when the function returns. This style of allocation is called **automatic allocation.** There is also a third way of allocating memory that permits you to acquire new memory when you need it and to free it explicitly when it is no longer needed. The process of acquiring new storage while the program is running is called **dynamic allocation.**

When a program is loaded into memory, it usually occupies only a fraction of the available storage. In most systems, you can allocate some of the unused storage to the program whenever it needs more memory. For example, if you need space for a new array while the program is running, you can reserve part of the unallocated memory, leaving the rest for subsequent allocations. The pool of unallocated memory available to a program is called the **heap.**

As part of the ANSI `stdlib` library, C provides several functions for allocating new memory from the heap. The most common function is `malloc`, which allocates a block of memory of a particular size given in bytes. For example, if you want to allocate 10 bytes of memory, you call

```
malloc(10)
```

which returns a pointer to a block of storage 10 bytes in size. In order to use the newly allocated storage, you must store the result of `malloc` in a pointer variable, after which you can use that pointer variable just like an array.

The type `void *`

Before giving examples of the use of `malloc`, it is important to clear up a few potentially thorny issues. In C, pointers have types. If you declare a variable `ip` by writing

```
int *ip;
```

that variable has the conceptual type pointer-to-`int`. The declaration

```
char *cp;
```

introduces a variable `cp` whose type is pointer-to-`char`. In ANSI C, these types are distinct, and the compiler will issue a warning message if you try to assign one pointer to a pointer variable with a different base type.

The idea that pointers have types raises the question of what type `malloc` returns. The `malloc` function is used to allocate new storage for any type of value that the caller desires and must therefore return a "general" pointer of an as-yet-unspecified type. In C, the general pointer type is indicated as if were a pointer to the nonexistent type `void`, which is also used to indicate a function that returns no value or an empty parameter list. If you declare a pointer to be of type pointer-to-`void`, as in

```
void *vp;
```

you can store a pointer value of any type in that variable. You are not, however, allowed to use the `*` operator to dereference `vp`. The compiler has no idea what base type to use for `vp`, so there is no meaningful way to talk about the value to which `vp` points.

The type `void *` is nonetheless useful because it allows functions—`malloc`, in particular—to return general pointers whose actual types the caller can establish later. The `malloc` function takes one argument, which is the number of bytes required.[2] Because it returns a pointer value of type `void *`, its prototype looks like this:

---

[2] The argument type to `malloc` is actually the type `size_t`, which is defined in the `stddef.h` header file. On some machines, the type `int` may not be large enough to represent the size of a large block of memory. In any event, the argument is conceptually an integer.

```
void *malloc(int nBytes);
```

Note that the result type of this function prototype is declared in much the same way that a pointer variable is. The * indicating that the result is a pointer is syntactically associated with the function name, and not with the base type, even though the conceptual association works the other way around. C's syntax for functions that return pointer values can be confusing until you get used to it.

ANSI C performs automatic conversions between the type pointer-to-**void** and pointer types that specify an explicit base type. For example, if you declare the character pointer **cp** as

```
char *cp;
```

you can assign the result of **malloc** to it directly, using the statement

```
cp = malloc(10);
```

Partly for historical reasons and partly because doing so makes the conversion between pointer types explicit, many programmers write this statement using a type cast to convert the result of **malloc** to a character pointer before making the assignment, as follows:

```
cp = (char *) malloc(10);
```

Whether or not the explicit type cast is used, this statement has the effect of allocating 10 bytes of new memory space and storing the address of the first byte in **cp**.

Coping with memory limitations

Although they are getting larger all the time, computer memory systems are finite in size. As a result, the heap will eventually run out of space. When this occurs, **malloc** returns the pointer **NULL** to indicate that it is unable to allocate a block of the requested size. If you are a conscientious programmer, you should check for this possibility on every call to **malloc**. Thus, when you allocate storage in the heap, you need to write something like

```
cp = malloc(10);
if (cp == NULL) Error("No memory available");
```

Because dynamic allocation is used frequently in a wide class of programs, error checking—as important as it is—can become tedious. It also has a tendency to obscure the structure of the algorithm by cluttering the code with error messages. When you run out of memory, there is usually nothing you can do about it; having the program display an error message and halt is often the only reasonable option. Thus, it probably makes sense to define a new function that combines the action of **malloc** with the test for the **NULL** result. That function is provided as part of the **genlib** library under the name **GetBlock**. If **GetBlock** detects the out-of-memory condition, it simply calls the **Error** function. Thus, you can replace the preceding two lines of code with

```
cp = GetBlock(10);
```

One way to help ensure that you don't run out of memory is to free any storage you have allocated when you are finished using it. The standard ANSI libraries provide a function **free**, which takes a pointer previously allocated by **malloc** and returns the memory associated with that pointer to the heap. If, for example, you determine that you are completely finished using the storage allocated for **arr**, you can free that storage for later reuse by calling

```
free(arr);
```

For symmetry with the **GetBlock** function, however, the **genlib** library includes a **FreeBlock** function, which is identical in operation to **free**. Because **GetBlock** and **FreeBlock** streamline the memory allocation operations and make the programs that use them easier to read, this text generally uses these function in preference to **malloc** and **free**.

Knowing when to free a piece of memory is not always an easy task, particularly as programs become large. If several parts of a program share some data structure that has been allocated in the heap, it may not be possible for any single part to recognize that the memory can be freed. Given the size of memories today, however, you can often allocate whatever memory you need without ever bothering to free it again. The problem of limited memory typically becomes critical only when you design an application that needs to run for a long period of time, such as the operating system on which all the other facilities of the system depend. In these applications, it is important to free memory when you no longer need it.

Some languages, including Java, support a system for dynamic allocation that actively goes through memory to see what parts of it are in use, freeing any storage that is no longer needed. This strategy is called **garbage collection.** Garbage-collecting allocators exist for C, and it is likely that their use will increase in coming years, particularly as people become more familiar with their advantages. If it does, the policy of ignoring deallocation will become reasonable even in long-running applications because you can rely on the garbage collector to perform the deallocation operations automatically.

For the most part, this text assumes that your applications fall into the class of problems for which allocating memory whenever you need it is a workable strategy. This assumption will simplify your life considerably and make it easier for you to concentrate on algorithmic details.

Dynamic arrays

From a conceptual perspective, an assignment of the form

```
cp = GetBlock(10);
```

creates the following configuration in memory:

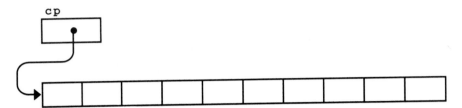

The variable `cp` points to a set of 10 consecutive bytes that have been allocated in the heap. Because pointers and arrays are freely interchangeable in C, the variable now acts exactly as if it had been declared as an array of 10 characters.

Arrays that you allocate on the heap and reference using a pointer variable are called **dynamic arrays** and play a significant role in modern programming. The principal differences between declared arrays and dynamic arrays are that

- The memory associated with a declared array is allocated automatically as part of the declaration process. When the frame for the function declaring the array is created, all the elements of that array are allocated as part of the frame. In the case of a dynamic array, the actual memory is not allocated until you call the `malloc` function.
- The size of a declared array must be a constant in the program. In contrast, because their memory comes from the heap, dynamic arrays can be of any size. Moreover, you can adjust the size of a dynamic array according to the amount of data. If you know you need an array with precisely N elements, you can reserve just the right amount of storage.

You can allocate a dynamic array using the standard `malloc` function. For example, if you wanted to initialize the variable `darray` to a dynamic array of `n` values of type `double`, you would declare `darray` using the line

```
double *darray;
```

and then execute the following code:

```
darray = malloc(n * sizeof(double));
if (darray == NULL) Error("No memory available");
```

To make this process as clean as possible conceptually, the `genlib` library defines a function `NewArray`, which takes the number of elements and the base type and then uses `GetBlock` to return a pointer to a dynamic array of the specified size.[3] Thus, the preceding lines of code can be replaced by

```
darray = NewArray(n, double);
```

---

[3] In actuality, both the **NewArray** function and the **New** function in the next section are implemented as *preprocessor macros* rather than as functions, although the distinction is not relevant to you as a programmer. For the actual definitions, see the text of the header file `genlib.h`.

Dynamic records

Dynamic memory allocation is just as useful for records as it is for arrays. If you declare a pointer to a record, you can allocate memory to store the actual data in the record by calling `GetBlock` or `malloc`. For example, if the type `employeeRecordT` is defined as

```
typedef struct {
    string name;
    string title;
    string ssnum;
    double salary;
    int withholding;
} employeeRecordT;
```

you can assign space for a newly allocated record to the variable `empPtr` as follows:

```
employeeRecordT *empPtr;

empPtr = GetBlock(sizeof(employeeRecordT));
```

In this example, the type name `employeeRecordT` corresponds to the record. Variables like `empPtr` are declared explicitly as pointers to that type. While this approach is certainly workable, it often makes more sense to define record types in a slightly different way. When you use the coding style in this most recent example, you have to think about two distinct types: the `employeeRecordT` record itself and the pointer to it. For the sake of conceptual economy, it would be better if there were only one type. In many applications, you never refer to a record type without using a pointer. In such cases, there is no reason to name the record type at all. You can instead define a type name that refers to the pointer, which then becomes the only type you need to consider.

To make this change in the employee example, you can change the type definition so that it defines `employeeT` as a pointer to a record, as follows:

```
typedef struct {
    string name;
    string title;
    string ssnum;
    double salary;
    int withholding;
} *employeeT;
```

The difference in the definition syntax is simply the asterisk before `employeeT`. The new definition indicates that a value of type `employeeT` points to a record of the given description, even though that record type itself has no explicit name.

Once you have established the new type definition, you can declare variables of type `employeeT` just like any other variable. The declaration

```
employeeT emp;
```

defines the variable `emp` to be of type `employeeT`. Because the definition of `employeeT` includes the pointer, the variable `emp` is automatically declared as a pointer value even though no asterisk appears in the declaration.

For types that are defined as pointers to records, the `genlib` library defines a function `New` that takes a pointer type as argument and returns a pointer to a newly allocated area of memory large enough to hold the underlying value. Thus, if you write

```
emp = New(employeeT);
```

the system allocates space in the heap for the unnamed employee record and returns a pointer to it.

Most of the new types defined in this text, including all the abstract data types introduced in Parts Three and Four, define the pointer as the principal type rather than the underlying record. The major reason for doing so is to emphasize the fact that this data value is a single entity with integrity as a whole. Other programmers prefer to see the pointers made explicit, and you will see both coding disciplines in professional code.

▓▓ Summary

In this chapter, you have learned how to use the data structure definition capabilities of C to create new data types. The data structures presented in this chapter—pointers, arrays, and records—form the foundation for abstract data types, which are presented in Part Three of this text. The principal advantage of these structures is that you can use them to represent data in a way that reflects the real-world structure of an application. Moreover, by combining pointers, arrays, and records in the right way, you can create hierarchical structures that allow you to manage data complexity in much the same way that decomposing a large program into separate functions allows you to manage algorithmic complexity.

Important points in this chapter include:

- C allows you to define new atomic types by listing the elements that comprise the domain of the type. Such types are called *enumeration types* and are part of a more general class called *scalar types* that also includes characters and integers.
- The `typedef` keyword in C allows you to introduce new type names. If you take any variable declaration and precede it with the `typedef` keyword, the statement no longer declares variables but instead defines new names for the corresponding types.
- Data values inside a computer are represented as collections of bits that are organized into larger structures called *bytes* and *words*. Every byte in memory is associated with a numeric address that can be used to refer to the data contained at that location.
- Addresses of data in memory are themselves data values and can be manipulated as such by a program. A data value that is the address of some

other piece of data is called a *pointer*. Pointer variables are declared in C by writing an asterisk in front of the variable name in its declaration line.

■ The fundamental operations on pointers are & and *, which indicate the address of a stored value and the value stored at a particular address, respectively.

■ There is a special pointer value called NULL, which is used to indicate that a pointer does not refer to anything.

■ Pointers make it possible for a function to change the value of parameters passed by the caller. This technique is known as *call by reference*.

■ An *array* is an ordered, homogeneous collection of data values composed of elements indicated by an index number. In C, index numbers in an array always begin with 0. Arrays are declared by specifying a constant size in square brackets after the name of the array. The size specified in the declaration is called the *allocated size* of the array and is typically larger than the *effective size*, which is the number of elements actually in use.

■ When an array is passed as a parameter, the elements of the array are not copied. Instead, the function is given the address of the actual array. As a result, if a function changes the values of any elements of an array passed as a parameter, those changes will be visible to the caller, which is working with the same array.

■ If the operators + and − are applied to pointers, the pointer value is scaled by the size of the base type. This behavior increases the symmetry between pointers and arrays and allows C programmers to use these structures interchangeably.

■ A *record* is a heterogeneous collection of data values that forms a logically consistent unit. This text uses **typedef** to define a type name for each new record, which then serves as a template for any subsequent declarations.

■ The storage for arrays and records can be allocated dynamically from a pool of unused memory called the *heap*. Because dynamic allocation is viewed as a fundamental operation, this text uses the functions **NewArray**(*size, type*) and **New**(*type*) to allocate dynamic arrays and records, respectively. These functions are defined in the **genlib** library.

REVIEW QUESTIONS

1. Define each of the following terms: *pointer, array, record*.

2. What type definition would you use to define a new enumeration type **polygonT** consisting of the following elements: **Triangle, Square, Pentagon, Hexagon, Octagon**? How would you change the definition so that internal representation for each constant name corresponded to the number of sides for that polygon?

3. What three advantages are cited in the text for defining a new enumeration type as opposed to using **#define** to achieve an equivalent effect?

4. True or false: In C, you may apply any operation defined on integers to values of any scalar type.

5. At first glance, the following function looks very much like `RightFrom`, which is defined in the section on "Scalar types":

```
directionT LeftFrom(directionT dir)
{
    return ((dir - 1) % 4);
}
```

The `RightFrom` implementation works fine, but this one has a small bug. Identify the problem, and then rewrite the function so that it correctly calculates the compass direction that is 90 degrees to the left of `dir`.

6. In your own words, explain how the keyword `typedef` operates.

7. Define the following terms: *bit, byte, word, address.*

8. True or false: In C, a value of type `int` always requires four bytes of memory.

9. True or false: In C, a value of type `char` always requires one byte of memory.

10. What is the purpose of the `sizeof` operator? How do you use it?

11. What four reasons for using pointers are cited in this chapter?

12. What is an lvalue?

13. What are the types of the variables introduced by the following declaration:

```
int *  p1, p2;
```

14. What declaration would you use to declare a variable named `pFlag` as a pointer to a Boolean value?

15. What are the two fundamental pointer operations? Which one corresponds to the term *dereferencing?*

16. Explain the difference between pointer assignment and value assignment.

17. Draw diagrams showing the contents of memory after each line of the following code:

```
v1 = 10; v2 = 25; p1 = &v1; p2 = &v2;
*p1 += *p2;
p2 = p1;
*p2 = *p1 + *p2;
```

18. What is the internal representation of the constant `NULL`?

19. What does the phrase *call by reference* mean?

20. Write array declarations for the following array variables:

    a.   An array `realArray` consisting of 100 floating-point values

b. An array `inUse` consisting of 16 Boolean values

c. An array `lines` that can hold up to 1000 strings

Remember that the upper bounds for these arrays should be defined as constants to make them easier to change.

21. Write the variable declaration and `for` loop necessary to create and initialize the following integer array:

squares

0	1	4	9	16	25	36	49	64	81	100
0	1	2	3	4	5	6	7	8	9	10

22. What is the difference between allocated size and effective size?

23. Assuming that the base address for `rectangular` is 1000 and that values of type `int` require four bytes of memory, draw a diagram that shows the address of each element in the array declared as follows:

```
int rectangular[2] [3];
```

24. Write a variable declaration that you could use to record the state of a chessboard, which consists of an 8×8 array of squares, each of which may contain any one of the following symbols:

k   white king   K   black king
q   white queen   Q   black queen
r   white rook   R   black rook
b   white bishop   B   black bishop
n   white knight   N   black knight
p   white pawn   P   black pawn
-    empty square

Explain how you could initialize this array so that it holds the standard starting position for a chess game:

R	N	B	Q	K	B	N	R
P	P	P	P	P	P	P	P
-	-	-	-	-	-	-	-
-	-	-	-	-	-	-	-
-	-	-	-	-	-	-	-
-	-	-	-	-	-	-	-
p	p	p	p	p	p	p	p
r	n	b	q	k	b	n	r

25. Assuming that `intArray` is declared as

    ```
    int intArray[10];
    ```

    and that `j` is an integer variable, describe the steps the computer would take to determine the value of the following expression:

    ```
    &intArray[j + 3];
    ```

26. If `arr` is declared to be an array, describe the distinction between the expressions

    ```
    arr[2]
    ```

    and

    ```
    arr + 2
    ```

27. Assume that variables of type `double` take up eight bytes on the computer system you are using. If the base address of the array `doubleArray` is 1000, what is the address value of `doubleArray + 5`?

28. True or false: If `p` is a pointer variable, the expression `p++` adds 1 to the internal representation of `p`.

29. What steps are necessary to declare a record variable?

30. If the variable `p` is declared as a pointer to a record that contains a field called `cost`, what is wrong with the expression

    ```
    *p.cost
    ```

    as a means of following the pointer from `p` to its value and then selecting the `cost` field? What expression would you write in C to accomplish this dereference-and-select operation?

31. What is the heap?

32. What is the purpose of the type `void *`?

33. Describe the effect of the following functions from the `genlib` library: `GetBlock`, `FreeBlock`, `New`, and `NewArray`.

34. What is meant by the term *garbage collection?*

PROGRAMMING EXERCISES

1. Define an enumeration type `weekdayT` whose elements are the days of the week. Write functions `NextDay` and `PreviousDay` that take a value of type `weekdayT` and return the day of the week that comes after or before the specified day, respectively. For example, `PreviousDay(Sunday)` should

return `Saturday`. Also write a function `IncrementDay(startDay, delta)` that returns the day of the week that comes `delta` days after `startDay`. Thus, `IncrementDay(Thursday, 4)` should return `Monday`. Your implementation of `IncrementDay` should work if the value of `delta` is negative, in which case it should proceed backward in time.

2. Write a program that computes the surface area and volume of a cylinder, given the height (h) and radius of the base (r) as shown in the following diagram:

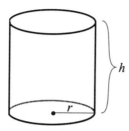

The formulas for calculating surface area and volume are

$$A = 2\pi\,h\,r$$
$$V = \pi\,h\,r^2$$

In this exercise, design your main program so that it consists of three function calls: one to read the input data, one to compute the results, and one to display the answers. When appropriate, use call by reference to communicate data between the functions and the main program.

3. Because individual judges may have some bias, it is common practice to throw out the highest and lowest score before computing the average. Modify the `gymjudge.c` program from Figure 2-2 to discard the highest and lowest scores before computing the average score.

4. Write a predicate function `IsSorted(array, n)` that takes an integer array and its effective size as parameters and returns `TRUE` if the array is sorted in nondecreasing order.

5. In the third century B.C., the Greek astronomer Eratosthenes developed an algorithm for finding all the prime numbers up to some upper limit N. To apply the algorithm, you start by writing down a list of the integers between 2 and N. For example, if N were 20, you would begin by writing down the following list:

2 3 4 5 6 7 8 9 10 11 12 13 14 15 16 17 18 19 20

Next you circle the first number in the list, indicating that you have found a prime. You then go through the rest of the list and cross off every multiple of the value you have just circled, since none of those multiples can be prime.

Thus, after executing the first step of the algorithm, you will have circled the number 2 and crossed off every multiple of two, as follows:

From this point, you simply repeat the process by circling the first number in the list that is neither crossed off nor circled, and then crossing off its multiples. In this example, you would circle 3 as a prime and cross off all multiples of 3 in the rest of the list, which would result in the following state:

② ③✗ 5 ✗ 7 ✗✗ ✗ 11 ✗ 13 ✗ ✗ ✗ 17 ✗ 19 ✗

Eventually, every number in the list will either be circled or crossed out, as shown in this diagram:

②③✗⑤✗⑦✗✗ ✗ ⑪ ✗ ⑬ ✗ ✗ ✗ ⑰ ✗ ⑲ ✗

The circled numbers are the primes; the crossed-out numbers are composites. This algorithm for generating a list of primes is called the *sieve of Eratosthenes*.

Write a program that uses the sieve of Eratosthenes to generate a list of the primes between 2 and 1000.

6. A *histogram* is a graphical way of displaying data by dividing the data into separate ranges and then indicating how many data values fall into each range. For example, given the set of exam scores

$$100, 95, 47, 88, 86, 92, 75, 89, 81, 70, 55, 80$$

a traditional histogram would have the following form:

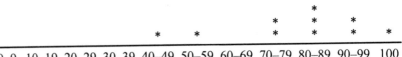

0–9 10–19 20–29 30–39 40–49 50–59 60–69 70–79 80–89 90–99 100

The asterisks in the histogram indicate one score in the 40s, one score in the 50s, five scores in the 80s, and so forth.

When you generate histograms using a computer, however, it is usually much easier to display them sideways on the page, as in this sample run:

```
   0:
  10:
  20:
  30:
  40: *
  50: *
  60:
  70: **
  80: *****
  90: **
 100: *
```

Write a program that reads in an array of integers and then displays a histogram of those numbers, divided into the ranges 0–9, 10–19, 20–29, and so forth, up to the range containing only the value 100. Your program should generate output that looks as much like the sample run as possible.

7. Rewrite the histogram program from the preceding exercise so that it displays the histogram in a more traditional vertical orientation, like this:

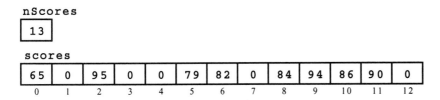

8. Write a function `RemoveZeroElements(array, n)` that goes through an array of integers and eliminates any elements whose value is 0. Because this operation changes the effective size of the array, `RemoveZeroElements` should return the new effective size as a result. For example, suppose that `scores` contains an array of scores on an optional exam and that `nScores` indicates the effective size of the array, as shown:

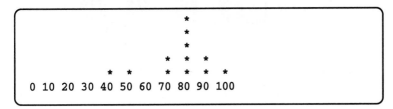

At this point, the statement

```
nScores = RemoveZeroElements(scores, nScores);
```

should remove the 0 scores, compressing the array into the following configuration:

nScores

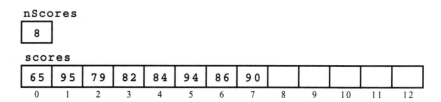

65	95	79	82	84	94	86	90					
0	1	2	3	4	5	6	7	8	9	10	11	12

9. The initial state of a checkers game is shown in the following diagram:

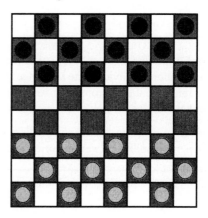

The dark squares in the bottom three rows are occupied by red checkers; the dark squares in the top three rows contain black checkers. The two center rows are unoccupied.

If you want to store the state of a checkerboard in a computer program, you need a two-dimensional array indexed by rows and columns. The elements of the array could be of various different types, but a reasonable approach—as illustrated by the tic-tac-toe example—is to use characters. For example, you could use the letter *r* to represent a red checker and the letter *b* to represent a black checker. Empty squares could be represented as spaces or hyphens depending on whether the color of the square was light or dark.

Implement a function **InitCheckerboard** that initializes a checkerboard array so that it corresponds to the starting position of a checkers game. Implement a second function **DisplayCheckerboard** that displays the current state of a checkerboard on the screen, as follows:

```
   b   b   b   b
 b   b   b   b
   b   b   b   b
 -   -   -   -
   -   -   -   -
 r   r   r   r
   r   r   r   r
 r   r   r   r
```

10. Design a function prototype that would allow a single function to find and return simultaneously both the lowest and highest values in an array of type `double`. Implement and test your function as shown in the following sample run:

```
Enter the elements of the array, one per line.
Use -1 to signal the end of the list.
   ? 67.↵
   ? 78.↵
   ? 75.↵
   ? 70.↵
   ? 71.↵
   ? 80.↵
   ? 69.↵
   ? 86.↵
   ? 65.↵
   ? 54.↵
   ? 76.↵
   ? 78.↵
   ? 70.↵
   ? 68.↵
   ? 77.↵
   ? -1.↵
The range of values is 54-86
```

11. Write a function `IndexArray(n)` that returns a pointer to a dynamically allocated integer array with `n` elements, each of which is initialized to its own index. For example, assuming that `ip` is declared as

    ```
    int *ip;
    ```

    the statement

    ```
    ip = IndexArray(10);
    ```

    should produce the following memory configuration:

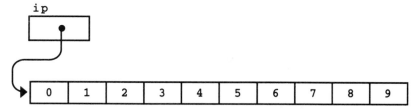

12. Design a new type called `payrollT` that is capable of holding the data for a list of employees, each of which is represented using the `employeeT` type introduced in the section on "Dynamic records" at the end of the chapter. The type `payrollT` should be a pointer type whose underlying value is a record

containing the number of employees and a dynamic array of the actual `employeeT` values, as illustrated by the following data diagram:

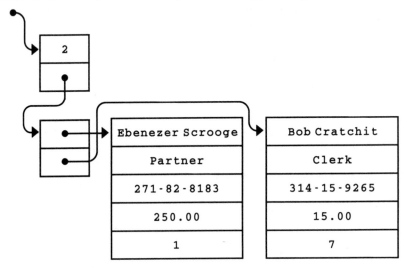

After writing the types that define this data structure, write a function `GetPayroll` that reads in a list of employees, as shown in the following sample run:

```
How many employees: 2↵
Employee #1:
  Name: Ebenezer Scrooge↵
  Title: Partner↵
  SSNum: 271-82-8183↵
  Salary: 250.00↵
  Withholding exemptions: 1↵
Employee #2:
  Name: Bob Cratchit↵
  Title: Clerk↵
  SSNum: 314-15-9265↵
  Salary: 15.00↵
  Withholding exemptions: 7↵
```

After the input values have been entered, the `GetPayroll` function should return a value of type `payrollT` that matches the structure shown in the diagram.

13. Write a program that generates the weekly payroll for a company whose employment records are stored using the type `payrollT`, as defined in the preceding exercise. Each employee is paid the salary given in the employee record, after deducting taxes. Your program should compute taxes as follows:

- Deduct $1 from the salary for each withholding exemption. This figure is the *adjusted income.* (If the result of the calculation is less than 0, use 0 as the adjusted income.)
- Multiply the adjusted income by the *tax rate,* which you should assume is a flat 25 percent.

For example, Bob Cratchit has a weekly income of $15. Because he has seven dependents, his adjusted income is $15 − (7 × $1), or $8. Twenty-five percent of $8 is $2, so Mr. Cratchit's net pay is $15 − $2, or $13.

The payroll listing should consist of a series of lines, one per employee, each of which contains the employee's name, gross pay, tax, and net pay. The output should be formatted in columns, as shown in the following sample run:

```
Name                    Gross    Tax      Net
------------------------------------------------
Ebenezer Scrooge        250.00 - 62.25 = 187.75
Bob Cratchit             15.00 -  2.00 =  13.00
```

14. Suppose that you have been assigned the task of computerizing the card catalog system for a library. As a first step, your supervisor has asked you to develop a prototype capable of storing the following information for each of 1000 books:

- The title
- A list of up to five authors
- The Library of Congress catalog number
- A list of up to five subject headings
- The publisher
- The year of publication
- Whether the book is circulating or noncirculating

Design the data structures that would be necessary to keep all the information required for this prototype library database. Given your definition, it should be possible to write the declaration

```
libraryT libdata;
```

and have the variable `libdata` contain all the information you would need to keep track of up to 1000 books. Remember that the actual number of books will usually be less than this upper bound.

Write an additional procedure `SearchBySubject` that takes as parameters the library database and a subject string. For each book in the library that lists the subject string as one of its subject headings, `SearchBySubject` should display the title, the name of the first author, and the Library of Congress catalog number of the book.

15. Write a function

    ```
    int *GetDynamicIntegerArray(int sentinel, int *pN);
    ```

    that returns a dynamically allocated array of integers read in from the user.
    The **sentinel** argument indicates the value used to signal the end of the input.
    The second argument is a pointer to an integer variable, which is used to return
    the effective size of the array. Note that it is impossible to know in advance
    how many values the user will enter. As a result, the implementation must
    allocate new array space as needed.

16. Suppose that the C libraries did not provide a **malloc** function for dynamic
    allocation. To a certain extent, you could achieve the same result by allocating
    a large global array at the beginning of a program and giving out pieces of that
    array to clients who need to use additional storage.

    Design and implement a function **myalloc** to simulate the dynamic
    allocation process. Calling **myalloc(nBytes)** should return a pointer to a
    block of memory that is **nBytes** long. Each new memory block is taken from
    the large global array, beginning wherever the last block left off. Make sure
    your implementation includes any static initialization necessary for the first
    call to **myalloc** to succeed.

    Consider the memory you allocate to be assigned for the lifetime of the
    program. Designing an allocation facility that allows clients to free memory is
    considerably more difficult.

CHAPTER 3

Libraries and Interfaces

My library / Was dukedom large enough.

— Shakespeare, *The Tempest, c.* 1612

Objectives

- To appreciate the importance of interfaces to modern programming and to understand the terminology used in interface-based programming.

- To recognize the criteria used to evaluate the design of an interface.

- To learn the syntactic rules and conventions required to write an interface file.

- To be able to use the facilities provided by the `random.h` interface.

- To understand how strings are represented inside the computer.

- To appreciate the relationship between the abstraction model used in the `string.h` and `strlib.h` interfaces and be able to manipulate strings using each of these models.

- To learn how to use the `stdio.h` functions to read and write data files.

In modern programming, it is impossible to write interesting programs without calling library functions. In fact, as the science of programming advances, programmers depend more and more on library functions. Today, it is not at all unusual for 90 percent or more of a program to consist of library code, with only a few parts specifically tailored for a particular application. As a programmer, you must understand not only how to write new code but also how to avoid doing so by making appropriate use of existing libraries.

The main purpose of this chapter is to encourage you to think about libraries in a way that emphasizes the distinction between the library itself and other programs that make use of it, which are called its **clients.** To do so, the chapter focuses on the boundary between a library and its clients, which is called the **interface.** An interface provides a channel of communication but also acts as a barrier that prevents complex details on one side from affecting the other. Interfaces are central to a modern treatment of libraries, and it is important—even if you've done a lot of programming—for you to understand libraries from this perspective.

3.1 The concept of an interface

In English, the word *interface* means a common boundary between two distinct entities. The surface of a pond, for example, is the interface between the water and the air. In programming, an interface constitutes a conceptual boundary rather than a physical one: an interface is the boundary between the implementation of a library and its clients. The purpose of the interface is to provide each client with the information it needs to use the library without revealing the details required by the implementation. Thus, it is important to think of an interface not only as a channel for communication between client and implementation, but also as a barrier that keeps them separated, as illustrated by the following diagram:

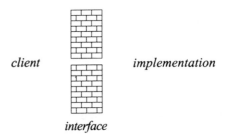

client   *implementation*

interface

By mediating the communication between the two sides, an interface reduces the conceptual complexity of the programming process by ensuring that details that lie on one side of the interface boundary do not escape to complicate the code on the other side.

Interfaces and implementations

In computer science, an interface is a conceptual entity. It consists of an understanding between the programmer who implements a library and the programmer who uses it, spelling out the information that is required by both sides.

When you write a C program, however, you must have some way to represent the conceptual interface as part of the actual program. In C, an interface is represented by a **header file,** which traditionally has the same name as the file that implements it with the .c extension replaced by .h.

As an example, suppose that you have created a collection of functions that you want to make available to clients as a library. To do so, you need to create two files: an interface that you might call **mylib.h** and the corresponding implementation **mylib.c**. The code for each of your functions goes in the **mylib.c** implementation file. The **mylib.h** interface contains only the function prototypes, which contain the information the compiler needs to interpret any calls to those functions. Putting the prototypes in the interface makes them available to clients and is called **exporting** those functions.

Although function prototypes are the most common component of an interface, interfaces can export other definitions as well. In particular, interfaces often export data types and constants. A single definition exported by an interface is called an **interface entry.**

Once you have written the interface and implementation for a library, you—or some other programmer with whom you are collaborating—can then write separate source files that act as clients of the **mylib.h** interface. The relationship between the files representing the client, interface, and implementation is illustrated in the following diagram:

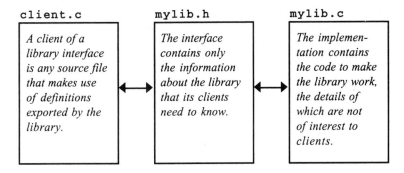

The distinction between the abstract concept of an interface and the header file that represents it may at first seem subtle. In many ways, the distinction is the same as that between an algorithm and a program that implements it. The algorithm is an abstract strategy; the program is the concrete realization of that algorithm. Similarly, in C, header files provide a concrete realization of an interface.

Packages and abstractions

The same distinction between a general concept and its programming manifestation also comes up in the definition of two other terms that are often used in discussions of interfaces. In computer science, you will often hear the term *package* used to describe the software that defines a library. If you are assigned to develop a library, part of your job consists of producing a .h file to serve as the library interface and a corresponding .c file that provides the underlying implementation. Those files constitute the **package.** To get a full understanding of a library, however, you must look beyond the software. Libraries embody a specific conceptual approach that transcends the package itself. The conceptual basis of a library is called an **abstraction.**

The relationship between an abstraction and a package is best illustrated by an example. The programs in the first two chapters of this text use the `printf` function in the `stdio.h` interface for all output operations. For input operations, however, those programs use functions exported by the `simpio.h` interface such as `GetInteger`, `GetReal`, and `GetLine`. The `stdio.h` interface provides functions for accepting user input, but they are more difficult for beginning programmers to use than their counterparts in `simpio.h`. The two libraries embody different approaches to input operations: the `stdio.h` interface emphasizes power and flexibility, while the `simpio.h` interface emphasizes simplicity of structure and ease of use. The approach used in each of these interfaces is part of the abstraction. The associated packages implement those abstractions and make them real, in the sense that they can then be used by programmers.

Principles of good interface design

Programming is hard because programs reflect the complexity of the problems they solve. As long as we use computers to solve problems of ever-increasing sophistication, the process of programming will need to keep becoming more sophisticated as well.

Writing a program to solve a large or difficult problem forces you to manage an enormous amount of complexity. There are algorithms to design, special cases to consider, user requirements to meet, and innumerable details to get right. To make programming manageable, you must reduce the complexity of the programming process as much as possible.

One of the primary purposes of defining new functions is to reduce complexity by dividing up the entire program into more manageable pieces. Interfaces offer a similar reduction in programming complexity but at a higher level of detail. A function gives its caller access to a set of steps that together implement a single operation. An interface gives its client access to a set of functions that together implement a programming abstraction. The extent to which the interface simplifies the programming process, however, depends largely on how well it is designed.

To design an effective interface, you must balance several criteria. In general, you should try to develop interfaces that are

- *Unified.* A single interface should define a consistent abstraction with a clear unifying theme. If a function does not fit within that theme, it should be defined in a separate interface.
- *Simple.* To the extent that the underlying implementation is itself complex, the interface must hide as much of that complexity from the client as possible.
- *Sufficient.* When clients use an abstraction, the interface must provide sufficient functionality to meet their needs. If some critical operation is

missing from an interface, clients may decide to abandon it and develop their own, more powerful abstraction. As important as simplicity is, the designer must avoid simplifying an interface to the point that it becomes useless.

- *General.* A well-designed interface should be flexible enough to meet the needs of many different clients. An interface that performs a narrowly defined set of operations for one client is not as useful as one that can be used in many different situations.

- *Stable.* The functions defined in an interface should continue to have precisely the same structure and effect, even if their underlying implementation changes. Making changes in the behavior of an interface forces clients to change their programs, which compromises the value of the interface.

Because it is important to maintain stable interfaces, the designer of an interface must exercise special care to get it right. As more and more clients start to depend on a particular interface, the cost of changing that interface increases. In fact, it is quite common to discover interfaces that cannot be changed at all, even if they have serious design flaws. Certain functions in the ANSI standard libraries, for example, exhibit behaviors that are widely considered flaws by the C programming community. Even so, it is impossible to change the design of these functions because too many clients depend on the current behavior.

Some interface changes, however, are more drastic than others. For example, adding an entirely new function to an interface is usually a relatively straightforward process, since no clients already depend on that function. Changing an interface in a way that requires no changes to existing programs is called **extending** the interface. If you find that you need to make evolutionary changes over the lifetime of an interface, it is usually best to make those changes by extension.

3.2 Random numbers

The easiest way to illustrate the structure of an interface is to provide a simple example. Chapter 8 of *The Art and Science of C* introduces an interface called `random.h` that makes it easier for client programs to simulate random processes like flipping a coin or rolling a die. Getting a computer—which ordinarily operates deterministically in the sense that running the same program with the same input always produces the same result—to behave in a random way involves a certain amount of complexity. For the benefit of client programmers, you want to hide this complexity behind an interface so that the client has access to the capabilities it needs without having to confront the complexity of the complete implementation.

The structure of the `random.h` interface

Figure 3-1 shows the `random.h` interface, which exports the following functions: `RandomInteger`, `RandomReal`, `RandomChance`, and `Randomize`. For each of these functions, the interface contains a one-line prototype along with a comment that describes the purpose of the function from the perspective of the client. As is typical for the interfaces defined in this text, comments comprise most of the interface and

FIGURE 3-1 The random.h interface

```
/*
 * File: random.h
 * --------------
 * This interface provides several functions for generating
 * pseudorandom numbers.
 */

#ifndef _random_h
#define _random_h

#include "genlib.h"

/*
 * Function: RandomInteger
 * Usage: n = RandomInteger(low, high);
 * -------------------------------------
 * This function returns a random integer in the range low to high,
 * inclusive.
 */

int RandomInteger(int low, int high);

/*
 * Function: RandomReal
 * Usage: d = RandomReal(low, high);
 * ----------------------------------
 * This function returns a random real number in the half-open
 * interval [low, high), meaning that the result is always
 * greater than or equal to low but strictly less than high.
 */

double RandomReal(double low, double high);

/*
 * Function: RandomChance
 * Usage: if (RandomChance(p)) . . .
 * ----------------------------------
 * The RandomChance function returns TRUE with the probability
 * indicated by p, which should be a floating-point number between
 * 0 (meaning never) and 1 (meaning always).  For example, calling
 * RandomChance(.30) returns TRUE 30 percent of the time.
 */

bool RandomChance(double p);
```

```
/*
 * Function: Randomize
 * Usage: Randomize();
 * ---------------------
 * This function initializes the random-number generator so that
 * its results are unpredictable.  If this function is not called,
 * the other functions will return the same values on each run.
 */

void Randomize(void);

#endif
```

provide all the information clients need. If the comments in an interface are well designed, clients should be able to rely on them without having to read the underlying implementation.

After the initial comment that describes the interface, the `random.h` interface includes a somewhat cryptic set of lines that is part of the conventional syntax for an interface. The lines

```
#ifndef _random_h
#define _random_h
```

operate in conjunction with the last line of the interface, which is

```
#endif
```

These three lines are often referred to as **interface boilerplate.** When you design your own interfaces, you should be sure to include similar boilerplate lines, substituting the name of your own interface for the name `random` in this example.

The purpose of the interface boilerplate is to prevent the compiler from reading the same interface many times during a single compilation. The line

```
#ifndef _random_h
```

causes the compiler to skip any text up to the `#endif` line if the symbol `_random_h` has been previously defined. When the compiler reads this interface for the first time, `_random_h` is undefined, which means that the compiler goes ahead and reads the contents of the file. The compiler immediately thereafter encounters the definition

```
#define _random_h
```

which defines the symbol `_random_h`. If the compiler reads the `random.h` interface a second time, the symbol `_random_h` has already been defined, which means that the compiler ignores the entire contents of the file on the second pass.

The next line in the source file is

```
#include "genlib.h"
```

which is part of every C program you have seen in this text. Interfaces sometimes need to include other interfaces, but only if the compiler needs those definitions to compile the interface itself. The `random.h` interface must include `genlib.h` because the interface itself uses the type `bool` as part of the prototype for `RandomChance`. Because `bool` is defined in `genlib.h`, the compiler must have access to that definition when it reads `random.h`.

The remainder of the interface consists of function prototypes and their associated comments. The first prototype is for the function `RandomInteger(low, high)`, which returns a randomly chosen integer in the range between `low` and `high`, inclusive. For example, calling `RandomInteger(1, 6)` would return 1, 2, 3, 4, 5, or 6 and could be used to simulate rolling a die. Calling `RandomInteger(0, 36)` returns an integer between 0 and 36 and could be used to model a European roulette wheel, which is marked with those 37 numbers.

The function `RandomReal(low, high)` is similar to `RandomInteger` and returns a floating-point value r subject to the condition that $low \leq r < high$. For example, calling `RandomReal(0, 1)` returns a random number that can be as small as 0 but is always strictly less than 1. In mathematics, a range of real numbers that can be equal to one endpoint but not the other is called a **half-open interval.** On a number line, a half-open interval is marked using an open circle to show that the endpoint is excluded, like this:

In text, the standard convention is to use square brackets to indicate closed ends of intervals and parentheses to indicate open ones, so that the notation [0, 1) indicates the half-open interval corresponding to this diagram.

The function `RandomChance(p)` is used to simulate random events that occur with some fixed probability. To be consistent with the conventions of statistics, a probability is represented as a number between 0 and 1, where 0 means that the event never occurs and 1 means that it always does. The function `RandomChance` returns `TRUE` with probability p, so that `RandomChance(0.75)` returns `TRUE` 75 percent of the time. You can use `RandomChance` to simulate flipping a coin, as illustrated by the following function, which returns either `"heads"` or `"tails"`:

```
string FlipCoin(void)
{
    if (RandomChance(0.50)) {
        return ("heads");
    } else {
        return ("tails");
    }
}
```

The last function in the `random.h` interface requires a little more explanation. Because computers are deterministic machines, random numbers are usually computed by going through a deterministic calculation that nonetheless appears random to the user. Random numbers computed in this way are called **pseudorandom numbers.** If you take no special action, the computer always applies the same process to generate its sequence of random numbers, which means that the results will be the same every time the program is run. The purpose of the `Randomize` function is to initialize the internal pseudorandom number generator so that each run of the program produces a different sequence, which is what you want if you are writing a program that plays a game.

At first, it may seem hard to understand why a random number package should return the same values on each run. After all, deterministic behavior of this sort seems to defeat the whole purpose of the package. There is, however, a good reason behind this behavior: programs that behave deterministically are easier to debug. To illustrate this fact, suppose you have just written a program to play an intricate game, such as Monopoly™. As is always the case with newly written programs, the odds are good that your program has a few bugs. In a complex program, bugs can be relatively obscure, in the sense that they only occur in rare situations. Suppose you are playing the game and discover that the program is starting to behave in a bizarre way. As you begin to debug the program, it would be very convenient if you could regenerate the same state and take a closer look at what is going on. Unfortunately, if the program is running in a nondeterministic way, a second run of the program will behave differently from the first. Bugs that showed up the first time may not occur on the second pass.

In general, it is extremely difficult to reproduce the conditions that cause a program to fail if the program is behaving in a truly random fashion. If, on the other hand, the program is operating deterministically, it will do the same thing each time it is run. This behavior makes it possible for you to recreate the conditions under which the problem occurred. When you write a program that works with random numbers, it is usually best to leave out the call to `Randomize` during the debugging phase. When the program seems to be working well, you can insert a call to `Randomize` at the beginning of the main program to make the program change its behavior from one run to the next.

Constructing a client program

Once you know what the interface looks like, you can immediately begin to code applications that use it. The interface provides all the information that any client needs to know. From the client's perspective, the important questions are what the functions in the library do and how to call them. The details of how they work are important only for the implementation.

As a simple illustration of how clients can use the random number package, let's consider the `craps.c` program shown in Figure 3-2, which simulates the casino game of craps. Because the program uses the random number library to simulate rolling the dice, the `craps.c` file needs to include the `random.h` interface. Moreover, in order to ensure that the outcome is not the same every time, the

FIGURE 3-2 A program to play the game of craps

```c
/*
 * File: craps.c
 * -------------
 * This program plays the casino game called craps, which is
 * played using a pair of dice.  At the beginning of the game,
 * you roll the dice and compute the total.  If your first roll
 * is 7 or 11, you win with what gamblers call a "natural."
 * If your first roll is 2, 3, or 12, you lose by "crapping
 * out."  In any other case, the total from the first roll
 * becomes your "point," after which you continue to roll
 * the dice until you roll your point again, in which case
 * you win, or until you roll a 7, in which case you lose.
 * Other rolls, including 2, 3, 11, and 12, have no effect
 * during this phase of the game.
 */

#include <stdio.h>
#include "genlib.h"
#include "random.h"

/* Function prototypes */

static int TryToMakePoint(int point);
static int RollTwoDice(void);

/* Main program */

main()
{
    int point;

    Randomize();
    printf("This program plays a game of craps.\n");
    point = RollTwoDice();
    switch (point) {
      case 7: case 11:
        printf("That's a natural.  You win.\n");
        break;
      case 2: case 3: case 12:
        printf("That's craps.  You lose.\n");
        break;
      default:
        printf("Your point is %d.\n", point);
        if (TryToMakePoint(point)) {
            printf("You made your point.  You win.\n");
        } else {
            printf("You rolled a seven.  You lose.\n");
        }
    }
}
```

```
/*
 * Function: TryToMakePoint
 * Usage: flag = TryToMakePoint(point);
 * -------------------------------------
 * This function is responsible for the part of the game
 * during which you roll the dice repeatedly until you either
 * make your point or roll a 7.  The function returns TRUE if
 * you make your point and FALSE if a 7 comes up first.
 */

static bool TryToMakePoint(int point)
{
    int total;

    while (TRUE) {
        total = RollTwoDice();
        if (total == point) return (TRUE);
        if (total == 7) return (FALSE);
    }
}

/*
 * Function: RollTwoDice
 * Usage: total = RollTwoDice();
 * -----------------------------
 * This function rolls two dice and returns their sum.  As part
 * of the implementation, the result is displayed on the screen.
 */

static int RollTwoDice(void)
{
    int d1, d2, total;

    printf("Rolling the dice . . .\n");
    d1 = RandomInteger(1, 6);
    d2 = RandomInteger(1, 6);
    total = d1 + d2;
    printf("You rolled %d and %d -- that's %d.\n", d1, d2, total);
    return (total);
}
```

program calls `Randomize` at the beginning of its operation. The rest of the program
is simply an encoding of the rules of the game, which are outlined in the comments
at the beginning of the program.

The ANSI functions for random numbers

Although you can design the `craps.c` program by relying on the interface
description, you cannot run the program until you have an implementation for the
random number library. To make sense of that implementation, you first need to
understand the facilities provided by the standard ANSI libraries for generating

random numbers. The basic tools are already provided in the form of a small set of functions exported by the `stdlib.h` interface. Unfortunately, that interface is not well suited to the needs of clients, largely because the results returned by the functions differ from machine to machine. One of the advantages of `random.h` is that it provides clients with a machine-independent interface that is considerably easier to use than the underlying facilities on which it is based.

The `random.c` implementation is based on a more primitive random number facility provided as part of the standard ANSI library interface `stdlib.h`. The function on which the implementation depends is called `rand` and has the following prototype:

```
int rand(void);
```

Unlike most functions, `rand` returns a different result each time it is called. The result of `rand` is guaranteed to be nonnegative and no larger than the constant RAND_MAX, which is also defined in the `stdlib.h` interface. Thus, each time `rand` is called, it returns a different integer between 0 and RAND_MAX, inclusive.

The value of RAND_MAX depends on the computer system. When you write programs that work with random numbers, you should not make any assumptions about the precise value of RAND_MAX. Instead, your programs should be prepared to use whatever value of RAND_MAX the system defines.

You can get a sense of how `rand` behaves on your own system by running the program

```
#define NTrials 10

main()
{
    int i;

    printf("On this computer, RAND_MAX is %d.\n", RAND_MAX);
    printf("The first %d calls to rand return:\n", NTrials);
    for (i = 0; i < NTrials; i++) {
        printf("%10d\n", rand());
    }
}
```

On the computer in my office, the program generates the following output:

```
On this computer, RAND_MAX is 32767.
The first 10 calls to rand return:
     16838
      5758
     10113
     17515
     31051
      5627
     23010
      7419
     16212
      4086
```

You can see that the program is generating integers, all of which are positive and none of which is greater than 32,767, which the sample run shows as the value of RAND_MAX for this machine. Because the numbers are pseudorandom, you know that there must be some pattern, but it is unlikely that you can discern one. From your point of view, the numbers appear to be random, because you don't know what the underlying pattern is.

The rand function generates each new random value by applying a set of mathematical calculations to the last value it produced. Because you don't know what those calculations are, it is best to think of the entire operation as a black box where old numbers go in on one side and new pseudorandom numbers pop out on the other. Since, the first call to rand produces the number 16838, the second call to rand corresponds to putting 16838 into one end of the black box and having 5758 pop out on the other side:

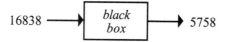

Similarly, on the next call to rand, the implementation puts 5758 into the black box, which returns 10113:

This same process is repeated on each call to rand. The computation inside the black box is designed so that (1) the numbers are uniformly distributed over the legal range, and (2) the sequence goes on for a long time before it begins to repeat.

But what about the first call to rand—the one that returns 16838? The implementation must have a starting point. There must be an integer, s_0, that goes into the black box and produces 16838:

This initial value—the value that is used to get the entire process started—is called a **seed** for the random number generator. The ANSI library implementation sets the initial seed to a constant value every time a program is started, which is why the library always generates the same sequence of values. To change the sequence, you need to set the seed to a different value, which is done by calling the function srand(*seed*).

The srand function is essential to the implementation of Randomize, which resets the seed so that the sequence of random numbers is different each time. The usual strategy is to use the value of the internal system clock as the initial seed. Because the time keeps changing, the random number sequence will change as well. You can retrieve the current value of the system clock by calling the function time, which is defined in the ANSI library interface time.h, and then converting the result to an integer. This technique allows you to write the following statement, which has the effect of initializing the pseudorandom number generator to some unpredictable point:

```
srand((int) time(NULL));
```

Although it requires only a single line, the operation to set the random seed to an unpredictable value based on the system clock is relatively obscure. If this line were to appear in the client program, the client would have to understand the concept of a random number seed, along with the functions `srand` and `time`. To make things simpler for the client, it is much better to give this operation a simple name like `Randomize` and make it part of the random number library. By doing so, the client simply needs to call

```
Randomize();
```

which is certainly easier to explain.

The `random.c` implementation

The ANSI functions described in the preceding section provide all the tools you need to implement the `random.h` interface. The implementation is contained in a separate source file called `random.c`, which is shown in Figure 3-3.

After the initial comment, the implementation file lists the `#include` files it needs. The `stdio.h` and `genlib.h` interfaces are standard, but the implementation also needs `stdlib.h` and `time.h` so that it has access to the functions `rand`, `srand`, and `time`. Finally, every implementation needs to include its own interface so the compiler can check the prototypes against the actual definitions.

The rest of the file consists of the functions exported by the interface, along with any comments that would be useful to the programmers who may need to maintain this program in the future. Like all other forms of expository writing, comments must be written with their audience in mind. When you write comments, you must put yourself in the role of the reader so that you can understand what information that reader will want to see. Comments in the `.c` file have a different audience than their counterparts in the `.h` file. The comments in the implementation are written for another implementor who may have to modify the implementation in some way. They therefore must explain how the implementation works and provide any details that later maintainers would want to know. Comments in the interface, on the other hand, are written for the client. A client should never have to read the comments inside the implementation. The comments in the interface should suffice.

The use of comments to explain the operation of the code are best illustrated by the `RandomInteger` implementation, which converts a random number in the range 0 to `RAND_MAX` into one that lies in the interval between the parameters `low` and `high`. As the comments indicate, the implementation uses the following four-step process:

- *Normalization.* The first step in the process is to convert the integer result from `rand` into a floating-point number d in the half-open interval [0, 1).

FIGURE 3-3 The implementation of the random number library

```
/*
 * File: random.c
 * --------------
 * This file implements the random.h interface.
 */

#include <stdio.h>
#include <stdlib.h>
#include <time.h>
#include "genlib.h"
#include "random.h"

/*
 * Function: RandomInteger
 * -----------------------
 * This function begins by using rand to select an integer
 * in the interval [0, RAND_MAX] and then converts it to the
 * desired range by applying the following steps:
 *
 * 1. Normalize the value to a real number in the interval [0, 1)
 * 2. Scale the resulting value to the appropriate range size
 * 3. Truncate the scaled value to an integer
 * 4. Translate the integer to the appropriate starting point
 */

int RandomInteger(int low, int high)
{
    int k;
    double d;

    d = (double) rand() / ((double) RAND_MAX + 1);
    k = (int) (d * (high - low + 1));
    return (low + k);
}

/*
 * Function: RandomReal
 * --------------------
 * The implementation of RandomReal is similar to that
 * of RandomInteger, without the truncation step.
 */

double RandomReal(double low, double high)
{
    double d;

    d = (double) rand() / ((double) RAND_MAX + 1);
    return (low + d * (high - low));
}
```

```
/*
 * Function: RandomReal
 * --------------------
 * The implementation of RandomReal is similar to that
 * of RandomInteger, without the truncation step.
 */

double RandomReal(double low, double high)
{
    double d;

    d = (double) rand() / ((double) RAND_MAX + 1);
    return (low + d * (high - low));
}

/*
 * Function: RandomChance
 * ----------------------
 * This function uses RandomReal to generate a real number
 * in the interval [0, 1) and then compares that value to p.
 */

bool RandomChance(double p)
{
    return (RandomReal(0, 1) < p);
}

/*
 * Function: Randomize
 * -------------------
 * This function operates by setting the random number
 * seed to the current time.  The srand function is
 * provided by the <stdlib.h> library and requires an
 * integer argument.  The time function is exported by
 * the <time.h> interface.
 */

void Randomize(void)
{
    srand((int) time(NULL));
}
```

To do so, all you need to do is convert the result of `rand` to a `double` and then divide it by the number of elements in the range. Because `RAND_MAX` is often the largest integer the machine can hold, it is important to convert it to a `double` before adding the constant 1, which ensures that the division produces a value that is strictly less than 1.

- *Scaling.* The second step consists of multiplying the value `d` by the size of the desired range, so that it spans the correct number of integers. Because the desired range includes both the endpoints, `low` and `high`, the number of integers in the range is given by the expression `high - low + 1`.

- *Truncation.* The third step consists of using a type cast to convert the number back to an integer by throwing away any fraction. This step gives you a random integer with a lower bound of 0.
- *Translation.* The final step consists of adding the value `low` so that the range begins at the desired lower bound.

The steps in this process are illustrated by the diagram in Figure 3-4, which shows how a call to `RandomInteger(1, 6)` converts the result of `rand` into an integer in the desired range of 1 to 6.

3.3 Strings

Although Chapter 2 includes an extensive discussion of arrays, it does not mention one of the most important applications of the array concept: using arrays of characters to represent strings. While it is perfectly legal to manipulate strings like any other array, it is more convenient to use library functions that provide the operations you want when you work with string data. By introducing string manipulation in the discussion of libraries, this chapter can give you a better sense of how to work with strings in C.

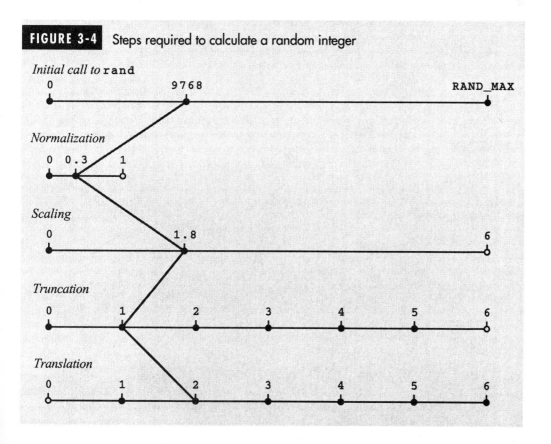

FIGURE 3-4 Steps required to calculate a random integer

The underlying representation of a string

Internally, strings are represented as arrays of characters. Whenever a string is stored in memory, its characters are assigned to consecutive bytes. Storing the characters themselves, however, is not sufficient to represent all the important information about a string. Programs that manipulate strings must have a way to determine where a string ends. In C, the end of a string is marked by storing the **null character**—the character whose internal code is 0 and which is represented by the escape sequence \0 in string and character constants—at the end of each string. Thus, if you include the string constant **"Hello"** in a program, the C compiler reserves six bytes of memory space and initializes them as follows:

H	e	l	l	o	\0

In C, you can use any character array to hold string data. For example, you can declare the array **str** and initialize it to hold the string **"Hello"** with the declaration

```
char str[6] = { 'H', 'e', 'l', 'l', 'o', '\0' };
```

or, more compactly,

```
char str[6] = "Hello";
```

Because a string is an array, it is also possible to choose the ith character from a string **str** using the notation for array selection, as follows:

```
str[i]
```

As with any array, index numbers in a string begin at 0. Thus, if **str** contains the string **"Hello"**, then **str[0]** has the value **'H'**, **str[1]** has the value **'e'**, and so on.

If you use array notation, the standard idiom for processing every character in a string looks like this[1]:

```
for (i = 0; str[i] != '\0'; i++) {
    body of loop that manipulates str[i]
}
```

---

[1] As you will discover if you read existing C code, many C programmers use an idiom for processing strings that is even more compact than this example. Because C treats the value zero as **FALSE** and any nonzero value as **TRUE**, many C programmers leave the comparison out of the **for** loop control line, as follows:

```
for (i = 0; str[i]; i++)
```

Even though you will often encounter this shorthand form in existing C programs and therefore need to recognize it, this text always includes the comparison explicitly to emphasize the conceptual distinction between Boolean and integer data.

On each loop cycle, the selection expression `str[i]` refers to the ith character in the string. Because the purpose of the loop is to process every character, the loop continues until `str[i]` selects the null character marking the end of the string. Thus, you can count the number of spaces in a string using the following function:

```
static int CountSpaces(char str[])
{
    int i, nSpaces;

    nSpaces = 0;
    for (i = 0; str[i] != '\0'; i++) {
        if (str[i] == ' ') nSpaces++;
    }
    return (nSpaces);
}
```

Like any array in C, a character array can also be interpreted as a pointer to its first element. Thus, you could reimplement the `CountSpaces` function like this:

```
static int CountSpaces(char *str)
{
    int nSpaces;
    char *cp;

    nSpaces = 0;
    for (cp = str; *cp != '\0'; cp++) {
        if (*cp == ' ') nSpaces++;
    }
    return (nSpaces);
}
```

In this case, the `for` loop control line

```
    for (cp = str; *cp != '\0'; cp++) {
```

begins by initializing the pointer variable `cp` to the address of the first character in `str` and advances it along the string until it points to the null character at the end.

The data type `string`

Even though C allows you to work with strings either as arrays of characters or as a pointer to a character, it often makes sense to look at strings from a more abstract perspective. If you want to refer to the individual characters in a string, you need to pay attention to its representation. If, however, you can think of the string as a unified whole, you can ignore the details details of the representation and can therefore write programs that are easier to understand.

The `genlib.h` library defines the type name `string` to emphasize that strings make sense as a conceptually distinct type. The definition in `genlib.h` is

```
typedef char *string;
```

which makes string identical to the type char *. The two types mean exactly the same thing to the compiler. The two type names, however, send different messages to human readers. If you declare a variable to be of type char *, you reveal its underlying representation as a pointer. On the other hand, if you declare the same variable to be of type string, you focus the reader's attention on the string as a whole.

In Chapter 1, you learned that a data type is defined by two properties: a domain and a set of operations. If you think about strings as a separate data type, the domain is easy to identify; the domain of type string is the set of all sequences of characters. The more interesting problem is to identify an appropriate set of operations. At the level of the language itself, C provides very few string operations, all of which require you to consider the underlying representation. If you want to maintain a high-level view of strings as a distinct type, you need a string library that exports a set of operations that allow you to manipulate a string as a whole.

This text presents two such libraries: the ANSI library defined by the string.h interface and a dynamic string library developed for *The Art and Science of C*, which is defined by the strlib.h interface. The relationship between those interfaces is illustrated by the following diagram, which represents what computer scientists call a **layered abstraction:**

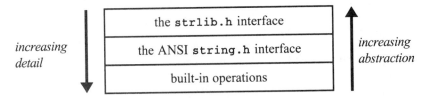

The language provides low-level operations that allow you to select individual characters from a string and then manipulate them arithmetically using their ASCII codes. While these operations are in fact sufficient for writing string-processing applications, they are not particularly convenient and force you to work at a very detailed level. The string.h interface provides a more advanced set of operations that allow you to work with an entire string in a single function call. Unfortunately, these functions still force you to be aware of the underlying representation, which makes it harder to maintain an abstract perspective. The strlib.h interface presents the most abstract view of string data, in the sense that you no longer need to think in terms of how a string is represented and can therefore regard the type string as a separate entity with an integrity of its own.

The biggest difference between the two string libraries lies in how they allocate memory for the characters in a string. In the case of the strlib.h interface, the functions dynamically allocate whatever memory is required. As a client, you don't have to worry about the details of that allocation, which makes the strlib.h interface considerably easier to use. The functions in the string.h interface shift the burden of allocating memory to the client. If you are using this interface, you are responsible for allocating all string storage. This allocation not only represents a burden on you as a programmer, but also increases the likelihood of introducing bugs into the code.

Despite its disadvantages, the `string.h` interface is important because it is an ANSI standard. If you work as a programmer, you will certainly encounter programs that use it, which means that you need to be familiar with its operation. Computer science, however, is moving increasingly toward the abstraction model used in `strlib.h`. In the programming language Java, for example, strings are defined in a way that is extremely close to the abstraction provided by the `strlib.h` interface. By learning to think about strings from a high-level perspective, it will be easier for you to make the transition to programming languages that support abstract operations on strings.

The details of these libraries are covered in the next two sections.

The ANSI string library

The `string.h` interface exports a large number of functions, many of which are useful only in certain relatively specialized applications. The most important functions exported by `string.h` are shown in Table 3-1.

Many of the functions in the ANSI string library are quite simple in their operation and do not require you to think about the internal representation. For example, you can determine the length of a string `s` by calling the function `strlen(s)` or check whether two strings are equal by using the following `if` statement:

```
if (strcmp(s1, s2) == 0) . . .
```

In general, functions that examine the contents of their string arguments without changing them cause relatively little trouble. Things begin to get confusing when the functions in the string library need to change the values of those parameter strings. Because arrays in C—including strings, which are implemented as arrays of characters—are always passed by reference, the functions in the string library are free to change the elements of the strings that are passed to them. As it is designed, however, the `string.h` interface places considerable responsibility on the client for making sure that these operations work correctly.

To make the operation of the string library more clear, it helps to differentiate two types of string parameters. Strings whose contents are never changed by the function to which they are passed are called **read-only parameters** and are used to provide string data to the function. For example, the arguments to `strcmp` are both read-only parameters. Strings whose contents are changed by the function are called **writable parameters** and are used to return string results. The `strcpy` and `strcat` functions, for example, take a parameter of each kind. In a call of the form

```
strcpy(dst, src);
```

which copies characters from `src` to `dst`, the first argument is a writable parameter and the second is read-only.

TABLE 3-1	Common functions exported by `string.h`
`strlen(s)`	This function returns the length of the string *s*.
`strcpy(dst, src)`	This function copies characters from *src* to *dst* up to and including the first null character. As with most functions in the ANSI string library, it is the client's responsibility to ensure that there is sufficient memory space in the destination string.
`strncpy(dst, src, n)`	This function is similar to `strcpy` except that it never copies more than *n* characters, which makes it much easier to avoid overflowing the buffer used for *dst*. The ANSI definition requires `strncpy` to initialize all unused positions in the *dst* string to the null character, which leads to unnecessary inefficiency.
`strcat(dst, src)`	This function appends the characters from *src* to the end of *dst*. As with `strcpy`, this function provides no protection against overflowing the end of *dst* buffer.
`strncat(dst, src, n)`	This function appends at most *n* characters from *src* to the end of *dst*. Because the available buffer space depends on the number of characters already in the *dst* buffer as well as on the length of the *src* string, this function does not provide much help in avoiding buffer overflow.
`strcmp(s₁, s₂)`	This function compares the strings s_1 and s_2 and returns an integer that is less than 0 if s_1 comes before s_2 in lexicographic order, 0 if they are equal, and greater than 0 if s_1 comes after s_2.
`strncmp(s₁, s₂, n)`	This function is like `strcmp` but looks only at the first *n* characters of the two strings.
`strchr(s, ch)`	This function searches the string *s* for the character *ch* and returns a pointer to the first character position in which it appears. If *ch* does not appear in *s*, the function returns NULL.
`strrchr(s, ch)`	This function is similar to `strchr` except that it returns a pointer to the last position at which the character *ch* exists.
`strstr(s₁, s₂)`	This function searches for the string s_1 to see if it contains s_2 as a substring. If it does, `strstr` returns a pointer to the character position in s_1 at which the match begins. If not, it returns NULL.

As a client of the `string.h` interface, it is your responsibility to make sure that there is storage available for any writable parameter. You must not, for example, write code like this:

```
string src = "Hello";
string dst;

strcpy(dst, src);
```

There is no memory assigned to dst.

In this program fragment, the variable `dst` is declared as a pointer to a character, but there is no memory allocated to hold the actual characters. What you need to do instead when you work with the `string.h` interface is allocate a character array to hold the destination string. Arrays that are preallocated and later used as a repository for data are called **buffers.** Thus, if you wanted to use `strcpy` to copy a string, you would need to declare a destination buffer, like this:

```
string src = "Hello";
char dst[BufferSize];

strcpy(dst, src);
```

The value of the constant `BufferSize` must be large enough to hold all the characters copied from the source string. In this simple example, where you know what the source string is, the code will work as long as `BufferSize` is at least six: five for the characters in `"Hello"` and one for the terminating null character. But what happens if you don't know how large the source string is? How can you choose an appropriate value of `BufferSize`?

When you use the ANSI string library, there are no good answers to this question. If you call `strcpy` with a source string that is longer than the destination buffer, the function will go ahead and copy characters right on past the end of the buffer, overwriting any data that happened to be there. Writing data past the end of an buffer is a common programming error called **buffer overflow.**

If you think the space you have allocated to the destination buffer might not be sufficient, you have an obligation to check the length of the source string before you copy it using `strcpy`. The following code, for example, catches the buffer overflow condition and reports it as an error:

```
if (strlen(str) >= BufferSize) Error("Buffer overflow");
strcpy(dst, src);
```

The code in Figure 3-5 provides a more extensive example of how you can use the `string.h` interface to perform simple string manipulation. The principal function is `PigLatin`, which converts an English word to Pig Latin by applying the following rules:

- If the word contains no vowels, no translation is done, which means that the translated word is the same as the original.
- If the word begins with a vowel, the function adds the string `"way"` to the end of the original word. Thus, the Pig Latin equivalent of *any* is *anyway.*
- If the word begins with a consonant, the function extracts the string of consonants up to the first vowel, moves that collection of consonants to the end of the word, and adds the string `"ay"`. For example, the Pig Latin equivalent of *trash* is *ashtray.*

Because this version of the `PigLatin` function uses the ANSI string library, it makes sense to design it in a way that is consistent with the abstraction presented by the `string.h` interface. Logically, the function takes one string and returns another,

FIGURE 3-5 Implementation of Pig Latin translation using the `string.h` interface

```
/*
 * Function: PigLatin
 * Usage: PigLatin(word, buffer, bufferSize);
 * -------------------------------------------
 * This function translates a word from English to Pig Latin.  The
 * translated word is written into the array buffer, which has an
 * allocated size of bufferSize.  The code checks for buffer
 * overflow and generates an error if it occurs.
 */

static void PigLatin(char *word, char buffer[], int bufferSize)
{
    char *vp;
    int wordLength;

    vp = FindFirstVowel(word);
    wordLength = strlen(word);
    if (vp == word) {
        wordLength += 3;
    } else if (vp != NULL) {
        wordLength += 2;
    }
    if (wordLength >= bufferSize) Error("Buffer overflow");
    if (vp == NULL) {
        strcpy(buffer, word);
    } else if (vp == word) {
        strcpy(buffer, word);
        strcat(buffer, "way");
    } else {
        strcpy(buffer, vp);
        strncat(buffer, word, vp - word);
        strcat(buffer, "ay");
    }
}

/*
 * Function: FindFirstVowel
 * Usage: vp = FindFirstVowel(word);
 * ---------------------------------
 * This function returns a pointer of the first vowel in word.
 * If word does not contain a vowel, FindFirstVowel returns NULL.
 */

static char *FindFirstVowel(char *word)
{
    char *cp;

    for (cp = word; *cp != '\0'; cp++) {
        if (IsVowel(*cp)) return (cp);
    }
    return (NULL);
}
```

which means that it needs to have a read-only string parameter for the English word and a writable one for the Pig Latin equivalent. Moreover, if you want the function to test for buffer overflow—as indeed you should—it needs to know the buffer size. Thus, the prototype for `PigLatin` might look like this:

```
void PigLatin(char *word, char buffer[], int bufferSize);
```

The code that calls `PigLatin` is responsible for allocating the buffer for the translated word. For example, the following main program reads in an English word and displays its Pig Latin translation:

```
main()
{
    string word;
    char translationBuffer[MaxWord + 1];

    printf("Enter a word: ");
    word = GetLine();
    PigLatin(word, translationBuffer, MaxWord + 1);
    printf("Pig Latin: %s\n", translationBuffer);
}
```

The constant `MaxWord` specifies the maximum length of the translated word; because the buffer must also have room for the terminating null character, the appropriate value for the buffer size is `MaxWord + 1`.

The `PigLatin` implementation uses `strcpy` and `strcat` to copy characters from the appropriate part of the string `word` into the buffer that holds the translated word. Almost half the code in the function, however, is concerned with making sure that the buffer space does not overflow. Writing the code to determine how many characters will be in the translated word and comparing that length against the size of the buffer can seem quite tedious. Many C programmers get frustrated by this part of the coding process and leave out such checking entirely, even though failure to check for buffer overflow can have dire consequences. In 1988, a graduate student at Cornell University released a program that spread like a virus through computers connected to a worldwide network called the Internet. This program, which became known as the *Internet worm,* took advantage of the fact that a system utility program used on many Internet computers failed to check whether character storage in an internal buffer had been exhausted by the input data. By providing enough input data to use up the allocated storage, the Internet worm was able to overwrite the system program itself and cause it to execute commands on its behalf.

The code for the implementation of `FindFirstVowel` also follows the conventions of the `string.h` interface and returns a pointer to the first vowel in the string `word`, or `NULL` if no vowel exists. To test whether the vowel appears at the beginning of the word, the `PigLatin` function checks the following condition:

```
if (vp == word) . . .
```

Note that this test does not check whether the *strings* are equal but rather whether the *pointers* are equal. If **vp** and **word** point to the same character, then the vowel appears at the beginning of the word.

The `strlib.h` interface

As the example in the preceding section makes clear, the ANSI string library can be very cumbersome, particularly if you are careful to check for buffer overflow conditions. Because the complexity imposed by the **string.h** interface tends to get in the way of understanding more critical algorithmic issues, this text adds another abstraction layer to hide most of that complexity. That interface is called **strlib.h**, and is presented in its complete form in Figure 3-6.

FIGURE 3-6 Interface to the dynamic string library

```
/*
 * File: strlib.h
 * --------------
 * The strlib.h file defines the interface for a dynamic string
 * library.  In the context of this package, strings are treated as
 * an abstract type, which means that the client relies only on the
 * exported operations and not on the underlying representation.
 */

#ifndef _strlib_h
#define _strlib_h

#include "genlib.h"

/* Exported entries */

/*
 * Function: Concat
 * Usage: s = Concat(s1, s2);
 * --------------------------
 * This function concatenates two strings by joining them end to end.
 * For example, Concat("ABC", "DE") returns the string "ABCDE".
 */

string Concat(string s1, string s2);
```

```
/*
 * Function: IthChar
 * Usage: ch = IthChar(s, i);
 * -------------------------
 * This function returns the character at position i in the string
 * s.  It is included in the library to make the type string a true
 * abstract type in the sense that all the necessary operations
 * can be invoked using functions. Calling IthChar(s, i) is like
 * selecting s[i], except that IthChar checks to see whether i is
 * within the range of legal index positions, which extend from 0
 * to StringLength(s). Calling IthChar(s, StringLength(s)) returns
 * the null character at the end of the string.
 */

char IthChar(string s, int i);

/*
 * Function: SubString
 * Usage: t = SubString(s, p1, p2);
 * --------------------------------
 * SubString returns a copy of the substring of s consisting of
 * the characters between index positions p1 and p2, inclusive.
 * The following special cases apply:
 *
 * 1. If p1 is less than 0, it is assumed to be 0.
 * 2. If p2 is greater than StringLength(s) - 1, then p2 is assumed
 *    to be StringLength(s) - 1.
 * 3. If p2 < p1, SubString returns the empty string.
 */

string SubString(string s, int p1, int p2);

/*
 * Function: CharToString
 * Usage: s = CharToString(ch);
 * ----------------------------
 * This function takes a single character and returns a one-character
 * string consisting of that character.  The CharToString function
 * is useful, for example, if you need to concatenate a string and
 * a character.  Since Concat requires two strings, you must first
 * convert the character into a string.
 */

string CharToString(char ch);

/*
 * Function: StringLength
 * Usage: len = StringLength(s);
 * ----------------------------
 * This function returns the length of s.
 */

int StringLength(string s);
```

```
/*
 * Function: CopyString
 * Usage: newstr = CopyString(s);
 * --------------------------------
 * CopyString copies the string s into dynamically allocated
 * memory and returns the new string.  This function is not required
 * if you use this library on its own, but is sometimes necessary
 * if you are working with the ANSI string library as well.
 */

string CopyString(string s);

/*
 * Function: StringEqual
 * Usage: if (StringEqual(s1, s2)) . . .
 * ----------------------------------------
 * This function returns TRUE if the strings s1 and s2 are equal.
 * For the strings to be considered equal, every character in one
 * string must precisely match the corresponding character in the
 * other.  Uppercase and lowercase characters are different.
 */

bool StringEqual(string s1, string s2);

/*
 * Function: StringCompare
 * Usage: if (StringCompare(s1, s2) < 0) . . .
 * -------------------------------------------------
 * This function returns a number less than 0 if string s1 comes
 * before s2 in alphabetical order, 0 if they are equal, and a
 * number greater than 0 if s1 comes after s2.  The order is
 * determined by the internal representation used for characters.
 */

int StringCompare(string s1, string s2);

/*
 * Function: FindChar
 * Usage: p = FindChar(ch, text, start);
 * ----------------------------------------
 * Beginning at position start in the string text, this
 * function searches for the character ch and returns the
 * first index at which it appears or -1 if no match is
 * found.
 */

int FindChar(char ch, string text, int start);
```

```
/*
 * Function: FindString
 * Usage: p = FindString(str, text, start);
 * -------------------------------------------
 * Beginning at position start in the string text, this
 * function searches for the string str and returns the
 * first index at which it appears or -1 if no match is
 * found.
 */

int FindString(string str, string text, int start);

/*
 * Function: ConvertToLowerCase
 * Usage: s = ConvertToLowerCase(s);
 * ----------------------------------
 * This function returns a new string with all
 * alphabetic characters converted to lower case.
 */

string ConvertToLowerCase(string s);

/*
 * Function: ConvertToUpperCase
 * Usage: s = ConvertToUpperCase(s);
 * ----------------------------------
 * This function returns a new string with all
 * alphabetic characters converted to upper case.
 */

string ConvertToUpperCase(string s);

/*
 * Function: IntegerToString
 * Usage: s = IntegerToString(n);
 * -------------------------------
 * This function converts an integer into the corresponding
 * string of digits.  For example, IntegerToString(123)
 * returns "123" as a string.
 */

string IntegerToString(int n);

/*
 * Function: StringToInteger
 * Usage: n = StringToInteger(s);
 * -------------------------------
 * This function converts a string of digits into an integer.
 * If the string is not a legal integer or contains extraneous
 * characters, StringToInteger signals an error condition.
 */

int StringToInteger(string s);
```

```
/*
 * Function: RealToString
 * Usage: s = RealToString(d);
 * ---------------------------
 * This function converts a floating-point number into the
 * corresponding string form.  For example, calling
 * RealToString(23.45) returns "23.45".  The conversion is
 * the same as that used for "%G" format in printf.
 */

string RealToString(double d);

/*
 * Function: StringToReal
 * Usage: d = StringToReal(s);
 * ---------------------------
 * This function converts a string representing a real number
 * into its corresponding value.  If the string is not a
 * legal floating-point number or if it contains extraneous
 * characters, StringToReal signals an error condition.
 */

double StringToReal(string s);

#endif
```

The principal advantage of the `strlib.h` interface is that strings are treated as abstract values. When a function needs to return a string to its caller, it does so by returning a string as its value. Any storage for that string is allocated dynamically by the library itself, which frees the client from having to worry about the details of memory allocation. This change in the abstraction leads to a considerable simplification of the code. Buffer overflow, for example, is no longer possible. Strings can be allocated at whatever lengths are necessary until the entire heap runs out of memory.

The extent of the simplification is illustrated by the code in Figure 3-7, which shows how to solve the Pig Latin translation problem using the approach to string manipulation supported by the `strlib.h` interface. In this model, the `PigLatin` function can simply return its result as a string, which in turn simplifies the main program to look like this:

```
main()
{
    string word;

    printf("Enter a word: ");
    word = GetLine();
    printf("Pig Latin: %s\n", PigLatin(word));
}
```

FIGURE 3-7 Implementation of Pig Latin translation using the `strlib.h` interface

```
/*
 * Function: PigLatin
 * Usage: translation = PigLatin(word);
 * ------------------------------------
 * This function translates a word from English to Pig Latin using
 * the rules specified in Chapter 3.  The translated word is
 * returned as the value of the function.
 */

static string PigLatin(string word)
{
    int vp;
    string head, tail;

    vp = FindFirstVowel(word);
    if (vp == -1) {
        return (word);
    } else if (vp == 0) {
        return (Concat(word, "way"));
    } else {
        head = SubString(word, 0, vp - 1);
        tail = SubString(word, vp, StringLength(word) - 1);
        return (Concat(tail, Concat(head, "ay")));
    }
}

/*
 * Function: FindFirstVowel
 * Usage: k = FindFirstVowel(word);
 * --------------------------------
 * This function returns the index position of the first vowel
 * in word.  If word does not contain a vowel, FindFirstVowel
 * returns -1.
 */

static int FindFirstVowel(string word)
{
    int i;

    for (i = 0; i < StringLength(word); i++) {
        if (IsVowel(IthChar(word, i))) return (i);
    }
    return (-1);
}
```

The new implementation of `PigLatin` uses the `SubString` function to extract pieces of the original word and the `Concat` function to reassemble them at the end. The `FindFirstVowel` function has also changed to be consistent with the discipline used in this interface. Instead of returning a pointer to a character, the implementation in Figure 3-7 returns the integer index of the first vowel, or –1 if no vowel appears.

Many of the functions in the `strlib.h` interface are implemented by calling similar functions in the underlying `string.h` interface, which forms the next level of the abstraction hierarchy. The complete implementation appears in *The Art and Science of C* and is available from the Addison-Wesley FTP (file transfer protocol) site at the following location:

> `ftp://aw.com/aw.computer.science/Roberts.CS1.C`

Even though this text relies extensively on the functions in the `strlib.h` interface, it is not necessary to understand that code from the implementation side. The programs in this book are invariably clients of `strlib.h`. The whole point of interfaces is that they protect clients from the complexity of the implementation. As you continue with your programming career, you will often make use of libraries even though you have no understanding of their implementation, so it is best to become comfortable with that process as early as you can.

3.4 The standard I/O library

The most commonly used library in the ANSI collection is the standard I/O library, which is defined by the `stdio.h` interface. Every program in the text includes this interface, mostly because it exports the `printf` function. The `stdio.h` interface, however, includes several additional functions that make it possible to read and write files, which in turn enable you to store data values that persist even after your program completes its operation.

Data files

Whenever you want to store information on the computer for longer than the running time of a program, the usual approach is to collect the data into a logically cohesive whole and store it on a permanent storage medium as a file. Ordinarily, a file is stored on a disk, either a removable floppy disk or a hard disk built into the machine. Occasionally, files are stored in another medium, such as a magnetic tape or a compact disc (CD), but the basic principles and modes of operation are the same. The important point is that the permanent data objects you store on the computer—documents, games, executable programs, source code, and the like—are all stored in the form of files.

On most systems, files come in a variety of types. For example, in the programming domain, you work with source files, object files, and executable files, each of which has a distinct representation. When you use a file to store data for use by a program, that file usually consists of text and is therefore called a **text file.** You can think of a text file as a sequence of characters stored in a permanent medium and identified by a file name. The name of the file and the characters it contains have the same relationship as the name of a variable and its contents.

As an example, the following text file contains the first stanza of Lewis Carroll's nonsense poem "Jabberwocky," which appears in *Through the Looking Glass:*

jabber.txt

```
'Twas brillig, and the slithy toves
Did gyre and gimble in the wabe;
All mimsy were the borogoves,
And the mome raths outgrabe.
```

When you look at a file, it is often convenient to regard it as a two-dimensional structure—a sequence of lines composed of individual characters. Internally, however, text files are represented as a one-dimensional sequence of characters. In addition to the printing characters you can see, files also contain the newline character '\n', which marks the end of each line. The file system also keeps track of the length of the file so programs that read files can recognize where the file ends.

In many respects, text files are similar to strings. They both consist of an ordered collection of characters with a specified endpoint. On the other hand, strings and files differ in several important respects. Of these, the most important difference is the permanence of the data. A string is stored temporarily in the computer's memory during the time that a program runs; a file is stored on a long-term storage device and continues to exist until it is explicitly deleted or overwritten. But there is also a difference in the way you use data in strings and files. A string is an array of characters. You can select characters in any order by specifying the appropriate index. In the context of a program, a file is usually read or written in a sequential fashion. When a program reads an existing file, it starts at the beginning and reads characters until it reaches the end. When a program creates a new file, it starts by writing the first character and continues in order with each subsequent character.

Using files in C

To read or write a file as part of a C program, you must use the following steps:

1. *Declare a file pointer variable.* The **stdio.h** interface exports a type called **FILE**, which keeps track of the information the system needs to manage file processing activity. Each file manipulated by the program is identified by a variable of type **FILE ***. Thus, if you are writing a program that reads an input file and creates a second file for output, you need to declare two **FILE *** variables, as follows:

```
FILE *infile, *outfile;
```

2. *Open the file.* Before you can use a file pointer variable, you need to establish an association between that variable and an actual file. This operation is called **opening** the file and is performed by calling the **fopen** function. The

`fopen` call requires you to specify the name of the file and to indicate the mode of data transfer, which is ordinarily one of the following:

"r" The file is open for *reading*. The file pointer variable returned by `fopen` can be used only in input operations. The file must already exist.

"w" The file is open for *writing*. The resulting file pointer variable can be used only for output operations. If the file does not yet exist, a new file is created with the specified name. If there is already a file with that name, its contents are erased.

"a" The file is open for *appending*. This mode is similar to **"w"** mode in that the resulting file pointer is available for output operations. The only difference occurs if the specified file already exists, in which case any new information written to the file appears at the end of the existing data.

For example, if you wanted to read the text of the `jabber.txt` file, you would execute the statement

```
infile = fopen("jabber.txt", "r");
```

If a requested input file is missing, the `fopen` function returns the pointer value **NULL** to indicate that an error has occurred. As a programmer, you have a responsibility to check for this error and report it to the user.

3. *Transfer the data.* Once you have opened the data files, you then call the appropriate functions in `stdio.h` to perform the actual I/O operations. For an input file, these functions read data from the file into your program; for an output file, the functions transfer data from the program to the file. To perform the actual transfers, you can choose any of several strategies, depending on the application. At the simplest level, you can read or write files character by character, using the functions `getc` and `putc`. In some cases, however, it is more convenient to process files line by line. For that purpose, the `stdio.h` interface provides the functions `fgets` and `fputs`, but it is usually simpler to use the function `ReadLine` from `simpio.h`, which solves a number of problems that arise when using the `stdio.h` functions. At a still higher level, you can choose to read and write formatted data using `fscanf` and `fprintf`. Doing so allows you to intermix numeric data with strings and other data types. The functions mentioned in this paragraph are described in separate sections later in the chapter.

4. *Close the file.* When you have finished all data transfers, you need to indicate that fact to the file system by calling `fclose`. This operation, called **closing** the file, breaks the association between a `FILE *` variable and the actual file.

Standard files

The standard I/O library defines three special identifiers—**stdin**, **stdout**, and **stderr**—that act as **FILE *** constants and are available to all programs. These constants are referred to as **standard files.** The constant **stdin** designates the standard input file, which is the source for user input. The constant **stdout** indicates standard output and represents the device on which output data is written to the user. The constant **stderr** represents the standard error file and is used to report any error messages the user should see. Typically, the standard files all refer to the computer console. When you read data from **stdin**, the input comes from the keyboard; when you write data to **stdout** or **stderr**, the output appears on the screen.

Character I/O

The simplest approach to file processing is to go through files character by character. The **stdio.h** interface defines a function **getc(infile)** that reads the next character in a file and returns it to its caller.

Although the idea of **getc** seems simple enough, there is a confusing aspect in its design. If you look at the formal definition of **getc**, its prototype looks like this:

```
int getc(FILE *infile);
```

At first glance, the result type seems odd. The prototype indicates that **getc** returns an integer, even though conceptually the function returns a character. The reason for this design decision is that returning a character would make it impossible for a program to detect the end-of-file mark. There are only 256 possible character codes, and a data file might contain any of those values. There is no value—or at least no value of type **char**—that you could use as a sentinel to indicate the end-of-file condition. By extending the definition so that **getc** returns an integer, the implementation can return a value outside the range of legal character codes to indicate the end-of-file condition. That value is given the symbolic name of **EOF** in **stdio.h**.

To write a single character, you use the function **putc(ch, outfile)**, which writes its first argument to the specified output file. As an example of the use of **getc** and **putc**, you can copy one file to another by calling the following function:

```
void CopyFile(FILE *infile, FILE *outfile)
{
    int ch;

    while ((ch = getc(infile)) != EOF) {
        putc(ch, outfile);
    }
}
```

The **while** loop in **CopyFile** is highly idiomatic and deserves some consideration. The test expression for the **while** loop uses embedded assignment to combine the operations of reading in a character and testing for the end-of-file condition. When the program evaluates the `while` condition, it begins by evaluating the subexpression

```
ch = getc(infile)
```

which reads a character and assigns it to `ch`. Before executing the loop body, the program then goes on to make sure the result of the assignment is not `EOF`. The parentheses around the assignment are required; without them, the expression would incorrectly assign to `ch` the result of comparing the character against `EOF`.

Rereading characters from an input file

When you are reading data from an input file, you will often find yourself in the position of not knowing that you should stop reading characters until you have already read more than you need. For example, suppose that you are asked to write a program that copies a program from one file to another, removing all comments as it does so. As you know, a comment in C begins with the character sequence `/*` and ends with the sequence `*/`. A program to remove them must copy characters until it detects the initial `/*` sequence and then read characters without copying them until it detects the `*/` at the end. The only aspect of this problem that poses any difficulty is the fact that the comment markers are two characters long. If you are copying the file a character at a time, what do you do when you encounter a slash? It might be the beginning of a comment, in which case you should not copy it to the output file. On the other hand, it might be the division operator. The only way to determine which of these cases applies is to look at the next character. If it is an asterisk, you need to ignore both characters and make note of the fact that a comment is in progress. If it not, however, what you would most like to do is forget that you ever read that character and then treat it normally on the next cycle of the loop.

The `stdio.h` interface provides a function that allows you to do just that. The function is called `ungetc` and has the following form:

```
ungetc(ch, infile);
```

The effect of this call is to "push" the character `ch` back into the input stream so that it is returned on the next call to `getc`. The C libraries only guarantee the ability to push back one character into the input file, so you should not rely on being able to read several characters ahead and then push them all back. Fortunately, being able to push back one character is sufficient in the vast majority of cases.

An implementation of a function `CopyRemovingComments` that uses `ungetc` is shown in Figure 3-8. This implementation copies characters from the input file to the output file, deleting comments as it goes.

Updating a file

The `CopyRemovingComments` function makes it easy to copy the contents of one file to another, removing comments as you go. In many file-processing applications, you are not interested in creating a new file but instead want to modify the contents of an existing one. The process of changing a file is called **updating** the file and is

| FIGURE 3-8 | Function to copy a file, removing any comments |

```
void CopyRemovingComments(FILE *infile, FILE *outfile)
{
    int ch, nch;
    bool commentFlag;

    commentFlag = FALSE;
    while ((ch = getc(infile)) != EOF) {
        if (commentFlag) {
            if (ch == '*') {
                nch = getc(infile);
                if (nch == '/') {
                    commentFlag = FALSE;
                } else {
                    ungetc(nch, infile);
                }
            }
        } else {
            if (ch == '/') {
                nch = getc(infile);
                if (nch == '*') {
                    commentFlag = TRUE;
                } else {
                    ungetc(nch, infile);
                }
            }
            if (!commentFlag) putc(ch, outfile);
        }
    }
}
```

not as simple as it might seem. On most systems, it is not legal to open a file for output if that file is already open for input. Depending on how files are implemented on a particular system, the call to `fopen` may fail or, in some cases, destroy the contents of the file altogether.

The most common way to update a file is to write the new data into a temporary file and then replace the original file with the temporary one after you have written the entire contents of the updated file. Thus, if you want to write a program to update an existing file, that program consists of the following steps:

1. Open the original file for input.
2. Open a temporary file for output with a different name.
3. Copy the input file to the temporary file, performing any updates as you go.
4. Close both files.
5. Delete the original file.
6. Rename the temporary file so that it once again has the original name.

To implement this strategy, you need to use three new functions from the `stdio.h` interface: `tmpnam`, `remove`, and `rename`.

Although you are certainly free to choose your own name for a temporary file, the `stdio.h` interface includes a function called `tmpnam` that generates temporary file names. The conventions for naming files differ from machine to machine. Calling the function `tmpnam(NULL)` returns a string whose value is a temporary file name suitable for use on that machine.[2] Thus, you can create and open a new temporary file using the following code:

```
temp = tmpnam(NULL);
outfile = fopen(temp, "w");
```

To delete a file, all you have to do is call the function **remove**(*name*), where *name* is the name of the file. Renaming a file is just as simple and is accomplished by calling **rename**(*old name*, *new name*). Like many functions in the ANSI libraries, **remove** and **rename** return 0 if they are successful and a nonzero value if they fail. Although you will certainly encounter code in which these functions are used as if they were procedures, it is safer to test their return value to make sure the operation has succeeded.

These three functions give you everything you need to write a main program that uses `CopyRemovingComments` to remove the comments from an existing file, as follows:

```
main()
{
    string filename, temp;
    FILE *infile, *outfile;

    printf("This program removes comments from a file.\n");
    while (TRUE) {
        printf("File name: ");
        filename = GetLine();
        infile = fopen(filename, "r");
        if (infile != NULL) break;
        printf("File %s not found -- try again.\n", filename);
    }
    temp = tmpnam(NULL);
    outfile = fopen(temp, "w");
    if (outfile == NULL) Error("Can't open temporary file");
    CopyRemovingComments(infile, outfile);
    fclose(infile);
    fclose(outfile);
    if (remove(filename) != 0 || rename(temp, filename) != 0) {
        Error("Unable to rename temporary file");
    }
}
```

---

[2] When it is called with **NULL** as its argument, the `tmpnam` function returns a pointer to memory that is private to the implementation of the standard I/O library. As a result, it is not safe to use `tmpnam` to generate a second temporary file name before you have finished with the first. If you need to do so, you can copy the result of `tmpnam` into new memory using `CopyString` or `strcpy`.

Line-oriented I/O

Because files are usually subdivided into individual lines, it is often useful to read an entire line of data at a time. The function in **stdio.h** that performs this operation is called **fgets** and has the following prototype:

```
string fgets(char buffer[], int bufSize, FILE *infile);
```

The effect of this function is to copy the next line of the file into the character array **buffer**. Ordinarily, **fgets** stops after reading the first newline character but returns earlier if the size of the buffer, as specified by the parameter **bufSize**, would otherwise be exceeded. Thus, the last character in **buffer** before the terminating null character will be a newline unless the line from the file is too long to fit in the buffer. Irrespective of whether it reads the entire line or a part of it, **fgets** ordinarily returns a pointer to the character array given as the first argument. If **fgets** is called at the end of the file, it returns **NULL**.

The corresponding function for output is called **fputs** and has the prototype

```
void fputs(string str, FILE *outfile);
```

Calling **fputs** copies characters from the string to the output file until the end of the string is reached.

You can use **fgets** and **fputs** to implement the **CopyFile** function introduced in the section on "Character I/O" earlier in this chapter, as follows:

```
static void CopyFile(FILE *infile, FILE *outfile)
{
    char buffer[MaxLine];

    while (fgets(buffer, MaxLine, infile) != NULL) {
        fputs(buffer, outfile);
    }
}
```

Because the **fgets** function requires the client to allocate buffer space, it is usually easier to use the **ReadLine** function defined in **simpio.h**. The **ReadLine** function is similar in operation to the **GetLine** function introduced in Chapter 1. The only difference is that the input comes from a file supplied as an argument instead of from the console. **ReadLine** offers the following advantages over **fgets**:

- **ReadLine** allocates its own heap memory as needed, making it impossible to overflow the buffer.
- **ReadLine** removes the newline character used to signal the end of the line, so that the data returned consists simply of the characters on the line.
- Each string returned by **ReadLine** is stored in its own memory, so that no confusion can occur as to whether a string needs to be copied before it is stored.

The **ReadLine** function returns **NULL** when it encounters the end of the input file.

Formatted I/O

Of all the facilities provided by the standard I/O library, none are more emblematic of C than the formatted I/O functions `printf` and `scanf`. You have used `printf` since Chapter 1 but have only scratched the surface of what you can do with it.

The `printf` function comes in three different forms:

```
printf (control string, . . .);
fprintf (output stream, control string, . . .);
sprintf (character array, control string, . . .);
```

The `printf` form always writes its output to standard output. The `fprintf` function is identical, except that it takes a `FILE` pointer argument as its first argument and writes its output to that file. The `sprintf` form takes a character array as its first argument and writes into that array the characters that would have been displayed by a `printf` call. It is the responsibility of the caller to ensure that there is sufficient space in the array to contain the output data.

Other than the destination to which the output is directed, all three forms of `printf` work in the same way: they take a string called the *control string* and copy it, character by character, to the indicated destination. If the string contains a percent sign (`%`), that character is treated as the beginning of a format code, which is replaced by a string representation of the next available argument in the `printf` call. The nature of the formatting is indicated by the letter that comes at the end of the format code, which may also include modifiers that specify field width, precision, and alignment. The most common `printf` options are described in the section on "Simple input and output" in Chapter 1.

A very useful feature of `printf` that is not covered in Chapter 1 is that the field width and precision indicators in a format code can be replaced by an asterisk, which means that the field width is taken from the next argument to the `printf` call, which must be an integer. For example, the statement

```
printf("%*d\n", fieldWidth, value);
```

displays `value` in a decimal field whose width is given by the variable `fieldWidth`. This feature will be used in several programs later in the text to ensure proper alignment.

The `scanf` functions

The `scanf` functions provide an input counterpart to `printf` that is intended to make it easier for programs to read in values of the various basic types. Like `printf`, `scanf` comes in three different forms:

```
scanf (control string, . . .)
fscanf (input stream, control string, . . .)
sscanf (character string, control string, . . .)
```

The first reads values from standard input, the second from the FILE pointer indicated by the input stream parameter, and the third from the specified character string. Each of these forms reads characters from the source and converts them according to the specifications in the control string. The data values themselves are stored in memory provided by the caller through additional arguments.

Because scanf must return information to its caller, the arguments after the control string must use call by reference, as described in Chapter 2. Each of the arguments after the control string must therefore be a pointer. In most cases, you simply include the address-of operator (&) in front of a variable name to convert that variable to its address, but it is important to remember that the names of character arrays are already pointers and therefore do not require the &.

The control string for scanf consists of three different classes of characters:

- Characters that appear as blank space, such as the space, tab, and newline characters. These characters cause scanf to skip ahead to the next nonblank character.
- A percent sign followed by a conversion specification.
- Any other character, which must match the next character in the input. This facility allows the program to check for required punctuation, such as a comma between two numbers, and so forth.

Conversion specifications are structurally similar to their printf analogues, but the set of available options is different. A conversion specification for scanf is composed of the following options, listed in the order in which you must specify them:

- An optional assignment-suppression flag indicated by an asterisk (*), which specifies that the value from the input should be discarded rather than stored through one of the argument pointers.
- An optional numeric field width indicating the maximum number of characters to be read for the field.
- An optional size specification consisting of either the letter h, which indicates an integer value of type short, or the letter l, which indicates either an integer value of type long or a floating-point value of type double.
- A conversion specification letter, which is ordinarily one of those shown in Table 3-2.

All forms of scanf return the number of conversions successfully performed, not counting those that were suppressed using the * specification. If the end-of-file condition is detected before any conversions occur, scanf returns the value EOF.

The scanf functions have not worked out well in practice and are used infrequently in commercial applications. P. J. Plauger, who chaired the committee to standardize the ANSI C libraries, issues the following warning:

> You will find that the scan conversion specifications are not as complete as the print conversion specifications. Too often, you want to exercise control over an input scan. Or you may find it impossible to determine

TABLE 3-2 Conversion specifications for scanf

%d	The next value from the input is scanned as a decimal integer. That integer value is then stored in the memory cell addressed by the next pointer argument. It is crucial that the size of the variable match the size indicated by the specification.
%f %e %g	The next input value is scanned as a floating-point value and stored in the memory cell indicated by the next pointer in the argument list. The %e and %g codes are identical to %f and are included for symmetry with printf. In the simple form of these conversion specifications, the target of the pointer must be of type float. To read a value of type double, the key letter must be preceded by the letter l.
%c	The next character is read and stored at the address indicated by the next argument, which must be a character pointer. In contrast to the other specifications, the %c specification does not skip whitespace characters before conversion.
%s	Characters are read from the input and stored in successive elements of the character array indicated by the next argument. The caller must ensure that enough space has been allocated in the array to accommodate the value being read. Input is terminated by the first whitespace character.
%[...] %[^...]	The conversion specification may consist of a set of characters enclosed in square brackets. In this case, a string is read up to the first character that is not in the bracketed set. The string is stored at the address specified by the next argument to scanf, which must be a character array. If the set of characters begins with a circumflex (^), the characters that follow are instead interpreted as those that are *not* permitted in the input. For example, the specification %[0123456789] reads in the next sequence of digits as a string; the specification %[^.!?] reads in a string of characters up to the next end-of-sentence mark (period, exclamation point, or question mark).
%%	No conversion is done; a percent sign must follow in the input.

where a scan failed well enough to recover properly from the failure. . . .
Be prepared . . . to give up on the scan functions beyond a point. Their usefulness, over the years, has proved to be limited.

Because of their limited utility in practical work, this text does not use the scanf functions and relies instead on the facilities provided by the simpio.h interface described in Chapter 1.

◼ 3.5 Other ANSI libraries

In addition to the string.h and stdio.h interfaces described earlier in this chapter, there are a few other interfaces in the standard ANSI library that are important for you to know. The most important of these are the stdlib.h, ctype.h and math.h

TABLE 3-3	Common functions exported by `ctype.h`
`isupper`(*ch*) `islower`(*ch*) `isalpha`(*ch*)	These functions return **TRUE** if *ch* is an uppercase letter, a lowercase letter, or any type of letter, respectively.
`isdigit`(*ch*)	This function returns **TRUE** if *ch* is one of the digit characters.
`isalnum`(*ch*)	This function returns **TRUE** if *ch* is **alphanumeric,** which means that it is either a letter or a digit.
`ispunct`(*ch*)	This function returns **TRUE** if *ch* is a punctuation symbol.
`isspace`(*ch*)	This function returns **TRUE** if *ch* is a **whitespace character.** These characters are `' '` (the space character), `'\t'`, `'\n'`, `'\f'`, or `'\v'`, all of which appear as blank space on the screen.
`isprint`(*ch*)	This function returns **TRUE** if *ch* is any printable character, including the whitespace characters.
`toupper`(*ch*) `tolower`(*ch*)	These functions first test *ch* to see if it is a letter. If so, *ch* is converted to the desired case, so that `tolower('A')` returns `'a'`. If *ch* is not a letter, its value is returned unchanged.

interfaces. The `stdlib.h` interface exports several standard definions including the constant **NULL**, the `malloc` and `free` functions for dynamic allocation, and the `abs` function for taking the absolute value of an integer. Other functions in the `stdlib.h` interface will be introduced in subsequent chapters as they become useful. The most important functions exported by the `ctype.h` and `math.h` interfaces are shown in Tables 3-3 and 3-4, respectively.

In some cases, the functions in these interfaces are easy to implement on your own. Even so, it is good programming practice to use the library functions instead of writing your own. There are three principal reasons for doing so.

1. Because the library functions are standard, programs you write will be easier for other programmers to read. Assuming that the programmers are at all experienced in C, they will recognize these functions and know exactly what they mean.

2. It is easier to rely on library functions for correctness than on your own. Because the ANSI C libraries are used by millions of client programmers, there is considerable pressure on the implementors to get the functions right. If you rewrite library functions yourself, the chance of introducing a bug is much larger.

3. The library implementations of functions are often more efficient than those you can write yourself. Because these libraries are standard and their performance affects many clients, the implementors have a large incentive to optimize the performance of the libraries as much as possible.

TABLE 3-4 Common functions in the `math` library	
`fabs`(*x*)	This function returns the absolute value of a real number *x*. (Note: The function `abs`, which takes the absolute value of an integer, is exported by `stdlib.h`.)
`floor`(*x*)	This function returns the floating-point representation of the largest integer less than or equal to *x*.
`ceil`(*x*)	This function returns the floating-point representation of the smallest integer greater than or equal to *x*.
`fmod`(*x*, *y*)	This function returns the floating-point remainder of *x* / *y*.
`sqrt`(*x*)	This function returns the square root of *x*.
`pow`(*x*, *y*)	This function returns x^y.
`exp`(*x*)	This function returns e^x.
`log`(*x*)	This function returns the natural logarithm of *x*.
`sin`(*theta*) `cos`(*theta*)	These functions return the trigonometric sine and cosine of the angle *theta*, which is expressed in radians. You can convert from degrees to radians by multiplying by π / 180.
`atan`(*x*)	This function returns the trigonometric arctangent of the value *x*. The result is an angle expressed in radians between $-\pi/2$ and $+\pi/2$.
`atan2`(*y*, *x*)	This function returns the angle formed between the *x*-axis and the line extending from the origin through the point (*x*, *y*). As with the other trigonometric functions, the angle is expressed in radians.

Summary

In this chapter, you have learned about *interfaces,* which are the points of connection between the client of a library abstraction and the corresponding implementation. Interfaces are one of the central themes of modern programming and will be used extensively throughout the rest of this text. You have also learned how to use several specific interfaces including `random.h`, `strlib.h`, `string.h`, `stdio.h`, `ctype.h`, and `math.h`.

Important points in this chapter include:

- An interface provides a channel of communication between a client of a library and its implementation but also acts as a barrier to keep unnecessary information from crossing the boundary between the two sides.
- Interfaces in C are represented using header files.

- The definitions exported by an interface are called *interface entries*. The most common interface entries are function prototypes, constant definitions, and type definitions. The interface should contain extensive comments for each entry so that the client can understand how to use that entry but should not expose details that are relevant only to the implementation.

- A well-designed interface must be *unified, simple, sufficient, general,* and *stable.* Because these criteria sometimes conflict with one another, you must learn to strike an appropriate balance in your interface design.

- You can use the `random.h` interface to generate pseudorandom numbers that appear to be random even though they are generated deterministically. The `random.h` interface exports four entries: `RandomInteger`, `RandomReal`, `RandomChance`, and `Randomize`.

- In C, a string is represented internally as an array of characters terminated by a null character. Like any array, strings can be manipulated using either array or pointer operations.

- The interfaces `string.h` and `strlib.h` form a layered abstraction that allow you to think about strings from an increasingly abstract perspective. The `string.h` interface requires clients to allocate storage explicitly. The `strlib.h` interface allocates memory dynamically and is therefore easier to use.

- The `stdio.h` interface exports functions that allow you to read and write data files. The process of using a data file consists of four steps: declaring a file pointer variable, opening the file, transferring data, and closing the file.

REVIEW QUESTIONS

1. Define the following terms: *interface, package, abstraction, implementation, client.*

2. In your own words, describe the difference in perspective between a programmer who writes the implementation of a library and one who writes programs that are clients of that library.

3. How are interfaces represented in C?

4. What are the most common interface entries?

5. What are the five criteria for good interface design listed in this chapter?

6. Why is it important for an interface to be stable?

7. What is meant by the term *extending an interface?*

8. Why are comments particularly important in interfaces?

9. True or false: The comments in an interface should explain in detail how each of the exported functions is implemented.

10. If you were defining an interface named `magic.h`, what would the interface boilerplate look like? What is the purpose of these lines?

11. Why are the values generated by the `rand` function called *pseudorandom numbers?*

12. How would you use `RandomInteger` to generate a random four-digit number?

13. Could you use the multiple assignment statement

```
d1 = d2 = RandomInteger(1, 6);
```

to simulate the process of rolling two dice?

14. The `rand` function ordinarily generates the same sequence of random numbers every time a program is run. What is the reason for this behavior?

15. What is meant by the term *seed* in the context of random numbers?

16. What four steps are necessary to convert the result of `rand` into an integer value between the limits `low` and `high`?

17. When a string is stored in memory, how can you tell where it ends?

18. What idiom can you use to process each character in a string that you view as an array of characters? How does the idiom change if you instead regard the string as a pointer to a character?

19. What is the principal difference between the abstraction models presented by the `string.h` and `strlib.h` interfaces?

20. Assuming that `s1` and `s2` are strings, describe the effect of the conditional test in the following `if` statement:

```
if (s1 == s2) . . .
```

21. If you call `strcpy(s1, s2)`, which argument is the source and which is the destination?

22. What is meant by the term *buffer overflow?*

23. When you are using the ANSI string library, how do you accomplish the effect of the `StringEqual` function?

24. What is the result of calling each of the following functions from the `strlib.h` interface?

a.	`StringLength("ABCDE")`	f.	`CharToString('2')`
b.	`StringLength("")`	g.	`SubString("ABCDE", 0, 3)`
c.	`StringLength("\a")`	h.	`SubString("ABCDE", 4, 1)`
d.	`IthChar("ABC", 2)`	i.	`SubString("ABCDE", 3, 9)`
e.	`Concat("12", ".00")`	j.	`SubString("ABCDE", 3, 3)`

25. What is the result of calling each of the following functions? (For calls to StringCompare, simply indicate the sign of the result.)

    a.   StringEqual("ABCDE", "abcde")

    b.   StringCompare("ABCDE", "ABCDE")

    c.   StringCompare("ABCDE", "ABC")

    d.   StringCompare("ABCDE", "abcde")

    e.   FindChar('a', "Abracadabra", 0)

    f.   FindString("ra", "Abracadabra", 3)

    g.   FindString("is", "This is a test.", 0)

    h.   FindString("This is a test", "this", 0)

    i.   ConvertToLowerCase("Catch-22")

    j.   RealToString(3.140)

26. What is the purpose of the type FILE *? Is understanding the underlying structure of this type important to most programmers?

27. What is meant by the phrase *opening a file?*

28. The second argument to fopen is usually one of the following strings: "r", "w", or "a". What is the significance of this argument and what do each of these values mean?

29. How does the fopen function report failure to its caller?

30. The stdio.h interface automatically defines three standard files. What are their names? What purpose does each one serve?

31. When you are using the getc function, how do you detect the end of a file?

32. What is the purpose of the ungetc function?

33. What steps are involved in the process of updating a file?

34. What are the differences between the functions ReadLine and fgets?

35. What does it mean if you use an asterisk as the field width or precision specification in a printf control string?

36. True or false: Over the years, the scanf function has proven to be an extremely valuable feature of the standard I/O library.

37. What is the result of each of the following calls from ctype.h:

    a.   isdigit(7)   d.   toupper('7')

    b.   isdigit('7')   e.   toupper('A')

    c.   isalnum('7')   f.   tolower('A')

38. When using the trigonometric functions in the math.h interface, how can you convert an angle from degrees to radians?

PROGRAMMING EXERCISES

1. Write a program that repeatedly generates a random real number between 0 and 1 and then displays the average after a certain number of runs, as illustrated by the following sample run:

```
This program averages a series of random numbers
between 0 and 1.
How many trials: 10000.⏎
The average value after 10000 trials is 0.501493
```

If the random number generator is working well, the average should get closer to 0.5 as the number of trials increases.

2.   Heads. . . .
        Heads. . . .
        Heads. . . .
        A weaker man might be moved to re-examine his faith, if
        in nothing else at least in the law of probability.

        — Tom Stoppard, Rosencrantz and Guildenstern Are Dead, 1967

Write a program that simulates flipping a coin repeatedly and continues until three *consecutive* heads are tossed. At that point, your program should display the total number of coin flips that were made. The following is one possible sample run of the program:

```
tails
heads
heads
tails
tails
heads
tails
heads
heads
heads
It took 10 flips to get 3 consecutive heads.
```

3. In casinos from Monte Carlo to Las Vegas, one of the most common gambling devices is the slot machine—the "one-armed bandit." A typical slot machine has three wheels that spin around behind a narrow window. Each wheel is marked with the following symbols: CHERRY, LEMON, ORANGE, PLUM, BELL, and BAR. The window, however, allows you to see only one symbol on each wheel at a time. For example, the window might show the following configuration:

| BELL | ORANGE | BAR |

If you put a dollar into a slot machine and pull the handle on its side, the wheels spin around and eventually come to rest in some new configuration. If the configuration matches one of a set of winning patterns printed on the front of the slot machine, you get back some money. If not, you're out a dollar. The following table shows a typical set of winning patterns, along with their associated payoffs:

BAR	BAR	BAR	*pays*	$250
BELL	BELL	BELL/BAR	*pays*	$20
PLUM	PLUM	PLUM/BAR	*pays*	$14
ORANGE	ORANGE	ORANGE/BAR	*pays*	$10
CHERRY	CHERRY	CHERRY	*pays*	$7
CHERRY	CHERRY	—	*pays*	$5
CHERRY	—	—	*pays*	$2

The notation BELL/BAR means that either a BELL or a BAR can appear in that position, and the dash means that any symbol at all can appear. Thus, getting a CHERRY in the first position is automatically good for $2, no matter what appears on the other wheels. Note that there is never any payoff for the LEMON symbol, even if you happen to line up three of them.

Write a program that simulates playing a slot machine. Your program should provide the user with an initial stake of $50 and then let the user play until the money runs out or the user decides to quit. During each round, your program should take away a dollar, simulate the spinning of the wheels, evaluate the result, and pay the user any appropriate winnings. For example, a user might be lucky enough to see the following sample run:

```
Would you like instructions? no.↵
You have $50.  Would you like to play? yes.↵
PLUM    LEMON   LEMON   -- You lose
You have $49.  Would you like to play? yes.↵
BAR     PLUM    PLUM    -- You lose
You have $48.  Would you like to play? yes.↵
CHERRY CHERRY ORANGE -- You win $5
You have $52.  Would you like to play? yes.↵
LEMON   ORANGE BAR     -- You lose
You have $51.  Would you like to play? yes.↵
BELL    BELL    BELL    -- You win $20
You have $70.  Would you like to play? yes.↵
ORANGE PLUM    BELL    -- You lose
You have $69.  Would you like to play? yes.↵
BAR     BAR     BAR     -- You win $250
You have $318.  Would you like to play? no.↵
```

Even though it's not realistic (and, if true, would make the slot machine unprofitable for the casino), you should assume that each of the six symbols is equally likely on each wheel.

4. Write two implementations of the function `strcmp` from the ANSI `string.h` interface that work directly with the internal representation of strings and call no string functions. One implementation should consider the string as an array of characters and the other as a pointer to a character.

5. Using the string model from the `strlib.h` interface, implement a function `Capitalize(str)` that returns a string in which the initial character is capitalized (if it is a letter) and all other letters are converted so that they appear in lowercase form. Characters other than letters are not affected. For example, `Capitalize("BOOLEAN")` and `Capitalize("boolean")` should each return the string `"Boolean"`.

6. A **palindrome** is a word that reads identically backward and forward, such as *level* or *noon*. Write a predicate function `IsPalindrome(str)` that returns `TRUE` if the string `str` is a palindrome. In addition, design and write a test program that calls `IsPalindrome` to demonstrate that it works.

7. One of the simplest types of codes used to make it harder for someone to read a message is a **letter-substitution cipher,** in which each letter in the original message is replaced by some different letter in the coded version of that message. A particularly simple type of letter-substitution cipher is a **cyclic cipher,** in which each letter is replaced by its counterpart a fixed distance ahead in the alphabet. The word *cyclic* refers to the fact that if the operation of moving ahead in the alphabet would take you past *Z,* you simply circle back to the beginning and start over again with *A.*

   Using the string functions provided by the `strlib.h` interface, implement a function `EncodeString(str, key)` that returns the new string formed by shifting every letter in `str` forward the number of letters indicated by the integer `key`, cycling back to the beginning of the alphabet if necessary. For example, if `key` has the value 4, the letter *A* becomes *E, B* becomes *F,* and so on up to *Z,* which becomes *D* because the coding cycles back to the beginning. If `key` is negative, letter values should be shifted toward the beginning of the alphabet instead of the end.

   After you have implemented `EncodeString`, write a test program that duplicates the examples shown in the following sample run:

```
This program encodes messages using a cyclic cipher.
To stop, enter 0 as the key.
Enter the key: 4↵
Enter a message: ABCDEFGHIJKLMNOPQRSTUVWXYZ.↵
Encoded message: EFGHIJKLMNOPQRSTUVWXYZABCD
Enter the key: 13↵
Enter a message: This is a secret message.↵
Encoded message: Guvf vf n frperg zrffntr.
Enter the key: -1↵
Enter a message: IBM-9000.↵
Encoded message: HAL-9000
Enter the key: 0.↵
```

Note that the coding operation applies only to letters; any other character is included unchanged in the output. Moreover, the case of letters is unaffected: lowercase letters come out as lowercase, and uppercase letters come out as uppercase.

8. Using only functions from the `string.h` interface, implement the function `SubString(s, p1, p2)` from the `strlib` library, which returns the substring of `s`, beginning at position `p1` and ending at position `p2`. Make sure that your function correctly applies the following rules:

   a. If `p1` is negative, it is set to 0 so that it indicates the first character in the string.
   b. If `p2` is greater than `strlen(s) - 1`, it is set to `strlen(s) - 1` so that it indicates the last character.
   c. If `p1` ends up being greater than `p2`, `SubString` returns the empty string.

9. Write a program `wc.c` that reads a file and reports how many lines, words, and characters appear in it. For the purposes of this program, a word consists of a consecutive sequence of any characters except whitespace characters. For example, if the file `twinkle.txt` contains the following verse from *Alice in Wonderland,*

   ```
   Twinkle, twinkle, little bat!
   How I wonder what you're at!
   Up above the world you fly,
   Like a teatray in the sky.
   ```

   your program should be able to generate the following sample run:

   ```
   File: twinkle.txt↵
   Lines:    4
   Words:   22
   Chars:  114
   ```

10. In the 1960s, entertainer Steve Allen often played a game called *madlibs* as part of his comedy routine. Allen would ask the audience to supply words that fit specific categories—a verb, an adjective, or a plural noun, for example—and then use these words to fill in blanks in a previously prepared text that he would then read back to the audience. The results were usually nonsense, but often very funny nonetheless.

    In this exercise, your task is to write a program that plays madlibs with the user. The text for the story comes from a text file that includes occasional placeholders enclosed in angle brackets. For example, suppose the input file `carroll.txt` contains the following excerpt from Lewis Carroll's poem "The Walrus and the Carpenter," with a few key words replaced by placeholders as shown:

```
"The time has come," the <animal> said,
"To talk of many things:"
"Of shoes—and ships—and sealing <sticky substance>—
Of <plural vegetable name>—and kings—
And why the <body of water> is boiling hot—
And whether <plural animal name> have wings."
```

Your program must read this file and display it on the console, giving the user the chance to fill in the placeholders with new strings. If Carroll himself had used the program, he would likely have obtained the following sample run:

```
Input file: carroll.txt⏎
   animal: Walrus⏎
   sticky substance: wax⏎
   plural vegetable name: cabbages⏎
   body of water: sea⏎
   plural animal name: pigs⏎

"The time has come," the Walrus said,
"To talk of many things:"
"Of shoes—and ships—and sealing wax—
Of cabbages—and kings—
And why the sea is boiling hot—
And whether pigs have wings."
```

Note that the user must provide all the substitutions before any of the text is displayed. This design complicates the program structure slightly because it is impossible to display the output text as you go. The simplest strategy is to write the output to a temporary file first and then copy the contents of the temporary file back to the screen.

11. Design and implement an interface called **card.h** that exports the following interface entries:

- A type **rankT** that allows you to represent the rank of a card. The values of type **rankT** include the integers between 2 and 10 but should also include the constants **Ace**, **Jack**, **Queen**, and **King**.
- A type **suitT** consisting of the four suits: **Clubs**, **Diamonds**, **Hearts**, and **Spades**.
- A type **cardT** that combines a rank and a suit.
- A function **NewCard**(*rank, suit*) that creates a **cardT** from the rank and suit values.
- Two functions, **Rank**(*card*) and **Suit**(*card*), that allow the client to select the rank and suit of a **cardT** value. These functions could easily be replaced by code that selected the appropriate components of the card, but defining them as functions means that the client need not pay attention to the underlying structure of the type.

- A function `CardName` (*card*) that returns a string identifying the card. The result of `CardName` begins with a rank indicator (which is one of A, 2, 3, 4, 5, 6, 7, 8, 9, 10, J, Q, or K), followed by a one-character suit (C, D, H, or S). Note that the result is usually a two-character string, but contains three characters if the rank is a 10.

12. Using the `card.h` interface from the preceding exercise, write a program that initializes a complete deck of 52 cards, shuffles it, and then displays the shuffled values, as shown in the following sample run:

```
This program initializes, shuffles, and displays
a deck of playing cards.

AH 10C  5D  4H  JS  AD  KH  3C  4C  2D  6C  AC  JD
2H  KS  9H  5S  AS  6S  6D  8S  KD  2S  7H  8H  5C
8C  QH  4S  9S  QS  9D  6H  7S  9C  7D  3H  JH 10D
KC 10H  8D  2C  7C  QD  JC  5H  QC  4D 10S  3D  3S
```

One of the easiest ways to shuffle the contents of an array is to adopt the strategy represented by the following pseudocode:

```
for  (each position p₁ in the array)  {
    Pick a random position p₂ between p₁ and the end of the array.
    Exchange the values at positions p₁ and p₂.
}
```

$$\text{for } (each\ position\ p_1\ in\ the\ array)\ \{$$

13. Write a program that plays the game of hangman. In hangman, the computer begins by selecting a secret word at random from a list of possibilities. It then prints out a row of dashes—one for each letter in the secret word—and asks the user to guess a letter. If the user guesses a letter that appears in the word, the word is redisplayed with all instances of that letter shown in the correct positions, along with any letters guessed correctly on previous turns. If the letter does not appear in the word, the player is charged with an incorrect guess. The player keeps guessing letters until either (1) the player has correctly guessed all the letters in the word or (2) the player has made eight incorrect guesses. A sample run of the hangman program is shown in Figure 3-9.

   To separate the process of choosing a secret word from the rest of the game, define and implement an interface called `randword.h` that exports two functions: `InitDictionary` and `ChooseRandomWord`. `InitDictionary` should take the name of a data file containing a list of words, one per line, and read it into an array declared as a static global variable in the implementation. `ChooseRandomWord` takes no arguments and returns a word chosen at random from the internally maintained array.

   For extra practice, implement the hangman program twice, once using the ANSI `string.h` interface and once using `strlib.h`.

FIGURE 3-9   Sample run of the hangman program

```
Welcome to Hangman!
I will guess a secret word.  On each turn, you guess a letter.
If the letter is in the secret word, I will show you where it
appears; if not, a part of your body gets strung up on the
scaffold.  The object is to guess the word before you are hung.
The word now looks like this: ---------
You have 8 guesses left.

Guess a letter: E↵
That guess is correct.
The word now looks like this: -------E-
You have 8 guesses left.

Guess a letter: A↵
There are no A's in the word.
The word now looks like this: -------E-
You have 7 guesses left.

Guess a letter: I↵
There are no I's in the word.
The word now looks like this: -------E-
You have 6 guesses left.

Guess a letter: O↵
That guess is correct.
The word now looks like this: -O----E-
You have 6 guesses left.

Guess a letter: T↵
That guess is correct.
The word now looks like this: -O---TE-
You have 6 guesses left.

Guess a letter: R↵
That guess is correct.
The word now looks like this: -O---TER
You have 6 guesses left.

Guess a letter: P↵
That guess is correct.
The word now looks like this: -O-P-TER
You have 6 guesses left.

Guess a letter: C↵
That guess is correct.
The word now looks like this: CO-P-TER
You have 6 guesses left.

Guess a letter: M↵
That guess is correct.
The word now looks like this: COMP-TER
You have 6 guesses left.

Guess a letter: U↵
That guess is correct.
You guessed the word: COMPUTER
You win.
```

PART TWO

Recursion and Algorithmic Analysis

Overview

In your study of computer science, one of the most important concepts you need to learn is recursion, a programming strategy in which you solve large problems by breaking them down into simpler problems of the same form. Recursion is an enormously powerful idea. Once you understand it, you will be able to solve many problems that initially seem extremely difficult. For a while, however, recursion will seem like magic. To master it, you need to work through enough examples to develop confidence in the recursive process. The four chapters in Part Two contain many examples of recursion designed to bring you to the point where you begin to think recursively. In addition, Chapter 7 introduces you to the technique of algorithmic analysis, which enables you to assess the relative efficiency of algorithmic strategies.

C H A P T E R   4

Introduction to Recursion

And often enough, our faith beforehand in a certain result is the only thing
that makes the result come true.

— William James, *The Will To Believe,* 1897

Objectives

- To be able to define the concept of recursion as a programming strategy distinct from other forms of algorithmic decomposition.

- To recognize the paradigmatic form of a recursive function.

- To understand the internal implementation of recursive calls.

- To appreciate the importance of the recursive leap of faith.

- To understand the concept of wrapper functions in writing recursive programs.

- To be able to write and debug simple recursive functions at the level of those presented in this chapter.

Most algorithmic strategies used to solve programming problems have counterparts outside the domain of computing. When you perform a task repeatedly, you are using iteration. When you make a decision, you exercise conditional control. Because these operations are familiar, most people learn to use the control statements `for`, `while`, and `if` with relatively little trouble.

Before you can solve many sophisticated programming tasks, however, you will have to learn to use a powerful problem-solving strategy that has few direct counterparts in the real world. That strategy, called **recursion,** is defined as any solution technique in which large problems are solved by reducing them to smaller problems *of the same form.* The italicized phrase is crucial to the definition, which otherwise describes the basic strategy of stepwise refinement. Both strategies involve decomposition. What makes recursion special is that the subproblems in a recursive solution have the same form as the original problem.

If you are like most beginning programmers, the idea of breaking a problem down into subproblems of the same form does not make much sense when you first hear it. Unlike repetition or conditional testing, recursion is not a concept that comes up in day-to-day life. Because it is unfamiliar, learning how to use recursion can be difficult. To do so, you must develop the intuition necessary to make recursion seem as natural as all the other control structures. For most students of programming, reaching that level of understanding takes considerable time and practice. Even so, learning to use recursion is definitely worth the effort. As a problem-solving tool, recursion is so powerful that it at times seems almost magical. In addition, using recursion often makes it possible to write complex programs in simple and profoundly elegant ways.

◼ 4.1 A simple example of recursion

To gain a better sense of what recursion is, let's imagine you have been appointed as the funding coordinator for a large charitable organization that is long on volunteers and short on cash. Your job is to raise $1,000,000 in contributions so the organization can meet its expenses.

If you know someone who is willing to write a check for the entire million, your job is easy. On the other hand, you may not be lucky enough to have friends who are generous millionaires. In that case, you must raise the million in smaller amounts. If the average contribution to your organization is $100, you might choose a different tack: call 10,000 friends and ask each of them for $100. But then again, you probably don't have 10,000 friends. So what can you do?

As is often the case when you are faced with a task that exceeds your own capacity, the answer lies in delegating part of the work to others. Your organization has a reasonable supply of volunteers. If you could find 10 dedicated supporters in different parts of the country and appoint them as regional coordinators, each of those 10 people could then take responsibility for raising $100,000.

Raising $100,000 is simpler than raising $1 million, but it hardly qualifies as easy. What should your regional coordinators do? If they adopt the same strategy, they will in turn delegate parts of the job. If they each recruit 10 fundraising volunteers, those people will only have to raise $10,000. The delegation process can continue until the volunteers are able to raise the money on their own; because the average contribution is $100, the volunteer fundraisers can probably raise $100 from a single donor, which eliminates the need for further delegation.

If you express this fundraising strategy in pseudocode, it has the following structure:

```
void CollectContributions(int n)
{
    if (n <= 100) {
        Collect the money from a single donor.
    } else {
        Find 10 volunteers.
        Get each volunteer to collect n/10 dollars.
        Combine the money raised by the volunteers.
    }
}
```

The most important thing to notice about this pseudocode translation is that the line

   Get each volunteer to collect `n/10` *dollars.*

is simply the original problem reproduced at a smaller scale. The basic character of the task—raise *n* dollars—remains exactly the same; the only difference is that *n* has a smaller value. Moreover, because the problem is the same, you can solve it by calling the original function. Thus, the preceding line of pseudocode would eventually be replaced with the following line:

```
CollectContributions(n / 10);
```

It's important to note that the `CollectContributions` function ends up calling itself if the contribution level is greater than $100. In the context of programming, having a function call itself is the defining characteristic of recursion.

The structure of the `CollectContributions` procedure is typical of recursive functions. In general, the body of a recursive function has the following form:

```
if (test for simple case) {
    Compute a simple solution without using recursion.
} else {
    Break the problem down into subproblems of the same form.
    Solve each of the subproblems by calling this function recursively.
    Reassemble the solutions to the subproblems into a solution for the whole.
}
```

This structure provides a template for writing recursive functions and is therefore called the **recursive paradigm.** You can apply this technique to programming problems as long as they meet the following conditions:

1. You must be able to identify **simple cases** for which the answer is easily determined.
2. You must be able to identify a **recursive decomposition** that allows you to break any complex instance of the problem into simpler problems of the same form.

The `CollectContributions` example illustrates the power of recursion. As in any recursive technique, the original problem is solved by breaking it down into smaller subproblems that differ from the original only in their scale. Here, the original problem is to raise $1,000,000. At the first level of decomposition, each subproblem is to raise $100,000. These problems are then subdivided in turn to create smaller problems until the problems are simple enough to be solved immediately without recourse to further subdivision. Because the solution depends on dividing hard problems into simpler ones, recursive solutions are often called **divide-and-conquer** strategies.

4.2 The factorial function

Although the `CollectContributions` example illustrates the concept of recursion, it gives little insight into how recursion is used in practice, because the steps that make up the solution, such as finding 10 volunteers and collecting money, are not easily represented in a C program. To get a practical sense of the nature of recursion, you need to consider problems that fit more easily into the programming domain.

For most people, the best way to understand recursion is to start with simple mathematical functions in which the recursive structure follows directly from the statement of the problem and is therefore easy to see. Of these, the most common is the factorial function—traditionally denoted in mathematics as *n*!—which is defined as the product of the integers between 1 and *n*. In C, the equivalent problem is to write an implementation of a function with the prototype

```
int Fact(int n);
```

that takes an integer n and returns its factorial.

As you probably discovered in an earlier programming course, it is easy to implement the `Fact` function using a `for` loop, as illustrated by the following implementation:

```
int Fact(int n)
{
    int product, i;

    product = 1;
    for (i = 1; i <= n; i++) {
        product *= i;
    }
    return (product);
}
```

This implementation uses a `for` loop to cycle through each of the integers between 1 and n. In the recursive implementation this loop does not exist. The same effect is generated instead by the cascading recursive calls.

Implementations that use looping (typically by using `for` and `while` statements) are said to be **iterative.** Iterative and recursive strategies are often seen as opposites because they can be used to solve the same problem in rather different ways. These strategies, however, are not mutually exclusive. Recursive functions sometimes employ iteration internally, and you will see examples of this technique in Chapter 5.

The recursive formulation of Fact

The iterative implementation of **Fact**, however, does not take advantage of an important mathematical property of factorials. Each factorial is related to the factorial of the next smaller integer in the following way:

$$n! = n \times (n-1)!$$

Thus, 4! is $4 \times 3!$, 3! is $3 \times 2!$, and so on. To make sure that this process stops at some point, mathematicians define 0! to be 1. Thus, the conventional mathematical definition of the factorial function looks like this:

$$n! = \begin{cases} 1 & \text{if } n = 0 \\ n \times (n-1)! & \text{otherwise} \end{cases}$$

This definition is recursive, because it defines the factorial of n in terms of the factorial of $n-1$. The new problem—finding the factorial of $n-1$—has the same form as the original problem, which is the fundamental characteristic of recursion. You can then use the same process to define $(n-1)!$ in terms of $(n-2)!$. Moreover, you can carry this process forward step by step until the solution is expressed in terms of 0!, which is equal to 1 by definition.

From your perspective as a programmer, the practical impact of the mathematical definition is that it provides a template for a recursive implementation. In C, you can implement a function **Fact** that computes the factorial of its argument as follows:

```
int Fact(int n)
{
    if (n == 0) {
        return (1);
    } else {
        return (n * Fact(n - 1));
    }
}
```

If **n** is 0, the result of **Fact** is 1. If not, the implementation computes the result by calling **Fact(n - 1)** and then multiplying the result by n. This implementation follows directly from the mathematical definition of the factorial function and has precisely the same recursive structure.

Tracing the recursive process

If you work from the mathematical definition, writing the recursive implementation of **Fact** is straightforward. On the other hand, even though the definition is easy to write, the brevity of the solution may seem suspicious. When you are learning about recursion for the first time, the recursive implementation of **Fact** seems to leave something out. Even though it clearly reflects the mathematical definition, the recursive formulation makes it hard to identify where the actual computational steps occur. When you call **Fact**, for example, you want the computer to give you the answer. In the recursive implementation, all you see is a formula that transforms one call to `Fact` into another one. Because the steps in that calculation are not explicit, it seems somewhat magical when the computer gets the right answer.

If you follow through the logic the computer uses to evaluate any function call, however, you discover that no magic is involved. When the computer evaluates a call to the recursive `Fact` function, it goes through the same process it uses to evaluate any other function call. To visualize the process, suppose that you have executed the statement

```
f = Fact(4);
```

as part of the function `main`. When `main` calls `Fact`, the computer creates a new stack frame and copies the argument value into the formal parameter n. The frame for `Fact` temporarily supersedes the frame for `main`, as shown in the following diagram:

```
main
   Fact
                        → if  (n  ==  0)  {
         n                    return  (1);
       ┌─────┐          }  else  {
       │  4  │                return  (n  *  Fact(n  -  1));
       └─────┘          }
```

In the diagram, the code for the body of `Fact` is shown inside the frame to make it easier to keep track of the current position in the program, which is indicated by an arrow. In the current diagram, the arrow appears at the beginning of the code because all function calls start at the first statement of the function body.

The computer now begins to evaluate the body of the function, starting with the `if` statement. Because n is not equal to 0, control proceeds to the `else` clause, where the program must evaluate and return the value of the expression

```
n * Fact(n - 1)
```

Evaluating this expression requires computing the value of `Fact(n - 1)`, which introduces a recursive call. When that call returns, all the program has to do is to multiply the result by n. The current state of the computation can therefore be diagrammed as follows:

```
main
   Fact
                        if  (n  ==  0)  {
         n                    return  (1);
       ┌─────┐          }  else  {
       │  4  │                return  (n  *  Fact(n  -  1));
       └─────┘          }                     ─────────────
                                                    └ ?
```

As soon as the call to `Fact(n - 1)` returns, the result is substituted for the expression underlined in the diagram, allowing computation to proceed.

The next step in the computation is to evaluate the call to `Fact(n - 1)`, beginning with the argument expression. Because the current value of n is 4, the argument expression n - 1 has the value 3. The computer then creates a new frame for `Fact` in which the formal parameter is initialized to this value. Thus, the next frame looks like this:

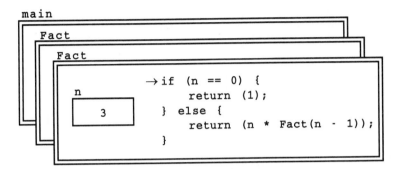

There are now two frames labeled `Fact`. In the most recent one, the computer is just starting to calculate `Fact(3)`. In the preceding frame, which the newly created frame hides, the `Fact` function is awaiting the result of the call to `Fact(n - 1)`.

The current computation, however, is the one required to complete the topmost frame. Once again, n is not 0, so control passes to the `else` clause of the `if` statement, where the computer must evaluate `Fact(n - 1)`. In this frame, however, n is equal to 3, so the required result is that computed by calling `Fact(2)`. As before, this process requires the creation of a new stack frame, as shown:

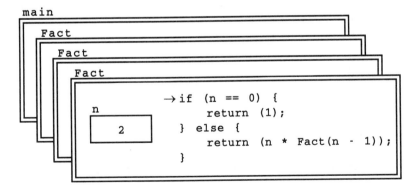

Following the same logic, the program must now call `Fact(1)`, which in turn calls `Fact(0)`, thereby creating two new stack frames. The resulting stack configuration looks like this:

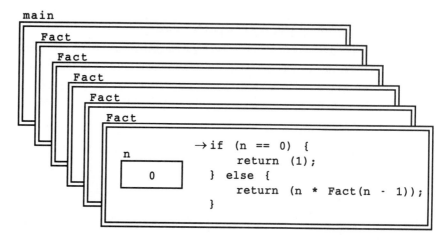

At this point, however, the situation changes. Because the value of n is 0, the function can return its result immediately by executing the statement

```
return (1);
```

The value 1 is returned to the calling frame, which resumes its position on top of the stack, as shown:

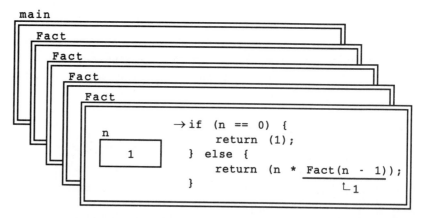

From this point, the computation proceeds back through each of the recursive calls, completing the calculation of the return value at each level. In this frame, for example, the call to Fact (n - 1) can be replaced by the value 1, so that the result at this level can be expressed as follows:

```
return (n *  1 ));
```

In this stack frame, n has the value 1, so the result of this call is simply 1. This result gets propagated back to its caller, which is represented by the top frame in the following diagram:

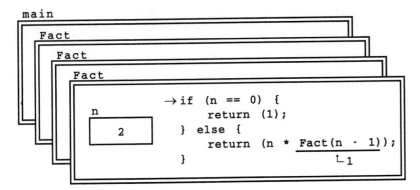

Because **n** is now 2, evaluating the **return** statement causes the value 2 to be passed back to the previous level, as follows:

```
main
 Fact
  Fact
   Fact
                  → if  (n  ==  0)  {
       n                 return  (1);
                  } else {
            3              return  (n  *  Fact(n  -  1));
                  }                           └₂
```

At this stage, the program returns 3×2 to the previous level, so that the frame for the initial call to **Fact** looks like this:

```
main
 Fact
                  → if  (n  ==  0)  {
       n                 return  (1);
                  } else {
            4              return  (n  *  Fact(n  -  1));
                  }                           └₆
```

The final step in the calculation process consists of calculating 4×6 and returning the value 24 to the main program.

The recursive leap of faith

The point of the long **Fact(4)** example in the preceding section is to show you that the computer treats recursive functions just like all other functions. When you are faced with a recursive function, you can—at least in theory—mimic the operation of the computer and figure out what it will do. By drawing all the frames and keeping track of all the variables, you can duplicate the entire operation and come up with the answer. If you do so, however, you will usually find that the complexity of the process ends up making the problem much harder to understand.

When you try to understand a recursive program, you must be able to put the underlying details aside and focus instead on a single level of the operation. At that level, you are allowed to assume that any recursive call automatically gets the right answer as long as the arguments to that call are simpler than the original arguments in some respect. This psychological strategy—assuming that any simpler recursive call will work correctly—is called the **recursive leap of faith.** Learning to apply this strategy is essential to using recursion in practical applications.

As an example, consider what happens when this implementation is used to compute `Fact(n)` with n equal to 4. To do so, the recursive implementation must compute the value of the expression

```
n * Fact(n - 1)
```

By substituting the current value of n into the expression, you know that the result is

```
4 * Fact(3)
```

Stop right there. Computing `Fact(3)` is simpler than computing `Fact(4)`. Because it is simpler, the recursive leap of faith allows you to assume that it works. Thus, you should assume that the call to `Fact(3)` will correctly compute the value of 3!, which is 3 × 2 × 1, or 6. The result of calling `Fact(4)` is therefore 4 × 6, or 24.

As you look at the examples in the rest of this chapter, try to focus on the big picture instead of the morass of detail. Once you have made the recursive decomposition and identified the simple cases, be satisfied that the computer can handle the rest.

■ 4.3 The Fibonacci function

In a mathematical treatise entitled *Liber Abbaci* published in 1202, the Italian mathematician Leonardo Fibonacci proposed a problem that has had a wide influence on many fields, including computer science. The problem was phrased as an exercise in population biology—a field that has become increasingly important in recent years. Fibonacci's problem concerns how the population of rabbits would grow from generation to generation if the rabbits reproduced according to the following, admittedly fanciful, rules:

- Each pair of fertile rabbits produces a new pair of offspring each month.
- Rabbits become fertile in their second month of life.
- Old rabbits never die.

If a pair of newborn rabbits is introduced in January, how many pairs of rabbits are there at the end of the year?

You can solve Fibonacci's problem simply by keeping a count of the rabbits at each month during the year. At the beginning of January, there are no rabbits, since the first pair is introduced sometime in that month, which leaves one pair of rabbits on February 1. Since the initial pair of rabbits is newborn, they are not yet fertile in February, which means that the only rabbits on March 1 are the original pair of rabbits. In March, however, the original pair is now of reproductive age, which means that a new pair of rabbits is born. The new pair increases the colony's population—counting by pairs—to two on April 1. In April, the original pair goes right on reproducing, but the rabbits born in March are as yet too young. Thus, there are three pairs of rabbits at the beginning of May. From here on, with more and more rabbits becoming fertile each month, the rabbit population begins to grow more quickly.

Computing terms in the Fibonacci sequence

At this point, it is useful to record the population data so far as a sequence of terms, indicated here by the subscripted value t_i, each of which shows the number of rabbit pairs at the beginning of the ith month from the start of the experiment on January 1. The sequence itself is called the **Fibonacci sequence** and begins with the following terms, which represent the results of our calculation so far:

t_0	t_1	t_2	t_3	t_4
0	1	1	2	3

You can simplify the computation of further terms in this sequence by making an important observation. Because rabbits in this problem never die, all the rabbits that were around in the previous month are still around. Moreover, all of the fertile rabbits have produced a new pair. The number of fertile rabbit pairs capable of reproduction is simply the number of rabbits that were alive in the month before the previous one. The net effect is that each new term in the sequence must simply be the sum of the preceding two. Thus, the next several terms in the Fibonacci sequence look like this:

t_0	t_1	t_2	t_3	t_4	t_5	t_6	t_7	t_8	t_9	t_{10}	t_{11}	t_{12}
0	1	1	2	3	5	8	13	21	34	55	89	144

The number of rabbit pairs at the end of the year is therefore 144.

From a programming perspective, it helps to express the rule for generating new terms in the following, more mathematical form:

$$t_n = t_{n-1} + t_{n-2}$$

An expression of this type, in which each element of a sequence is defined in terms of earlier elements, is called a **recurrence relation.**

The recurrence relation alone is not sufficient to define the Fibonacci sequence. Although the formula makes it easy to calculate new terms in the sequence, the process has to start somewhere. In order to apply the formula, you need to have at least two terms in hand, which means that the first two terms in the sequence—t_0

and t_1—must be defined explicitly. The complete specification of the terms in the Fibonacci sequence is therefore

$$t_n = \begin{cases} n & \text{if } n \text{ is 0 or 1} \\ t_{n-1} + t_{n-2} & \text{otherwise} \end{cases}$$

This mathematical formulation is an ideal model for a recursive implementation of a function `Fib(n)` that computes the nth term in the Fibonacci sequence. All you need to do is plug the simple cases and the recurrence relation into the standard recursive paradigm. The recursive implementation of `Fib(n)` is shown in Figure 4-1, which also includes a test program that displays the terms in the Fibonacci sequence between two specified indices.

Gaining confidence in the recursive implementation

Now that you have a recursive implementation of the function `Fib`, how can you go about convincing yourself that it works? You can always begin by tracing through the logic. Consider, for example, what happens if you call `Fib(5)`. Because this is not one of the simple cases enumerated in the `if` statement, the implementation computes the result by evaluating the line

```
return (Fib(n - 1) + Fib(n - 2));
```

which is in this case equivalent to

```
return (Fib(4) + Fib(3));
```

At this point, the computer calculates the result of `Fib(4)`, adds that to the result of calling `Fib(3)`, and returns the sum as the value of `Fib(5)`.

But how does the computer go about evaluating `Fib(4)` and `Fib(3)`? The answer, of course, is that it uses precisely the same strategy. The essence of recursion is to break problems down into simpler ones that can be solved by calls to exactly the same function. Those calls get broken down into simpler ones, which in turn get broken down into even simpler ones, until at last the simple cases are reached.

On the other hand, it is best to regard this entire mechanism as irrelevant detail. Remember the recursive leap of faith. Your job at this level is to understand how the call to `Fib(5)` works. In the course of walking though the execution of that function, you have managed to transform the problem into computing the sum of `Fib(4)` and `Fib(3)`. Because the argument values are smaller, each of these calls represents a simpler case. Applying the recursive leap of faith, you can assume that the program correctly computes each of these values, without going through all the steps yourself. For the purposes of validating the recursive strategy, you can just look the answers up in the table. `Fib(4)` is 3 and `Fib(3)` is 2, so the result of calling `Fib(5)` is $3 + 2$, or 5, which is indeed the correct answer. Case closed. You don't need to see all the details, which are best left to the computer.

FIGURE 4-1   Recursive implementation of the Fibonacci function

```
/*
 * File: fib.c
 * -----------
 * This program lists the terms in the Fibonacci sequence with
 * indices ranging from MinIndex to MaxIndex.
 */

#include <stdio.h>
#include "genlib.h"

/* Constants */

#define MinIndex  0
#define MaxIndex 12

/* Private function prototypes */

int Fib(int n);

/* Main program */

main()
{
    int i;

    printf("This program lists the Fibonacci sequence.\n");
    for (i = MinIndex; i <= MaxIndex; i++) {
        printf("Fib(%d)", i);
        if (i < 10) printf(" ");
        printf(" = %4d\n", Fib(i));
    }
}

/*
 * Function: Fib
 * Usage: t = Fib(n);
 * ------------------
 * This function returns the nth term in the Fibonacci sequence
 * using a recursive implementation of the recurrence relation
 *
 *      Fib(n) = Fib(n - 1) + Fib(n - 2)
 */

int Fib(int n)
{
    if (n < 2) {
        return (n);
    } else {
        return (Fib(n - 1) + Fib(n - 2));
    }
}
```

Efficiency of the recursive implementation

If you do decide to go through the details of the evaluation of the call to `Fib(5)`, however, you will quickly discover that the calculation is extremely inefficient. The recursive decomposition makes many redundant calls, in which the computer ends up calculating the same term in the Fibonacci sequence several times. This situation is illustrated in Figure 4-2, which shows all the recursive calls required in the calculation of `Fib(5)`. As you can see from the diagram, the program ends up making one call to `Fib(4)`, two calls to `Fib(3)`, three calls to `Fib(2)`, five calls to `Fib(1)`, and three calls to `Fib(0)`. Given that the Fibonacci function can be implemented efficiently using iteration, the enormous explosion of steps required by the recursive implementation is more than a little disturbing.

Recursion is not to blame

On discovering that the implementation of `Fib(n)` given in Figure 4-1 is highly inefficient, many people are tempted to point their fingers at recursion as the culprit. The problem in the Fibonacci example, however, has nothing to do with recursion per se but rather the way in which recursion is used. By adopting a different strategy, it is possible to write a recursive implementation of the `Fib` function in which the large-scale inefficiencies revealed in Figure 4-2 disappear completely.

As is often the case when using recursion, the key to finding a more efficient solution lies in adopting a more general approach. The Fibonacci sequence is not the only sequence whose terms are defined by the recurrence relation

$$t_n = t_{n-1} + t_{n-2}$$

FIGURE 4-2 Steps in the calculation of `Fib(5)`

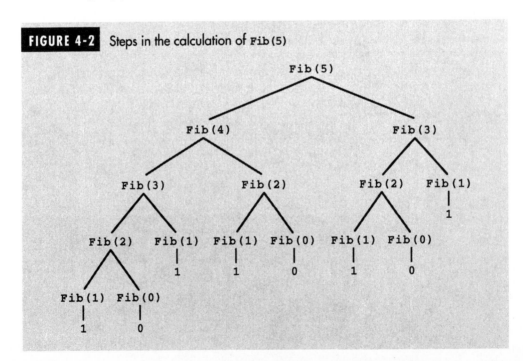

Depending on how you choose the first two terms, you can generate many different sequences. The traditional Fibonacci sequence

$$0, 1, 1, 2, 3, 5, 8, 13, 21, 34, 55, 89, 144, \ldots$$

comes from defining $t_0 = 0$ and $t_1 = 1$. If, for example, you defined $t_0 = 3$ and $t_1 = 7$, you would get this sequence instead:

$$3, 7, 10, 17, 27, 44, 71, 115, 186, 301, 487, 788, 1275, \ldots$$

Similarly, defining $t_0 = -1$ and $t_1 = 2$ gives rise to the following sequence:

$$-1, 2, 1, 3, 4, 7, 11, 18, 29, 47, 76, 123, 199, \ldots$$

These sequences all use the same recurrence relation, which specifies that each new term is the sum of the previous two. The only way the sequences differ is in the choice of the first two terms. As a general class, the sequences that follow this pattern are called **additive sequences.**

This concept of an additive sequence makes it possible to convert the problem of finding the nth term in the Fibonacci sequence into the more general problem of finding the nth term in an additive sequence whose initial terms are t_0 and t_1. Such a function requires three arguments and might be expressed in C as a function with the following prototype:

```
int AdditiveSequence(int n, int t0, int t1);
```

If you had such a function, it would be easy to implement **Fib** using it. All you would need to do is supply the correct values of the first two terms, as follows:

```
int Fib(int n)
{
    return (AdditiveSequence(n, 0, 1));
}
```

The body consists of a single line of code that does nothing but call another function, passing along a few extra arguments. Functions of this sort, which simply return the result of another function, often after transforming the arguments in some way, are called **wrapper** functions. Wrapper functions are extremely common in recursive programming. In most cases, a wrapper function is used—as it is here—to supply additional arguments to a subsidiary function that solves a more general problem.

From here, the only remaining task is to implement the function **AdditiveSequence**. If you think about this more general problem for a few minutes, you will discover that additive sequences have an interesting recursive character of their own. The simple case for the recursion consists of the terms t_0 and t_1, whose values are part of the definition of the sequence. In the C implementation, the values of these terms are passed as arguments. If you need to compute t_0, for example, all you have to do is return the argument **t0**.

But what if you are asked to find a term that appears later in the sequence? Suppose, for example, that you want to find t_6 in the additive sequence whose initial terms are 3 and 7. By looking at the list of terms in the sequence

t_0	t_1	t_2	t_3	t_4	t_5	t_6	t_7	t_8	t_9	
3	7	10	17	27	44	71	115	186	301	...

you can see that the correct value is 71. The interesting question, however, is how you can use recursion to determine this result.

The key insight you need to discover is that the nth term in any additive sequence is simply the $n-1^{st}$ term in the additive sequence which begins one step further along. For example, t_6 in the sequence shown in the most recent example is simply t_5 in the additive sequence

t_0	t_1	t_2	t_3	t_4	t_5	t_6	t_7	t_8	
7	10	17	27	44	71	115	186	301	...

that begins with 7 and 10.

This discovery makes it possible to implement the function `AdditiveSequence` as follows:

```
int AdditiveSequence(int n, int t0, int t1)
{
    if (n == 0) return (t0);
    if (n == 1) return (t1);
    return (AdditiveSequence(n - 1, t1, t0 + t1));
}
```

If you trace through the steps in the calculation of `Fib(5)` using this technique, you will discover that the calculation involves none of the redundant computation that plagued the earlier recursive formulation. The steps lead directly to the solution, as shown in the following diagram:

```
Fib(5)
   = AdditiveSequence(5, 0, 1)
      = AdditiveSequence(4, 1, 1)
         = AdditiveSequence(3, 1, 2)
            = AdditiveSequence(2, 2, 3)
               = AdditiveSequence(1, 3, 5)
               = 5
```

Even though the new implementation is entirely recursive, it is comparable in efficiency to the standard iterative version of the Fibonacci function.

4.4 Other examples of recursion

Although the factorial and Fibonacci functions provide excellent examples of how recursive functions work, they are both mathematical in nature and may therefore convey the incorrect impression that recursion is applicable only to mathematical functions. In fact, you can apply recursion to any problem that can be decomposed into simpler problems of the same form. It is useful to consider a few additional examples, including several that are far less mathematical in their character.

Detecting palindromes

A **palindrome** is a string that reads identically backward and forward, such as "level" or "noon". Although it is easy to check whether a string is a palindrome by iterating through its characters, palindromes can also be defined recursively. The insight you need to do so is that any palindrome longer than a single character must contain a shorter palindrome in its interior. For example, the string "level" consists of the palindrome "eve" with an "l" at each end. Thus, to check whether a string is a palindrome—assuming the string is sufficiently long that it does not constitute a simple case—all you need to do is

1. Check to see that the first and last characters are the same.
2. Check to see whether the substring generated by removing the first and last characters is itself a palindrome.

If both conditions apply, the string is a palindrome.

The only other question you must consider before writing a recursive solution to the palindrome problem is what the simple cases are. Clearly, any string with only a single character is a palindrome because reversing a one-character string has no effect. The one-character string therefore represents a simple case, but it is not the only one. The empty string—which contains no characters at all—is also a palindrome, and any recursive solution must operate correctly in this case as well.

Figure 4-3 contains a recursive implementation of the predicate function IsPalindrome(str) that returns TRUE if the string str is a palindrome. The function first checks to see whether the length of the string is less than 2. If it is, the string is certainly a palindrome. If not, the function checks to make sure that the string meets both of the criteria listed earlier.

This implementation in Figure 4-3, which makes extensive use of the functions in the strlib.h library, is rather inefficient, even though the recursive decomposition is easy to follow. You can write a more efficient implementation of IsPalindrome by making the following changes:

- *Calculate the length of the argument string only once.* The initial implementation calculates the length of the string at every level of the recursive decomposition, even though the structure of the solution guarantees that the length of the string decreases by two on every recursive call. By calculating the length of the string at the beginning and passing it down through each of the recursive calls, you can eliminate redundant calls to StringLength (or strlen, if you are using the ANSI string.h interface). To avoid changing the prototype for IsPalindrome, you need to define IsPalindrome as a wrapper function and have it pass the length to a second recursive function that does all the actual work.

FIGURE 4-3 Recursive implementation of `IsPalindrome` using `strlib.h`

```
/*
 * Function: IsPalindrome
 * Usage: if (IsPalindrome(str)) . . .
 * -------------------------------------
 * This function returns TRUE if the string is a palindrome.
 * This implementation operates recursively by noting that all
 * strings of length 0 or 1 are palindromes (the simple case)
 * and that longer strings are palindromes only if their first
 * and last characters match and the remaining substring is a
 * palindrome.
 */
bool IsPalindrome(string str)
{
    int len;

    len = StringLength(str);
    if (len <= 1) {
        return (TRUE);
    } else {
        return (IthChar(str, 0) == IthChar(str, len - 1)
                && IsPalindrome(SubString(str, 1, len - 2)));
    }
}
```

- *Take advantage of the fact that strings are represented internally as arrays of characters.* Instead of calling `IthChar` to extract the first and last characters from the argument string, it is more efficient to use array indexing to compare the characters at positions 0 and $len - 1$.
- *Use pointer arithmetic to "remove" the first character of the string.* In C, an array is always treated as a pointer to its initial element. If you add 1 to that address, C's rules for pointer arithmetic return the address of an array that begins one element further along. Thus, the call

    ```
    CheckPalindrome(str + 1, len - 2)
    ```

    has the effect of calling `CheckPalindrome` on a string that begins one character later and ends one character earlier than the original value of `str`.

The revised implementation of `IsPalindrome` appears in Figure 4-4.

Binary search

When you work with arrays in programming, one of the most common algorithmic operations consists of searching the array for a particular element. For example, if

FIGURE 4-4 More efficient implementation of `IsPalindrome` using `string.h`

```
/*
 * Function: IsPalindrome
 * Usage: if (IsPalindrome(str)) . . .
 * ------------------------------------
 * This function returns TRUE if the character string str
 * is a palindrome.  This level of the implementation is
 * just a wrapper for the CheckPalindrome function, which
 * does the real work.
 */

bool IsPalindrome(char str[])
{
    return (CheckPalindrome(str, strlen(str)));
}

/*
 * Function: CheckPalindrome
 * Usage: if (CheckPalindrome(str, len)) . . .
 * --------------------------------------------
 * This function returns TRUE if the next len characters
 * in the character array str form a palindrome.  The
 * implementation uses the recursive insight that all
 * strings of length 0 or 1 are palindromes (the simple
 * case) and that longer strings are palindromes only if
 * their first and last characters match and the remaining
 * substring is a palindrome.  Extracting the substring
 * is performed by array arithmetic.  The new substring
 * begins at str+1 and proceeds for len-2 characters.
 */

static bool CheckPalindrome(char str[], int len)
{
    if (len <= 1) {
        return (TRUE);
    } else {
        return (str[0] == str[len - 1]
                && CheckPalindrome(str + 1, len - 2));
    }
}
```

you were working with arrays of strings, it would be extremely useful to have a function

```
int FindStringInArray(string key, string array[], int n);
```

that searches through each of the n elements of `array`, looking for an element whose value is equal to `key`. If such an element is found, `FindStringInArray` returns the index at which it appears (if the key appears more than once in the array, the index of any matching is fine). If no matching element exists, the function returns –1.

If you have no specific knowledge about the order of elements within the array, the implementation of `FindStringInArray` must simply check each of the elements in turn until it either finds a match or runs out of elements. This strategy, which is called the **linear search algorithm,** can be time-consuming if the arrays are large. On the other hand, if you know that the elements of the array are arranged in alphabetical order, you can adopt a much more efficient approach. All you have to do is divide the array in half and compare the key you're trying to find against the element closest to the middle of the array, using the order defined by the ASCII character codes, which is called **lexicographic order.** If the key you're looking for precedes the middle element, then the key—if it exists at all—must be in the first half. Conversely, if the key follows the middle element in lexicographic order, you only need to look at the elements in the second half. This strategy is called the **binary search algorithm.** Because binary search makes it possible for you to discard half the possible elements at each step in the process, it turns out to be much more efficient than linear search for sorted arrays.

The binary search algorithm is also a perfect example of the divide-and-conquer strategy. It is therefore not surprising that binary search has a natural recursive implementation, which is shown in Figure 4-5. Note that the function `FindStringInSortedArray` is implemented as a wrapper, leaving the real work to the recursive function `BinarySearch`, which takes two indices—`low` and `high`—that limit the range of the search. The simple cases for `BinarySearch` are

1. *There are no elements in the active part of the array.* This condition is marked by the fact that the index `low` is greater than the index `high`, which means that there are no elements left to search.
2. *The middle element (or an element to one side of the middle if the array contains an even number of elements) matches the specified key.* Since the key has just been found, `FindStringInSortedArray` can simply return the index of the middle value.

If neither of these cases applies, however, the implementation can simplify the problem by choosing the appropriate half of the array and call itself recursively with an updated set of search limits.

Mutual recursion

In each of the examples considered so far, the recursive functions have called themselves directly, in the sense that the body of the function contains a call to itself. Although most of the recursive functions you encounter are likely to adhere to this style, the definition of *recursion* is actually somewhat broader. To be recursive, a function must call itself at some point during its evaluation. If a function is subdivided into subsidiary functions, the recursive call can actually occur at a deeper level of nesting. For example, if a function *f* calls a function *g*, which in turn calls *f*, the function calls are still considered to be recursive. Because the functions *f* and *g* call each other, this type of recursion is called **mutual recursion.**

FIGURE 4-5   Divide-and-conquer implementation of binary search

```
/*
 * Function: FindStringInSortedArray
 * Usage: index = FindStringInSortedArray(key, array, n);
 * --------------------------------------------------------
 * This function searches the array looking for the specified
 * key. The argument n specifies the effective size of the
 * array, which must be sorted according to the lexicographic
 * order imposed by StringCompare. If the key is found, the
 * function returns the index in the array at which that key
 * appears.  (If the key appears more than once in the array,
 * any of the matching indices may be returned).  If the key
 * does not exist in the array, the function returns -1.  In
 * this implementation, FindStringInSortedArray is simply a
 * wrapper; all the work is done by the recursive function
 * BinarySearch.
 */

int FindStringInSortedArray(string key, string array[], int n)
{
    return (BinarySearch(key, array, 0, n - 1));
}

/*
 * Function: BinarySearch
 * Usage: index = BinarySearch(key, array, low, high);
 * ----------------------------------------------------
 * This function does the work for FindStringInSortedArray.
 * The only difference is that BinarySearch takes both the
 * upper and lower limit of the search.
 */

static int BinarySearch(string key, string array[],
                        int low, int high)
{
    int mid, cmp;

    if (low > high) return (-1);
    mid = (low + high) / 2;
    cmp = StringCompare(key, array[mid]);
    if (cmp == 0) return (mid);
    if (cmp < 0) {
        return (BinarySearch(key, array, low, mid - 1));
    } else {
        return (BinarySearch(key, array, mid + 1, high));
    }
}
```

As a simple example, let's investigate how to use recursion to test whether a number is even or odd. If you limit the domain of possible values to the set of **natural numbers,** which are defined simply as the set of nonnegative integers, the even and odd numbers can be characterized as follows:

- A number is *even* if its predecessor is odd.
- A number is *odd* if is not even.
- The number 0 is even by definition.

Even though these rules seem simplistic, they constitute the basis of an effective, if inefficient, strategy for distinguishing odd and even numbers. A mutually recursive implementation of the predicate functions `IsEven` and `IsOdd` appears in Figure 4-6.

FIGURE 4-6 Mutually recursive definitions of `IsEven` and `IsOdd`

```
/*
 * Function: IsEven
 * Usage: if (IsEven(n)) . . .
 * -------------------------
 * This function returns TRUE if n is even.  The number 0
 * is considered even by definition; any other number is
 * even if its predecessor is odd.  Note that this function
 * is defined to take an unsigned argument and is therefore
 * not applicable to negative integers.
 */

bool IsEven(unsigned n)
{
    if (n == 0) {
        return (TRUE);
    } else {
        return (IsOdd(n - 1));
    }
}

/*
 * Function: IsOdd
 * Usage: if (IsOdd(n)) . . .
 * -------------------------
 * This function returns TRUE if n is odd, where a number
 * is defined to be odd if it is not even.  Note that this
 * function is defined to take an unsigned argument and is
 * therefore not applicable to negative integers.
 */

bool IsOdd(unsigned n)
{
    return (!IsEven(n));
}
```

4.5 Thinking recursively

For most people, recursion is not an easy concept to grasp. Learning to use it effectively requires considerable practice and forces you to approach problems in entirely new ways. The key to success lies in developing the right mindset—learning how to think recursively. The remainder of this chapter is designed to help you achieve that goal.

Maintaining a holistic perspective

In Chapter 2 of *The Art and Science of C,* I devote one section to the philosophical concepts of holism and reductionism. Simply stated, **reductionism** is the belief that the whole of an object can be understood merely by understanding the parts that make it up. Its antithesis is **holism,** the position that the whole is often greater than the sum of its parts. As you learn about programming, it helps to be able to interleave these two perspectives, sometimes focusing on the behavior of a program as a whole, and at other times delving into the details of its execution. When you try to learn about recursion, however, this balance seems to change. Thinking recursively requires you to think holistically. In the recursive domain, reductionism is the enemy of understanding and invariably gets in the way.

To maintain the holistic perspective, you must become comfortable adopting the recursive leap of faith, which was introduced in its own section earlier in this chapter. Whenever you are writing a recursive program or trying to understand the behavior of one, you must get to the point where you ignore the details of the individual recursive calls. As long as you have chosen the right decomposition, identified the appropriate simple cases, and implemented your strategy correctly, those recursive calls will simply work. You don't need to think about them.

Unfortunately, until you have had extensive experience working with recursive functions, applying the recursive leap of faith does not come easily. The problem is that it requires you to suspend disbelief and make assumptions about the correctness of your programs that fly in the face of your experience. After all, when you write a program, the odds are good—even if you are an experienced programmer—that your program won't work the first time. In fact, it is quite likely that you have chosen the wrong decomposition, messed up the definition of the simple cases, or somehow messed things up trying to implement your strategy. If you have done any of these things, your recursive calls won't work.

When things go wrong—as they inevitably will—you have to remember to look for the error in the right place. The problem lies somewhere in your recursive implementation, not in the recursive mechanism itself. If there is a problem, you should be able to find it by looking at a single level of the recursive hierarchy. Looking down through additional levels of recursive calls is not going to help. If the simple cases work and the recursive decomposition is correct, the subsidiary calls will work correctly. If they don't, there is something you need to fix in the definition of the recursive function itself.

Avoiding the common pitfalls

As you gain experience with recursion, the process of writing and debugging recursive programs will become more natural. At the beginning, however, finding out what you need to fix in a recursive program can be difficult. The following is a checklist that will help you identify the most common sources of error.

- *Does your recursive implementation begin by checking for simple cases?* Before you attempt to solve a problem by transforming it into a recursive subproblem, you must first check to see if the problem is so simple that such decomposition is unnecessary. In almost all cases, recursive functions begin with the keyword `if`. If your function doesn't, you should look carefully at your program and make sure that you know what you're doing.[1]

- *Have you solved the simple cases correctly?* A surprising number of bugs in recursive programs arise from having incorrect solutions to the simple cases. If the simple cases are wrong, the recursive solutions to more complicated problems will inherit the same mistake. For example, if you had mistakenly defined `Fact(0)` as 0 instead of 1, calling `Fact` on any argument would end up returning 0.

- *Does your recursive decomposition make the problem simpler?* For recursion to work, the problems have to get simpler as you go along. More formally, there must be some **metric**—a standard of measurement that assigns a numeric difficulty rating to the problem—that gets smaller as the computation proceeds. For mathematical functions like `Fact` and `Fib`, the value of the integer argument serves as a metric. On each recursive call, the value of the argument gets smaller. For the `IsPalindrome` function, the appropriate metric is the length of the argument string, because the string gets shorter on each recursive call. If the problem instances do not get simpler, the decomposition process will just keep making more and more calls, giving rise to the recursive analogue of the infinite loop, which is called **nonterminating recursion.**

- *Does the simplification process eventually reach the simple cases, or have you left out some of the possibilities?* A common source of error is failing to include simple case tests for all the cases that can arise as the result of the recursive decomposition. For example, in the `IsPalindrome` implementation presented in Figure 4-3, it is critically important for the function to check the zero-character case as well as the one-character case, even if the client never intends to call `IsPalindrome` on the empty string. As the recursive decomposition proceeds, the string arguments get shorter by two characters at each level of the recursive call. If the original argument string is even in length, the recursive decomposition will never get to the one-character case.

- *Do the recursive calls in your function represent subproblems that are truly identical in form to the original?* When you use recursion to break down a

---

[1] At times, as in the case of the `IsPalindrome` implementation, it may be necessary to perform some calculations prior to making the simple-case test. The point is that the simple-case test must precede any recursive decomposition.

problem, it is essential that the subproblems be of the same form. If the recursive calls change the nature of the problem or violate one of the initial assumptions, the entire process can break down. As several of the examples in this chapter illustrate, it is often useful to define the publicly exported function as a simple wrapper that calls a more general recursive function which is private to the implementation. Because the private function has a more general form, it is usually easier to decompose the original problem and still have it fit within the recursive structure.

- *When you apply the recursive leap of faith, do the solutions to the recursive subproblems provide a complete solution to the original problem?* Breaking a problem down into recursive subinstances is only part of the recursive process. Once you get the solutions, you must also be able to reassemble them to generate the complete solution. The way to check whether this process in fact generates the solution is to walk through the decomposition, religiously applying the recursive leap of faith. Work through all the steps in the current function call, but assume that every recursive call generates the correct answer. If following this process yields the right solution, your program should work.

◼ Summary

This chapter has introduced the idea of *recursion,* a powerful programming strategy in which complex problems are broken down into simpler problems of the same form. The important points presented in this chapter include:

- Recursion is similar to stepwise refinement in that both strategies consist of breaking a problem down into simpler problems that are easier to solve. The distinguishing characteristic of recursion is that the simpler subproblems must have the same form as the original.

- In C, recursive functions typically have the following paradigmatic form:

```
if (test for simple case) {
    Compute a simple solution without using recursion.
} else {
    Break the problem down into subproblems of the same form.
    Solve each of the subproblems by calling this function recursively.
    Reassemble the solutions to the subproblems into a solution for the whole.
}
```

- To use recursion, you must be able to identify *simple cases* for which the answer is easily determined and a *recursive decomposition* that allows you to break any complex instance of the problem into simpler problems of the same type.

- Recursive functions are implemented using exactly the same mechanism as any other function call. Each call creates a new stack frame that contains the local variables for that call. Because the computer creates a separate stack frame for each function call, the local variables at each level of the recursive decomposition remain separate.

- Before you can use recursion effectively, you must learn to limit your analysis to a single level of the recursive decomposition and to rely on the correctness of all simpler recursive calls without tracing through the entire computation. Trusting these simpler calls to work correctly is called the *recursive leap of faith.*

- Mathematical functions often express their recursive nature in the form of a *recurrence relation,* in which each element of a sequence is defined in terms of earlier elements.

- Although some recursive functions may be less efficient than their iterative counterparts, recursion itself is not the problem. As is typical with all types of algorithms, some recursive strategies are more efficient than others.

- In order to ensure that a recursive decomposition produces subproblems that are identical in form to the original, it is often necessary to generalize the problem. As a result, it is often useful to implement the solution to a specific problem as a simple *wrapper* function whose only purpose is to call a subsidiary function that handles the more general case.

- Recursion need not consist of a single function that calls itself but may instead involve several functions that call each other in a cyclical pattern. Recursion that involves more than one function is called *mutual recursion.*

- You will be more successful at understanding recursive programs if you can maintain a holistic perspective rather than a reductionistic one.

Thinking about recursive problems in the right way does not come easily. Learning to use recursion effectively requires practice and more practice. For many students, mastering the concept takes years. But because recursion will turn out to be one of the most powerful techniques in your programming repertoire, that time will be well spent.

REVIEW QUESTIONS

1. Define the terms *recursive* and *iterative.* Is it possible for a function to employ both strategies?

2. What is the fundamental difference between recursion and stepwise refinement?

3. In the pseudocode for the `CollectContributions` function, the `if` statement looks like this:

   ```
   if (n <= 100)
   ```

   Why is it important to use the `<=` operator instead of simply checking whether `n` is exactly equal to 100?

4. What is the standard recursive paradigm?

5. What two properties must a problem have for recursion to make sense as a solution strategy?

6. Why is the term *divide and conquer* appropriate to recursive techniques?

7. What is meant by the *recursive leap of faith?* Why is this concept important to you as a programmer?

8. In the section entitled "Tracing the recursive process," the text goes through a long analysis of what happens internally when `Fact(4)` is called. Using this analysis as a model, trace through the execution of `Fib(4)`, sketching out each stack frame created in the process.

9. Modify Fibonacci's rabbit problem by introducing the additional rule that rabbit pairs stop reproducing after giving birth to three litters. How does this assumption change the recurrence relation? What changes do you need to make in the simple cases?

10. How many times is `Fib(1)` called when calculating `Fib(n)` using the recursive implementation given in Figure 4-1?

11. What would happen if you eliminated the `if (n == 1)` check from the function `AdditiveSequence`, so that the implementation looked like this:

```
static int AdditiveSequence(int n, int t0, int t1)
{
    if (n == 0) return (t0);
    return (AdditiveSequence(n - 1, t1, t0 + t1));
}
```

Would the function still work? Why or why not?

12. What is a wrapper function? Why are they often useful in writing recursive functions?

13. Why is it important that the implementation of `IsPalindrome` in Figure 4-3 check for the empty string as well as the single character string? What would happen if the function didn't check for the single character case and instead checked only whether the length is 0? Would the function still work correctly?

14. Explain the effect of the function call

```
CheckPalindrome(str + 1, len - 2)
```

in the `IsPalindrome` implementation given in Figure 4-4.

15. What is mutual recursion?

16. What would happen if you defined `IsEven` and `IsOdd` as follows:

```
bool IsEven(unsigned n)
{
    return (!IsOdd(n));
}
```

```
bool IsOdd(unsigned n)
{
    return (!IsEven(n));
}
```

Which of the errors explained in the section "Avoiding the common pitfalls" is illustrated in this example?

17. The following definitions of `IsEven` and `IsOdd` are also incorrect:

```
bool IsEven(unsigned n)
{
    if (n == 0) {
        return (TRUE);
    } else {
        return (IsOdd(n - 1));
    }
}
```

```
bool IsOdd(unsigned n)
{
    if (n == 1) {
        return (TRUE);
    } else {
        return (IsEven(n - 1));
    }
}
```

Give an example that shows how this implementation can fail. What common pitfall is illustrated here?

PROGRAMMING EXERCISES

1. Spherical objects, such as cannonballs, can be stacked to form a pyramid with one cannonball at the top, sitting on top of a square composed of four cannonballs, sitting on top of a square composed of nine cannonballs, and so forth. Write a recursive function `Cannonball` that takes as its argument the height of the pyramid and returns the number of cannonballs it contains. Your function must operate recursively and must not use any iterative constructs, such as `while` or `for`.

2. Unlike many programming languages, C does not include a predefined operator that raises a number to a power. As a partial remedy for this deficiency, write a recursive implementation of a function

```
int RaiseIntToPower(int n, int k)
```

that calculates n^k. The recursive insight that you need to solve this problem is the mathematical property that

$$n^k = \begin{cases} 1 & \text{if } k = 0 \\ n \times n^{k-1} & \text{otherwise} \end{cases}$$

3. The **greatest common divisor** (g.c.d.) of two nonnegative integers is the largest integer that divides evenly into both. In the third century B.C., the Greek mathematician Euclid discovered that the greatest common divisor of x and y can always be computed as follows:

   - If x is evenly divisible by y, then y is the greatest common divisor.
   - Otherwise, the greatest common divisor of x and y is always equal to the greatest common divisor of y and the remainder of x divided by y.

   Use Euclid's insight to write a recursive function **GCD(x, y)** that computes the greatest common divisor of x and y.

4. Write an iterative implementation of the function **Fib(n)**.

5. For each of the two recursive implementations of the function **Fib(n)** presented in this chapter, write a recursive function (you can call these **CountFib1** and **CountFib2** for the two algorithms) that counts the number of function calls made during the evaluation of the corresponding Fibonacci calculation. Write a main program that uses these functions to display a table showing the number of calls made by each algorithm for various values of **n**, as shown in the following sample run:

```
This program compares the performance of two
algorithms to compute the Fibonacci sequence.

Number of calls:
  N      Fib1    Fib2
  --     ----    ----
   0       1       2
   1       1       3
   2       3       4
   3       5       5
   4       9       6
   5      15       7
   6      25       8
   7      41       9
   8      67      10
   9     109      11
  10     177      12
  11     287      13
  12     465      14
  13     753      15
  14    1219      16
  15    1973      17
```

6. Write a recursive function `DigitSum(n)` that takes a nonnegative integer and returns the sum of its digits. For example, calling `DigitSum(1729)` should return $1 + 7 + 2 + 9$, which is 19.

    The recursive implementation of `DigitSum` depends on the fact that it is very easy to break an integer down into two components using division by 10. For example, given the integer 1729, you can divide it into two pieces as follows:

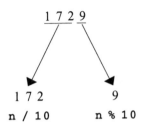

Each of the resulting integers is strictly smaller than the original and thus represents a simpler case.

7. The **digital root** of an integer n is defined as the result of summing the digits repeatedly until only a single digit remains. For example, the digital root of 1729 can be calculated using the following steps:

Step 1:	$1 + 7 + 2 + 9$	$\rightarrow$	19
Step 2:	$1 + 9$	$\rightarrow$	10
Step 3:	$1 + 0$	$\rightarrow$	1

Because the total at the end of step 3 is the single digit 1, that value is the digital root.

    Write a function `DigitalRoot(n)` that returns the digital root of its argument. Although it is easy to implement `DigitalRoot` using the `DigitSum` function from exercise 6 and a `while` loop, part of the challenge of this problem is to write the function recursively without using any explicit loop constructs.

8. The mathematical function C(*n*, *k*) is usually defined in terms of factorials, as follows:

$$C(n, k) \quad = \quad \frac{n!}{k! \times (n-k)!}$$

The values of C(*n*, *k*) can also be arranged geometrically to form a triangle in which *n* increases as you move down the triangle and *k* increases as you move from left to right. The resulting structure, which is called **Pascal's Triangle** after the French mathematician Blaise Pascal, is arranged like this:

$$C(0, 0)$$
$$C(1, 0) \quad C(1, 1)$$
$$C(2, 0) \quad C(2, 1) \quad C(2, 2)$$
$$C(3, 0) \quad C(3, 1) \quad C(3, 2) \quad C(3, 3)$$
$$C(4, 0) \quad C(4, 1) \quad C(4, 2) \quad C(4, 3) \quad C(4, 4)$$

Pascal's Triangle has the interesting property that every entry is the sum of the two entries above it, except along the left and right edges, where the values are always 1. Consider, for example, the circled entry in the following display of Pascal's Triangle:

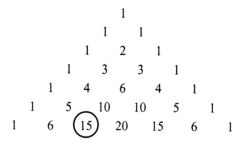

This entry, which corresponds to $C(6, 2)$, is the sum of the two entries—5 and 10—that appear above it to either side. Use this relationship between entries in Pascal's Triangle to write a recursive implementation of the $C(n, k)$ that uses no loops, no multiplication, and no calls to **Fact**.

9. Write a recursive function that takes a string as argument and returns the reverse of that string. The prototype for this function should be

```
string Reverse(string str);
```

and the statement

```
printf("%s\n", Reverse("program"));
```

should display

```
margorp
```

Your solution should be entirely recursive and should not use any iterative constructs such as **while** or **for**.

10. The **string.h** library contains a function **IntegerToString**, which is implemented using the **sprintf** function, as follows:

```
#define MaxDigits 30

string IntegerToString(int n)
{
    char buffer[MaxDigits];

    sprintf(buffer, "%d", n);
    return (CopyString(buffer));
}
```

This implementation, however, hides all the work inside the `sprintf` function and gives no insight at all into how the computer actually goes about the process of converting an integer into its string representation. As it turns out, the easiest way to implement this function is to use the recursive decomposition of an integer outlined in exercise 6.

Rewrite the `IntegerToString` implementation so that it operates recursively. Your function may call any of the functions in the `strlib.h` library except for `IntegerToString` or `RealToString` but may not use any other library functions such as `sprintf`. Moreover, your function must operate recursively and must not use any of the iterative constructs such as `while` and `for`.

11. The second implementation of the `IsPalindrome` function, as presented in Figure 4-4, uses pointer arithmetic to derive the starting address of the substring that gets passed in the recursive call. By using this same technique, write a recursive implementation of `FindStringInSortedArray` that does not use a subsidiary function.

CHAPTER 5

Recursive Procedures

Nor would I consider the magnitude and complexity of my plan as any argument of its impracticability.

— Mary Shelley, *Frankenstein*, 1818

Objectives

- To become familiar with several classic examples of recursive programming, including the Tower of Hanoi puzzle and the problem of generating permutations.

- To recognize that recursion can sometimes offer concise solutions to problems that are difficult to solve by any other means.

- To appreciate how recursion can be applied to the problem of generating graphical displays.

When a recursive decomposition follows directly from a mathematical definition, as it does in the case of the `Fact` and `Fib` functions in Chapter 4, applying recursion is not particularly hard. In most cases, you can translate the mathematical definition directly into a recursive implementation by plugging the appropriate expressions into the standard recursive paradigm. The situation changes, however, as you begin to solve more complex problems.

This chapter introduces several programming problems that seem—at least on the surface—much more difficult than those in Chapter 4. In fact, if you try to solve these problems without using recursion, relying instead on more familiar iterative techniques, you will find them quite difficult to solve. Even so, each of the problems has a recursive solution that is surprisingly short. If you exploit the power of recursion, a few lines of code are sufficient for each task.

The brevity of these solutions endows them with a deceptive aura of simplicity. The hard part of solving these problems does not lie in the intricacy or length of the code. What makes these programs difficult is identifying the appropriate recursive decomposition in the first place. Doing so occasionally requires some cleverness, but what you need even more is confidence. You have to accept the recursive leap of faith. As you develop your solution, you must strive to come to a point at which you are faced with a problem that is identical to the original in form but simpler in scale. When you do, you have to be willing to stop and declare the problem solved, without trying to trace the program further.

5.1 The Tower of Hanoi

The first example in this chapter is a simple puzzle that has come to be known as the **Tower of Hanoi.** Invented by French mathematician Edouard Lucas in the 1880s, the Tower of Hanoi puzzle quickly became popular in Europe. Its success was due in part to the legend that grew up around the puzzle, which was described as follows in *La Nature* by the French mathematician Henri De Parville (as translated by the mathematical historian W. W. R. Ball):

> In the great temple at Benares beneath the dome which marks the center of the world, rests a brass plate in which are fixed three diamond needles, each a cubit high and as thick as the body of a bee. On one of these needles, at the creation, God placed sixty-four disks of pure gold, the largest disk resting on the brass plate and the others getting smaller and smaller up to the top one. This is the Tower of Brahma. Day and night unceasingly, the priests transfer the disks from one diamond needle to another according to the fixed and immutable laws of Brahma, which require that the priest on duty must not move more than one disk at a time and that he must place this disk on a needle so that there is no smaller disk below it. When all the sixty-four disks shall have been thus transferred from the needle on which at the creation God placed them to one of the other needles, tower, temple and Brahmins alike will crumble into dust, and with a thunderclap the world will vanish.

Over the years, the setting has shifted from India to Vietnam, but the puzzle and its legend remain the same.

1. Move the entire stack consisting of the top seven disks from spire A to spire C.
2. Move the bottom disk from spire A to spire B.
3. Move the stack of seven disks from spire C to spire B.

Executing the first step takes you to the following position:

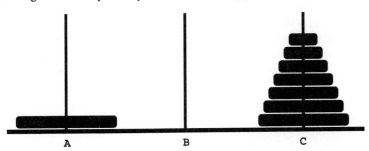

Once you have gotten rid of the seven disks on top of the largest disk, the second step is simply to move that disk from spire A to spire B, which results in the following configuration:

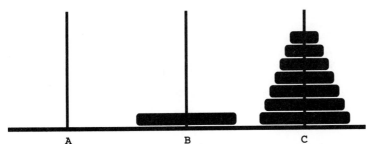

All that remains is to move the tower of seven disks back from spire C to spire B, which is again a smaller problem of the same form. This operation is the third step in the recursive strategy, and leaves the puzzle in the desired final configuration:

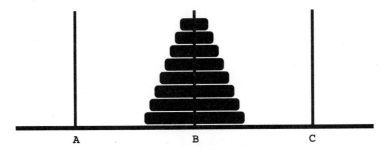

That's it! You're finished. You've reduced the problem of moving a tower of size eight to one of moving a tower of size seven. More importantly, this recursive strategy generalizes to towers of size N, as follows:

1. Move the top *N*–1 disks from the start spire to the temporary spire.
2. Move a single disk from the start spire to the finish spire.
3. Move the stack of *N*–1 disks from the temporary spire back to the finish spire.

At this point, it is hard to avoid saying to yourself, "Okay, I can reduce the problem to moving a tower of size *N*–1, but how do I accomplish that?" The answer, of course, is that you move a tower of size *N*–1 in precisely the same way. You break that problem down into one that requires moving a tower of size *N*–2, which further breaks down into the problem of moving a tower of size *N*–3, and so forth, until there is only a single disk to move. Psychologically, however, the important thing is to avoid asking that question altogether. The recursive leap of faith should be sufficient. You've reduced the scale of the problem without changing its form. That's the hard work. All the rest is bookkeeping, and it's best to let the computer take care of that.

Once you have identified the simple cases and the recursive decomposition, all you need to do is plug them into the standard recursive paradigm, which results in the following pseudocode procedure:

```
void MoveTower(int n, char start, char finish, char temp)
{
    if (n == 1) {
        Move a single disk from start to finish.
    } else {
        Move a tower of size n - 1 from start to temp.
        Move a single disk from start to finish.
        Move a tower of size n - 1 from temp to finish.
    }
}
```

Validating the strategy

Although the pseudocode strategy is in fact correct, the derivation up to this point has been a little careless. Whenever you use recursion to decompose a problem, you must make sure that the new problems are identical in form to the original. The task of moving *N*–1 disks from one spire to another certainly sounds like an instance of the same problem and fits the `MoveTower` prototype. Even so, there is a subtle but important difference. In the original problem, the destination and temporary spires are empty. When you move a tower of size *N*–1 to the temporary spire as part of the recursive strategy, you've left a disk behind on the starting spire. Does the presence of that disk change the nature of the problem and thus invalidate the recursive solution?

To answer this question, you need to think about the subproblem in light of the rules of the game. If the recursive decomposition doesn't end up violating the rules, everything should be okay. The first rule—that only one disk can be moved at a time—is not an issue. If there is more than a single disk, the recursive decomposition breaks the problem down to generate a simpler case. The steps in the pseudocode that actually transfer disks move only one disk at a time. The second rule—that you are not allowed to place a larger disk on top of a smaller one—is the critical one. You need to convince yourself that you will not violate this rule in the recursive decomposition.

The important observation to make is that, as you move a subtower from one spire to the other, the disk you leave behind on the original spire—and indeed any disk left behind at any previous stage in the operation—must be larger than anything in the current subtower. Thus, as you move those disks among the spires, the only disks below them will be larger in size, which is consistent with the rules.

Coding the solution

To complete the Tower of Hanoi solution, the only remaining step is to substitute function calls for the remaining pseudocode. The task of moving a complete tower requires a recursive call to the `MoveTower` function. The only other operation is moving a single disk from one spire to another. For the purposes of writing a test program that displays the steps in the solution, all you need is a function that records its operation on the console. For example, you can implement the function `MoveSingleDisk` as follows:

```
void MoveSingleDisk(char start, char finish)
{
    printf("%c -> %c\n", start, finish);
}
```

The `MoveTower` code itself looks like this:

```
void MoveTower(int n, char start, char finish, char temp)
{
    if (n == 1) {
        MoveSingleDisk(start, finish);
    } else {
        MoveTower(n - 1, start, temp, finish);
        MoveSingleDisk(start, finish);
        MoveTower(n - 1, temp, finish, start);
    }
}
```

Tracing the recursive process

The only problem with this implementation of `MoveTower` is that it seems like magic. If you're like most students learning about recursion for the first time, the solution seems so short that there must be something missing. Where is the strategy? How can the computer know which disk to move first and where it should go?

The answer is that the recursive process—breaking a problem down into smaller subproblems of the same form and then providing solutions for the simple cases—is all you need to solve the problem. If you trust the recursive leap of faith, you're done. You can skip this section of the book and go on to the next. If you're still suspicious, it may be necessary for you to go through the steps in the complete process and watch what happens.

To make the problem more managable, consider what happens if there are only three disks in the original tower. The main program call is therefore

```
MoveTower(3, 'A', 'B', 'C');
```

To trace how this call computes the steps necessary to transfer a tower of size 3, all you need to do is keep track of the operation of the program, using precisely the same strategy as in the factorial example from Chapter 4. For each new function call, you introduce a stack frame that shows the values of the parameters for that call. The initial call to **MoveTower**, for example, creates the following stack frame:

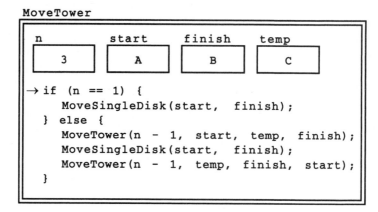

As the arrow in the code indicates, the function has just been called, so execution begins with the first statement in the function body . The current value of **n** is not equal to 1, so the program skips ahead to the **else** clause and executes the statement

```
MoveTower(n - 1, start, temp, finish);
```

As with any function call, the first step is to evaluate the arguments. To do so, you need to determine the values of the variables **n**, **start**, **temp**, and **finish**. Whenever you need to find the value of a variable, you use the value as it is defined in the current stack frame. Thus, the **MoveTower** call is equivalent to

```
MoveTower(2, 'A', 'C', 'B');
```

This operation, however, indicates another function call, which means that the current operation is suspended until the new function call is complete. To trace the operation of the new function call, you need to generate a new stack frame and repeat the process. As always, the parameters in the new stack frame are initialized by copying the calling arguments in the order in which they appear. Thus, the new stack frame looks like this:

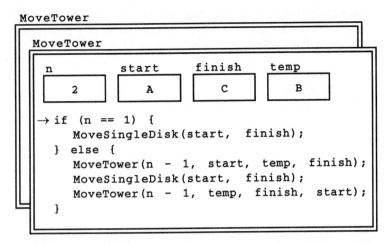

As the diagram illustrates, the new stack frame has its own set of variables, which temporarily supersede the variables in frames that are further down on the stack. Thus, as long as the program is executing in this stack frame, n will have the value 2, start will be 'A', finish will be 'C', and temp will be 'B'. The old values in the previous frame will not reappear until the subtask represented by this call is created and the function returns.

The evaluation of the recursive call to MoveTower proceeds exactly like the original one. Once again, n is not 1, which requires another call of the form

```
MoveTower(n - 1, start, temp, finish);
```

If you evaluate the arguments in the context of the current stack frame, you discover that this function call is equivalent to MoveTower(1, 'A', 'B', 'C'), which introduces yet another stack frame for the MoveTower function, as follows:

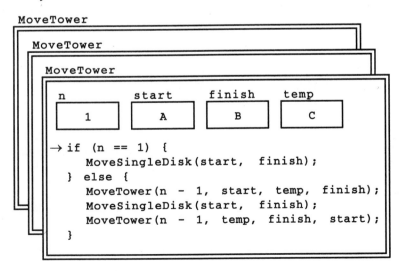

This call to `MoveTower`, however, does represent the simple case. Since `n` is 1, the program calls the `MoveSingleDisk` function to move a disk from A to B, leaving the puzzle in the following configuration:

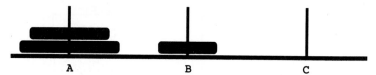

At this point, the most recent call to `MoveTower` is complete and the function returns. In the process, its stack frame is discarded, which brings the execution back to the previous stack frame, having just completed the first statement in the `else` clause:

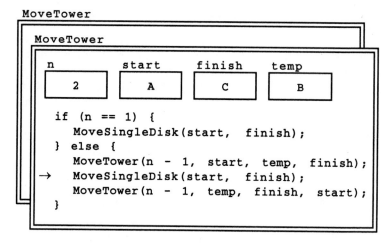

The call to `MoveSingleDisk` again represents a simple operation, which leaves the puzzle in the following state:

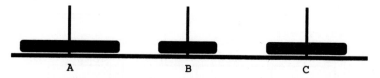

With the `MoveSingleDisk` operation completed, the only remaining step required to finish the current call to `MoveTower` is the last statement in the function:

```
MoveTower(n - 1, temp, finish, start);
```

Evaluating these arguments in the context of the current frame reveals that this call is equivalent to

```
MoveTower(1, 'B', 'C', 'A');
```

Once again, this call requires the creation of a new stack frame. By this point in the process, however, you should be able to see that the effect of this call is simply to move a tower of size 1 from B to C, using A as a temporary repository. Internally, the function determines that n is 1 and then calls MoveSingleDisk to reach the following configuration:

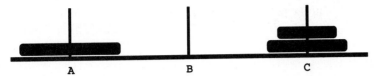

This operation again completes a call to MoveTower, allowing it to return to its caller having completed the subtask of moving a tower of size 2 from A to C. Discarding the stack frame from the just-completed subtask reveals the stack frame for the original call to MoveTower, which is now in the following state:

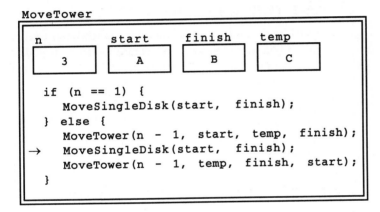

The next step is to call MoveSingleDisk to move the largest disk from A to B, which results in the following position:

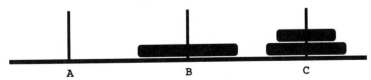

The only operation that remains is to call

```
MoveTower(n - 1, temp, finish, start);
```

with the arguments from the current stack frame, which are

```
MoveTower(2, 'C', 'B', 'A');
```

If you're still suspicious of the recursive process, you can draw the stack frame created by this function call and continue tracing the process to its ultimate conclusion. At some point, however, it is essential that you trust the recursive process enough to see that function call as a single operation that has the effect of the following command in English:

Move a tower of size 2 from C to B, using A as a temporary repository.

If you think about the process in this holistic form, you can immediately see that completion of this step will move the tower of two disks back from C to B, leaving the desired final configuration:

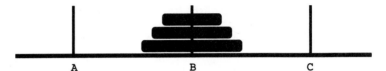

■■■ 5.2 Generating permutations

Many word games such as Scrabble™ require the ability to rearrange a set of letters to form a word. Thus, if you wanted to write a Scrabble program, it would be useful to have a facility for generating all possible arrangements of a particular set of tiles. In word games, such arrangements are generally called **anagrams.** In mathematics, they are known as **permutations.**

Let's suppose you want to write a function `ListPermutations(s)` that displays all permutations of the string `s`. For example, if you call

```
ListPermutations("ABC");
```

your program should display the six arrangements of `"ABC"`, as follows:

```
ABC
ACB
BAC
BCA
CBA
CAB
```

The order of the output is unimportant, but each of the possible arrangements should appear exactly once.

How would you go about implementing the `ListPermutations` function? If you are limited to iterative control structures, finding a general solution that works for strings of any length is difficult. Thinking about the problem recursively, on the other hand, leads to a relatively straightforward solution.

As is usually the case with recursive programs, the hard part of the solution process is figuring out how to divide the original problem into simpler instances of the same problem. In this case, to generate all permutations of a string, you need to discover how being able to generate all permutations of a shorter string might contribute to the solution.

Stop and think about this problem for a few minutes. When you are first learning about recursion, it is easy to look at a recursive solution and believe that you could have generated it on your own. Without trying it first, however, it is hard to know whether you would have come up with the same insight.

To give yourself more of a feel for the problem, you need to consider a concrete case. Suppose you want to generate all permutations of a five-character string, such as **"ABCDE"**. In your solution, you can apply the recursive leap of faith to generate all permutations of any shorter string. Just assume that the recursive calls work and be done with it. Once again, the critical question is how being able to permute shorter strings helps you solve the problem of permuting the original five-character string.

The recursive insight

The key to solving the permutation problem is recognizing that the permutations of the five-character string **"ABCDE"** consist of the following strings:

- The character **'A'** followed by every possible permutation of **"BCDE"**
- The character **'B'** followed by every possible permutation of **"ACDE"**
- The character **'C'** followed by every possible permutation of **"ABDE"**
- The character **'D'** followed by every possible permutation of **"ABCE"**
- The character **'E'** followed by every possible permutation of **"ABCD"**

More generally, to display all permutations of a string of length n, you can take each of the n characters in turn and display that character followed by every possible permutation of the remaining $n - 1$ characters.

The only difficulty with this solution strategy is that the recursive subproblem does not have exactly the same form as the original. The original problem requires you to display all permutations of a string. The subproblem requires you to display a character from a string followed by all permutations of the remaining letters. As the recursion proceeds, the character in front will become two characters, then three, and so forth. The general subproblem, therefore, is to generate all permutations of a string, leaving some characters at the beginning of the string fixed in their positions.

As discussed in Chapter 4, the easiest way to solve the problem of asymmetry between the original problem and its recursive subproblems is to define **ListPermutations** as a simple wrapper function that calls a subsidiary function to solve the more general case. In this example, the general problem can be solved by a new procedure **RecursivePermute**, which generates all permutations of a string with the first k letters fixed. When k is 0, all the letters are free to change, which gives you the original problem. As k increases, the problem becomes simpler. When k is the length of the string, there are no characters to interchange, and the string can be displayed exactly as it appears. The original problem, of course, leaves no letters fixed, so that the definition of **ListPermutations** itself looks like this:

```
static void ListPermutations(string str)
{
    RecursivePermute(str, 0);
}
```

The `RecursivePermute` procedure follows the outline of the recursive permutation algorithm and has the following pseudocode form:

```
static void RecursivePermute(string str, int k)
{
    if (k is equal to the length of the string) {
        Display the string.
    } else {
        For each character position i between k and the end of the string {
            Exchange the characters in positions i and k.
            Use recursion to generate permutations with the first k+1 characters fixed.
            Restore the original string by again exchanging positions i and k.
        }
    }
}
```

Translating this function from pseudocode to C is reasonably simple, particularly if you define a function `ExchangeCharacters` to exchange two characters in a string. The full definition of `RecursivePermute` looks like this:

```
static void RecursivePermute(string str, int k)
{
    int i;

    if (k == StringLength(str)) {
        printf("%s\n", str);
    } else {
        for (i = k; i < StringLength(str); i++) {
            ExchangeCharacters(str, k, i);
            RecursivePermute(str, k + 1);
            ExchangeCharacters(str, k, i);
        }
    }
}
```

The only remaining step is to complete the stepwise refinement by defining the function `ExchangeCharacters`, as follows:

```
static void ExchangeCharacters(string str, int p1, int p2)
{
    char tmp;

    tmp = str[p1];
    str[p1] = str[p2];
    str[p2] = tmp;
}
```

■ 5.3 Graphical applications of recursion

In *The Art and Science of C*, I introduced a simple graphics library that makes it possible to construct simple drawings on a computer display using line segments and circular arcs. Using the graphics library makes programming more fun, but it also has proven to be useful in illustrating the concepts of recursion. Many of the figures you can create with the graphics library are fundamentally recursive in nature and provide excellent examples of recursive programming.

The remainder of this chapter includes an overview of the graphics library, followed by two illustrations of how recursion can be applied in the graphics domain. This material is not essential to learning about recursion, and you can skip it if you don't have ready access to the graphics library. On the other hand, working through these examples might make recursion seem a lot more powerful, not to mention more fun.

The graphics library

The `graphics.h` interface provides you with access to a collection of functions that enable you to create simple line drawings on the computer screen. When you initialize the graphics package, a new rectangular window called the **graphics window** is created on the screen and used as the drawing surface. Whenever you call procedures and functions in the graphics library, the results are displayed in the graphics window.

To specify points within the graphics window, the graphics library uses an approach that should be familiar from high-school geometry or algebra. All drawing in the graphics window takes place on a conceptual grid, as illustrated in Figure 5-1.

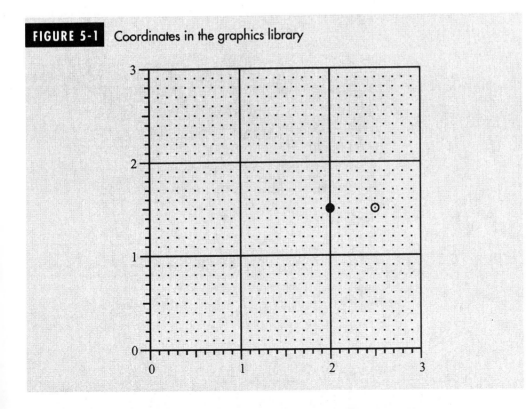

FIGURE 5-1 Coordinates in the graphics library

As in traditional geometry, points are identified by specifying their position relative to the **origin,** which is the point at the lower left corner of the graphics window. The horizontal and vertical lines that emanate from the origin along the edges of the graphics window are called the **axes;** the x-axis runs along the bottom of the window, and the y-axis runs up the left side. Every point in the graphics window is identified by a pair of values, usually written as (x, y), that specifies the position of that point along the x and y axes. These values are called the **coordinates** of the point. Coordinates are measured in inches relative to the origin, which is the point $(0, 0)$. From there, x values increase as you move to the right, and y values increase as you move up.

Coordinates in the graphics library come in two forms:

- **Absolute coordinates** specify a point in the window by giving its coordinates with respect to the origin. For example, the solid dot in Figure 5-1 is at absolute coordinates $(2.0, 1.5)$.
- **Relative coordinates** specify a position in the window by indicating how far away that point is along each axis from the last position specified. For example, the open dot in Figure 5-1 has absolute coordinates $(2.5, 1.5)$. If, however, you express its coordinates in relation to the solid dot, this point is shifted by the relative coordinates $(0.5, 0.0)$. If you want to connect these dots with a line, the standard approach is to specify the first point in absolute coordinates and the endpoint of the line in relative coordinates.

The best mental model to use for the drawing process is to imagine that there is a pen positioned over a piece of transparent graph paper covering the screen. You can move the pen to any location on the screen by specifying the absolute coordinates. You then draw a straight line by moving the pen to a new point specified using relative coordinates, making sure that the pen continuously touches the graph paper as you draw the line. From there, you can start another line beginning where the last one ended.

The functions exported by the `graphics.h` interface are shown in Table 5-1. Graphics applications begin by calling `InitGraphics`, after which the image itself is created by calls to `MovePen`, `DrawLine`, and `DrawArc`. The remaining functions— `GetWindowWidth`, `GetWindowHeight`, `GetCurrentX`, and `GetCurrentY`—make it possible to retrieve information about the dimensions and state of the graphics window. These functions come up less frequently, but are nonetheless useful enough that it makes sense to include them in the interface.

To get a better sense of how the graphics library works, consider the following program, which draws a simple archway:

```
main()
{
    InitGraphics();
    MovePen(2.0, 0.5);
    DrawLine(1.0, 0.0);
    DrawLine(0.0, 1.0);
    DrawArc(0.5, 0, 180);
    DrawLine(0.0, -1.0);
}
```

TABLE 5-1 Functions exported by `graphics.h`	
`InitGraphics()`	This procedure creates the graphics window on the screen. The call to `InitGraphics` must precede any output operations of any kind and is usually the first statement in the function `main`.
`MovePen(x, y)`	This procedure picks up the pen and moves it—without drawing any lines—to the position (x, y), which is specified in absolute coordinates.
`DrawLine(dx, dy)`	This procedure draws a line extending from the current point by moving the pen dx inches in the x direction and dy inches in the y direction. The final position becomes the new current point.
`DrawArc(r, start, sweep)`	This procedure draws a circular arc, which always begins at the current point. The arc itself has radius r, and starts at the angle specified by the parameter *start,* relative to the center of the circle. This angle is measured in degrees counterclockwise from the 3 o'clock position along the x-axis, as in traditional mathematics. For example, if *start* is 0, the arc begins at the 3 o'clock position; if *start* is 90, the arc begins at the 12 o'clock position; and so on. The fraction of the circle drawn is specified by the parameter *sweep,* which is also measured in degrees. If *sweep* is 360, `DrawArc` draws a complete circle; if *sweep* is 90, it draws a quarter of a circle. If the value of *sweep* is positive, the arc is drawn counterclockwise from the current point; if *sweep* is negative, the arc is drawn clockwise. The current point at the end of the `DrawArc` operation is the final position of the pen along the arc.
`GetWindowWidth()` `GetWindowHeight()`	These functions return the width and height of the graphics window, respectively.
`GetCurrentX()` `GetCurrentY()`	These functions return the absolute coordinates of the current point.

The program begins, like all graphics programs, with a call to `InitGraphics`, which creates an empty graphics window. The next two statements then move the pen to the point (2.0, 0.5) and draw a line with the relative coordinates (1.0, 0.0). The effect of these statements is to draw a 1-inch horizontal line near the bottom of the window. The next call to `DrawLine` adds a vertical line that begins where the first line ended. Thus, at this point, the graphics window looks like this:

The next statement

```
DrawArc(0.5, 0, 180);
```

draws a circular arc with a radius of 0.5 inches. Because the second argument is 0, the arc begins at the 0 degree mark, which corresponds to the 3 o'clock position. From there, the third argument indicates that the arc proceeds in the positive direction (counterclockwise) for a total of 180 degrees, or halfway around the circle. Adding this semicircle to the line segments generated earlier makes the following figure:

The last statement in the program draws a 1-inch vertical line in the downward direction, which completes the archway, as shown:

An example from computer art

In the early part of the twentieth century, a controversial artistic movement arose in Paris, largely under the influence of Pablo Picasso and Georges Braque. The Cubists—as they were called by their critics—rejected classical artistic notions of perspective and representationalism and instead produced highly fragmented works based on primitive geometrical forms. Strongly influenced by Cubism, the Dutch painter Piet Mondrian (1872–1944) produced a series of compositions based on horizontal and vertical lines, such as the one shown in Figure 5-2.

Because of its simplicity and regularity of form, Mondrian's style has been of interest to computer scientists exploring the question of whether a computer can generate "art." It is certainly possible to generate geometrical patterns on the computer that resemble Mondrian's compositions. Whether such computer-generated compositions have any artistic value is an aesthetic, philosophical question. However, such designs certainly have pedagogical value as an illustration of how recursion plays a role in computer graphics.

FIGURE 5-2 Grid pattern from Piet Mondrian, "Composition with Grid 6," 1

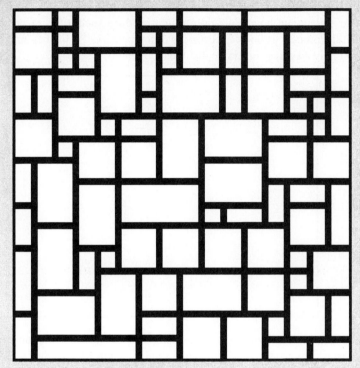

Suppose that you want to generate compositions such as the following, which—like much of Mondrian's work—consists only of horizontal and vertical lines:

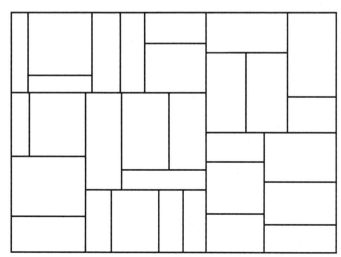

How would you go about designing a general strategy to create such a figure using the graphics library?

To understand how a program might produce such a figure, it helps to think about the process as one of successive decomposition. At the beginning, the canvas was simply an empty rectangle that looked like this:

If you want to subdivide the canvas using a series of horizontal and vertical lines, the easiest way to start is by drawing a single line that divides the rectangle in two:

If you're thinking recursively, the thing to notice at this point is that you now have two empty rectangular canvases, each of which is smaller in size. The task of subdividing these rectangles is the same as before, so you can perform it by using a recursive implementation of the same procedure. Since the new rectangles are taller than they are wide, you might choose to use a horizontal dividing line, but the basic process remains the same.

At this point, the only thing needed for a complete recursive strategy is a simple case. The process of dividing up rectangles can't go on indefinitely. As the rectangles get smaller and smaller, at some point the process has to stop. One approach is to look at the area of each rectangle before you start. Once the area of a rectangle falls below some threshold, you needn't bother to subdivide it any further.

The `mondrian.c` program shown in Figure 5-3 implements the recursive algorithm, using the entire graphics window as the initial canvas.

FIGURE 5-3   Program to generate a Mondrian-style drawing

```
/*
 * File: mondrian.c
 * ----------------
 * This program creates a random line drawing in a style reminiscent
 * of the Dutch painter Piet Mondrian.  The picture is generated by
 * recursively subdividing the canvas into successively smaller
 * rectangles with randomly chosen horizontal and vertical lines.
 */

#include <stdio.h>
#include "genlib.h"
#include "random.h"
#include "graphics.h"

/*
 * Constants
 * ---------
 * MinArea -- Smallest square that will be split
 * MinEdge -- Minimum fraction on each side of dividing line
 */

#define MinArea  0.5
#define MinEdge  0.15

/* Private function prototypes */

static void SubdivideCanvas(double x, double y,
                            double width, double height);

/* Main program */

main()
{
    InitGraphics();
    Randomize();
    SubdivideCanvas(0, 0, GetWindowWidth(), GetWindowHeight());
}
```

```
/*
 * Function: SubdivideCanvas
 * Usage: SubdivideCanvas(x, y, width, height);
 * ---------------------------------------------
 * This function decomposes a canvas by recursive subdivision.  The
 * lower left corner of the canvas is the point (x, y), and the
 * dimensions are given by the width and height parameters.  The
 * function first checks for the simple case, which is obtained
 * when the size of the rectangular canvas is too small to subdivide
 * (area < MinArea).  In the simple case, the function does nothing.
 * If the area is larger than the minimum, the function first
 * decides whether to split the canvas horizontally or vertically,
 * choosing the larger dimension.  The function then chooses a
 * random dividing line, making sure to leave at least MinEdge on
 * each side.  The program then uses a divide-and-conquer strategy
 * to subdivide the two new rectangles.
 */

static void SubdivideCanvas(double x, double y,
                            double width, double height)
{
    double divider;

    if (width * height >= MinArea) {
        if (width > height) {
            divider = width * RandomReal(MinEdge, 1 - MinEdge);
            MovePen(x + divider, y);
            DrawLine(0, height);
            SubdivideCanvas(x, y, divider, height);
            SubdivideCanvas(x + divider, y, width - divider, height);
        } else {
            divider = height * RandomReal(MinEdge, 1 - MinEdge);
            MovePen(x, y + divider);
            DrawLine(width, 0);
            SubdivideCanvas(x, y, width, divider);
            SubdivideCanvas(x, y + divider, width, height - divider);
        }
    }
}
```

In mondrian.c, the recursive function SubdivideCanvas does all the work. The arguments give the position and dimensions of the current rectangle on the canvas. At each step in the decomposition, the function simply checks to see whether the rectangle is large enough to split. If it is, the function checks to see which dimension—width or height—is larger and accordingly divides the rectangle with a vertical or horizontal line. In each case, the function draws only a single line; all remaining lines in the figure are drawn by subsequent recursive calls.

Fractals

In the late 1970s, a researcher at IBM named Benoit Mandelbrot generated a great deal of excitement by publishing a book on **fractals,** which are geometrical structures in which the same pattern is repeated at many different scales. Although mathematicians have known about fractals for a long time, there was a resurgence of interest in the subject during the 1980s, partly because the development of computers made it possible to do so much more with fractals than had ever been possible before.

One of the earliest examples of fractal figures is called the **Koch snowflake** after its inventor, Helge von Koch. The Koch snowflake begins with an equilateral triangle like this:

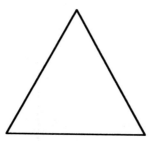

This triangle, in which the sides are straight lines, is called the Koch fractal of order 0. The figure is then revised in stages to generate fractals of successively higher orders. At each stage, every straight-line segment in the figure is replaced by one in which the middle third consists of a triangular bump protruding outward from the figure. Thus, the first step is to replace each line segment in the triangle with a line that looks like this:

Applying this transformation to each of the three sides of the original triangle generates the Koch fractal of order 1, as follows:

If you then replace each line segment in this figure with a new line that again includes a triangular wedge, you create the following order 2 Koch fractal:

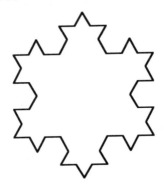

Replacing each of these line segments gives the order 3 fractal shown in the following diagram, which has started to resemble a snowflake:

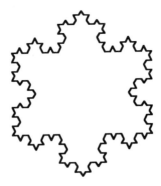

Because figures like the Koch fractal are much easier to draw by computer than by hand, it makes sense to write a program that uses the graphics library to generate this design. Before designing the program itself, however, it helps to introduce a new procedure that will prove useful in a variety of graphical applications. The DrawLine primitive in the graphics library requires you to specify the relative coordinates of the new endpoint as a pair of values, *dx* and *dy*. In many graphical applications, it is much easier to think of lines as having a length and a direction. For example, the solid line in the following diagram can be identified by its length (r) and its angle from the horizontal (θ):

In mathematics, the parameters r and θ are called the **polar coordinates** of the line. Converting from polar coordinates to the more traditional Cartesian coordinates used in the graphics library requires a little trigonometry, as shown in the following implementation of the procedure `DrawPolarLine`, which draws a line of length `r` in the direction `theta`, measured in degrees counterclockwise from the x-axis:

```
#define Pi 3.1415926535

static void DrawPolarLine(double r, double theta)
{
    double radians;

    radians = theta / 180 * Pi;
    DrawLine(r * cos(radians), r * sin(radians));
}
```

If you don't understand trigonometry, don't worry. You don't need to understand the implementation of `DrawPolarLine` to use it. If you have had a trigonometry course, most of this implementation should be straightforward; the only complexity comes from the fact that the library functions `sin` and `cos` are defined to take their arguments in radian measure, which means that the implementation must convert the `theta` parameter from degrees to radians prior to calling the trigonometric functions.

Given `DrawPolarLine`, it is very easy to draw the equilateral triangle that represents the Koch snowflake of order 0. If `size` is the length of one side of the triangle, all you need to do is position the pen at the lower left corner of the figure and make the following calls:

```
DrawPolarLine(size, 0);
DrawPolarLine(size, 120);
DrawPolarLine(size, 240);
```

But how would you go about drawing a more complicated Koch fractal, that is, one of a higher order? The first step is simply to replace each of the calls to `DrawPolarLine` with a call to a new procedure that draws a fractal line of a specified order. Thus, the three calls in the main program look like this:

```
DrawFractalLine(size, 0, order);
DrawFractalLine(size, 120, order);
DrawFractalLine(size, 240, order);
```

The next task is to implement `DrawFractalLine`, which is easy if you think about it recursively. The simple case for `DrawFractalLine` occurs when `order` is 0, in which case the function simply draws a straight line with the specified length and direction. If `order` is greater than 0, the fractal line is broken down into four components, each of which is itself a fractal line of the next lower order. Thus, the implementation of `DrawFractalLine` looks like this:

```
static void DrawFractalLine(double len, double theta, int order)
{
    if (order == 0) {
        DrawPolarLine(len, theta);
    } else {
        DrawFractalLine(len/3, theta, order - 1);
        DrawFractalLine(len/3, theta - 60, order - 1);
        DrawFractalLine(len/3, theta + 60, order - 1);
        DrawFractalLine(len/3, theta, order - 1);
    }
}
```

The complete implementation of the koch.c program is shown in Figure 5-4.

FIGURE 5-4   Program to draw a Koch fractal snowflake

```
/*
 * File: koch.c
 * ----------------
 * This program draws a Koch fractal.
 */

#include <stdio.h>
#include <math.h>
#include "genlib.h"
#include "simpio.h"
#include "graphics.h"

/* Mathematical constants */

#define Pi 3.1415926535

/* Private function prototypes */

static void KochFractal(double size, int order);
static void DrawFractalLine(double len, double theta, int order);
static void DrawPolarLine(double r, double theta);

/* Main program */

main()
{
    double size;
    int order;

    InitGraphics();
    printf("Program to draw Koch fractals\n");
    printf("Enter edge length in inches: ");
    size = GetReal();
    printf("Enter order of fractal: ");
    order = GetInteger();
    KochFractal(size, order);
}
```

```
/*
 * Function: KochFractal
 * Usage: KochFractal(size, order);
 * ---------------------------------
 * This function draws a Koch fractal snowflake centered in
 * the graphics window of the indicated size and order.
 */

static void KochFractal(double size, int order)
{
    double x0, y0;

    x0 = GetWindowWidth() / 2 - size / 2;
    y0 = GetWindowHeight() / 2 - sqrt(3) * size / 6;
    MovePen(x0, y0);
    DrawFractalLine(size, 0, order);
    DrawFractalLine(size, 120, order);
    DrawFractalLine(size, 240, order);
}


/*
 * Function: DrawFractalLine
 * Usage: DrawFractalLine(len, theta, order);
 * ------------------------------------------
 * This function draws a fractal line of the given length, starting
 * from the current point and moving in direction theta.  If order
 * is 0, the fractal line is just a straight line.  If order is
 * greater than zero, the line is divided into four line segments,
 * each of which is a fractal line of the next lower order.  The
 * four segments connect the same endpoints as the straight line,
 * but include a triangular wedge replacing the center third of
 * the segment.
 */

static void DrawFractalLine(double len, double theta, int order)
{
    if (order == 0) {
        DrawPolarLine(len, theta);
    } else {
        DrawFractalLine(len/3, theta, order - 1);
        DrawFractalLine(len/3, theta - 60, order - 1);
        DrawFractalLine(len/3, theta + 60, order - 1);
        DrawFractalLine(len/3, theta, order - 1);
    }
}
```

```
/*
 * Function: DrawPolarLine
 * Usage: DrawPolarLine(r, theta);
 * --------------------------------
 * This function draws a line of length r in the direction
 * specified by the angle theta.  As in the DrawArc function,
 * theta is measured in degrees counterclockwise from the +x
 * axis.  This style of measurement is called "polar coordinates."
 */

static void DrawPolarLine(double r, double theta)
{
    double radians;

    radians = theta / 180 * Pi;
    DrawLine(r * cos(radians), r * sin(radians));
}
```

Summary

Except for the discussion of the graphics library in the section entitled "Graphical applications of recursion" earlier in this chapter, relatively few new concepts have been introduced in Chapter 5. The fundamental precepts of recursion were introduced in Chapter 4. The point of Chapter 5 is to raise the sophistication level of the recursive examples to the point at which the problems become difficult to solve in any other way. Because of this increase in sophistication, beginning students often find these problems much harder to comprehend than those in the preceding chapter. Indeed, they are harder, but recursion is a tool for solving hard problems. To master it, you need to practice with problems at this level of complexity.

The important points in this chapter include:

- Whenever you want to apply recursion to a programming problem, you have to devise a strategy that transforms the problem into simpler instances of the same problem. Until you find the correct insight that leads to the recursive strategy, there is no way to apply recursive techniques.
- Once you identify a recursive approach, it is important for you to check your strategy to ensure that it does not violate any conditions imposed by the problem.
- When the problems you are trying to solve increase in complexity, the importance of accepting the recursive leap of faith increases.
- Recursion is not magical. If you need to do so, you can simulate the operation of the computer yourself by drawing the stack frames for every procedure that is called in the course of the solution. At the same time, it is critical to get beyond the skepticism that forces you to look at all the underlying details.

- Wrapper functions are useful in complex recursive procedures, just as they are for the simple recursive functions presented in Chapter 4.
- The `graphics.h` library makes it possible to display simple graphical drawings, many of which have an interesting recursive structure.

REVIEW QUESTIONS

1. In your own words, describe the recursive insight necessary to solve the Tower of Hanoi puzzle.

2. What is wrong with the following strategy for solving the recursive case of the Tower of Hanoi puzzle:

   a. Move the top disk from the start spire to the temporary spire.
   b. Move a stack of $N-1$ disks from the start spire to the finish spire.
   c. Move the top disk now on the temporary spire back to the finish spire.

3. If you call

   ```
   MoveTower(16, 'A', 'B', 'C')
   ```

   what line is displayed by **MoveSingleDisk** as the first step in the solution? What is the last step in the solution?

4. What is a permutation?

5. In your own words, explain the recursive insight necessary to enumerate the permutations of the characters in a string.

6. How many permutations are there of the string **"WXYZ"**?

7. Why is it necessary to define both **ListPermutations** and **RecursivePermute** in the permutation problem?

8. Where is the origin located in the graphics window?

9. What is the difference between absolute and relative coordinates?

10. What are the eight functions exported by the **graphics.h** interface?

11. What simple case is used to terminate the recursion in **mondrian.c**?

12. Draw a picture of the order 1 Koch fractal.

13. How many line segments appear in the order 2 Koch fractal?

14. From the caller's point of view, describe the effect of the function **DrawPolarLine**.

PROGRAMMING EXERCISES

1. Following the logic of the `MoveTower` function, write a recursive function `NHanoiMoves(n)` that calculates the number of individual moves required to solve the Tower of Hanoi puzzle for n disks.

2. To make the operation of the program somewhat easier to explain, the implementation of `MoveTower` in this chapter uses

   ```
   if (n == 1)
   ```

   as its simple case test. Whenever you see a recursive program use 1 as its simple case, it pays to be a little skeptical; in most applications, 0 is a more appropriate choice. Rewrite the Tower of Hanoi program so that the `MoveTower` function checks whether n is 0 instead. What happens to the length of the `MoveTower` implementation?

3. As presented in the text, the function `RecursivePermute` takes a string and an integer, which indicates how far the permutation process has progressed. You could also design the program so that `RecursivePermute` takes two strings: (1) a fixed prefix that is always included as part of the output and (2) a suffix whose characters can still be permuted. For example, if you call the redesigned `RecursivePermute` function on the strings `"AB"` and `"CD"`, the output should be

   ```
   ABCD
   ABDC
   ```

   which is all strings beginning with `"AB"` followed by some permutation of `"CD"`.

   Rewrite the permutation program so that it uses this new design and, moreover, uses only functions in the `strlib.h` interface (`Concat`, `IthChar`, `SubString`, and so forth) to manipulate strings. In particular, your implementation may not use array notation to select or change characters inside a string.

4. Once you have revised the implementation of the permutation program as described in exercise 3, it is reasonably straightforward to generate the correct list of permutations even if the string contains repeated letters. For example, if you call `ListPermutations` on the string `"AABB"`, your program should not generate as many permutations as it does for the string `"ABCD"` because some of the strings generated by the standard algorithm would be indistinguishable from others. Your program should instead generate the following six:

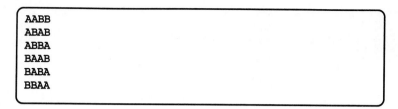

```
AABB
ABAB
ABBA
BAAB
BABA
BBAA
```

Write a new implementation of **ListPermutations** that works correctly even if the string contains duplicated letters. In writing this implementation, you should not merely keep a list of the permutations that have already been encountered and avoid generating duplicates. Instead, you should think carefully about the recursive structure of the problem and find a way to avoid generating the extra permutations in the first place.

5. On the standard Touch-Tone™ telephone dial, the digits are mapped onto the alphabet (minus the letters *Q* and *Z*) as shown in the diagram below:

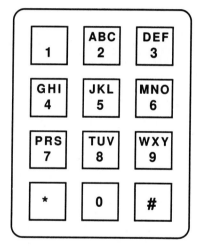

In order to make their phone numbers more memorable, service providers like to find numbers that spell out some word (called a **mnemonic**) appropriate to their business that makes that phone number easier to remember. For example, the phone number for a recorded time-of-day message in some localities is 637-8687 (NERVOUS).

Imagine that you have just been hired by a local telephone company to write a function **ListMnemonics** that will generate all possible letter combinations that correspond to a given number, represented as a string of digits. For example, if you call

```
ListMnemonics("723")
```

your program should generate the following 27 possible letter combinations that correspond to that prefix:

PAD	PBD	PCD	RAD	RBD	RCD	SAD	SBD	SCD
PAE	PBE	PCE	RAE	RBE	RCE	SAE	SBE	SCE
PAF	PBF	PCF	RAF	RBF	RCF	SAF	SBF	SCF

6. Using the `ListPermutations` example as a starting point, write a function `ListSubsets` that generates all possible subsets of a given set, where the set is represented by a string of letters. For example, if you call the function

   ```
   ListSubsets("ABC");
   ```

   your function should produce the following output:

   ```
   This program lists all subsets of a set.
   Enter a string representing a set: ABC↵
   {ABC}
   {AB}
   {AC}
   {A}
   {BC}
   {B}
   {C}
   {}
   ```

   Like permutations, the subset problem has a recursive formulation. If you represent a set of characters using a string that either contains or does not contain a given letter, you can calculate all possible subsets by (1) including the first character in the subset and concatenating it onto the front of all subsets of the remaining N–1 characters and then (2) displaying the subsets of the remaining N–1 without this character.

7. Inside a computer system, integers are represented as a sequence of bits, each of which is a single digit in the binary number system and can therefore have only the value 0 or 1. With N bits, you can represent 2^N distinct integers. For example, three bits are sufficient to represent the eight (2^3) integers between 0 and 7, as follows:

0 0 0	→	0
0 0 1	→	1
0 1 0	→	2
0 1 1	→	3
1 0 0	→	4
1 0 1	→	5
1 1 0	→	6
1 1 1	→	7

   Each entry in the left side of the table is written in its standard binary representation, in which each bit position counts for twice as much as the position to its right. For instance, you can demonstrate that the binary value

110 represents the decimal number 6 by following the logic shown in the following diagram:

$$
\begin{array}{ccccc}
\textit{place value} \longrightarrow & 4 & & 2 & & 1 \\
& \times & & \times & & \times \\
\textit{binary digits} \longrightarrow & \mathbf{1} & & \mathbf{1} & & \mathbf{0} \\
& \| & & \| & & \| \\
& 4 & + & 2 & + & 0 & = & 6
\end{array}
$$

Write a recursive function `GenerateBinaryCode(nBits)` that generates the bit patterns for the standard binary representation of all integers that can be represented using the specified number of bits. For example, calling `GenerateBinaryCode(3)` should produce the following output:

```
000
001
010
011
100
101
110
111
```

8. Although the binary coding used in exercise 7 is ideal for most applications, it has certain drawbacks. As you count in standard binary notation, there are some points in the sequence at which several bits change at the same time. For example, in the three-bit binary code, the value of every bit changes as you move from 3 (**011**) to 4 (**100**).

In some applications, this instability in the bit patterns used to represent adjacent numbers can lead to problems. Imagine for the moment that you are using some hardware measurement device that produces a three-bit value from some real-world phenomenon that happens to be varying between 3 and 4. Sometimes, the device will register **011** to indicate the value 3; at other times, it will register **100** to indicate 4. For this device to work correctly, the transitions for each of the individual bits must occur simultaneously. If the first bit changes more quickly than the others, for example, there may be an intermediate state in which the device reads **111**, which would be a highly inaccurate reading.

It is interesting to discover that you can avoid this problem simply by changing the numbering system. If instead of using binary representation in the traditional way, you can assign three-bit values to each of the numbers 0 through 7 with the highly useful property that only one bit changes in the representation between every pair of adjacent integers. Such an encoding is called a **Gray code** (after its inventor, the mathematician Frank Gray) and looks like this:

0 0 0	→	0
0 0 1	→	1
0 1 1	→	2
0 1 0	→	3
1 1 0	→	4
1 1 1	→	5
1 0 1	→	6
1 0 0	→	7

Note that, in the Gray code representation, the bit patterns for 3 and 4 differ only in their leftmost bit. If the hardware measurement device used Gray codes, a value oscillating between 3 and 4 would simply turn that bit on and off, eliminating any problems with synchronization.

The recursive insight that you need to create a Gray code of N bits is summarized in the following informal procedure:

1. Write down the Gray code for $N-1$ bits.
2. Copy that same list *in reverse order* below the original one.
3. Add a **0** bit in front of the codings in the original half of the list and a **1** bit in front of those in the reversed copy.

This procedure is illustrated in the following derivation of the Gray code for three bits:

3-bit Gray code   *2-bit Gray code*   *1-bit Gray code*

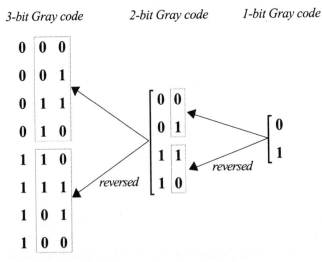

Write a recursive function **GenerateGrayCode(nBits)** that generates the Gray code patterns for the specified number of bits.

9. Given a set of numbers, the *partition problem* is to find a subset of the numbers that add up to a specific target number. For example, there are two ways to partition the set {1, 3, 4, 5} so that the remaining elements add up to 5:

- Select the 1 and the 4
- Select just the 5

By contrast, there is no way to partition the set {1, 3, 4, 5} to get 11.

Write a function `NumberOfPartitions` that takes an array of integers, the length of that array, and a target number, and returns the number of partitions of that set of integers which add up to the target. For example, suppose that the array `sampleSet` has been initialized as follows:

```
int sampleSet[] = {1, 3, 4, 5};
```

Given this definition of `sampleSet`, calling

```
NumberOfPartitions(sampleSet, 4, 5);
```

should return 2 (there are two ways to make 5), and calling

```
NumberOfPartitions(sampleSet, 4, 11)
```

should return 0 (there are no ways to make 11).

The prototype for `NumberOfPartitions` is

```
int NumberOfPartitions(int array[], int length, int target);
```

In order to see the recursive nature of this problem, think about any specific element in the set, such as the first element. If you think about all the partitions of a particular target number, some of them will include the first element and some won't. If you count those that do include the first element and then add that total to the number of those which leave out that element, you get the total number of partitions. Each of these two computations, however, can be expressed as a problem in the same form as the outer partition problem and can therefore be solved recursively.

10.
> I am the only child of parents who weighed, measured, and priced everything; for whom what could not be weighed, measured, and priced had no existence.
>
> —Charles Dickens, *Little Dorrit*, 1857

In Dickens's time, merchants measured many commodities using weights and a two-pan balance—a practice that continues in many parts of the world today. If you are using a limited set of weights, however, you can only measure certain quantities accurately.

For example, suppose that you have only two weights: a 1-ounce weight and a 3-ounce weight. With these you can easily measure out 4 ounces, as shown:

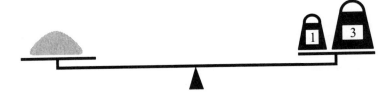

It is somewhat more interesting to discover that you can also measure out 2 ounces by shifting the 1-ounce weight to the other side, as follows:

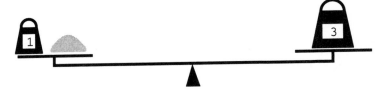

Write a recursive function

```
bool IsMeasurable(int target, int weights[], int nWeights)
```

that determines whether it is possible to measure out the desired target amount with a given set of weights. The available weights are stored in the array `weights`, which has `nWeights` as its effective size. For instance, the sample set of two weights illustrated above could be represented using the following pair of variables:

```
static int sampleWeights[] = { 1, 3 };
static int nSampleWeights = 2;
```

Given these values, the function call

```
IsMeasurable(2, sampleWeights, nSampleWeights)
```

should return TRUE because it is possible to measure out 2 ounces using the sample weight set as illustrated in the preceding diagram. On the other hand, calling

```
IsMeasurable(5, sampleWeights, nSampleWeights)
```

should return FALSE because it is impossible to use the 1- and 3-ounce weights to add up to 5 ounces.

The fundamental observation you need to make for this problem is that you can use each weight in any of the following three ways:

1. You can put it on the opposite side of the balance from the sample.
2. You can put it on the same side of the balance as the sample.
3. You can leave it off the balance entirely.

If you consider one of the weights in the array and determine how choosing one of these three options affects the rest of the problem, you should be able to come up with the recursive insight you need to solve the problem.

11. In countries like the United States that still use the traditional English system of measurement, each inch on a ruler is marked off into fractions using tick marks that look like this:

The longest tick mark falls at the half-inch position, two smaller tick marks indicate the quarter inches, and even smaller ones are used to mark the eighths and sixteenths. Write a recursive program that draws a 1-inch line at the center of the graphics window and then draws the tick marks shown in the diagram. Assume that the length of the tick mark indicating the half-inch position is given by the constant definition

```
#define HalfInchTick 0.2
```

and that each smaller tick mark is half the size of the next larger one.

12. One of the reasons that fractals have provoked so much interest is that they turn out to be useful in some surprising practical contexts. For example, the most successful techniques for drawing computer images of mountains and certain other landscape features involve using fractal geometry.

   As a simple example of where this issue comes up, consider the problem of connecting two points A and B with a fractal that looks like a coastline on a map. The simplest possible strategy would be to draw a straight line between the two points:

A •————————————————————————• B

This is the order 0 coastline and represents the base case of the recursion.

   Of course, a real coastline will have small peninsulas or inlets somewhere along its length, so you would expect a realistic drawing of a coastline to jut in or out occasionally like a real one. As a first approximation, you could replace the straight line with precisely the same fractal line used to create the Koch snowflake in the program described in the section on "Fractals" earlier in the chapter, as follows:

This process gives the order 1 coastline. However, in order to give the feeling of a traditional coastline, it is important for the triangular wedge in this line sometimes to point up and sometimes down, with equal probability.

If you then replace each of the straight line segments in the order 1 fractal with a fractal line in a random direction, you get the order 2 coastline, which might look like this:

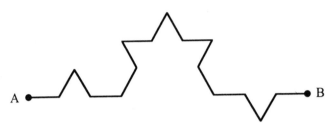

Continuing this process eventually results in a drawing that conveys a remarkably realistic sense, as in this order 5 coastline:

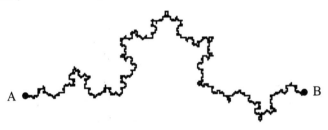

Write a function `DrawCoastline` that fits the following interface description:

```
/*
 * Function: DrawCoastline
 * Usage: DrawCoastline(length, theta, order);
 * ------------------------------------------------
 * The DrawCoastline function starts at the current (x, y)
 * position and draws a fractal coastline of the specified
 * length moving in the direction given by the angle theta
 * (as defined in the definition of DrawPolarLine in the
 * preceding problem).  The parameter order gives the number
 * of recursive subdivisions into which each segment will be
 * divided.
 */

void DrawCoastline(double length, double theta, int order);
```

13. Recursive decomposition can also be used to draw a stylized representation of a tree. The tree begins as a simple trunk indicated by a straight vertical line, as follows:

The trunk may branch at the top to form two lines that veer off at an angle, as shown:

These branches may themselves split to form new branches, which split to form new ones, and so on. If the decision to branch is made randomly at each step of the process, the tree will eventually become unsymmetrical and will end up looking a little more like trees in nature, as illustrated by the following diagram:

If you think about this process recursively, however, you can see that all trees constructed in this way consist of a trunk, optionally topped by two trees that veer off at an angle. If the probability of branching is a function of the length of the current branch, the process will eventually terminate as the branches get progressively shorter.

Write a program `drawtree.c` that uses this recursive strategy and the graphics library to draw a stylized line drawing of a tree.

CHAPTER 6

Backtracking Algorithms

Truth is not discovered by proofs but by exploration. It is always experimental.

— Simone Weil, *The New York Notebook,* 1942

Objectives

- To appreciate how backtracking can be used as a solution strategy.

- To recognize the problem domains for which backtracking strategies are appropriate.

- To understand how recursion applies to backtracking problems.

- To be able to implement recursive solutions to problems involving backtracking.

- To comprehend the minimax strategy as it applies to two-player games.

- To appreciate the importance of developing abstract solutions that can be applied to many different problem domains.

For many real-world problems, the solution process consists of working your way through a sequence of decision points in which each choice leads you further along some path. If you make the correct set of choices, you end up at the solution. On the other hand, if you reach a dead end or otherwise discover that you have made an incorrect choice somewhere along the way, you have to backtrack to a previous decision point and try a different path. Algorithms that use this approach are called **backtracking algorithms.**

If you think about a backtracking algorithm as the process of repeatedly exploring paths until you encounter the solution, the process appears to have an iterative character. As it happens, however, most problems of this form are easier to solve recursively. The fundamental recursive insight is simply this: a backtracking problem has a solution if and only if at least one of the smaller backtracking problems that results from making each possible initial choice has a solution. The examples in this chapter are designed to illustrate this process and demonstrate the power of recursion in this domain.

■■■ 6.1 Solving a maze by recursive backtracking

Once upon a time, in the days of Greek mythology, the Mediterranean island of Crete was ruled by a tyrannical king named Minos. From time to time, Minos demanded tribute from the city of Athens in the form of young men and women, whom he would sacrifice to the Minotaur—a fearsome beast with the head of a bull and the body of a man. To house this deadly creature, Minos forced his servant Daedelus (the engineering genius who later escaped the island by constructing a set of wings) to build a vast underground labyrinth at Knossos. The young sacrifices from Athens would be led into the labyrinth, where they would be eaten by the Minotaur before they could find their way out. This tragedy continued until young Theseus of Athens volunteered to be one of the sacrifices. Following the advice of Minos's daughter Ariadne, Theseus entered the labyrinth with a sword and a ball of string. After slaying the monster, Theseus was able to find his way back to the exit by unwinding the string as he went along.

The right-hand rule

Theseus's strategy represents an algorithm for escaping from a maze, but not everyone in such a predicament is lucky enough to have a ball of string or an accomplice clever enough to suggest such an effective approach. Fortunately, there are other strategies for escaping from a maze. Of these strategies, the best known is called the **right-hand rule,** which can be expressed in the following pseudocode form:

> *Put your right hand against a wall.*
> **while** (*you have not yet escaped from the maze*) **{**
>   *Walk forward keeping your right hand on a wall.*
> **}**

As you walk, the requirement that you keep your right hand touching the wall may force you to turn corners and occasionally retrace your steps. Even so, following the right-hand rule guarantees that you will always be able to find an opening to the outside of any maze.

To visualize the operation of the right-hand rule, imagine that Theseus has successfully dispatched the Minotaur and is now standing in the position marked by the first character in Theseus's name, the Greek letter theta (Θ):

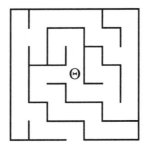

If Theseus puts his right hand on the wall and then follows the right-hand rule from there, he will trace out the path shown by the dashed line in this diagram:

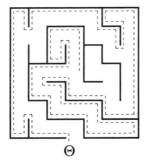

Finding a recursive approach

As the `while` loop in its pseudocode form makes clear, the right-hand rule is an *iterative* strategy. You can, however, also think about the process of solving a maze from a *recursive* perspective. To do so, you must adopt a different mindset. You can no longer think about the problem in terms of finding a complete path. Instead, your goal is to find a recursive insight that simplifies the problem, one step at a time. Once you have made the simplification, you can use the same procedure to solve each of the resulting subproblems.

Let's go back to the initial configuration of the maze shown in the illustration of the right-hand rule. Put yourself in Theseus's position. From the initial configuration, you have three choices, as indicated by the arrows in the following diagram:

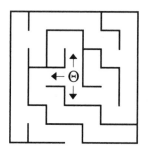

The exit, if any, must lie along one of those paths. Moreover, if you choose the correct direction, you will be one step closer to the solution. The maze has therefore become simpler along that path, which is the key to a recursive solution. This observation suggests the necessary recursive insight. The original maze has a solution if and only if it is possible to solve at least one of the new mazes shown in Figure 6-1. The × in each diagram marks the original starting square and is off-limits for any of the recursive solutions because the optimal solution will never have to backtrack through this square.

By looking at the mazes in Figure 6-1, it is easy to see—at least from your global vantage point—that the submazes labeled (a) and (c) represent dead-end paths and that the only solution begins in the direction shown in the submaze (b). If you are thinking recursively, however, you don't need to carry on the analysis all the way to the solution. You have already decomposed the problem into simpler instances. All you need to do is rely on the power of recursion to solve the individual subproblems, and you're home free. You still have to identify a set of simple cases so that the recursion can terminate, but the hard work has been done.

Identifying the simple cases

What constitutes the simple case for a maze? One possibility is that you might already be standing outside the maze. If so, you're finished. Clearly, this situation represents one simple case. There is, however, another possibility. You might also reach a blind alley where you've run out of places to move. For example, if you try

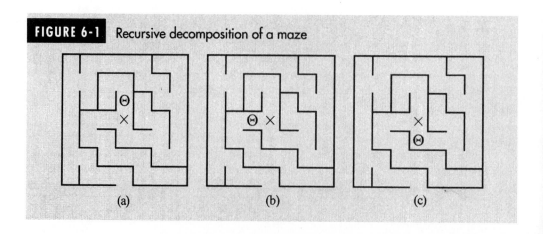

FIGURE 6-1   Recursive decomposition of a maze

(a)   (b)   (c)

to solve the sample maze by moving north and then continue to make recursive calls along that path, you will eventually be in the position of trying to solve the following maze:

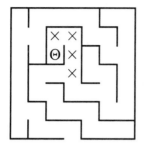

At this point, you've run out of room to maneuver. Every path from the new position is either marked or blocked by a wall, which makes it clear that the maze has no solution from this point. Thus, the maze problem has a second simple case in which every direction from the current square is blocked, either by a wall or a marked square.

It is easier to code the recursive algorithm if, instead of checking for marked squares as you consider the possible directions of motion, you go ahead and make the recursive calls on those squares. If you check at the beginning of the procedure to see whether the current square is marked, you can terminate the recursion at that point. After all, if you find yourself positioned on a marked square, you must be retracing your path, which means that the solution must lie in some other direction.

Thus, the two simple cases for this problem are as follows:

1. If the current square is outside the maze, the maze is solved.
2. If the current square is marked, the maze is unsolvable.

Coding the maze solution algorithm

Although the recursive insight and the simple cases are all you need to solve the problem on a conceptual level, writing a complete program to navigate a maze requires you to consider a number of implementation details as well. For example, you need to decide on a representation for the maze itself that allows you, for example, to figure out where the walls are, keep track of the current position, indicate that a particular square is marked, and determine whether you have escaped from the maze. While designing an appropriate data structure for the maze is an interesting programming challenge in its own right, it has very little to do with understanding the recursive algorithm, which is the focus of this discussion. If anything, the details of the data structure are likely to get in the way and make it more difficult for you to understand the algorithmic strategy as a whole.

Fortunately, it is possible to put such details aside by introducing a new abstraction layer. The purpose of the abstraction is to provide the main program with access to the information it needs to solve a maze, even though the details are hidden behind an interface. An interface that provides the necessary functionality is the **mazelib.h** interface shown in Figure 6-2.

```
/*
 * File: mazelib.h
 * --------------
 * This interface provides a library of primitive operations
 * to simplify the solution to the maze problem.
 */

#ifndef _mazelib_h
#define _mazelib_h

#include "genlib.h"

/*
 * Type: pointT
 * ------------
 * The type pointT is used to encapsulate a pair of integer
 * coordinates into a single value with x and y components.
 */

typedef struct {
    int x, y;
} pointT;

/*
 * Type: directionT
 * ----------------
 * This type is used to represent the four compass directions.
 */

typedef enum { North, East, South, West } directionT;

/*
 * Function: ReadMazeMap
 * Usage: ReadMazeMap(filename);
 * -----------------------------
 * This function reads in a map of the maze from the specified
 * file and stores it in private data structures maintained by
 * this module.  In the data file, the characters '+', '-', and
 * '|' represent corners, horizontal walls, and vertical walls,
 * respectively; spaces represent open passageway squares.  The
 * starting position is indicated by the character 'S'.  For
 * example, the following data file defines a simple maze:
 *
 *      +-+-+-+-+-+
 *      |       |
 *      + +-+ + +-+
 *      |S |   |
 *      +-+-+-+-+-+
 *
 * Coordinates are numbered starting at (0,0) in the lower left.
 */

void ReadMazeMap(string filename);
```

```
/*
 * Function: GetStartPosition
 * Usage: pt = GetStartPosition();
 * --------------------------------
 * This function returns a pointT indicating the coordinates of
 * the start square.
 */

pointT GetStartPosition(void);

/*
 * Function: OutsideMaze
 * Usage: if (OutsideMaze(pt)) . . .
 * --------------------------------
 * This function returns TRUE if the specified point is outside
 * the boundary of the maze.
 */

bool OutsideMaze(pointT pt);

/*
 * Function: WallExists
 * Usage: if (WallExists(pt, dir)) . . .
 * --------------------------------------
 * This function returns TRUE if there is a wall in the indicated
 * direction from the square at position pt.
 */

bool WallExists(pointT pt, directionT dir);

/*
 * Functions: MarkSquare, UnmarkSquare, IsMarked
 * Usage: MarkSquare(pt);
 *        UnmarkSquare(pt);
 *        if (IsMarked(pt)) . . .
 * --------------------------------
 * These functions mark, unmark, and test the status of the
 * square specified by the coordinates pt.
 */

void MarkSquare(pointT pt);
void UnmarkSquare(pointT pt);
bool IsMarked(pointT pt);

#endif
```

Once you have access to the `mazelib.h` interface, writing a program to solve a maze becomes much simpler. The essence of the problem is to write a function `SolveMaze` that uses recursive backtracking to solve a maze whose specific characteristics are maintained by the `mazelib` module. The argument to `SolveMaze` is the starting position, which changes for each of the recursive subproblems. To ensure that the recursion can terminate when a solution is found, the `SolveMaze` function must also return some indication of whether it has succeeded. The easiest

way to convey this information is to define `SolveMaze` as a predicate function that returns **TRUE** if a solution has been found, and **FALSE** otherwise. Thus, the prototype for `SolveMaze` looks like this:

```
bool SolveMaze(pointT pt);
```

Given this definition, the main program is simply

```
main()
{
    ReadMazeMap(MazeFile);
    if (SolveMaze(GetStartPosition())) {
        printf("The marked squares show a solution path.\n");
    } else {
        printf("No solution exists.\n");
    }
}
```

The code for the `SolveMaze` function itself turns out to be extremely short and is shown in Figure 6-3. The entire algorithm fits into approximately 10 lines of code with the following pseudocode structure:

> *If the current square is outside, return TRUE to indicate that a solution has been found.*
> *If the current square is marked, return FALSE to indicate that this path has been tried.*
> *Mark the current square.*
> **for** *(each of the four compass directions)* {
>   **if** *(this direction is not blocked by a wall)* {
>   *Move one step in the indicated direction from the current square.*
>   *Try to solve the maze from there by making a recursive call.*
>   *If this call shows the maze to be solvable, return TRUE to indicate that fact.*
>   }
> }
> *Unmark the current square.*
> *Return FALSE to indicate that none of the four directions led to a solution.*

The only function called by `SolveMaze` that is not exported by the `mazelib.h` interface is the function `AdjacentPoint(pt, dir)`, which returns the coordinates of the square that is one step away from `pt` in the direction `dir`. The following is a simple implementation of `AdjacentPoint` that copies the original point and then adjusts the appropriate coordinate value:

```
pointT AdjacentPoint(pointT pt, directionT dir)
{
    pointT newpt;

    newpt = pt;
    switch (dir) {
      case North: newpt.y++; break;
      case East:  newpt.x++; break;
      case South: newpt.y--; break;
      case West:  newpt.x--; break;;
    }
    return (newpt);
}
```

FIGURE 6-3   Function for solving a maze

```
/*
 * Function: SolveMaze
 * Usage: if (SolveMaze(pt)) . . .
 * --------------------------------
 * This function attempts to generate a solution to the current
 * maze from point pt.  SolveMaze returns TRUE if the maze has
 * a solution and FALSE otherwise.  The implementation uses
 * recursion to solve the submazes that result from marking the
 * current square and moving one step along each open passage.
 */

static bool SolveMaze(pointT pt)
{
    directionT dir;

    if (OutsideMaze(pt)) return (TRUE);
    if (IsMarked(pt)) return (FALSE);
    MarkSquare(pt);
    for (dir = North; dir <= West; dir++) {
        if (!WallExists(pt, dir)) {
            if (SolveMaze(AdjacentPoint(pt, dir))) {
                return (TRUE);
            }
        }
    }
    UnmarkSquare(pt);
    return (FALSE);
}
```

The code to unmark the current square at the end of the `for` loop is not strictly necessary in this implementation and in fact can reduce the performance of the algorithm if there are loops in the maze (see exercise 3). The principal advantage of including it is that doing so means that the solution path ends up being recorded by a chain of marked squares from the original starting position to the exit. If you are using a graphical implementation of this algorithm, erasing the marks as you retreat down a path makes it much easier to see the current path.

Convincing yourself that the solution works

In order to use recursion effectively, at some point you must be able to look at a recursive function like the `SolveMaze` example in Figure 6-3 and say to yourself something like this: "I understand how this works. The problem is getting simpler because more squares are marked each time. The simple cases are clearly correct. This code must do the job." For most of you, however, that confidence in the power of recursion will not come easily. Your natural skepticism makes you want to see the steps in the solution. The problem is that, even for a maze as simple as the one shown earlier in this chapter, the complete history of the steps involved in the solution is far too large to think about comfortably. Solving that maze, for example, requires 66 calls to `SolveMaze` that are nested 27 levels deep when the solution is finally discovered. If you attempt to trace the code in detail, you will inevitably get lost.

If you are not yet ready to accept the recursive leap of faith, the best you can do is track the operation of the code in a more general sense. You know that the code first tries to solve the maze by moving one square to the north, because the `for` loop goes through the directions in the order defined by the `directionT` enumeration. Thus, the first step in the solution process is to make a recursive call that starts in the following position:

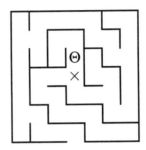

At this point, the same process occurs again. The program again tries to move north and makes a new recursive call in the following position:

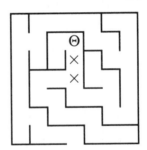

At this level of the recursion, moving north is no longer possible, so the `for` loop cycles through the other directions. After a brief excursion southward, upon which the program encounters a marked square, the program finds the opening to the west and proceeds to generate a new recursive call. The same process occurs in this new square, which in turn leads to the following configuration:

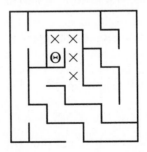

In this position, none of the directions in the `for` loop do any good; every square is either blocked by a wall or already marked. Thus, when the `for` loop at this level exits at the bottom, it unmarks the current square and returns to the previous level. It turns out that all the paths have also been explored in this position, so the program once again unmarks the square and returns to the next higher level in the recursion. Eventually, the program backtracks all the way to the initial call, having completely exhausted the possibilities that begin by moving north. The `for` loop then tries the eastward direction, finds it blocked, and continues on to explore the southern corridor, beginning with a recursive call in the following configuration:

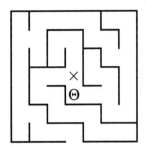

From here on, the same process ensues. The recursion systematically explores every corridor along this path, backing up through the stack of recursive calls whenever it reaches a dead end. The only difference along this route is that eventually—after descending through an additional recursive level for every step on the path—the program makes a recursive call in the following position:

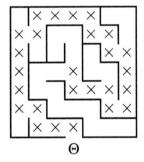

At this point, Theseus is outside the maze. The simple case kicks in and returns TRUE to its caller. This value is then propagated back through all 27 levels of the recursion, at which point the original call to `SolveMaze` returns to the main program.

■ 6.2 Backtracking and games

Although backtracking is easiest to illustrate in the context of a maze, the strategy is considerably more general. For example, you can apply backtracking to most two-player strategy games. The first player has several choices for an initial move. Depending on which move is chosen, the second player then has a particular set of responses. Each of these responses leads in turn to new options for the first player, and this process continues until the end of the game. The different possible positions at each turn in the game form a branching structure in which each option opens up more and more possibilities.

If you want to program a computer to take one side of a two-player game, one approach is simply to have the computer follow all the branches in the list of possibilities. Before making its first move, the computer would try every possible choice. For each of these choices, it would then try to determine what its opponent's response would be. To do so, it would follow the same logic: try every possibility and evaluate the possible counterplays. If the computer can look far enough ahead to discover that some move would leave its opponent in a hopeless position, it should make that move.

In theory, this strategy can be applied to any two-player strategy game. In practice, the process of looking at all the possible moves, potential responses, responses to those responses, and so on requires too much time and memory, even for modern computers. There are, however, several interesting games that are simple enough to solve by looking at all the possibilities, yet complex enough so that the solution is not immediately obvious to the human player.

The game of nim

To see how recursive backtracking applies to two-player games, it helps to consider a simple example such as the game of nim. The word *nim* actually applies to a large class of games in which players take turns removing objects from some initial configuration. In this particular version, the game begins with a pile of 13 coins in the center of a table. On each turn, players take either one, two, or three coins from the pile and put them aside. The object of the game is to avoid being forced to take the last coin. Figure 6-4 shows a sample game between the computer and a human player.

How would you go about writing a program to play a winning game of nim? The mechanical aspects of the game—keeping track of the number of coins, asking the player for a legal move, determining the end of the game, and so forth—are a straightforward programming task. The interesting part of the program consists of figuring out how to give the computer a strategy for playing the best possible game.

Finding a successful strategy for nim is not particularly hard, particularly if you work backward from the end of the game. The rules of nim state that the loser is the player who takes the last coin. Thus, if you ever find yourself with just one coin on the table, you're in a bad position. You have to take that coin and lose. On the other hand, things look good if you find yourself with two, three, or four coins. In any of these cases, you can always take all but one of the remaining coins, leaving your opponent in the unenviable position of being stuck with just one coin. But what if there are five coins on the table? What can you do then? After a bit of thought, it's easy to see that you're also doomed if you're left with five coins. No matter what you do, you have to leave your opponent with two, three, or four coins—situations that you've just discovered represent good positions from your opponent's perspective. If your opponent is playing intelligently, you will surely be left with a single coin on your next turn. Since you have no good moves, being left with five coins is clearly a bad position.

FIGURE 6-4   Sample game of nim

```
Hello.  Welcome to the game of nim.
In this game, we will start with a pile of
13 coins on the table.  On each turn, you
and I will alternately take between 1 and
3 coins from the table.  The player who
takes the last coin loses.

There are 13 coins in the pile.
How many would you like? 2↵
There are 11 coins in the pile.
I'll take 2.
There are 9 coins in the pile.
How many would you like? 3↵
There are 6 coins in the pile.
I'll take 1.
There are 5 coins in the pile.
How many would you like? 1↵
There are 4 coins in the pile.
I'll take 3.
There is only one coin left.
I win.
```

This informal analysis reveals an important insight about the game of nim. On each turn, you are looking for a good move. A move is good if it leaves your opponent in a bad position. But what is a bad position? A bad position is one in which there is no good move. Although these definitions of *good move* and *bad position* are circular, they nonetheless constitute a complete strategy for playing a perfect game of nim. All you have to do is rely on the power of recursion. If you have a function `FindGoodMove` that takes the number of coins as its argument, all it has to do is try every possibility, looking for one that leaves a bad position for the opponent. You can then assign the job of determining whether a particular position is bad to the predicate function `IsBadPosition`, which calls `FindGoodMove` to see if there is one. The two functions call each other back and forth, evaluating all possible branches as the game proceeds.

The `FindGoodMove` function has the following pseudocode formulation:

```
int FindGoodMove(int nCoins)
{
      for (each possible move) {
            Evaluate the position that results from making that move.
            If the resulting position is bad, return that move.
      }
      Return a sentinel value indicating that no good move exists.
}
```

The legal values returned by `FindGoodMove` are 1, 2, and 3. The sentinel indicating that no good move exists can be any integer value outside that range. For example, you can define the constant `NoGoodMove` as follows:

```
#define NoGoodMove    -1
```

The code for `FindGoodMove` then looks like this:

```
static int FindGoodMove(int nCoins)
{
    int nTaken;

    for (nTaken = 1; nTaken <= MaxTake; nTaken++) {
        if (IsBadPosition(nCoins - nTaken)) return (nTaken);
    }
    return (NoGoodMove);
}
```

The code for the `IsBadPosition` function is even easier. After checking for the simple case that occurs when there is only a single coin to take, the function simply calls `FindGoodMove` to see if a good move exists. The code for `IsBadPosition` is therefore simply

```
static bool IsBadPosition(int nCoins)
{
    if (nCoins == 1) return (TRUE);
    return (FindGoodMove(nCoins) == NoGoodMove);
}
```

This function encapsulates the following ideas:

- Being left with a single coin indicates a bad position.
- A position is bad if there are no good moves.

The functions `FindGoodMove` and `IsBadPosition` provide all the strategy that the nim program needs to play a perfect game. The rest of the program just takes care of the mechanics of playing nim with a human player, as shown in Figure 6-5.

A generalized program for two-player games

The code in Figure 6-5 is highly specific to the game of nim. The `FindGoodMove` function, for example, is written so that it incorporates directly into the structure of the code the knowledge that the computer may take one, two, or three coins. The basic idea, however, is far more general. Many two-player games can be solved using the same overall strategy, even though different games clearly require different codings of the details.

FIGURE 6-5	Program to play the game of nim

```
/*
 * File: nim.c
 * ----------
 * This program simulates a simple variant of the game of nim.
 * In this version, the game starts with a pile of 13 coins
 * on a table.  Players then take turns removing 1, 2, or 3
 * coins from the pile.  The player who takes the last coin
 * loses.  This simulation allows a human player to compete
 * against the computer.
 */

#include <stdio.h>
#include "genlib.h"
#include "simpio.h"
#include "strlib.h"

/*
 * Constants
 * ---------
 * InitialCoins -- Initial number of coins
 * MaxTake      -- The maximum number of coins a player may take
 * NoGoodMove   -- Sentinel indicating no good move is available
 */

#define InitialCoins 13
#define MaxTake       3
#define NoGoodMove   -1

/*
 * Type: playerT
 * -------------
 * This enumeration type distinguishes the turns for the human
 * player from those for the computer.
 */

typedef enum { Human, Computer } playerT;

/* Private function prototypes */

static void GiveInstructions(void);
static void AnnounceWinner(int nCoins, playerT whoseTurn);
static int GetUserMove(int nCoins);
static bool MoveIsLegal(int nTaken, int nCoins);
static int ChooseComputerMove(int nCoins);
static int FindGoodMove(int nCoins);
static bool IsBadPosition(int nCoins);
```

```
/*
 * Main program
 * ------------
 * This program plays the game of nim.  In this implementation,
 * the human player always goes first.
 */

main()
{
    int nCoins, nTaken;
    playerT whoseTurn;

    GiveInstructions();
    nCoins = InitialCoins;
    whoseTurn = Human;
    while (nCoins > 1) {
        printf("There are %d coins in the pile.\n", nCoins);
        switch (whoseTurn) {
          case Human:
            nTaken = GetUserMove(nCoins);
            whoseTurn = Computer;
            break;
          case Computer:
            nTaken = ChooseComputerMove(nCoins);
            printf("I'll take %d.\n", nTaken);
            whoseTurn = Human;
            break;
        }
        nCoins -= nTaken;
    }
    AnnounceWinner(nCoins, whoseTurn);
}

/*
 * Function: GiveInstructions
 * Usage: GiveInstructions();
 * --------------------------
 * This function explains the rules of the game to the user.
 */

static void GiveInstructions(void)
{
    printf("Hello.  Welcome to the game of nim.\n");
    printf("In this game, we will start with a pile of\n");
    printf("%d coins on the table.  ", InitialCoins);
    printf("On each turn, you\n");
    printf("and I will alternately take between 1 and\n");
    printf("%d coins from the table.  ", MaxTake);
    printf("The player who\n");
    printf("takes the last coin loses.\n");
    printf("\n");
}
```

```
/*
 * Function: AnnounceWinner
 * Usage: AnnounceWinner(nCoins, whoseTurn);
 * -------------------------------------------
 * This function announces the final result of the game.
 */

static void AnnounceWinner(int nCoins, playerT whoseTurn)
{
    if (nCoins == 0) {
        printf("You took the last coin.  You lose.\n");
    } else {
        printf("There is only one coin left.\n");
        switch (whoseTurn) {
          case Human:    printf("I win.\n"); break;
          case Computer: printf("I lose.\n"); break;
        }
    }
}

/*
 * Function: GetUserMove
 * Usage: nTaken = GetUserMove(nCoins);
 * -------------------------------------
 * This function is responsible for the human player's turn.
 * It takes the number of coins left in the pile as an argument,
 * and returns the number of coins that the player removes
 * from the pile.  The function checks the move for legality
 * and gives the player repeated chances to enter a legal move.
 */

static int GetUserMove(int nCoins)
{
    int nTaken, limit;

    while (TRUE) {
        printf("How many would you like? ");
        nTaken = GetInteger();
        if (MoveIsLegal(nTaken, nCoins)) break;
        limit = (nCoins < MaxTake) ? nCoins : MaxTake;
        printf("That's cheating!  Please choose a number");
        printf(" between 1 and %d.\n", limit);
        printf("There are %d coins in the pile.\n", nCoins);
    }
    return (nTaken);
}
```

```
/*
 * Function: MoveIsLegal
 * Usage: if (MoveIsLegal(nTaken, nCoins)) . . .
 * ------------------------------------------------
 * This predicate function returns TRUE if it is legal to take
 * nTaken coins from a pile of nCoins.
 */

static bool MoveIsLegal(int nTaken, int nCoins)
{
    return (nTaken > 0 && nTaken <= MaxTake && nTaken <= nCoins);
}

/*
 * Function: ChooseComputerMove
 * Usage: nTaken = ChooseComputerMove(nCoins);
 * ------------------------------------------------
 * This function figures out what move is best for the computer
 * player and returns the number of coins taken.  The function
 * first calls FindGoodMove to see if a winning move exists.
 * If none does, the program takes only one coin to give the
 * human player more chances to make a mistake.
 */

static int ChooseComputerMove(int nCoins)
{
    int nTaken;

    nTaken = FindGoodMove(nCoins);
    if (nTaken == NoGoodMove) nTaken = 1;
    return (nTaken);
}

/*
 * Function: FindGoodMove
 * Usage: nTaken = FindGoodMove(nCoins);
 * ----------------------------------------
 * This function looks for a winning move, given the specified
 * number of coins.  If there is a winning move in that
 * position, the function returns that value; if not, the
 * function returns the constant NoWinningMove.  This function
 * depends on the recursive insight that a good move is one
 * that leaves your opponent in a bad position and a bad
 * position is one that offers no good moves.
 */

static int FindGoodMove(int nCoins)
{
    int nTaken;

    for (nTaken = 1; nTaken <= MaxTake; nTaken++) {
        if (IsBadPosition(nCoins - nTaken)) return (nTaken);
    }
    return (NoGoodMove);
}
```

```
/*
 * Function: IsBadPosition
 * Usage: if (IsBadPosition(nCoins)) . . .
 * ----------------------------------------
 * This function returns TRUE if nCoins is a bad position.
 * A bad position is one in which there is no good move.
 * Being left with a single coin is clearly a bad position
 * and represents the simple case of the recursion.
 */

static bool IsBadPosition(int nCoins)
{
    if (nCoins == 1) return (TRUE);
    return (FindGoodMove(nCoins) == NoGoodMove);
}
```

One of the principal ideas in this text is the notion of **abstraction,** which is the process of separating out the general aspects of a problem so that they are no longer obscured by the details of a specific domain. You may not be terribly interested in a program that plays nim; after all, nim is rather boring once you figure it out. What you would probably enjoy more is a program that is general enough to be adapted to play nim, or tic-tac-toe, or any other two-player strategy game you choose.

The first step in creating such a generalization lies in recognizing that there are several concepts that are common to all games. The most important such concept is **state.** For any game, there is some collection of data that defines exactly what is happening at any point in time. In the nim game, for example, the state consists of the number of coins on the table and whose turn it is to move. For a game like chess, the state would instead include what pieces were currently on which squares. Whatever the game, however, it should be possible to combine all the relevant data together into a single record structure and then refer to it using a single variable. Another common concept is that of a **move.** In nim, a move consists of an integer representing the number of coins taken away. In chess, a move might consist of a pair indicating the starting and ending coordinates of the piece that is moving, although this approach is in fact complicated by the need to represent various esoteric moves like castling or the promotion of a pawn. In any case, a move can also be represented by a single structure that includes whatever information is appropriate to that particular game. The process of abstraction consists partly of defining these concepts as general types, with names like `stateT` and `moveT`, that transcend the details of any specific game. The internal structure of these types will be different for different games, but the abstract algorithm can refer to these concepts in a generic form.

Consider, for example, the following main program, which comes from the tic-tac-toe example introduced in Figure 6-6 at the end of this chapter:

```
main()
{
    stateT state;
    moveT move;

    GiveInstructions();
    state = NewGame();
    while (!GameIsOver(state)) {
        DisplayGame(state);
        switch (WhoseTurn(state)) {
          case Human:
            move = GetUserMove(state);
            break;
          case Computer:
            move = ChooseComputerMove(state);
            DisplayMove(move);
            break;
        }
        MakeMove(state, move);
    }
    AnnounceResult(state);
}
```

At this level, the program is easy to read. It begins by giving instructions and then calls **NewGame** to initialize a new game, storing the result in the variable **state**. It then goes into a loop, taking turns for each side until the game is over. On the human player's turns, it calls a function **GetUserMove** to read in the appropriate move from the user. On its own turns, the program calls **ChooseComputerMove**, which has the task of finding the best move in a particular state. Once the move has been determined by one of these two functions, the main program then calls **MakeMove**, which updates the state of the game to show that the indicated move has been made and that it is now the other player's turn. At the end, the program displays the result of the game and exits.

It is important to notice that the main program gives no indication whatsoever about what the actual game is. It could just as easily be nim or chess as tic-tac-toe. Each game requires its own definitions for **stateT**, **moveT**, and the various functions like **GiveInstructions**, **MakeMove**, and **GameIsOver**. Even so, the implementation of the main program is general enough to work for many different games.

The minimax strategy

The main program, however, is hardly the most interesting part of a game. The real challenge consists of providing the computer with an effective strategy. In the general program for two-player games, the heart of the computer's strategy is the function **FindBestMove**, which is called by the function **ChooseComputerMove** in the main program. Given a particular state of the game, the role of **FindBestMove** is to return the optimal move in that position.

From the discussion of nim earlier in this chapter, you should already have some sense of what constitutes an optimal move. The best move in any position is simply the one that leaves your opponent in the worst position. The worst position is likewise the one that offers the weakest best move. This idea—finding the position that leaves your opponent with the worst possible best move—is called the **minimax** strategy because the goal is to find the move that minimizes your opponent's maximum opportunity.

The best way to visualize the operation of the minimax strategy is to think about the possible future moves in a game as forming a branching diagram that expands on each turn. Because of their branching character, such diagrams are called **game trees.** The current state is represented by a dot at the top of the game tree. If there are, for example, three possible moves from this position, there will be three lines emanating down from the current state to three new states that represent the results of these moves, as shown in the following diagram:

For each of these new positions, your opponent will also have options. If there are again three options from each of these positions, the next generation of the game tree looks like this:

Which move do you choose in the initial position? Clearly, your goal is to achieve the best outcome. Unfortunately, you only get to control half of the game. If you were able to select your opponent's move as well as your own, you could select the path to the state two turns away that left you in the best position. Given the fact that your opponent is also trying to win, the best thing you can do is choose the initial move that leaves your opponent with as few winning chances as possible.

In order to get a sense of how you should proceed, it helps to add some quantitative data to the analysis. Determining whether a particular move is better than some alternative is much easier if it is possible to assign a numeric score to each possible move. The higher the numeric score, the better the move. Thus, a move that had a score of +7, for example, is better than a move with a rating of –4. In addition to rating each possible move, it makes sense to assign a similar numeric rating to each position in the game. Thus, one position might have a rating of +9 and would therefore be better than a position with a score of only +2.

Both positions and moves are rated from the perspective of the player having the move. Moreover, the rating system is designed to be symmetric around 0, in the sense that a position that has a score of +9 for the player to move would have a score of –9 from the opponent's point of view. This interpretation of rating numbers captures the idea that a position that is good for one player is therefore a bad position for the opponent, as you saw in the discussion of the nim game earlier in this chapter. More importantly, defining the rating system in this way makes it easy to express the relationship between the scores for moves and positions. The score for any move is simply the negative of the score for the resulting position when rated by your opponent. Similarly, the rating of any position can be defined as the rating of its best move.

To make this discussion more concrete, let's consider a simple example. Suppose that you have looked two steps ahead in the game, covering one move by you and the possible responses from your opponent. In computer science, a single move for a single player is called a **ply** to avoid the ambiguity associated with the words *move* and *turn,* which sometimes imply that both players have a chance to play. If you rate the positions at the conclusion of the two-ply analysis, the game tree might look like this:

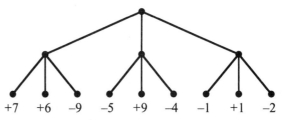

Because the positions at the bottom of this tree are again positions in which—as at the top of the tree—you have to move, the rating numbers in those positions are assigned from your perspective. Given these ratings of the potential positions, what move should you make from the original configuration? At first glance, you might be attracted by the fact that the leftmost branch has the most positive total score or that the center one contains a path that leads to a +9, which is an excellent outcome for you. Unfortunately, none of these considerations matter much if your opponent is playing rationally. If you choose the leftmost branch, your opponent will surely take the rightmost option from there, which leaves you with a –9 position. The same thing happens if you choose the center branch; your opponent finds the worst possible position, which has a rating of –5. The best you can do is choose the rightmost branch, which only allows your opponent to end up with a –2 rating. While this position is hardly ideal, it is better for you than the other outcomes.

The situation becomes easier to follow if you add the ratings for each of your opponent's responses at the second level of the tree. The rating for a move—from the perspective of the player making it—is the negative of the resulting position. Thus, the move ratings from your opponent's point of view look like this:

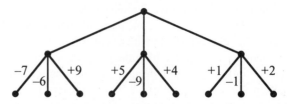

In these positions, your opponent will seek to play the move with the best score. By choosing the rightmost path, you minimize the maximum score available to your opponent, which is the essence of the *minimax* strategy.

Implementing the minimax algorithm

The minimax algorithm is quite general and can be implemented in a way that does not depend on the specific characteristics of the game. In many respects, the implementation of the minimax algorithm is similar to the strategy section in `nim.c` because it consists of two mutually recursive functions, one that finds the best move and another than evaluates the quality of a position. If you want to make your algorithm as general as possible, however, you must modify the approach used in the nim program to accommodate the following extensions:

- *It must be possible to limit the depth of the recursive search.* For games that involve any significant level of complexity, it is impossible to search the entire game tree in a reasonable amount of time. If you try to apply this approach to chess, for example, a program running on the fastest computers available would require many times the lifetime of the universe to make the first move. As a result, a practical implementation of the minimax algorithm must include a provision for cutting off the search at a certain point. One possible approach is to limit the depth of the recursion to a certain number of moves. You could, for example, allow the recursion to proceed until each player had made three moves and then evaluate the position at that point using some nonrecursive approach.

- *It must be possible to assign ratings to moves and positions.* Every position in nim is either good or bad; there are no other options. In a more complex game, it is necessary—particularly if you can't perform a complete analysis—to assign ratings to positions and moves so that the algorithm has a standard for comparing them against other possibilities. The rating scheme used in this implementation assigns integers to positions and moves. Those integers extend in both the positive and the negative direction and are centered on zero, which means that a rating of –5 for one player is equivalent to a rating of +5 from the opponent's point of view. Zero is therefore the neutral rating and is given the name `NeutralPosition`. The maximum positive rating is the constant `WinningPosition`, which indicates a position in which the player whose turn it is to move will invariably win; the corresponding extreme in the negative direction is `LosingPosition`, which indicates that the player will always lose.

Taking these general considerations into account requires some changes in the design of the mutually recursive functions that implement the minimax algorithm, which are called `FindBestMove` and `EvaluatePosition`. Both functions take the state of the game as an argument, but each also requires the current depth of the recursion so that the recursive search can be restricted if necessary. Moreover, in order to avoid a considerable amount of redundant calculation, it is extremely useful if `FindBestMove` can return a rating along with the best move. One possibility is to design `FindBestMove` to return a structure containing both a `moveT` and an integer rating, but doing so makes the program a bit harder to read. The approach used in this implementation is to use call-by-reference to obtain the rating value. The caller passes a pointer to an integer variable; before returning, `FindBestMove` stores the rating of the move in that location. Given these design decisions, the prototypes for `FindBestMove` and `EvaluatePosition` look like this:

```
moveT FindBestMove(stateT state, int depth, int *pRating);
int EvaluatePosition(stateT state, int depth);
```

The strategy for `FindBestMove` can be expressed using the following pseudocode:

```
moveT FindBestMove(stateT state, int depth, int *pRating)
{
    for (each possible move or until you find a forced win) {
        Make the move.
        Evaluate the resulting position, adding one to the depth indicator.
        Keep track of the minimum rating so far, along with the corresponding move.
        Retract the move to restore the original state.
    }
    Store the move rating using the pointer provided by the client.
    Return the best move.
}
```

The corresponding implementation, which follows this pseudocode outline, looks like this:

```
moveT FindBestMove(stateT state, int depth, int *pRating)
{
    moveT moveArray[MaxMoves], move, bestMove;
    int i, nMoves, rating, minRating;

    nMoves = GenerateMoveList(state, moveArray);
    if (nMoves == 0) Error("No moves available");
    minRating = WinningPosition + 1;
    for (i = 0; i < nMoves && minRating != LosingPosition; i++) {
        move = moveArray[i];
        MakeMove(state, move);
        rating = EvaluatePosition(state, depth + 1);
        if (rating < minRating) {
            bestMove = move;
            minRating = rating;
        }
        RetractMove(state, move);
    }
    *pRating = -minRating;
    return (bestMove);
}
```

The function `GenerateMoveList(state, moveArray)` is implemented separately for each game and has the effect of filling the elements in `moveArray` with a list of the legal moves in the current position; the result of the function is the number of available moves. The only other parts of this function that require some comment are the line

```
minRating = WinningPosition + 1;
```

which initializes the value of `minRating` to a number large enough to guarantee that this value will be replaced on the first cycle through the `for` loop, and the line

```
*pRating = -minRating;
```

which stores the rating of the best move in the variable supplied by the client. The negative sign is included because the perspective has shifted: the positions were evaluated from the point of view of your opponent, whereas the ratings express the value of a move from your own point of view. A move that leaves your opponent with a negative position is good for you and therefore has a positive value.

The `EvaluatePosition` function is considerably simpler. The simple cases that allow the recursion to terminate occur when the game is over or when the maximum allowed recursive depth has been achieved. In these cases, the program must evaluate the current state as it exists without recourse to further recursion. This evaluation is performed by the function `EvaluateStaticPosition`, which is coded separately for each game. In the general case, however, the rating of a position is simply the rating of the best move available, given the current state. Thus, the following code is sufficient to the task:

```
int EvaluatePosition(stateT state, int depth)
{
    int rating;

    if (GameIsOver(state) || depth >= MaxDepth) {
        return (EvaluateStaticPosition(state));
    }
    (void) FindBestMove(state, depth, &rating);
    return (rating);
}
```

Using the general strategy to solve a specific game

The minimax strategy embodied in the functions `FindBestMove` and `EvaluatePosition` takes care of the conceptually complicated work of finding the best move from a given position. Moreover, because it is written in an abstract way, the code does not depend on the details of a particular game. Once you have these functions, the task of coding a new two-player strategy game is reduced to the problem of designing `moveT` and `stateT` structures that are appropriate to the game and then writing code for the functions that must be supplied independently for each game.

The long program in Figure 6-6 illustrates how to use the general minimax facility to construct a program that plays tic-tac-toe.[1] The implementations of the main program and the functions `FindBestMove` and `EvaluatePosition` are completely independent of the details of tic-tac-toe, even though they are responsible for calculating most of the strategy. What makes this program play tic-tac-toe is the definition of the types and functions that surround the basic framework.

The types `moveT` and `stateT` are defined so that they are appropriate for tic-tac-toe. If you number the squares in the board like this:

1	2	3
4	5	6
7	8	9

a move can be represented as a single integer, which means that the appropriate definition for the type `moveT` is simply

```
typedef int moveT;
```

The state of the tic-tac-toe game is determined by the symbols on the nine squares of the board and whose turn it is to move. Thus, you can represent the essential components of the state as follows:

```
typedef struct {
    char board[(3 * 3) + 1];
    playerT whoseTurn;
} *stateT;
```

The board is represented as a single-dimensional array to correspond with the numbering of the squares from 1 to 9; the fact that position 0 is unused makes it necessary to add an extra element to the array. As the complete program shows, adding a `turnsTaken` component to the state makes it much easier to determine whether the game is complete.

The rules of tic-tac-toe are expressed in the implementation of functions like `GenerateMoveList`, `MoveIsLegal`, and `EvaluateStaticPosition`, each of which is coded specifically for this game. Even though these functions require some thought, they tend to be less conceptually complex than those that implement the minimax strategy. By coding the difficult functions once and then reusing them in various different game programs, you can avoid having to go through the same logic again and again.

---

[1] For readers from cultures in which children do not usually play this game, tic-tac-toe is played on a 3 × 3 grid of squares. Players take turns placing letters in empty squares. The first player traditionally marks squares with an X, the second with an O. The object of the game is to line up three of your letters in a row, which may be either horizontal, vertical, or diagonal.

FIGURE 6-6 Program to play tic-tac-toe

```c
/*
 * File: tictac.c
 * --------------
 * This program plays a game of tic-tac-toe with the user.
 * The program is designed to emphasize the separation between
 * those aspects of the code that are common to all games and
 * those that are specific to tic-tac-toe.
 */

#include <stdio.h>
#include "genlib.h"
#include "simpio.h"
#include "strlib.h"

/*
 * Constants: WinningPosition, NeutralPosition, LosingPosition
 * -----------------------------------------------------------
 * These constants define a rating system for game positions.
 * A rating is an integer centered at 0 as the neutral score:
 * ratings greater than 0 are good for the cuurent player,
 * ratings less than 0 are good for the opponent.  The
 * constants WinningPosition and LosingPosition are opposite
 * in value and indicate a position that is a forced win or
 * loss, respectively.  In a game in which the analysis is
 * complete, no intermediate values ever arise.  If the full
 * tree is too large to analyze, the EvaluatePosition function
 * returns integers that fall between the two extremes.
 */

#define WinningPosition   1000
#define NeutralPosition   0
#define LosingPosition    (-WinningPosition)

/*
 * Type: playerT
 * --------------
 * This type is used to distinguish the human and computer
 * players and keep track of who has the current turn.
 */

typedef enum { Human, Computer } playerT;
```

```
/*
 * Type: moveT
 * -----------
 * For any particular game, the moveT type must keep track of the
 * information necessary to describe a move.  For tic-tac-toe,
 * a moveT is simply an integer identifying the number of one of
 * the nine squares.
 */

typedef int moveT;

/*
 * Type: stateT
 * ------------
 * For any game, the stateT structure records the current state
 * of the game.  For tic-tac-toe, the main component of the
 * state record is the board, which is an array of characters
 * using 'X' for the first player, 'O' for the second, and ' '
 * for empty squares.  Although the board array is logically
 * a two-dimensional structure, it is stored as a linear array
 * so that its indices match the numbers used by the human
 * player to refer to the squares, as follows:
 *
 *        1 | 2 | 3
 *       ---+---+---
 *        4 | 5 | 6
 *       ---+---+---
 *        7 | 8 | 9
 *
 * Note that element 0 is not used, which requires allocation
 * of an extra element.
 *
 * In addition to the board array, the code stores a playerT
 * value to indicate whose turn it is.  In this example, the
 * stateT structure also contains the total number of moves
 * so that functions can check this entry without counting
 * the number of occupied squares.
 */

typedef struct {
    char board[(3 * 3) + 1];
    playerT whoseTurn;
    int turnsTaken;
} *stateT;
```

```
/*
 * Constant: MaxMoves
 * ------------------
 * This constant indicates the maximum number of legal moves
 * available on a turn and is used to allocate array space for
 * the legal move list.  This constant will change according
 * to the specifics of the game.  For tic-tac-toe, there are
 * never more than nine possible moves.
 */

#define MaxMoves 9

/*
 * Constant: MaxDepth
 * ------------------
 * This constant indicates the maximum depth to which the
 * recursive search for the best move is allowed to proceed.
 * The use of a very large number for this constant ensures
 * that the analysis is carried out to the end of the game.
 */

#define MaxDepth 10000

/*
 * Constant: FirstPlayer
 * ---------------------
 * This constant indicates whether the human or the computer
 * player goes first and should be one of the enumerated
 * constants: Human or Computer.
 */

#define FirstPlayer Computer

/*
 * Private variable: winningLines
 * ------------------------------
 * This two-dimensional array contains the index numbers of
 * the cells in each of the winning combinations.  Although
 * it is easy for the program to compute these values as it
 * runs, storing them in advance speeds up the execution.
 */

static int winningLines[][3] = {
    { 1, 2, 3 },
    { 4, 5, 6 },
    { 7, 8, 9 },
    { 1, 4, 7 },
    { 2, 5, 8 },
    { 3, 6, 9 },
    { 1, 5, 9 },
    { 3, 5, 7 }
};
static int nWinningLines = sizeof winningLines
                              / sizeof winningLines[0];
```

```
/* Private function prototypes */

static moveT FindBestMove(stateT state, int depth, int *pRating);
static int EvaluatePosition(stateT state, int depth);
static stateT NewGame(void);
static void DisplayGame(stateT state);
static void DisplayMove(moveT move);
static void GiveInstructions(void);
static char PlayerMark(playerT player);
static moveT GetUserMove(stateT state);
static bool MoveIsLegal(moveT move, stateT state);
static moveT ChooseComputerMove(stateT state);
static int GenerateMoveList(stateT state, moveT moveArray[]);
static void MakeMove(stateT state, moveT move);
static void RetractMove(stateT state, moveT move);
static void AnnounceResult(stateT state);
static bool GameIsOver(stateT state);
static int EvaluateStaticPosition(stateT state);
static bool CheckForWin(stateT state, playerT player);
static playerT WhoseTurn(stateT state);
static playerT Opponent(playerT player);

/*
 * Main program
 * ------------
 * The main program, along with the functions FindBestMove and
 * EvaluatePosition, are general in their design and can be
 * used with most two-player games.  The specific details of
 * tic-tac-toe do not appear in these functions and are instead
 * encapsulated in the stateT and moveT data structures and a
 * a variety of subsidiary functions.
 */

main()
{
    stateT state;
    moveT move;

    GiveInstructions();
    state = NewGame();
    while (!GameIsOver(state)) {
        DisplayGame(state);
        switch (WhoseTurn(state)) {
          case Human:
            move = GetUserMove(state);
            break;
          case Computer:
            move = ChooseComputerMove(state);
            DisplayMove(move);
            break;
        }
        MakeMove(state, move);
    }
    AnnounceResult(state);
}
```

```
/*
 * Function: FindBestMove
 * Usage: move = FindBestMove(state, depth, pRating);
 * --------------------------------------------------------
 * This function finds the best move for the current player, given
 * the specified state of the game.  The depth parameter and the
 * constant MaxDepth are used to limit the depth of the search
 * for games that are too difficult to analyze in full detail.
 * The function returns the best move and stores its rating in
 * the integer variable to which pRating points.
 */

static moveT FindBestMove(stateT state, int depth, int *pRating)
{
    moveT moveArray[MaxMoves], move, bestMove;
    int i, nMoves, rating, minRating;

    nMoves = GenerateMoveList(state, moveArray);
    if (nMoves == 0) Error("No moves available");
    minRating = WinningPosition + 1;
    for (i = 0; i < nMoves && minRating != LosingPosition; i++) {
        move = moveArray[i];
        MakeMove(state, move);
        rating = EvaluatePosition(state, depth + 1);
        if (rating < minRating) {
            bestMove = move;
            minRating = rating;
        }
        RetractMove(state, move);
    }
    *pRating = -minRating;
    return (bestMove);
}

/*
 * Function: EvaluatePosition
 * Usage: rating = EvaluatePosition(state, depth);
 * --------------------------------------------------
 * This function evaluates a position by finding the rating of
 * the best move in that position.  The depth parameter and the
 * constant MaxDepth are used to limit the depth of the search.
 */

static int EvaluatePosition(stateT state, int depth)
{
    int rating;

    if (GameIsOver(state) || depth >= MaxDepth) {
        return (EvaluateStaticPosition(state));
    }
    (void) FindBestMove(state, depth, &rating);
    return (rating);
}
```

```
/*
 * Function: NewGame
 * Usage: state = NewGame();
 * -------------------------
 * This function starts a new game and returns a stateT that
 * has been initialized to the defined starting configuration.
 */

static stateT NewGame(void)
{
    stateT state;
    int i;

    state = New(stateT);
    for (i = 1; i <= 9; i++) {
        state->board[i] = ' ';
    }
    state->whoseTurn = FirstPlayer;
    state->turnsTaken = 0;
    return (state);
}

/*
 * Function: DisplayGame
 * Usage: DisplayGame(state);
 * --------------------------
 * This function displays the current state of the game.
 */

static void DisplayGame(stateT state)
{
    int row, col;

    if (GameIsOver(state)) {
        printf("\nThe final position looks like this:\n\n");
    } else {
        printf("\nThe game now looks like this:\n\n");
    }
    for (row = 0; row < 3; row++) {
        if (row != 0) printf("---+---+---\n");
        for (col = 0; col < 3; col++) {
            if (col != 0) printf("|");
            printf(" %c ", state->board[row * 3 + col + 1]);
        }
        printf("\n");
    }
    printf("\n");
}
```

```
/*
 * Function: DisplayMove
 * Usage: DisplayMove(move);
 * ------------------------
 * This function displays the computer's move.
 */

static void DisplayMove(moveT move)
{
    printf("I'll move to square %d.\n", move);
}

/*
 * Function: GiveInstructions
 * Usage: GiveInstructions();
 * --------------------------
 * This function gives the player instructions about how to
 * play the game.
 */

static void GiveInstructions(void)
{
    printf("Welcome to tic-tac-toe.  The object of the game\n");
    printf("is to line up three symbols in a row, vertically,\n");
    printf("horizontally, or diagonally.  You'll be %c and\n",
            PlayerMark(Human));
    printf("I'll be %c.\n", PlayerMark(Computer));
}

/*
 * Function: PlayerMark
 * Usage: mark = PlayerMark(player);
 * ---------------------------------
 * This function returns the mark used on the board to indicate
 * the specified player.  By convention, the first player is
 * always X, so the mark used for each player depends on who
 * goes first.
 */

static char PlayerMark(playerT player)
{
    if (player == FirstPlayer) {
        return ('X');
    } else {
        return ('O');
    }
}
```

```
/*
 * Function: GetUserMove
 * Usage: move = GetUserMove(state);
 * ------------------------------------
 * This function allows the user to enter a move and returns the
 * number of the chosen square.  If the user specifies an illegal
 * move, this function gives the user the opportunity to enter
 * a legal one.
 */

static moveT GetUserMove(stateT state)
{
    moveT move;

    printf("Your move.\n");
    while (TRUE) {
        printf("What square? ");
        move = GetInteger();
        if (MoveIsLegal(move, state)) break;
        printf("That move is illegal.  Try again.\n");
    }
    return (move);
}

/*
 * Function: MoveIsLegal
 * Usage: if (MoveIsLegal(move, state)) . . .
 * --------------------------------------------------
 * This function returns TRUE if the specified move is legal
 * in the current state.
 */

static bool MoveIsLegal(moveT move, stateT state)
{
    return (move >= 1 && move <= 9 && state->board[move] == ' ');
}

/*
 * Function: ChooseComputerMove
 * Usage: move = ChooseComputerMove(state);
 * --------------------------------------------
 * This function chooses the computer's move and is primarily
 * a wrapper for FindBestMove.  This function also makes it
 * possible to display any game-specific messages that need
 * to appear at the beginning of the computer's turn.  The
 * rating value returned by FindBestMove is simply discarded.
 */

static moveT ChooseComputerMove(stateT state)
{
    int rating;

    printf("My move.\n");
    return (FindBestMove(state, 0, &rating));
}
```

```
/*
 * Function: GenerateMoveList
 * Usage: n = GenerateMoveList(state, moveArray);
 * -------------------------------------------------
 * This function generates a list of the legal moves available in
 * the specified state.  The list of moves is returned in the
 * array moveArray, which must be allocated by the client.  The
 * function returns the number of legal moves.
 */

static int GenerateMoveList(stateT state, moveT moveArray[])
{
    int i, nMoves;

    nMoves = 0;
    for (i = 1; i <= 9; i++) {
        if (state->board[i] == ' ') {
            moveArray[nMoves++] = (moveT) i;
        }
    }
    return (nMoves);
}

/*
 * Function: MakeMove
 * Usage: MakeMove(state, move);
 * -----------------------------
 * This function changes the state of the game by making the
 * indicated move.
 */

static void MakeMove(stateT state, moveT move)
{
    state->board[move] = PlayerMark(state->whoseTurn);
    state->whoseTurn = Opponent(state->whoseTurn);
    state->turnsTaken++;
}

/*
 * Function: RetractMove
 * Usage: RetractMove(state, move);
 * --------------------------------
 * This function changes the state of the game by "unmaking" the
 * indicated move.
 */

static void RetractMove(stateT state, moveT move)
{
    state->board[move] = ' ';
    state->whoseTurn = Opponent(state->whoseTurn);
    state->turnsTaken--;
}
```

```
/*
 * Function: AnnounceResult
 * Usage: AnnounceResult(state);
 * -----------------------------
 * This function announces the result of the game.
 */

static void AnnounceResult(stateT state)
{
    DisplayGame(state);
    if (CheckForWin(state, Human)) {
        printf("You win\n");
    } else if (CheckForWin(state, Computer)) {
        printf("I win\n");
    } else {
        printf("Cat's game\n");
    }
}

/*
 * Function: GameIsOver
 * Usage: if (GameIsOver(state)) . . .
 * -----------------------------------
 * This function returns TRUE if the game is complete.
 */

static bool GameIsOver(stateT state)
{
    return (state->turnsTaken == 9
            || CheckForWin(state, state->whoseTurn)
            || CheckForWin(state, Opponent(state->whoseTurn)));
}

/*
 * Function: EvaluateStaticPosition
 * Usage: rating = EvaluateStaticPosition(state);
 * ----------------------------------------------
 * This function gives the rating of a position without looking
 * ahead any further in the game tree.  Although this function
 * duplicates much of the computation of GameIsOver and therefore
 * introduces some runtime inefficiency, it makes the algorithm
 * somewhat easier to follow.
 */

static int EvaluateStaticPosition(stateT state)
{
    if (CheckForWin(state, state->whoseTurn)) {
        return (WinningPosition);
    }
    if (CheckForWin(state, Opponent(state->whoseTurn))) {
        return (LosingPosition);
    }
    return (NeutralPosition);
}
```

```
/*
 * Function: CheckForWin
 * Usage: if (CheckForWin(state, player)) . . .
 * -----------------------------------------------
 * This function returns TRUE if the specified player has won
 * the game.  The check on turnsTaken increases efficiency,
 * because neither player can win the game until the fifth move.
 */

static bool CheckForWin(stateT state, playerT player)
{
    int i;
    char mark;

    if (state->turnsTaken < 5) return (FALSE);
    mark = PlayerMark(player);
    for (i = 0; i < nWinningLines; i++) {
        if (mark == state->board[winningLines[i][0]]
                && mark == state->board[winningLines[i][1]]
                && mark == state->board[winningLines[i][2]]) {
            return (TRUE);
        }
    }
    return (FALSE);
}

/*
 * Function: WhoseTurn
 * Usage: player = WhoseTurn(state);
 * ---------------------------------
 * This function returns whose turn it is, given the current
 * state of the game.
 */

static playerT WhoseTurn(stateT state)
{
    return (state->whoseTurn);
}

/*
 * Function: Opponent
 * Usage: opp = Opponent(player);
 * -------------------------------
 * This function returns the playerT value corresponding to the
 * opponent of the specified player.
 */

static playerT Opponent(playerT player)
{
    switch (player) {
      case Human:    return (Computer);
      case Computer: return (Human);
    }
}
```

▇▇ **Summary**

In this chapter, you have learned to solve problems that require making a sequence of choices as you search for a goal, as illustrated by finding a path through a maze or a winning strategy in a two-player game. The basic strategy is to write programs that can backtrack to previous decision points if those choices lead to dead ends. By exploiting the power of recursion, however, you can avoid coding the details of the backtracking process explicitly and develop general solution strategies that apply to a wide variety of problem domains.

Important points in this chapter include:

- You can solve most problems that require backtracking by adopting the following recursive approach:

    > *If you are already at a solution, report success.*
    > **for** (*every possible choice in the current position*) {
    >   *Make that choice and take one step along the path.*
    >   *Use recursion to solve the problem from the new position.*
    >   *If the recursive call succeeds, report the success to the next higher level.*
    >   *Back out of the current choice to restore the original state.*
    > }
    > *Report failure.*

- The complete history of recursive calls in a backtracking problem—even for relatively simple applications—is usually too complex to understand in detail. For problems that involve any significant amount of backtracking, it is essential to accept the recursive leap of faith.
- You can often find a winning strategy for two-player games by adopting a recursive-backtracking approach. Because the goal in such games involves minimizing the winning chances for your opponent, the conventional strategic approach is called the *minimax algorithm.*
- It is possible to code the minimax algorithm in a general way that keeps the details of any specific game separate from the implementation of the minimax strategy itself. This approach makes it easier to adapt an existing program to new games and illustrates the power of abstraction.

 REVIEW QUESTIONS

1. What is the principal characteristic of a backtracking algorithm?

2. Using your own words, state the right-hand rule for escaping from a maze. Would a left-hand rule work equally well?

3. What is the insight that makes it possible to solve a maze by recursive backtracking?

4. What are the simple cases that apply in the recursive implementation of `SolveMaze`?

5. Why is important to mark squares as you proceed through the maze? What would happen in the `SolveMaze` function if you never marked any squares?

6. What is the purpose of the `UnmarkSquare` call at the end of the `for` loop in the `SolveMaze` implementation? Is this statement essential to the algorithm?

7. What is the purpose of the Boolean result returned by `SolveMaze`?

8. In your own words, explain how the backtracking process actually takes place in the recursive implementation of `SolveMaze`.

9. In the simple nim game, the human player plays first and begins with a pile of 13 coins. Is this a good or a bad position? Why?

10. Write a simple C expression based on the value of `nCoins` that has the value `TRUE` if the position is good for the current player and `FALSE` otherwise. (*Hint:* Use the `%` operator.)

11. What is the minimax algorithm? What does its name signify?

12. When you are analyzing a game, what is meant by the word *ply?*

13. Suppose you are in a position in which the analysis for the next two ply shows the following rated outcomes from your point of view:

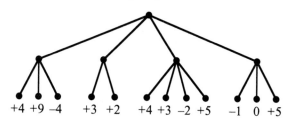

If you adopt the minimax strategy, what is the best move to make in this position? What is the rating of that move from your perspective?

14. Why is it useful to develop an abstract implementation of the minimax algorithm?

15. What two data structures are used to make the minimax implementation independent of the specific characteristics of a particular game?

16. What is the role of each of the three arguments to the `FindBestMove` function?

17. Explain the role of the `EvaluateStaticPosition` function in the minimax implementation.

PROGRAMMING EXERCISES

1. The `SolveMaze` function shown in Figure 6-3 implements a recursive algorithm for solving a maze but is not complete as it stands. The solution depends on several functions exported by the `mazelib.h` interface, which is specified in Figure 6-2 but never actually implemented.

   Write a file `mazelib.c` that implements this interface. Your implementation should store the data representing the maze as part of the private state of the module. This design requires you to declare static global variables within the implementation that are appropriate to the data you need to implement the operations. If you design the data structure well, most of the individual function definitions in the interface are quite simple. The hard parts of this exercise are designing an appropriate internal representation and implementing the function `ReadMapFile`, which initializes the internal structures from a data file formatted as described in the interface documentation.

2. In many mazes, there are multiple paths. For example, the diagrams below show three solutions for the same maze:

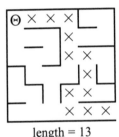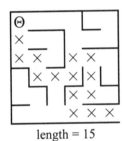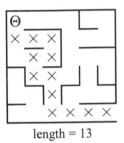

length = 13   length = 15   length = 13

   None of these solutions, however, is optimal. The shortest path through the maze has a path length of 11:

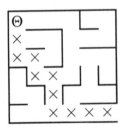

   Write a function

   ```
   int ShortestPathLength(pointT pt);
   ```

   that returns the length of the shortest path in the maze from the specified position to any exit. If there is no solution to the maze, `ShortestPathLength` should return the constant `NoSolution`, which is defined to have a value larger than the maximum permissible path length, as follows:

```
#define NoSolution 10000
```

3. As implemented in Figure 6-3, the `SolveMaze` function unmarks each square as it discovers there are no solutions from that point. Although this design strategy has the advantage that the final configuration of the maze shows the solution path as a series of marked squares, the decision to unmark squares as you backtrack has a considerable cost in terms of the overall efficiency of the algorithm. If you've marked a square and then backtracked through it, you've already explored the possibilities leading from that square. If you come back to it by some other path, you might as well rely on your earlier analysis instead of exploring the same options again.

   To give yourself a sense of how much these unmarking operations cost in terms of efficiency, extend the `SolveMaze` program so that it records the number of recursive calls as it proceeds. Use this program to calculate how many recursive calls are required to solve the following maze if the call to `UnmarkSquare` remains part of the program:

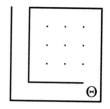

   Run your program again, this time without the call to `UnmarkSquare`. What happens to the number of recursive calls?

4. As the result of the preceding exercise makes clear, the idea of keeping track of the path through a maze by using the `MarkSquare` facility in `mazelib.h` has a substantial cost. A more practical approach is to change the definition of the recursive function so that it keeps track of the current path as it goes. Following the logic of `SolveMaze`, write a function

```
int FindPath(pointT pt, pointT path[], int pathSize);
```

   that takes, in addition to the coordinates of the starting position, an array of `pointT` values called `path` whose allocated size is `pathSize`. When `FindPath` returns to the calling program, the elements of the `path` array should be initialized to a sequence of coordinates beginning with the starting position and ending with the coordinates of the first square that lies outside the maze. The function returns the number of points in the actual path, or 0 if no path exists.

   For example, if you use `FindPath` with the following main program, it will display the coordinates of the points in the solution path on the screen.

```
main()
{
    pointT path[MaxPath];
    int i, len;

    ReadMazeMap(MazeFile);
    len = FindPath(GetStartPosition(), path, MaxPath);
    if (len == 0) {
        printf("No solution exists.\n");
    } else {
        printf("The following path is a solution:\n");
        for (i = 0; i < len; i++) {
            printf("   (%d, %d)\n", path[i].x, path[i].y);
        }
    }
}
```

For this exercise, it is sufficient for **FindPath** to find any solution path. It need not find the shortest one.

5. If you have access to the graphics library described in Section 5.3, extend the **maze.c** program so that, in addition to keeping track of the internal data structures for the maze, it also displays a diagram of the maze on the screen and shows the final solution path.

6. Most drawing programs for personal computers make it possible to fill an enclosed region on the screen with a solid color. Typically, you invoke this operation by selecting a paint-bucket tool and then clicking the mouse, with the cursor somewhere in your drawing. When you do, the paint spreads to every part of the picture it can reach without going through a line.

   For example, suppose you have just drawn the following picture of a house:

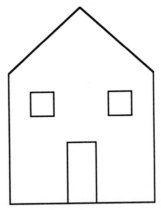

If you select the paint bucket and click inside the door, the drawing program fills the area bounded by the door frame as shown at the left side of the following diagram. If you instead click somewhere on the front wall of the house, the program fills the entire wall space except for the windows and doors, as shown on the right:

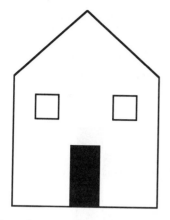 

In order to understand how this process works, it is important to understand that the screen of the computer is actually broken down into an array of tiny dots called **pixels.** On a monochrome display, pixels can be either white or black. The paint-fill operation consists of painting black the starting pixel (i.e., the pixel you click while using the paint-bucket tool) along with any pixels connected to that starting point by an unbroken chain of white pixels. Thus, the patterns of pixels on the screen representing the preceding two diagrams would look like this:

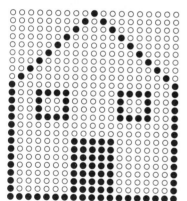 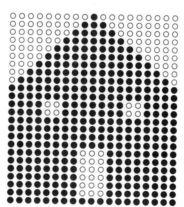

Write a program that simulates the operation of the paint-bucket tool. To simplify the problem, assume that you have access to the enumerated type

```
typedef enum { White, Black } pixelStateT;
```

and the following functions:

```
pixelStateT GetPixelState(pointT pt);
void SetPixelState(pointT pt, pixelStateT state);
bool OutsidePixelBounds(pointT pt);
```

The first function is used to return the state of any pixel, given its coordinates in the pixel array. The second allows you to change the state of any pixel to a new value. The third makes it possible to determine whether a particular coordinate is outside the pixel array altogether, so that the recursion can stop at the edges of the screen.

7. In chess, a knight moves in an L-shaped pattern: two squares in one direction horizontally or vertically, and then one square at right angles to that motion. For example, the black knight in the following diagram can move to any of the eight squares marked with a black cross:

The mobility of the knight decreases toward the edges of the board, as illustrated by the position of the white knight, which can move only to the three squares marked by white crosses.

It turns out that a knight can visit all 64 squares on a chessboard without ever moving to the same square twice. A path for the knight that moves through all the squares without repeating a square is called a **knight's tour.** One such tour is shown in the following diagram, in which the numbers in the squares indicate the order in which they were visited:

52	47	56	45	54	5	22	13
57	44	53	4	23	14	25	6
48	51	46	55	26	21	12	15
43	58	3	50	41	24	7	20
36	49	42	27	62	11	16	29
59	2	37	40	33	28	19	8
38	35	32	61	10	63	30	17
1	60	39	34	31	18	9	64

Write a program that uses backtracking recursion to find a knight's tour.

8. The most powerful piece in the game of chess is the queen, which can move any number of squares in any direction, horizontally, vertically, or diagonally. For example, the queen shown in this chessboard can move to any of the marked squares:

Even though the queen can cover a large number of squares, it is possible to place eight queens on a 8×8 chessboard so that none of them attacks any of the others, as shown in the following diagram:

Write a program that solves the more general problem of whether it is possible to place N queens on an $N \times N$ chessboard so that none of them can move to a square occupied by any of the others in a single turn. Your program should either display a solution if it finds one or report that no solutions exist.

9. In the 1960s, a puzzle called *Instant Insanity* was popular for some years before it faded from view. The puzzle consisted of four cubes whose faces were each painted with one of the colors red, blue, green, and white, represented in the rest of this problem by their initial letter. The goal of the

puzzle was to arrange the cubes into a line so that if you looked at the line from any of its edges, you would see no duplicated colors.

Cubes are hard to draw in two dimensions, but the following diagram shows what the cubes would look like if you unfolded them and placed them flat on the page:

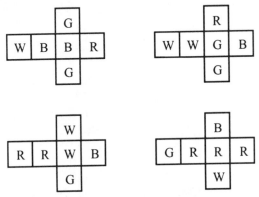

Write a program that uses backtracking to solve the Instant Insanity puzzle.

10. Rewrite the simple nim game from Figure 6-5 so that it uses the more general structure developed for tic-tac-toe. Your new program should not change the implementations of **main**, **FindBestMove**, and **EvaluatePosition**, which should remain exactly as they appear in Figure 6-6. Your job is to come up with appropriate definitions of **stateT**, **moveT**, and the various game-specific functions in the implementation so that the program plays nim instead of tic-tac-toe.

11. Modify the code for the simple nim game you wrote for exercise 10 so that it plays a different variant of nim. In this version, the pile begins with 17 coins. On each turn, players alternate taking one, two, three, or four coins from the pile. In the simple nim game, the coins the players took away were simply ignored; in this game, the coins go into a pile for each player. The player whose pile contains an even number of coins after the last one is taken wins the game.

12. In the most common variant of nim, the coins are not combined into a single pile but are instead arranged in three rows like this:

A move in this game consists of taking any number of coins, subject to the condition that all the coins must come from the same row. The player who takes the last coin loses.

Write a program that uses the minimax algorithm to play a perfect game of three-pile nim. The starting configuration shown here is a typical one, but your program should be general enough so that you can easily change the number of coins in each row.

13. The tic-tac-toe program in Figure 6-6 uses a large value for the constant `MaxDepth` to ensure that the minimax strategy is carried out all the way to the end of the game. As a result, the program plays the best possible game but tends to move slowly at the beginning. You can increase the speed of the computer's play in such a game by reducing the depth of the search, although you then run the risk of having the computer miss some line of play in which it would lose. To guard against this possibility of loss, you have two choices: you can either pay the time cost of the deeper search or improve your program's ability to analyze a static position.

    Because `MaxDepth` has been set so that every game will be analyzed all the way to the end, the `EvaluateStaticPosition` function in Figure 6-6 is never called except at the end of the game. If it were called before the game was over, it would always return `NeutralPosition`, which provides no strategic information to help the computer choose its move. `EvaluateStaticPosition` could, however, be coded so that it gives higher ratings to positions that offer winning chances. For example, you could make the function look for lines in the tic-tac-toe board that still provide a chance to win. If some line contains two of your symbols and an empty square, you can give that position a higher rating.

    Rewrite the `EvaluateStaticPosition` function so that the tic-tac-toe program never loses a game even if `MaxDepth` is set to 4.

CHAPTER 7

Algorithmic Analysis

Without analysis, no synthesis.

— Friedrich Engels, *Herr Eugen Duhring's Revolution in Science,* 1878

Objectives

- To recognize that algorithms for solving a problem vary widely in their performance.

- To understand the concept of computational complexity as a qualitative measure of how running time changes in proportion to the size of a problem.

- To learn to express computational complexity using big-O notation.

- To appreciate how divide-and-conquer techniques can improve the efficiency of sorting algorithms.

- To be able to identify the most common complexity classes and understand the performance characteristics of each class.

- To know how to prove simple properties using mathematical induction.

In Chapter 4, you were introduced to two different recursive implementations of the function `Fib(n)`, which computes the nth Fibonacci number. The first is based directly on the mathematical definition

$$\texttt{Fib(n)} = \begin{cases} \texttt{n} & \textit{if } \texttt{n} \textit{ is 0 or 1} \\ \texttt{Fib(n - 1) + Fib(n - 2)} & \textit{otherwise} \end{cases}$$

and turns out to be wildly inefficient. The second implementation, which uses the notion of additive sequences to produce a version of `Fib(n)` that is comparable in efficiency to traditional iterative approaches, demonstrates that recursion is not really the root of the problem. Even so, examples like the simple recursive implementation of the Fibonacci function have such high execution costs that recursion sometimes gets a bad name as a result.

As you will see in this chapter, the ability to think recursively about a problem often leads to new strategies that are considerably *more* efficient than anything that would come out of an iterative design process. The power of recursive divide-and-conquer algorithms is enormous and has a profound impact on many problems that arise in practice. By using recursive algorithms of this form, it is possible to achieve dramatic increases in efficiency that can cut the solution times, not by factors of two or three, but by factors of a thousand or more.

Before looking at these algorithms, however, it is important to ask a few questions. What does the term *efficiency* mean in an algorithmic context? How would you go about measuring that efficiency? These questions form the foundation for the subfield of computer science known as **analysis of algorithms.** Although a detailed understanding of algorithmic analysis requires a reasonable facility with mathematics and a lot of careful thought, you can get a sense of how it works by investigating the performance of a few simple algorithms.

■■■ 7.1 The sorting problem

The easiest way to illustrate the analysis of algorithms is to consider a problem domain in which different algorithms vary widely in their performance. Of these, one of the most interesting is the problem of **sorting,** which consists of reordering the elements in an array so that they fall in some defined sequence. For example, suppose you have stored the following integers in the variable `array`, whose effective size is stored in the variable `n`:

array   n

56	25	37	58	95	19	73	30		8
----	----	----	----	----	----	----	----		---
0	1	2	3	4	5	6	7

Your mission is to write a function `SortIntegerArray(array, n)` that rearranges the elements into ascending order, like this:

19	25	30	37	56	58	73	95
0	1	2	3	4	5	6	7

The selection sort algorithm

There are many algorithms you could choose to sort an array of integers into ascending order. One of the simplest is called **selection sort.** Given an array of N items, the selection sort algorithm goes through each element position and finds the value which should occupy that position in the sorted array. When it finds the appropriate element, the algorithm exchanges it with the value which previously occupied the desired position to ensure that no elements are lost. Thus, on the first cycle, the algorithm finds the smallest element and swaps it with the first array position. On the second cycle, it finds the smallest remaining element and swaps it with the second position. Thereafter, the algorithm continues this strategy until all positions in the array are correctly ordered. An implementation of `SortIntegerArray` that uses selection sort is shown in Figure 7-1.

FIGURE 7-1 Implementation of the selection sort algorithm

```
/*
 * Function: SortIntegerArray
 * --------------------------
 * This implementation uses an algorithm called selection sort,
 * which can be described in English as follows.  With your left
 * hand (lh), point at each element in the array in turn,
 * starting at index 0.  At each step in the cycle:
 *
 * 1. Find the smallest element in the range between your left
 *    hand and the end of the array, and point at that element
 *    with your right hand (rh).
 *
 * 2. Move that element into its correct position by exchanging
 *    the elements indicated by your left and right hands.
 */

void SortIntegerArray(int array[], int n)
{
    int lh, rh, i, temp;

    for (lh = 0; lh < n; lh++) {
        rh = lh;
        for (i = lh + 1; i < n; i++) {
            if (array[i] < array[rh]) rh = i;
        }
        temp = array[lh];
        array[lh] = array[rh];
        array[rh] = temp;
    }
}
```

For example, given the initial array

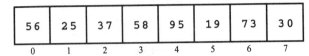

the first cycle through the outer `for` loop identifies the 19 in index position 5 as the smallest value in the entire array and then swaps it with the 56 in index position 0 to leave the following configuration:

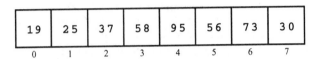

On the second cycle, the algorithm finds the smallest element between positions 1 and 7, which turns out to be the 25 in position 1. The program goes ahead and performs the exchange operation, leaving the array unchanged from the preceding diagram. On each subsequent cycle, the algorithm performs a swap operation to move the next smallest value into its appropriate final position. When the `for` loop is complete, the entire array is sorted.

Empirical measurements of performance

How efficient is the selection sort algorithm as a strategy for sorting arrays? To answer this question, it helps to collect empirical data about how long it takes the computer to sort an array of various sizes. When I did this experiment on my own computer—the actual running times, after all, depend on the speed of the computer—I observed the following timing data for selection sort, where N represents the number of elements in the array:

N	Running time
10	0.12 msec
20	0.39 msec
40	1.46 msec
100	8.72 msec
200	33.33 msec
400	135.42 msec
1000	841.67 msec
2000	3.35 sec
4000	13.42 sec
10,000	83.90 sec

For an array of 10 integers, the selection sort algorithm completes its work in a fraction of a millisecond. Even for 1000 integers, `SortIntegerArray` takes less than a second, which certainly seems fast enough in terms of our human sense of time. As the array sizes get larger, however, the performance of selection sort begins to go downhill. For an array of 10,000 integers, the algorithm requires over a minute of computing time. If you're sitting in front of your computer waiting for it to reply, a minute seems like an awfully long time.

Even more disturbing is the fact that the performance of selection sort rapidly gets worse as the array size increases. As you can see from the timing data, every time you double the number of values in the array, the running time increases by about a factor of four. Similarly, if you multiply the number of values by 10, the time required to sort the array goes up a hundredfold. If this pattern continues, sorting a list of 100,000 numbers would take two and a half hours. Sorting an array of a million numbers by this method would take approximately 10 days. Thus, if your business required you to solve sorting problems on this scale, you would have no choice but to find a more efficient approach.

Analyzing the performance of selection sort

What makes selection sort perform so badly as the number of values to be sorted becomes large? To answer this question, it helps to think about what the algorithm has to do on each cycle of the outer loop. To correctly determine the first value in the array, the selection sort algorithm must consider all N elements as it searches for the smallest value. Thus, the time required on the first cycle of the loop is presumably proportional to N. For each of the other elements in the array, the algorithm performs the same basic steps but looks at one fewer element each time. It looks at $N-1$ elements on the second cycle, $N-2$ on the third, and so on, so the total running time is roughly proportional to

$$N + N{-}1 + N{-}2 + \ldots + 3 + 2 + 1$$

Because it is difficult to work with an expression in this expanded form, it is useful to simplify it by applying a bit of mathematics. As you may have learned in an algebra course, the sum of the first N integers is given by the formula

$$\frac{N\,(N+1)}{2}$$

or, multiplying out the numerator,

$$\frac{N^2 + N}{2}$$

You will learn how to prove that this formula is correct in the section on "Mathematical induction" later in this chapter. For the moment, all you need to know is that the sum of the first N integers can be expressed in this more compact form.

If you write out the values of the function

$$\frac{N^2 + N}{2}$$

for various values of N, you get a table that looks like this:

N	$\dfrac{N^2 + N}{2}$
10	55
20	210
40	820
100	5050
200	20,100
400	80,200
1000	500,500
2000	2,001,000
4000	8,002,000
10,000	50,005,000

Because the running time of the selection sort algorithm is presumably related to the amount of work the algorithm needs to do, the values in this table should be roughly proportional to the observed execution time of the algorithm, which turns out to be true. If you look at the measured timing data for selection sort, for example, you discover that the algorithm requires 83.90 seconds to sort 10,000 numbers. In that time, the selection sort algorithm has to perform 50,005,000 operations in its innermost loop. Assuming that there is indeed a proportionality relationship between these two values, dividing the time by the number of operations gives the following estimate of the proportionality constant:

$$\frac{83.90 \text{ seconds}}{50,005,000} = 0.00167 \text{ msec}$$

If you then apply this same proportionality constant to the other entries in the table, you discover that the formula

$$0.00167 \text{ msec} \times \frac{N^2 + N}{2}$$

is indeed a good approximation of the running time, at least for large values of N. The observed times and the estimates calculated using this formula are shown in Table 7-1, along with the relative error between the two.

■ 7.2 Computational complexity

The problem with carrying out a detailed analysis like the one shown in Table 7-1 is that you end up with too much information. Although it is occasionally useful to have a formula for predicting exactly how long a program will take, you can usually get away with more qualitative measures. The reason that selection sort is impractical for large values of N has little to do with the precise timing characteristics of a particular implementation running on a specific machine. The problem is much simpler and more fundamental. At its essence, the problem with selection sort is that doubling the size of the input array increases the running time

body of the loop is executed n times. Because no part of the code is executed more often than this, you can predict that the computational complexity will be $O(N)$.

The selection sort function can be analyzed in a similar way. The most frequently executed part of the code is the comparison in the statement

```
if (array[i] < array[rh]) rh = i;
```

That statement is nested inside two **for** loops whose limits depend on the value of N. The inner loop runs N times as often as the outer loop, which implies that the inner loop body is executed $O(N^2)$ times. Algorithms like selection sort that exhibit $O(N^2)$ performance are said to run in **quadratic time.**

Worst-case versus average-case complexity

In some cases, the running time of an algorithm depends not only on the size of the problem but also on the specific characteristics of the data. For example, consider the function

```
int LinearSearch(int key, int array[], int n)
{
    int i;

    for (i = 0; i < n; i++) {
        if (key == array[i]) return (i);
    }
    return (-1);
}
```

which returns the first index position in **array** at which the value **key** appears, or –1 if the value **key** does not appear anywhere in the array. Because the **for** loop in the implementation executes n times, you expect the performance of **LinearSearch**— as its name implies—to be $O(N)$.

On the other hand, some calls to **LinearSearch** can be executed very quickly. Suppose, for example, that the key element you are searching for happens to be in the first position in the array. In that case, the body of the **for** loop will run only once. If you're lucky enough to search for a value that always occurs at the beginning of the array, **LinearSearch** will run in constant time.

When you analyze the computational complexity of a program, you're usually not interested in the minimum possible time. In general, computer scientists tend to be concerned about the following two types of complexity analysis:

- *Worst-case complexity.* The most common type of complexity analysis consists of determining the performance of an algorithm in the worst possible case. Such an analysis is useful because it allows you to set an upper bound on the computational complexity. If you analyze for the worst case, you can guarantee that the performance of the algorithm will be at least as good as your analysis indicates. You might sometimes get lucky, but you can be confident that the performance will not get any worse.

- *Average-case complexity.* From a practical point of view, it is often useful to consider how well an algorithm performs if you average its behavior over all possible sets of input data. Particularly if you have no reason to assume that the specific input to your problem is in any way atypical, the average-case analysis provides the best statistical estimate of actual performance. The problem, however, is that average-case analysis is usually much more difficult to carry out and typically requires considerable mathematical sophistication.

The worst case for the `LinearSearch` function occurs when the key is not in the array at all. When the key is not there, the function must complete all n cycles of the `for` loop, which means that its performance is $O(N)$. If the key is known to be in the array, the `for` loop will be executed about half as many times on average, which implies that average-case performance is also $O(N)$. As you will discover in the section on "The Quicksort algorithm" later in this chapter, the average-case and worst-case performances of an algorithm sometimes differ in qualitative ways, which means that in practice it is often important to take both performance characteristics into consideration.

A formal definition of big-O

Because understanding big-O notation is critical to modern computer science, it is important to offer a somewhat more formal definition to help you understand why the intuitive model of big-O works and why the suggested simplifications of big-O formulas are in fact justified. In mathematics, big-O notation is used to express the relationship between two functions, in an expression like this:

$$t(N) = O(f(N))$$

The formal meaning of this expression is that $f(N)$ is an approximation of $t(N)$ with the following characteristic: it must be possible to find a constant N_0 and a positive constant C so that for every value of $N \geq N_0$, the following condition holds:

$$t(N) \leq C \times f(N)$$

In other words, as long as N is "large enough," the function $t(N)$ is always bounded by a constant multiple of the function $f(N)$.

When it is used to express computational complexity, the function $t(N)$ represents the actual running time of the algorithm, which is usually difficult to compute. The function $f(N)$ is a much simpler formula that nonetheless provides a reasonable qualitative estimate for how the running time changes as a function of N, because the condition expressed in the mathematical definition of big-O ensures that the actual running time cannot grow faster than $f(N)$.

To see how the formal definition applies, it is useful to go back to the selection sorting example. Analyzing the loop structure of selection sort showed that the operations in the innermost loop were executed

$$\frac{N^2 + N}{2}$$

times and that the running time was presumably roughly proportional to this formula. When this complexity was expressed in terms of big-O notation, the constants and low-order terms were eliminated, leaving only the assertion that the execution time was $O(N^2)$, which is in fact an assertion that

$$\frac{N^2 + N}{2} = O(N^2)$$

To show that this expression is indeed true under the formal definition of big-O, all you need to do is find constants C and N_0 so that

$$\frac{N^2 + N}{2} \leq C \times N^2$$

for all values of $N \geq N_0$. This particular example is extremely simple. All you need to do to satisfy the constraints is to set the constants C and N_0 both to 1. After all, as long as N is no smaller than 1, you know that $N^2 \geq N$. It must therefore be the case that

$$\frac{N^2 + N}{2} \leq \frac{N^2 + N^2}{2}$$

But the right side of this inequality is simply N^2, which means that

$$\frac{N^2 + N}{2} \leq N^2$$

for all values of $N \geq 1$, as required by the definition.

You can use a similar argument to show that any polynomial of degree k, which can be expressed in general terms as

$$a_k N^k + a_{k-1} N^{k-1} + a_{k-2} N^{k-2} + \ldots + a_2 N^2 + a_1 N + a_0$$

is $O(N^k)$. To do so, your goal is to find constants C and N_0 so that

$$a_k N^k + a_{k-1} N^{k-1} + a_{k-2} N^{k-2} + \ldots + a_2 N^2 + a_1 N + a_0 \leq C \times N^k$$

for all values of $N \geq N_0$.

As in the preceding example, start by letting N_0 be 1. For all values of $N \geq 1$, each successive power of N is at least as large as its predecessor, so

$$N^k \geq N^{k-1} \geq N^{k-2} \geq \ldots \geq N^2 \geq N \geq 1$$

This property in turn implies that

$$a_k N^k + a_{k-1} N^{k-1} + a_{k-2} N^{k-2} + \ldots + a_2 N^2 + a_1 N + a_0$$
$$\leq \left| a_k \right| N^k + \left| a_{k-1} \right| N^k + \left| a_{k-2} \right| N^k + \ldots + \left| a_2 \right| N^k + \left| a_1 \right| N^k + \left| a_0 \right| N^k$$

where the vertical bars surrounding the coefficients on the right side of the equation indicate absolute value. By factoring out N^k, you can simplify the right side of this inequality to

$$\left(\left| a_k \right| + \left| a_{k-1} \right| + \left| a_{k-2} \right| + \ldots + \left| a_2 \right| + \left| a_1 \right| + \left| a_0 \right| \right) N^k$$

Thus, if you define the constant C to be

$$\left| a_k \right| + \left| a_{k-1} \right| + \left| a_{k-2} \right| + \ldots + \left| a_2 \right| + \left| a_1 \right| + \left| a_0 \right|$$

you have established that

$$a_k N^k + a_{k-1} N^{k-1} + a_{k-2} N^{k-2} + \ldots + a_2 N^2 + a_1 N + a_0 \leq C \times N^k$$

This result proves that the entire polynomial is $O(N^k)$.

If all this mathematics scares you, try not to worry. It is much more important for you to understand what big-O means in practice than it is to follow all the steps in the formal derivation.

■ 7.3 Recursion to the rescue

At this point, you know considerably more about complexity analysis than you did when you started the chapter. However, you are no closer to solving the practical problem of how to write a sorting algorithm that is more efficient for large arrays. The selection sort algorithm is clearly not up to the task, because the running time increases in proportion to the square of the input size. The same is true for most sorting algorithms that process the elements of the array in a linear order. To develop a better sorting algorithm, you need to adopt a qualitatively different approach.

The power of divide-and-conquer strategies

Oddly enough, the key to finding a better sorting strategy lies in recognizing that the quadratic behavior of algorithms like selection sort has a hidden virtue. The basic characteristic of quadratic complexity is that, as the size of a problem doubles, the running time increases by a factor of four. The reverse, however, is also true. If you divide the size of a quadratic problem by two, you decrease the running time by that same factor of four. This fact suggests that dividing an array in half and then applying a recursive divide-and-conquer approach might reduce the required sorting time.

To make this idea more concrete, suppose you have a large array that you need to sort. What happens if you divide the array into two halves and then use the selection sort algorithm to sort each of those pieces? Because selection sort is quadratic, each of the subarrays requires one quarter of the original time. You need to sort both halves, of course, but the total time required to sort the two subarrays is still only half the time that would have been required to sort the original array. If it turns out that sorting two halves of an array simplifies the problem of sorting the complete array, you will be able to reduce the total time substantially. More importantly, once you discover how to improve performance at one level, you can use the same algorithm recursively to sort each subarray.

To determine whether a divide-and-conquer strategy is applicable to the sorting problem, you need to answer the question of whether dividing an array into two smaller arrays and then sorting each one helps to solve the general problem. As a way to gain some insight into this question, suppose that you start with an array containing the following eight elements:

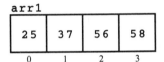

array

56	25	37	58	95	19	73	30
0	1	2	3	4	5	6	7

If you divide the array of eight elements into two arrays of length four and then sort each of those smaller arrays—remember that the recursive leap of faith means you can assume that the recursive calls work correctly—you get the following sorted subarrays:

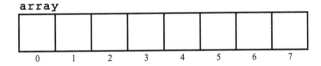

arr1

25	37	56	58
0	1	2	3

arr2

19	30	73	95
0	1	2	3

How useful is this decomposition? Remember that your goal is to take the values out of these smaller arrays and put them back into the original array in the correct order. In other words, you need to copy the values from the subarrays into the slots in the following diagram:

array

0	1	2	3	4	5	6	7

What would you do?

Merging two arrays

As it happens, reconstructing the complete array from the smaller sorted arrays is a much simpler problem than sorting itself. The required technique, called **merging,** depends on the fact that the first element in the complete ordering must be either the first element in **arr1** or the first element in **arr2**, whichever is smaller. In this example, the first element in the new array is the 19 in **arr2**. If you put that element into `array[0]` and, in effect, cross it out of `arr2`, you get the following configuration:

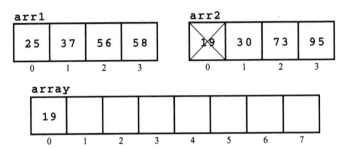

Once again, the next element can only be the first unused element in one of the two smaller arrays. You compare the 25 from `arr1` against the 30 in `arr2` and choose the former:

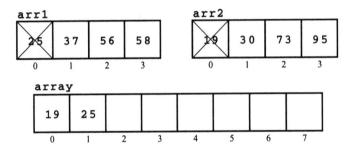

You can easily continue this process of choosing the smaller value from `arr1` or `arr2` until the entire array is filled.

The merge sort algorithm

The merge operation, combined with recursive decomposition, gives rise to a new sorting algorithm called **merge sort,** which you can implement in a straightforward way. The basic idea of the algorithm can be outlined as follows:

1. Check to see if the array is empty or has only one element. If so, it must already be sorted, and the function can return without doing any work. This condition defines the simple case for the recursion.
2. Divide the array into two new subarrays, each of which is half the size of the original.
3. Sort each of the subarrays recursively.
4. Merge the two subarrays back into the original one.

The code for the merge sort algorithm, shown in Figure 7-2, is divided into three functions: `SortIntegerArray`, `Merge`, and `CopySubArray`. The code for `SortIntegerArray` follows directly from the outline of the algorithm. After checking for the special case, the algorithm divides the array into two smaller

FIGURE 7-2 Implementation of the merge sort algorithm

```
/*
 * Function: SortIntegerArray
 * Usage: SortIntegerArray(array, n);
 * ------------------------------------
 * This function sorts the first n elements of array into
 * increasing numerical order using the merge sort algorithm,
 * which requires (1) dividing the array into two halves,
 * (2) sorting each half, and (3) merging the halves together.
 */

void SortIntegerArray(int array[], int n)
{
    int n1, n2, *arr1, *arr2;

    if (n <= 1) return;
    n1 = n / 2;
    n2 = n - n1;
    arr1 = CopySubArray(array, 0, n1);
    arr2 = CopySubArray(array, n1, n2);
    SortIntegerArray(arr1, n1);
    SortIntegerArray(arr2, n2);
    Merge(array, arr1, n1, arr2, n2);
    FreeBlock(arr1);
    FreeBlock(arr2);
}

/*
 * Function: Merge
 * Usage: Merge(array, arr1, n1, arr2, n2);
 * -----------------------------------------
 * This function merges two sorted arrays (arr1 and arr2) into a
 * single output array.  Because the input arrays are sorted, the
 * implementation can always select the first unused element in
 * one of the input arrays to fill the next position in array.
 */

static void Merge(int array[], int arr1[], int n1,
                                int arr2[], int n2)
{
    int p, p1, p2;

    p = p1 = p2 = 0;
    while (p1 < n1 && p2 < n2) {
        if (arr1[p1] < arr2[p2]) {
            array[p++] = arr1[p1++];
        } else {
            array[p++] = arr2[p2++];
        }
    }
    while (p1 < n1) array[p++] = arr1[p1++];
    while (p2 < n2) array[p++] = arr2[p2++];
}
```

```
/*
 * Function: CopySubArray
 * Usage: CopySubArray(array, start, n);
 * ----------------------------------------
 * This function makes a copy of a subset of an integer array
 * and returns a pointer to a new dynamic array containing the
 * new elements. The array begins at the indicated start
 * position in the original array and continues for n elements.
 */

static int *CopySubArray(int array[], int start, int n)
{
    int i, *result;

    result = NewArray(n, int);
    for (i = 0; i < n; i++) {
        result[i] = array[start + i];
    }
    return (result);
}
```

arrays, `arr1` and `arr2`, whose effective sizes are `n1` and `n2`, respectively. In this implementation, the task of creating those subarrays is given to the `CopySubArray` function, which exists only to make the `SortIntegerArray` implementation easier to read. Once `arr1` and `arr2` have been created, the rest of the function sorts these arrays recursively and then calls `Merge` to reassemble the complete solution. Before returning, the function calls `FreeBlock` on `arr1` and `arr2` to release the storage associated with the temporary arrays.

Most of the work is done by the `Merge` function, which takes the destination array, along with the smaller arrays `arr1` and `arr2`, coupled with their effective sizes, `n1` and `n2`. The indices `p1` and `p2` mark the progress through each of the subarrays, and `p` is the index in `array`. On each cycle of the loop, the function selects an element from `arr1` or `arr2`—whichever is smaller—and copies that value into `array`. As soon as the elements in either subarray are exhausted, the function can simply copy the elements from the other array without bothering to test them. In fact, because one of the subarrays is already exhausted when the first `while` loop exits, the function can simply copy the rest of each array to the destination. One of these subarrays will be empty, and the corresponding `while` loop will not be executed at all.

The computational complexity of merge sort

You now have an implementation of the `SortIntegerArray` function based on the strategy of divide-and-conquer. How efficient is it? You can measure its efficiency by sorting arrays of numbers and timing the result, but it is helpful to start by thinking about the algorithm in terms of its computational complexity.

When you call the merge sort implementation of `SortIntegerArray` on a list of N numbers, the running time can be divided into two components:

1. The amount of time required to execute the operations at the current level of the recursive decomposition
2. The time required to execute the recursive calls

At the top level of the recursive decomposition, the cost of performing the nonrecursive operations is proportional to N. The two calls to `CopySubArray` together account for N cycles, and the call to `Merge` has the effect of filling up the original N positions in the array. If you add these operations and ignore the constant factor, you discover that the complexity of any single call to `SortIntegerArray`—not counting the recursive calls within it—requires $O(N)$ operations.

But what about the cost of the recursive operations? To sort an array of size N, you must recursively sort two subarrays of size $N/2$. Each of these operations requires some amount of time. If you apply the same logic, you quickly determine that sorting each subarray requires time proportional to $N/2$ at that level, plus whatever time is required by its own recursive calls. The same process then continues until you reach the simple case in which the subarrays consist of a single element or no elements at all.

The total time required to solve the problem is the sum of the time required at each level of the recursive decomposition. In general, the decomposition has the structure shown in Figure 7-3. As you move down through the recursive hierarchy, the arrays get smaller, but more numerous. The amount of work done at each level, however, is always directly proportional to N. Determining the total amount of work is therefore a question of finding out how many levels there will be.

FIGURE 7-3 Recursive decomposition of merge sort

Sorting an array of size N

N

requires sorting two arrays of size N / 2

$2 \times N/2$

which requires sorting four arrays of size N / 4

$4 \times N/4$

which requires sorting eight arrays of size N / 8

$8 \times N/8$

and so on.

At each level of the hierarchy, the value of N is divided by 2. The total number of levels is therefore equal to the number of times you can divide N by 2 before you get down to 1. Rephrasing this problem in mathematical terms, you need to find a value of k such that

$$N = 2^k$$

Solving the equation for k gives

$$k = \log_2 N$$

Because the number of levels is $\log_2 N$ and the amount of work done at each level is proportional to N, the total amount of work is proportional to $N \log_2 N$.

Unlike other scientific disciplines, in which logarithms are expressed in terms of powers of 10 (common logarithms) or the mathematical constant e (natural logarithms), computer science tends to use **binary logarithms,** which are based on powers of 2. Logarithms computed using different bases differ only by a constant factor, and it is therefore traditional to omit the logarithmic base when you talk about computational complexity. Thus, the computational complexity of merge sort is usually written as

$$O(N \log N)$$

Comparing N^2 and $N \log N$ performance

But how good is $O(N \log N)$? You can compare its performance to that of $O(N^2)$ by looking at the values of these functions for different values of N, as follows:

N	N^2	$N \log N$
10	100	33
100	10,000	664
1000	1,000,000	9965
10,000	100,000,000	132,877

The numbers in both columns grow as N becomes larger, but the N^2 column grows much faster than the $N \log N$ column. Sorting algorithms based on an $N \log N$ algorithm are therefore useful over a much larger range of array sizes.

It is interesting to verify these results in practice. Because big-O notation discards constant factors, it may be that selection sort is more efficient for some problem sizes. Running the selection and merge sort algorithms on arrays of varying sizes and measuring the actual running times results in the timing data shown in Table 7-2. For 10 items, this implementation of merge sort is more than four times slower than selection sort. At 40 items, selection sort is still faster, but not by very much. By the time you get up to 10,000 items, merge sort is almost 100 times faster than selection sort. On my computer, the selection sort algorithm requires almost a minute and a half to sort 10,000 items while merge sort takes a little under a second. For large arrays, merge sort clearly represents a significant improvement.

TABLE 7-2 Empirical comparison of selection and merge sorts

N	Selection sort	Merge sort
10	0.12 msec	0.54 msec
20	0.39 msec	1.17 msec
40	1.46 msec	2.54 msec
100	8.72 msec	6.90 msec
200	33.33 msec	14.84 msec
400	135.42 msec	31.25 msec
1000	841.67 msec	84.38 msec
2000	3.35 sec	179.17 msec
4000	13.42 sec	383.33 msec
10,000	83.90 sec	997.67 msec

■ 7.4 Standard complexity classes

In programming, most algorithms fall into one of several common complexity classes. The most important complexity classes are shown in Table 7-3, which gives the common name of the class along with the corresponding big-O expression and a representative algorithm in that class.

The classes in Table 7-3 are presented in strictly increasing order of complexity. If you have a choice between one algorithm that requires $O(\log N)$ time and another that requires $O(N)$ time, the first will always outperform the second as N grows large. For small values of N, terms that are discounted in the big-O calculation may allow a theoretically less efficient algorithm to do better against one that has a lower computational complexity. On the other hand, as N grows larger, there will always be a point at which the theoretical difference in efficiency becomes the deciding factor.

The differences in efficiency between these classes are in fact profound. You can begin to get a sense of how the different complexity functions stand in relation to one another by looking at the graph in Figure 7-4, which plots these complexity

TABLE 7-3 Standard complexity classes

Class	Notation	Example
constant	$O(1)$	Returning the first element in an array
logarithmic	$O(\log N)$	Binary search in a sorted array
linear	$O(N)$	Linear search in an array
$N \log N$	$O(N \log N)$	Merge sort
quadratic	$O(N^2)$	Selection sort
cubic	$O(N^3)$	Conventional algorithms for matrix multiplication
exponential	$O(2^N)$	Tower of Hanoi

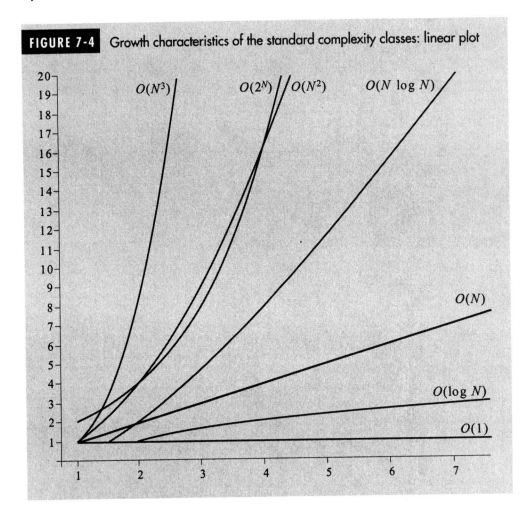

FIGURE 7-4   Growth characteristics of the standard complexity classes: linear plot

functions on a traditional linear scale. Unfortunately, this graph tells an incomplete and somewhat misleading part of the story, because the values of N are all very small. Complexity analysis, after all, is primarily relevant as the values of N become large. Figure 7-5 shows the same data plotted on a logarithmic scale, which gives you a better sense of how these functions grow.

Algorithms that fall into the constant, linear, quadratic, and cubic complexity classes are all part of a more general family called **polynomial algorithms** that execute in time N^k for some constant k. One of the useful properties of the logarithmic plot shown in Figure 7-5 is that the graph of any function N^k always comes out as a straight line whose slope is proportional to k. From looking at the figure, it is immediately clear that the function N^k—no matter how big k happens to be—will invariably grow more slowly than the exponential function represented by 2^N, which continues to curve upward as the value of N increases. This property has important implications in terms of finding practical algorithms for real-world

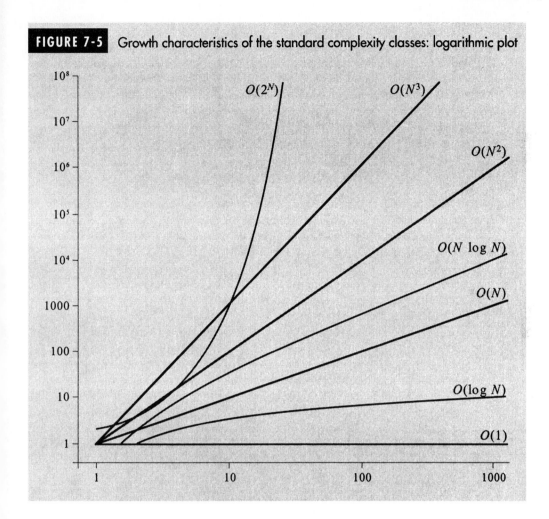

FIGURE 7-5 Growth characteristics of the standard complexity classes: logarithmic plot

problems. Even though the selection sort example makes it clear that quadratic algorithms have substantial performance problems for large values of N, algorithms whose complexity is $O(2^N)$ are considerably worse. As a general rule of thumb, computer scientists classify problems that can be solved using algorithms that run in polynomial time as **tractable,** in the sense that they are amenable to implementation on a computer. Problems for which no polynomial time algorithm exists are regarded as **intractable.**

Unfortunately, there are many commercially important problems for which all known algorithms require exponential time. For example, suppose you are a member of the sales force for a business and need to find a way to start at your home office, visit a list of cities, and return home, in a way that minimizes the cost of travel. This problem has become a classic in computer science and is called the **traveling salesman problem.** As far as anyone knows, it is not possible to solve the traveling salesman problem in polynomial time. The best-known approaches all have exponential performance in the worst case and are equivalent in efficiency to generating all possible routings and comparing the cost. In general, the number of possible routes in a connected network of N cities grows in proportion to 2^N, which gives rise to the exponential behavior. On the other hand, no one has been able to prove conclusively that no polynomial-time algorithm for this problem exists. There might be some clever algorithm that makes this problem tractable. There are many open questions as to what types of problems can actually be solved in polynomial time, which makes this topic an exciting area of active research.

7.5 The Quicksort algorithm

Even though the merge sort algorithm presented earlier in this chapter performs well in theory and has a worst-case complexity of $O(N \log N)$, it is not used much in practice. Instead, most sorting programs in use today are based on an algorithm called Quicksort, developed by the British computer scientist C. A. R. (Tony) Hoare.

Both Quicksort and merge sort employ a divide-and-conquer strategy. In the merge sort algorithm, the original array is divided into two halves, each of which is sorted independently. The resulting sorted subarrays are then merged together to complete the sort operation for the entire array. Suppose, however, that you took a different approach to dividing up the array. What would happen if you started the process by making an initial pass through the array, changing the positions of the elements so that "small" values came at the beginning of the array and "large" values came at the end, for some appropriate definition of the words *large* and *small?*

For example, suppose that the original array you wanted to sort was the following one, presented earlier in the discussion of merge sort:

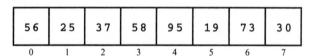

Half of these elements are larger than 50 and half are smaller, so it might make sense to define *small* in this case as being less than 50 and *large* as being 50 or more. If you could then find a way to rearrange the elements so that all the small elements came at the beginning and all the large ones at the end, you would wind up with an array that looks something like the following diagram, which shows one of many possible orderings that fit the definition:

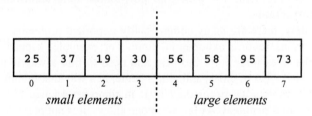

When the elements are divided into two subarrays in this fashion, all that remains to be done is to sort each of the subarrays, using a recursive call to the function that does the sorting. Since all the elements on the left side of the boundary line are smaller than all those on the right, the final result will be a completely sorted array:

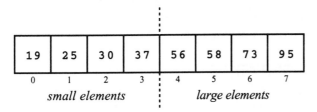

If you could always choose the optimal boundary between the small and large elements on each cycle, this algorithm would divide the array in half each time and end up demonstrating the same qualitative characteristics as merge sort. In practice, the Quicksort algorithm selects some existing element in the array and uses that value as the dividing line between the small and large elements. For example, a common approach is to pick the first element, which was 56 in the original array, and use it as the demarcation point between small and large elements. When the array is reordered, the boundary is therefore at a particular index position rather than between two positions, as follows:

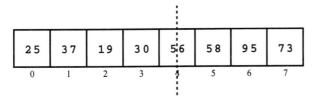

From this point, the recursive calls must sort the subarray between positions 0 and 3 and the subarray between positions 5 and 7, leaving index position 4 right where it is.

As in merge sort, the simple case of the Quicksort algorithm is an array with 0 or 1 elements, which must already be sorted. The recursive part of the Quicksort algorithm consists of the following steps:

1. *Choose an element to serve as the boundary between the small and large elements.* This element is traditionally called the **pivot.** For the moment, it is sufficient to choose any element for this purpose, and the simplest strategy is to select the first element in the array.
2. *Rearrange the elements in the array so that large elements are moved toward the end of the array and small elements toward the beginning.* More formally, the goal of this step is to divide the elements around a boundary position so that all elements to the left of the boundary are less than the pivot

and all elements to the right are greater than or possibly equal to the pivot.[2] This processing is called **partitioning** the array and is discussed in detail in the next section.

3. *Sort the elements in each of the subarrays.* Because all elements to the left of the pivot boundary are strictly less than all those to the right, sorting each of the subarrays must leave the entire array in sorted order. Moreover, since the algorithm uses a divide-and-conquer strategy, these subarrays can be sorted using a recursive application of Quicksort.

Partitioning the array

In the partition step of the Quicksort algorithm, the goal is to rearrange the elements so that they are divided into three classes: those that are smaller than the pivot; the pivot element itself, which is situated at the boundary position; and those elements that are at least as large as the pivot. The tricky part about partition is to rearrange the elements without using any extra array storage, which is typically done by swapping pairs of elements.

Tony Hoare's original approach to partitioning is fairly easy to explain in English. Because the pivot value has already been selected when you start the partitioning phase of the algorithm, you can tell immediately whether a value is large or small relative to that pivot. To make things easier, let's assume that the pivot value is stored in the initial element position. Hoare's partitioning algorithm proceeds as follows:

1. For the moment, ignore the pivot element at index position 0 and concentrate on the remaining elements. Use two index values, `lh` and `rh`, to record the index positions of the first and last elements in the rest of the array, as shown:

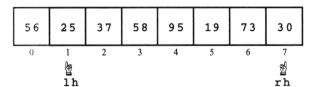

2. Move the `rh` index to the left until it either coincides with `lh` or points to an element containing a value that is small with respect to the pivot. In this example, the value 30 in position 7 is already a small value, so the `rh` index does not need to move.

3. Move the `lh` index to the right until it coincides with `rh` or points to an element containing a value that is larger than or equal to the pivot. In this example, the `lh` index must move to the right until it points to an element larger than 56, which leads to the following configuration:

---

[2] The subarray to the right of the boundary will contain values equal to the pivot only if the pivot value appears more than once in the array.

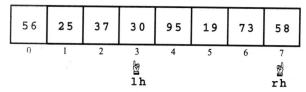

4. If the `lh` and `rh` index values have not yet reached the same position, exchange the elements in those positions in the array, which leaves the array looking like this:

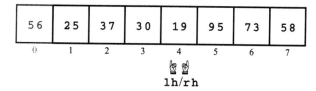

5. Repeat steps 2 through 4 until the `lh` and `rh` positions coincide. On the next pass, for example, the exchange operation in step 4 swaps the 19 and the 95. As soon as that happens, the next execution of step 2 moves the `rh` index to the left, where it ends up matching the `lh`, as follows:

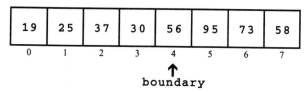

6. In most cases, the element at the point where the `lh` and `rh` index positions coincide will be the small value that is furthest to right in the array. If that position in fact contains a large value, the pivot must have been the smallest element in the entire array, so the boundary is at position 0. If that position contains a small value, as it usually does, the only remaining step is to exchange that value in this position with the pivot element at the beginning of the array, as shown:

19	25	37	30	56	95	73	58
0	1	2	3	4	5	6	7

↑
boundary

Note that this configuration meets the requirements of the partitioning step. The pivot value is at the marked boundary position, with every element to the left being smaller and every element to the right being at least that large.

A simple implementation of **SortIntegerArray** using the Quicksort algorithm is shown in Figure 7-6.

FIGURE 7-6   Implementation of Hoare's Quicksort algorithm

```
/*
 * Implementation notes: SortIntegerArray
 * ---------------------------------------
 * This implementation of SortIntegerArray uses the Quicksort
 * algorithm, which begins by "partitioning" the array so that
 * all elements smaller than a designated pivot element appear
 * to the left of a boundary and all equal or larger values
 * appear to the right.  Sorting the subarrays to the left and
 * right of boundary ensures that the entire array is sorted.
 */

void SortIntegerArray(int array[], int n)
{
    int boundary;

    if (n < 2) return;
    boundary = Partition(array, n);
    SortIntegerArray(array, boundary);
    SortIntegerArray(array + boundary + 1, n - boundary - 1);
}

/*
 * Function: Partition
 * Usage: boundary = Partition(array, n);
 * ---------------------------------------
 * This function rearranges the elements of array relative to
 * a pivot value, which is taken from array[0].  The Partition
 * function returns a boundary index such that array[i] < pivot
 * for all i < boundary, array[i] == pivot for i == boundary,
 * and array[i] >= pivot for all i > boundary.
 */

static int Partition(int array[], int n)
{
    int lh, rh, pivot, temp;

    pivot = array[0];
    lh = 1;
    rh = n - 1;
    while (TRUE) {
        while (lh < rh && array[rh] >= pivot) rh--;
        while (lh < rh && array[lh] < pivot) lh++;
        if (lh == rh) break;
        temp = array[lh];
        array[lh] = array[rh];
        array[rh] = temp;
    }
    if (array[lh] >= pivot) return (0);
    array[0] = array[lh];
    array[lh] = pivot;
    return (lh);
}
```

Analyzing the performance of Quicksort

As you can see from Table 7-4, this implementation of Quicksort tends to run several times faster than the implementation of merge sort given in Figure 7-2, which is one of the reasons why programmers use it more frequently in practice. Moreover, the running times for both algorithms appear to grow in roughly the same way.

The empirical results presented in Table 7-4, however, obscure an important point. As long as the Quicksort algorithm chooses a pivot that is close to the median value in the array, the partition step will divide the array into roughly equal parts. If the algorithm chooses poorly, one of the two subarrays may be much larger than the other, which defeats the purpose of the divide-and-conquer strategy. In a randomly chosen array, Quicksort tends to perform well and has an average-case complexity of $O(N \log N)$. In the worst case—which paradoxically consists of an array that is already sorted—the performance degenerates to $O(N^2)$. Despite this inferior behavior in the worst case, Quicksort is so much faster in practice than most other algorithms that it has become the standard choice for general sorting procedures.

There are several strategies you can use to increase the likelihood that the pivot is in fact close to the median value in the array. One simple approach is to have the Quicksort implementation choose the pivot element at random. Although it is still possible that the random process will choose a poor pivot value, it is unlikely that it would make the same mistake repeatedly at each level of the recursive decomposition. Moreover, there is no distribution of the original array that is always bad. Given any input, choosing the pivot randomly ensures that the average-case performance for that array would be $O(N \log N)$. Another possibility, which is explored in more detail in exercise 7, is to select a few values, typically three or five, from the array and choose the median of those values as the pivot.

You do have to be somewhat careful as you try to improve the algorithm in this way. Picking a good pivot improves performance, but also costs some time. If the algorithm spends more time choosing the pivot than it gets back from making a

TABLE 7-4 Empirical comparison of merge sort and Quicksort

N	Merge sort	Quicksort
10	0.54 msec	0.10 msec
20	1.17 msec	0.26 msec
40	2.54 msec	0.52 msec
100	6.90 msec	1.76 msec
200	14.84 msec	4.04 msec
400	31.25 msec	8.85 msec
1000	84.38 msec	26.04 msec
2000	179.17 msec	56.25 msec
4000	383.33 msec	129.17 msec
10,000	997.67 msec	341.67 msec

good choice, you will end up slowing down the implementation rather than speeding it up.

■ 7.6 Mathematical induction

Earlier in the chapter, I asked you to rely on the fact that the sum

$$N + N{-}1 + N{-}2 + \ldots + 3 + 2 + 1$$

could be simplified to the more manageable formula

$$\frac{N(N+1)}{2}$$

If you were skeptical about this simplification, how would you go about proving that the simplified formula is indeed correct?

There are, in fact, several different proof techniques you could try. One possibility is to represent the original extended sum in a geometric form. Suppose, for example, that N is 5. If you then represent each term in the summation with a row of dots, those dots form the following triangle:

If you make a copy of this triangle and flip it upside down, the two triangles fit together to form a rectangle, shown here with the lower triangle in gray:

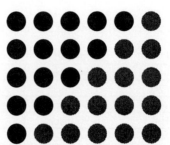

Since the pattern is now rectangular, the total number of dots—both black and gray—is easy to compute. In this picture, there are five rows of six dots each, so the total collection of dots, counting both colors, is 5×6, or 30. Since the two triangles are identical, exactly half of these dots are black; thus the number of black dots is

30 / 2, or 15. In the more general case, there are N rows containing $N+1$ dots each, and the number of black dots from the original triangle is therefore

$$\frac{N\,(N+1)}{2}$$

Proving that a formula is correct in this fashion, however, has some potential drawbacks. For one thing, geometrical arguments presented in this style are not as formal as many computer scientists would like. More to the point, constructing this type of argument requires that you come up with the right geometrical insight, which is different for each problem. It would be better to adopt a more general proof strategy that would apply to many different problems.

The technique that computer scientists generally use to prove propositions like

$$N\;+\;N\!-\!1\;+\;N\!-\!2\;+\;.\;.\;.+\;3\;+\;2\;+\;1\;\;=\;\;\frac{N\,(N+1)}{2}$$

is called **mathematical induction.** Mathematical induction applies when you want to show that a proposition is true for all values of an integer N beginning at some initial starting point. This starting point is called the **basis** of the induction and is typically 0 or 1. The process consists of the following steps:

- *Prove the base case.* The first step is to establish that the proposition holds true when N has the basis value. In most cases, this step is a simple matter of plugging the basis value into a formula and showing that the desired relationship holds.
- *Prove the inductive case.* The second step is to demonstrate that, if you assume the proposition to be true for N, it must also be true for $N+1$.

As an example, here is how you can use mathematical induction to prove the proposition that

$$N\;+\;N\!-\!1\;+\;N\!-\!2\;+\;.\;.\;.+\;3\;+\;2\;+\;1\;\;=\;\;\frac{N\,(N+1)}{2}$$

is indeed true for all N greater than or equal to 1. The first step is to prove the base case, when N is equal to 1. That part is easy. All you have to do is substitute 1 for N in both halves of the formula to determine that

$$1\;=\;\frac{1\times(1+1)}{2}\;=\;\frac{2}{2}\;=\;1$$

To prove the inductive case, you begin by assuming that the proposition

$$N\;+\;N\!-\!1\;+\;N\!-\!2\;+\;.\;.\;.+\;3\;+\;2\;+\;1\;\;=\;\;\frac{N\,(N+1)}{2}$$

is indeed true for N. This assumption is called the **inductive hypothesis.** Your goal is now to verify that the same relationship holds for $N+1$. In other words, what you need to do to establish the truth of the current formula is to show that

$$N+1 + N + N{-}1 + N{-}2 + \ldots + 3 + 2 + 1 = \frac{(N+1)(N+2)}{2}$$

If you look at the left side of the equation, you should notice that the sequence of terms beginning with N is exactly the same as the left side of your inductive hypothesis. Since you have assumed that the inductive hypothesis is true, you can substitute the equivalent closed-form expression, so that the left side of the proposition you're trying to prove looks like this:

$$N+1 + \frac{N(N+1)}{2}$$

From here on, the rest of the proof is simple algebra:

$$N+1 + \frac{N(N+1)}{2}$$

$$= \frac{2N+2}{2} + \frac{N^2+N}{2}$$

$$= \frac{N^2+3N+2}{2}$$

$$= \frac{(N+1)(N+2)}{2}$$

The last line in this derivation is precisely the result you were looking for and therefore completes the proof.

Many students need time to get used to the idea of mathematical induction. At first glance, the inductive hypothesis seems to be "cheating" in some sense; after all, you get to assume precisely the proposition that you are trying to prove. In fact, the process of mathematical induction is nothing more than an infinite family of proofs, each of which proceeds by the same logic. The base case in a typical example establishes that the proposition is true for $N = 1$. Once you have proved the base case, you can adopt the following chain of reasoning:

Now that I know the proposition is true for $N = 1$, I can prove it is true for $N = 2$.
Now that I know the proposition is true for $N = 2$, I can prove it is true for $N = 3$.
Now that I know the proposition is true for $N = 3$, I can prove it is true for $N = 4$.
Now that I know the proposition is true for $N = 4$, I can prove it is true for $N = 5$.
And so on. . . .

At each step in this process, you could write out a complete proof by applying the logic you used to establish the inductive case. The power of mathematical induction comes from the fact that you don't actually need to write out the details of each step individually.

In a way, the process of mathematical induction is like the process of recursion viewed from the opposite direction. If you try to explain a typical recursive decomposition in detail, the process usually sounds something like this:

To calculate this function for $N = 5$, I need to know its value for $N = 4$.
To calculate this function for $N = 4$, I need to know its value for $N = 3$.
To calculate this function for $N = 3$, I need to know its value for $N = 2$.
To calculate this function for $N = 2$, I need to know its value for $N = 1$.
The value $N = 1$ represents a simple case, so I can return the result immediately.

Both induction and recursion require you to make a leap of faith. When you write a recursive function, this leap consists of believing that all simpler instances of the function call will work without your paying any attention to the details. Making the inductive hypothesis requires much the same mental discipline. In both cases, you have to restrict your thinking to one level of the solution and not get sidetracked trying to follow the details all the way to the end.

Summary

The most valuable concept to take with you from this chapter is that algorithms for solving a problem can vary widely in their performance characteristics. Choosing an algorithm that has better computational properties can often reduce the time required to solve a problem by many orders of magnitude. The difference in behavior is illustrated dramatically by the tables presented in this chapter that give the actual running times for various sorting algorithms. When sorting an array of 10,000 integers, for example, the Quicksort algorithm outperforms selection sort by a factor of almost 250; as the array sizes get larger, the difference in efficiency between these algorithms will become even more pronounced.

Other important points in this chapter include:

- Most algorithmic problems can be characterized by an integer N that represents the size of the problem. For algorithms that operate on large integers, the size of the integer provides an effective measure of problem size; for algorithms that operate on arrays, it usually makes sense to define the problem size as the number of elements in the array.
- The most useful qualitative measure of efficiency is *computational complexity,* which is defined as the relationship between problem size and algorithmic performance as the problem size becomes large.
- *Big-O notation* provides an intuitive way of expressing computational complexity because it allows you to highlight the most important aspects of the complexity relationship in the simplest possible form.
- When you use big-O notation, you can simplify the formula by eliminating any term in the formula that becomes insignificant as N becomes large, along with any constant factors.

- You can often predict the computational complexity of a program by looking at the nesting structure of the loops it contains.

- Two useful measures of complexity are *worst-case* and *average-case* analysis. Average-case analysis is usually much more difficult to conduct.

- Divide-and-conquer strategies make it possible to reduce the complexity of sorting algorithms from $O(N^2)$ to $O(N \log N)$, which is a significant reduction.

- Most algorithms fall into one of several common *complexity classes*, which include the *constant, logarithmic, linear, N log N, quadratic, cubic,* and *exponential* classes. Algorithms whose complexity class appears earlier in this list are more efficient than those that come afterward when the problems being considered are sufficiently large.

- Problems that can be solved in *polynomial time,* which is defined to be $O(N^k)$ for some constant value *k,* are considered to be *tractable.* Problems for which no polynomial-time algorithm exists are considered *intractable* because solving such problems requires prohibitive amounts of time even for problems of relatively modest size.

- Because it tends to perform extremely well in practice, most sorting programs are based on the *Quicksort algorithm* developed by Tony Hoare, even though its worst-case complexity is $O(N^2)$.

- Mathematical induction provides a general technique for proving that a property holds for all values of N greater than or equal to some *base* value. To apply this technique, your first step is to demonstrate that the property holds in the base case. In the second step, you must prove that, if the formula holds for a specific value N, then it must also hold for $N+1$.

REVIEW QUESTIONS

1. The simplest recursive implementation of the Fibonacci function is considerably less efficient than the iterative version. Does this fact allow you to make any general conclusions about the relative efficiency of recursive and iterative solutions?

2. What is the sorting problem?

3. The implementation of `SortIntegerArray` shown in Figure 7-1 runs through the code to exchange the values at positions `lh` and `rh` even if these values happen to be the same. If you change the program so that it checks to make sure `lh` and `rh` are different before making the exchange, it is likely to run more slowly than the original algorithm. Why might this be so?

4. Suppose that you are using the selection sort algorithm to sort an array of 250 values and find that it takes 50 milliseconds to complete the operation. What would you expect the running time to be if you used the same algorithm to sort an array of 1000 values on the same machine?

5. What is the closed-form expression that computes the sum of the series

   $$N + N{-}1 + N{-}2 + \ldots + 3 + 2 + 1$$

6. In your own words, define the concept of computational complexity.

7. True or false: Big-O notation was invented as a means to express computational complexity.

8. What are the two rules presented in this chapter for simplifying big-O notation?

9. Is it technically correct to say that selection sort runs in

   $$O\left(\frac{N^2 + N}{2}\right)$$

   time? What, if anything, is wrong with doing so?

10. Is it technically correct to say that selection sort runs in $O(N^3)$ time? Again, what, if anything, is wrong with doing so?

11. Why is it customary to omit the base of the logarithm in big-O expressions such as $O(N \log N)$?

12. What is the computational complexity of the following function:

```
int Mystery1(int n)
{
    int i, j, sum;

    sum = 0;
    for (i = 0; i < n; i++) {
        for (j = 0; j < i; j++) {
            sum += i * j;
        }
    }
    return (sum);
}
```

13. What is the computational complexity of this function:

```
int Mystery2(int n)
{
    int i, j, sum;

    sum = 0;
    for (i = 0; i < 10; i++) {
        for (j = 0; j < i; j++) {
            sum += j * n;
        }
    }
    return (sum);
}
```

14. Explain the difference between worst-case and average-case complexity. In general, which of these measures is harder to compute?

15. State the formal definition of big-O.

16. In your own words, explain why the **Merge** function runs in linear time.

17. The last two lines of the **Merge** function are

    ```
    while (p1 < n1) array[p++] = arr1[p1++];
    while (p2 < n2) array[p++] = arr2[p2++];
    ```

    Would it matter if these two lines were reversed? Why or why not?

18. What are the seven complexity classes identified in this chapter as the most common classes encountered in practice?

19. What does the term *polynomial algorithm* mean?

20. What criterion do computer scientists use to differentiate tractable and intractable problems?

21. In the Quicksort algorithm, what conditions must be true at the conclusion of the partitioning step?

22. What are the worst- and average-case complexities for Quicksort?

23. Describe the two steps involved in a proof by mathematical induction.

24. In your own words, describe the relationship between recursion and mathematical induction.

PROGRAMMING EXERCISES

1. It is easy to write a recursive function

   ```
   double RaiseToPower(double x, int n)
   ```

   that calculates x^n, by relying on the recursive insight that

   $$x^n = x \times x^{n-1}$$

   Such a strategy leads to an implementation that runs in linear time. You can, however, adopt a recursive divide-and-conquer strategy which takes advantage of the fact that

   $$x^{2n} = x^n \times x^n$$

   Use this fact to write a recursive version of **RaiseToPower** that runs in $O(\log N)$ time.

2. There are several other sorting algorithms that exhibit the $O(N^2)$ behavior of selection sort. Of these, one of the most important is **insertion sort,** which operates as follows. You go through each element in the array in turn, as with the selection sort algorithm. At each step in the process, however, the goal is not to find the smallest remaining value and switch it into its correct position, but rather to ensure that the values considered so far are correctly ordered with respect to each other. Although those values may shift as more elements are processed, they form an ordered sequence in and of themselves.

For example, if you consider again the data used in the sorting examples from this chapter, the first cycle of the insertion sort algorithm requires no work, because an array of one element is always sorted:

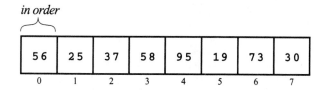

On the next cycle, you need to put 25 into the correct position with respect to the elements you have already seen, which means that you need to exchange the 56 and 25 to reach the following configuration:

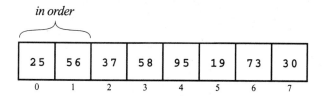

On the third cycle, you need to find where the value 37 should go. To do so, you need to move backward through the earlier elements—which you know are in order with respect to each other—looking for the position where 37 belongs. As you go, you need to shift each of the larger elements one position to the right, which eventually makes room for the value you're trying to insert. In this case, the 56 gets shifted by one position, and the 37 winds up in position 1. Thus, the configuration after the third cycle looks like this:

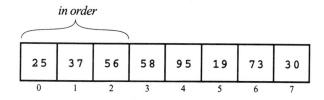

After each cycle, the initial subarray is always sorted, which implies that cycling through all the positions in this way will sort the entire array.

The insertion sort algorithm is important in practice because it runs in linear time if the array is already more or less in the correct order. It therefore makes sense to use insertion sort to restore order to a large array in which only a few elements are out of sequence.

Write an implementation of **SortIntegerArray** that uses the insertion sort algorithm. Construct an informal argument to show that the worst-case behavior of insertion sort is $O(N^2)$.

3. Write a function that keeps track of the elapsed time as it executes the **SortIntegerArray** procedure on a randomly chosen array. Use that function to write a program that produces a table of the observed running times for a predefined set of array sizes, as shown in the following sample run:

```
 N | Time (msec)
-------+-------------
   10 |       0.54
   20 |       1.17
   40 |       2.54
  100 |       6.90
  200 |      14.84
  400 |      31.25
 1000 |      84.38
 2000 |     179.17
 4000 |     383.33
10000 |     997.67
```

The best way to measure elapsed system time for programs of this sort is to use the ANSI **clock** function, which is exported by the **time.h** interface. The **clock** function takes no arguments and returns the amount of time the processing unit of the computer has used in the execution of the program. The unit of measurement and even the type used to store the result of **clock** differ depending on the type of machine, but you can always convert the system-dependent clock units into seconds by using the following expression:

(double) clock() / CLOCKS_PER_SEC

If you record the starting and finishing times in the variables **start** and **finish**, you can use the following code to compute the time required by a calculation:

```
double start, finish, elapsed;

start = (double) clock() / CLOCKS_PER_SEC;
Perform some calculation.
finish = (double) clock() / CLOCKS_PER_SEC;
elapsed = finish - start;
```

Unfortunately, calculating the time requirements for a program that runs quickly requires some subtlety because there is no guarantee that the system clock unit is precise enough to measure the elapsed time. For example, if you used this strategy to time the process of sorting 10 integers, the odds are good that the time value of `elapsed` at the end of the code fragment would be 0. The reason is that the processing unit on most machines can execute many instructions in the space of a single clock tick—almost certainly enough to get the entire sorting process done for an array of 10 elements. Because the system's internal clock may not tick in the interim, the values recorded for `start` and `finish` are likely to be the same.

The best way to get around this problem is to repeat the calculation many times between the two calls to the `clock` function. For example, if you want to determine how long it takes to sort 10 numbers, you can perform the sort-10-numbers experiment 1000 times in a row and then divide the total elapsed time by 1000. This strategy gives you a timing measurement that is much more accurate.

4. Suppose you know that all the values in an integer array fall into the range 0 to 9999. Show that it is possible to write a $O(N)$ algorithm to sort arrays with this restriction. Implement your algorithm and evaluate its performance by taking empirical measurements using the strategy outlined in exercise 3. Explain why the performance of the algorithm is so bad for small values of N.

5. In the merge sort implementation shown in Figure 7-2, each level of the recursive decomposition allocates two new subarrays. Since the combined size of the two subarrays is N and the same process is repeated at every level, this implementation requires $O(N \log N)$ extra storage. One of the major drawbacks of the merge sort algorithm is that it always requires some amount of additional allocated space, but $O(N \log N)$ is excessive.

Revise the merge sort implementation so that the amount of allocated space used by the recursive process is $O(N)$. A useful strategy to get you started is to define `SortIntegerArray` as a wrapper function which allocates a temporary array of size N and then passes that temporary array to the recursive function which does the work. If the recursive function itself does no allocation, this one temporary array will serve for all levels in the decomposition.

6. Write a program that generates a table which compares the performance of two algorithms—linear and binary search—when used to find a randomly chosen integer key in a sorted integer array. The linear search algorithm simply goes through each element of the array in turn until it finds the desired one or determines that the key does not appear. The binary search algorithm, which is implemented for string arrays in Figure 4-5, uses a divide-and-conquer strategy by checking the middle element of the array and then deciding which of the two remaining subarrays to search.

The table you generate in this problem, rather than computing the time as in exercise 3, should instead calculate the number of comparisons made against elements of the array. To ensure that the results are not completely random, your program should average the results over several independent trials. A sample run of the program might look like this:

```
   N |   Linear  |   Binary
-------+-----------+-----------
   10 |     5.7   |     2.8
   20 |     8.4   |     3.7
   40 |    18.0   |     4.5
  100 |    49.3   |     5.3
  200 |    93.6   |     6.6
  400 |   193.2   |     7.9
 1000 |   455.7   |     8.9
 2000 |   924.1   |    10.0
 4000 |  2364.2   |    11.2
10000 |  5078.1   |    12.4
```

7. Change the implementation of the Quicksort algorithm so that, instead of picking the first element in the array as the pivot, the `Partition` function chooses the median of the first, middle, and last elements.

8. Although $O(N \log N)$ sorting algorithms are clearly more efficient than $O(N^2)$ algorithms for large arrays, the simplicity of quadratic algorithms like selection sort often means that they perform better for small values of N. This fact raises the possibility of developing a strategy that combines the two algorithms, using Quicksort for large arrays but selection sort whenever the arrays become smaller than some threshold called the **crossover point.** Approaches that combine two different algorithms to exploit the best features of each are called **hybrid strategies.**

   Reimplement `SortIntegerArray` using a hybrid of the Quicksort and selection sort strategies. Experiment with different values of the crossover point below which the implementation chooses to use selection sort, and determine what value gives the best performance. The value of the crossover point depends on the specific timing characteristics of your computer and will change from system to system.[3]

9. Another interesting hybrid strategy for the sorting problem is to start with a recursive Quicksort that simply returns when the size of the array falls below a certain threshold. When this function returns, the array is not sorted, but all the elements are relatively close to their final positions. At this point, you can use the insertion sort algorithm presented in exercise 2 on the entire array to fix any remaining problems. Because insertion sort runs in linear time on arrays that are mostly sorted, you may be able to save some time using this approach.

10. Suppose you have two functions, f and g, for which $f(N)$ is less than $g(N)$ for all values of N. Use the formal definition of big-O to prove that

$$15f(N) + 6g(N)$$

   is $O(g(N))$.

---

[3] In fact, if your computer executes procedure calls quickly but takes a relatively long time to perform array selections, Quicksort may always come out being more efficient than selection sort even for small arrays. If this is true, no appropriate crossover point exists.

11. Use the formal definition of big-O to prove that N^2 is $O(2^N)$.

12. Use mathematical induction to prove that the following properties hold for all positive values of N.

   a. $1 + 3 + 5 + 7 + \ldots + 2N{-}1 = N^2$

   b. $1^2 + 2^2 + 3^2 + 4^2 + \ldots + N^2 = \dfrac{N\,(N+1)\,(2N+1)}{6}$

   c. $1^3 + 2^3 + 3^3 + 4^3 + \ldots + N^3 = (1 + 2 + 3 + 4 + \ldots + N)^2$

   d. $2^0 + 2^1 + 2^2 + 2^3 + \ldots + 2^N = 2^{N+1} - 1$

13. Exercise 1 shows that it is possible to compute x^n in $O(\log N)$ time. This fact in turn makes it possible to write an implementation of the function `Fib(n)` that also runs in $O(\log N)$ time, which is much faster than the traditional iterative version. To do so, you need to rely on the somewhat surprising fact that the Fibonacci function is closely related to a value called the **golden ratio,** which has been known since the days of Greek mathematics. The golden ratio, which is usually designated by the Greek letter ϕ, is defined to be the value that satisfies the equation

   $$\phi^2 - \phi - 1 = 0$$

   Because this is a quadratic equation, it actually has two roots. If you apply the quadratic formula, you will discover that these roots are

   $$\phi = \frac{1 + \sqrt{5}}{2}$$

   $$\hat{\phi} = \frac{1 - \sqrt{5}}{2}$$

   In 1718, the French mathematician Abraham de Moivre discovered that the nth Fibonacci number can be represented in closed form as

   $$\frac{\phi^n - \hat{\phi}^n}{\sqrt{5}}$$

   Moreover, since $\hat{\phi}^n$ is always very small, the formula can be simplified to

   $$\frac{\phi^n}{\sqrt{5}}$$

   rounded to the nearest integer.

Use this formula and the `RaiseToPower` function from exercise 1 to write an implementation of `Fib(n)` that runs in $O(\log N)$ time. Once you have verified empirically that the formula seems to work for the first several terms in the sequence, use mathematical induction to prove that the formula

$$\frac{\phi^n - \hat{\phi}^n}{\sqrt{5}}$$

actually computes the nth Fibonacci number.

14. If you're ready for a real algorithmic challenge, write the function

```
int MajorityElement(int array[], int n);
```

that returns the **majority element** in the array, which is defined to be a value that occurs in an absolute majority (at least 50 percent plus one) of the element positions in `array`. If no majority element exists, the function should return the constant `NoMajorityElement`, which you can define so that it has any value that cannot appear in the array. Your function must also meet the following conditions:

- It must run in $O(N)$ time.
- It must use $O(1)$ additional space. In other words, it may use individual temporary variables but may not allocate any additional arrays. Moreover, this condition rules out recursive solutions, because the space required to store the stack frames would grow with the depth of the recursion.
- It may not change any of the values in the array.

The hard part about this problem is coming up with the algorithm, not implementing it. Play with some sample arrays and see if you can come up with the right strategy.

Data Abstraction

Overview

Interfaces are important to modern programming because they make it possible to reduce the complexity of large software projects. As a client of an interface, you can look beyond the details of how a particular module is implemented and focus instead on the more abstract question of what that module does. The chapters in Part Three show you how to apply the principle of abstraction to data structures. Chapter 8 introduces the idea of an abstract data type, which is defined by its behavior rather than its underlying representation. Part Three also defines several abstract data types—particularly stacks, queues, and symbol tables—that you will use over and over again as tools in your own programming.

CHAPTER 8

Abstract Data Types

Nothing remained in whose reality she could believe, save those abstract ideas.

— Virginia Woolf, *Night and Day,* 1919

Objectives

- To appreciate the concept and purpose of abstract data types, or ADTs.

- To understand both the abstract behavior and the underlying implementation of the stack data type.

- To be able to use the incomplete type mechanism in ANSI C to define ADTs.

- To recognize that ADTs provide an attractive alternative to maintaining encapsulated state within a module.

- To understand the design and implementation of a scanner abstraction based on ADTs.

As you know from your programming experience, data structures can be assembled to form hierarchies. The atomic data types—such as `int`, `char`, `double`, and enumerated types—occupy the lowest level in the hierarchy. To represent more complex information, you combine the atomic types to form larger structures. These larger structures can then be assembled into even larger ones in an open-ended process. You build each new level in the hierarchy by using one of the three primitives for type construction: arrays, records, and pointers. Given an existing type, you can define an array of that type, include it as a field of a record, or declare a pointer to it. These facilities constitute the mortar of the data hierarchy and allow you to build arbitrarily complex structures.

As you learn more about programming, however, you will discover that particular data structures can be extremely useful and are worth studying in their own right. For example, a string is represented internally as an array of characters, which is in turn represented as a pointer to the first address in the array. But a string also has an abstract behavior that transcends its representation. When you use a string, its representation is often unimportant; what matters most is how it behaves. A type defined in terms of its behavior rather than its representation is called an **abstract data type,** which is often abbreviated to **ADT.**

Most abstract data types are defined by an interface that exports the ADT along with a collection of functions that define the behavior of that type. This technique has the following advantages:

- *Simplicity.* Hiding the internal representation of a type from the client means that there are fewer details for the client to understand.
- *Flexibility.* Because an ADT is defined in terms of its behavior, the programmer who implements one is free to change its underlying representation. As with any abstraction, it is appropriate to change the implementation as long as the interface remains the same.
- *Security.* The interface boundary acts as a wall that protects the implementation and the client from each other. If a client program has access to the representation of a type, it can change the values in the underlying data structure in unexpected ways. Using an ADT prevents the client from making such changes.

■ 8.1 Stacks

To understand the concept of abstract data types, it helps to consider a specific data structure and see how the standard principles of abstraction can be applied to data types. In this section, you will learn about a data structure called a **stack,** which provides storage for a collection of data values, subject to the restriction that values can only be removed from a stack in the opposite order from which they were added.

In computer science, stacks have acquired their own terminology. The values stored in a stack are called its **elements.** Adding a new element to a stack is called **pushing** that element; removing the most recent item from a stack is called **popping** the stack. Moreover, the defining behavior of stacks—that the elements are processed in a "last in, first out" fashion—is sometimes abbreviated as **LIFO.**

The basic stack metaphor

The conventional (and possibly apocryphal) explanation for the words *stack, push,* and *pop* is that they come from the following metaphor. In many cafeterias, plates for the food are placed in spring-loaded columns that make it easy for people in the cafeteria line to take the top plate, as illustrated in the following diagram:

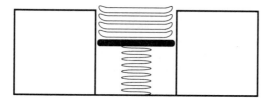

When a dishwasher adds a new plate, it goes on the top of the stack, pushing the others down slightly as the spring is compressed, as shown:

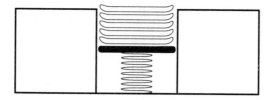

Customers can only take plates from the top of the stack. When they do, the remaining plates pop back up. The last plate added to the stack is the first one a customer takes.

Stacks and function calls

As you have already seen, stacks also play an important role in programming because nested function calls behave in a stack-oriented fashion. For example, if the main program calls a function named **F**, a stack frame for **F** gets pushed on top of the stack frame for **main**.

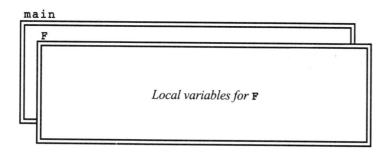

If F calls G, a new stack frame for G is pushed on top of the frame for F.

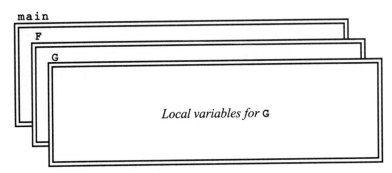

When G returns, its frame is popped off the stack, restoring F to the top of the stack as shown in the original diagram.

Stacks and pocket calculators

In addition to their importance to the internal structure of programming languages, stacks prove useful in other contexts as well. One of the most common applications is in electronic calculators, where stacks are often used to store intermediate results. Although stacks play a central role in the operation of most calculators, their role is easiest to see in scientific calculators that require users to enter expressions in a form called **reverse Polish notation, or RPN.**

In reverse Polish notation, operators are entered after the operands to which they apply. For example, to compute the result of the C expression

```
50.0 * 1.5 + 3.8 / 2.0
```

on an RPN calculator, you would enter the operations in the following order:

50.0 (ENTER) 1.5 (x) 3.8 (ENTER) 2.0 (/) (+)

When the **ENTER** button is pressed, the calculator takes the previous value and pushes it on a stack. When an operator button is pressed, the calculator first checks whether the user has just entered a value and, if so, automatically pushes it on the stack. It then computes the result of applying the operator by

- Popping the top two values from the stack
- Applying the arithmetic operation indicated by the button to these values
- Pushing the result back on the stack

Except when the user is actually typing in a number, the calculator display shows the value at the top of the stack. Thus, at each point in the operation, the calculator display and stack contain the values shown:

| Buttons | 50.0 (ENTER) 1.5 | (X) | 3.8 (ENTER) 2.0 | (/) | (+) |

Buttons	50.0	ENTER	1.5	X		3.8	ENTER	2.0	/	+
Display	50.0	50.0	1.5	75.0	3.8	3.8	2.0	1.9	76.9
Stack					3.8	3.8	1.9		
	50.0	50.0	75.0	75.0	75.0	75.0	75.0	76.9

■■■ 8.2 Defining a stack ADT

The RPN calculator exemplifies the use of stacks in a context that is relatively easy to implement. Before you can do so, however, you need to have a way to represent the stack on which the calculator is based. Moreover, because stacks are useful in a variety of application domains, it makes sense to define a general stack abstraction for use by clients, and not one that is suitable only for the RPN calculator.

As with most general abstractions, the best way to provide several clients with a tool for executing stack operations is to define a `stack.h` interface, which exports a stack data type and various functions clients will need to manipulate stacks. Those functions implement the primitive operations for the abstract stack type, which include, for example, creating a new stack, pushing an element onto an existing stack, and popping the top element from a stack.

Defining the types for the stack abstraction

Before defining the primitive operations, it is important to think for a moment about the data types that are involved in the stack abstraction. There are two types you need to consider: the type of element stored in the stack and the type of the stack itself. What data type should you use to represent each of these conceptual entities? This question is more subtle than it first appears. To answer it, you need to think carefully about the relationship between the stack abstraction and its clients. In particular, you must decide whether each type is part of the implementation or part of the client's domain.

It helps to begin by thinking about the values stored in the stack. All values in C have types. What then is the type of a stack element? The answer depends entirely on how the stack is used. If you are implementing a calculator, the stack elements are presumably floating-point numbers. If you are instead simulating the nested structure of function calls, the elements of the stack must represent the contents of a stack frame. Thus, the stack element type is a property of the client. To a large extent, it doesn't matter to the stack abstraction what values are stored in the stack, because the basic stack operations remain the same. When the client pushes a value on a stack, all the implementation has to do is store that value in the internal data structure. When the client later pops that element off the stack, the implementation can return the stored value to the client.

Even so, C requires that you specify the element type so that the functions exported by the package can declare parameters that refer to stack elements. For the purpose of the stack abstraction and similar abstract types that contain client-supplied data values, it would be ideal if C included a data type called **any** that would match any type at all. Some languages include this facility, which makes it easy to define functions that take values of arbitrary types. The ability to apply the same function to objects of different types is called **polymorphism.**

Unfortunately, true polymorphism is not possible in ANSI C. The closest thing the language provides is the type **void ***, which is defined to be compatible with any pointer type. For example, if you define the stack abstraction to use the type **void *** for the values in the stack, you can use stacks to store data of any pointer type. You could, for example, push strings on one stack and pointers to integers on another. You could even push values of different pointer types on the same stack, although you would then have to make sure your application has enough information to know which types are which.

In some cases, however, forcing the client to use pointers as data values imposes an unacceptable level of overhead. Imagine, for example, that you are implementing the calculator program described in the section entitled "Stacks and pocket calculators" earlier in this chapter. In that application, the stack needs to store values of type **double**, which are not pointers and are therefore incompatible with the type **void ***. If the **stack.h** interface is defined to use **void *** as the value type, you have to adopt the following strategy to push a value of type **double** on the stack:

1. Allocate space for a value of type **double** using **GetBlock** or **New**.
2. Assign the value you're trying to push into the newly allocated memory.
3. Push the address of the newly allocated **double** on the stack.

The address of a **double** is a valid pointer and is therefore compatible with the **void *** type used in the stack abstraction. When you later pop the value from the stack, you get back a pointer that must be dereferenced to obtain the actual value. The allocation and dereferencing operations complicate the structure of the calculator and make it harder for you to use the **stack.h** interface as a tool.

If you provide clients access to the source code for the stack package, you can increase the flexibility of the interface by using **typedef** to introduce a new name for the client-supplied type. For example, instead of referring to specific type names like **double** and **void ***, you can define all the prototypes in the **stack.h** interface in terms of the type name **stackElementT**. By changing the **typedef** line that defines **stackElementT**, you can create a stack that holds any type of value you need. For example, in the calculator example, you can add the following line to the **stack.h** interface:

```
typedef double stackElementT;
```

For other applications, you can substitute definitions of **stackElementT** appropriate to each particular domain.

Although allowing clients to change the definition of **stackElementT** offers additional flexibility, the strategy has important drawbacks that make it inappropriate in certain contexts. The most significant problem is that clients who wish to use a particular type of stack must edit the **stack.h** interface to change the definition of **stackElementT**. Allowing clients to change an interface violates the basic principles of abstraction that prompted the use of interfaces in the first place. Moreover, adopting this approach means that clients must have access to the implementation of the stack package so that they can compile it with the appropriate definition of `stackElementT`. If would be impossible, for example, to put a precompiled version of the stack package in a library and still allow clients to redefine the element type.

The problem, however, is that there really isn't an optimal design strategy in C. You would like to make it possible for clients to define the element type stored in a stack. At the same time, you would like to maintain the stability of the `stack.h` interface. Because of C's limitations, you cannot achieve both these goals simultaneously. The best you can do in this case is adopt the following compromise:

1. Define the `stack.h` interface in terms of the type `stackElementT`, thereby allowing clients with access to the source code to change the element type.
2. Export a "standard" version of the `stack.h` interface in which the type `stackElementT` is bound to `void *`.

The advantage of this approach is that clients who are content to work with stacks containing pointer values can simply use the exported version of the stack interface in which `stackElementT` is defined to be `void *`. On the other hand, clients who insist on greater efficiency can easily go back to the source code and build a version of the stack package that uses some other element type.

Opaque types

The next question is how to represent the stack itself. Unlike stack elements, which are in the *client's* domain, the stack itself is definitely the property of the *implementation*. Your package is responsible for being able to push values of `stackElementT` onto a stack and later retrieve them in a last-in/first-out order whenever the stack is popped. The implementation you write has to choose a representation for stacks that allows it to perform these operations. If possible, the client should be spared the implementation details.

In C, you can define a type in an interface so that its underlying representation remains hidden from clients. Because it is impossible for the client to look beyond the abstract type to its underlying representation, such types are said to be **opaque.** Exporting opaque types in an interface hides the details of data type representation in much the same way that exporting function prototypes hides the details of their underlying implementation.

To define an opaque type in C, you include in the interface an abstract type definition of the form

```
typedef struct nameCDT *nameADT;
```

where *name*ADT is the name of the abstract type, and *name*CDT is the name of the corresponding concrete type. For example, to define `stackADT` as an abstract type, the interface would include the following line:

```
typedef struct stackCDT *stackADT;
```

As far as C's syntax is concerned, this line defines the type `stackADT` as a pointer to a structure identified by the name `stackCDT`, which has not yet been defined. Because pointers are always the same size, the C compiler allows you to work with pointers to structures even if it does not know the details of the structure itself. In ANSI C, a structure that has not yet been defined is called an **incomplete type.**

In the implementation, you complete the type by writing the actual structure definition, which looks like this:

```
struct nameCDT {
    field declarations
};
```

The two definitions are linked by the identifier *name*CDT, which is called the **structure tag.** The abstract definition in the interface indicates that the type *name*ADT points to structures with the tag *name*CDT, which is defined only in the implementation. Clients of the interface see only the abstract type. Clients can declare variables of the abstract type and then manipulate the values of those variables as if they were atomic types. But because the compiler has no information about the underlying representation, clients are not able to dereference the abstract type to see how it is constructed. The implementation, on the other hand, defines the concrete type as well, which means that it is free to dereference the ADT pointer and gain access to the underlying representation.

Partly because it was not possible to do so in earlier implementations of C, many programmers do not bother to separate the underlying representation of a type from its abstract definition. If you include the concrete definition of a type in the interface, the program will still work correctly. In doing so, however, you lose both security and flexibility. If the client is permitted to cross the abstraction boundary and manipulate the internal representation directly, the client can destroy data the implementation needs. Using an abstract type denies the client access to that representation and protects the underlying data. Moreover, by taking the representation completely outside the client's domain, use of the abstract type mechanism makes it easier to modify the underlying representation.

Defining the `stack.h` interface

Because the client of an ADT has no direct access to the underlying representation, an abstract type is useful only if the interface also exports operations that define its behavior. Thus, in order to complete the design of the stack abstraction, you need to specify a set of functions that perform the basic stack operations.

Before you can push objects on a stack, you must first create one. Because the client does not have any knowledge of the underlying representation, the implementation must provide a function that creates a new `stackADT` and returns it to the client. As a general convention throughout this text, the names of functions that create new values of an abstract type begin with **New** to emphasize that dynamic allocation is involved. Thus, the function to create a new stack has the following prototype:

```
stackADT NewStack(void);
```

Whenever an interface defines a function for allocating a new value of an abstract type, it is customary for the interface to provide an additional function that frees the storage once the client no longer needs to use it. Because the client has no idea what storage may have been allocated within the internal representation, the only way to free that storage—should it become necessary to do so—is to let the implementation handle the task. Thus, in addition to the function `NewStack`, you need a symmetric function

```
void FreeStack(stackADT stack);
```

that takes a buffer and relinquishes any dynamically allocated storage it contains.

The `Push` function takes a stack and adds a new element, so its prototype is

```
void Push(stackADT stack, stackElementT element);
```

The `Pop` function takes a stack, removes its top element, and returns that element to the caller. It therefore has this prototype:

```
stackElementT Pop(stackADT stack);
```

In addition to these primitive operations, it is often necessary to determine the number of elements a stack contains, or at least whether the stack is empty or full. These operations are provided by the functions `StackDepth`, `StackIsEmpty`, and `StackIsFull`, which have the following prototypes:

```
int StackDepth(stackADT stack);
bool StackIsEmpty(stackADT stack);
bool StackIsFull(stackADT stack);
```

Finally, it is sometimes useful—particularly when writing code to help debug an application—to be able to look at stack elements without changing their values. The function `GetStackElement`, defined by the prototype

```
stackElementT GetStackElement(stackADT stack, int index);
```

takes a stack and an index and returns the element which is at that level in the stack. Because index 0 is defined to be at the top, `GetStackElement(stack, 0)` returns the top element in a stack without removing it, `GetStackElement(stack, 1)` returns the next element down, and so on. Calling `GetStackElement` on an index that is outside the range of previously pushed values generates an error.

The prototypes given above, together with the English descriptions of the behavior of those functions, are pretty much all you need to write the interface for the `stack.h` abstraction, which is shown in Figure 8-1. This version of the interface defines `stackElementT` to be `double`, making it appropriate to the calculator application. For other applications, you can edit the `typedef` line and create a new abstraction that corresponds to the requirements of that application.

FIGURE 8-1 Interface for the stack abstraction

```
/*
 * File: stack.h
 * -------------
 * This interface defines an abstraction for stacks.  In any
 * single application that uses this interface, the values in
 * the stack are constrained to a single type, although it
 * is easy to change that type by changing the definition of
 * stackElementT in this interface.
 */

#ifndef _stack_h
#define _stack_h

#include "genlib.h"

/*
 * Type: stackElementT
 * -------------------
 * The type stackElementT is used in this interface to indicate
 * the type of values that can be stored in the stack.  Here the
 * stack is used to store values of type double, but that can
 * be changed by editing this definition line.
 */

typedef double stackElementT;

/*
 * Type: stackADT
 * --------------
 * The type stackADT represents the abstract type used to store
 * the elements that have been pushed.  Because stackADT is
 * defined only as a pointer to a concrete structure that is not
 * itself defined in the interface, clients have no access to
 * the underlying fields.
 */

typedef struct stackCDT *stackADT;

/*
 * Function: NewStack
 * Usage: stack = NewStack();
 * --------------------------
 * This function allocates and returns a new stack, which is
 * initially empty.
 */

stackADT NewStack(void);
```

```
/*
 * Function: FreeStack
 * Usage: FreeStack(stack);
 * ------------------------
 * This function frees the storage associated with the stack.
 */

void FreeStack(stackADT stack);

/*
 * Function: Push
 * Usage: Push(stack, element);
 * ----------------------------
 * This function pushes the specified element onto the stack.
 */

void Push(stackADT stack, stackElementT element);

/*
 * Function: Pop
 * Usage: element = Pop(stack);
 * ----------------------------
 * This function pops the top element from the stack and returns
 * that value.  The first value popped is always the last one
 * that was pushed.  If the stack is empty when Pop is called,
 * the function calls Error with an appropriate message.
 */

stackElementT Pop(stackADT stack);

/*
 * Functions: StackIsEmpty, StackIsFull
 * Usage: if (StackIsEmpty(stack)) . . .
 *        if (StackIsFull(stack)) . . .
 * -------------------------------------
 * This functions test whether the stack is empty or full.
 */

bool StackIsEmpty(stackADT stack);
bool StackIsFull(stackADT stack);

/*
 * Function: StackDepth
 * Usage: depth = StackDepth(stack);
 * ---------------------------------
 * This function returns the number of elements currently pushed
 * on the stack.
 */

int StackDepth(stackADT stack);
```

```
/*
 * Function: GetStackElement
 * Usage: element = GetStackElement(stack, index);
 * ------------------------------------------------
 * This function returns the element at the specified index in
 * the stack, where the top of the stack is defined as index 0.
 * For example, calling GetStackElement(stack, 0) returns the top
 * element on the stack without removing it.  If the caller tries
 * to select an out-of-range element, GetStackElement calls Error.
 * Note: This function is not a fundamental stack operation and
 * is instead provided principally to facilitate debugging.
 */

stackElementT GetStackElement(stackADT stack, int index);

#endif
```

■ 8.3 Using stacks in an application

Completing the specification of the stack interface represents a significant milestone, and it is important not to underrate the importance of this achievement. Once the interface is complete, you can immediately shift your focus to application programs, because you now have names and prototypes for all the relevant operations. For example, you could use the structure provided by the interface to write a program that simulates the operation of the RPN calculator introduced earlier in this chapter in the section entitled "Stacks and pocket calculators."

The code for the calculator application appears in Figure 8-2. A sample run of the program looks like this:

```
RPN Calculator Simulation (type H for help)
> 50.0↵
> 1.5↵
> *↵
75
> 3.8↵
> 2.0↵
> /↵
1.9
> +↵
76.9
> Q↵
```

Because the user enters each number on a separate line terminated with the Return key, there is no need for any counterpart to the calculator's ENTER button, which really serves only to indicate that a number is complete. The calculator program can just push all numbers on the stack as the user enters them. When the calculator reads an operator, it simply pops the top two elements from the stack, applies the operator, displays the result, and then pushes the result back on the stack.

FIGURE 8-2   Implementation of a calculator that uses reverse Polish notation

```c
/*
 * File: rpncalc.c
 * ---------------
 * This program simulates an electronic calculator that uses
 * reverse Polish notation, in which the operators come after
 * the operands to which they apply.
 */

#include <stdio.h>
#include <ctype.h>
#include "genlib.h"
#include "simpio.h"
#include "strlib.h"
#include "stack.h"

/* Private function prototypes */

static void ApplyOperator(char op, stackADT operandStack);
static void HelpCommand(void);
static void ClearStack(stackADT operandStack);
static void DisplayStack(stackADT operandStack);

/* Main program */

main()
{
    stackADT operandStack;
    string line;
    char ch;

    printf("RPN Calculator Simulation (type H for help)\n");
    operandStack = NewStack();
    while (TRUE) {
        printf("> ");
        line = GetLine();
        ch = toupper(line[0]);
        switch (ch) {
          case 'Q': exit(0);
          case 'H': HelpCommand(); break;
          case 'C': ClearStack(operandStack); break;
          case 'S': DisplayStack(operandStack); break;
          default:
            if (isdigit(ch)) {
                Push(operandStack, StringToReal(line));
            } else {
                ApplyOperator(ch, operandStack);
            }
            break;
        }
    }
}
```

```
/* Private functions */

/*
 * Function: ApplyOperator
 * Usage: ApplyOperator(op, operandStack);
 * -----------------------------------------
 * This function applies the operator to the top two elements on
 * the operand stack.  Because the elements on the stack are
 * popped in reverse order, the right operand is popped before
 * the left operand.
 */

static void ApplyOperator(char op, stackADT operandStack)
{
    double lhs, rhs, result;

    rhs = Pop(operandStack);
    lhs = Pop(operandStack);
    switch (op) {
      case '+': result = lhs + rhs; break;
      case '-': result = lhs - rhs; break;
      case '*': result = lhs * rhs; break;
      case '/': result = lhs / rhs; break;
      default:  Error("Illegal operator %c", op);
    }
    printf("%g\n", result);
    Push(operandStack, result);
}


/*
 * Function: HelpCommand
 * Usage: HelpCommand();
 * ---------------------
 * This function generates a help message for the user.
 */

static void HelpCommand(void)
{
    printf("Enter expressions in Reverse Polish Notation,\n");
    printf("in which operators follow the operands to which\n");
    printf("they apply.  Each line consists of a number, an\n");
    printf("operator, or one of the following commands:\n");
    printf("  Q -- Quit the program\n");
    printf("  H -- Display this help message\n");
    printf("  C -- Clear the calculator stack\n");
    printf("  S -- Display all values in the stack\n");
}
```

```
/*
 * Function: ClearStack
 * Usage: ClearStack(stack);
 * ------------------------
 * This function clears the stack by popping elements until it is
 * empty.
 */

static void ClearStack(stackADT stack)
{
    while (!StackIsEmpty(stack)) {
        (void) Pop(stack);
    }
}

/*
 * Function: DisplayStack
 * Usage: DisplayStack(stack);
 * ---------------------------
 * This function displays the contents of a stack.
 */

static void DisplayStack(stackADT stack)
{
    int i, depth;

    printf("Stack: ");
    depth = StackDepth(stack);
    if (depth == 0) {
        printf("empty\n");
    } else {
        for (i = depth - 1; i >= 0; i--) {
            if (i < depth - 1) printf(", ");
            printf("%g", GetStackElement(stack, i));
        }
        printf("\n");
    }
}
```

In addition to numbers and operators, the calculator program accepts the following commands from the user:

- The letter Q, which causes the program to quit[1]
- The letter H, which prints a help message
- The letter C, which clears any values left on the stack
- The letter S, which displays the entire contents of the calculator stack

---

[1] The Q command is implemented by calling the ANSI function `exit`, which is exported by the `stdlib.h` interface. The argument to `exit` indicates the termination status, with 0 indicating normal termination. This function is often useful when you need to exit from the program at some deeply nested point in the code.

The program checks explicitly for each of these command letters. If the first character on the command line is one of these letters, the program calls a function to perform the corresponding operation. If the first character is a digit, the program calls `StringToReal` to convert the input string to a `double` and then pushes the resulting value on the stack. In all other cases, the program calls the function `ApplyOperator`, which checks to see that the operator is legal and, if so, performs the necessary calculation.

■ 8.4 Implementing the stack abstraction

Before you can run the `rpncalc.c` program, however, someone—this might be you or some other programmer if you're working in a larger team—needs to supply the code to implement the `stack.h` interface. As with any interface, implementing `stack.h` consists of writing a module, presumably named `stack.c`, that supplies the code for the exported functions and the representational details of the abstract type.

Defining the concrete type

The first thing you need to do is provide some concrete representation for the abstract type `stackADT`. The most common approach is to use an array to hold the elements currently on the stack and then to specify a count indicating the number of elements currently in the stack. This design suggests the following representation:

```
#define MaxStackSize 100

struct stackCDT {
    stackElementT elements[MaxStackSize];
    int count;
};
```

As elements are pushed on the stack, you store the new element in the next available space in the array and increment the count. As elements are popped, you decrement the count and return the top element. Since all operations happen at the end of the array, the execution cost of the stack operations is independent of the number of elements already on the stack. Thus, the stack operations `Push` and `Pop` are each $O(1)$.

Implementing the stack operations

As you can see from the implementation in Figure 8-3, the operations in the stack abstraction are all extremely simple. None of the functions implemented in `stack.c` requires more than four lines of code, and several are implemented using only a single line. For example, the `StackDepth` function has the following, rather short definition:

```
int StackDepth(stackADT stack)
{
    return (stack->count);
}
```

FIGURE 8-3   Simple implementation of the stack abstraction

```
/*
 * File: stack.c
 * -------------
 * This file implements the stack.h interface.  Note that the
 * implementation is independent of the type of value stored
 * in the stack.  That type is defined by the interface as
 * the type name stackElementT.
 */

#include <stdio.h>
#include "genlib.h"
#include "stack.h"

/*
 * Constant: MaxStackSize
 * ----------------------
 * This constant specifies the amount of space to allocate for
 * the array that holds the stack elements.  Attempts to push
 * more than this many values will result in an error.
 */

#define MaxStackSize 100

/*
 * Type: stackCDT
 * --------------
 * The type stackCDT is the concrete representation of the type
 * stackADT defined by the interface.  In this implementation,
 * the elements are stored in an array.  Because this type
 * definition appears only in the implementation and not in the
 * interface, the definition can be changed as long as the
 * abstract behavior of the type remains the same.
 */

struct stackCDT {
    stackElementT elements[MaxStackSize];
    int count;
};

/* Exported entries */

stackADT NewStack(void)
{
    stackADT stack;

    stack = New(stackADT);
    stack->count = 0;
    return (stack);
}
```

```
void FreeStack(stackADT stack)
{
    FreeBlock(stack);
}

void Push(stackADT stack, stackElementT element)
{
    if (StackIsFull(stack)) Error("Stack size exceeded");
    stack->elements[stack->count++] = element;
}

stackElementT Pop(stackADT stack)
{
    if (StackIsEmpty(stack)) Error("Pop of an empty stack");
    return (stack->elements[--stack->count]);
}

bool StackIsEmpty(stackADT stack)
{
    return (stack->count == 0);
}

bool StackIsFull(stackADT stack)
{
    return (stack->count == MaxStackSize);
}

int StackDepth(stackADT stack)
{
    return (stack->count);
}

stackElementT GetStackElement(stackADT stack, int index)
{
    if (index < 0 || index >= stack->count) {
        Error("Non-existent stack element");
    }
    return (stack->elements[stack->count - index - 1]);
}
```

The advantages of opaque types

To beginning programmers, defining a one-line function like **StackDepth** sometimes seems wasteful. If the concrete type structure had been defined in the interface, you could eliminate this function entirely and simply have the client write

```
stack->count
```

instead of

```
StackDepth(stack)
```

Given that the first form is shorter and easier to type, you might argue that removing this function would simplify both the implementation and the client code. This argument, however, is shortsighted and fails to give sufficient weight to the importance of abstraction boundaries to good software engineering.

The expression

```
stack->count
```

represents a violation of the `stackADT` abstraction. As a client, you shouldn't know what fields exist in the record that lies underneath the pointer variable `stack`. If clients use the name `count` in their programs, those programs now depend on the specific structure of the `stackADT` representation. If someone wanted to change that implementation in the future—something that the implementor should feel free to do as long as the abstract interface remains unchanged—all the programs that relied on this piece of "forbidden knowledge" would break. By using the

```
StackDepth(stack)
```

form, you provide a layer of insulation between the client and the implementation. An implementor's decision to change the representation should not affect clients of the `StackDepth` function at all, as long as the implementor guarantees to preserve its behavior as advertised in the interface. Change is a fact of life in software engineering, and it is always best to prepare for it as well as you can.

Improving the `stack.c` implementation

One useful change that you might decide to make in the stack implementation is to remove the arbitrary limitation on the size of the array. The easiest way to do so is to make the array dynamic and reallocate space for a new, larger array whenever space in the old array is exhausted. You therefore need to change the concrete type structure so that it provides a pointer to a dynamic array whose elements are of type `stackElementT`. In addition, because the size of the array is no longer constant, the structure will need to keep track of the allocated size. The new concrete representation is therefore

```
struct stackCDT {
    stackElementT *elements;
    int count;
    int size;
};
```

This change in representation requires a change in the implementation of several functions, starting with `NewStack`. With the new representation, it is no longer sufficient to create only the concrete type structure and return that pointer. You now need to allocate initial space to the array. The easiest approach is to use the `NewArray` function from `genlib.h`, which creates a dynamic array of a given size and base type. If you assume that the initial stack size is given by the constant `InitialStackSize`, the updated definition of `NewStack` is

```
stackADT NewStack(void)
{
    stackADT stack;

    stack = New(stackADT);
    stack->elements = NewArray(InitialStackSize, stackElementT);
    stack->count = 0;
    stack->size = InitialStackSize;
    return (stack);
}
```

Once you have made this change, you also need to change the definition of
FreeStack. The new concrete structure contains internal storage that is allocated
from the heap, which needs to be freed along with the storage for the block itself.
The new definition is then

```
void FreeStack(stackADT stack)
{
    FreeBlock(stack->elements);
    FreeBlock(stack);
}
```

The other major change is the definition of **Push**, which must now expand the stack
if necessary. Implementing this change is easiest if you define an auxiliary function
ExpandStack to do the actual expansion. If you adopt this approach, the **Push**
function looks like this:

```
void Push(stackADT stack, stackElementT element)
{
    if (stack->count == stack->size) ExpandStack(stack);
    stack->elements[stack->count++] = element;
}
```

where **ExpandStack** is given by

```
static void ExpandStack(stackADT stack)
{
    stackElementT *array;
    int i, newSize;

    newSize = stack->size * 2;
    array = NewArray(newSize, stackElementT);
    for (i = 0; i < stack->size; i++) {
        array[i] = stack->elements[i];
    }
    FreeBlock(stack->elements);
    stack->elements = array;
    stack->size = newSize;
}
```

Here, the **ExpandStack** function simply doubles the size of the stack. It allocates a
new array of the larger size, copies items from the old array into the new one, frees

the storage occupied by the old array, and then stores the pointer to the new array in the stack structure.

The final required change is in the function `StackIsFull`. In the dynamic stack implementation, stacks are never full. On the other hand, you can't simply eliminate this function from the interface, because existing clients may call it. You should instead rewrite the function so that it always returns `FALSE`, as follows:

```
bool StackIsFull(stackADT stack)
{
    return (FALSE);
}
```

Making these changes to the implementation requires you to modify the definition of the concrete type used for the `stackCDT` structure. Such changes are feasible only if the type is private to the implementation and not part of the interface. If the concrete type is exported, some client will almost certainly write code that depends on a specific detail of that structure. Because this client's program would then be invalidated by the change in representation, the process of upgrading the interface would be much more difficult.

■ 8.5 Defining a scanner ADT

When you read text on a page, you don't ordinarily pay much attention to the individual letters. Your eye instead groups letters together to form words, which it then recognizes as independent units. A program that does the same thing is called a **scanner.** Chapter 10 of *The Art and Science of C* introduces a simple scanner abstraction that divides a string into its component **tokens,** which are defined to be either

- A sequence of consecutive alphanumeric characters (letters or digits), or
- A single-character string consisting of a space or punctuation mark

For example, if the scanner were initialized to extract tokens from the string

```
This line contains 10 tokens.
```

successive calls to the scanner package would return the individual tokens shown here in boxes:

| This | | line | | contains | | 10 | | tokens | . |

The dangers of encapsulated state

Although the design of the scanner module made sense given the level of the earlier text, its use of global variables—even though they are declared as `static` and are therefore private to the module—limits the utility of the scanner package. Those global variables were introduced because the scanner needed to maintain state between function calls. Information that is maintained privately within a module in this way is called **encapsulated state.** Although encapsulated state is not always bad, it has a significant drawback: any module that uses it can have only one copy of the state information available at any particular time. In the case of the scanner, this restriction means that, as long as you are using the scanner in one part of your program and need to preserve the active state, you cannot use the scanner again in some other part of your code.

This problem presents the greatest danger in a large application that is designed at many different levels of abstraction. For instance, suppose you are working on a large project for which your particular responsibility is designing a simple interface that provides tools for dividing the name of a file into its component parts. Such an interface might export a function `RootName` that returns the part of its argument string prior to the first dot, so that `RootName("test.dat")` returns the string `"test"`. You could, of course, implement such a function using string operations, but you might be tempted to call the scanner into service instead. After all, the scanner module will happily divide the string `"test.dat"` into these three tokens:

If you carry through with this design, you will end up creating a layered abstraction hierarchy in which your module sits on top of the scanner module as a client, as follows:

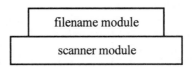

Layered abstractions are often very useful. In this case, however, the fact that the scanner module relies on encapsulated state creates dependencies that may be hard for clients to recognize. Suppose, for example, that some other programmer working on your project decides to use your filename module. That decision has an unexpected cost, because it rules out using the scanner simultaneously. Calling the entries in the filename module—if these entries are indeed implemented using the scanner package—will destroy the internal state maintained by the scanner if it is being used by some other client. Such hidden dependencies complicate the problem of maintaining the system and can lead to bugs that are extremely hard to find.

Abstract data types as an alternative to encapsulated state

Abstract data types make it possible to avoid the problems associated with encapsulated state and provide a much cleaner basis for the design of a package like the scanner. Instead of maintaining private data within the implementation module in global variables, the scanner can define a new abstract type called `scannerADT` that is capable of storing the same information. Because `scannerADT` is an abstract type, the details of the representation are hidden from the client, which means that the integrity of the internal representation has not been compromised in any way. The principal difference is that this new design allows multiple instances of the scanner data. Whenever a client wants to use the scanner abstraction, all it needs to do is ask for a new value of type **scannerADT** from the scanner package. Thereafter, all calls to the scanner module executed on behalf of that client will pass in that same value, so the scanner can have access to the private state information that is relevant to the client's operation.

An interface that uses this design, called **scanadt.h** to avoid confusion with the more primitive **scanner.h** interface from *The Art and Science of C*, is shown in Figure 8-4. To use the **scanadt.h** interface, you must go through the following steps:

1. *Create a new scanner instance.* Before you can make any other calls on the scanner package, your first responsibility is to call the function **NewScanner**, which returns a new **scannerADT** instance that you can save in a variable using a statement like

    ```
    myScanner = NewScanner();
    ```

    In all subsequent calls to the scanner package, you need to pass **myScanner** as an argument so the scanner can distinguish your use of the scanner from that of all the other clients.

2. *Initialize the scanner string.* Once you have a scanner instance, you can then initialize your scanner by calling

    ```
    SetScannerString(myScanner, str);
    ```

    where **str** is the string from which the tokens are scanned.

3. *Read tokens from the scanner.* Once you have initialized the scanner string, you can process each of its tokens individually by calling **ReadToken(myScanner)** for each token in the stored string. When all the tokens have been consumed, the function **MoreTokensExist(myScanner)** returns **FALSE**, which means that the standard idiom for iterating through each token in turn looks like this:

    ```
    while (MoreTokensExist(myScanner)) {
        token = ReadToken(myScanner);
        Do something with the token you've found.
    }
    ```

    Because it is often more convenient to check for a sentinel value than to call **MoreTokensExist**, the **ReadToken** function returns the empty string if it is called after the last token has been read.

4. *Free the scanner instance when all processing is complete.* You can use the same scanner instance many times by calling **SetScannerString** for each string you want to process. When you are entirely finished, you can free the storage associated with the scanner by calling **FreeScanner(myScanner)**.

FIGURE 8-4   Interface for the scanner abstraction

```
/*
 * File: scanadt.h
 * ---------------
 * This file is the interface to a module that exports an abstract
 * data type to facilitate dividing a string into logical units
 * called "tokens," which are either
 *
 * 1. Strings of consecutive letters and digits representing words
 * 2. One-character strings representing punctuation or separators
 *
 * To use this package, you must first create an instance of a
 * scannerADT by calling
 *
 *     scanner = NewScanner();
 *
 * All other calls to the scanner package take this variable as their
 * first argument to identify a particular instance of the abstract
 * scanner type.
 *
 * You initialize the scanner to hold a particular string by calling
 *
 *     SetScannerString(scanner, str);
 *
 * where str is the string from which tokens should be read.  To
 * retrieve each individual token, you make the following call:
 *
 *     token = ReadToken(scanner);
 *
 * To determine whether any tokens remain to be read, you can call
 * the predicate function MoreTokensExist(scanner).  The ReadToken
 * function returns the empty string after the last token is read.
 *
 * The following code fragment serves as an idiom for processing
 * each token in the string inputString:
 *
 *     scanner = NewScanner();
 *     SetScannerString(scanner, inputString);
 *     while (MoreTokensExist(scanner)) {
 *         token = ReadToken(scanner);
 *         . . . process the token . . .
 *     }
 *
 * This version of scanadt.h also supports the following extensions,
 * which are documented later in the interface:
 *
 *    SaveToken
 *    SetScannerSpaceOption
 */

#ifndef _scanadt_h
#define _scanadt_h
```

```
#include "genlib.h"

/*
 * Type: scannerADT
 * ----------------
 * This type is the abstract type used to represent a single instance
 * of a scanner.  As with any abstract type, the details of the
 * internal representation are hidden from the client.
 */

typedef struct scannerCDT *scannerADT;

/*
 * Function: NewScanner
 * Usage: scanner = NewScanner();
 * ------------------------------
 * This function creates a new scanner instance.  All other functions
 * in this interface take this scanner value as their first argument
 * so that they can identify what particular instance of the scanner
 * is in use.  This design makes it possible for clients to have more
 * than one scanner process active at the same time.
 */

scannerADT NewScanner(void);

/*
 * Function: FreeScanner
 * Usage: FreeScanner(scanner);
 * ----------------------------
 * This function frees the storage associated with scanner.
 */

void FreeScanner(scannerADT scanner);

/*
 * Function: SetScannerString
 * Usage: SetScannerString(scanner, str);
 * --------------------------------------
 * This function initializes the scanner so that it will start
 * extracting tokens from the string str.
 */

void SetScannerString(scannerADT scanner, string str);

/*
 * Function: ReadToken
 * Usage: token = ReadToken(scanner);
 * ----------------------------------
 * This function returns the next token from scanner.  If
 * ReadToken is called when no tokens are available, it returns
 * the empty string.  The token returned by ReadToken is always
 * allocated in the heap, which means that clients can call
 * FreeBlock when the token is no longer needed.
 */

string ReadToken(scannerADT scanner);
```

```
/*
 * Function: MoreTokensExist
 * Usage: if (MoreTokensExist(scanner)) . . .
 * -----------------------------------------
 * This function returns TRUE as long as there are additional
 * tokens for the scanner to read.
 */

bool MoreTokensExist(scannerADT scanner);

/*
 * Function: SaveToken
 * Usage: SaveToken(scanner, token);
 * ---------------------------------
 * This function stores the token in the scanner data structure
 * in such a way that the next time ReadToken is called, it will
 * return that token without reading any additional characters
 * from the input.
 */

void SaveToken(scannerADT scanner, string token);

/*
 * Functions: SetScannerSpaceOption, GetScannerSpaceOption
 * Usage: SetScannerSpaceOption(scanner, option);
 *        option = GetScannerSpaceOption(scanner);
 * ------------------------------------------------------
 * The SetScannerSpaceOption function controls whether the scanner
 * ignores whitespace characters or treats them as valid tokens.
 * By default, the ReadToken function treats whitespace characters,
 * such as spaces and tabs, just like any other punctuation mark.
 * If, however, you call
 *
 *    SetScannerSpaceOption(scanner, IgnoreSpaces);
 *
 * the scanner will skip over any white space before reading a token.
 * You can restore the original behavior by calling
 *
 *    SetScannerSpaceOption(scanner, PreserveSpaces);
 *
 * The GetScannerSpaceOption function returns the current setting
 * of this option.
 */

typedef enum { PreserveSpaces, IgnoreSpaces } spaceOptionT;

void SetScannerSpaceOption(scannerADT scanner, spaceOptionT option);
spaceOptionT GetScannerSpaceOption(scannerADT scanner);

#endif
```

Primarily because they are useful in later chapters, the `scanadt.h` interface supports the following extensions:

- *The interface provides the option of ignoring whitespace characters in tokens.* When a scanner is used to read program text in a language like C, spaces and tabs are used only to separate individual tokens and have no other significance. If you were using the scanner abstraction to write a C compiler, for example, it would be useful for it to discard such characters automatically. The `scanadt.h` interface includes a function `SetScannerSpaceOption` that allows the client to control how the scanner treats whitespace characters, for which the `isspace` function in the ANSI `ctype.h` interface returns `TRUE`. By default, a scanner returns spaces just like other punctuation characters. If, however, you call the function

      SetScannerSpaceOption(scanner, IgnoreSpaces);

  the scanner will ignore whitespace characters in any subsequent calls.

- *The interface allows the client to save a token in the scanner stream.* When you are writing applications that use the scanner package, you can often simplify the structure of your code if the scanner package allows you to "unread" a token by putting it back in the scanner input stream. In the `scanadt.h` interface, clients can save tokens by calling

      SaveToken(scanner, *token*);

  which sets the internal data structure of the scanner so that it returns *token* on the next call to `ReadToken`. This function is conceptually similar to the `ungetc` function in the standard I/O library, which makes it possible to back up one character if you discover that you've read too far ahead.

Implementing the scanner abstraction

The implementation of the `scanadt.h` interface is similar to the one used to implement the more primitive scanner interface from *The Art and Science of C*. The most significant difference is that the new implementation maintains its private state in the record used as the concrete counterpart of the `scannerADT` type. The definition of the `scannerCDT` type looks like this:

```
struct scannerCDT {
    string str;
    int len;
    int cp;
    string savedToken;
    spaceOptionT spaceOption;
};
```

The complete implementation of the scanner package is shown in Figure 8-5. Most of it is straightforward. The only function that is at all complicated is `ReadToken`, but even its logic follows directly from the definition of what constitutes a token.

FIGURE 8-5 Implementation of the scanner

```
/*
 * File: scanadt.c
 * ---------------
 * This file implements the scanadt.h interface.
 */

#include <stdio.h>
#include <ctype.h>
#include "genlib.h"
#include "strlib.h"
#include "scanadt.h"

/*
 * Type: scannerCDT
 * ----------------
 * This structure is the concrete representation of the type
 * scannerADT, which is exported by this interface.  Its purpose
 * is to maintain the state of the scanner between calls.  The
 * details of the representation are invisible to the client,
 * but consist of the following fields:
 *
 * str         -- Copy of string passed to SetScannerString
 * len         -- Length of string, saved for efficiency
 * cp          -- Current character position in the string
 * savedToken  -- String saved by SaveToken (NULL indicates none)
 * spaceOption -- Setting of the space option extension
 */

struct scannerCDT {
    string str;
    int len;
    int cp;
    string savedToken;
    spaceOptionT spaceOption;
};

/* Private function prototypes */

static void SkipSpaces(scannerADT scanner);
static int ScanToEndOfIdentifier(scannerADT scanner);

/* Exported entries */

scannerADT NewScanner(void)
{
    scannerADT scanner;

    scanner = New(scannerADT);
    scanner->str = NULL;
    scanner->spaceOption = PreserveSpaces;
    return (scanner);
}
```

```
void FreeScanner(scannerADT scanner)
{
    if (scanner->str != NULL) FreeBlock(scanner->str);
    FreeBlock(scanner);
}

void SetScannerString(scannerADT scanner, string str)
{
    if (scanner->str != NULL) FreeBlock(scanner->str);
    scanner->str = CopyString(str);
    scanner->len = StringLength(str);
    scanner->cp = 0;
    scanner->savedToken = NULL;
}

string ReadToken(scannerADT scanner)
{
    char ch;
    string token;
    int start, finish;

    if (scanner->str == NULL) {
        Error("SetScannerString has not been called");
    }
    if (scanner->savedToken != NULL) {
        token = scanner->savedToken;
        scanner->savedToken = NULL;
        return (token);
    }
    if (scanner->spaceOption == IgnoreSpaces) SkipSpaces(scanner);
    start = finish = scanner->cp;
    if (start >= scanner->len) return (CopyString(""));
    ch = scanner->str[scanner->cp];
    if (isalnum(ch)) {
        finish = ScanToEndOfIdentifier(scanner);
    } else {
        scanner->cp++;
    }
    return (SubString(scanner->str, start, finish));
}

bool MoreTokensExist(scannerADT scanner)
{
    if (scanner->str == NULL) {
        Error("SetScannerString has not been called");
    }
    if (scanner->savedToken != NULL) {
        return (!StringEqual(scanner->savedToken, ""));
    }
    if (scanner->spaceOption == IgnoreSpaces) SkipSpaces(scanner);
    return (scanner->cp < scanner->len);
}
```

```c
void SaveToken(scannerADT scanner, string token)
{
    if (scanner->str == NULL) {
        Error("SetScannerString has not been called");
    }
    if (scanner->savedToken != NULL) {
        Error("Token has already been saved");
    }
    scanner->savedToken = token;
}

void SetScannerSpaceOption(scannerADT scanner, spaceOptionT option)
{
    scanner->spaceOption = option;
}

spaceOptionT GetScannerSpaceOption(scannerADT scanner)
{
    return (scanner->spaceOption);
}

/* Private functions */

/*
 * Function: SkipSpaces
 * Usage: SkipSpaces(scanner);
 * -----------------------------
 * This function advances the position of the scanner until the
 * current character is not a whitespace character.
 */

static void SkipSpaces(scannerADT scanner)
{
    while (isspace(scanner->str[scanner->cp])) {
        scanner->cp++;
    }
}

/*
 * Function: ScanToEndOfIdentifier
 * Usage: finish = ScanToEndOfIdentifier(scanner);
 * -----------------------------------------------------
 * This function advances the position of the scanner until it
 * reaches the end of a sequence of letters or digits that make
 * up an identifier.  The return value is the index of the last
 * character in the identifier; the value of the stored index
 * cp is the first character after that.
 */

static int ScanToEndOfIdentifier(scannerADT scanner)
{
    while (isalnum(scanner->str[scanner->cp])) {
        scanner->cp++;
    }
    return (scanner->cp - 1);
}
```

A few subtleties in the code are worth special mention. At two places in the scanner implementation, the code calls the `CopyString` function in the `strlib.h` library. The first call occurs in `SetScannerString`, which initializes the string in the ADT using the line

```
scanner->str = CopyString(str);
```

Why is it important to copy the value of `str` in this context? The basic answer is that doing so preserves the separation between the client and the implementation. If you consider the situation from the implementation side, you realize that you have no control over what the client does with the string passed to `SetScannerString`. That string might be a statically allocated character buffer, in which case the situation on the client's side of the interface might look like this:

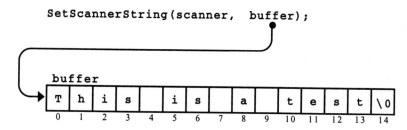

The value passed to `SetScannerString` as the parameter `str` is the address of `buffer`, which is part of the client domain. If the scanner package simply stores the value of that pointer in the data structure for the ADT, the string the scanner package thinks it has will change if the client ever overwrites the contents of `buffer`. On the other hand, if the `SetScannerString` function copies the string provided by the client, this problem goes away. The client is then free to change the contents of buffer because doing so has no effect on the copy of its original contents stored in the scanner data structures.

The second occurrence of `CopyString` appears in the following line of the `ReadToken` function:

```
if (cp >= scanner->len) return (CopyString(""));
```

This line ensures that the scanner returns the empty string if no input characters remain in the string. The interesting question is why the implementation bothers to copy the empty string before returning it to the client. Wouldn't it be just as good to return the empty string itself as a constant?

There are two reasons for returning a copy in this case. First, doing so protects the implementation from careless or malicious clients. Returning a pointer to storage in your own domain represents a security loophole because it allows a client to overwrite the target of that pointer, which can have unpredictable and potentially disastrous consequences. The second reason, however, is perhaps more important because it affects even those well-disciplined clients who are not trying to change data within the scanner package. If you look carefully at the code, you will see that

`ReadToken` always returns a newly allocated string, because the result is produced by calling a function that allocates new storage, such as `SubString` or `CharToString`. By being careful to allocate the empty string as well, the `ReadToken` function can guarantee the client that the storage is always newly allocated, which in turn means that the client is always entitled to call `FreeBlock` on any token returned by `ReadToken`.

Summary

In this chapter, you have learned how to use abstract data types, or ADTs, which are defined by their behavior instead of their representation. In most cases, an ADT is exported by an interface along with a set of functions that allow the client to create and manipulate values of the abstract type. The interface exports the ADT using the idiom

```
typedef struct nameCDT *nameADT;
```

which defines the ADT as a pointer to an incomplete structure whose representation is unspecified. In the implementation, the concrete structure is revealed using a definition of the following form:

```
struct nameCDT {
    field declarations
}
```

Because the implementation has access to the underlying representation, the code for the functions on the implementation side of the interface boundary can select the fields in the underlying structure. The code on the client side of the interface has no access to the definition of the concrete structure and therefore cannot refer to these fields.

Hiding the underlying representation of an ADT from the client has three critical advantages as a software engineering technique:

1. *Simplicity.* The representation of the underlying type is left unspecified, which means that there are fewer details for the client to understand.
2. *Flexibility.* The implementor is free to enhance the underlying representation as long as the functions in the interface continue to behave in the same way.
3. *Security.* The interface barrier prevents the client from making unexpected changes in the internal structure.

Other important points in this chapter include:

- A *stack* is a programming structure whose abstract behavior is defined by the property that items are removed from a stack in the opposite order from which they were added: the last element in is the first element out. Adding a new value to a stack is called *pushing* that value; removing the most recent item is called *popping* the stack.

- The type of data value in a stack must be determined by the client. Unfortunately, ANSI C provides no ideal mechanism for defining a polymorphic interface that allows the same interface to work with many different types. It is possible to obtain a degree of polymorphism by using the type **void *** as the base type, although doing so limits the client to using pointer types. Another approach is to define the interface in terms of a new type name like **stackElementT** so that any dependence on the base type is limited to a single definition.
- Defining stacks as an ADT makes it possible to change their underlying representation without forcing clients to change their code. In this chapter, for example, stacks are implemented using both static and dynamic arrays.
- Using ADTs is usually preferable to the technique of maintaining encapsulated state using global variables in a module. The principal advantage of the ADT approach is that it allows clients to make more than one copy of the ADT. Each ADT value identifies a particular instance of the abstraction and provides a structure in which the private data for each instance can be kept separately.
- The ADT approach provides an ideal basis for implementing a token scanner that divides a line into its component parts.

REVIEW QUESTIONS

1. True or false: An abstract type is defined only in terms of its representation, not its behavior.

2. What are the three advantages cited in this chapter for using ADTs?

3. Assuming that the operations apply to an abstract stack that is initially empty, draw a diagram showing the contents of the stack at each stage in the following sequence of operations:

   push *A*
   push *B*
   pop
   push *C*
   push *D*
   pop
   pop
   push *E*
   pop
   pop

   What is the value generated at each **pop** operation? What is the final state of the stack?

4. Give an example of how stacks are useful in programming.

5. What does the abbreviation *RPN* stand for? What does it mean?

6. What is meant by the term *polymorphism?*

7. Although C offers no way to achieve true polymorphism, the chapter adopts a strategy for the `stack.h` interface that provides clients some flexibility in defining the element type. Describe that strategy, along with its advantages and limitations.

8. What type is used for stack elements in the exported version of `stack.h`?

9. What is the standard syntax for an ADT exported by an interface? What does the corresponding concrete definition look like in the implementation?

10. What is a structure tag?

11. What are the seven functions exported by the `stack.h` interface?

12. What is the computational complexity of the `Push` and `Pop` functions in the stack implementation shown in Figure 8-3?

13. Why would it be bad programming practice for a client programmer to use an expression like

    ```
    stack->count
    ```

    to determine the number of items in a stack? If you use the `stack.h` interface shown in Figure 8-1, is it possible for the client to make this mistake?

14. In the section entitled "Improving the `stack.c` implementation," the underlying representation of the stack is changed from a static array to a dynamic one. What is the reason for this change?

15. What is meant by the term *encapsulated state?*

16. Why is it usually better to maintain state information in ADTs than to keep it in global variables within a module?

17. What are the standard steps involved in using the scanner package?

18. What does `ReadToken` return if it is called when no characters remain in the input string?

19. What is the purpose of the calls to `CopyString` in the scanner implementation shown in Figure 8-5?

PROGRAMMING EXERCISES

1. Write a program that uses a stack ADT to reverse a sequence of integers read in one per line from the console, as shown in the following sample run:

```
Enter a list of integers, ending with 0:
> 1⏎
> 2⏎
> 3⏎
> 4⏎
> 0⏎
Those integers in reverse order are:
   4
   3
   2
   1
```

2. Rewrite the program from the preceding exercise so that it uses recursion instead of a stack ADT. Your program should match the output from exercise 1 without declaring any array storage or using the stack abstraction. As the user enters the list of values, where are the previous input values stored?

3. Rewrite the Tower of Hanoi program from Chapter 4 so that it uses an explicit stack of pending tasks instead of recursion. In this context, a task can be represented as a pointer to a structure containing the number of disks to move and the names of the spires used for the start, finish, and temporary repositories. At the beginning of the process, you push onto your stack a single task that describes the process of moving the entire tower. The program then repeatedly pops the stack and executes the task found there until no tasks are left. Except for the simple cases, the process of executing a task results in the creation of more tasks that get pushed onto the stack for later execution.

4. Write a program that uses a character stack to check whether the bracketing operators (parentheses, brackets, and curly braces) in a string are properly matched. As an example of proper matching, consider the string

```
{ s = 2 * (a[2] + 3); x = (1 + (2)); }
```

If you go through the string carefully, you discover that all the bracketing operators are correctly nested, with each open parenthesis matched by a close parenthesis, each open bracket matched by a close bracket, and so on. On the other hand, the following strings are all unbalanced for the reasons indicated:

(([ ])	*The line is missing a close parenthesis.*
) (	*The close parenthesis comes before the open parenthesis.*
{ (})	*The bracketing operators are improperly nested.*

5. Reimplement the reverse Polish notation calculator given in Figure 8-2 so that it uses the exported version of the `stack.h` interface, in which `stackElementT` is defined to be `void *` instead of `double`. Your revised implementation must allocate space dynamically for each value it pushes and dereference each pointer value it pops.

6. Because the exported implementation of the stack package requires the client to use pointer values, it is convenient to define a general interface that allows

the client to create pointers to values of the built-in types and then later recover the underlying values. The `ref.h` interface that appears in Figure 8-6 defines such functions for every predefined type that is not already a pointer type. Implement this interface and then use it to produce a more compact solution to exercise 5.

7. For certain applications, it is useful to be able to generate a series of names that form a sequential pattern. For example, if you were writing a program to number figures in a paper, having some mechanism to return the sequence of strings `"Figure 1"`, `"Figure 2"`, `"Figure 3"`, and so on, would be very handy. However, you might also need to number points in a geometric diagram, in which case you would want to be able to maintain a similar but independent set of labels for points such as `"P0"`, `"P1"`, `"P2"`, and so forth.

If you think about this problem more generally, the tool you need is a label generator that allows the client to define arbitrary sequences of labels, each of which consists of a prefix string (`"Figure "` or `"P"` for the examples in the preceding paragraph) coupled with an integer used as a sequence number. Because the client may want different sequences to be active simultaneously, it makes sense to define the label generator as an abstract type called `labelGeneratorADT`. To initialize a new generator, the client provides the prefix string and the initial index as arguments to the `NewLabelGenerator` function. Once the generator has been created, the client can return new labels in the sequence by calling `GetNextLabel` on the `labelGeneratorADT`.

As an illustration of how the interface works, the program

```
main()
{
    labelGeneratorADT figureNumbers, pointNumbers;
    int i;

    figureNumbers = NewLabelGenerator("Figure ", 1);
    pointNumbers = NewLabelGenerator("P", 0);
    printf("Figure numbers: ");
    for (i = 0; i < 3; i++) {
        if (i > 0) printf(", ");
        printf("%s", GetNextLabel(figureNumbers));
    }
    printf("\nPoint numbers:  ");
    for (i = 0; i < 5; i++) {
        if (i > 0) printf(", ");
        printf("%s", GetNextLabel(pointNumbers));
    }
    printf("\nMore figures:   ");
    for (i = 0; i < 3; i++) {
        if (i > 0) printf(", ");
        printf("%s", GetNextLabel(figureNumbers));
    }
    printf("\n");
    FreeLabelGenerator(figureNumbers);
    FreeLabelGenerator(pointNumbers);
}
```

FIGURE 8-6   The ref.h interface

```
/*
 * File: ref.h
 * -----------
 * This interface exports several simple functions for allocating
 * pointers to the atomic types.
 */

#ifndef _ref_h
#define _ref_h

/*
 * Part 1 -- Functions to create pointers from basic types
 * -------------------------------------------------------
 * These functions take a value of one of the built-in types and
 * copy it into dynamically allocated memory.  The result is a
 * pointer to the newly allocated value.  For example, calling
 * NewRefInt(i) returns a pointer to a copy of the integer i.
 */

void *NewRefInt(int value);
void *NewRefShort(short value);
void *NewRefLong(long value);
void *NewRefFloat(float value);
void *NewRefDouble(double value);
void *NewRefChar(char value);
void *NewRefBool(bool value);
void *NewRefUnsigned(unsigned value);
void *NewRefUnsignedShort(unsigned short value);
void *NewRefUnsignedLong(unsigned long value);
void *NewRefUnsignedChar(unsigned char value);

/*
 * Part 2 -- Functions to dereference generic pointers
 * ---------------------------------------------------
 * These functions take a generic pointer of type void * and return
 * the value to which it points, which must be of the type indicated
 * by the function name.  For example, RefToInt(ref) interprets ref
 * as a pointer to an int and returns the integer at that address.
 */

int RefToInt(void *ref);
short RefToShort(void *ref);
long RefToLong(void *ref);
float RefToFloat(void *ref);
double RefToDouble(void *ref);
char RefToChar(void *ref);
bool RefToBool(void *ref);
unsigned RefToUnsigned(void *ref);
unsigned short RefToUnsignedShort(void *ref);
unsigned long RefToUnsignedLong(void *ref);
unsigned char RefToUnsignedChar(void *ref);

#endif
```

produces the following sample run:

```
Figure numbers: Figure 1, Figure 2, Figure 3
Point numbers:  P0, P1, P2, P3, P4
More figures:   Figure 4, Figure 5, Figure 6
```

Write the files `labelgen.h` and `labelgen.c` that define and implement this interface.

8. Probably because solving problems by computer can generate such intense frustration, computer science courses seem to generate more than their share of plagiarism. In several universities, the situation has gotten so bad that computer science departments have had to develop software to help detect cases of academic misconduct. The usual approach taken in such programs is to compare the structure of two programs, ignoring differences that are easy for students to change, such as the names of variables and procedures.

Consider, for example, the two program fragments shown below, each of which sums the elements in an integer array.

`student1.dat`

```
int Total(int array[], int n)
{
    int i, sum;

    sum = 0;
    for (i = 0; i < n; i++) {
        sum += array[i];
    }
    return (total);
}
```

`student2.dat`

```
int Sum(int list[], int nl)
{
    int j, total;

    total= 0;
    for (j = 0; j < nl; j++) {
        total += list[j];
    }
    return (total);
}
```

The names of the functions and many of the variables are different, but the two programs are otherwise exactly the same. In code samples this short, it is entirely possible that the programs were created independently, but one would start to get suspicious if the structural similarity went on for page after page.

Write a program that uses two instances of the `scannerADT` to perform a line-by-line comparison of two input files. The output of the program should be the percentage of lines in the files that "match." Two lines are defined as matching if their corresponding tokens match all the way across. Two tokens match if either of the following is true:

- The tokens are the same string.
- The tokens both begin with a letter.

For example, the tokens `"sum"` and `"total"` match because both begin with a letter. In the `student1.dat` and `student2.dat` sample files, every line matches perfectly under this definition, so the program should report that 100 percent of the lines match.

9. Add the necessary code to the scanner package to implement the extension shown in Figure 8-7, which allows the scanner to read quoted strings as a single token. By default, the scanner should continue to treat double-quotation marks just like any other punctuation mark. However, if the client calls

```
SetScannerStringOption(scanner, ScanQuotesAsStrings);
```

the scanner will instead recognize a quoted string as a single unit. For example, the input line

```
"Hello, world."
```

would be scanned as the following single token:

> `"Hello, world."`

Note that the quotation marks are preserved as part of the token so that the client can differentiate a string token from other token types.

FIGURE 8-7 Interface extension allowing the scanner to recognize quoted strings

```
/*
 * Functions: SetScannerStringOption, GetScannerStringOption
 * Usage: SetScannerStringOption(scanner, option);
 *        option = GetScannerStringOption(scanner);
 * -------------------------------------------------
 * This function controls how the scanner treats double quotation
 * marks in the input.  The default behavior for the scanner is
 * to treat quotes just like any other punctuation character.
 * If, however, you call
 *
 *     SetScannerStringOption(scanner, ScanQuotesAsStrings);
 *
 * a token beginning with a quotation mark will be scanned up to
 * the closing quotation mark.  The quotation marks are returned
 * as part of the scanned token so that clients can differentiate
 * strings from other token types.  The original behavior can be
 * restored by calling
 *
 *     SetScannerStringOption(scanner, ScanQuotesAsPunctuation);
 *
 * When scanning a string, the scanner recognizes the standard
 * escape sequences from ANSI C, such as \n and \t.
 */
typedef enum {
    ScanQuotesAsPunctuation,
    ScanQuotesAsStrings
} stringOptionT;

void SetScannerStringOption(scannerADT scanner, stringOptionT option);
stringOptionT GetScannerStringOption(scannerADT scanner);
```

As an extra challenge, extend the string-recognition code in the scanner so that the scanner correctly interprets the standard escape sequences from ANSI C, such as \n and \t. A complete list of these escape sequences appears in Table 1-2.

10. Add the necessary code to the scanner package to implement the extension shown in Figure 8-8, which allows the scanner to read numbers as single tokens. Note that this option has two different forms. If SetScannerNumberOption is

---

FIGURE 8-8 Interface extension allowing the scanner to recognize numbers

```
/*
 * Functions: SetScannerNumberOption, GetScannerNumberOption
 * Usage: SetScannerNumberOption(scanner, option);
 *        option = GetScannerNumberOption(scanner);
 * --------------------------------------------------------
 * This function controls whether the scanner treats numeric values
 * specially.  The default behavior for the scanner is to treat
 * digits as equivalent to letters.  If you call
 *
 *     SetScannerNumberOption(scanner, ScanNumbersAsIntegers);
 *
 * a token beginning with a digit will end at the first nondigit.
 * (Note that digits can still be scanned as part of a token as in
 * the token "x1".)  If you call
 *
 *     SetScannerNumberOption(scanner, ScanNumbersAsReals);
 *
 * the scanner will return the longest token string that represents
 * a real number, if the next character to be scanned is a digit.
 * The format for a real number is a sequence of digit characters
 * that may include at most one decimal point, optionally followed
 * by the letter 'E' in either upper- or lowercase, an optional sign,
 * and an exponent.  You can restore the default behavior by calling
 *
 *     SetScannerNumberOption(scanner, ScanNumbersAsLetters);
 *
 * Even if the number options are enabled, ReadToken always returns
 * its result as a string, which means that you need to call
 * StringToInteger or StringToReal to convert the token to a number.
 */

typedef enum {
    ScanNumbersAsLetters,
    ScanNumbersAsIntegers,
    ScanNumbersAsReals
} numberOptionT;

void SetScannerNumberOption(scannerADT scanner, numberOptionT option);
numberOptionT GetScannerNumberOption(scannerADT scanner);
```

called with `ScanNumbersAsIntegers`, the package will divide the string
`"3.14"` into three tokens, as follows:

$\boxed{3}\ \boxed{.}\ \boxed{14}$

If the `ScanNumbersAsReals` option is set instead, the same string would be
scanned as a single token:

$\boxed{3.14}$

  The process of scanning to the end of an integer is reasonably
straightforward and follows the structure of the existing scanner code. The
only difference is that a string like `"3rd"` that begins with a digit but also
includes letters will be read as one token by the original scanner but as two if
the `ScanNumbersAsIntegers` option is set. The hard part is implementing the
`ScanNumbersAsReals` option. The specification for a legal real number is
given in the comments in Figure 8-8. It is often easier, however, to understand
the idea of scanning a number in terms of a structure that computer scientists
call a **finite-state machine,** which is usually represented diagrammatically as
a collection of circles representing the possible states of the machine. The
circles are then connected by a set of labeled arcs that indicate how the process
moves from one state to another. A finite-state machine for scanning a real
number, for example, looks like this:

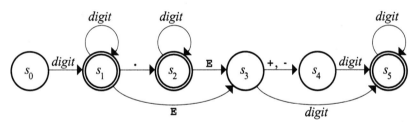

You start scanning a number in state s_0 and then follow the labeled arcs for
each character in the input until there is no arc that matches the input
character. If you end up in a state marked by a double circle, you have
successfully scanned a number. These states are called **final states.**
  To illustrate the operation of this finite-state machine, suppose that the
scanner string is

  `3.14-17.5E-9`

and that the number option has been set to `ScanNumbersAsReals`. The
intended result is that the scanner divide this string into two numbers and an
operator as follows:

$\boxed{3.14}\ \boxed{-}\ \boxed{17.5E-9}$

When the scanner encounters the digit 3 at the beginning of the input, it starts the numeric scanner in state s_0. From there, it makes the following state transitions:

State	Input
s_0	3
s_1	.
s_2	1
s_2	4
s_2	–

Because there is no transition from state s_2 labeled with a minus sign and because s_2 is a final state, the process ends at this point, having successfully recognized the numeric string **"3.14"** as a token. The next token is simply the minus sign, which is returned as a single-character string. The final token on the line is scanned by making the following transitions:

State	Input
s_0	1
s_1	7
s_1	.
s_2	5
s_2	E
s_3	–
s_4	9
s_5	*none*

11. Using the scanner extension from exercise 10, rewrite the RPN calculator in Figure 8-2 so that the input expressions appear on single lines, as illustrated by the following sample run:

```
RPN Calculator Simulation
> 1 2 3 * +↵
7
> 50.0 1.5 * 3.8 2.0 / +↵
76.9
> quit↵
```

12. If you are writing programs to play word games, you need to have some fast way to determine whether a string of characters represents a legal English word. One approach is to define a new abstract data type for a word list, or **lexicon,** that makes it easy for clients to look up words. A simple version of the **lexicon.h** interface is shown in Figure 8-9.

Write a file **lexicon.c** that implements the **lexicon.h** interface. As you do so, think carefully about how to design the underlying representation. For most applications of the lexicon, it is worth sacrificing some efficiency in **AddWordToLexicon** if doing so makes **IsWord** run more quickly.

FIGURE 8-9   The lexicon.h interface

```
/*
 * File: lexicon.h
 * ---------------
 * This file is the interface to an abstraction that allows
 * the client to keep track of a list of words.  The difference
 * between the lexicon abstraction and a symbol table or
 * dictionary is that the lexicon does not provide a mechanism
 * for storing the definitions of words; a lexicon merely
 * indicates whether a given string is a legal word.
 */

#ifndef _lexicon_h
#define _lexicon_h

#include "genlib.h"

/*
 * Type: lexiconADT
 * ----------------
 * This type represents the ADT for a lexicon.  The type is
 * a purely abstract type in this interface, defined entirely
 * in terms of the operations.  Because the type is represented
 * as a pointer to an incomplete structure type, the client has
 * no access to the underlying record structure.
 */

typedef struct lexiconCDT *lexiconADT;

/* Operations */

/*
 * Function: NewLexicon
 * Usage: lexicon = NewLexicon();
 * ------------------------------
 * This function creates a new lexicon and initializes it to
 * be empty.
 */

lexiconADT NewLexicon(void);

/*
 * Function: FreeLexicon
 * Usage: FreeLexicon(lexicon);
 * ----------------------------
 * This function frees the storage associated with the lexicon.
 */

void FreeLexicon(lexiconADT lexicon);
```

```
/*
 * Function: ClearLexicon
 * Usage: ClearLexicon(lexicon);
 * -----------------------------
 * This function removes all words from the lexicon and resets
 * it to its initial state.
 */

void ClearLexicon(lexiconADT lexicon);

/*
 * Function: ReadLexiconFile
 * Usage: ReadLexiconFile(lexicon, filename);
 * ------------------------------------------
 * This function initializes the lexicon to the set of words
 * stored in the file with the specified name.  If the file
 * does not exist or memory space is exhausted, this function
 * calls Error with an appropriate message.
 */

void ReadLexiconFile(lexiconADT lexicon, string filename);

/*
 * Function: AddWordToLexicon
 * Usage: AddWordToLexicon(lexicon, word);
 * ---------------------------------------
 * This function adds the specified word to the lexicon.
 */

void AddWordToLexicon(lexiconADT lexicon, string word);

/*
 * Function: WordsInLexicon
 * Usage: n = WordsInLexicon(lexicon);
 * -----------------------------------
 * This function returns the number of words in the lexicon.
 */

long WordsInLexicon(lexiconADT lexicon);

/*
 * Function: IsWord
 * Usage: flag = IsWord(lexicon, word);
 * ------------------------------------
 * This function looks up the specified word in the lexicon
 * and returns TRUE if the word is a valid entry.
 */

bool IsWord(lexiconADT lexicon, string word);

#endif
```

13. In exercise 5 from Chapter 5, you were asked to write a program that generates all possible mnemonics for a telephone number. Use the `lexicon.h` interface from the preceding exercise to extend the `mnemonic.c` program so that it only lists the mnemonics that are valid English words.

14. Extend the `lexicon.h` interface from exercise 12 so that it supports two additional functions, `IsPrefix` and `GetWordFromPrefix`. The `IsPrefix` function has the prototype

    ```
    bool IsPrefix(lexiconADT lexicon, string prefix);
    ```

    and returns `TRUE` if the string `prefix` is either a valid word or the prefix of a valid word in the lexicon. For example, calling `IsPrefix(lexicon, "hel")` on a lexicon containing all English words would return `TRUE` because `"hel"` is a prefix of such words as `"help"`, `"hello"`, and `"helicopter"`. The function

    ```
    string GetWordFromPrefix(lexiconADT lexicon, string prefix);
    ```

    returns any valid word in the lexicon beginning with `prefix`, or `NULL` if no such word exists.

15. Using the extended `lexicon.h` interface from the preceding exercise, write a program that plays the game of ghost. In ghost, each player in turn adds a new letter to the end of a string, which is initially empty. The object is to avoid making a word on your turn while always being able to find a longer word that starts with the current set of letters. Words of one or two letters don't count.

    For example, suppose that you have the first play and pick the letter P. The computer might respond with the letter R, so that the current letters are PR. You can't at this point add an O or a Y because PRO and PRY are words. You might add an I hoping to make PRINCE, which would end on the computer's turn. Unfortunately, for you, the computer might add a Z to make the string PRIZ. You can forestall an immediate loss by adding an I instead of an E, but if the computer adds an N, you have no choice but to complete the word PRIZING and lose.

    The easiest way to make sure that your program plays a good game of ghost is to start with the general minimax code presented for the tic-tac-toe game in Figure 6-6 and then adapt it to the specific structure of ghost.

16. The game of Boggle™ is played with a set of 16 letter cubes, which are rolled and then put into a 4 × 4 square that might turn out like this:

E	E	C	A
A	L	E	P
H	N	B	O
Q	T	T	Y

The object of the game is to find as many words as possible by starting at one letter and then moving to adjacent letters to form a word that meets the following conditions:

- The word must be at least four letters long.
- The path traced out by the letters in the word must be connected horizontally, vertically, or diagonally. You can't skip over intervening cubes to get the next letter.
- Each cube may be used only once in a given word.

For instance, the sample pattern contains the word **PEACE** as follows:

The pattern, however, does not contain the word **PLACE**, which would require jumping from the **P** to the **L** and then back to the **A**. Similarly, it is not possible to make the word **POPE**, because doing so would require reusing the **P**.

Write a program that generates a 4 × 4 array of random letters and then finds all the legal Boggle words it contains. Assume that you have access to the extended `lexicon.h` interface from exercise 14 as well as a data file containing all English words.

CHAPTER 9

Efficiency and ADTs

Time granted does not necessarily coincide with time that can be most fully used.

— Tillie Olsen, *Silences*, 1965

Objectives

- To learn that different strategies for representing data can have a profound effect on the efficiency of your code.

- To be able to compare the computational complexity of different representation strategies.

- To understand the concept of a linked list and how it can be used to provide a basis for efficient insertion and deletion operations.

- To appreciate that representations which are efficient in terms of their execution time may be inefficient in their use of memory.

This chapter brings together two ideas that might at first seem to have little to do with each other: the notion of algorithmic efficiency presented in Chapter 7 and the idea of abstract data types from Chapter 8. Up to now, efficiency has been closely linked with the study of algorithms. If you choose a more efficient algorithm, you can reduce the running time of a program substantially, particularly if the new algorithm is in a different complexity class. In some cases, choosing a different underlying representation for an abstract data type can have an equally dramatic effect. To illustrate this idea, this chapter looks at a specific abstract data type that can be represented in several different ways and contrasts the efficiency of those representations.

■■ 9.1 The concept of an editor buffer

Whenever you create a source file or use a word processor to edit text, you are using a piece of software called an **editor,** which allows you to make changes to a text file. Internally, an editor maintains a sequence of characters, which is usually called a **buffer.** The editor application allows you to make changes to the contents of the buffer, usually by some combination of the following operations:

- Moving the cursor to the point in the text at which editing needs to take place.
- Typing in new text, which is then inserted at the current cursor position.
- Deleting characters using a delete or backspace key.

Modern editors usually provide a highly sophisticated editing environment, complete with such fancy features as using a mouse to position the cursor or commands that search for a particular text string. Moreover, they tend to show the results of all editing operations precisely as they are performed. Editors that display the current contents of the buffer throughout the editing process are called **wysiwyg** (pronounced "wizzy-wig") editors, which is an acronym for "what you see is what you get." Such editors are very easy to use, but their advanced features sometimes make it harder to see how an editor works on the inside.

In the early days of computing, editors were much simpler. Lacking access to a mouse or a sophisticated graphics display, editors were designed to respond to commands entered on the keyboard. For example, with a typical keyboard-based editor, you insert new text by typing the command letter I, followed by a sequence of characters. Additional commands perform other editing functions, such as moving the cursor around in the buffer. By entering the right combinations of these commands, you can make any desired set of changes.

To make the idea of the editor buffer as concrete as possible, let's suppose that your task is to build an editor that can execute the six commands shown in Table 9-1. Except for the I command, which also takes the characters to be inserted, every editor command consists of a single letter read in on a line. The editor program itself simply reads a sequence of commands from the user. The program updates the state of the buffer after each command and displays the contents on the screen, marking the position of the cursor with a carat symbol (∧) on the next line.

	TABLE 9-1	Commands implemented by the editor

Command	Operation
F	Moves the editing cursor forward one character position
B	Moves the editing cursor backward one character position
J	Jumps to the beginning of the buffer (before the first character)
E	Moves the cursor to the end of the buffer (after the last character)
I*xxx*	Inserts the characters *xxx* at the current cursor position
D	Deletes the character just after the current cursor position

The following sample run illustrates the operation of the editor, along with annotations that describe each action. In this session, the user first inserts the characters **axc** and then corrects the contents of the buffer to **abc**.

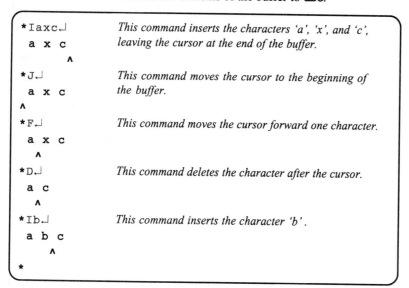

▊ 9.2 Defining the buffer abstraction

In creating an editor that can execute the commands from Table 9-1, your main task is to design a data structure that maintains the state of the editor buffer. This data structure must keep track of the characters in the buffer and the position of the cursor. It must also be able to update the buffer contents whenever an editing operation is performed. In other words, what you want to do is define a new abstraction that represents the editor buffer. In programming terms, defining the abstraction consists of defining a **buffer.h** interface that exports the types and functions necessary to implement the required editing operations.

Even at this early stage, you probably have some ideas about what data structures might be appropriate. Because the buffer is clearly an ordered sequence of characters, one seemingly obvious choice is to use an array of characters for the buffer. Although using an array to represent the buffer is certainly a reasonable approach to the problem, there are other representations that offer interesting possibilities. The fundamental lesson in this chapter—and indeed in much of this book—is that you should not be so quick to choose a particular representation. In the case of the editor buffer, arrays are only one of several options, each of which has certain advantages and disadvantages. After evaluating the tradeoffs, you might decide to use one strategy in a certain set of circumstances and a different strategy in another. At the same time, it is important to note that, no matter what representation you choose, the editor must always be able to perform the same set of commands. Thus, the external behavior of an editor buffer must remain the same, even if the underlying representation changes.

In order to make your interface as flexible as possible, it makes sense to define a new abstract data type to represent an editor buffer. The principal advantage of using an ADT in this context is that doing so allows you to separate the specification of behavior and representation. Because you understand the operations to which it must respond, you already know how an editor buffer behaves. If you define an ADT for the editor buffer that implements the required set of operations, you will then be free to change the underlying representation of that type without requiring your clients to make any changes in their programs.

As you know from Chapter 8, you can define an abstract type in ANSI C by declaring it to be a pointer to a concrete type that is defined only in the implementation. Thus, in the interface that defines the buffer abstraction, you can define the abstract buffer type using a line of the form

```
typedef struct bufferCDT *bufferADT;
```

Clients work entirely with the `bufferADT` type and have no access to the underlying representation.

Functions in the `buffer.h` interface

The remainder of the interface consists of prototypes for the functions that implement the primitive operations on an editor buffer. What operations do you need to define? If nothing else, you need functions for each of the six editor commands. As with any abstract type, however, you will also need to define a function that allocates a new buffer and returns it to the client program. The prototype for such a function might be

```
bufferADT NewBuffer(void);
```

Moreover, just as with the stack ADT introduced in Chapter 8, you also need to provide the function

```
void FreeBuffer(bufferADT buffer);
```

which takes a buffer and relinquishes its storage. These eight functions—the six operations and the `NewBuffer`/`FreeBuffer` pair—form the core of the `buffer.h` interface, which appears in Figure 9-1.

FIGURE 9-1   Interface for the editor buffer abstraction

```c
/*
 * File: buffer.h
 * ---------------
 * This file defines the interface for an editor buffer abstraction.
 */

#ifndef _buffer_h
#define _buffer_h

#include "genlib.h"

/*
 * Type: bufferADT
 * ---------------
 * This type defines the abstract type used to represent
 * an editor buffer.
 */

typedef struct bufferCDT *bufferADT;

/* Exported entries */

/*
 * Function: NewBuffer
 * Usage: buffer = NewBuffer();
 * -----------------------------
 * This function dynamically allocates enough memory for the
 * underlying representation of a bufferADT and initializes
 * it to represent an empty buffer.
 */

bufferADT NewBuffer(void);

/*
 * Function: FreeBuffer
 * Usage: FreeBuffer(buffer);
 * ---------------------------
 * This function frees the storage associated with the buffer.
 */

void FreeBuffer(bufferADT buffer);

/*
 * Functions: MoveCursorForward, MoveCursorBackward
 * Usage: MoveCursorForward(buffer);
 *        MoveCursorBackward(buffer);
 * -------------------------------------
 * These functions move the cursor forward or backward one
 * character, respectively.  If you call MoveCursorForward
 * at the end of the buffer or MoveCursorBackward at the
 * beginning, the function call has no effect.
 */

void MoveCursorForward(bufferADT buffer);
void MoveCursorBackward(bufferADT buffer);
```

```
/*
 * Functions: MoveCursorToStart, MoveCursorToEnd
 * Usage: MoveCursorToStart(buffer);
 *        MoveCursorToEnd(buffer);
 * --------------------------------------
 * These functions move the cursor to the start or the
 * end of the buffer, respectively.
 */

void MoveCursorToStart(bufferADT buffer);
void MoveCursorToEnd(bufferADT buffer);

/*
 * Function: InsertCharacter
 * Usage: InsertCharacter(buffer, ch);
 * --------------------------------------
 * This function inserts the single character ch into the
 * buffer at the current cursor position.  The cursor is
 * positioned after the inserted character, which allows
 * for consecutive insertions.
 */

void InsertCharacter(bufferADT buffer, char ch);

/*
 * Function: DeleteCharacter
 * Usage: DeleteCharacter(buffer);
 * -------------------------------
 * This function deletes the character immediately after
 * the cursor.  If the cursor is at the end of the buffer,
 * this function has no effect.
 */

void DeleteCharacter(bufferADT buffer);

/*
 * Function: DisplayBuffer
 * Usage: DisplayBuffer(buffer);
 * -----------------------------
 * This function displays the current contents of the buffer
 * on the console.
 */

void DisplayBuffer(bufferADT buffer);

#endif
```

The last function in the `buffer.h` interface is `DisplayBuffer`, which displays the contents of the buffer on the screen. This function is used in the editor application, but does not represent a primitive operation on the `bufferADT` type in the way that the other functions in the interface do. Even so, it is useful to include such display functions in an abstract interface, because having them available simplifies the debugging process. As you search for a problem in your application code, you can use the display functions to trace the execution of your program.

Coding the editor application

Once you have defined the `buffer.h` interface, you are free to go back and write the editor application, even though you have not yet implemented the buffer abstraction or settled on an appropriate internal representation. When you're writing the editor application, the only important consideration is what each of the functions does. At this level, the implementation details are unimportant.

As long as you limit yourself to the commands in Table 9-1, writing the editor application is relatively easy. The necessary code appears in Figure 9-2. The main program simply allocates a new buffer and then enters a loop in which it reads a series of editor commands. Whenever the user enters a command, the program looks at the first character in the command name and performs the requested operation by calling the appropriate function in the `buffer.h` interface.

FIGURE 9-2   Simple implementation of a command-driven editor

```
/*
 * File: editor.c
 * --------------
 * This program implements a simple character editor, which
 * is used to test the buffer abstraction.  The editor reads
 * and executes simple commands entered by the user.
 */

#include <stdio.h>
#include <ctype.h>
#include "genlib.h"
#include "buffer.h"
#include "simpio.h"

/* Private function prototypes */

static void ExecuteCommand(bufferADT buffer, string line);
static void HelpCommand(void);

/* Main program */

main()
{
    bufferADT buffer;

    buffer = NewBuffer();
    while (TRUE) {
        printf("*");
        ExecuteCommand(buffer, GetLine());
        DisplayBuffer(buffer);
    }
    FreeBuffer(buffer);
}
```

```
/*
 * Function: ExecuteCommand
 * Usage: ExecuteCommand(buffer, line);
 * -------------------------------------
 * This function parses the user command in the string line
 * and executes it on the buffer.
 */

static void ExecuteCommand(bufferADT buffer, string line)
{
    int i;

    switch (toupper(line[0])) {
      case 'I': for (i = 1; line[i] != '\0'; i++) {
                    InsertCharacter(buffer, line[i]);
                }
                break;
      case 'D': DeleteCharacter(buffer); break;
      case 'F': MoveCursorForward(buffer); break;
      case 'B': MoveCursorBackward(buffer); break;
      case 'J': MoveCursorToStart(buffer); break;
      case 'E': MoveCursorToEnd(buffer); break;
      case 'H': HelpCommand(); break;
      case 'Q': exit(0);
      default:  printf("Illegal command\n"); break;
    }
}


/*
 * Function: HelpCommand
 * Usage: HelpCommand();
 * ----------------------
 * This function lists the available editor commands.
 */

static void HelpCommand(void)
{
    printf("Use the following commands to edit the buffer:\n");
    printf(" I...   Inserts text up to the end of the line\n");
    printf(" F      Moves forward a character\n");
    printf(" B      Moves backward a character\n");
    printf(" J      Jumps to the beginning of the buffer\n");
    printf(" E      Jumps to the end of the buffer\n");
    printf(" D      Deletes the next character\n");
    printf(" H      Generates a help message\n");
    printf(" Q      Quits the program\n");
}
```

9.3 Implementing the editor using arrays

As noted earlier in the section on "Defining the buffer abstraction," one of the possible representations for the buffer is an array of characters. Although this design is not the only option for representing the editor buffer, it is nonetheless a useful starting point. After all, the characters in the buffer form an ordered, homogeneous sequence, which is precisely the sort of data that arrays are intended to represent.

Defining the concrete type

Representing the editor buffer as an array is simple, but not necessarily as simple as it might at first appear. There are a couple of details to consider, and it is worth spending a little time to get them right.

In terms of the characters themselves, the simplest solution is to store the characters from the buffer in consecutive elements of the array. Thus, the array component of the buffer is very much like the internal representation of a string. Because strings seem like an appropriate model, you could choose to mark the end of the buffer by storing a null character at the end, as in a string. Such an approach, however, is time-consuming because you must search for that null character whenever you need to know the length of the buffer. An alternative strategy would be to store the current length in a separate field within the buffer structure. Thus, a buffer containing the characters

H E L L O

would be represented using the following structure:

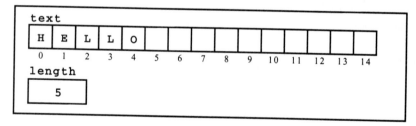

In addition to these fields, the buffer structure must also contain an indication of the current location of the cursor. Because the cursor is essentially a character position, you can represent it by including another integer field called `cursor` in the buffer structure. If you look at the display screen, however, you will realize that the cursor does not actually appear at a character position but instead sits between two characters. Thus, you have to establish a convention relating the index position stored in the `cursor` field to the logical position of the cursor in the buffer. The easiest convention to choose is that the `cursor` field records the index position of the character that follows the cursor. Thus, if the buffer contains

H E L | L O

with the cursor sitting between the two L characters, the internal structure of the buffer would look like this:

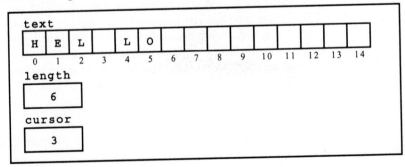

Using this representation, the cursor is at the beginning of the buffer when the cursor field is 0 and at the end of the buffer when the cursor field is equal to the length field.

The structure diagram makes it easy to write down the concrete definition for the buffer, as follows:

```
struct bufferCDT {
    char text[MaxBuffer];
    int length;
    int cursor;
};
```

Implementing the buffer operations

As you can see from the arraybuf.c implementation in Figure 9-3, implementing the editor operations using an array-based representation of the buffer is quite simple. Several of the functions consist of a single line of code. Moving to the beginning of the buffer, for example, requires nothing more than assigning the value 0 to the buffer's cursor field.

The only operations that are at all tricky are the InsertCharacter and DeleteCharacter operations. Suppose, for example, that you wanted to insert the character X at the cursor position in the buffer containing

$$H \quad E \quad L \mid L \quad O$$

To do so in the array representation of the buffer, you need to make room for the new character at the appropriate position. The only way to get that space is to shift all the remaining characters one position to the right, as follows:

FIGURE 9-3   Implementation of the editor buffer using an array

```
/*
 * File: arraybuf.c
 * ----------------
 * This file implements the buffer.h abstraction using an
 * array to represent the buffer.
 */

#include <stdio.h>
#include "genlib.h"
#include "buffer.h"

/*
 * Type: bufferCDT
 * ---------------
 * In this representation of the buffer, the characters are stored
 * in an array embedded within a structure that also holds the
 * length of the buffer and the cursor position as integers.
 * The cursor indicates the index position of the character that
 * follows where the cursor would appear on the screen.
 */

#define MaxBuffer 100

struct bufferCDT {
    char text[MaxBuffer];
    int length;
    int cursor;
};

/* Exported entries */

bufferADT NewBuffer(void)
{
    bufferADT buffer;

    buffer = New(bufferADT);
    buffer->length = buffer->cursor = 0;
    return (buffer);
}

void FreeBuffer(bufferADT buffer)
{
    FreeBlock(buffer);
}

void MoveCursorForward(bufferADT buffer)
{
    if (buffer->cursor < buffer->length) buffer->cursor++;
}

void MoveCursorBackward(bufferADT buffer)
{
    if (buffer->cursor > 0) buffer->cursor--;
}
```

```
void MoveCursorToStart(bufferADT buffer)
{
    buffer->cursor = 0;
}

void MoveCursorToEnd(bufferADT buffer)
{
    buffer->cursor = buffer->length;
}

/*
 * Implementation notes: InsertCharacter and DeleteCharacter
 * ---------------------------------------------------------
 * Each of the functions that inserts or deletes characters must
 * shift all subsequent characters in the array, either to make
 * room for new insertions or to close up space left by deletions.
 */

void InsertCharacter(bufferADT buffer, char ch)
{
    int i;

    if (buffer->length == MaxBuffer) Error("Buffer size exceeded");
    for (i = buffer->length; i > buffer->cursor; i--) {
        buffer->text[i] = buffer->text[i - 1];
    }
    buffer->text[buffer->cursor] = ch;
    buffer->length++;
    buffer->cursor++;
}

void DeleteCharacter(bufferADT buffer)
{
    int i;

    if (buffer->cursor < buffer->length) {
        for (i = buffer->cursor+1; i < buffer->length; i++) {
            buffer->text[i - 1] = buffer->text[i];
        }
        buffer->length--;
    }
}

void DisplayBuffer(bufferADT buffer)
{
    int i;

    for (i = 0; i < buffer->length; i++) {
        printf(" %c", buffer->text[i]);
    }
    printf("\n");
    for (i = 0; i < buffer->cursor; i++) {
        printf("  ");
    }
    printf("^\n");
}
```

The resulting gap in the array gives you the space you need to insert the X, after which the cursor advances so that it follows the newly inserted character, leaving the following configuration:

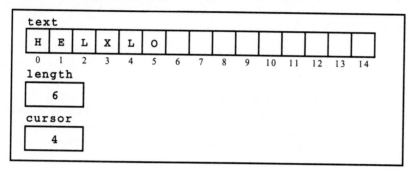

The `DeleteCharacter` operation is similar in that it requires a loop to close the gap left by the deleted character.

The computational complexity of the array implementation

In order to establish a baseline for comparison with other representations, it is useful to evaluate the computational complexity of the array-based implementation of the editor. As usual, the goal of the complexity analysis is to understand how the execution time required for the editing operations varies qualitatively as a function of the problem size. In the editor example, the problem size is best measured by the number of characters in the buffer. For the editor buffer, you therefore need to determine how each of the editing operations is affected by the number of characters in the buffer.

Let's start with an easy case. How is the efficiency of the `MoveCursorForward` operation affected by N, the number of characters? When you use the array-based representation for buffers shown in Figure 9-3, the function `MoveCursorForward` has the following implementation:

```
void MoveCursorForward(bufferADT buffer)
{
    if (buffer->cursor < buffer->length) buffer->cursor++;
}
```

Even though the function does indeed check the length of the buffer, it doesn't take long to realize that the execution time of the function is independent of the buffer length. This function executes precisely the same operations no matter how long the buffer is: there is one test and, in almost all cases, one increment operation. Because the execution time is independent of N, the `MoveCursorForward` operation runs in $O(1)$ time. The same analysis also applies to the functions `MoveCursorBackward`, `MoveCursorToStart`, and `MoveCursorToEnd`, none of which involve any operations that depend on the length of the buffer.

But what about `InsertCharacter`? In `arraybuf.c`, `InsertCharacter` contains the following `for` loop:

```
for (i = buffer->length; i > buffer->cursor; i--) {
    buffer->text[i] = buffer->text[i - 1];
}
```

If you insert a character at the end of the buffer, this function runs pretty quickly, because there is no need to shift characters to make room for the new one. On the other hand, if you insert a character at the beginning of the buffer, every character in the buffer must be shifted one position rightward in the array. Thus, in the worst case, the running time for `InsertCharacter` is proportional to the number of characters in the buffer and is therefore $O(N)$. Because the `DeleteCharacter` operation has a similar structure, its complexity is also $O(N)$. These results are summarized in Table 9-2.

The fact that the last two operations in the table require linear time has important performance implications for the editor program. If an editor uses arrays to represent its internal buffer, it will start to run more slowly as the number of characters in the buffer becomes large. Because this problem seems serious, it makes sense to explore other representational possibilities.

■ 9.4 Implementing the editor using stacks

The problem with the array implementation of the editor buffer is that insertions and deletions run slowly when they occur near the beginning of the buffer. When those same operations are applied at the end of the buffer, they run relatively quickly because there is no need to shift the characters in the internal array. This property suggests an approach to making things faster: force all insertions and deletions to occur at the end of the buffer. While this approach is completely impractical from the user's point of view, it does contain the seed of a workable idea.

The key insight necessary to make insertions and deletions faster is that you can divide the buffer at the cursor boundary and store the characters before and after the cursor in separate structures. Because all changes to the buffer occur at the cursor position, each of those structures behaves like a stack and can be represented by the `stackADT` type defined in Chapter 8. The characters that precede the cursor are pushed on one stack so that the beginning of the buffer is at the base and the

TABLE 9-2 Complexity of the editor operations (array representation)

Function	Complexity
MoveCursorForward	$O(1)$
MoveCursorBackward	$O(1)$
MoveCursorToStart	$O(1)$
MoveCursorToEnd	$O(1)$
InsertCharacter	$O(N)$
DeleteCharacter	$O(N)$

character just before the pointer is at the top. The characters after the cursor are stored in the opposite direction, with the end of the buffer at the base of the stack and the character just after the pointer at the top.

The best way to illustrate this structure is with a diagram. Suppose that the buffer contains the string

H E L | L O

with the cursor sitting between the two L characters as shown. The two-stack representation of the buffer looks like this:

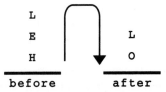

To read the contents of the buffer, you need to read up the characters in the **before** stack and then down the characters in the **after** stack, as indicated by the arrow.

Defining the concrete structure for the stack-based buffer

Using this strategy, the concrete representation of the editor buffer structure is simply a pair of stacks, one to hold the character before the cursor and another to hold the ones that come after it. Because you already have the stack abstraction developed in Chapter 8, you might as well go ahead and use it, making sure to define **stackElementT** to be **char**. The concrete structure is then

```
struct bufferCDT {
    stackADT before;
    stackADT after;
};
```

Note that the cursor is not explicitly represented in this model but is instead simply the boundary between the two stacks.

Implementing the buffer operations

In the stack model, most of the operations for the editor are surprisingly easy to implement. For example, moving backward consists of popping a character from the **before** stack and pushing it back on the **after** stack. Thus, if you were to call **MoveCursorBackward** in the position shown in the preceding diagram, the buffer would be left in the following position:

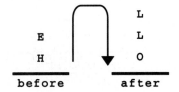

Moving forward is entirely symmetrical. Inserting a character consists of pushing that character on the `before` stack. Deleting a character is accomplished by popping a character from the `after` stack and throwing it away.

This conceptual outline makes it easy to code the following operations, each of which appears in Figure 9-4:

- `MoveCursorForward`
- `MoveCursorBackward`
- `InsertCharacter`
- `DeleteCharacter`

Each of these operations runs in constant time. None of the implementations contain any sort of loop, and all stack operations called by these functions are themselves constant-time operations.

But what about the last two operations? Implementing `MoveCursorToStart` and `MoveCursorToEnd` requires the program to transfer the entire contents from one of the stacks to the other. Given the operations provided by the stack abstraction, the only way to accomplish this operation is to pop values from one stack and push them back on the other stack, one value at a time, until the original stack becomes empty. For example, `MoveCursorToEnd` has the following implementation:

```
void MoveCursorToEnd(bufferADT buffer)
{
    while (!StackIsEmpty(buffer->after)) {
        Push(buffer->before, Pop(buffer->after));
    }
}
```

These implementations have the desired effect, but require $O(N)$ time in the worst case.

Comparing computational complexities

Table 9-3 shows the computational complexity of the editor operations for both the array- and the stack-based implementation of the editor. Each of the last two columns in Table 9-3 includes some entries that run in constant time and others that run in linear time.

TABLE 9-3 Relative performance of the array and stack representations

Function	Array	Stack
MoveCursorForward	$O(1)$	$O(1)$
MoveCursorBackward	$O(1)$	$O(1)$
MoveCursorToStart	$O(1)$	$O(N)$
MoveCursorToEnd	$O(1)$	$O(N)$
InsertCharacter	$O(N)$	$O(1)$
DeleteCharacter	$O(N)$	$O(1)$

FIGURE 9-4   Implementation of the editor buffer using a pair of stacks

```
/*
 * File: stackbuf.c
 * -----------------
 * This file implements the buffer.h abstraction using a pair of
 * stacks to represent the buffer.
 */

#include <stdio.h>
#include "genlib.h"
#include "buffer.h"
#include "stack.h"

/*
 * Type: bufferCDT
 * ---------------
 * In this representation of the buffer, all characters are stored
 * in one of two stacks.  Characters before the cursor are pushed
 * on the before stack; those after the cursor are pushed on the
 * after stack.  The cursor is represented implicitly by the
 * boundary between the stacks.  Characters are at deeper levels on
 * their respective stack if they are farther from the cursor.  As
 * an example, the buffer containing ABCDE with the cursor between
 * the C and the D would look like this:
 *
 *          C
 *          B         D
 *          A         E
 *        ------     -----
 *        before     after
 */

struct bufferCDT {
    stackADT before;
    stackADT after;
};

/* Exported entries */

bufferADT NewBuffer(void)
{
    bufferADT buffer;

    buffer = New(bufferADT);
    buffer->before = NewStack();
    buffer->after = NewStack();
    return (buffer);
}

void FreeBuffer(bufferADT buffer)
{
    FreeStack(buffer->before);
    FreeStack(buffer->after);
    FreeBlock(buffer);
}
```

```
void MoveCursorForward(bufferADT buffer)
{
    if (!StackIsEmpty(buffer->after)) {
        Push(buffer->before, Pop(buffer->after));
    }
}

void MoveCursorBackward(bufferADT buffer)
{
    if (!StackIsEmpty(buffer->before)) {
        Push(buffer->after, Pop(buffer->before));
    }
}

void MoveCursorToStart(bufferADT buffer)
{
    while (!StackIsEmpty(buffer->before)) {
        Push(buffer->after, Pop(buffer->before));
    }
}

void MoveCursorToEnd(bufferADT buffer)
{
    while (!StackIsEmpty(buffer->after)) {
        Push(buffer->before, Pop(buffer->after));
    }
}

void InsertCharacter(bufferADT buffer, char ch)
{
    Push(buffer->before, ch);
}

void DeleteCharacter(bufferADT buffer)
{
    if (!StackIsEmpty(buffer->after)) {
        (void) Pop(buffer->after);
    }
}

void DisplayBuffer(bufferADT buffer)
{
    int i;

    for (i = StackDepth(buffer->before) - 1; i >= 0; i--) {
        printf(" %c", GetStackElement(buffer->before, i));
    }
    for (i = 0; i < StackDepth(buffer->after); i++) {
        printf(" %c", GetStackElement(buffer->after, i));
    }
    printf("\n");
    for (i = 0; i < StackDepth(buffer->before); i++) {
        printf("  ");
    }
    printf("^\n");
}
```

Which implementation is better? Without some knowledge of the usage pattern, it is impossible to answer this question. Knowing a little about the way that people use editors, however, suggests that the stack-based strategy might well be more efficient because the slow operations for the array implementation (insertion and deletion) are used much more frequently than the slow operations for the stack implementation (moving the cursor a long distance).

While this tradeoff seems reasonable given the relative frequency of the operations involved, it makes sense to ask whether it is possible to do even better. After all, it is now true that each of the six fundamental editing operations runs in constant time in at least one of the two editor implementations. Insertion is slow given the array implementation but fast when using the stack approach. By contrast, moving to the front of the buffer is fast in the array case but slow in the stack case. None of the operations, however, seems to be *fundamentally* slow, since there is always some implementation which makes that operation fast. Is it possible to develop an implementation in which all the operations are fast? The answer to this question turns out to be "yes," but discovering the key to the puzzle will require you to learn a new approach to representing ordering relationships in a data structure.

■ 9.5 Implementing the editor using linked lists

As an initial step toward finding a more efficient representation for the editor buffer, it makes sense to examine why the previous approaches have failed to provide efficient service for certain operations. In the case of the array implementation, the answer is obvious: the problem comes from the fact that you have to move a large number of characters whenever you need to insert some new text near the beginning of the buffer. For example, suppose that you were trying to enter the alphabet and instead typed

```
A C D E F G H I J K L M N O P Q R S T U V W X Y Z
```

When you discovered that you'd left out the letter B, you would have to shift each of the next 24 characters one position to the right in order to make room for the missing letter. A modern computer could handle this shifting operation relatively quickly as long as the buffer did not grow too long; even so, the delay would eventually become noticeable if the number of characters in the buffer became sufficiently large.

Suppose, however, that you were writing before the invention of modern computers. What would happen if you were instead using a typewriter and had already typed the complete line? To avoid giving the impression that you had slighted one of the letters in the alphabet, you could simply take out a pen and make the following notation:

```
  B
A C D E F G H I J K L M N O P Q R S T U V W X Y Z
  ^
```

The result is perhaps a trifle inelegant, but nonetheless acceptable in such desperate circumstances.

One advantage of this human editing notation is that it allows you to suspend the rule that says all letters are arranged in sequence in precisely the form in which they appear on the printed page. The carat symbol below the line tells your eyes that, after reading the **A**, you have to then move up, read the **B**, come back down, read the **c**, and then continue with the sequence. It is also important to notice another advantage of using this insertion strategy. No matter how long the line is, all you have to draw is the new character and the carat symbol. Using pencil and paper, insertion runs in constant time.[1]

The concept of a linked list

You can adopt a similar approach in designing a computer-based representation of the editing buffer. In fact, you can even generalize the idea so that, instead of representing the buffer mostly as an array with occasional deviations from the normal sequence, you simply draw an arrow from each letter in the buffer to the letter that follows it. The original buffer contents might then be represented as follows:

A→C→D→E→F→G→H→I→J→K→L→M→N→O→P→Q→R→S→T→U→V→W→X→Y→Z

If you then need to add the character **B** after the character **A**, all you need to do is (1) write the **B** down somewhere, (2) draw an arrow from **B** to the letter to which **A** is pointing (which is currently the **c**) so that you don't lose track of the rest of the string, and (3) change the arrow pointing from the **A** so that it now points to the **B**, like this:

A C→D→E→F→G→H→I→J→K→L→M→N→O→P→Q→R→S→T→U→V→W→X→Y→Z

Given the symbols used to draw these diagrams, it is probably not surprising to discover that the principal tool for implementing the new strategy in C is the pointer. One of the great advantages of pointers is that they make it possible for one data object to include a pointer to a second object. You can use this pointer to indicate an ordering relationship, much like the ordering relationship implied by the arrows in the foregoing diagram. Pointers used in this way are often referred to as **links.** When such links are used to create a linearly ordered data structure in which each element points to its successor, that structure is called a **linked list.**

---

[1] This technique for inserting missing text was used twice in the U.S. Declaration of Independence. The first instance, for example, occurs in the list of charges against King George III and looks like this:

He has dissolved Representative Houses repeatedly,

Designing a linked-list data structure

If you want to apply this pointer-based strategy to the design of the editor buffer, what you need is a linked list of characters. You have to associate each character in the buffer with a pointer that indicates the next character in the list. That pointer, however, cannot be a simple character pointer; what you really need is a pointer to the next character/link combination. To make a linked list work, you have to combine in a single record a piece of data relevant to the application (in this case, the character) and a pointer to another such record, which is then used to indicate the internal ordering. This combination of the application data and the pointer becomes the basic building block for the linked list, which is often referred to as a **cell.**

To make the idea of a cell a little easier to visualize, it often helps to start with a structure diagram before moving to an actual definition. In the editor buffer, a cell has two components: a character and link to the following cell. A single cell can therefore be diagrammed as follows:

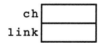

You can then represent a sequence of characters by linking several of these cells together. For example, the character sequence **ABC** could be represented as a linked list containing the following collection of cells:

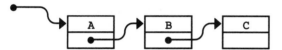

If the **C** is the last character in the sequence, you need to indicate that fact by putting a special value in the `link` field of that cell to indicate that there are no additional characters in the list. When programming in C, it is customary to use the special pointer value **NULL** for this purpose. In list structure diagrams, however, it is common to indicate the **NULL** value with a diagonal line across the box, as follows:

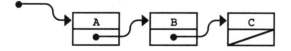

To represent these cell structure diagrams in C, you need to define an appropriate record type. In doing so, however, you must be a little careful. If you tried to define a record type called `cellT` that follows the structure of the diagram, you would probably write a type definition that looked something like this:

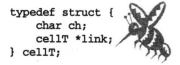

```
typedef struct {
    char ch;
    cellT *link;
} cellT;
```

This definition does not work in C.

The conceptual idea behind the definition is entirely correct: the `cellT` structure should include a `ch` field for the character and a `link` field that points to the next cell. There is, however, a problem in the line

```
cellT *link;
```

You want this line to tell the C compiler that the `link` field is a pointer to a `cellT`. The problem is that the type `cellT` has not yet been defined. The compiler does not know that it is defining the type `cellT` until it gets to the final line of the definition. At the time the compiler reads the definition of the `link` field, the name `cellT` is completely mysterious, and the compiler has no choice but to flag it as an error.

The essence of the problem is that the `cellT` type is defined in terms of itself and is therefore a **recursive type.** In C, whenever you define a structure that is part of a recursive type, you need to include a structure tag—as defined in the section on "Opaque types" in Chapter 8—so that you can refer to the type within the body of the definition. Thus, the following type definition correctly represents the conceptual structure of a cell:

```
typedef struct cellT {
    char ch;
    struct cellT *link;
} cellT;
```

In this definition, the `link` component is defined as a pointer to the type `struct cellT`. Because the compiler has already encountered the definition of `struct cellT` two lines earlier, the definition of the `link` field is no longer a problem.

Although the use of structure tags complicates the syntax of the type definition, you should not let it complicate your conceptual understanding. This text does not use structure tags outside of type definitions and always uses `typedef` to create a single name for each new structured type. As soon as the definition is complete, you can ignore the structure tag and use only the defined type name.

Using a linked list to represent the buffer

You are now in a position to consider the question of how you might use linked lists to represent the editor buffer. One possibility is simply to have the initial pointer in the linked list be the buffer, but this approach ignores the fact that you must also represent the cursor. The need to indicate a current buffer position suggests that the `bufferADT` type must contain two pointers: one to indicate where the buffer starts and one to indicate the current cursor position:

```
struct bufferCDT {
    cellT *start;
    cellT *cursor;
};
```

Thus, if your buffer contained the text `ABC`, you could take the character list

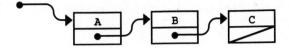

and store its initial pointer in the **start** field.

But what about the **cursor** field? Your hope, of course, is that the **cursor** field can also be a pointer to one of these three cells, depending on the position of the abstract cursor. Unfortunately, there's a bit of a problem. There are four possible positions of the cursor in this buffer:

On the other hand, there are only three cells to which the **cursor** field might point. Thus, it is not immediately clear how you would be able to represent each of the possible cursor locations.

There are many tactical approaches to solving this problem, but the one that usually turns out to be the best is to allocate an extra cell so that the list contains one cell for each possible insertion point. Typically, this cell goes at the beginning of the list and is called a **dummy cell.** The value of the **ch** field in the dummy cell is irrelevant and is indicated in diagrams by filling the value field with a gray background, as follows:

When you use the dummy cell approach, the **cursor** field points to the cell immediately before the logical insertion point. For example, a buffer containing **ABC** with the cursor at the beginning of the buffer would look like this:

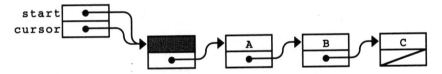

Both **start** and **cursor** point to the dummy cell, which means that insertions in this buffer will occur immediately after this cell. If the **cursor** field instead indicates the end of the buffer, the diagram looks like this:

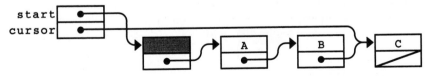

The dummy cell approach, while extremely useful, is not necessary and is certainly not part of all linked-list structures. The principal advantage of using a dummy cell is that doing so reduces the number of special cases you need to consider in your code when you are performing insertions or deletions at arbitrary points in the list.

Insertion into a linked-list buffer

No matter where the cursor is positioned, the insertion operation for a linked list consists of precisely the steps outlined for the conceptual arrow model earlier, written here in the terminology used in the buffer data structure:

1. Allocate space for a new cell, and store the pointer to this cell in the temporary variable `cp`.
2. Copy the character to be inserted into the `ch` field of the new cell (`cp->ch`).
3. Go to the cell indicated by the `cursor` field of the buffer and copy its link field (`buffer->cursor->link`) to the `link` field of the new cell (`cp->link`). This operation makes sure that you don't lose the characters that lie beyond the current cursor position.
4. Change the `link` field in the cell addressed by the cursor so that it points to the new cell.
5. Change the `cursor` field in the buffer so that it also points to the new cell. This operation ensures that the next character will be inserted after this one in repeated insertion operations.

To illustrate this process, suppose that you want to insert the letter B into a buffer that currently contains

$$A \mid C \quad D$$

with the cursor between the A and the C as shown. The situation prior to the insertion looks like this:

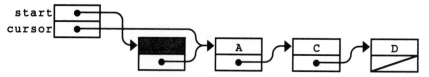

The first step in the insertion strategy is to allocate a new cell and store a pointer to it in the variable `cp`, as shown:

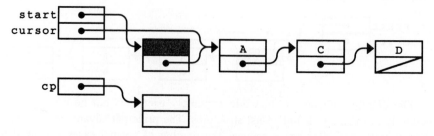

Step 2 is to put the character B into the `ch` field of the new cell, which leaves the following configuration:

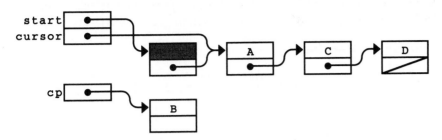

In step 3, you copy the `link` field from the cell whose address appears in the `cursor` field into the `link` field of the new cell. That `link` field points to the cell containing C, so the resulting diagram looks like this:

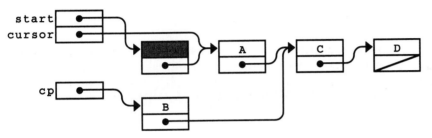

In step 4, you change the `link` field in the current cell addressed by the cursor so that it points to the newly allocated cell, as follows:

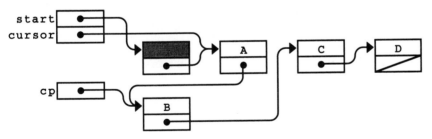

Note that the buffer now has the correct contents. If you follow the arrows from the dummy cell at the beginning of the buffer, you encounter the cells containing A, B, C, and D, in order along the path.

The final step consists of changing the `cursor` field in the buffer structure so that it also points to the new cell, which results in the following configuration:

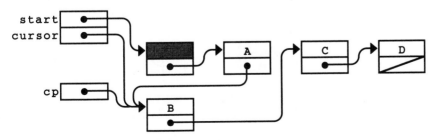

When the program returns from the `InsertCharacter` function, the temporary variable `cp` is released, which results in the following final buffer state:

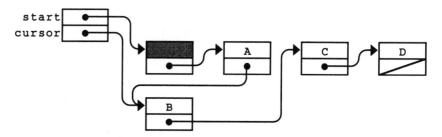

which represents the buffer contents

A B|C D

The following implementation of the `InsertCharacter` function is a simple translation into C code of the informal steps illustrated in the last several diagrams:

```
void InsertCharacter(bufferADT buffer, char ch)
{
    cellT *cp;

    cp = New(cellT *);
    cp->ch = ch;
    cp->link = buffer->cursor->link;
    buffer->cursor->link = cp;
    buffer->cursor = cp;
}
```

Because there are no loops inside this function, the `InsertCharacter` function now runs in constant time.

Deletion in a linked-list buffer

To delete a cell in a linked list, all you have to do is remove it from the pointer chain. Let's assume that the current contents of the buffer are

A|B C

which has the following graphical representation:

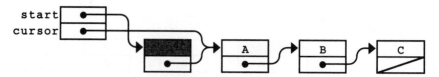

Deleting the character after the cursor means that you need to eliminate the cell containing the B by changing the `link` field of the cell containing A so that it points to the following character. To find that character, you need to follow the `link` field from the current cell and continue on to the following `link` field. The necessary statement is therefore

```
buffer->cursor->link = buffer->cursor->link->link;
```

Executing this statement leaves the buffer in the following state:

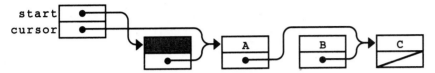

Because the cell containing `B` is no longer accessible through the linked-list structure, it is good policy to free its storage by calling `FreeBlock`, as shown in the following implementation of `DeleteCharacter`:

```
void DeleteCharacter (bufferADT buffer)
{
    cellT *cp;

    if (buffer->cursor->link != NULL) {
        cp = buffer->cursor->link;
        buffer->cursor->link = cp->link;
        FreeBlock (cp) ;
    }
}
```

Note that you need a variable like `cp` to hold a copy of the pointer to the cell about to be freed while you adjust the chain pointers. If you do not save this value, there will be no way to refer to that cell when you want to call `FreeBlock`.

Cursor motion in the linked-list representation

The remaining operations in the `buffer.h` interface simply move the cursor. How would you go about implementing these operations in the linked-list buffer? It turns out that two of these operations (`MoveCursorForward` and `MoveCursorToStart`) are easy to perform in the linked-list model. To move the cursor forward, for example, all you have to do is pick up the `link` field from the current cell and make that pointer be the new current cell by storing it in the `cursor` field of the buffer. The statement necessary to accomplish this operation is simply

```
buffer->cursor = buffer->cursor->link;
```

As an example, suppose that the editor buffer contains

$$|\ \text{A B C}$$

with the cursor at the beginning as shown. The list structure diagram for the buffer is then

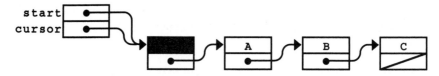

and the result of executing the `MoveCursorForward` operation is

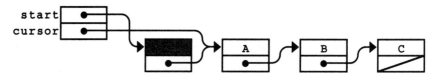

Of course, when you reach the end of the buffer, you can no longer move forward. The implementation of `MoveCursorForward` should check for this condition, so the complete function definition looks like this:

```
void MoveCursorForward(bufferADT buffer)
{
    if (buffer->cursor->link != NULL) {
        buffer->cursor = buffer->cursor->link;
    }
}
```

Moving the cursor to the beginning of the buffer is equally easy. No matter where the cursor is, you can always restore it to the beginning of the buffer by copying the `start` field into the `cursor` field. Thus, the implementation of `MoveCursorToStart` is simply

```
void MoveCursorToStart(bufferADT buffer)
{
    buffer->cursor = buffer->start;
}
```

The operations `MoveCursorBackward` and `MoveCursorToEnd`, however, are more complicated. Suppose, for example, that the cursor is sitting at the end of a buffer containing the characters **ABC** and that you want to move back one position. In its graphical representation, the buffer looks like this:

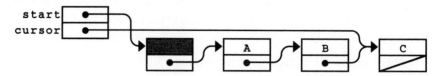

Given the structure of the `bufferADT`, there is no constant time strategy for backing up the pointer. The problem is that you have no easy way—given the information you can see—to find out what cell precedes the current one. Pointers allow you to follow a chain from the pointer to the object to which it points, but there is no way to reverse the direction. Given only the address of a cell, it is impossible to find out what cells point to it. With respect to the pointer diagrams, the effect of this restriction is that you can move from the dot at the base of an arrow to the cell to which the arrow points, but you can never go from an arrowhead back to its base.

In the list-structure representation of the buffer, you have to implement every operation in terms of the data that you can see from the buffer structure itself, which contains the `start` and the `cursor` pointers. Looking at just the `cursor` field and following the links that are accessible from that position does not seem promising, because the only cell reachable on that chain is the very last cell in the buffer, as illustrated in the following diagram:

If you instead consider the `start` pointer, the entire buffer is accessible on the linked-list chain:

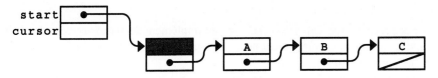

On the other hand, without looking at the `cursor` field, you no longer have any indication of the current buffer position.

Before you abandon hope, you need to recognize that it is possible in this case to find the cell which precedes the current cell. It is just not possible to do so in constant time. If you start at the beginning of the buffer and follow the links through all its cells, you will eventually hit a cell whose `link` field points to the same cell as the `cursor` field in the `bufferADT` structure itself. This cell must be the preceding cell in the list. Once you find it, you can simply change the `cursor` field in the `bufferADT` to point to that cell, which has the effect of moving the cursor backward.

Moving through the values of a linked list, one cell at a time, by following link pointers is a very common operation, which is usually called **traversing** or **walking** the list. To traverse the list representing the buffer, you first declare a pointer variable and initialize it to the beginning of the list. Thus, in this instance, you might write

```
cellT *cp;

cp = buffer->start;
```

To find the character preceding the cursor, you want to walk down the list as long as `cp`'s `link` field does not match the cursor, moving `cp` from cell to cell by following each `link` field. You might therefore continue the code by adding the following `while` loop:

```
cp = buffer->start;
while (cp->link != buffer->cursor) {
    cp = cp->link;
}
```

When the `while` loop exits, `cp` is set to the cell prior to the cursor. As with moving forward, you need to protect this loop against trying to move past the limits of the buffer, so the complete code for `MoveCursorBackward` would be

```
void MoveCursorBackward(bufferADT buffer)
{
    cellT *cp;

    if (buffer->cursor != buffer->start) {
        cp = buffer->start;
        while (cp->link != buffer->cursor) {
            cp = cp->link;
        }
        buffer->cursor = cp;
    }
}
```

For precisely the same reasons, you can implement `MoveCursorToEnd` only by walking through the entire linked list until you detect the `NULL` pointer, as illustrated by the following code:

```
void MoveCursorToEnd(bufferADT buffer)
{
    while (buffer->cursor->link != NULL) {
        MoveCursorForward(buffer);
    }
}
```

Linked-list idioms

Many C programmers, however, will not use a `while` in the `MoveCursorBackward` implementation to walk through the elements of a list. In C, whenever you have a repetitive operation in which you can easily specify an initialization, a test to see whether you should continue, and a sequencing operation that moves from one cycle to the next, the iterative construct of choice is the `for` loop, which allows you to put all these ideas together in one place. In the `MoveCursorBackward` example, you have all three of these pieces and might therefore have coded the internal loop as follows:

```
for (cp = buffer->start; cp->link != buffer->cursor; cp = cp->link);
```

The first thing to notice about this loop is that the body performs no operations at all. The `for` loop is executed entirely for its effect on the pointer variable `cp`, and there are no other operations to perform. In C, such situations come up surprisingly often. In this example, the body of the loop is the empty statement indicated by the semicolon at the end of the `for` line. Although the use of the semicolon as an empty loop body is common practice and you need to recognize it, this text will always use a comment to make it easier to see that the loop body has no effect, as in the following example:

```
for (cp = buffer->start; cp->link != buffer->cursor; cp = cp->link) {
    /* Empty */
}
```

Because the `for` loop is so useful when working with linked lists, it is important to recognize the standard `for` loop idioms used to manipulate list structure. In C programs, such idioms are often as important as those used with arrays. For example, the idiom for performing an operation on every element in an array whose effective size is n looks like this:

```
for (i = 0; i < N; i++) {
    code using a[i]
}
```

For linked lists, the corresponding idiom is

```
for (cp = list; cp != NULL; cp = cp->link) {
    code using cp
}
```

Completing the buffer implementation

The complete `buffer.h` interface contains three functions that have yet to be implemented: `NewBuffer`, `FreeBuffer`, and `DisplayBuffer`. In `NewBuffer`, the only wrinkle is that you need to remember the existence of the dummy cell when you write the code. In addition to allocating space for the buffer itself, the code must also allocate the dummy cell that is present even in the empty buffer. Once you remember this detail, however, the code for `NewBuffer` is fairly straightforward:

```
bufferADT NewBuffer(void)
{
    bufferADT buffer;

    buffer = New(bufferADT);
    buffer->start = buffer->cursor = New(cellT *);
    buffer->start->link = NULL;
    return (buffer);
}
```

The implementation of `FreeBuffer` is slightly more subtle. When `FreeBuffer` is called, it is responsible for freeing any memory allocated by the abstraction, which includes not only the `bufferADT` itself, but also every cell in the linked-list chain. Given the earlier discussion of the `for` loop idiom, you might be tempted to code `FreeBuffer` as follows:

```
void FreeBuffer(bufferADT buffer)
{
    cellT *cp;

    for (cp = buffer->start; cp != NULL; cp = cp->link) {
        FreeBlock(cp);
    }
    FreeBlock(buffer);
}
```

This code refers to memory that has already been freed.

The problem here is that the code tries to use the `link` pointer inside each block after that block has been freed. Once you call `FreeBlock` on a pointer to a record, you are no longer allowed to look inside that record. Doing so is likely to cause errors. To avoid this problem, you need to maintain your position in the list in a separate variable as you free each cell; in essence, you need a place to stand. Thus, the correct code for `FreeBuffer` is slightly more convoluted and has the following form:

```
void FreeBuffer(bufferADT buffer)
{
    cellT *cp, *next;

    cp = buffer->start;
    while (cp != NULL) {
        next = cp->link;
        FreeBlock(cp);
        cp = next;
    }
    FreeBlock(buffer);
}
```

The complete code for the linked-list implementation of the buffer abstraction appears in Figure 9-5.

Computational complexity of the linked-list buffer

From the discussion in the preceding section, it is easy to add another column to the complexity table showing the cost of the fundamental editing operations as a function of the number of characters in the buffer. The new table, which includes the data for all three implementations, appears in Table 9-4.

TABLE 9-4 Relative efficiency of the buffer representations

Function	Array	Stack	List
MoveCursorForward	$O(1)$	$O(1)$	$O(1)$
MoveCursorBackward	$O(1)$	$O(1)$	$O(N)$
MoveCursorToStart	$O(1)$	$O(N)$	$O(1)$
MoveCursorToEnd	$O(1)$	$O(N)$	$O(N)$
InsertCharacter	$O(N)$	$O(1)$	$O(1)$
DeleteCharacter	$O(N)$	$O(1)$	$O(1)$

FIGURE 9-5   Implementation of the editor buffer using a linked list

```
/*
 * File: listbuf.c
 * ---------------
 * This file implements the buffer.h abstraction using a linked
 * list to represent the buffer.
 */

#include <stdio.h>
#include "genlib.h"
#include "strlib.h"
#include "buffer.h"

/* Types */

typedef struct cellT {
    char ch;
    struct cellT *link;
} cellT;

struct bufferCDT {
    cellT *start;
    cellT *cursor;
};

/*
 * Implementation notes: NewBuffer
 * -------------------------------
 * This function allocates an empty editor buffer, represented
 * as a linked list.  To simplify the link list operation, this
 * implementation adopts the useful programming tactic of
 * keeping an extra "dummy" cell at the beginning of each list,
 * so that the empty buffer has the following representation:
 *
 *      +-------+          +------+
 *      |   o---+-----====>|      |
 *      +-------+    /      +------+
 *      |   o---+---/       | NULL |
 *      +-------+          +------+
 */

bufferADT NewBuffer(void)
{
    bufferADT buffer;

    buffer = New(bufferADT);
    buffer->start = buffer->cursor = New(cellT *);
    buffer->start->link = NULL;
    return (buffer);
}
```

```
/*
 * Implementation notes: FreeBuffer
 * --------------------------------
 * FreeBuffer must free every cell in the buffer as well as
 * the buffer storage itself.  Note that the loop structure
 * is not exactly the standard idiom for processing every
 * cell within a linked list, because it is not legal to
 * free a cell and later look at its link field.  To avoid
 * selecting fields in the structure after it has been freed,
 * you have to copy the link pointer before calling FreeBlock.
 */

void FreeBuffer(bufferADT buffer)
{
    cellT *cp, *next;

    cp = buffer->start;
    while (cp != NULL) {
        next = cp->link;
        FreeBlock(cp);
        cp = next;
    }
    FreeBlock(buffer);
}

void MoveCursorForward(bufferADT buffer)
{
    if (buffer->cursor->link != NULL) {
        buffer->cursor = buffer->cursor->link;
    }
}

void MoveCursorBackward(bufferADT buffer)
{
    cellT *cp;

    if (buffer->cursor != buffer->start) {
        cp = buffer->start;
        while (cp->link != buffer->cursor) {
            cp = cp->link;
        }
        buffer->cursor = cp;
    }
}

void MoveCursorToStart(bufferADT buffer)
{
    buffer->cursor = buffer->start;
}

void MoveCursorToEnd(bufferADT buffer)
{
    while (buffer->cursor->link != NULL) {
        MoveCursorForward(buffer);
    }
}
```

```
void InsertCharacter(bufferADT buffer, char ch)
{
    cellT *cp;

    cp = New(cellT *);
    cp->ch = ch;
    cp->link = buffer->cursor->link;
    buffer->cursor->link = cp;
    buffer->cursor = cp;
}

void DeleteCharacter(bufferADT buffer)
{
    cellT *cp;

    if (buffer->cursor->link != NULL) {
        cp = buffer->cursor->link;
        buffer->cursor->link = cp->link;
        FreeBlock(cp);
    }
}

void DisplayBuffer(bufferADT buffer)
{
    cellT *cp;

    for (cp = buffer->start->link; cp != NULL; cp = cp->link) {
        printf(" %c", cp->ch);
    }
    printf("\n");
    for (cp = buffer->start; cp != buffer->cursor; cp = cp->link) {
        printf("  ");
    }
    printf("^\n");
}
```

Unfortunately, the table for the list structure representation still contains two $O(N)$ operations, `MoveCursorBackward` and `MoveCursorToEnd`. The problem with this representation is that the link pointers impose a directionality on the implementation: moving forward is easy because the pointers move in the forward direction.

Doubly linked lists

The good news is that this problem is quite easy to solve. To get around the problem that the links run only in one direction, all you need to do is make the pointers symmetrical. In addition to having a pointer from each cell that indicates the next one, you can also include a pointer to the previous cell. The resulting structure is called a **doubly linked list.**

Each cell in the doubly linked list has two link fields, a **prev** field that points to the previous cell and a **next** field that points to the next one. For reasons that will become clear when you implement the primitive operations, it simplifies the manipulation of the structure if the **prev** field of the dummy cell points to the end of the buffer and the **next** field of the last cell points back to the dummy cell. If this design is used, the doubly linked representation of the buffer containing the text

A | B C

looks like this:

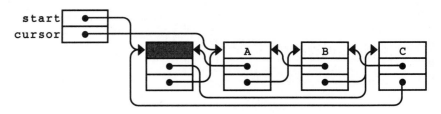

There are quite a few pointers in this diagram, which makes it is easy to get confused. On the other hand, the structure has all the information you need to implement each of the fundamental editing operations in constant time. The actual implementation, however, is left as an exercise so that you can refine your understanding of linked lists.

Time-space tradeoffs

The discovery that you can implement a buffer that has these good computational properties is an important theoretical result. Unfortunately, that result may not in fact be so useful in practice, at least in the context of the editor application. By the time you get around to adding the **prev** field to each cell for the doubly linked list, you will end up using at least nine bytes of memory to represent each character. You may be able to perform editing operations very quickly, but you will use up memory at an extravagant rate. At this point, you face what computer scientists call a **time-space tradeoff.** You can improve the computational efficiency of your algorithm, but waste space in doing so. Wasting this space could matter a lot, if, for example, it meant that the maximum size of the file you could edit on your machine were only one-tenth of what it would have been if you had chosen the array representation.

When such situations arise in practice, it is usually possible to develop a hybrid strategy that allows you to select a point somewhere in the middle of the time-space tradeoff curve. For example, you could combine the array and linked-list strategies by representing the buffer as a doubly linked list of lines, where each line was represented using the array form. In this case, insertion at the beginning of a line would be a little slower, but only in proportion to the length of the line and not to the length of the entire buffer. On the other hand, this strategy requires link pointers for each line rather than for each character. Since a line typically contains many characters, using this representation would reduce the storage overhead considerably.

Getting the details right on hybrid strategies can be a challenge, but it is important to know that such strategies exist and that there are ways to take advantage of algorithmic time improvements which are not prohibitively expensive in terms of their storage requirements.

◼ Summary

Even though this chapter focused its attention on implementing an abstract data type representing an editor buffer, the buffer itself is not the main point. Text buffers that maintain a cursor position are useful in a relatively small number of application domains. The individual techniques used to improve the buffer representation— particularly the concept of a linked list—are fundamental ideas that you will use over and over again.

Important points in this chapter include:

- The strategy used to represent a type can have a significant effect on the computational complexity of the operations used to manipulate the type.
- Although an array provides a workable representation for an editor buffer, you can improve its performance by using other representation strategies. Using a pair of stacks, for example, reduces the cost of insertion and deletion at the cost of making it harder to move the cursor a long distance.
- You can indicate the order of elements in a sequence by storing a pointer with each value linking it to the one that follows it. In programming, structures designed in this way are called *linked lists*. The pointers that connect that connect one value to the next are called *links,* and the individual records used to store the values and link fields together are called *cells*.
- The conventional way to mark the end of a linked list is to store the pointer constant **NULL** in the link field of the last cell.
- If you are inserting and deleting values from a linked list, it is often convenient to allocate an extra dummy cell at the beginning of the list. The advantage of this technique is that the existence of the dummy cell reduces the number of special cases you need to consider in your code.
- Insertions and deletions at specified points in a linked list are constant-time operations.
- You can iterate through the cells of a linked list by using the following idiom:

```
for (cp = list; cp != NULL; cp = cp->link) {
    code using cp
}
```

- Doubly linked lists make it possible to traverse a list efficiently in both directions.

- Linked lists tend to be efficient in execution time but inefficient in their use of memory. In some cases, you may be able to design a hybrid strategy that allows you to combine the execution efficiency of linked lists with the space advantages of arrays.

REVIEW QUESTIONS

1. True or false: The computational complexity of a program depends only on its algorithmic structure, not on the structures used to represent the data.

2. What does *wysiwyg* stand for?

3. In your own words, describe the purpose of the buffer abstraction used in this chapter.

4. What are the six commands implemented by the editor application? What are the corresponding functions in the `buffer.h` interface?

5. In addition to the functions that correspond to the editor commands, what other functions are exported by the `buffer.h` interface?

6. Which editor operations require linear time in the array representation of the editor buffer? What makes those operations slow?

7. Draw a diagram showing the contents of the `before` and `after` stack in the two-stack representation of a buffer that contains the following text, with the cursor positioned as shown:

$$A \quad B \quad C \quad D \mid G \quad H \quad I \quad J$$

8. How is the cursor position indicated in the two-stack representation of the editor buffer?

9. Which editor operations require linear time in the two-stack representation?

10. Define each of the following terms: *cell, link, linked list, dummy cell.*

11. What is the conventional way to mark the end of a linked list?

12. Why is a structure tag required in the type definition of a linked-list cell?

13. What is the purpose of a dummy cell in a linked list?

14. Does the dummy cell go at the beginning or the end of a linked list? Why?

15. What are the five steps required to insert a new character into the linked-list buffer?

16. Draw a diagram showing all the cells in the linked-list representation of a buffer that contains the following text, with the cursor positioned as shown:

H   E   L $|$ L   O

17. Modify the diagram you drew in the preceding exercise to show what happens if you insert the character **X** at the cursor position.

18. What is meant by the phrase *traversing a list?*

19. What is the standard idiom used in C to traverse a linked list?

20. Which editor operations require linear time in the linked-list representation of the editor buffer? What makes those operations slow?

21. What modification can you make to the linked-list structure so that all six of the editor operations run in constant time?

22. What is a time-space tradeoff?

23. What is the major drawback to the solution you offered in your answer to question 21? What can you do to improve the situation?

PROGRAMMING   EXERCISES

1. The array implementation of the buffer abstraction in Figure 9-3 imposes an arbitrary upper limit on the buffer size. By replacing the explicit character array with a dynamically allocated one, rewrite the **arraybuf.c** implementation so that it expands the buffer space if an insertion would otherwise overflow the existing buffer boundaries.

2. Even if the stacks used in the **stackbuf.c** implementation of the buffer abstraction (see Figure 9-4) expand dynamically, the amount of character space required in the stacks is likely to be twice as large as that required in the corresponding array implementation. The problem is that each stack must be able to accommodate all the characters in the buffer. Suppose, for example, that you are working with a buffer containing N characters. If you're at the beginning of the buffer, those N characters are in the **after** stack; if you move to the end of the buffer, those N characters move to the **before** stack. As a result, each of the stacks must have a capacity of N characters.

   You can reduce the storage requirement in the two-stack implementation of the buffer by storing the two stacks at opposite ends of the same internal array. The **before** stack starts at the beginning of the array, while the **after** stack starts at the end. The two stacks then grow toward each other as indicated by the arrows in the following diagram:

before $\longrightarrow$　　　　　　　　$\longleftarrow$ after

Reimplement the buffer abstraction using this design. Make sure that your program continues to have the same computational efficiency as the two-stack implementation in the text and that it expands the buffer space dynamically if necessary.

3. Rewrite the editor application given in Figure 9-2 so that the F, B, and D commands take a repetition count specified by a string of digits before the command letter. Thus, the command 17F would move the cursor forward 17 character positions.

4. Extend the numeric argument facility from exercise 3 so that the numeric argument can be preceded with a negative sign. For the F and B commands, this facility is not particularly useful because the -4F command is the same as 4B. For the D command, however, this extension allows you to delete characters backward using a command like -3D, which deletes the three characters before the current cursor position. What changes, if any, do you need to make to the buffer.h interface to implement this operation?

5. Extend the editor application so that the F, B, and D commands can be preceded with the letter W to indicate word motion. Thus, the command WF should move forward to the end of the next word, WB should move backward to the beginning of the preceding word, and WD should delete characters through the end of the next word. For the purposes of this exercise, a word consists of a consecutive sequence of alphanumeric characters (i.e., letters or digits) and includes any adjacent nonalphanumeric characters between the cursor and the word. This interpretation is easiest to see in the context of the following example:

```
*IThis is a test.↵                    Insert some text.
  T h i s   i s   a   t e s t .
                              ^

*WB↵                                  Back up one word.  Note
  T h i s   i s   a   t e s t .       that the period is skipped.
                          ^

*J↵                                   Jump to the beginning.
  T h i s   i s   a   t e s t .
  ^

*WF↵                                  Move forward to the end
  T h i s   i s   a   t e s t .       of the word.
        ^

*WF↵                                  Move forward to the end
  T h i s   i s   a   t e s t .       of the word.
              ^

*WD↵                                  Delete the space and the
  T h i s   i s   t e s t .           next word.
              ^
```

To complete this exercise, you will have to extend the `buffer.h` interface in some way. As you design that extension, try to keep in mind the principles of good interface design that were introduced in Chapter 3. After you have designed the interface extension, add the necessary code to `arraybuf.c`, `stackbuf.c`, and `listbuf.c` to implement your changes for each of the representations used in this chapter.

6. Most modern editors provide a facility that allows the user to copy a section of the buffer text into an internal storage area and then paste it back in at some other position. For each of the three representations of the buffer given in this chapter, implement the function

```
void CopyFromBuffer(bufferADT buffer, int count);
```

which stores a copy of the next `count` characters somewhere in the internal structure for the buffer, and the function

```
void PasteIntoBuffer(bufferADT buffer);
```

which inserts those saved characters back into the buffer at the current pointer position. Calling `PasteIntoBuffer` does not affect the saved text, which means that you can insert multiple copies of the same text by calling `PasteIntoBuffer` more than once. Test your implementation by adding the commands C and P to the editor application for the copy and paste operations, respectively. The C command should take a numeric argument to specify the number of characters using the technique described in exercise 3.

7. Editors that support the copy/paste facility described in the preceding exercise usually provide a third operation called *cut* that copies the text from the buffer and then deletes it. Implement a new editor command called x that implements the cut operation without making any changes to the `buffer.h` interface beyond those you needed to solve exercise 6.

8. For each of the three representations of the buffer given in this chapter, implement the function

```
bool SearchBuffer(bufferADT buffer, string str);
```

When this function is called, it should start searching from the current cursor position, looking for the next occurrence of the string `str`. If it finds it, `SearchBuffer` should leave the cursor after the last character in `str` and return the value TRUE. If `str` does not occur between the cursor and the end of the buffer, then `SearchBuffer` should leave the cursor unchanged and return FALSE.

To illustrate the operation of `SearchBuffer`, suppose that you have added the s command to the `editor.c` program so that it calls the `SearchBuffer` function, passing it the rest of the input line. Your program should then be able to match the following sample run:

```
*ITo Erik Roberts.↵              Insert some text.
  T  o     E  r  i  k     R  o  b  e  r  t  s
                                             ∧

*J.↵                             Jump back to the start.
  T  o     E  r  i  k     R  o  b  e  r  t  s
∧

*SErik.↵                         Find "Erik"; put cursor
  T  o     E  r  i  k     R  o  b  e  r  t  s    at the end of the string.
                      ∧

*B.↵                             Back up one character.
  T  o     E  r  i  k     R  o  b  e  r  t  s
                   ∧

*D.↵                             Delete the "k".
  T  o     E  r  i     R  o  b  e  r  t  s
                   ∧

*Ic.↵                            Insert the "c".
  T  o     E  r  i  c     R  o  b  e  r  t  s
                   ∧

*SErik.↵                         Finding "Erik" again has
Search failed.                   no effect because there
  T  o     E  r  i  c     R  o  b  e  r  t  s    are no more matches.
                   ∧
```

9. Without making any further changes to the **buffer.h** interface beyond those required for exercise 8, add an **R** command to the editor application that replaces the next occurrence of one string with another, where the two strings are specified after the **R** command separated by a slash, as shown:

```
*ITo Erik Roberts↵
  T  o     E  r  i  k     R  o  b  e  r  t  s
                                             ∧

*J.↵
  T  o     E  r  i  k     R  o  b  e  r  t  s
∧
*RErik/Eric.↵
  T  o     E  r  i  c     R  o  b  e  r  t  s
                   ∧
```

10. For each of the three representations of the buffer given in this chapter, implement the function

```
string BufferToString(bufferADT buffer);
```

which returns the entire contents of the buffer as a string of characters.

11. The dummy cell strategy described in the text is useful because it reduces the number of special cases in the code. On the other hand, it is not strictly necessary. Write a new implementation of `listbuf.c` in which you make the following changes to the design:

    - The linked list contains no dummy cell—just a cell for every character.
    - A buffer in which the cursor occurs before the first character is indicated by storing `NULL` in the cursor field.
    - Every function that checks the position of the cursor makes a special test for `NULL` and performs whatever special actions are necessary in that case.

12. Implement the buffer abstraction using the strategy described in the section entitled "Doubly linked lists" earlier in this chapter. Be sure to test your implementation as thoroughly as you can. In particular, make sure that you can move the cursor in both directions across parts of the buffer where you have recently made insertions and deletions.

13. The biggest problem with using a doubly linked list to represent the editor buffer is that it is terribly inefficient in terms of space. With two pointers in each cell and only one character, pointers take up 89 percent of the storage, which is likely to represent an unacceptable level of overhead.

    The best way around this problem is to combine the array and linked-list models so that the actual structure consists of a doubly linked list of units called *blocks,* where each block contains the following:

    - The `prev` and `next` pointers required for the doubly linked list
    - The number of characters currently stored in the block
    - A fixed-size array capable of holding several characters rather than a single one

    By storing several data characters in each block, you reduce the storage overhead, because the pointers take up a smaller fraction of the data. However, since the blocks are of a fixed maximum size, the problem of inserting a new character never requires shifting more than k characters, where k is the **block size** or maximum number of characters per block. Because the block size is a constant, the insertion operation remains $O(1)$. As the block size gets larger, the storage overhead decreases, but the time required to do an insertion increases. In the examples that follow, the block size is assumed to be four characters, although a larger block size would make more sense in practice.

    To get a better idea of how this new buffer representation works, consider how you would represent the character data in a block-based buffer. The characters in the buffer are stored in individual blocks, and each block is chained to the blocks that precede and follow it by link pointers. Because the blocks need not be full, there are many possible representations for the contents of a buffer, depending on how many characters appear in each block. For example, the buffer containing the text `"ABCDGHIJ"` might be divided into three blocks, as follows:

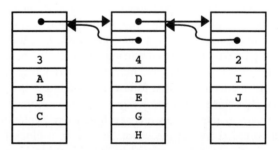

In this diagram, what you see are three blocks, each of which contains a pointer to the next block, a pointer to the previous block, the number of characters currently stored in the block, and four bytes of character storage. The actual definition of the concrete buffer type and the contents of two link fields missing in this diagram (the first backward link and the last forward one) depend on your representation of the concrete structure of the buffer, which is up to you to design. In particular, your buffer structure must include some way to represent the cursor position, which presumably means that the actual **bufferCDT** structure definition will include a pointer to the current block, as well as an index showing the current position within that block.

Assume for the moment that the cursor in the previous example follows the **D**, so the buffer contents are

A B C D | G H I J

Suppose you want to insert the missing letters, **E** and **F**. Inserting the **E** is a relatively simple matter because the active block has only three characters, leaving room for an extra one. Inserting the **E** into the buffer requires shifting the **G** and the **H** toward the end of the block, but does not require any changes to the pointers linking the blocks themselves. The configuration after inserting the **E** therefore looks like this:

If you now try to insert the missing **F**, however, the problem becomes more complicated. At this point, the current block is full. To make room for the **F**, you need to split the block into two pieces. A simple strategy is to split the block in two, putting half of the characters into each block. After splitting (but before inserting the **F**), the buffer looks like this:

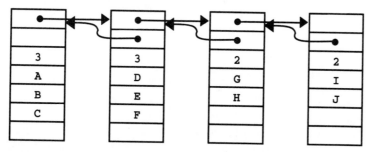

From this point, it is a simple matter to insert the **F** in the second block:

Reimplement the `buffer.h` interfaces so that the concrete representation of the buffer is a linked list of blocks, where each block can hold up to `MaxCharsPerBlock` characters. In writing your implementation, you should be sure to remember the following points:

- It is your responsibility to design the data structure for the `bufferCDT` type. Think hard about the design of your data structure before you start writing the code. Draw pictures. Figure out what the empty buffer looks like. Consider carefully how the data structures change as blocks are split.
- You should choose a strategy for representing the cursor that allows you to represent the possible states of a buffer in a consistent, understandable way. To get a sense of whether your representation works well, make sure that you can answer basic questions about your representation. How does your buffer structure indicate that the cursor is at the beginning of the buffer? What about a cursor at the end? What about a cursor that falls between characters in different blocks? Is there a unique representation for such circumstances, or is there ambiguity in your design? In general, it will help a great deal if you try to simplify your design and avoid introducing lots of special case handling.
- If you have to insert a character into a block that is full, you should divide the block in half before making the insertion. This policy helps ensure that neither of the two resulting blocks starts out being filled, which might immediately require another split when the next character came along.
- If you delete the last character in a block, your program should free the storage associated with that block unless it is the only block in the buffer.

- You should convince yourself that `FreeBuffer` works, in the sense that all allocated memory is freed and that you never reference data in memory that has been returned to the heap.
- Important design decisions should be documented explicitly in your code.

CHAPTER 10

Linear Structures

It does not come to me in quite so direct a line as that; it takes a bend or two, but nothing of consequence.

— Jane Austen, *Persuasion*, 1818

Objectives

- To recognize that stacks can be implemented using linked lists.

- To appreciate the relationship between the stack and queue abstractions.

- To learn how to implement queues using both arrays and linked lists as the underlying representation.

- To understand the concepts of models and simulations.

- To be able to write simple simulations that depend on the notion of discrete time.

The stack ADT introduced in Chapter 8 is an example of a general class of abstract data types called **linear structures,** in which the elements form a conceptual straight line. This chapter introduces a related abstract type called a *queue,* in which the internal elements have this same linear arrangement. The difference between these abstract structures lies in the operations they support. The *push* and *pop* operations defined by the stack abstraction require you to process elements in a last-in/first-out order. The corresponding operations for a queue are *enqueue* and *dequeue,* which allow you to process elements in a first-come/first-served fashion.

Because the elements in a linear structure are arranged in an array-like order, using arrays to represent them seems like an obvious choice. Indeed, the stack ADT presented in Chapter 8 is implemented using an array as the underlying representation. Arrays, however, are not the only option. Both stacks and queues can also be implemented using a linked list much like the one used to implement the editor buffer in Chapter 9. By focusing on the linked-list implementation of these structures, you will increase your understanding, not only of how linked lists work, but also of how you can apply them in practical programming contexts.

This chapter has another purpose as well. After you've learned how queues are implemented, the final section shows you how you can use queues in the context of a larger application. Like most of the other abstract types introduced in this text, stacks and queues act as tools that you can apply to a variety of useful contexts. Creating such tools, however, is only part of the programming process. As a programmer, you will spend most of your time building application programs. If the tools you build are well designed, they will simplify your work considerably. At the same time, it is important to remember that programming tools are a means to an end rather than an end in themselves. Thus, as you learn about new interfaces and tools, it is important to think about how you can use those tools and not focus entirely on how they are constructed.

■■ 10.1 Stacks revisited

Before examining the queue ADT in detail, it is useful to go back and take another look at stacks. While arrays are the most common underlying representation for stacks, it is also possible to implement the `stack.h` interface using linked lists. If you do so, the conceptual representation for the empty stack is simply the NULL pointer:

When you push a new element onto the stack, the element is simply added to the front of the linked-list chain. Thus, if you push the element e_1 onto an empty stack, that element is stored in a new cell which becomes the only link in the chain:

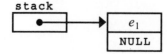

Pushing a new element onto the stack adds that element at the beginning of the chain. The steps involved are the same as those required to insert a character into a linked-list buffer. You first allocate a new cell, then enter the data, and, finally, update the link pointers so that the new cell becomes the first element in the chain. Thus, if you push the element e_2 on the stack, you get the following configuration:

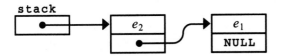

In the linked-list representation, the `Pop` operation consists of removing the first cell in the chain and returning the value stored there. Thus, a `Pop` operation from the stack shown in the preceding diagram returns e_2 and restores the previous state of the stack, as follows:

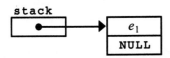

These diagrams, however, are overly simplistic. They suggest that the abstract type for the stack might simply be a pointer to a cell. The empty stack would be represented by **NULL**, and nonempty stacks by a pointer to the cell containing the topmost stack element. This definition has a certain elegance in theory but fails to work in practice.

Consider, for the moment, what would happen in you tried to define the type **stackADT** as a pointer to a cell, using the following definition:

```
typedef struct cellT *stackADT;
```

This definition fails.

Given this definition, the implementation of the procedure **NewStack** would be:

```
stackADT NewStack(void)
{
    return (NULL);
}
```

The client cannot use stacks initialized in this way.

There is no problem with the **NewStack** procedure itself. You can go ahead and declare a **stackADT** variable **myStack** in the client and initialize it by calling

```
myStack = NewStack();
```

After executing this statement, the variable **myStack** is initialized to **NULL**, which represents the empty stack.

```
myStack
NULL
```

Up to now, everything seems fine. The problem becomes apparent only when you try to use the stack. Imagine, for example, that you try to call

```
Push(myStack, e₁);
```

where e_1 is the value you want to push onto the stack. This call generates a new frame for **Push** whose parameter variables are initialized as follows:

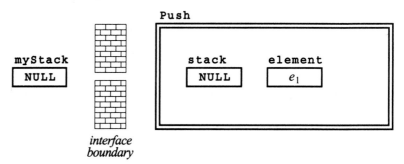

The important thing to notice in this diagram is that the value of **stack** inside the implementation is a *copy* of the value of **myStack** in the client. For **Push** to have the correct effect, it would need to change—not the value of the parameter variable **stack**, which it is perfectly free to do—but the value of **myStack** on the client side of the interface boundary. Given C's semantics, however, the **Push** function cannot change the value of **myStack**, which makes it impossible to use this representation strategy in its current form.

As a general rule, if a function exported by an interface needs to change the value of any data associated with an ADT, the data must be accessible from the implementation side of the abstraction boundary. The usual strategy for ensuring that the implementation has access to the data it requires is to make sure that the concrete type consists of a record whose address never changes. Any memory locations whose values change in response to operations performed by the implementation—such as the pointer to the stack chain in this example—must be embedded within the record used as the concrete type. What you need to do in this case is define the type **stackADT** as a pointer to its concrete **stackCDT** counterpart and then define **stackCDT** as a record with a single field used to store the linked list representing the stack. The interface therefore contains the standard abstract definition

```
typedef struct stackCDT *stackADT;
```

The implementation then defines **stackCDT** like this:

```
struct stackCDT {
    cellT *start;
};
```

This change seems innocuous, but the additional level of nesting in the record definition makes this structure work, even though the previous design failed. To see why, it helps to work through the design of the functions in the `stack.h` interface and determine how they change to accommodate the revised record structure.

The first function that needs to change is `NewStack`, which must allocate space for the `stackCDT` record and initialize the `start` field to `NULL`, like this:

```
stackADT NewStack(void)
{
    stackADT stack;

    stack = New(stackADT);
    stack->start = NULL;
    return (stack);
}
```

Given this revised representation, calling

```
myStack = NewStack();
```

has an effect that can be diagrammed as follows:

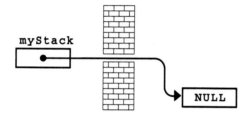

The variable `myStack` contains a pointer to a record that lives on the implementation side of the interface boundary, which means that the client has no direct access to the record itself. However, if the client calls

```
Push(myStack, e₁);
```

the implementation receives a copy of this pointer, which it can use to access the underlying structure. The stack frame after the call looks like this:

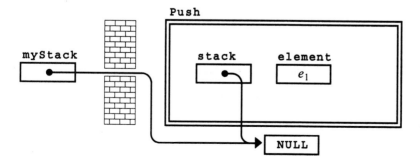

The implementation now has no trouble changing the `start` field of the stack record, because that field is accessible through the pointer passed as the parameter

stack. For example, the `Push` implementation simply allocates a new cell, initializes it, and assigns it to `stack->start`. The resulting configuration looks like this:

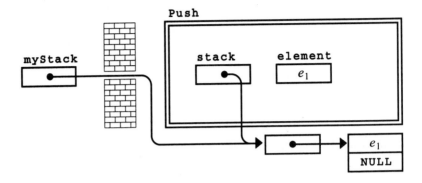

When the `Push` function returns, its stack frame goes away, leaving the following configuration:

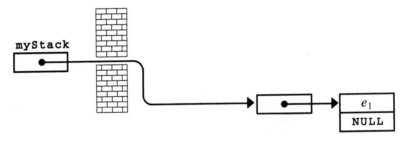

This diagram makes it clear that adding an extra level of pointer nesting in the data structure has made it possible for the `Push` function to insert e_1 at the correct position in the linked-list chain.

The complete implementation of the stack abstraction using linked lists is shown in Figure 10-1.

■ 10.2 Queues

The defining feature of a stack is that the last item pushed is always the first item popped. As noted in Chapter 8, this behavior is often referred to in computer science as **LIFO**, which is an acronym for the phrase "last in, first out." The LIFO discipline is useful in programming contexts because it reflects the operation of function calls; the most recently called function is the first to return. In real-world situations, however, its usefulness is more limited. In human society, our collective notion of fairness assigns some priority to being first, as expressed in the maxim "first come, first served." In programming, the usual phrasing of this ordering strategy is "first in, first out," which is traditionally abbreviated as **FIFO**. A data structure that stores items using a FIFO discipline is called a **queue.**

FIGURE 10-1 Implementation of the stack abstraction using linked lists

```c
/*
 * File: stack.c
 * -------------
 * This file implements the stack.h interface using linked lists.
 */

#include <stdio.h>
#include "genlib.h"
#include "stack.h"

/*
 * Type: cellT
 * -----------
 * This type defines the linked list cell used for the stack.
 */

typedef struct cellT {
    stackElementT element;
    struct cellT *link;
} cellT;

/*
 * Type: stackCDT
 * --------------
 * This type defines the concrete structure of a stack.
 */

struct stackCDT {
    cellT *start;
};

/* Exported entries */

stackADT NewStack(void)
{
    stackADT stack;

    stack = New(stackADT);
    stack->start = NULL;
    return (stack);
}

void FreeStack(stackADT stack)
{
    cellT *cp, *next;

    cp = stack->start;
    while (cp != NULL) {
        next = cp->link;
        FreeBlock(cp);
        cp = next;
    }
    FreeBlock(stack);
}
```

```
void Push(stackADT stack, stackElementT element)
{
    cellT *cp;

    cp = New(cellT *);
    cp->element = element;
    cp->link = stack->start;
    stack->start = cp;
}

stackElementT Pop(stackADT stack)
{
    stackElementT result;
    cellT *cp;

    if (StackIsEmpty(stack)) Error("Pop of an empty stack");
    cp = stack->start;
    result = cp->element;
    stack->start = cp->link;
    FreeBlock(cp);
    return (result);
}

bool StackIsEmpty(stackADT stack)
{
    return (stack->start == NULL);
}

bool StackIsFull(stackADT stack)
{
    return (FALSE);
}

int StackDepth(stackADT stack)
{
    int n;
    cellT *cp;

    n = 0;
    for (cp = stack->start; cp != NULL; cp = cp->link) n++;
    return (n);
}

stackElementT GetStackElement(stackADT stack, int depth)
{
    int i;
    cellT *cp;

    if (depth < 0 || depth >= StackDepth(stack)) {
        Error("Non-existent stack element");
    }
    cp = stack->start;
    for (i = 0; i < depth; i++) cp = cp->link;
    return (cp->element);
}
```

The fundamental operations on a queue—which are analogous to the **Push** and **Pop** operations for stacks—are called **Enqueue** and **Dequeue**. The **Enqueue** operation adds a new element to the end of the queue, which is traditionally called its **tail.** The **Dequeue** operation removes the element at the beginning of the queue, which is called its **head.**

The conceptual difference between these structures can be illustrated most easily with a diagram. In a stack, the client must add and remove elements from the same end of the internal data structure, as follows:

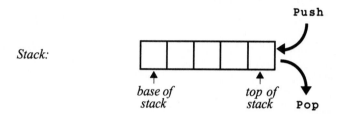

In a queue, the client adds elements at one end and removes them from the other, like this:

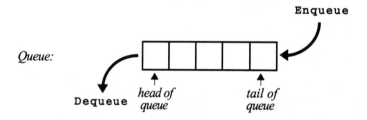

The structure of the queue.h interface

Because queues represent a general programming structure whose applicability extends beyond any specific application, it makes sense to define the queue interface as generally as possible. In particular, it is probably best to adopt the strategy used in **stack.h** to represent the element type, which means that the interface as a whole should be defined in terms of a type **queueElementT** that can be changed for particular applications. For many applications, the appropriate definition for **queueElementT** is the generic pointer type **void ***, which allows the queue elements to be any pointer type. A complete **queue.h** interface that uses **void *** as the definition of **queueElementT** is shown in Figure 10-2.

Array-based implementation of queues

As with stacks, it is possible to implement the queue abstraction using either arrays or linked lists for the underlying representation. The array implementation of a queue is more complicated than the corresponding implementation of a stack, because the action is no longer confined to one end of the array. Items are enqueued

FIGURE 10-2 The interface to the queue abstraction

```
/*
 * File: queue.h
 * --------------
 * This interface defines an abstraction for queues.  In any
 * single application that uses this interface, the values in
 * the queue are constrained to a single type, although it
 * is easy to change that type by changing the definition of
 * queueElementT in this interface.
 */

#ifndef _queue_h
#define _queue_h

#include "genlib.h"

/*
 * Type: queueElementT
 * -------------------
 * The type queueElementT is used in this interface to indicate
 * the type of values that can be stored in the queue.  Here the
 * queue is used to store values of type void *, but that can
 * be changed by editing this definition line.
 */

typedef void *queueElementT;

/*
 * Type: queueADT
 * --------------
 * The queueADT type is defined as a pointer to its concrete
 * counterpart, which is available only to the implementation,
 * not to clients.
 */

typedef struct queueCDT *queueADT;

/*
 * Function: NewQueue
 * Usage: queue = NewQueue();
 * --------------------------
 * This function allocates and returns an empty queue.
 */

queueADT NewQueue(void);

/*
 * Function: FreeQueue
 * Usage: FreeQueue(queue);
 * ------------------------
 * This function frees the storage associated with queue.
 */

void FreeQueue(queueADT queue);
```

Suppose now that five customers arrive, indicated by the letters *A* through *E*. Those customers are enqueued in order, which gives rise to the following configuration:

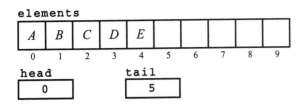

The value 0 in the **head** field indicates that the first customer in the queue is stored in position 0 of the array; the value 5 in **tail** indicates that the next customer will be placed in position 5. So far, so good. At this point, suppose that you alternately serve a customer at the beginning of the queue and then add a new customer to the end. For example, customer *A* is dequeued and customer *F* arrives, which leads to the following situation:

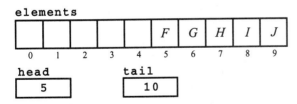

Imagine that you continue to serve one customer just before the next customer arrives and that this trend continues until customer *J* arrives. The internal structure of the queue then looks like this:

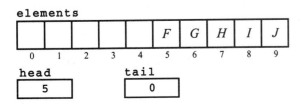

At this point, you've got a bit of a problem. There are only five customers in the queue, but you have used up all the available space. The **tail** field is pointing beyond the end of the array. On the other hand, you now have unused space at the beginning of the array. Thus, instead of incrementing **tail** so that it indicates the nonexistent position 10, you can "wrap around" from the end of the array back to position 0, as follows:

From this position, you have space to enqueue customer *K* in position 0, which leads to the following configuration:

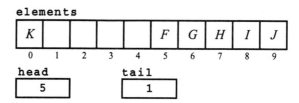

If you allow the elements in the queue to wrap around from the end of the array to the beginning, the active elements always extend from the `head` index up to the position immediately preceding the `tail` index, as illustrated in this diagram:

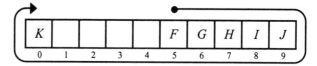

Because the ends of the array act as if they were joined together, programmers call this representation a **ring buffer.**

The only remaining issue you need to consider before you can write the code for **Enqueue** and **Dequeue** is how to check whether the queue is completely full. Testing for a full queue is trickier than you might expect. To get a sense of where complications might arise, suppose that three more customers arrive before any additional customers are served. If you enqueue the customers *L, M,* and *N,* the data structure looks like this:

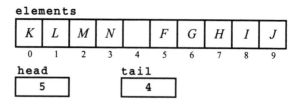

At this point, it appears as if there is one extra space. What happens, though, if customer *O* arrives at this moment? If you followed the logic of the earlier enqueue operations, you would end up in the following configuration:

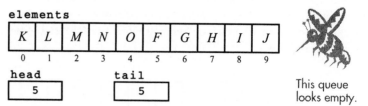

This queue looks empty.

The queue array is now completely full. Unfortunately, whenever the `head` and `tail` fields have the same value, as they do in this diagram, the queue is considered to be empty. There is no way to tell from the contents of the queue structure itself which of the two conditions—empty or full—actually applies, because the data values look the same in each case. Although you can fix this problem by adopting a different definition for the empty queue and writing some special-case code, the traditional approach is to limit the number of elements in the queue to one less than the number of elements in the array.

The code for the array implementation of `queue.h` is shown in Figure 10-3. It is important to notice that the code does not explicitly test the array indices to see whether they wrap around from the end of the array to the beginning. Instead, the code makes use of the `%` operator to compute the correct index automatically. The technique of using remainders to reduce the result of a computation to a small, cyclical range of integers is an important mathematical technique called **modular arithmetic.**

Linked-list representation of queues

The queue ADT also has a simple representation using list structure. To illustrate the basic approach, the elements of the queue are stored in a list beginning at the head of the queue and ending at the tail. To allow both **Enqueue** and **Dequeue** to run in constant time, the `queueCDT` structure must keep a pointer to both ends of the queue. For example, the queue containing the customers *A, B,* and *C* has the following diagrammatic structure:

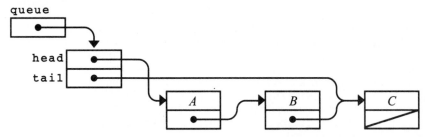

On the whole, the code is reasonably straightforward, particularly if you use the linked-list implementation of stacks as a model. The diagram of the internal structure provides the essential insights you need to understand how to implement each of the queue operations. The **Enqueue** operation, for example, adds a new cell after the one marked by the **tail** pointer and then updates the **tail** pointer so that it continues to indicate the end of the list. The **Dequeue** operation consists of removing the cell addressed by the **head** pointer and returning the value in that cell.

The only place where the implementation gets tricky is in the representation of the empty queue. The most straightforward approach is to indicate an empty queue by storing **NULL** in the **head** pointer, as follows:

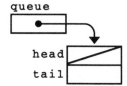

FIGURE 10-3 Implementation of queues using ring buffers

```c
/*
 * File: qarray.c
 * --------------
 * This file implements the queue.h abstraction using an array.
 */

#include <stdio.h>
#include "genlib.h"
#include "queue.h"

/*
 * Constants:
 * ----------
 * MaxQueueSize   -- Maximum number of elements in the queue
 * QueueArraySize -- Size of the internal array
 */

#define MaxQueueSize   100
#define QueueArraySize (MaxQueueSize + 1)

/*
 * Type: queueCDT
 * --------------
 * This type defines the concrete representation of a queue.
 * This implementation uses a ring buffer to implement the
 * queue.  The next item to be dequeued is found at the array
 * element indexed by head.  The tail index indicates the next
 * free position.  When head and tail are equal, the queue is
 * empty.  The head and tail indices each move from the end of
 * the array back to the beginning, giving rise to the name
 * "ring buffer."  The functions use modular arithmetic to
 * implement this wrap-around behavior.
 */

struct queueCDT {
    queueElementT elements[QueueArraySize];
    int head;
    int tail;
};

/* Exported entries */

queueADT NewQueue(void)
{
    queueADT queue;

    queue = New(queueADT);
    queue->head = queue->tail = 0;
    return (queue);
}
```

```
void FreeQueue(queueADT queue)
{
    FreeBlock(queue);
}

void Enqueue(queueADT queue, queueElementT element)
{
    if (QueueIsFull(queue)) Error("Enqueue: queue is full");
    queue->elements[queue->tail] = element;
    queue->tail = (queue->tail + 1) % QueueArraySize;
}

queueElementT Dequeue(queueADT queue)
{
    queueElementT result;

    if (QueueIsEmpty(queue)) Error("Dequeue: queue is empty");
    result = queue->elements[queue->head];
    queue->head = (queue->head + 1) % QueueArraySize;
    return (result);
}

bool QueueIsEmpty(queueADT queue)
{
    return (queue->head == queue->tail);
}

bool QueueIsFull(queueADT queue)
{
    return ((queue->tail + 1) % QueueArraySize == queue->head);
}

/*
 * Implementation note: QueueLength
 * --------------------------------
 * This function determines the number of elements by computing
 * (tail - head) % size.  The size of the queue is added in at
 * the beginning to ensure that the left operand to % is always
 * positive.
 */

int QueueLength(queueADT queue)
{
    return ((QueueArraySize + queue->tail - queue->head)
                % QueueArraySize);
}

queueElementT GetQueueElement(queueADT queue, int index)
{
    if (index < 0 || index >= QueueLength(queue)) {
        Error("Queue element is out of range");
    }
    return (queue->elements[(queue->head + index)
                            % QueueArraySize]);
}
```

The `Enqueue` implementation must check for the empty queue as a special case. If the `head` pointer is `NULL`, `Enqueue` must set both the `head` and `tail` pointers so that they point to the cell containing the new element. Thus, if you were to enqueue the customer *A* into an empty queue, the internal structure of the pointers at the end of the `Enqueue` operation would look like this:

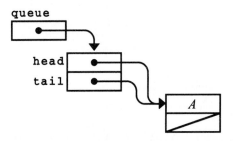

If you make another call to `Enqueue`, the `head` pointer is no longer `NULL`, which means that the implementation no longer has to perform the special-case action for the empty queue. Instead, the `Enqueue` implementation uses the `tail` pointer to find the end of the linked-list chain and adds the new cell at that point. For example, if you enqueue the customer *B* after customer *A*, the resulting structure looks like this:

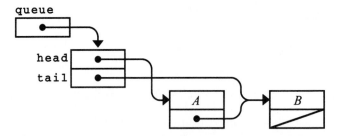

Figure 10-4 shows the complete code for the linked-list implementation of queues.

■ 10.3 Simulations involving queues

The queue data structure has many applications in programming. Not surprisingly, queues turn up in many situations in which it is important to maintain a first-in/first-out discipline in order to ensure that service requests are treated fairly. For example, if you are working in an environment in which a single printer is shared among several computers, the printing software is usually designed so that all print requests are entered in a queue. Thus, if several users decide to enter print requests, the queue structure ensures that each user's request is processed in the order received.

Queues are also common in programs that simulate the behavior of waiting lines. For example, if you wanted to decide how many cashiers you needed in a supermarket, it might be worth writing a program that could simulate the behavior of customers in the store. Such a program would almost certainly involve queues, because a checkout line operates in a first-in/first-out way. Customers who have completed their purchases arrive in the checkout line and wait for their turn to pay.

FIGURE 10-4   Implementation of queues using linked lists

```c
/*
 * File: qlist.c
 * -------------
 * This file implements the queue.h abstraction using a linked
 * list of cells.
 */

#include <stdio.h>
#include "genlib.h"
#include "queue.h"


/*
 * Type: cellT
 * -----------
 * This type defines the cells used for the linked list that
 * stores the items in the queue.
 */

typedef struct cellT {
    queueElementT value;
    struct cellT *link;
} cellT;

/*
 * Type: queueCDT
 * --------------
 * This type defines the concrete representation of a queue.
 * In this representation, the queue is a linked list of cells.
 * The next item to be dequeued is found at the cell addressed
 * by the head field.  The tail field points to the last element
 * in the queue, which allows Enqueue to operate in constant time.
 * The empty queue is indicated by a NULL head pointer.
 */

struct queueCDT {
    cellT *head;
    cellT *tail;
};

/* Exported entries */

queueADT NewQueue(void)
{
    queueADT queue;

    queue = New(queueADT);
    queue->head = NULL;
    return (queue);
}
```

```
void FreeQueue(queueADT queue)
{
    cellT *cp, *next;

    cp = queue->head;
    while (cp != NULL) {
        next = cp->link;
        FreeBlock(cp);
        cp = next;
    }
    FreeBlock(queue);
}

void Enqueue(queueADT queue, queueElementT element)
{
    cellT *cp;

    cp = New(cellT *);
    cp->value = element;
    cp->link = NULL;
    if (queue->head == NULL) {
        queue->head = cp;
    } else {
        queue->tail->link = cp;
    }
    queue->tail = cp;
}

queueElementT Dequeue(queueADT queue)
{
    queueElementT result;
    cellT *cp;

    cp = queue->head;
    if (cp == NULL) {
        Error("Dequeue: queue is empty");
    }
    result = cp->value;
    queue->head = cp->link;
    FreeBlock(cp);
    return (result);
}

bool QueueIsEmpty(queueADT queue)
{
    return (queue->head == NULL);
}

bool QueueIsFull(queueADT queue)
{
    return (FALSE);
}
```

```
int QueueLength(queueADT queue)
{
    int n;
    cellT *cp;

    n = 0;
    for (cp = queue->head; cp != NULL; cp = cp->link) n++;
    return (n);
}

queueElementT GetQueueElement(queueADT queue, int index)
{
    int i;
    cellT *cp;

    if (index < 0 || index >= QueueLength(queue)) {
        Error("Queue element is out of range");
    }
    cp = queue->head;
    for (i = 0; i < index; i++) cp = cp->link;
    return (cp->value);
}
```

Each customer eventually reaches the front of the line, at which point the cashier totals up the purchases and collects the money. Because simulations of this sort represent an important class of application programs, it is worth spending a little time understanding how such simulations work.

Simulations and models

Beyond the world of programming, there is a endless variety of real-world events and processes that—although they are undeniably important—are nonetheless too complicated to understand completely. For example, it would be very useful to know how various pollutants affect the ozone layer and how the resulting changes in the ozone layer affect the global climate. Similarly, if economists and political leaders had a more complete understanding of exactly how the national economy works, it would be possible to evaluate whether a cut in the capital-gains tax would spur investment or whether it would exacerbate the existing disparities of wealth and income.

When faced with such large-scale problems, it is usually necessary to come up with an idealized **model,** which is a simplified representation of some real-world process. Most problems are far too complex to allow for a complete understanding. There are just too many details. The reason to build a model is that, despite the complexity of a particular problem, it is often possible to make certain assumptions that allow you to simplify a complicated process without affecting its fundamental character. If you can come up with a reasonable model for a process, you can often translate the dynamics of the model into a program that captures the behavior of that model. Such a program is called a **simulation.**

It is important to remember that creating a simulation is usually a two-step process. The first step consists of designing a conceptual model for the real-world behavior you are trying to simulate. The second consists of writing a program that implements the conceptual model. Because errors can occur in both steps of the process, maintaining a certain skepticism about simulations and their applicability to the real world is probably wise. In a society conditioned to believe the "answers" delivered by computers, it is critical to recognize that the simulations can never be better than the models on which they are based.

The waiting-line model

Suppose that you want to design a simulation that models the behavior of a supermarket waiting line. By simulating the waiting line, you can determine some useful properties of waiting lines that might help a company make such decisions as how many cashiers are needed, how much space needs to be reserved for the line itself, and so forth.

The first step in the process of writing a checkout-line simulation is to develop a model for the waiting line, detailing the simplifying assumptions. For example, to make the initial implementation of the simulation as simple as possible, you might begin by assuming that there is one cashier who serves customers from a single queue. You might then assume that customers arrive with a random probability and enter the queue at the end of the line. Whenever the cashier is free and someone is waiting in line, the cashier begins to serve that customer. After an appropriate service period—which you must also model in some way—the cashier completes the transaction with the current customer and is free to serve the next customer in the queue.

Discrete time

Another assumption often required in a model is some limitation on the level of accuracy. Consider, for example, the time that a customer spends being served by the cashier. One customer might spend two minutes; another might spend six. It is important, however, to consider whether measuring time in minutes allows the simulation to be sufficiently precise. If you had a sufficiently accurate stopwatch, you might discover that a customer actually spent 3.141592 minutes. The question you need to resolve is how accurate you need to be.

For most models, and particularly for those intended for simulation, it is useful to introduce the simplifying assumption that all events within the model happen in discrete integral time units. Using discrete time assumes that you can find a time unit that—for the purpose of the model—you can treat as indivisible. In general, the time units used in a simulation must be small enough that the probability of more than one event occurring during a single time unit is negligible. In the checkout-line simulation, for example, minutes may not be accurate enough; two customers could easily arrive in the same minute. On the other hand, you could probably get away with using seconds as the time unit and discount the possibility that two customers arrive in precisely the same second.

Although the checkout-line example assumes that simulation time is measured in seconds, in general, there is no reason you have to measure time in conventional units. When you write a simulation, you can define the unit of time in any way that fits the structure of the model. For example, you could define a time unit to be five seconds and then run the simulation as a series of 5-second intervals.

Events in simulated time

The real advantage of using discrete time units is not that it makes it possible to work with variables of type `int` instead of being forced to use type `double`. The most important property of discrete time is that it allows you to structure the simulation as a loop in which each time unit represents a single cycle. When you approach the problem in this way, a simulation program has the following form:

```
for (time = 0; time < SimulationTime; time++) {
    Execute one cycle of the simulation.
}
```

Within the body of the loop, the program performs the operations necessary to advance through one unit of simulated time.

Think for a moment about what events might occur during each time unit of the checkout-line simulation. One possibility is that a new customer might arrive. Another is that the cashier might finish with the current customer and go on the serve the next person in line. These events bring up some interesting issues. To complete the model, you need to say something about how often customers arrive and how much time they spend at the cash register. You could (and probably should) gather approximate data by watching a real checkout line in a store. Even if you collect that information, however, you will need to simplify it to a form that (1) captures enough of the real-world behavior to be useful and (2) is easy to understand in terms of the model. For example, your surveys might show that customers arrive at the line on average once every 20 seconds. This average arrival rate is certainly useful input to the model. On the other hand, you would not have much confidence in a simulation in which customers arrived exactly once every 20 seconds. Such an implementation would violate the real-world condition that customer arrivals have some random variability and that they sometimes bunch together.

For this reason, an arrival process is usually modeled by specifying the probability that an arrival takes place in any discrete time unit instead of the average time between arrivals. For example, if your studies indicated that a customer arrived once every 20 seconds, the average probability of a customer arriving in any particular second would be 1/20 or 0.05. If you assume that arrivals occur randomly with an equal probability in each unit of time, the arrival process forms a pattern that mathematicians call a **Poisson distribution.**

You might also choose to make simplifying assumptions about how long it takes to serve a particular customer. For example, the program is easier to write if you assume that the service time required for each customer is uniformly distributed within a certain range. If you do, you can use the `RandomInteger` function from the `random.h` interface to pick the service time.

Implementing the simulation

The code for the simulation program itself is reasonably easy to write and is shown in Figure 10-5. The core of the simulation is a loop that runs for the number of seconds indicated by the parameter `SimulationTime`. In each second, the simulation performs the following operations:

1. Determine whether a new customer has arrived and, if so, add that person to the queue.
2. If the cashier is busy, note that the cashier has spent another second with the current customer. Eventually, the required service time will be complete, which will free the cashier.
3. If the cashier is free, serve the next customer in the waiting line.

The simulation is controlled by the following parameters:

- `SimulationTime`—This parameter specifies the duration of the simulation.
- `ArrivalProbability`—This parameter indicates the probability that a new customer will arrive at the checkout line during a single unit of time. In keeping with standard statistical convention, the probability is expressed as a real number between 0 and 1.
- `MinServiceTime, MaxServiceTime`—These parameters define the legal range of customer service time. For any particular customer, the amount of time spent at the cashier is determined by picking a random integer in this range.

When the simulation is complete, the program reports the simulation parameters along with the following results:

- The number of customers served
- The average amount of time customers spent in the waiting line
- The average length of the waiting line

For example, the following sample run shows the results of the simulation for the indicated parameter values:

```
Simulation results given the following parameters:
   SimulationTime:     2000
   ArrivalProbability:   0.05
   MinServiceTime:        5
   MaxServiceTime:       15

Customers served:      117
Average waiting time:  15.24
Average line length:    0.90
```

FIGURE 10-5 Program to simulate a checkout line

```
/*
 * File: checkout.c
 * -----------------
 * This program simulates a checkout line, such as one you
 * might encounter in a grocery store.  Customers arrive at
 * the checkout stand and get in line.  Those customers wait
 * in the line until the cashier is free, at which point
 * they are served and occupy the cashier for some period
 * of time.  After the service time is complete, the cashier
 * is free to serve the next customer in the line.
 *
 * In each unit of time, up to the parameter SimulationTime,
 * the following operations are performed:
 *
 * 1. Determine whether a new customer has arrived.
 *    New customers arrive randomly, with a probability
 *    determined by the parameter ArrivalPercentage.
 *
 * 2. If the cashier is busy, note that the cashier has
 *    spent another minute with that customer.  Eventually,
 *    the customer's time request is satisfied, which frees
 *    the cashier.
 *
 * 3. If the cashier is free, serve the next customer in line.
 *    The service time is taken to be a random period between
 *    MinServiceTime and MaxServiceTime.
 *
 * At the end of the simulation, the program displays the
 * parameters and the following computed results:
 *
 * o  The number of customers served
 * o  The average time spent in line
 * o  The average number of people in line
 */

#include <stdio.h>
#include <stdlib.h>
#include "genlib.h"
#include "strlib.h"
#include "random.h"
#include "queue.h"

/* Simulation parameters */

#define SimulationTime       2000
#define ArrivalProbability    0.1
#define MinServiceTime          5
#define MaxServiceTime         15
```

```
/*
 * Type: customerT
 * ---------------
 * A customer is represented using a pointer to a record
 * containing the following information:
 *
 * o The customer number (for debugging traces)
 * o The arrival time (to compute the waiting time)
 * o The time required for service
 */

typedef struct {
    int customerNumber;
    int arrivalTime;
    int serviceTime;
} *customerT;


/*
 * Type: simDataT
 * --------------
 * This type stores the data required for the simulation.  The
 * main program declares a variable of this type and then passes
 * it by reference to every other function in the program.
 */

typedef struct {
    queueADT queue;
    customerT activeCustomer;
    int time;
    int numCustomers;
    int numServed;
    long totalWaitTime;
    long totalLineLength;
} simDataT;


/*
 * Debugging option: traceFlag
 * ---------------------------
 * This variable controls whether the simulation produces a
 * debugging trace.
 */

static bool traceFlag = FALSE;

/* Private function declarations */

static void InitializeSimulation(simDataT *sdp);
static void RunSimulation(simDataT *sdp);
static void EnqueueCustomer(simDataT *sdp);
static void ProcessQueue(simDataT *sdp);
static void ServeCustomer(simDataT *sdp);
static void DismissCustomer(simDataT *sdp);
static void ReportResults(simDataT *sdp);
```

```
/* Main program */

main()
{
    simDataT simData;

    Randomize();
    InitializeSimulation(&simData);
    RunSimulation(&simData);
    ReportResults(&simData);
}

/*
 * Function: InitializeSimulation
 * Usage: InitializeSimulation(&simData);
 * ---------------------------------------
 * This function initializes the simulation data block whose
 * address is passed as the argument.
 */

static void InitializeSimulation(simDataT *sdp)
{
    sdp->queue = NewQueue();
    sdp->activeCustomer = NULL;
    sdp->numServed = 0;
    sdp->totalWaitTime = 0;
    sdp->totalLineLength = 0;
}

/*
 * Function: RunSimulation
 * Usage: RunSimulation(&simData);
 * --------------------------------
 * This function runs the actual simulation.  In each time unit,
 * the program first checks to see whether a new customer arrives.
 * Then, if the cashier is busy (indicated by having a non-NULL
 * pointer in the activeCustomer field), the program decrements
 * the service time counter for that customer.  Finally, if the
 * cashier is free, it serves another customer from the queue
 * and updates the necessary bookkeeping data.
 */

static void RunSimulation(simDataT *sdp)
{
    for (sdp->time = 0; sdp->time < SimulationTime; sdp->time++) {
        if (RandomChance(ArrivalProbability)) {
            EnqueueCustomer(sdp);
        }
        ProcessQueue(sdp);
    }
}
```

```
/*
 * Function: EnqueueCustomer
 * Usage: EnqueueCustomer(&simData);
 * ----------------------------------
 * This function simulates the arrival of a new customer.
 */

static void EnqueueCustomer(simDataT *sdp)
{
    customerT c;

    sdp->numCustomers++;
    c = New(customerT);
    c->customerNumber = sdp->numCustomers;
    c->arrivalTime = sdp->time;
    c->serviceTime = RandomInteger(MinServiceTime, MaxServiceTime);
    Enqueue(sdp->queue, c);
    if (traceFlag) {
        printf("%4d: Customer %d arrives and gets in line\n",
               sdp->time, sdp->numCustomers);
    }
}

/*
 * Function: ProcessQueue
 * Usage: ProcessQueue(&simData);
 * ------------------------------
 * This function processes a single time cycle for the queue.
 */

static void ProcessQueue(simDataT *sdp)
{
    if (sdp->activeCustomer == NULL) {
        if (!QueueIsEmpty(sdp->queue)) {
            ServeCustomer(sdp);
        }
    } else {
        if (sdp->activeCustomer->serviceTime == 0) {
            DismissCustomer(sdp);
        } else {
            sdp->activeCustomer->serviceTime--;
        }
    }
    sdp->totalLineLength += QueueLength(sdp->queue);
}

/*
 * Function: ServeCustomer
 * Usage: ServeCustomer(&simData);
 * ----------------------------------
 * This function is called when the cashier is free and a
 * customer is waiting.  The effect is to serve the first
 * customer in the line and update the total waiting time.
 */
```

```
static void ServeCustomer(simDataT *sdp)
{
    customerT c;

    c = Dequeue(sdp->queue);
    sdp->activeCustomer = c;
    sdp->numServed++;
    sdp->totalWaitTime += (sdp->time - c->arrivalTime);
    if (traceFlag) {
        printf("%4d: Customer %d reaches cashier\n",
                sdp->time, c->customerNumber);
    }
}

/*
 * Function: DismissCustomer
 * Usage: DismissCustomer(&simData);
 * ----------------------------------
 * This function is called when the active customer's service
 * time has dropped to 0. The cashier becomes free and the
 * program no longer needs to hold the customer's storage.
 */

static void DismissCustomer(simDataT *sdp)
{
    if (traceFlag) {
        printf("%4d: Customer %d leaves cashier\n",
                sdp->time, sdp->activeCustomer->customerNumber);
    }
    FreeBlock(sdp->activeCustomer);
    sdp->activeCustomer = NULL;
}

/*
 * Function: ReportResults
 * Usage: ReportResults(&simData);
 * -------------------------------
 * This function reports the results of the simulation.
 */

static void ReportResults(simDataT *sdp)
{
    printf("Simulation results given the following parameters:\n");
    printf("  SimulationTime:    %4d\n", (int) SimulationTime);
    printf("  ArrivalProbability: %7.2f\n",
                                  (double) ArrivalProbability);
    printf("  MinServiceTime:    %4d\n", (int) MinServiceTime);
    printf("  MaxServiceTime:    %4d\n", (int) MaxServiceTime);
    printf("\n");
    printf("Customers served:    %4d\n", sdp->numServed);
    printf("Average waiting time: %7.2f\n",
            (double) sdp->totalWaitTime / sdp->numServed);
    printf("Average line length:  %7.2f\n",
            (double) sdp->totalLineLength / SimulationTime);
}
```

The behavior of the simulation depends significantly on the values of its parameters. Suppose, for example, that the probability of a customer arriving increases from 0.05 to 0.10. Running the simulation with these parameters gives the following results:

```
Simulation results given the following parameters:
   SimulationTime:      2000
   ArrivalProbability:     0.10
   MinServiceTime:         5
   MaxServiceTime:        15

Customers served:        166
Average waiting time:    237.47
Average line length:      23.35
```

As you can see, doubling the probability of arrival causes the average waiting time to grow from approximately 15 seconds to nearly four minutes, which is obviously a dramatic increase. The reason for the poor performance is that the arrival rate in the second run of the simulation means that new customers arrive at the same rate at which they are served. When this arrival level is reached, the length of the queue and the average waiting time begin to grow very quickly. Simulations of this sort make it possible to experiment with different parameter values, which in turn makes it possible to identify potential sources of trouble in the corresponding real-world systems.

▉ Summary

In this chapter, you have learned that stacks are closely related to another abstract structure called *queues*. Stacks and queues are both used to represent an ordered list of items in which the primitive operations are adding an element to the list and removing the one that is positioned at the conceptual head of the line. The only difference between the structures is in the discipline used to order the elements within the list. Stacks use a last-in/first-out (LIFO) discipline in which items are removed from a stack in an order opposite to the order of their insertion. Queues use the more familiar first-in/first-out (FIFO) discipline, in which elements are removed in the order of their arrival. The fundamental operations for stacks are called *push* and *pop;* their counterparts for queues are *enqueue* and *dequeue*.

In addition to the queue structure itself, this chapter introduces the idea of simulation. A simulation is a computational implementation of a real-world process, which is usually simplified by adopting an idealized model for that process that makes simulation more feasible. Both the design of the model and the implementation of the corresponding simulation introduce the risk of error, and it is important to remember that the results of a simulation can never be more accurate than the underlying model.

Important points in this chapter include:

- Stacks can be implemented using a linked-list structure in addition to the more traditional array-based representation.
- As a general rule, if a function exported by an interface needs to change the value of any data associated with an ADT, the data must be accessible from the implementation side of the abstraction boundary. For example, the underlying representation for a `stackADT` must be a record that contains the pointer to the chain of linked elements. You could not use the chain pointer itself as the `stackADT` type because it would then be impossible for clients to change its value.
- The array-based implementation of queues is somewhat more complex than its stack counterpart. The traditional implementation uses a structure called a *ring buffer,* in which the elements logically wrap around from the end of the array to the beginning. Modular arithmetic makes it easy to implement the ring buffer concept.
- In the ring-buffer implementation used in this chapter, a queue is considered empty when its head and tail indices are the same. This representation strategy means that the maximum capacity of the queue is one element less than the allocated size of the array. Attempting to fill all the elements in the array makes a full queue indistinguishable from an empty one.
- Queues can also be represented using a singly linked list marked by two pointers, one to the head of the queue and another to the tail.
- One of the most important simplifying assumptions used in simulation models is the concept of *discrete time,* in which all events are assumed to occur at specific instants measured in some integral unit of time. Using discrete time means that most simulation programs can be written with the following loop structure:

```
for (time = 0; time < SimulationTime; time++) {
    code for one time unit of the simulation
}
```

REVIEW QUESTIONS

1. Assuming that `stackElementT` is defined to be `char`, draw a linked-list diagram of the stack `myStack` after the following operations are performed:

```
myStack = NewStack();
Push(myStack, 'A');
Push(myStack, 'B');
Push(myStack, 'C');
```

2. What problem arises if you try to use the linked-list cell itself as the underlying representation for the `stackADT` type? What strategy is traditionally used to avoid this problem?

3. Rephrase your answer to the preceding question as a general rule applicable to all abstract types.

4. What are the expanded forms of the acronyms LIFO and FIFO? Which of these disciplines pertains to the queue abstraction?

5. What are the names of the fundamental queue operations?

6. If you use an array to store the underlying elements in a queue, what is the definition of the concrete `queueCDT` structure?

7. What is a ring buffer? How does the ring-buffer concept apply to queues?

8. How can you tell if an array-based queue is empty? How can you tell if it is full?

9. Assuming that `queueElementT` is `char` and that `QueueArraySize` has the value 5, draw a diagram showing the underlying representation of the array-based queue `myQueue` after the following sequence of operations:

```
myQueue = NewQueue();
Enqueue(myQueue, 'A');
Enqueue(myQueue, 'B');
Enqueue(myQueue, 'C');
(void) Dequeue(myQueue);
(void) Dequeue(myQueue);
Enqueue(myQueue, 'D');
Enqueue(myQueue, 'E');
(void) Dequeue(myQueue);
Enqueue(myQueue, 'F');
```

10. Explain how modular arithmetic is useful in the array-based implementation of queues.

11. Describe what is wrong with the following implementation of `QueueLength` for the array-based representation of queues:

```
int QueueLength(queueADT queue)
{
    return ((queue->tail - queue->head)
            % QueueArraySize);
}
```

12. Draw a diagram showing the internal structure of a linked-list queue after the computer finishes the set of operations in question 9.

13. How can you tell if a linked-list queue is empty?

14. What is the difference between a simulation and a model?

15. Why is it important to maintain some skepticism about the results of computerized simulations?

16. What is meant by the concept of discrete time? How does that concept apply to simulation programs?

PROGRAMMING EXERCISES

1. One of the principal reasons that stacks are usually implemented using arrays is that linked lists impose a significant memory overhead to store the pointers. You can, however, reduce this cost by adopting a hybrid approach similar to the one described in Chapter 9, exercise 13. The idea is to represent the stack as a linked list of blocks, each of which contains a fixed array of elements. Whenever a stack block is exhausted, a new block can be added to the front of a chain in the data structure to open up the necessary additional space. For example, if there were four elements per block, a stack into which the integers 1 through 9 had been pushed in numerical order would look like this:

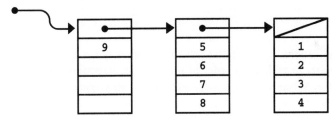

   Write a new implementation of the `stack.h` interface that uses this design. Note that the `stackCDT` structure itself is not shown in the diagram and is left for you to design.

2. The array implementation for queues introduced in Figure 10-3 imposes a maximum bound on the number of elements. Rewrite the array-based implementation of queues to use a dynamic array that expands when the original space is exhausted.

3. Because the ring-buffer implementation of queues makes it impossible to tell the difference between an empty queue and one that is completely full, the capacity of the queue is one less than the allocated size of the array. You can avoid this restriction by changing the internal representation so that the concrete structure of the queue keeps track of the number of elements in the queue instead of the index of the tail element. Given the index of the head element and the number of data values in the queue, you can easily calculate the tail index, which means that you don't need to store this value explicitly. Rewrite the `queue.c` implementation so that it uses this representation.

4.
   And the first one now
   Will later be last
   For the times they are a-changin'.
   — Bob Dylan, "The Times They Are A-Changin," 1963

   In keeping with the spirit expressed in Dylan's song (which is paraphrased from Matthew 19:30), implement a function

```
void ReverseQueue(queueADT queue);
```

that reverses the elements in the queue. Implement this function for both the list and array versions of the queue. In both cases, write the functions so that they use the original memory cells and do not allocate any additional storage.

After you have written the array and list versions, go back and rewrite a new implementation of `ReverseQueue` from the client side of the abstraction boundary. More specifically, in writing this version of the implementation, you are allowed to call only functions exported by an interface and may not rely on the characteristics of the underlying representation. Moreover, because `GetQueueElement` makes this part of the exercise too easy, write your implementation of `ReverseQueue` without using `GetQueueElement` or its counterpart in `stack.h`.

5. In the queue abstraction presented in this chapter, new items are always added at the end of the queue and wait their turn in line. For some programming applications, it is useful to extend the simple queue abstraction into a **priority queue,** in which the order of the items is determined by a numeric priority value. When an item is enqueued in a priority queue, it is inserted in the list ahead of any lower priority items. If two items in a queue have the same priority, they are processed in the standard first-in/first-out order.

Extend the linked-list implementation of queues from Figure 10-4 so that it supports priority queues. To do so, you need to add a new function to the interface with the following prototype:

```
void PriorityEnqueue(queueADT queue, queueElementT element,
                     int priority);
```

The parameters `queue` and `element` are the same as for `Enqueue`; the additional `priority` argument is an integer representing the priority. As in conventional English usage, smaller integers correspond to higher priorities, so that priority 1 comes before priority 2, and so forth.

Keep in mind that you are implementing an extension to an existing interface. Clients who do not use the `PriorityEnqueue` extension should not need to make any changes in their code.

6. The checkout-line simulation in Figure 10-5 can be extended to investigate important practical questions about how waiting lines behave. As a first step, rewrite the simulation so that there are several independent queues, as is usually the case in supermarkets. A customer arriving at the checkout area finds the checkout line with the fewest customers and enters that queue. Your revised simulation should calculate the same results as the simulation in the chapter.

7. As a second extension to the checkout-line simulation, change the program from the previous exercise so that there is a single waiting line served by multiple cashiers—a practice that has become more common in recent years.

In each cycle of the simulation, any cashier that becomes idle serves the next customer in the queue. If you compare the data produced by this exercise and the preceding one, what can you say about the relative advantages of these two strategies?

8. If waiting lines become too long, customers can easily become frustrated and may decide to take their business elsewhere. Simulations may make it possible to reduce the risk of losing customers by allowing managers to determine how many cashiers are required to reduce the average waiting time below a predetermined threshold. Rewrite the checkout-line simulation from exercise 7 so that the program itself determines how many cashiers are needed. To do so, your program must run the complete simulation several times, holding all parameters constant except the number of cashiers. When it finds a staffing level that reduces the average wait to an acceptable level, your program should display the number of cashiers used on that simulation run.

9. Queues come up quite often in computing applications. As noted in the chapter, the software that runs a printer typically uses a queue to keep track of pending print requests. Write a simulation of a printer queue that incorporates the following assumptions:

   ▪ In each unit of time, the simulation checks to see whether a new print request has been issued. As in the `checkout.c` program from Figure 10-5, assume that the probability of a new request in any time unit is given by the constant `ArrivalProbability`.
   ▪ Whenever it is idle, the printer takes the next request from the queue and processes it. Processing a print request requires a random amount of time, uniformly chosen between `MinPrintTime` and `MaxPrintTime`.

   So far, this exercise is essentially the same as `checkout.c`. What makes this problem more interesting is to compare the behavior of the first-come/first-served strategy used by a traditional queue with the alternative strategy of always printing the shortest job first.

   Using the priority queue mechanism from exercise 5, rewrite the simulation so that print requests are enqueued in shortest-job-first order. If you run the two simulations with the same pattern of print requests, which strategy yields the lowest average waiting time?

10. Write a program to simulate the following experiment, which was the subject of a short film many years ago. The setting is a large cubical box, the bottom of which is complete covered with an array of 100 mousetraps. Each of the mousetraps is initially loaded with two ping-pong balls. At the beginning of the simulation, an additional ping-pong ball is released from the top of the box and falls on one of the mousetraps. That mousetrap springs and shoots its two ping-pong balls into the air. The ping-pong balls bounce around the sides of the box and eventually land on the floor, where they are likely to set off more mousetraps.

In writing this simulation, you should make the following simplifying assumptions:

- Every ping-pong ball that falls always lands on a mousetrap, chosen randomly from the array. If the trap is loaded, its balls are released into the air. If the trap has already been sprung, having a ball fall on it has no effect.
- Once a ball falls on a mousetrap—whether or not the trap is sprung—that ball stops and takes no further role in the simulation.
- Balls launched from a mousetrap bounce around the room and land again after a random number of simulation cycles have gone by. That random interval is chosen independently for each ball and is always between one and four cycles.

Your simulation should run until there are no balls in the air. At that point, your program should report how many time units have elapsed since the beginning and what percentage of the traps have been sprung.

11. As linear structures go, stacks and queues are both quite restrictive. Although each of these types maintains an ordered sequence of values as part of its internal state, the client cannot make arbitrary changes to that sequence. Instead, all updates to the internal structure are mediated by the exported functions, which allow the client to perform only a few, highly constrained operations on each type.

    The restrictions on stacks and queues simplify their conceptual structure and make it possible to implement them quite efficiently but are in no sense fundamental to the concept of linear structures. There is nothing to prevent you from defining a more flexible abstraction that allows clients to perform much more extensive manipulations on the internal collection of elements. The programming language Java, for example, defines a linear structure called a *vector* that allows the client to insert and delete elements at any index position. A scaled-down version of a similar interface for C appears in Figure 10-6.

    Write two separate implementations of the **vector.h** interface, one that uses dynamic arrays as the underlying representation and one that uses linked lists.

12. Test the **vector.h** interface from the preceding exercise by writing a program that reads in a list of strings and inserts them into a vector in such a way that the elements of the vector are always in alphabetical order. The heart of your program should be the function

    ```
    int InsertSorted(vectorADT vec, string str);
    ```

    which inserts a string into a vector in the correct alphabetical position.

FIGURE 10-6   The vector.h interface

```
/*
 * File: vector.h
 * --------------
 * This interface defines an abstraction for an ordered collection
 * of objects that supports insertion and deletion operations.
 * The abstraction is called a "vector" primarily because that is
 * the name used for a similar concept in Java.
 */

#ifndef _vector_h
#define _vector_h

#include "genlib.h"

/*
 * Type: vectorElementT
 * --------------------
 * The type vectorElementT is used in this interface to indicate
 * the type of values that can be stored in the vector.  Here the
 * vector is used to store values of type void *, but that can
 * be changed by editing this definition line.
 */

typedef void *vectorElementT;

/*
 * Type: vectorADT
 * ---------------
 * The type vectorADT is the abstract type used to represent
 * the vector itself.
 */

typedef struct vectorCDT *vectorADT;

/*
 * Function: NewVector
 * Usage: vec = NewVector();
 * -------------------------
 * This function allocates and returns a new vector, which is
 * initially empty.
 */

vectorADT NewVector(void);

/*
 * Function: FreeVector
 * Usage: FreeVector(vec);
 * -----------------------
 * This function frees the storage associated with the vector.
 */

void FreeVector(vectorADT vec);
```

```
/*
 * Function: VectorLength
 * Usage: n = VectorLength(vec);
 * -------------------------------
 * This function returns the number of elements in the vector.
 */

int VectorLength(vectorADT vec);

/*
 * Function: NthElement
 * Usage: element = NthElement(vec, n);
 * --------------------------------------
 * This function returns the element at position n in the vector
 * vec, where the position numbers begin at 0.  Thus, calling
 * NthElement(vec, 0) returns the initial element in the vector;
 * calling NthElement(vec, VectorLength(vec) - 1) returns the
 * last.  The vector is unchanged by this operation, which
 * generates an error if n is outside the range [0, N-1].
 */

vectorElementT NthElement(vectorADT vec, int n);

/*
 * Function: InsertElement
 * Usage: InsertElement(vec, element, pos);
 * ------------------------------------------
 * This function inserts the element into the vector before
 * the specified position.  Position numbers start at 0 and
 * go up to the length of the vector, which is used to signify
 * an insertion at the end of the vector.  The function generates
 * an error if pos is outside the range [0, N].
 */

void InsertElement(vectorADT vec, vectorElementT element, int pos);

/*
 * Function: DeleteElement
 * Usage: DeleteElement(vec, pos);
 * -------------------------------
 * This function deletes the element at the specified position.
 * The function generates an error if pos is outside the range
 * [0, N-1].
 */

void DeleteElement(vectorADT vec, int pos);

#endif
```

CHAPTER 11

Symbol Tables

Yea, from the table of my memory
I'll wipe away all trivial fond records

— Shakespeare, *Hamlet*, 1602

Objectives

- To become familiar with the concept of a symbol table and the design of its interface.

- To understand the technique of hashing and how it applies to symbol tables.

- To appreciate that pointers to functions can be interpreted as data values in C.

- To be able to use function pointers in the implementation of callback and mapping functions.

- To recognize the value of iterators as a tool for stepping through the values in an ADT.

- To learn how symbol tables and function pointers together provide a good solution to the command-dispatch problem.

So far, you have encountered several abstract data types that can be applied in a variety of programming domains. This chapter focuses on another programming structure called a **symbol table,** which is conceptually similar to a dictionary. A dictionary allows you to look up a word to find its meaning. A symbol table is a generalization of this idea that provides a mapping between an identifying tag called a **key** and an associated **value,** which may be a much larger and more complicated structure. In the dictionary example, the key is the word you're looking up, and the value is its definition.

Symbol tables have many applications in programming. For example, an interpreter for a programming language needs to be able to assign values to variables, which can then be referenced by name. A symbol table makes it easy to maintain the association between the name of a variable and its corresponding value.

■■■ 11.1 Defining a symbol table abstraction

The goal of this chapter is to define an abstraction for symbol tables that is flexible enough for use in a wide variety of applications while retaining a high level of implementation efficiency. As in the last few chapters, it is best to start this process by defining the interface, which exports a new abstract type called symtabADT along with a collection of functions that define its behavior.

The interface definition of the abstract type, as always, is simply a pointer to a concrete structure defined only in the implementation. Thus, in specifying the interface, all you need to write to declare the abstract type is

```
typedef struct symtabCDT *symtabADT;
```

In order to complete the interface, you must consider what operations are required for symbol tables. As with all abstract types, you need to have a constructor function **NewSymbolTable** that allows you to allocate new symbol tables. Moreover, in keeping with the interfaces you have seen in the preceding chapters, it is useful to provide a function **FreeSymbolTable** so that clients can deallocate the space used to represent the table when it is no longer required. Neither of these functions, however, are specific to the symbol table application. The defining property of a symbol table is that you can associate keys with values and later look up the value associated with a particular key. Thus, you expect to call a procedure like

```
Enter(table, key, value);
```

when you want to define a particular value for the specified key and a function like

```
value = Lookup(table, key);
```

when you want to find out what value was last entered for the specified key.

Choosing types for values and keys

Before you write the prototypes for these functions, however, you need to think for a moment about the types involved. For example, what type should you use to represent keys? What type should you use for the corresponding values? On the one hand, you would like to choose a representation that offers maximum flexibility and convenience to the client. On the other, the representation you select must make it possible to implement the desired behavior with reasonable efficiency.

Deciding how to represent values turns out to be easier than deciding how to represent keys. The value stored in a symbol table is entirely a client-controlled concept. You would like to allow the client of the symbol table package to store any type of value in the symbol table. From your perspective as the implementor, you don't care what the type is because you never have to do anything with the value field other than store it away and later return it when the client looks up the corresponding key. Thus, the type used to represent values should be as general as possible.

To allow clients the most flexibility, you could adopt the same strategy used for the linear structures in Chapter 10 and define a special type for values that individual clients could change. This strategy is always a little cumbersome but has two additional drawbacks in the case of symbol tables:

1. Symbol tables come up much more frequently in applications than stacks or queues. Moreover, it is quite common for a single application to use several symbol tables, each of which has a different value type. The need to represent different types in symbol tables is inconsistent with the strategy of defining a specific type to represent all values.

2. It is important for the symbol table abstraction to specify a sentinel value that `Lookup` can return to indicate that a key is undefined. As with any sentinel, the value used to indicate the undefined condition must be in the domain used for the value type. For atomic types like `int`, there is no appropriate value to use for this purpose because any integer might be a legal data value. As a result, an approach that allows the client to define the value type as `int` makes it harder for the abstraction to report undefined values in a consistent way.

A strategy that gets around both of these problems is to use the general pointer type `void *` as the value field. Although this approach forces all values to be pointers, clients are free to use pointers of any type. Moreover, as you will discover in the next section, on "Representing an undefined entry," using `void *` makes it convenient for `Lookup` to indicate that a particular key is undefined.

But what about keys in a symbol table? At one level, many of the arguments presented earlier in this section about values apply equally well to keys. The client has a particular view of what constitutes a key, and it would be ideal if the implementation did not constrain that choice. Unfortunately, using `void *` to represent keys causes significant problems for the implementation. The reason is that keys and values are not treated symmetrically by the implementation. The implementation needs to know nothing about the representation of a value. The `Enter` function merely stores the value somewhere in the internal structure so that a subsequent call to `Lookup` can retrieve it. No operations other than assignment and retrieval are ever performed. With keys, the implementation must take a more active role. The client hands a key to the implementation, which must then be able to determine whether the key exists in the table and, if so, what value corresponds to that key. To do so, it must at least be able to compare one key with another.

Although you will have a chance to investigate an alternative approach in exercise 13, a simple strategy that works well in practice is to insist that the keys be of type `string`. Strings are certainly the most common type of key that arises in practice. Besides, if you want to use keys of some other type in an application, it is usually easy to convert those values into strings. For example, if you wanted to use integers as keys, you could simply call `IntegerToString` to create the string-valued key.

Deciding to use the type `string` to represent keys and `void *` to represent values enables you to complete the prototypes for the `Enter` and `Lookup` functions as follows:

```
void Enter(symtabADT table, string key, void *value);
void *Lookup(symtabADT table, string key);
```

Representing an undefined entry

Although you have specified the `Enter` and `Lookup` prototypes, there is an additional issue to resolve before you can complete the interface. The comments in the interface must describe what each functions returns and, in particular, must indicate any special conditions that can arise. To ensure that your comments provide all the information a client needs, you must specify what the `Lookup` function returns if no value has been entered for a particular key. Given the prototype for `Lookup`, the value used to represent an undefined entry must be a pointer, but not one that the client might actually want to store in the table.

In the past, whenever you needed to use a special pointer value as a sentinel, the obvious choice was the pointer constant `NULL`. This strategy is used, for example, by the `fopen` function, which returns `NULL` to indicate failure. In the symbol table, however, clients might very well want to store `NULL` as the value of a key. If you use `NULL` as the sentinel for an undefined entry, there will be no way to tell the difference between the following cases:

1. The client explicitly entered a `NULL` value.
2. The client never entered a value at all.

Because it is often important to make a distinction between these cases, `NULL` is not the best pointer for indicating that a particular key is undefined. Instead, what makes the most sense is to define a new pointer constant whose only role is to serve as a sentinel for undefined entries. The `genlib.h` interface defines the constant `UNDEFINED` for this purpose.[1] The `UNDEFINED` pointer is initialized to point to a variable inside the `genlib.c` implementation that is not exported to any clients, which means that its address never arises in the normal course of program operation.

---

[1] The symbol `UNDEFINED` appears in `genlib.h`—as opposed to `symtab.h`—because it represents a general concept that transcends its specific use in symbol tables. Exporting this symbol from a low-level interface makes it easier for other abstractions to share that definition.

A preliminary version of the symbol table interface

Figure 11-1 shows an initial version of the symtab.h interface, which takes the design decisions from the preceding sections into account. As the caption indicates, this interface is preliminary, in the sense that it is missing an important capability that will be added later in the chapter. Even in its current form, however, the symtab.h interface is quite useful, so it makes sense to investigate possible implementations of the fundamental operations before extending the interface.

FIGURE 11-1 Preliminary interface to the symbol table abstraction

```
/*
 * File: symtab.h
 * --------------
 * This interface exports a simple symbol table abstraction.
 */

#ifndef _symtab_h
#define _symtab_h

#include "genlib.h"

/*
 * Type: symtabADT
 * ---------------
 * This type is the ADT used to represent a symbol table.
 */

typedef struct symtabCDT *symtabADT;

/*
 * Function: NewSymbolTable
 * Usage: table = NewSymbolTable();
 * --------------------------------
 * This function allocates a new symbol table with no entries.
 */

symtabADT NewSymbolTable(void);

/*
 * Function: FreeSymbolTable
 * Usage: FreeSymbolTable(table);
 * ------------------------------
 * This function frees the storage associated with the symbol table.
 */

void FreeSymbolTable(symtabADT table);
```

```
/*
 * Function: Enter
 * Usage: Enter(table, key, value);
 * ---------------------------------
 * This function associates key with value in the symbol table.
 * Each call to Enter supersedes any previous definition for key.
 */

void Enter(symtabADT table, string key, void *value);

/*
 * Function: Lookup
 * Usage: value = Lookup(table, key);
 * ---------------------------------
 * This function returns the value associated with key in the symbol
 * table, or UNDEFINED, if no such value exists.
 */

void *Lookup(symtabADT table, string key);

#endif
```

As you will see if you solve exercise 1, you can easily implement the `symtab.h` interface by storing key/value pairs in an array. The code for `Lookup` simply scans the elements of the array until it finds a matching key, in which case it returns the corresponding value. If `Lookup` scans the entire array without finding a match, it returns `UNDEFINED`. The code for `Enter` is similar. If scanning the elements in the table reveals a matching key, `Enter` simply sets the corresponding value field. If not, `Enter` adds a new element to the array with the appropriate key and value fields.

Unfortunately, the simple array-based implementation of symbol tables is not very efficient. In the worst case—which occurs when a key does not appear in the table—both `Enter` and `Lookup` require $O(N)$ time because the code must search through every entry in the table. By using the binary search algorithm introduced in Chapter 4, you can reduce the complexity of `Lookup` to $O(\log N)$, although `Enter` still requires $O(N)$ time to keep the array in sorted order.

11.2 Hashing

Symbol tables are often used heavily in applications and can consume a considerable fraction of the total execution time. As a result, efficiency is a particularly important concern. In practice, even the $O(\log N)$ behavior of the implementation based on binary search may not suffice. You would prefer a strategy that allows, at least on average, a constant-time implementation for both `Lookup` and `Enter`. To achieve this bound, the usual approach is to use an algorithm called **hashing,** an algorithmic strategy that consists of mapping keys to integers and then using those integers as indices to locate keys quickly in an array. Hashing is used extensively in applications and deserves recognition as one of the cleverer inventions of computer science.

To understand the idea behind hashing, think for a moment about the dictionary analogy. If you were trying to find a word in a dictionary, you could start at the first entry, go on to the second, and then the third, until you found the word. This strategy represents the linear search algorithm, which is completely impractical in a dictionary of any size. Alternatively, you could use the binary search algorithm and open the dictionary exactly at the middle. By comparing the first entry on the page to the word you're searching for, you can easily determine whether your word appears in the first or second half. By recursively applying this algorithm to smaller and smaller parts of the dictionary, you could find your word much faster than you did by using the linear search technique. On the other hand, you probably don't use either of these strategies with a real dictionary. Most dictionaries have thumb tabs along the side that indicate where the entries for each letter appear. You look for words starting with A in the A section, words starting with B in the B section, and so on.

You can use the same strategy to implement a symbol table. In the symbol table, each key begins with some character value, although that character is not necessarily a letter as the interface is defined. If you wanted to duplicate the strategy of using thumb tabs for each first character, you could divide the symbol table into 256 independent lists of key/value pairs—one for each starting character. When `Lookup` or `Enter` is presented with a key, the code can choose the appropriate list on the basis of the first character in the key. If the characters used to form keys were uniformly distributed, this strategy would reduce the average search time by a factor of 256.

Unfortunately, keys in a symbol table—like words in a dictionary—are not uniformly distributed. In the dictionary case, for example, many more words begin with C than with X. In a symbol table used as part of a programming language system, it is extremely likely that most of the 256 characters will never appear at all. As a result, some of the lists will remain empty, while others become quite long. The increase in efficiency provided by this strategy therefore depends on how common the first character in the key happens to be.

Although selecting the appropriate internal list based on the first character of the key closely parallels the dictionary example, there is no reason that your implementation has to adopt an approach that is, after all, designed for humans. What you want is any function f that transforms a key into an integer index that selects one of the internal lists. For example, if applying f to some key returns the value 17, both the `Lookup` and the `Enter` function will try to find or insert that key only in list 17. A function that reduces a search key to an integer in a fixed range is called a **hash function**. The value of the hash function for a particular key is called its **hash code**. Symbol tables that use this approach are called **hash tables**.

Implementing the hash table strategy

The code in Figure 11-2 shows how you can construct an implementation of the `symtab.h` interface based on the hashing concept. The concrete type `symtabCDT` is represented as an array of linked lists, each of which is traditionally called a **bucket.** Whenever `Lookup` or `Enter` is called, the first step in the process is to select one of the buckets by calling a hash function that transforms a key into an integer between 0 and `NBuckets - 1`, where `NBuckets` is the number of buckets in the array. The array element identified by this bucket number contains a pointer to the first cell in a list of key/value pairs. Colloquially, computer scientists say that a key **hashes to a bucket** if the hash function applied to the key returns that bucket number. Thus, the common property that links all the keys in a single linked list is that they all hash to the same bucket. Having two or more keys hash to the same bucket is called **collision.**

To help you visualize the representation of a hash table, the following diagram shows a table with six key/value pairs distributed across a symbol table with 10 buckets. In the diagram, three entries (key_1, key_3, and key_6) hash to bucket 0, one (key_4) hashes to bucket 4, and two (key_2 and key_5) hash to bucket 7:

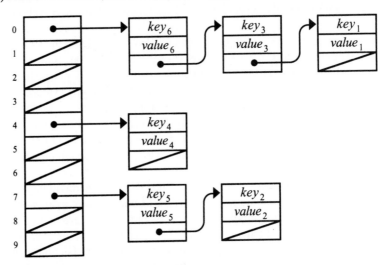

To represent the hash table structure in C, you need to define structure types for the individual cells and the concrete type for the table as a whole, as follows:

```
typedef struct cellT {
    string key;
    void *value;
    struct cellT *link;
} cellT;

struct symtabCDT {
    cellT *buckets[NBuckets];
};
```

The definition of `cellT` looks very much like the type definitions used for linked list cells in earlier chapters, except that each cell includes both a key and a value along with the link. The definition of `symtabCDT` is a structure containing an array of buckets, each of which is a pointer to the first cell in its chain.

FIGURE 11-2   Implementation of symbol tables using a hash table

```
/*
 * File: symtab.c
 * --------------
 * This file implements the symbol table abstraction.
 */

#include <stdio.h>
#include "genlib.h"
#include "strlib.h"
#include "symtab.h"

/*
 * Constants
 * ---------
 * NBuckets -- Number of buckets in the hash table
 */

#define NBuckets 101

/*
 * Type: cellT
 * -----------
 * This type defines a linked list cell for the symbol table.
 */

typedef struct cellT {
    string key;
    void *value;
    struct cellT *link;
} cellT;

/*
 * Type: symtabCDT
 * ---------------
 * This type defines the underlying concrete representation for a
 * symtabADT.  These details are not relevant to and therefore
 * not exported to the client.  In this implementation, the
 * underlying structure is a hash table organized as an array of
 * "buckets," in which each bucket is a linked list of elements
 * that share the same hash code.
 */

struct symtabCDT {
    cellT *buckets[NBuckets];
};

/* Private function declarations */

static void FreeBucketChain(cellT *cp);
static cellT *FindCell(cellT *cp, string s);
static int Hash(string s, int nBuckets);
```

```
/* Public entries */

symtabADT NewSymbolTable(void)
{
    symtabADT table;
    int i;

    table = New(symtabADT);
    for (i = 0; i < NBuckets; i++) {
        table->buckets[i] = NULL;
    }
    return (table);
}

void FreeSymbolTable(symtabADT table)
{
    int i;

    for (i = 0; i < NBuckets; i++) {
        FreeBucketChain(table->buckets[i]);
    }
    FreeBlock(table);
}

void Enter(symtabADT table, string key, void *value)
{
    int bucket;
    cellT *cp;

    bucket = Hash(key, NBuckets);
    cp = FindCell(table->buckets[bucket], key);
    if (cp == NULL) {
        cp = New(cellT *);
        cp->key = CopyString(key);
        cp->link = table->buckets[bucket];
        table->buckets[bucket] = cp;
    }
    cp->value = value;
}

void *Lookup(symtabADT table, string key)
{
    int bucket;
    cellT *cp;

    bucket = Hash(key, NBuckets);
    cp = FindCell(table->buckets[bucket], key);
    if (cp == NULL) return(UNDEFINED);
    return (cp->value);
}
```

```
/* Private functions */

/*
 * Function: FreeBucketChain
 * Usage: FreeBucketChain(cp);
 * ----------------------------
 * This function takes a chain pointer and frees all the cells
 * in that chain.  Because the package makes copies of the keys,
 * this function must free the string storage as well.
 */

static void FreeBucketChain(cellT *cp)
{
    cellT *next;

    while (cp != NULL) {
        next = cp->link;
        FreeBlock(cp->key);
        FreeBlock(cp);
        cp = next;
    }
}

/*
 * Function: FindCell
 * Usage: cp = FindCell(cp, key);
 * ------------------------------
 * This function finds a cell in the chain beginning at cp that
 * matches key.  If a match is found, a pointer to that cell is
 * returned.  If no match is found, the function returns NULL.
 */

static cellT *FindCell(cellT *cp, string key)
{
    while (cp != NULL && !StringEqual(cp->key, key)) {
        cp = cp->link;
    }
    return (cp);
}

/*
 * Function: Hash
 * Usage: bucket = Hash(key, nBuckets);
 * ------------------------------------
 * This function takes the key and uses it to derive a hash code,
 * which is an integer in the range [0, nBuckets - 1].  The hash
 * code is computed using a method called linear congruence.  The
 * choice of the value for Multiplier can have a significant effect
 * on the performance of the algorithm, but not on its correctness.
 */

#define Multiplier -1664117991L
```

```
static int Hash(string s, int nBuckets)
{
    int i;
    unsigned long hashcode;

    hashcode = 0;
    for (i = 0; s[i] != '\0'; i++) {
        hashcode = hashcode * Multiplier + s[i];
    }
    return (hashcode % nBuckets);
}
```

As you can see in Figure 11-2, the code for **Lookup** begins by calling the **Hash** function to convert the key into the index of a bucket. **Lookup** then calls **FindCell**, which searches for the key in the list associated with the designated bucket. If the key is found, **Lookup** returns the corresponding value. If not, **Lookup** returns the special pointer constant **UNDEFINED**.

The code for **Enter** is quite similar. Up through the call to **FindCell**, the code for the two functions is exactly the same. When **FindCell** returns, the **Enter** function must respond to two possible conditions. If **FindCell** found a cell whose key matched the argument, **cp** contains its address; if not, **cp** contains the value **NULL**. In the second case, **Enter** must add a new cell to the linked list associated with that bucket and initialize it with a copy of the key. At this point, the two cases merge, and the only remaining work is to update the value field in the cell.

Choosing a hash function

The preceding section describes the operation of every function in the **hash.c** implementation except the one that gives the method its name—the **Hash** function. In Figure 11-2, the **Hash** function has the following implementation, which is certainly rather cryptic:

```
#define Multiplier -1664117991L

int Hash(string s, int nBuckets)
{
    int i;
    unsigned long hashcode;

    hashcode = 0;
    for (i = 0; s[i] != '\0'; i++) {
        hashcode = hashcode * Multiplier + s[i];
    }
    return (hashcode % nBuckets);
}
```

Although there are many different strategies for writing hash functions, the code for **Hash** shown here is typical of the functions most often used in commercial practice. The code iterates through each character in the key, updating an integer value stored in the local variable `hashcode`. On each loop cycle, the `Hash` function multiplies the previous value of `hashcode` by a mysterious constant called `Multiplier` and then adds the ASCII value of the current character. At the end of the loop, the value of `hashcode` is reduced using the remainder operator to an integer between 0 and `nBuckets - 1`. It is also important to note that the variable `hashcode` is declared as an `unsigned long`. The `long` qualifier requests that the compiler allocate at least 32 bits to the integer value. The `unsigned` qualifier means that all 32 bits are considered to be part of a nonnegative number, which ensures that the remainder operator in the last line returns a positive value, as long as the value of `nBuckets` is also positive.

From the discussion in the preceding paragraph, you know that the `Hash` function will return a value in the desired range, but the gyrations it goes through to do so may nonetheless seem overly complex. What is the purpose of `Multiplier`, for example? Why does the implementation go to all this trouble? The answer is that the performance of a hash table depends significantly on how often keys collide.

Depending on the choice of hash function, collisions are more or less likely to occur. Poorly designed hash functions often map similar keys to the same bucket, which reduces the advantage of the hash table approach. For example, if you left `Multiplier` out of the computation, the `Hash` function would simply add up the ASCII values of the characters in the key. With this strategy, any keys that were permutations of each other would collide. Thus, `abc` and `cba` would hash to the same bucket. So would the keys `a3`, `b2`, and `c1`. If you were using this hash table in the context of a compiler, variable names that fit such patterns would all end up hashing to the same bucket.

At the cost of making the code for the `Hash` function more obscure, you can reduce the likelihood that similar keys will collide. Figuring out how to design such a function, however, requires some experience and a more advanced knowledge of computer science theory. The strategy used in Figure 11-2 is closely related to the technique used in a typical random number generator like the ANSI function `rand`. In both the hashing algorithms and the random number generator, the arithmetical properties of the calculation make the results harder to predict. In the hash table, the consequence of this unpredictability is that keys chosen by a programmer are unlikely to exhibit any higher level of collision than one would expect by random chance.

Even though careful choice of a hash function can reduce the number of collisions and thereby improve performance, it is important to recognize that the *correctness* of the algorithm is not affected by the collision rate. The only requirement is that the hash function deliver a result that lies in the range between 0 and `NBuckets - 1`. If it does, the symbol table implementation will still work. For example, if the hash function were

```
int Hash(string s, int nBuckets)
{
    return (0);
}
```

This implementation works but is extremely inefficient.

every key would end up in the chain attached to bucket 0. Programs that used such a hash function would run slowly because every key would be linked into the same chain, but they would nonetheless continue to give the correct results.

Determining the number of buckets

Although the design of the hash function is important, it is clear that the likelihood of collision also depends on the number of buckets. If the number is small, collisions occur more frequently. In particular, if there are more entries in the hash table than buckets, collisions are inevitable. Collisions affect the performance of the hash table strategy because they force **Lookup** and **Enter** to search through longer chains. As the hash table fills up, the number of collisions rises, which in turn reduces the performance of the hash table.

Remember that the goal of using a hash table is to implement a symbol table so that the **Lookup** and **Enter** run in constant time, at least in the average case. To achieve this goal, it is important that the linked-list chains emerging from each bucket remain fairly short. Thus, you want to make sure that the number of buckets is large enough to keep the chains relatively modest in length. If the hash function does a good job of distributing the keys evenly among the buckets, the average length of each bucket chain is given by the formula

$$\lambda = \frac{N_{\text{entries}}}{N_{\text{buckets}}}$$

For example, if the total number of symbols in the table is three times the number of buckets, the average chain will contain three entries, which in turn means that three string comparisons will be required, on average, to find a key in the table. The value λ is called the **load factor** of the hash table.

For good performance, you want to make sure that the value of λ remains relatively small. On the other hand, choosing a large value for **NBuckets** means that there are lots of empty buckets in the hash table array, which wastes a certain amount of space. Hash tables represent a good example of a time-space tradeoff, a concept introduced in Chapter 9. By increasing the amount of space, you can improve performance.

Of course, it may be difficult to choose a value of **NBuckets** that works well for all clients. If a client keeps entering more and more symbols into a symbol table, the performance will eventually decline. If you want to restore good performance in such a case, one approach is to allow the implementation to increase the number of buckets dynamically. For example, you can design the implementation so that it allocates a larger hash table if the load factor in the table ever reaches a certain threshold. Unfortunately, if you increase the number of buckets, the hash values all change, which means that the code to expand the table must reenter every key from the old table into the new one. This process is called **rehashing.** Although rehashing can be time-consuming, it is performed infrequently and therefore has minimal impact on the overall running time of the application. Rehashing is unnecessary for most application domains and is not included in the implementations of hashing used in this text.

There is one other consideration that comes up in choosing the value of NBuckets. Many of the common techniques used to generate hash functions—including the linear congruential method introduced in the preceding section—work better if the number of buckets is prime. If NBuckets is not prime, patterns that result in unbalanced bucket loads are more likely to emerge. The mathematical reasons for this behavior are beyond the scope of this text, but it is nonetheless useful to know that using prime values for NBuckets sometimes improves performance.

11.3 Limitations of the preliminary interface

The symtab.h file in Figure 11-1 was presented as a preliminary version of the interface. In order to understand what operations are missing, it helps to use the symbol table interface in an application. Suppose, for example, that you have been asked to write a program that tabulates how often words appear in a data file. For example, if the file macbeth.txt contains the lines

```
Tomorrow, and tomorrow, and tomorrow
Creeps in this petty pace from day to day
```

what you want is a program that produces the following output:

```
and         2
creeps      1
day         2
from        1
in          1
pace        1
petty       1
this        1
to          1
tomorrow    3
```

Most of the code required to tabulate word frequencies is quite straightforward. The basic framework for such a program, ignoring #include lines and function prototypes, appears in Figure 11-3. The main program opens the data file and then uses the scanner abstraction from Chapter 8 to divide each line of the file into words. To keep track of how often each word appears, the program uses a symbol table in which the key is the word—after converting all letters to lower case so that "Tomorrow" and "tomorrow" are not counted separately—and the value is a pointer to a record containing a count field. Each time the word appears in the file, the count field is incremented. Thus, when the program reaches the end of the file, the symbol table contains the correct count for each word.

The problem comes in writing the function DisplayWordFrequencies. The symbol table contains all the information you need. Unfortunately, the current version of the symtab.h interface offers no easy way to retrieve this information.

```
┌─────────────────┐
│ FIGURE 11-3 │ Framework for a word frequency program
└─────────────────┘
```

```
/*
 * Type: counterT
 * --------------
 * This type is used to record the count of each word in the
 * symbol table, which requires that values be pointers.
 */

typedef struct {
    int count;
} *counterT;

/* Main program */

main()
{
    FILE *infile;
    string line, token, filename;
    scannerADT scanner;
    symtabADT table;

    scanner = NewScanner();
    table = NewSymbolTable();
    printf("Input file: ");
    filename = GetLine();
    infile = fopen(filename, "r");
    if (infile == NULL) Error("Can't open %s", filename);
    while ((line = ReadLine(infile)) != NULL) {
        SetScannerString(scanner, ConvertToLowerCase(line));
        while (MoreTokensExist(scanner)) {
            token = ReadToken(scanner);
            if (isalpha(token[0])) RecordWord(table, token);
        }
    }
    fclose(infile);
    DisplayWordFrequencies(table);
}

static void RecordWord(symtabADT table, string word)
{
    counterT entry;

    entry = Lookup(table, word);
    if (entry == UNDEFINED) {
        entry = New(counterT);
        entry->count = 0;
        Enter(table, word, entry);
    }
    entry->count++;
}

static void DisplayWordFrequencies(symtabADT table)
{
    The implementation of this function requires a new technique described in Section 11.5.
}
```

What you need is some way to express the operation embodied in the following pseudocode implementation:

```
void DisplayWordFrequencies(symtabADT table)
{
      for  (each entry in the table)  {
           Display the key and the corresponding count.
      }
}
```

There are many strategies you could use to include this functionality in the symbol table abstraction. The best such strategies, however, depend on a general programming technique that you have not yet seen. This technique—which consists of using functions as part of the data structure—is extremely powerful and requires discussion in its own right. Section 11.4 outlines the basic approach, after which Section 11.5 returns to the question of how using functions as data helps solve the problem of displaying a table of word frequencies.

■■■ 11.4 Using functions as data

In the programming you have done up to this point, the concepts of functions and data structures have remained separate. Functions provide the means for representing an algorithm; data structures allow you to organize the information to which those algorithms are applied. Functions have only been part of the algorithmic structure, not part of the data structure. Being able to use functions as data values, however, often makes it much easier to design effective interfaces because doing so allows clients to specify operations as well as data. The next few sections offer several examples of how functions can be used as data that illustrate the importance of this technique.

A general plotting function

One of the easiest ways to illustrate the notion of functions as data is to design a simple plotting package that allows clients to plot graphs of mathematical functions. Suppose, for example, that you want to write a general function that plots the value of a function $f(x)$ for values of x between two specified limits. For example, if f is the trigonometric sine function and the limits are 0 and 2π, you get a graph like this:

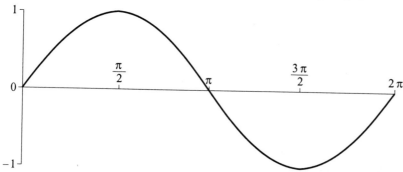

If f were the square root function plotted over the range 0 to 4, the shape of the resulting graph would instead look like this:

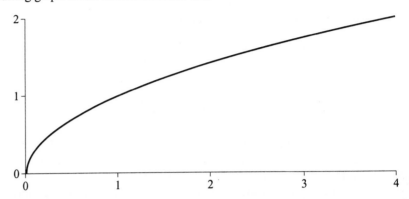

From a programming perspective, the interesting question is whether you can design a procedure `PlotFunction` that allows you to supply the function you want to plot as an argument. For example, assuming that `Pi` is defined to be the mathematical constant π, you would like to be able to call

```
PlotFunction(sin, 0, 2 * Pi);
```

to produce the first sample graph and

```
PlotFunction(sqrt, 0, 4);
```

to produce the second.

What would the prototype for `PlotFunction` look like? The two arguments indicating the range are easy to declare, but what is the type of the first argument? The implementation of `PlotFunction` clearly needs to know something about the function it is given. You would not expect just any old function to work. For example, you would have no idea what to expect if you called

```
PlotFunction(Concat, 0, 2 * Pi);
```
  This call is meaningless.

even though `Concat` is a perfectly legal C function. The problem, of course, is that `Concat` is a string function. For `PlotFunction` to make sense, its first argument must be a function that takes a real number (presumably a `double`) and returns one as well. Thus, you can say that the first argument to `PlotFunction` must be part of the general class of functions that map one `double` into another `double`.

Declaring pointers to functions and function classes

To make functions fit more comfortably into the existing data structure facilities, the designers of C took advantage of the fact that the code for a function is stored somewhere in memory and can therefore be identified by the address of its first instruction. Thus, it makes sense to define pointers to functions, using a syntactic form that turns out to be compatible with all other C declarations, even though it appears a bit odd at first. If you want, for example, to declare a variable `fn` to be a pointer to a function taking and returning a double, you can write

```
double (*fn) (double);
```

It's important to remember the parentheses around `*fn` in the declaration of a function pointer. The alternative

```
double *fn(double);
```

This line declares a function returning a pointer, not a pointer to a function.

declares `fn` as a function returning a pointer to a `double`.

In most cases, it makes more sense to use `typedef` to define an entire class of functions and then to define individual variables of that class. Thus, to define the name `doubleFnT` to indicate the class of functions (really pointers to functions) that take one `double` and return a `double`, you would write the following

```
typedef double (*doubleFnT) (double);
```

This definition means that you could write the prototype for `PlotFunction` as follows:

```
void PlotFunction(doubleFnT fn, double start, double finish);
```

Implementing `PlotFunction`

Once you have defined the prototype, you can write a primitive implementation of `PlotFunction` using the graphics library presented in Chapter 5, as follows:

```
void PlotFunction(doubleFnT fn, double start, double finish)
{
    double x;

    MovePen(start, fn(start));
    for (x = start + DeltaX; x <= finish; x += DeltaX) {
        DrawLineTo(x, fn(x));
    }
}
```

The constant `DeltaX`, which is defined as part of the plotting package, specifies how much `x` changes on each cycle of the loop. If you make `DeltaX` smaller, the plot representation becomes more accurate, although the program takes longer to run.

This implementation of `PlotFunction` does not have all the features you would want in a general package. For one thing, the implementation assumes that all the (x, y) coordinates generated by the function actually correspond to positions on the screen. If, for example, these values are negative or extend beyond the screen boundary, it would help to provide the client with some way to reposition and scale the output graph so that the values of the function are easy to see.

Even in its current form, however, `PlotFunction` illustrates the usefulness of functions as data. In the implementation, the parameter `fn` is a variable whose value is logically a function supplied by the caller. It can be `sin`, `sqrt`, or a user-defined function as long as its prototype matches the `doubleFnT` type class, which consists of all functions taking and returning a `double`. Inside the implementation, calls to `fn` are interpreted as calls to the function whose address is stored in the variable `fn`, which is declared as a function pointer. Thus, these calls end up invoking the function that the caller specified as the first argument to `PlotFunction`.

The `qsort` function

The various implementations of sorting functions presented in Chapter 7 make it clear that sorting is a complex problem that requires considerable care to implement efficiently. Because sorting is so important—and because its performance depends so heavily on its implementation—the designers of the standard ANSI libraries included a general function called `qsort` that implements the Quicksort algorithm. The `qsort` function allows clients to sort arrays of any type without having to worry about the details of writing a sorting procedure that is both efficient and correct.

The details of the Quicksort algorithm are discussed in detail in Chapter 7. The issue here is how a function like `qsort` can be written in a way that allows the element type of the array being sorted to vary from call to call. The solution used by the ANSI `qsort` function depends on function pointers for its generality and would not be possible in C without them.

In principle, sorting can be applied to data values of any ordered type. The structure of the sorting algorithm does not depend on the base type of the array. As long as the implementation can compare two values and move elements from one position in the array to another, it should be possible to use the same basic code to sort an array of any type. On the other hand, writing such a function is tricky because C requires function prototypes to declare the types of its parameters. How does `qsort`, for example, declare the type of the array being sorted?

When you are defining the prototype for `qsort`, what you would like is something that looks like this:

```
void qsort(any array[], int n);
```

No type any exists.

Unfortunately, no type `any` exists in C. In some abstractions, you can use the type `void *` to achieve a similarly polymorphic effect, but doing so constrains the individual values to be of some pointer type. Such a design would rule out using the `qsort` function on arrays consisting of nonpointer types, including `int` and `double`. Such a restriction clearly compromises the effectiveness of the interface.

In order to find a way out of this dilemma, it is important to remember that an array in C is treated as a pointer to its initial element. In implementing `qsort`, such a view turns out to be decidedly advantageous. If you think of the problem in terms of the internal arrangement of memory, the client might have passed any of the following arrays:

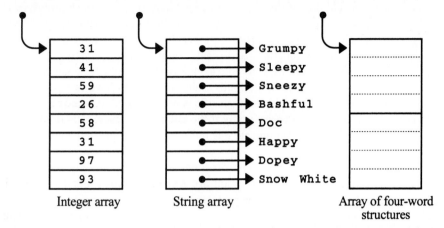

Integer array	String array	Array of four-word structures

The three arrays have different element types and potentially different element sizes, but in each case the pointer to the first element is the same. Thus, if you think of the array not as being of type "array of **any**" but as type "pointer to **any**," you can always refer to the first element in the array. You already know that the type **void *** acts as type "pointer to **any**," and you can therefore refine your prototype to be

```
void qsort(void *array, int n);
```

This approach is incomplete.

Unfortunately, this prototype is still not sufficient to solve the problem. While you can treat the array pointer as the address of the first element, you cannot find the address of the second element without knowing how large the element type is. Since the **qsort** function must have access to all the array elements, you must also pass the size of each element, as follows:

```
void qsort(void *array,
           int n,
           int elementSize,
```

This prototype is reasonably close but is still missing one important feature.

The **elementSize** parameter allows the **qsort** implementation to calculate the address of any element in the array. Given the parameters to **qsort** shown in the prototype, you can calculate the address of element **array[k]** like this:

```
(void *) ((char *) array + k * elementSize)
```

Converting the array address to a character pointer is essential because C does not allow you to perform address arithmetic on the type **void ***. Because **elementSize** is specified in terms of bytes (which in C are considered equivalent to characters), the address of the array must be converted to the type `char *` before adding in the offset for the kth element.

Even with the addition of the `elementSize` parameter, the `qsort` prototype is still not finished. The `qsort` function must be able to compare two elements in the array to see which should come before the other. In the case of sorting integers or real numbers, the `qsort` function has to make an arithmetic comparison. For the `Alphabetize` application, it must be able to call `StringCompare`. If the client has passed in some record structure, the fields within that record have to be compared against each other in some application-specific way. In general, the `qsort` function can perform the correct comparison only if the client, in essence, tells it how. The best way for the client to communicate this information is by passing a comparison function to `qsort`.

What does the class of comparison functions look like? The only comparison functions you have seen up to this point are `StringCompare` and its `strcmp` counterpart in the ANSI libraries. The prototype for `StringCompare` is

```
int StringCompare(string s1, string s2);
```

which suggests that comparison functions take two arguments representing the values to be compared and return an integer. The conventional interpretation of the integer result is that the return value is less than 0 when the first argument is less than the second, equal to 0 when the arguments are equal, and greater than 0 when the first argument is greater than the second.

Although the `StringCompare` function provides useful insights into the nature of comparison functions, its prototype is not general enough to be used as a template for a general function class. The `StringCompare` function defines its arguments as strings, which is certainly not true for comparison functions in general. The prototype for a general comparison function must be expressed in terms that are common to both the client and the implementation. Because it does not know the base type of the array, the implementation would be unable to use a function like `StringCompare` that depends on specific type information.

To achieve the necessary level of generality, the `qsort` implementation cannot pass the actual values from the array to the comparison function, because doing so would require it to specify their type. What the implementation must do instead is pass pointers to the two elements and then let the client use the pointer to retrieve the actual values. Thus, if you want to define a general comparison function, that function should take two `void *` pointers as arguments and return an integer. The function class for comparison functions therefore looks like this:

```
typedef int (*cmpFnT)(const void *p1, const void *p2);
```

The `const` keyword indicates that the comparison function is free to read the target of the pointer but not change it.[2]

---

[2] Unfortunately, several common C compilers do not handle the `const` keyword consistently, and I therefore avoid using it in most examples in the text. In this case, it is part of the ANSI definition of a comparison function, which means that many compilers require its use.

This type definition allows you to complete the prototype for **qsort**, as follows:

```
void qsort(void *array, int n, int elementSize, cmpFnT cmpFn);
```

The **qsort** implementation calls the function **cmpFn** on pointers to array elements and uses the result returned by the client's comparison function to determine the correct order.

The client-supplied comparison function makes it possible for the implementation to compare values of the specific type stored in the array. For example, to compare two integers, you would need to supply a function like the following:

```
int IntCmpFn(const void *p1, const void *p2)
{
    int v1, v2;

    v1 = *((int *) p1);
    v2 = *((int *) p2);
    if (v1 == v2) return (0);
    return ((v1 < v2) ? -1 : 1);
}
```

To sort an integer array of size **n**, you could then call

```
qsort(intArray, n, sizeof(int), IntCmpFn);
```

Similarly, to alphabetize a list of names, you need to write a function that takes two pointers to strings as arguments and then compares the underlying strings. Note that the arguments to a comparison function are pointers to strings and not pointers to characters, so the conventional **StringCompare** function is not appropriate. You need instead to define a function like this:

```
int StringCmpFn(const void *p1, const void *p2)
{
    return (StringCompare(*((string *) p1), *((string *) p2)));
}
```

You then call **qsort** with

```
qsort(strArray, n, sizeof(string), StringCmpFn);
```

Because comparison functions like **IntCmpFn** and **StringCmpFn** are useful in a variety of applications, it is convenient to implement comparison functions for the standard types and assemble them into a library. If such a library exists, you can rely on the library implementations of these functions whenever you need them. Figure 11-4 shows the interface for such a library. The corresponding implementation file is not reproduced in full, but consists of several short functions, each of which is similar in structure to **IntCmpFn**.

FIGURE 11-4 An interface that defines comparison functions for the predefined types

```
/*
 * File: cmpfn.h
 * -------------
 * This interface exports several comparison functions for use
 * with ANSI library functions like qsort and bsearch as well
 * as various functions in the extended library.
 */

#ifndef _cmpfn_h
#define _cmpfn_h

/*
 * Type: cmpFnT
 * ------------
 * This type defines the type space of comparison functions,
 * each of which take the addresses of their arguments and
 * return an integer from the set {-1, 0, +1} depending on
 * whether the first argument is less than, equal to, or
 * greater than the second.
 */

typedef int (*cmpFnT)(const void *p1, const void *p2);

/*
 * Standard comparison functions
 * -----------------------------
 * The remainder of this interface exports standard comparison
 * functions for the most common built-in types.
 */

int IntCmpFn(const void *p1, const void *p2);
int ShortCmpFn(const void *p1, const void *p2);
int LongCmpFn(const void *p1, const void *p2);
int UnsignedCmpFn(const void *p1, const void *p2);
int UnsignedShortCmpFn(const void *p1, const void *p2);
int UnsignedLongCmpFn(const void *p1, const void *p2);
int CharCmpFn(const void *p1, const void *p2);
int FloatCmpFn(const void *p1, const void *p2);
int DoubleCmpFn(const void *p1, const void *p2);
int StringCmpFn(const void *p1, const void *p2);
int PtrCmpFn(const void *p1, const void *p2);

#endif
```

Functions that are passed by clients to an implementation, such as the various comparison functions defined in cmpfn.h, are called **callback functions** because the implementation uses these functions to make calls back to the client. Because callback functions make it possible for the client to specify operations along with data, they play an important role in modern programming methodology and are an integral part of the implementation of object-oriented languages.

■ 11.5 Mapping functions

Callback functions make it possible to implement the one missing piece of the program in Figure 11-3, which counts how often words appear in a data file. That missing piece is the function `DisplayWordFrequencies`, which has the following pseudocode structure:

```
void DisplayWordFrequencies(symtabADT table)
{
    for (each entry in the table) {
        Display the key and the corresponding count.
    }
}
```

If you think about the pseudocode for `DisplayWordFrequencies`, it becomes clear that the task of displaying the symbol table must be shared by both the client and the implementation. Only the client knows how to display a word and its associated count, which means that the body of the loop is the client's responsibility. On the other hand, only the implementation knows what entries exist in the symbol table. Thus, the process of stepping through each entry in the table must be driven from the implementation side.

One strategy that makes it possible to manage this shared responsibility between the client and implementation is to have the `symtab.h` export a function that allows the client to execute a callback operation on every entry in the symbol table. Such a function is called a **mapping function**. For example, if `symtab.h` exported a function called `MapSymbolTable` that took a callback function as an argument, all you would have to do to complete the implementation of `DisplayWordFrequencies` is write a function `DisplayEntry` to display the value of a single entry and then use `MapSymbolTable` to apply `DisplayEntry` to the table as a whole.

Mapping over entries in a symbol table

The first step toward defining a function like `MapSymbolTable` is to decide on the structure of the callback function. If you were writing a callback function to process a single entry in the symbol table, you would probably assume that its arguments consist of a key and the corresponding value. Thus, you might expect the prototype for `DisplayEntry` to look like this:

```
void DisplayEntry(string key,
                  void *value);
```

This prototype is incomplete as it stands.

Although it is possible to define a mapping function for symbol tables that supplies only a key and a value, these two arguments alone are insufficient for many applications. As you will discover in the section on "Passing client data to callback functions" later in this chapter, it is often necessary for the client to pass additional information. The best way to communicate such information is through the parameter list. As a result, most callback functions are designed to include an additional parameter through which the client can pass a pointer to an arbitrary data structure. Thus, the complete prototype for `DisplayEntry` looks like this:

```
void DisplayEntry(string key, void *value, void *clientData);
```

If the client has no use for the `clientData` field, it can simply supply `NULL` as the `clientData` argument.

By generalizing from the prototype for `DisplayEntry`, it is easy to define a type that represents the class of functions you can use with `MapSymbolTable`. Each such function takes a key, a value, and the client data pointer, as follows:

```
typedef void (*symtabFnT)(string key, void *value,
                          void *clientData);
```

This definition enables you to write the interface description for `MapSymbolTable`, which appears as the last entry in the complete `symtab.h` interface shown in Figure 11-5.

FIGURE 11-5 Final version of the symtab.h interface

```
/*
 * File: symtab.h
 * --------------
 * This interface exports a simple symbol table abstraction.
 */

#ifndef _symtab_h
#define _symtab_h

#include "genlib.h"

/*
 * Type: symtabADT
 * ---------------
 * This type is the ADT used to represent a symbol table.
 */

typedef struct symtabCDT *symtabADT;

/*
 * Type: symtabFnT
 * ---------------
 * This type defines the class of functions that can be used to
 * map over the entries in a symbol table.
 */

typedef void (*symtabFnT)(string key, void *value,
                          void *clientData);
```

```
/* Exported entries */

/*
 * Function: NewSymbolTable
 * Usage: table = NewSymbolTable();
 * --------------------------------
 * This function allocates a new symbol table with no entries.
 */

symtabADT NewSymbolTable(void);

/*
 * Function: FreeSymbolTable
 * Usage: FreeSymbolTable(table);
 * --------------------------------
 * This function frees the storage associated with the symbol table.
 */

void FreeSymbolTable(symtabADT table);

/*
 * Function: Enter
 * Usage: Enter(table, key, value);
 * --------------------------------
 * This function associates key with value in the symbol table.
 * Each call to Enter supersedes any previous definition for key.
 */

void Enter(symtabADT table, string key, void *value);

/*
 * Function: Lookup
 * Usage: value = Lookup(table, key);
 * --------------------------------
 * This function returns the value associated with key in the symbol
 * table, or UNDEFINED, if no such value exists.
 */

void *Lookup(symtabADT table, string key);

/*
 * Function: MapSymbolTable
 * Usage: MapSymbolTable(fn, table, clientData);
 * --------------------------------------------------
 * This function goes through every entry in the symbol table
 * and calls the function fn, passing it the following arguments:
 * the current key, its associated value, and the clientData
 * pointer.  The clientData pointer allows the client to pass
 * additional state information to the function fn, if necessary.
 * If no clientData argument is required, this value should be NULL.
 */

void MapSymbolTable(symtabFnT fn, symtabADT table,
                    void *clientData);

#endif
```

Once you have the definition of `MapSymbolTable`, it is easy to implement the functions `DisplayWordFrequencies` and `DisplayEntry`, as follows:

```
void DisplayWordFrequencies(symtabADT table)
{
    printf("Word frequency table:\n");
    MapSymbolTable(DisplayEntry, table, NULL);
}

void DisplayEntry(string key, void *value, void *clientData)
{
    printf("%-15s%5d\n", key, ((counterT) value)->count);
}
```

`DisplayWordFrequencies` just calls the mapping function for symbol tables, which in turn calls `DisplayEntry` on each key/value pair. `DisplayEntry` displays the key along with the contents of the `count` field stored in the record that represents the value. However, only the client knows what the value record looks like, so `DisplayEntry` must convert the type from `void *` to `counterT` before selecting the `count` field. Because this example is simple enough that `DisplayEntry` doesn't need any other information besides the key and the value, `DisplayWordFrequencies` passes `NULL` as the value of `clientData`, which is completely ignored by `DisplayEntry`.

Implementing `MapSymbolTable`

The only remaining task is to add the code for `MapSymbolTable` to the `symtab.c` implementation. Because the hash table consists of an array of linked lists, mapping over the entries in the table is simply a matter of going through each of the buckets in the array and then iterating through every entry in the corresponding chain, as illustrated by the following implementation:

```
void MapSymbolTable(symtabFnT fn, symtabADT table,
                    void *clientData)
{
    int i;
    cellT *cp;

    for (i = 0; i < NBuckets; i++) {
        for (cp = table->buckets[i]; cp != NULL; cp = cp->link) {
            fn(cp->key, cp->value, clientData);
        }
    }
}
```

Putting all the code together leaves you with an implementation of the frequency-counting program that does almost everything you want. If you run the program in its current form on the `macbeth.txt` data file, the tabulation looks like this:

```
pace          1
to            1
day           2
tomorrow      3
petty         1
and           2
creeps        1
from          1
in            1
this          1
```

All the counts are correct. The only problem is that the words are not displayed in any recognizable order. The `MapSymbolTable` function simply cycled through the entries as they appear in the internal structure, which means that the order depends on how the keys are organized into the different buckets.

The fact that the keys are not processed in order is not the fault of `MapSymbolTable`, which is behaving exactly as it should. Trying to recode `MapSymbolTable` so that the keys were always delivered in alphabetical order would make the function more complex and less efficient. Because the keys are jumbled in the hash table, putting them back in order would require `MapSymbolTable` to sort the entries, which requires at least $O(N \log N)$ time. Because many clients of `MapSymbolTable` may not care about the order of the keys, it is better to assign the responsibility of sorting the keys to any clients that need to do so.

Passing client data to callback functions

There are several strategies that you might consider to ensure that the table of word frequencies appears in sorted order. If you wanted to solve the problem with as little additional programming as possible, you might just write the tabulation data to a file instead of to the console screen, because there are many utility programs that sort data files. To get the display you wanted, you would simply run the unsorted output of the current program through one of these utilities. This strategy, which demonstrates a good understanding of the value of software tools, often works quite well. To implement it for this example, you could just replace the function `DisplayWordFrequencies` with a function `DumpWordFrequencies` that takes the name of the output file as an additional argument, like this:

```
void DumpWordFrequencies(symtabADT table, string filename);
```

Unfortunately, writing `DumpWordFrequencies` is not quite as easy as it might seem. In order to write data to an output file, you have to open the file using a statement like

```
outfile = fopen(filename, "w");
```

The problem arises when you try to write the callback function. You can't simply write a function `DumpEntry` like this:

```
void DumpEntry(string key, void *value, void *clientData)
{
    fprintf(outfile, "%-15s%5d\n", key,
        ((counterT) value)->count);
}
```

The variable `outfile` is not declared.

The crux of the problem is that you can't use the variable `outfile` in `DumpEntry` because it is declared as a local variable in `DumpWordFrequencies`. When the compiler reads the function `DumpEntry`, it regards the variable `outfile` as undeclared. Moreover, since `DumpWordFrequencies` calls `MapSymbolTable`, which in turn calls `DumpEntry`, the value of `outfile` must be passed across the interface boundary to `MapSymbolTable` and then back again to `DumpEntry`. The easiest way to communicate this information is to use the `clientData` pointer, which allows the client to pass an arbitrary pointer through `MapSymbolTable` to the callback function.

Using the `clientData` strategy allows you to implement `DumpWordFrequencies` and `DumpEntry`, as follows:

```
void DumpWordFrequencies(symtabADT table, string filename)
{
    FILE *outfile;

    outfile = fopen(filename, "w");
    if (outfile == NULL) Error("Can't open output file");
    MapSymbolTable(DumpEntry, table, outfile);
    fclose(outfile);
}

void DumpEntry(string key, void *value, void *clientData)
{
    FILE *outfile;

    outfile = clientData;
    fprintf(outfile, "%-15s%5d\n", key,
        ((counterT) value)->count);
}
```

The `clientData` parameter also makes it possible to retain information between independent invocations to a callback function. If you need, for example, to update a variable every time the callback function is executed, you can pass a pointer to that variable using the `clientData` parameter. Each call then has access to the information in that variable. An example that uses this technique appears in exercise 14 at the end of this chapter.

■ 11.6 Iterators

The `DumpWordFrequencies` function in the preceding section shows how it is possible to use the `clientData` parameter to pass data from the client to the callback function. But although this technique makes mapping functions much more powerful, the need to pass data in this way is often inconvenient. If you think about the problem in its pseudocode form, it is clear that the `DumpWordFrequencies` function involves none of the complexity associated with passing data through the `clientData` field. The implementation you want looks more like this:

```
void DumpWordFrequencies(symtabADT table, string filename)
{
    FILE *outfile;

    outfile = fopen(filename, "w");
    if (outfile == NULL) Error("Can't open output file");
    for (each key in the table) {
        Write out the key and its associated count to the output file.
    }
    fclose(outfile);
}
```

If it were possible to implement a facility that captured the effect of the line

```
for (each key in the table)
```

you would no longer have to worry about passing the value of `outfile` through the `clientData` mechanism. Because this strategy keeps all relevant code in a single function, the implementation becomes much simpler. In modern programming practice, the usual approach to problems of this sort is to define a new type called an **iterator** that allows clients to step through values in some collection, such as the keys in a symbol table.

Using iterators

The technique of using iterators is illustrated by the following implementation of `DisplayWordFrequencies`:

```
static void DisplayWordFrequencies(symtabADT table)
{
    iteratorADT iterator;
    counterT entry;
    string key;

    printf("Word frequency table:\n");
    iterator = NewIterator(table);
    while (StepIterator(iterator, &key)) {
        entry = Lookup(table, key);
        printf("%-15s%5d\n", key, entry->count);
    }
    FreeIterator(iterator);
}
```

In this implementation, the line

```
iteratorADT iterator;
```

declares a new variable that serves as an iterator for the symbol table. To use the iterator, you must first call `NewIterator` to allocate a new instance of the iterator type. The `NewIterator` function takes the symbol table as its argument and initializes the internal representation to return keys from that table. The actual process of cycling through each of the keys is performed by the function `StepIterator`, which uses call by reference to store each new key in the address specified as the second argument. The `StepIterator` function itself returns a Boolean value. As long as there are more keys in the table, `StepIterator` stores the next key in the variable provided by the client and returns `TRUE`. Once the last key has been processed, `StepIterator` returns `FALSE`. The `FreeIterator` function frees any internal storage associated with the iterator.

These functions make it very easy to step through all the keys in a table. The general idiom for doing so looks like this:

```
iterator = NewIterator(table);
while (StepIterator(iterator, &key)) {
    code that uses the value of key
}
FreeIterator(iterator);
```

Defining the iterator interface

If you were content to work with iterators only in the context of symbol tables, it would make sense to include the iterator mechanism directly in the symbol table abstraction. The idea of an iterator, however, is considerably more general. As you will discover later in this text, there are other abstract types besides symbol tables for which iterators are extremely useful, and it is convenient to use the same mechanism for each of these ADTs. Thus, it makes sense to prepare for the future by defining a separate interface called `iterator.h`, which is shown in Figure 11-6.

For the moment, both the `iterator.h` interface and its implementation in the next section make specific reference to symbol tables and can be used only in that context. In Chapter 15, you will learn how to extend the interface to work with other types without having to make any client-level changes in existing code.

Implementing the iterator abstraction for symbol tables

There are many ways to implement the iterator abstraction. One of the most common approaches is to let `NewIterator` do the lion's share of the work. When the client calls

```
iterator = NewIterator(table);
```

you can set up the internal structure so that the iterator contains a complete list of all the keys in the table. Thereafter, each call to `StepIterator` consists only of taking the next value from the list and returning it to the client.

As a general approach, the strategy of assembling a complete list of values when `NewIterator` is called has the following advantages:

- *Iterators that assemble a complete list are easier to implement.* Particularly when the iterator abstraction is extended to other abstract types, keeping the structure simple makes it easier to reimplement iterators for new types.

FIGURE 11-6   Interface for the iterator abstraction

```
/*
 * File: iterator.h
 * ----------------
 * This file implements an iterator for the symbol table
 * abstraction.  In the chapter on "Sets," this package is
 * superseded by a more general polymorphic iterator that
 * works for other collection types as well.
 */

#ifndef _iterator_h
#define _iterator_h

#include "genlib.h"
#include "symtab.h"

/*
 * Type: iteratorADT
 * -----------------
 * This abstract type is used to iterate over the elements
 * in a symbol table.
 */

typedef struct iteratorCDT *iteratorADT;

/* Exported entries */

/*
 * Functions: NewIterator, StepIterator, FreeIterator
 * Usage: iterator = NewIterator(table);
 *        while (StepIterator(iterator, &key)) {
 *            . . . body of loop involving key . . .
 *        }
 *        FreeIterator(iterator);
 * ----------------------------------------------------
 * These functions make it possible to iterate over the keys
 * in a symbol table without having to call a mapping function.
 * The call to NewIterator creates a new iteratorADT that
 * contains all the keys in the table, arranged in ASCII order.
 * Each call to StepIterator advances the iterator and returns
 * the next key using the reference parameter.  StepIterator
 * returns TRUE until the keys are exhausted, after which it
 * returns FALSE.  The FreeIterator function releases any
 * storage associated with the iterator.
 */

iteratorADT NewIterator(symtabADT table);
bool StepIterator(iteratorADT iterator, string *pKey);
void FreeIterator(iteratorADT iterator);

#endif
```

- *Assembling a list reduces the overhead necessary to process the values in a logical order.* In the symbol table example, it is convenient to process the keys in alphabetical order, but only if the cost of sorting the keys can be kept moderate. Because `NewIterator` creates a list of values anyway, the additional cost of keeping the list in sorted order no longer seems so unreasonable.

- *The body of the loop in the client code can change the contents of the ADT on which the iteration is performed.* This point is more subtle than the others, but in some ways more important. Imagine for the moment that you have decided to build an iterator for symbol tables without making a complete list at the beginning. Such a strategy is certainly possible. All you have to do is keep track of the current bucket and the position in the current chain as part of the iterator's internal state. The situation, however, becomes confusing if the client adds new symbols to the table as part of the body of the loop. Those symbols are added into the existing structure and may or may not appear in the iteration depending upon where the new values fit into the table. By making a complete list at the time `NewIterator` is called, the package essentially takes a snapshot of the symbol table at that point. Subsequent insertions in the symbol table will not change the iteration at all.

An implementation of the iterator abstraction for symbol tables that uses the approach of creating a list at the beginning appears in Figure 11-7. To generate the list, `NewIterator` calls `MapSymbolTable` with a callback function that inserts each key into a sorted list. Once `NewIterator` has created the list, the rest of the operations in the `iterator.h` interface are straightforward examples of list manipulation.

FIGURE 11-7 Implementation of the iterator abstraction for symbol tables

```
/*
 * File: iterator.c
 * ----------------
 * This file implements an iterator for the symbol table
 * abstraction.  In Chapter 14, this package is superseded
 * by a more general polymorphic iterator that also works for
 * other types that represent collections.
 */

#include <stdio.h>
#include "genlib.h"
#include "strlib.h"
#include "symtab.h"
#include "iterator.h"
```

```
/*
 * Type: cellT
 * ----------
 * This type defines a linked list cell for the iterator.
 */

typedef struct cellT {
    string key;
    struct cellT *link;
} cellT;

/*
 * Type: iteratorCDT
 * -----------------
 * This type provides the concrete representation for the
 * iterator, which is simply a linked list.
 */

struct iteratorCDT {
    cellT *start;
};

/* Private function declarations */

static void InsertKey(string key, void *value, void *clientData);

/* Public entries */

iteratorADT NewIterator(symtabADT table)
{
    iteratorADT iterator;

    iterator = New(iteratorADT);
    iterator->start = NULL;
    MapSymbolTable(InsertKey, table, iterator);
    return (iterator);
}

bool StepIterator(iteratorADT iterator, string *pKey)
{
    cellT *cp;

    cp = iterator->start;
    if (cp == NULL) return (FALSE);
    *pKey = cp->key;
    iterator->start = cp->link;
    FreeBlock(cp);
    return (TRUE);
}
```

```
void FreeIterator(iteratorADT iterator)
{
    cellT *cp;

    while ((cp = iterator->start) != NULL) {
        iterator->start = cp->link;
        FreeBlock(cp);
    }
    FreeBlock(iterator);
}

/* Private functions */

/*
 * Function: InsertKey
 * Usage: MapSymbolTable(InsertKey, table, iterator);
 * -----------------------------------------------------
 * This function is a callback function called by MapSymbolTable
 * on every entry in a symbol table.  Its effect is to insert
 * the current key into the linked list so that the order of the
 * keys is maintained in sorted order.  The code is a simple
 * find-and-insert loop that ends with prev and next pointing to
 * the cells on each side of the insertion point.  As a special
 * case, a NULL value for prev indicates insertion at the beginning.
 */

static void InsertKey(string key, void *value, void *clientData)
{
    iteratorADT iterator;
    cellT *prev, *next, *cp;

    iterator = (iteratorADT) clientData;
    prev = NULL;
    next = iterator->start;
    while (next != NULL && StringCompare(key, next->key) > 0) {
        prev = next;
        next = next->link;
    }
    cp = New(cellT *);
    cp->key = key;
    cp->link = next;
    if (prev == NULL) {
        iterator->start = cp;
    } else {
        prev->link = cp;
    }
}
```

11.7 Command dispatch tables

Although modern application programs tend to be controlled by buttons and menus, many programs still include a command interpreter that accepts typed commands from the user and responds to them by invoking an appropriate operation. For example, typing `help` might generate a help message, typing `quit` might cause the program to exit, and so on. The process of translating a command name into the corresponding action is called **command dispatching.**

To get a concrete sense of how command dispatching works, imagine that you are interested in building an application that responds to the following commands:

```
clear
run
help
quit
```

What these commands actually do, of course, depends on the details of the application. For the moment, the relevant issue is how to find an implementation strategy that allows you to use the command name to invoke the corresponding function from the following list:

```
ClearCmd
RunCmd
HelpCmd
QuitCmd
```

To make the problem as specific as possible, the goal in the remainder of the chapter is to write a function

```
void ExecuteCommand(string cmd);
```

that calls the appropriate function if `cmd` matches one of the four predefined commands. If `cmd` does not match any of the options, `ExecuteCommand` displays a message to that effect.

The easiest way to implement `ExecuteCommand` is to write a cascading `if` statement that checks for each possibility, as follows:

```
static void ExecuteCommand(string cmd)
{
    if (StringEqual(cmd, "clear")) {
        ClearCmd();
    } else if (StringEqual(cmd, "run")) {
        RunCmd();
    } else if (StringEqual(cmd, "help")) {
        HelpCmd();
    } else if (StringEqual(cmd, "quit")) {
        QuitCmd();
    } else {
        printf("Undefined command: %s\n", cmd);
    }
}
```

Because the code skips over commands until it finds a match, programmers often call a control structure of this form a **skip chain.** Skip chains are effective if the number of commands is small, but quickly become both tedious and inefficient as the number of possibilities grows.

As an alternative, you can also solve the command-dispatch problem by using symbol tables and function pointers together. The basic idea is to use the commands as keys in a table in which the corresponding values include pointers to functions that implement the corresponding commands. The code for this approach to command dispatching appears in Figure 11-8.

FIGURE 11-8 Dispatch table using function pointers

```
/*
 * Type: commandFnT
 * ----------------
 * This type defines the class of command functions.
 */

typedef void (*commandFnT)(void);

/*
 * Type: commandEntryT
 * -------------------
 * This type consists of a structure containing only a command
 * function.  This extra level of structure is required because
 * function pointers are not compatible with void * in ANSI C.
 */

typedef struct {
    commandFnT fn;
} *commandEntryT;

/*
 * Private variable: commandTable
 * ------------------------------
 * The entries in this table are used to hold the commands and
 * their corresponding actions.
 */

static symtabADT commandTable;

/* Command table functions */

static void InitCommandTable(void)
{
    commandTable = NewSymbolTable();
    DefineCommand("clear", ClearCmd);
    DefineCommand("run", RunCmd);
    DefineCommand("help", HelpCmd);
    DefineCommand("quit", QuitCmd);
}
```

```
static void DefineCommand(string cmd, commandFnT fn)
{
    commandEntryT entry;

    entry = New(commandEntryT);
    entry->fn = fn;
    Enter(commandTable, cmd, entry);
}

static void ExecuteCommand(string cmd)
{
    commandEntryT entry;

    entry = Lookup(commandTable, cmd);
    if (entry == UNDEFINED) {
        printf("Undefined command: %s\n", cmd);
        return;
    }
    entry->fn();
}
```

The values stored for each key in this implementation consist of a structure of type `commandEntryT` that contains the function pointer as its only field. The reason for this additional level of structure is that the rules of ANSI C dictate that pointers to functions are not compatible with the type `void *`, even though most C compilers allow assignment between these types. Even if your compiler lets you use a function pointer directly as the value corresponding to a key, your programs will be more portable if you obey the rules by storing the function pointer in a structure and then storing the address of the structure in the table.

The solution to the command-dispatch problem shown in Figure 11-8 has the following advantages over the skip-chain approach:

- *The dispatch operation is more efficient.* The skip-chain strategy is inherently linear in its performance. As long as the internal hash table is sufficiently large, the symbol table strategy tends to operate in constant time.
- *The program structure is easier to read.* When you use the skip-chain strategy, the body of the function that executes a command quickly becomes long and unwieldy. The individual functions in Figure 11-8 are shorter and more readable.
- *The command table can be extended much more easily.* To add a new command to the command-dispatch implementation in Figure 11-8, all you have to do is write the function that implements it and then add a single line to the `InitCommandTable` function. What's more, it is easy to enter new commands into the table dynamically, even as the program runs.

■ Summary

The focus of this chapter has been a new abstract data type called a *symbol table,* which allows clients to define an association between a key and a value and later to retrieve the value associated with a key. As part of the discussion of symbol tables, the chapter also introduced the concept of using functions as data—a powerful general technique that has important applications in the symbol table domain.

Important points in this chapter include:

- Symbol tables make it possible to associate keys with values by providing the fundamental operations `Enter` and `Lookup`. To simplify the design of the `symtab.h` interface, this text uses the type `string` to represent keys and `void *` to represent values.
- To differentiate the case of a key that has been explicitly bound to the pointer constant `NULL`, from the case in which no value has ever been entered for a key, the `Lookup` function in the `symtab.h` interface uses the constant `UNDEFINED`, which indicates that a particular key does not appear in the table.
- Symbol tables can be implemented very efficiently using a strategy called *hashing,* in which keys are converted to an array index by a function that tends to distribute the keys uniformly throughout the array. As long as your implementation permits the table space to expand with the number of symbols, hashing allows both `Enter` and `Lookup` to operate in constant time on average.
- The detailed design of a hash function is subtle and requires mathematical analysis to achieve optimum performance. Even so, any hash function that delivers integer values in the specified range always produces correct results and usually performs well in practice.
- The `Enter` and `Lookup` functions alone are not sufficient for many applications of symbol tables. The client often needs the ability to perform some operation for all the keys defined in a table. This chapter presents two techniques—mapping functions and iterators—that provide this capability.
- C makes it possible to use a pointer to the code for a function as a data value. This facility makes it possible for the client of an interface to pass information to the implementation about how a particular data value behaves. The usual approach is for the client to supply a *callback function* that can then be invoked on the implementation side of the interface boundary.
- A common use of callback functions in practice is in the context of *mapping functions,* which allow clients to invoke an operation on all internal elements of an ADT.
- Callback functions are more flexible if they include a parameter—called `clientData` in this text—that allows the client to pass additional information to the callback function.
- Because the `clientData` mechanism is sometimes cumbersome, modern programming environments often define a separate abstract type called an

iterator that makes it easy for client functions to step through the values in an ADT without having to change their context by calling a mapping function. The fundamental operations on iterators are illustrated by the following idiom for processing all the keys in a table:

```
iterator = NewIterator(table);
while (StepIterator(iterator, &key)) {
    code that uses the value of key
}
FreeIterator(iterator);
```

- Symbol tables and pointers to functions together provide a convenient mechanism for solving the command-dispatch problem, which consists of translating a command name into a corresponding operation.

REVIEW QUESTIONS

1. Describe the relationship between dictionaries and symbol tables.

2. What does the term *key* mean in the context of a symbol table?

3. Name the two operations that define the characteristic behavior of a symbol table.

4. What types are used in the **symtab.h** interface to represent keys and values?

5. In each of the linear structures in Chapter 10, the element type is defined using a **typedef** statement that is easy for the client to change. For example, the elements of a **stackADT** are defined to be of type **stackElementT**. Why was this approach rejected in the case of symbol tables?

6. Why is it difficult to use the type **void *** to represent keys in a symbol table?

7. What simple strategy could you use if you wanted to use integers as keys, given the definition of the **symtab.h** interface used in this chapter?

8. What value is used to represent an undefined entry in a symbol table? What argument is given in the chapter against using **NULL** for this purpose?

9. True or false: If you represent a symbol table using an array sorted by keys, the binary search algorithm allows you to implement both **Lookup** and **Enter** in $O(\log N)$ time.

10. Describe the dictionary analogue to the hashing algorithm.

11. What disadvantages would you expect from using the ASCII value of the first character in a key as its hash code?

12. What is meant by the term *bucket* in the implementation of a hash table? What constitutes a collision?

13. Explain the operation of the `FindCell` function in the `symtab.c` implementation given in Figure 11-2.

14. What is the role of the constant `Multiplier` in the implementation of the function `Hash`?

15. The `Hash` function that appears in the text has an internal structure similar to that of a random-number generator. If you took that similarity too literally, however, you might be tempted to write the following `Hash` function:

```
int Hash(string s, int nBuckets)
{
    return (RandomInteger(0, nBuckets - 1));
}
```

Why would this approach fail?

16. What time-space tradeoff arises in the implementation of a hash table?

17. What is meant by the term *rehashing*?

18. The code for the word-frequency program in Figure 11-3 defines a type `counterT` to keep track of how many times each word appears. Why couldn't the implementation simply use an integer for that purpose?

19. What capability is missing from the preliminary version of the `symtab.c` interface in Figure 11-1?

20. What advantages are cited in the chapter for regarding functions as part of the data structure?

21. Explain in English the effect of the following definition:

```
typedef string (*stringFnT)(string);
```

Give an example of a library function that fits into this function class.

22. What `typedef` line would you use to define the class of functions that take no arguments and return no results?

23. Describe the parameters used by the `qsort` function in the ANSI library. Why is each of those parameters necessary?

24. Why is it illegal to pass `StringCompare` or `strcmp` to `qsort` as a comparison function?

25. Define the terms *callback function* and *mapping function*.

26. What is the purpose of the `clientData` parameter in a callback function?

27. Describe the differences between iterators and mapping functions. Why are iterators generally easier to use?

28. What is the idiom introduced in this chapter for using an iterator with a symbol table?

29. What advantages are cited in the text for computing the entire list of values at the time **NewIterator** is called?

30. Explain how function pointers can be used to solve the command-dispatch problem.

31. What is the reason behind the inclusion of the type **commandEntryT** in the dispatch table code in Figure 11-8?

32. What factors make the use of command dispatch tables preferable to using skip chains for the same purpose?

 PROGRAMMING EXERCISES

1. As discussed in the section entitled "A preliminary version of the symbol table interface," reimplement the **symtab.h** interface using an array of key/value pairs as the underlying representation. Make sure that your implementation expands the array storage dynamically if the initial allocation is exhausted.

2. Modify your solution to the preceding exercise so that **Enter** always keeps the keys in sorted order in the internal array. Maintaining the sorted array makes it possible to use binary search with both the **Lookup** and the **Enter** function.

3. Evaluate the performance of the hashing algorithm by writing a procedure called **DisplayHashTableStatistics** that counts the length of each hash chain and displays the mean and standard deviation of those lengths. The mean is equivalent to the traditional average. The standard deviation is a measure of the how much the individual values tend to differ from the mean. The formula for calculating the standard deviation is

$$\sigma = \sqrt{\frac{\sum_{i=1}^{N}(\text{len}_{avg} - \text{len}_i)^2}{N}}$$

where N is the number of buckets, len_i is the length of bucket chain i, and len_{avg} is the average chain length. If the hash function is working well, the standard deviation should be relatively small in comparison to the mean, particularly as the number of symbols increases.

4. Extend the **symtab.h** interface to include a function

```
void DeleteSymbol(symtabADT table, string key);
```

that deletes the entry containing the specified key from the symbol table.

5. In certain applications, it is useful to extend the symbol table interface so that you can insert a temporary definition for a particular key, hiding away any previous value associated with that key. Later in the program, you can delete

the temporary definition, restoring the next most recent one. For example, you could use such a mechanism to capture the effect of local variables, which come into existence when a function is called and disappear again when the function returns.

Implement such a facility by adding the function

```
void InsertSymbol(symtabADT table, string key, void *value);
```

to the **symtab.h** interface. Because the **Lookup** and **Enter** functions always find the first entry in the chain, you can ensure that **InsertSymbol** hides the previous definitions simply by adding each new entry at the beginning of the list for a particular hash bucket. Moreover, as long as the implementation of **DeleteSymbol** function from exercise 4 deletes the first occurrence of a symbol from its hash chain, you can use **DeleteSymbol** to remove the most recently inserted definition for a key.

6. Extend the implementation of the hash table from Figure 11-2 so that the internal table can expand dynamically. Your implementation should keep track of the load factor for the hash table and perform a rehashing operation if the load factor exceeds the limit indicated by a constant **RehashThreshold** defined in the implementation.

7. Although the bucket-chaining approach used in the text is extremely effective in practice, other strategies exist for resolving collisions in hash tables. In the early days of computing—when memories were small enough that the cost of introducing extra pointers was taken seriously—hash tables often used a more memory-efficient strategy called **open addressing,** in which the key/value pairs are stored directly in the array, like this:

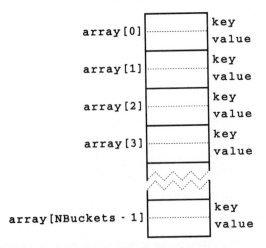

For example, if a key hashes to bucket 3, the open-addressing implementation of a hash table tries to put that key and its value directly into the entry at **array[3]**.

The problem with this approach is that `array[3]` may already be assigned to another key that hashes to the same bucket. The simplest approach to dealing with collisions of this sort is to store each new key in the first free cell at or after its expected hash position. Thus, if a key hashes to bucket 3, the `Lookup` and `Enter` functions first try to find or insert that key in `array[3]`. If that entry is filled with a different key, however, these functions move on to try `array[4]`, continuing the process until they find an empty entry or an entry with a matching key. As in the ring-buffer implementation of queues in Chapter 10, if the index advances past the end of the array, it should wrap back to the beginning. This strategy for resolving collisions is called **linear probing**.

Reimplement the `symtab.h` interface using open addressing with linear probing. Make sure your function generates an error if the client tries to enter a new key into a table that is already full. For an additional challenge, extend your implementation so that it supports the `DeleteSymbol` function defined in exercise 4.

8. When you design an interface that exports an ADT, it often makes sense to include a function that creates a copy of an existing ADT value by duplicating its internal data. For example, in the `symtab.h` interface, it would be useful to include a function

```
symtabADT CopySymbolTable(symtabADT oldTable);
```

that creates a new symbol table containing a copy of all the key/value pairs in `oldTable`. Thus, client code that wanted to make a snapshot of the contents of a symbol table named `varTable` could use the statement

```
saveTable = CopySymbolTable(varTable);
```

Later on, the client could restore the previous contents of the table by executing the following code:

```
FreeSymbolTable(varTable);
varTable = CopySymbolTable(saveTable);
```

Implement the `CopySymbolTable` function as an extension to the hash table code in Figure 11-2.

9. Modify the `PlotFunction` introduced in the section entitled "A general plotting function" so that it takes the following parameters:

```
void PlotFunction(doubleFnT fn, double xmin, double xmax,
                                 double ymin, double ymax);
```

where `xmin`, `xmax`, `ymin`, and `ymax` specify the desired dimensions of the graph, which is scaled to fill the entire graphics window. Thus, if you call

```
PlotFunction(sin, -Pi, Pi, -1, 1);
```

the program should produce a plot of the `sin` function that completely fills the graphics window, like this:

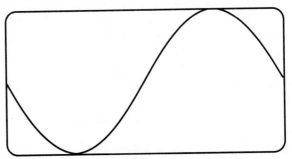

10. In calculus, the **definite integral** of a function is defined to be the area bounded horizontally by two specified limits and vertically by the x-axis and the value of the function.[3] For example, the definite integral of `sin` in the range 0 to π is the area of the shaded region in the following diagram:

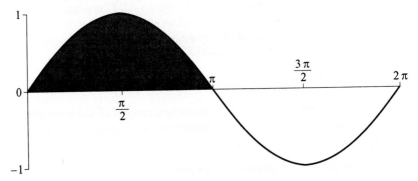

You can compute an approximation to this area by adding up the area of small rectangles of a fixed width, where the height is given by the value of the function at the midpoint of the rectangle:

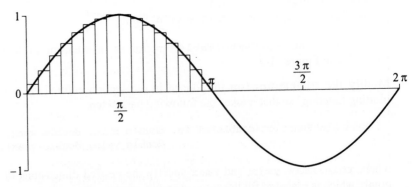

[3] Any region that falls below the x-axis is treated as negative area. Thus, if you computed the definite integral of `sin` from 0 to 2π, the result would be 0 because the areas above and below the x-axis cancel each other out.

Design the prototype (including any associated type definitions) and write the implementation for a function `Integrate` that calculates the definite integral by summing the areas of a set of rectangles. For example, to calculate the area of the shaded region in the earlier example, the client would write

```
value = Integrate(sin, 0, 3.1415926, 18);
```

where the last argument is the number of rectangles into which the area gets divided; the larger this value, the more accurate the approximation.

11. Write an implementation of the Quicksort algorithm, which is coded specifically for integers in Figure 7-6, so that its prototype corresponds to the one given in this chapter:

```
void qsort(void *array, int n, int elementSize,
           cmpFnT cmpFn);
```

12. Along with `qsort`, the `stdlib.h` interface in ANSI libraries exports a general implementation of the binary search algorithm with the following prototype:

```
void *bsearch(const void *key, const void *array, int n,
              int elementSize, cmpFnT cmpFn);
```

The `key` argument is a pointer to the value for which the function is searching, and the remaining arguments are equivalent to those used in `qsort`. The function returns the address of an array element containing the value addressed by `key`, assuming that the value appears in the array at all. If not, `bsearch` returns `NULL`.

13. Function pointers make it possible to design a more general symbol table interface that does not require keys to be of type `string`. If keys are represented instead as arbitrary pointers, the client must tell the implementation how to compare and hash individual keys by supplying pointers to appropriate functions.

Extend the symbol table package so that keys are declared as type `void *` and the interface exports the following additional function:

```
SetCompareAndHashFunctions(symtabADT table,
                           cmpFnT cmpFn, hashFnT hashFn);
```

By default, newly created symbol tables should be initialized to use functions appropriate to strings, so that the `symtab.h` interface ordinarily operates exactly as it did in the original version. If the client wants to change that behavior, it can call the function `SetCompareAndHashFunctions`, after which the package should use the client-supplied functions to compare two keys or derive a hash code. Designing a suitable definition for the type `hashFnT` is part of the exercise.

14. Use the `MapSymbolTable` capability to implement the function

    ```
    string LongestKey(symtabADT table);
    ```

    that returns the longest key (or any of the longest keys, if there are several with the same length) in the specified symbol table. After you get `LongestKey` working using this strategy, reimplement it using the `iterator.h` interface.

15. Use a command dispatch table to implement a test program for the symbol table package. Your program should accept the following commands:

enter *key* = *value*	Enter a new value for the specified key.
lookup *key*	Look up and display the value of the key.
list	Display all the key/value pairs in the table.
clear	Eliminate all entries by initializing a new table.
help	Display a list of commands for the program.
quit	Exit from the program.

    Your program should use the `scanadt.h` interface to divide the line into separate tokens, which means that the values are single-token strings. You should also implement the command dispatch mechanism by defining functions for each of the command names, as discussed in the section on "Command dispatch tables."

16. Design a general interface called `cmdscan.h` that allows you to associate commands with corresponding callback functions that implement them, much as in the preceding exercise. The difference here is that you are designing a general interface that clients can use to implement any sort of program that uses a command line scanner. Like most problems in interface design, this exercise is quite open-ended, and you need to think hard about what functions and types `cmdscan.h` needs to export and what facilities it should offer to clients.

Recursive Data

Overview

At first glance, the concepts of recursion and abstract data types seem completely independent. The purpose of Part Four is to bring these two ideas together. Up to this point, you have applied recursion only to functions. In Chapter 12, you will learn that data structures can also be recursive. Chapters 13 to 16 introduce several important abstract data types—including trees, sets, and graphs—that are recursive in their underlying structure. The last chapter in the book moves beyond the world of C to give you an overview of Java, an exciting new language that has created a revolution in modern computing. As you will discover, many of the topics covered in the earlier parts of the text—most notably interfaces, encapsulation, and abstract data types—play an even larger role in Java than they do in C.

CHAPTER 12

Recursive Lists

As some day it may happen that a victim must be found,
I've got a little list—I've got a little list.

— William S. Gilbert, *The Mikado,* 1885

Objectives

- To recognize that linked lists have a fundamentally recursive character.

- To learn how to write recursive functions that mirror the structure of recursive lists.

- To comprehend the design and implementation of a general `list.h` interface.

- To appreciate the importance of immutable types.

- To understand the concept of extended-precision arithmetic and how to implement it using recursive lists.

When you were first introduced to recursion in Chapter 4, you learned that a recursive function is one that calls itself in the process of computing its result. For example, the function

```
int Fact(int n)
{
    if (n == 0) {
        return (1);
    } else {
        return (n * Fact(n - 1));
    }
}
```

is recursive, because the implementation of the **Fact** function includes a call to **Fact**. The term *recursion,* however, can be applied to programming structures other than functions and procedures. In general, recursion occurs when anything is defined in terms of itself.

If you think about recursion in this expanded sense, it is clear that types can also be recursive. You have, in fact, already seen several recursive data types in the earlier chapters. Consider, for example, the following definition used in Chapter 9 to represent a cell in the linked-list implementation of the editor buffer:

```
typedef struct cellT {
    char ch;
    struct cellT *link;
} cellT;
```

The type **cellT** is defined so that the structure includes a reference to another value of this same type. Types that are defined in this way are called **recursive types.**

Learning how to use recursive data requires you to apply many of the same skills you needed to write recursive functions. In general, recursive solutions require you to think about problems in a more holistic way. It is not enough to look at the definition of a linked-list cell and notice that it contains a pointer to another cell. To understand how recursion applies to list structure, you must learn to think about lists in a more abstract way that makes their recursive structure clear. Looking at the concrete representation may help to provide insight, but the real challenge lies in moving beyond the details of representation to the conceptual nature of a list as a whole.

■■■ 12.1 The recursive formulation of a list

To get a sense of how recursion applies to lists, imagine that you have created a linked list containing the elements e_0, e_1, and e_2. In its internal representation, the list consists of three cells linked together like this:

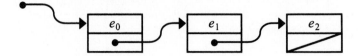

In order to identify the recursion in this diagram, it helps to shift your attention from the cells to the pointers. If you think about a list as a pointer to a cell, it quickly becomes clear that there is more than one list here. The initial pointer represents the entire list containing the elements e_0, e_1, and e_2. The link field of the leftmost cell, however, is also a list, which contains the elements e_1 and e_2. The pointer in the link field of the middle cell is also a list; in this case, the list contains the single element e_2. Moreover, if you extend this same style of reasoning to the rightmost cell, you can regard the NULL pointer in the final link field as a list containing no elements at all.

The observation that lists are composed of smaller sublists makes it possible to define lists recursively. The simple case is the constant NULL, which represents the **empty list.** The recursive case consists of nonempty lists, each of which consists of a pointer to a linked-list cell containing the first element and a list of the elements that follow. In the standard terminology for lists—which can be confusing because the words have a different meaning than they do for queues in Chapter 10—the first element of a list is called the **head.** The sublist that remains after removing the head of a list is called the **tail.** Thus, the list shown in the preceding diagram can be subdivided into head and tail components as follows:

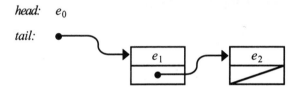

It is important to keep in mind that the head and tail of a list have distinct conceptual types. The head of a list is always a single element. The tail is always a list, even though that list may be empty.

When you use linked lists in programs, it is often easiest to manipulate them using recursion. The necessary recursive insight comes from the observation that every list fits into one of these two classes:

1. The empty list, represented by the constant NULL
2. A nonempty list, consisting of an element followed by a list

This recursive definition forms a template for recursive functions that manipulate lists. A recursive function that takes a list as its argument can usually be implemented by adopting the following pseudocode strategy:

```
if (the list is empty) {
      Compute the result for the empty list.
} else {
      Divide the list into its head and tail components.
      Use a recursive call to compute the result for the tail of the list.
      Compute the result at this level from the head of the list and the result
         of the recursive call.
}
```

The operations necessary to compute the result depend, of course, on what the recursive function you're writing is intended to do. Even so, the general recursive template will work for a wide variety of functions. Before presenting specific examples, however, it helps to define a general interface for manipulating lists that can serve as a framework for discussion.

12.2 Defining an abstract list type

The recursive formulation of a list presented in the preceding section makes it easy to define an abstract data type that represents a list. A simple interface that provides the basic operations is shown in Figure 12-1. In addition to the `listADT` type, the `list.h` interface exports three simple functions: `ListCons`, `ListHead`, and `ListTail`. The function `ListCons`(*head, tail*) creates a new list from the specified *head* and *tail* values.[1] The `ListHead` and `ListTail` functions each take an existing list and return the appropriate component from that list.

The three functions exported by the `list.h` interface are closely related in their operation. If you construct a new list by calling

```
newList = ListCons(head, tail);
```

calling `ListHead` and `ListTail` on the result will return the following values:

```
ListHead(newList)  → head
ListTail(newList)  → tail
```

Functions like `ListCons` that create new abstract data values are called **constructor functions.** Functions like `ListHead` and `ListTail` that return components of an abstract value are called **selector functions.** Both types of functions are common in interfaces that export ADTs.

The implementation of the list abstraction, which appears in Figure 12-2, is as simple as the interface. The longest implementation is only four lines long. It may at first seem silly to build an abstraction that involves so little code, but there are important reasons for doing so. Many interfaces used in modern programming export operations that are as simple as these. Although interfaces are often used to hide complexity, their main advantage lies in providing a barrier that separates the client and the implementation. Even if the code is relatively simple on both sides of the abstraction boundary, keeping the client and implementation separate makes it possible to think about each side independently.

---

[1] The name of the `ListCons` function is derived from the programming language LISP, which uses lists as its fundamental data type. The corresponding function in Lisp is called CONS, and it seems useful to borrow that terminology. The counterparts of `ListHead` and `ListTail`, on the other hand, are called CAR and CDR, after the names of internal registers in a now-ancient machine. These names seem a little obscure for a general introduction, but you will certainly encounter them again if you continue in computer science.

FIGURE 12-1   A simple interface for lists

```
/*
 * File: list.h
 * ------------
 * This interface defines an abstraction for an immutable list.
 */

#ifndef _list_h
#define _list_h

#include "genlib.h"

/*
 * Type: listElementT
 * ------------------
 * The type listElementT is used in this interface to indicate
 * the type of values that can be stored in the list.  Here the
 * list is used to store values of type void *, but that can
 * be changed by editing this definition line.
 */

typedef void *listElementT;

/*
 * Type: listADT
 * -------------
 * The type listADT represents the abstract type used to represent
 * the list itself.  The empty list is always represented by NULL.
 */

typedef struct listCDT *listADT;

/*
 * Function: ListCons
 * Usage: list = ListCons(head, tail);
 * -----------------------------------
 * This function allocates and returns a new list, which consists
 * of the element head followed by the list tail.
 */

listADT ListCons(listElementT head, listADT tail);

/*
 * Functions: ListHead, ListTail
 * Usage: head = ListHead(list);
 *        tail = ListTail(list);
 * -----------------------------
 * These functions return the head and tail of a list, where the
 * head is defined to be the first element and the tail is the
 * list that remains after removing the head of the list.
 */

listElementT ListHead(listADT list);
listADT ListTail(listADT list);

#endif
```

FIGURE 12-2   The implementation of the `list.h` interface

```
/*
 * File: list.c
 * ------------
 * This file implements the list.h interface, which defines
 * an immutable abstraction for manipulating lists of values.
 */

#include <stdio.h>
#include "genlib.h"
#include "list.h"

/*
 * Type: listCDT
 * -------------
 * The type listCDT is the concrete representation of the type
 * listADT defined by the interface.  Because the list exported
 * by this interface is immutable, there is no need for an extra
 * level of structure.  Thus, the concrete list type is just a
 * linked-list cell containing an element and another list.
 */

struct listCDT {
    listElementT head;
    listADT tail;
};

/* Exported entries */

listADT ListCons(listElementT head, listADT tail)
{
    listADT list;

    list = New(listADT);
    list->head = head;
    list->tail = tail;
    return (list);
}

listElementT ListHead(listADT list)
{
    if (list == NULL) Error("ListHead called on NULL list");
    return (list->head);
}

listADT ListTail(listADT list)
{
    if (list == NULL) Error("ListTail called on NULL list");
    return (list->tail);
}
```

Immutable types

If you contrast the `list.h` interface in Figure 12-1 with the interfaces used for stacks and queues, you may notice an apparent contradiction. The section entitled "Stacks revisited" in Chapter 10 explicitly proposes using a `NULL` pointer to represent the empty stack, but abandons that idea when it proves to be unworkable. By using `NULL` to represent the empty list, the `list.h` interface seems to return to this previously discredited strategy. Is it possible that this design works for lists but not for stacks? If so, what is the difference between the two interfaces that accounts for this asymmetry?

Look carefully at the implementation of the list abstraction in Figure 12-2. The functions exported by the interface make it possible for clients to *examine* the contents of a list cell but provide no opportunity for the client to *change* the internal structure. The `ListCons` function always generates a new list formed from its arguments; the values of the arguments themselves never change. Similarly, the functions `ListHead` and `ListTail` merely return the components of an existing list. Moreover, because `listADT` is defined as an abstract type, clients have no access to the underlying structure. The interface barrier stands in the way. The net effect of these design decisions is that, once a new `listADT` has been created, its fields will remain intact. Abstract types that prohibit clients from making any changes to the underlying representation are called **immutable types.**

On the other hand, the ADTs exported by the `stack.h` and `queue.h` interfaces are not immutable, even though the client cannot cross the abstraction boundary to change the underlying representation directly. In those ADTs, the functions in the interface change the underlying representation on the client's behalf. The `Push` and `Pop` functions from the `stack.h` interface, for example, change the values of fields within the `stackCDT` structure, even though the client cannot see the details of that change.

Immutable types have several important properties, of which the following are the most useful:

- *Immutable types typically have a straightforward internal structure.* At a conceptual level, the internal structure used to represent the stack data type in Figure 10-1 is similar to the immutable list type implemented in Figure 12-2. In both cases, the underlying representation is simply a linked list of cells. The fact that the list type is immutable, however, means that its underlying representation can be the cell structure itself. Such an approach is not possible for the stack because the `PUSH` and `POP` functions require that the internal structure of the stack change. To permit such changes, the concrete type for the stack must include an additional level of nesting. The `stackCDT` structure must therefore be a separate record whose only field is the initial pointer in the linked-list chain. In an immutable type, this additional level of structure is not required.

- *In an immutable type, you can use null pointers to indicate empty abstract values.* In the `list.h` interface, the constant `NULL` is a perfectly reasonable representation of the empty list. As discussed in Chapter 10, you could not use **NULL** to represent the empty stack because doing so would mean that the functions **Push** and **Pop** would have no access to the underlying structure. Because none of the functions in the **list.h** interface change the values of their arguments, this problem does not arise in the implementation of immutable lists.

- *Using immutable types often makes it easier to understand the behavior of a program.* If you are working with immutable types, you no longer have to consider the possibility that some client will change an abstract value unexpectedly. Suppose, for example, that you need to call a function written by some other programmer that takes a **stackADT** as its argument. You have no idea whether that function will change the stack by pushing new values on or popping values off. The implementation of the function you're calling is certainly free to do so. On the other hand, if you call a function that takes a **listADT** as its argument, you can be sure that any list you pass to that function will remain unchanged. Because the type is immutable, the function you're calling cannot possibly change its value.

- *Immutable types permit internal sharing of data.* Because clients are unable to change the underlying values associated with an immutable type, it is possible for several abstract data values to share parts of their internal structure. In the absence of immutability, such sharing is dangerous because a client who changes one value could inadvertently change some seemingly unrelated value. This property of immutable types is discussed in more detail in the section on "Internal sharing in immutable types" later in this chapter.

Functions that manipulate list structure

Given the **list.h** interface in Figure12-1, it is easy to define client-level functions that work with values of type **listADT**. As a simple example, the following function returns the length of a list:

```
int ListLength(listADT list)
{
    listADT cp;
    int n;

    n = 0;
    for (cp = list; cp != NULL; cp = ListTail(cp)) {
        n++;
    }
    return (n);
}
```

This implementation of **ListLength** uses a straightforward iteration to count the elements in the list. The **for** loop steps through each of the elements in the list, adding 1 to the element count on each cycle.

Although iterative techniques of this sort are perfectly suitable for lists, it is also possible to write recursive functions that more closely reflect the recursive structure of the underlying type. If you think about this function recursively, you can reduce the problem to the following rules:

1. The length of the empty list is 0.
2. The length of any nonempty list is 1 plus the length of its tail.

This observation leads directly to the following recursive implementation of ListLength:

```
int ListLength(listADT list)
{
    if (list == NULL) {
        return (0);
    } else {
        return (ListLength(ListTail(list)) + 1);
    }
}
```

The same recursive strategy can be applied to other functions as well. Suppose that you want to implement a function NthElement(list, n) that returns the nth element of the specified list, in which the elements are numbered starting at 0 in accordance with the standard conventions of C. For example, if the variable myList is bound to the list

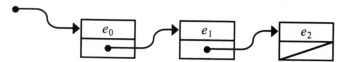

calling NthElement(myList, 1) returns the value e_1. In this function, there are two simple cases. If the list is empty, the NthElement function cannot succeed, because the list has no n^{th} element for any value of n. The second simple case occurs when n is 0. The 0th element of any nonempty list is just the head of the list. The recursive insight is that, for all values of n greater than 0, the nth element of a nonempty list is the $n-1^{st}$ element of its tail. Once again, the recursive decomposition leads directly to a corresponding implementation, as follows:

```
listElementT NthElement(listADT list, int n)
{
    if (list == NULL) {
        Error("NthElement: No such element");
    } else if (n == 0) {
        return (ListHead(list));
    } else {
        return (NthElement(ListTail(list), n - 1));
    }
}
```

The functions ListLength and NthElement do not depend on the specific definition of the type listElementT. Many functions, however, must be specifically tailored to the type of element the list contains. For example, if you want to write a function that displays the contents of a list on the computer screen, you need to know the element type so that you can display the values of the individual elements. If the lists you were working with contained strings, you would write one function. If they instead contained integers, you would write a function that has the same general structure but displays individual values in a different way.

In writing any function that depends on the element type, it is important to remember that you are working as a client of the `list.h` interface. It would be difficult, for example, to write a general `DisplayList` function and export it as part of the list package. If `DisplayList` is coded as part of the implementation, the client will have to supply a function pointer that makes it possible for the implementation to display an individual value. While such an approach is certainly possible, the fact that you are working at the client level means that you need not design solutions with this level of generality. As the client, you know what type of value a particular list contains. This knowledge makes it possible for you to implement list manipulation functions that provide you with exactly the capabilities you need.

Suppose then, that you are using the list package to manipulate lists of strings. How could you write a function `DisplayStringList(list)` that displays the contents of `list` on the screen? In computer science, the traditional format for displaying a list, which is derived from the programming language LISP, is to enclose the entire list in parentheses and to separate the elements by spaces. Thus, if you are working with a list of strings whose internal representation is

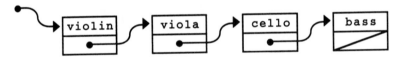

the list should be displayed as follows:

```
(violin viola cello bass)
```

If you use a wrapper function to supply the outer set of parentheses, it is easy to code a recursive implementation of `DisplayStringList`, as follows:

```
void DisplayStringList(listADT list)
{
    printf("(");
    RecDisplayList(list);
    printf(")\n");
}
```

```
static void RecDisplayList(listADT list)
{
    if (list != NULL) {
        printf("%s", ListHead(list));
        if (ListTail(list) != NULL) printf(" ");
        RecDisplayList(ListTail(list));
    }
}
```

Concatenating lists

Recursion can be used to create functions for list manipulation that are considerably more sophisticated than those described in the preceding section. For example, you can use recursion to implement the function ListConcat(list1, list2), which returns a list composed of all the elements in list1 followed by the elements in list2. To make sure that you understand the process, imagine that the lists you are trying to concatenate look like this:

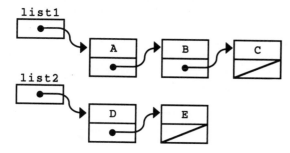

If you then call

```
list = ListConcat(list1, list2);
```

the intended result is that the variable list is set to the following five-element list:

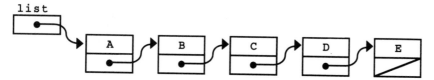

Let's think about this problem recursively. What happens in the simple cases? If a list is empty, concatenating it with another list returns the second list unchanged. Thus, if list1 is empty, the result of calling ListConcat(list1, list2) is simply list2. If list1 is nonempty, however, you need to apply recursive decomposition to express the result of ListConcat(list1, list2) in terms of simpler recursive calls.

To see how recursion applies, you start by dividing list1 into its head and tail components, as follows:

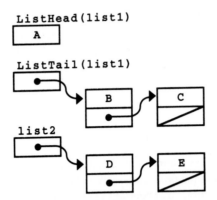

Because the tail of `list1` is shorter than the original list, you have simplified the problem. By depending once again on the recursive leap of faith, you can assume that a recursive call involving this shorter list will work. You can, for example, go ahead and concatenate `list2` onto the end of the tail of `list1` to reach the following configuration:

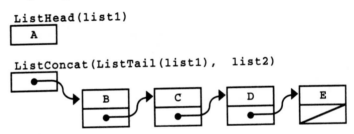

From this point, all you have to do is call `ListCons` to put the initial element back onto the front of the list, like this:

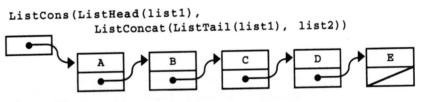

This strategy can be translated directly into the following recursive implementation:

```
listADT ListConcat(listADT list1, listADT list2)
{
    if (list1 == NULL) {
        return (list2);
    } else {
        return (ListCons(ListHead(list1),
                         ListConcat(ListTail(list1), list2)));
    }
}
```

Internal sharing in immutable types

If you follow carefully the logic of the `ListConcat` example in the preceding section, you will discover that the cells in `list2` are never actually copied as part of the concatenation process. Thus, the result of calling

```
list = ListConcat(list1, list2);
```

should in fact be diagrammed as follows:

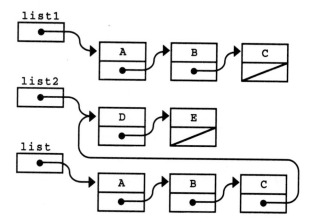

If you follow the link chains from each starting position, you can see that each list has the correct value: `list1` has the value (A B C), `list2` has the value (D E), and `list` has the value (A B C D E). On the other hand, `list` and `list2` share the same cells in their internal structure.

At first glance, this state of affairs appears dangerous. What would happen, for example, if the value in the first element of `list2` somehow changed? That change would also be reflected in the fourth element of `list`, which is stored in the same memory location. Fortunately, such problems cannot arise, because the `listADT` type is immutable. Once the cells are allocated, the client cannot change the internal contents of those cells at all. An important advantage of immutable types is that independent values can freely share their internal structure, because that structure will never change once it has been created.

There is, however, one interesting catch. You may have noticed that the `list.h` interface does not export a function to free a list. This omission was not an oversight. Adding a `FreeList` function would invalidate the immutability of the abstraction. Consider, for example, what would happen if the client called `FreeList(list2)` in the state represented by the preceding diagram. The cells in `list2` would be deallocated, even though those same cells are part of the value of `list`.

To work well, abstractions like the `listADT` abstraction that make use of internal sharing depend on having the memory allocation system discover for itself when memory can be reused. The technique of having the computer recognize that memory is no longer in use and then reclaim it for future allocation is called **garbage collection,** which was mentioned briefly in the section on "Coping with memory limitations" in Chapter 2. Garbage collection is becoming much more common in modern programming languages, and it is likely that the languages you use in the future will include it as a standard feature.

■ 12.3 Using lists to represent large integers

Before moving beyond the topic of recursive lists to introduce more sophisticated recursive structures, it makes sense to introduce an example showing how recursively defined lists can be used to solve a problem that at first appears to have nothing to do with lists. The problem consists of representing integers that are too large to store in one of C's integer types. Although the ANSI standard for C doesn't define the limits precisely, many computers store values of type `long` in 32-bit words. On such machines, the largest value that you can store in a variable of type `long` is $2^{31}-1$, which is 2,147,483,647. If your computer is more modern and uses 64 bits for values of type `long`, you could store values up to $2^{63}-1$, or 9,223,372,036,854,775,807. While this number seems enormous, there are certainly some applications that require even larger integers. For example, if you were asked to compute the number of possible arrangements for a deck of 52 cards, you would need to calculate 52!, which is

80,658,175,170,943,878,571,660,636,856,403,766,975,289,505,440,883,277,824,000,000,000,000

This number is much too large to fit into a value of type `long` on any commercially available machine. Even so, integers of this magnitude do arise in practical computing applications. Modern techniques for protecting digital data through encryption typically require the use of integers that are much larger than the types provided by the hardware.

The easiest way to circumvent the size limitations imposed by the hardware is to break large integers into smaller pieces, each of which fits into a single memory location. In general, this technique is called **multiple-** or **extended-precision arithmetic.** Multiple-precision arithmetic can be implemented in either hardware or software. If you want to implement it in software, you have to design a package that provides functions for the standard arithmetic operations—addition, subtraction, multiplication, division, and so forth—on integers that are stored as collections of smaller integer parts. It is even possible to design an extended-precision package that allows integers to grow dynamically. Such packages provide what programmers call **arbitrary-precision arithmetic,** which means that the precision is not restricted to any predetermined bound.

Commercial packages that implement extended-precision arithmetic exist for many computer systems. Making such packages run efficiently is a difficult task best left to expert designers who understand both the capabilities of the hardware and the mathematical foundations of machine arithmetic. On the other hand, building a simple package for arbitrary-precision arithmetic offers important advantages for you as a student. For one thing, it gives you a sense of how such packages operate. Moreover, because the solution strategy provides an excellent opportunity to use linked lists and recursion, writing a package to implement arbitrary-precision arithmetic also serves to reinforce the discussion of recursive lists presented in the earlier sections in this chapter.

The `bigint.h` interface

To illustrate the techniques used to implement arbitrary-precision arithmetic, it helps to begin by defining an interface that exports an abstract type representing an integer value of unbounded size, along with a few simple functions that implement basic arithmetic operations. An interface that exports a few such functions appears in Figure 12-3.

Because the goal of this example is to illustrate concepts rather than to build a practical tool, the definition of `bigint.h` shown in Figure 12-3 is quite restricted, which simplifies its design and implementation. The first major restriction is that the type `bigIntADT` cannot be used to represent negative integers. Although adding a sign to the internal representation is not particularly difficult, doing so complicates the code and obscures the recursive structure. The second restriction is that the interface defines only two arithmetic operations: addition and multiplication. Adding other operations like subtraction and division increases the size and complexity of the implementation without illustrating any new concepts. You will have an opportunity to add these features in the exercises.

In addition to the function `NewBigInt` that makes it possible to construct a new `bigIntADT` from an integer, the `bigint.h` interface exports two functions that make it possible to convert values back and forth between the type `bigIntADT` and strings of digits. The function `StringToBigInt` converts a string of digits into a `bigIntADT` and makes it possible to construct a `bigIntADT` whose value is larger than the maximum value of an integer. For example, to create a `bigIntADT` with the value 1234567890, you could simply call `StringToBigInt("1234567890")`. The function `BigIntToString` converts a `bigIntADT` into the corresponding string of digits and is therefore useful in displaying values of type `bigIntADT` on the screen. Thus, if `bn` is declared as a `bigIntADT`, you can display its value using the following statement:

```
printf("%s", BigIntToString(bn));
```

It is also important to notice that the type `bigIntADT`—as defined by this interface—is immutable. New values of type `bigIntADT` are returned by several functions in the interface, but none of them change the value of an existing `bigIntADT`. The fact that `bigIntADT` is an immutable type makes it easier to represent its internal structure.

Representing the type `bigIntADT`

The first question that arises in implementing the `bigint.h` interface is how to represent the concrete type corresponding to `bigIntADT`. The underlying representation must be expandable so that it can accommodate integers of any size. Although there are certainly other strategies that work, one possibility is to represent an integer as a linked list of its digits. Thus, the integer 1729 would be represented as a list containing the integers 1, 7, 2, and 9.

In designing the linked-list representation, it is important to think carefully about the order in which the digits appear. If you let yourself be influenced by the

FIGURE 12-3 An interface for manipulating large integers

```
/*
 * File: bigint.h
 * --------------
 * This interface is a primitive version of a facility intended
 * to support integers of an arbitrary size. This package has the
 * following limitations, which significantly reduce its utility:
 *
 * 1. The package does not support negative integers.
 * 2. The only operations are addition and multiplication.
 * 3. It is inefficient in terms of both space and time.
 */

#ifndef _bigint_h
#define _bigint_h

#include "genlib.h"

/*
 * Type: bigIntADT
 * ---------------
 * This type is the abstract type used to store a nonnegative
 * integer of arbitrary size.
 */

typedef struct bigIntCDT *bigIntADT;

/*
 * Function: NewBigInt
 * Usage: n = NewBigInt(i);
 * ------------------------
 * This function creates a new bigIntADT with the value i.  Use
 * StringToBigInt to create bigIntADTs larger than an integer.
 */

bigIntADT NewBigInt(int i);

/*
 * Functions: StringToBigInt, BigIntToString
 * Usage: n = StringToBigInt(str);
 *        str = BigIntToString(n);
 * -----------------------------------------
 * These functions convert between strings of digits and values
 * of type bigIntADT.
 */

bigIntADT StringToBigInt(string str);
string BigIntToString(bigIntADT n);
```

```
/*
 * Function: AddBigInt
 * Usage: n = AddBigInt(n1, n2);
 * ----------------------------
 * This function allocates a new bigIntADT n whose value is
 * the sum of n1 and n2.
 */

bigIntADT AddBigInt(bigIntADT n1, bigIntADT n2);

/*
 * Function: MultiplyBigInt
 * Usage: n = MultiplyBigInt(n1, n2);
 * ----------------------------------
 * This function allocates a new bigIntADT n whose value is
 * the product of n1 and n2.
 */

bigIntADT MultiplyBigInt(bigIntADT n1, bigIntADT n2);

#endif
```

traditional left-to-right ordering of the decimal system, you might be tempted to arrange the linked list of digits like this:

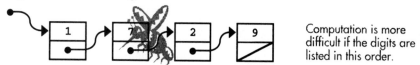

Computation is more difficult if the digits are listed in this order.

The problem with this arrangement is that it is difficult to determine what each digit means mathematically. What value, for example, does the digit 1 at the beginning of the number signify? The answer is that the value of this digit depends on the number of digits that follow it in the list. In this example, the 1 signifies 1000 because there are three digit positions after it, each of which contributes a factor of 10. Unfortunately, the only way to determine the value of the first digit is to count the remaining elements.

The situation is considerably better if you store the digits in the opposite order, so that the units digit appears first in the linked-list chain, followed by the tens digit, and so on through all the digits in the integer. In this representation, the integer 1729 will look like this:

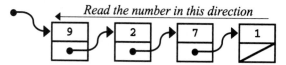

Read the number in this direction

In this representation, you can immediately determine the value of each digit as you step through the elements in the list. The digit 9 that appears as the initial element in the list represents the value 9. As you move through the cells in this list, each digit position is worth 10 times the previous one. Thus, the digit 2 represents 20, the 7 represents 700, and the 1 represents 1000. The integer value of the `bigIntADT` represented by the list is the sum of the individual digit values, which is indeed 1729 (9 + 20 + 700 + 1000).

If you think about the linked-list representation of an integer in mathematical terms, you may notice that its structure—like the `listADT` type defined by the `list.h` interface—has a simple recursive interpretation. If you divide the list representing a `bigIntADT` into its head and tail components, the head of the list is the final digit and the tail is a `bigIntADT` representing the leading digits of the original integer. Thus, if the mathematical value of a `bigIntADT` is the integer n, its head has the value n % 10 and its tail has the value n / 10.

The fact that the tail of a `bigIntADT` is itself a `bigIntADT` whose value is a smaller integer makes it easy to use recursion in the implementation of the `bigint.h` interface. If n is a `bigIntADT`, there are two possibilities:

1. The list used to represent n is empty, which means that its mathematical value is 0.
2. The list used to represent n is nonempty, which means that it can be divided into a head component specifying the final digit and a tail component specifying the leading digits of the original value.

Functions that operate on values of type `bigIntADT` can use these cases as an outline for their recursive subdivision.

Implementing the `bigint` package

The discussion of the underlying representation in the preceding section provides the information you need to begin the actual implementation of the `bigint.h` interface. The concrete structure corresponding to the type `bigIntADT` is similar to that of the `listADT` type defined in Figure 12-2 earlier in the chapter. Because the type is immutable, the concrete type can be the linked-list cell itself, which looks like this:

```
struct bigIntCDT {
    int finalDigit;
    bigIntADT leadingDigits;
};
```

Although the implementation can work directly with the fields in this record, it turns out to be useful to define counterparts of the functions `ListCons`, `ListHead`, and `ListTail` for this interface, even though these functions are not exported to clients. The implementation file uses the constructor function `DigitCons` to construct a new `bigIntADT` consisting of an existing `bigIntADT` followed by a new units digit. The implementation similarly uses the selector functions `FinalDigit` and `LeadingDigits` to select the head and tail components of a `bigIntADT`. Using functions instead of selecting fields directly makes it possible to centralize the special-case checking for the value `NULL`. The details are outlined in the comments associated with the code, which appears in Figure 12-4.

FIGURE 12-4	Implementation of the bigint package

```
/*
 * File: bigint.c
 * --------------
 * This file implements the bigint.h interface, which provides
 * addition and multiplication operations for nonnegative
 * integers of arbitrary size.
 */

#include <stdio.h>
#include <ctype.h>
#include "genlib.h"
#include "strlib.h"
#include "bigint.h"

/*
 * Type: bigIntCDT
 * ---------------
 * This type is the concrete counterpart of the abstract type
 * bigIntADT.  The underlying representation is a linked list
 * of cells, each of which contains a single digit.  The digits
 * in the list appear in reverse order, with the units digit at
 * the beginning of the list, the tens digit next, and so on.
 * In its recursive formulation, a bigIntADT is either
 *
 * 1. NULL, representing the integer 0, or
 * 2. A digit d and a bigIntADT n, representing 10 * n + d
 */

struct bigIntCDT {
    int finalDigit;
    bigIntADT leadingDigits;
};

/* Private function prototypes */

static bigIntADT AddWithCarry(bigIntADT n1, bigIntADT n2, int carry);
static bigIntADT MultiplyDigit(int digit, bigIntADT n);
static bigIntADT DigitCons(bigIntADT n, int digit);
static bigIntADT LeadingDigits(bigIntADT n);
static int FinalDigit(bigIntADT n);

/* Exported entries */

bigIntADT NewBigInt(int i)
{
    if (i < 0) Error("Negative integers are not permitted");
    if (i == 0) return (NULL);
    return (DigitCons(NewBigInt(i / 10), i % 10));
}
```

```
bigIntADT StringToBigInt(string str)
{
    int len;
    char ch;

    len = StringLength(str);
    if (len == 0) return (NULL);
    ch = str[len - 1];
    if (!isdigit(ch)) Error("Illegal digit %c", ch);
    return (DigitCons(StringToBigInt(SubString(str, 0, len - 2)),
                      ch - '0'));
}

string BigIntToString(bigIntADT n)
{
    string str;

    str = CharToString(FinalDigit(n) + '0');
    if (LeadingDigits(n) != NULL) {
        str = Concat(BigIntToString(LeadingDigits(n)), str);
    }
    return (str);
}

/*
 * Implementation notes: AddBigInt
 * --------------------------------
 * The AddBigInt function itself is a simple wrapper that calls
 * AddWithCarry to do the real work.   The third argument to
 * AddWithCarry is the carry from the preceding digit position.
 */

bigIntADT AddBigInt(bigIntADT n1, bigIntADT n2)
{
    return (AddWithCarry(n1, n2, 0));
}

static bigIntADT AddWithCarry(bigIntADT n1, bigIntADT n2, int carry)
{
    int sum;
    bigIntADT p1, p2;

    p1 = LeadingDigits(n1);
    p2 = LeadingDigits(n2);
    sum = FinalDigit(n1) + FinalDigit(n2) + carry;
    if (sum == 0 && p1 == NULL && p2 == NULL) return (NULL);
    return (DigitCons(AddWithCarry(p1, p2, sum / 10), sum % 10));
}
```

```
/*
 * Function: MultiplyBigInt
 * -----------------------
 * The MultiplyBigInt implementation uses the standard
 * elementary-school algorithm of multiplying by each
 * digit in turn, except that the algorithm is implemented
 * recursively here.  The recursive insight is that the
 * product of n1 and n2 is
 *
 *    FinalDigit(n1) * n2 + LeadingDigits(n1) * n2 * 10
 *
 * Note that multiplying by 10 is implemented simply by
 * adding a 0 to the number using DigitCons.  Single-digit
 * multiplication is implemented by recursive addition.
 */

bigIntADT MultiplyBigInt(bigIntADT n1, bigIntADT n2)
{
    if (n1 == NULL) return (NULL);
    return (AddBigInt(MultiplyDigit(FinalDigit(n1), n2),
                      MultiplyBigInt(LeadingDigits(n1),
                                     DigitCons(n2, 0))));
}

static bigIntADT MultiplyDigit(int digit, bigIntADT n)
{
    if (digit == 0) return (NULL);
    return (AddBigInt(n, MultiplyDigit(digit - 1, n)));
}

/*
 * Function: DigitCons
 * Usage: n = DigitCons(leadingDigits, finalDigit);
 * -----------------------------------------------
 * This low-level constructor function combines leadingDigits
 * and finalDigit to make a new bigIntADT.  Note that the
 * direction of this function is opposite to that of ListCons
 * in that finalDigit is added to the beginning of the linked
 * list.  The reason for using this argument order is that
 * doing so makes it easier to understand the function in
 * its arithmetic sense: finalDigit is added to the end of
 * leadingDigits.  The implementation also includes a check
 * to make sure that 0 is always represented as NULL.
 */

static bigIntADT DigitCons(bigIntADT leadingDigits, int finalDigit)
{
    bigIntADT cp;

    if (leadingDigits == NULL && finalDigit == 0) return (NULL);
    cp = New(bigIntADT);
    cp->finalDigit = finalDigit;
    cp->leadingDigits = leadingDigits;
    return (cp);
}
```

```
/*
 * Functions: LeadingDigits, FinalDigit
 * Usage: prefix = LeadingDigits(n);
 *        last = FinalDigit(n);
 * ----------------------------------------
 * These functions select the leading digits and final digit
 * of a bigIntADT, respectively. Because these functions are
 * defined locally in the implementation, callers could select
 * the fields directly. However, by making these functions,
 * the special-case handling of NULL as 0 becomes much easier
 * to implement.
 */

static bigIntADT LeadingDigits(bigIntADT n)
{
    return ((n == NULL) ? NULL : n->leadingDigits);
}

static int FinalDigit(bigIntADT n)
{
    return ((n == NULL) ? 0 : n->finalDigit);
}
```

Each of the exported functions in the `bigint.c` file is implemented recursively, using the division of an integer into its leading and final digits as the basis for the recursive decomposition. For simple functions like `NewBigInt`, the recursion is reasonably straightforward. The mathematical operations of addition and multiplication, however, may take some additional explanation. Both implementations, however, borrow heavily from the pencil-and-paper strategies for these operations that you learned in elementary school, which should make them easier to follow.

When you add two integers by hand, you start with the last pair of digits and compute their sum. This sum is sometimes a single digit, but it might also be 10 or more, in which case there would be a carry into the next position. Thus, in the general case, adding two integers must take into account the possibility of a carry coming in from the previous step. The recursive implementation of `AddBigInt` in Figure 12-4 follows precisely this logic. The `AddBigInt` function itself is implemented as a wrapper to the recursive function `AddWithCarry`. Before each recursive call, the function determines whether there is a carry from the current position and passes the carry value as an argument to the next recursive level.

Multiplication is slightly trickier, but still surprisingly simple. For concreteness, consider the following multiplication problem:

$$
\begin{array}{r}
3\ 4\ 2 \\
\times\ 1\ 7\ 3 \\
\hline
1\ 0\ 2\ 6 \\
2\ 3\ 9\ 4 \\
3\ 4\ 2 \\
\hline
5\ 9\ 1\ 6\ 6
\end{array}
$$

Each line in the expansion of the product comes from multiplying the number on the top row, which is called the **multiplicand,** by each digit in the number on the second row, which is called the **multiplier.** Each multiplier digit contributes 10 times as much to the product as the digit to its right. Thus the product of 342 and 173 can be expressed as the following sum:

$$342 \times 3 \; + \; 3420 \times 7 \; + \; 34200 \times 1$$

If you think about this process recursively, however, you will discover that you can proceed one digit at a time. The product can be expressed equally well as the sum of the following two terms:

$$342 \times 3 \; + \; 3420 \times 17$$

Computing the product of 3420 and 17 requires further decomposition, but the goal of a recursive solution is merely to reduce the original problem to a simpler case.

In general, the product of the integers m and n can be decomposed as follows:

$$m \times n = m \times \texttt{FinalDigit}(n) \; + \; (m \times 10) \times \texttt{LeadingDigits}(n)$$

You can multiply m by a single digit by repeated addition. Multiplying m by 10 is actually even easier. All you need to do is add a zero to the end of m by calling `DigitCons(m, 0)`. The recursive implementation of `MultiplyBigInt` follows directly from these observations.

Using the `bigint` package

The code in Figure 12-5 illustrates the use of the `bigint.h` interface by calculating a table of factorials. The output of the program looks like this:

```
 0! = 1
 1! = 1
 2! = 2
 3! = 6
 4! = 24
 5! = 120
 6! = 720
 7! = 5040
 8! = 40320
 9! = 362880
10! = 3628800
11! = 39916800
12! = 479001600
13! = 6227020800
14! = 87178291200
15! = 1307674368000
16! = 20922789888000
17! = 355687428096000
18! = 6402373705728000
19! = 121645100408832000
20! = 2432902008176640000
```

FIGURE 12-5 Program to display a table of factorials

```c
/*
 * File: bigfact.c
 * ---------------
 * This file defines the BigFact function, which calculates
 * the factorial of an integer but returns the result as a
 * bigIntADT so that the result can be arbitrarily large.
 * This file also includes a test program that prints the
 * factorials of the numbers between the limits LowerLimit
 * and UpperLimit, inclusive.
 */

#include <stdio.h>
#include "genlib.h"
#include "bigint.h"

/* Constants */

#define LowerLimit  0
#define UpperLimit 20

/* Private function prototypes */

static bigIntADT BigFact(int n);

/* Main program */

main()
{
    int i;

    for (i = LowerLimit; i <= UpperLimit; i++) {
        printf("%2d! = %s\n", i, BigIntToString(BigFact(i)));
    }
}

/*
 * Function: BigFact
 * Usage: b = BigFact(n);
 * ----------------------
 * This function returns the factorial of n, which is defined
 * as the product of all integers from 1 up to n.
 */

static bigIntADT BigFact(int n)
{
    if (n == 0) {
        return (NewBigInt(1));
    } else {
        return (MultiplyBigInt(NewBigInt(n), BigFact(n - 1)));
    }
}
```

■ Summary

The `listADT` type presented in Figure 12-1 differs in its structure from the other abstract types you have seen in two important ways. First, the abstraction is defined so that it emphasizes the recursive structure of linked lists. Second, the functions exported by the `list.h` interface make it impossible for clients to change any `listADT` value once it has been created by the package. An abstract type that exhibits this property is called an *immutable type*. Immutable types play an important role in modern programming, partly because the interface boundary is even more rigidly enforced than with traditional ADTs.

Important points in this chapter include:

- A list can be defined recursively as either (1) an empty list represented by the constant **NULL** or (2) an element followed by a list. The first element in a list is called the *head* of the list; the list that remains after the head is removed is called the *tail*. The `list.h` interface emphasizes this structure by exporting three functions—`ListHead`, `ListTail`, and `ListCons`—that provide a natural basis for higher-level list operations.

- Functions that manipulate lists can easily be defined recursively by taking advantage of the recursion inherent in the underlying structure. The standard idiom for implementing recursive functions on a list has the following pseudocode form:

  ```
  if (the list is empty) {
      Compute the result for the empty list.
  } else {
      Divide the list into its head and tail components.
      Use a recursive call to compute the result for the tail of the list.
      Compute the result at this level from the head of the list and the result
          of the recursive call.
  }
  ```

- Although using **NULL** proved unacceptable as a representation for an empty stack, this strategy works well in the `list.h` interface because the `listADT` type is immutable. In the stack abstraction, the problem was that the **NULL** pointer did not point to any memory that the implementation could update in responses to push and pop operations. This problem, however, does not arise with the `list.h` interface, because none of its exported functions change any of the internal data structures.

- The use of immutable types makes it possible for data values to share internal structure without running the risk that changes to one structure will cause unexpected changes in others. On the other hand, using immutable types makes it difficult for the client to free structures explicitly. Immutable types work best when the system includes an automatic garbage-collection facility that finds unused memory and returns it to the dynamically allocated heap.

- Recursive linked lists can be used to implement a package that performs arbitrary-precision arithmetic, in which integers are allowed to grow to a size that is limited only by the total memory of the machine rather than by the size of an individual machine word. The implementation of the `bigint.h` interface presented in the chapter is too inefficient to be used in practice, but nonetheless illustrates both the fundamental techniques of extended-precision arithmetic and the practical utility of recursive data.

REVIEW QUESTIONS

1. What does it mean for a data type to be recursive?

2. When you think about a list from a recursive perspective, what are the two possible forms for a list?

3. What are the three functions exported by the `list.h` interface? Which are constructor functions, and which are selector functions?

4. What is the fundamental difference between the `list.h` and `stack.h` interfaces that makes it possible to use **NULL** as the representation of an empty list even though this strategy failed for stacks?

5. What is an immutable type?

6. What are the four advantages of immutable types listed in this chapter?

7. What happens if you call **NthElement (list, n)** with a negative value of **n**? What about a value of **n** that is greater than or equal to the length of the list?

8. Assuming that `list1` and `list2` have the values

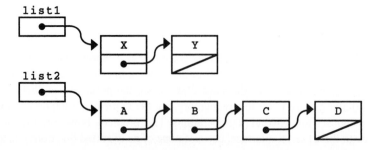

diagram the result of calling `ListConcat (list1, list2)`. How many new list cells are allocated during the operation?

9. True or false: If a type is immutable, it is possible for many different values to share parts of their internal structure without causing problems for clients.

10. Why doesn't the `list.h` interface export a function to free a list?

11. What is the largest value that can be stored in a variable of type `long` on a machine that uses 32-bit words to store values of type `long`?

12. Describe how the technique of multiple-precision arithmetic can be used to represent integers that are larger than the maximum size supported by the hardware.

13. What restrictions have been incorporated into the design of the `bigint.h` interface shown in Figure 12-3 to make it easier to implement?

14. Suppose that you wanted to use the constant 18,446,744,073,709,551,616 (2^{64}) in a program. How would you create a `bigIntADT` with that value?

15. Why does it make sense to design the internal representation for the type `bigIntADT` so that the linked list begins with the units digit?

16. Assuming that you are working in the context of the implementation and have access to the private functions in `bigint.c`, what is the easiest way to multiply a `bigIntADT` by 10?

 PROGRAMMING EXERCISES

1. Suppose that you are working as a client of the list abstraction shown in Figure 12-1 and know that the elements in the list are always strings. Write a recursive function

   ```
   int FindStringInList(string id, listADT list);
   ```

   that returns the index of the first occurrence of the string `id` in the specified list, where index numbers begin at 0 and increase as you continue through the elements in the list. If `id` does not appear in the list, `FindStringInList` should return −1.

2. Write a function

   ```
   listADT GetList(void);
   ```

   that reads in a list from the user. The format of the list is a sequence of tokens (as defined by the `scanadt.h` interface in Chapter 8) enclosed in parentheses. The tokens must be separated by at least one space, but the `GetList` function should ignore any extra spaces it finds. Thus, the main program

   ```
   main()
   {
       listADT list;

       printf("Enter a list: ");
       list = GetList();
       DisplayStringList(list);
   }
   ```

   should be able to produce the following sample run:

```
Enter a list: (Mercury Venus Earth Mars).↵
(Mercury Venus Earth Mars)
```

3. Write a recursive function

   ```
   listADT ReverseList(listADT list);
   ```

   that returns a new list consisting of the elements of `list` in reverse order.

4. Write a recursive function

   ```
   listADT SortStringList(listADT list);
   ```

   that takes a list of strings and returns a new list consisting of the elements of `list` in lexicographic order.

5. Write a recursive function

   ```
   void MapList(listFnT fn, listADT list, void *clientData);
   ```

   that calls `fn(element, clientData)` for each element in `list`. Part of this exercise is finding a suitable definition for the function type `listFnT`.

6. If `listElementT` is defined to be the generic pointer type `void *`, the elements of a `listADT` may be any pointer type, including other values of type `listADT`. The following diagram, for example, shows a three-element list, where each of the elements is a list of strings:

   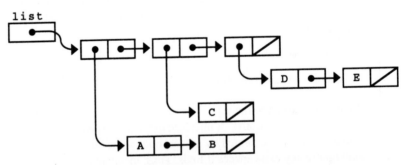

   Assuming that `list` is always a two-level list of this sort, write a recursive function `ExpandList` that returns a new list consisting of the elements of the subsidiary lists linked together in order. For example, given the value of `list` in the preceding diagram, `ExpandList(list)` should return the following:

   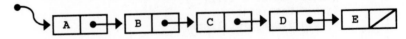

7. If you define `listElementT` to be the primitive type `char`, the resulting lists can be used to simulate strings. Implement an interface `clstring.h` that exports the functions

```
int CListLength(listADT s);
listADT CListConcat(listADT s1, listADT s2);
listADT CListSubString(listADT s, int n1, int n2);
char CListIthChar(listADT s, int i);
listADT CharToCList(char ch);
int CListCompare(listADT s1, listADT s2);
```

each of which is analogous to the similarly named function in the `strlib.h` interface. In addition, your interface should export the functions

```
listADT StringToCList(string str);
string CListToString(listADT s);
```

which convert back and forth between strings and lists of characters.

8. When you have completed the `clstring.h` interface described in the preceding exercise, use it to implement a function

```
listADT CListAcronym(listADT s);
```

that takes a `listADT` composed of characters and returns a new `listADT` formed by taking the first character in each word in `s`. For simplicity, you may assume that the words in the argument `s` are separated by a single space and that there are no extraneous spaces or punctuation marks. Your implementation of `CListAcronym` should use only the string-like functions exported by `clstring.h` and should not make any direct calls to the underlying `list.h` interface.

9. Use the `bigint.h` interface to write a program that lists the powers of two from 0 to 99. The last five lines of the output should look like this:

```
2 ^ 95 = 39614081257132168796771975168
2 ^ 96 = 79228162514264337593543950336
2 ^ 97 = 158456325028528675187087900672
2 ^ 98 = 316912650057057350374175801344
2 ^ 99 = 633825300114114700748351602688
```

10. As integers become large, they become very difficult to read if they are written as an unbroken sequence of digits. In English-speaking countries, the usual approach to making numbers more readable is to use commas to divide the digits in a number into groups of three. Write a function

```
string BigIntWithCommas(bigIntADT n);
```

that returns the string representation of the number `n` with commas inserted in the conventional places. For example, calling

```
BigIntWithCommas(StringToBigInt("12345678987654321"))
```

should return the string `"12,345,678,987,654,321"`.

11. Beyond making integers easier to read, the idea of grouping digits together can also increase the efficiency of the extended-precision package. You could, for example, change the underlying representation of a `bigIntADT` so that—instead of putting each digit in a cell of its own—each cell contained an integer from 0 to 999 representing three digits of the actual value. Thus, the internal representation of the integer 1,234,567,890 would look like this:

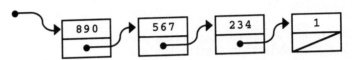

Rewrite the `bigint.c` implementation so that integers are stored in this more tightly packed form.

12. As it appears in Figure 12-3, the `bigint.h` interface is too restrictive to be used in many applications. As a first step toward designing a more powerful package, extend the interface and implementation so that they support negative integers and subtraction. To do so, the first step is to redefine the `bigIntCDT` structure so that it consists of a sign and a list of digits. You then need to redefine the functions so that they take the sign of their arguments into account.

13. After completing the extensions for negative integers described in the preceding exercise, write a function `CompareBigInt(n1, n2)` that takes two values of type `bigIntADT` and returns –1 if `n1` is less than `n2`, 0 if the two are equal, and +1 if `n1` is greater than `n2`.

14. Write a function `DivideBigInt(n1, n2)` that returns the quotient of two extended-precision integers. This exercise is considerably more challenging than the extensions in the preceding exercises. The hard part, however, is not so much the implementation but rather figuring out a recursive formulation that allows you to express the quotient in terms of simpler calculations. For inspiration, you should begin by reviewing the process of long division that you presumably learned in elementary school. What's really going on when you divide one multidigit number by another? Is there some way to implement the long-division algorithm that takes advantage of the recursive structure of a `bigIntADT`?

CHAPTER 13

Trees

I like trees because they seem more resigned to the way they have to live than other things do.

— Willa Cather, *O Pioneers!*, 1913

Objectives

- To understand the concept of trees and the standard terminology used to describe them.

- To appreciate the recursive nature of a tree and how that recursive structure is reflected in its underlying representation.

- To become familiar with the data structures and algorithms used to implement binary search trees.

- To recognize that it is possible to maintain balance in a binary search tree as new keys are inserted.

- To learn how binary search trees can be implemented as a general abstraction.

As you have seen in several earlier chapters, linked lists make it possible to represent an ordered collection of values without using arrays. The link pointers associated with each cell form a linear chain that defines the underlying order. Although linked lists require more memory space than arrays and are less efficient for operations such as selecting a value at a particular index position, they have the advantage that insertion and deletion operations can be performed in constant time.

The use of pointers to define the ordering relationship among a set of values is considerably more powerful than the linked-list example suggests and is by no means limited to creating linear structures. In this chapter, you will learn about a data structure that uses pointers to model hierarchical relationships. That structure is called a **tree,** which is defined to be a collection of individual entries called **nodes** for which the following properties hold:

- As long as the tree contains any nodes at all, there is a specific node called the **root** that forms the top of a hierarchy.
- Every other node is connected to the root by a unique line of descent.

Tree-structured hierarchies occur in many contexts outside of computer science. The most familiar example is the family tree, which is discussed in the next section. Other examples include

- *Game trees.* The game trees introduced in the section on "The minimax strategy" in Chapter 6 have a branching pattern that is typical of trees. The current position is the root of the tree. The various branches lead to positions that might occur later in the game.
- *Biological classifications.* The classification system for living organisms, which was developed in the eighteenth century by the Swedish botanist Carolus Linnaeus, is structured as a tree. The root of the tree is all living things. From there, the classification system branches to form separate kingdoms, of which animals and plants are the most familiar. The hierarchy continues down through several additional levels until it defines an individual species.
- *Organization charts.* Many companies are structured so that each employee reports to a single supervisor. The organization chart of such a company forms a tree that extends up to the company president, who represents the root.
- *Directory hierarchies.* On most modern computers, files are stored in directories that form a tree. There is a top-level directory that represents the root, which can contain files along with other directories. Those directories may contain subdirectories, which gives rise to the hierarchical structure representative of trees.

13.1 Family trees

Family trees provide a convenient way to represent the lines of descent from a single individual through a series of generations. For example, the diagram in Figure 13-1 shows the family tree of the House of Normandy, which ruled England after the Battle of Hastings in 1066, when William the Conquerer defeated Harold to become King William I. The structure of the diagram fits the definition of a tree given in the preceding section. William I is the root of the tree, and all the other individuals in the chart are connected to William I through a unique line of descent.

Terminology used to describe trees

The family tree in Figure 13-1 makes it easy to introduce the terminology computer scientists use to describe tree structures. Each node in a tree may have several **children,** but only a single **parent** in the tree. In the context of trees, the words **ancestor** and **descendant** have exactly the same meaning as they do in English. The line of descent through Henry I and Matilda shows that Henry II is a descendant of William I, which in turn implies that William I is an ancestor of Henry II. Similarly, the term **siblings** is used to refer to two nodes that share the same parent, such as Robert and Adela.

Although most of the terms used to describe trees come directly from the family-tree analogue, others—like the word *root*—come from the botanical metaphor instead. At the opposite end of the tree from the root, there are nodes that have no children, which are called **leaves.** Nodes that are neither the root nor a leaf are called **interior** nodes. For example, in Figure 13-1, Robert, William II, Stephen, William, and Henry II represent leaf nodes; Adela, Henry I, and Matilda represent interior nodes. The **height** of a tree is defined to be the length of the longest path from the root to a leaf. Thus, the height of the tree shown in Figure 13-1 is 4, because there are four nodes on the path from William I to Henry II, which is longer than any other path from the root.

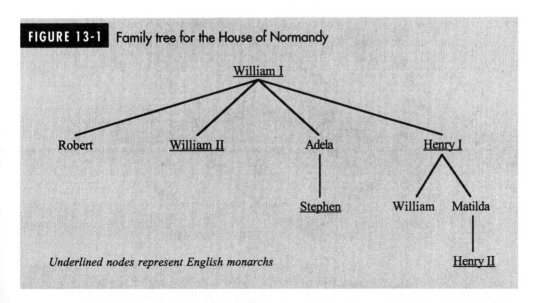

FIGURE 13-1   Family tree for the House of Normandy

Underlined nodes represent English monarchs

The recursive nature of a tree

One of the most important things to notice about any tree is that the same branching pattern occurs at every level of the decomposition. If you take any node in a tree together with all its descendants, the result fits the definition of a tree. For example, if you extract the portion of Figure 13-1 beginning at Henry I, you get the following tree:

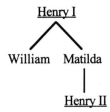

A tree formed by extracting a node and its descendants from an existing tree is called a **subtree** of the original one. The tree in this diagram, for example, is the subtree rooted at Henry I.

The fact that each node in a tree can be considered the root of its own subtree underscores the recursive nature of tree structures. If you think about trees from a recursive perspective, a tree is simply a node and a set—possibly empty in the case of a leaf node—of attached subtrees. The recursive character of trees is fundamental to their underlying representation as well as to most algorithms that operate on trees.

Representing family trees in C

In order to represent any type of tree in C, you need some way to model the hierarchical relationships among the data values. In most cases, the easiest way to represent the parent/child relationship is to include a pointer in the parent that points to the child. If you use this strategy, each node is a structure that contains—in addition to other data specific to the node itself—pointers to each of its children. In general, it works well to define a node as the structure itself and to define a tree as a pointer to that structure. This definition is mutually recursive even in its English conception because of the following relationship:

- Trees are pointers to nodes.
- Nodes are structures that contain trees.

How would you use this recursive insight to design a structure suitable for storing the data in a family tree such as the one shown in Figure 13-1? Each node consists of a name of a person and a set of pointers to its children. If you store the child pointers in an array, a node has the following structure:

```
typedef struct familyNodeT {
    string name;
    struct familyNodeT *children[MaxChildren];
} familyNodeT;
```

A family tree is simply a pointer to one of these nodes. You can define a type name for the tree itself by including the line

```
typedef familyNodeT *familyTreeT;
```

as a separate definition. It is easier, however, to define both types—the node and the tree—in a single **typedef** that looks like this:

```
typedef struct familyNodeT {
    string name;
    struct familyNodeT *children[MaxChildren];
} familyNodeT, *familyTreeT;
```

A diagram showing the internal representation of the royal family tree appears in Figure 13-2. This representation uses NULL pointers in the **children** array if there are fewer than **MaxChildren** for a particular node. Other strategies—such as maintaining a separate count of the number of children or storing the children in a linked list rather than an array—are more general, but complicate the basic design. You will have a chance to experiment with these alternative representations in the exercises at the end of this chapter.

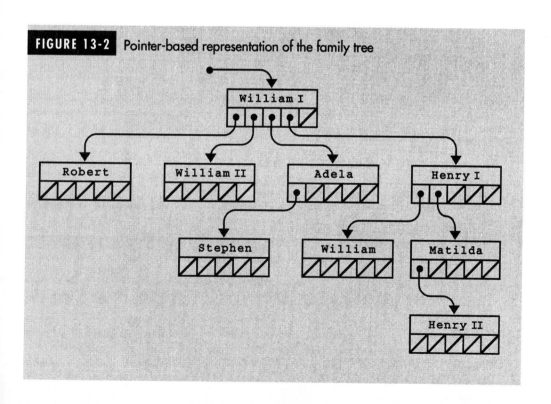

FIGURE 13-2   Pointer-based representation of the family tree

■ 13.2 Binary search trees

Although it is possible to illustrate tree algorithms using family trees, it is more effective to do so in a simpler environment that has more direct application to programming. The family-tree example provides a useful framework for introducing the terminology used to describe trees, but suffers in practice from the complication that each node can have an arbitrary number of children. In many programming contexts, it is reasonable to restrict the number of children to make the resulting trees easier to implement.

One of the most important subclasses of trees—which has many practical applications—is a **binary tree,** which is defined to be a tree in which the following additional properties hold:

- Each node in the tree has at most two children.
- Every node except the root is designated as either a *left child* or a *right child* of its parent.

The second condition emphasizes the fact that child nodes in a binary tree are ordered with respect to their parents. For example, the binary trees

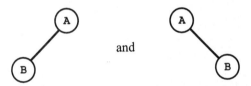

and

are different trees, even though they consist of the same nodes. In both cases, the node labeled B is a child of the root node labeled A, but it is a left child in the first tree and a right child in the second.

The fact that the nodes in a binary tree have a defined geometrical relationship makes it convenient to represent ordered collections of data using binary trees. The most common application uses a special class of binary tree called a **binary search tree,** which is defined by the following properties:

1. Every node contains—possibly in addition to other data—a special value called a *key* that defines the order of the nodes.
2. Key values are *unique,* in the sense that no key can appear more than once in the tree.
3. At every node in the tree, the key value must be greater than all the keys in the subtree rooted at its left child and greater than all the keys in the subtree rooted at its right child.

Although this definition is formally correct, it almost certainly seems confusing at first glance. To make sense of the definition and begin to understand why constructing a tree that meets these conditions might be useful, it helps to go back and look at a specific problem for which binary search trees represent a potential solution strategy.

The underlying motivation for using binary search trees

In Chapter 11, one of the strategies proposed for representing symbol tables—before the hashing algorithm made other options seem far less attractive—was to store the key/value pairs in an array. This strategy has a useful computational property: if you keep the keys in sorted order, you can write an implementation of **Lookup** that runs in $O(\log N)$ time. All you need to do is employ the binary search algorithm, which was introduced in Chapter 4. Unfortunately, the array-based representation does not offer any equally efficient way to code the **Enter** function. Although **Enter** can use binary search to determine where any new key fits into the array, maintaining the sorted order requires $O(N)$ time because each subsequent array element must be shifted to make room for the new entry.

This problem brings to mind a similar situation that arose in Chapter 9. When arrays were used to represent the editor buffer, inserting a new character was a linear-time operation. In that case, the solution was to replace the array with a linked list. Is it possible that a similar strategy would improve the performance of **Enter** in the symbol table abstraction? After all, inserting a new element into a linked list—as long as you have a pointer to the cell prior to the insertion point—is a constant-time operation.

The trouble with linked lists is that they do not support the binary search algorithm in any efficient way. Binary search depends on being able to find the middle element in constant time. In an array, finding the middle element is easy. In a linked list, the only way to do so is to iterate through all the link pointers in the first half of the list.

To get a more concrete sense of why linked lists have this limitation, suppose that you have a linked list containing the following seven elements:

Bashful → Doc → Dopey → Grumpy → Happy → Sleepy → Sneezy

The elements in this list appear in **lexicographic order**, which is an extension of alphabetical ordering that ranks characters according to their internal character codes.

Given a linked list of this sort, you can easily find the first element, because the initial pointer gives you its address. From there, you can follow the link pointer to find the second element. On the other hand, there is no easy way to locate the element that occurs halfway through the sequence. To do so, you have to walk through each chain pointer, counting up to $N/2$. This operation requires linear time, which completely negates the efficiency advantage of binary search. If binary search is to offer any improvement in efficiency, the data structure must enable you to find the middle element quickly.

Although it might at first seem silly, it is useful to consider what happens if you simply point at the middle of the list instead of the beginning:

Bashful → Doc → Dopey → Grumpy → Happy → Sleepy → Sneezy

In this diagram, you have no problem at all finding the middle element. It's immediately accessible through the list pointer. The problem, however, is that you've thrown away the first half of the list. The pointers in the structure provide access to `Grumpy` and any name that follows it in the chain, but there is no longer any way to reach `Bashful`, `Doc`, and `Dopey`.

If you think about the situation from `Grumpy`'s point of view, the general outline of the solution becomes clear. What you need is to have two chains emanating from the `Grumpy` cell: one that consists of the cells whose names precede `Grumpy` and another for the cells whose names follow `Grumpy` in the alphabet. In the conceptual diagram, all you need to do is reverse the arrows:

Each of the strings is now accessible, and you can easily divide the entire list in half.

At this point, you need to apply the same strategy recursively. The binary search algorithm requires you to find the middle of not only the original list but its sublists as well. You therefore need to restructure the lists that precede and follow `Grumpy`, using the same decomposition strategy. Every cell points in two directions: to the midpoint of the list that precedes it and to the midpoint of the list that follows it. Applying this process transforms the original list into the following binary tree:

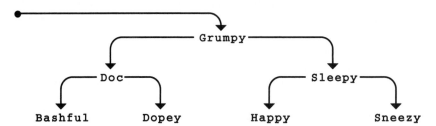

The most important feature about this particular style of binary tree is that it is ordered. For any particular node in the tree, the string it contains must follow all the strings in the subtree descending to the left and precede all strings in the subtree to the right. In this example, `Grumpy` comes after `Doc`, `Bashful`, and `Dopey` but before `Sleepy`, `Happy`, and `Sneezy`. The same rule, however, applies at each level, so the node containing `Doc` comes after the `Bashful` node but before the `Dopey` node. The formal definition of a binary search tree, which appears at the end of the preceding section, simply ensures that every node in the tree obeys this ordering rule.

Finding nodes in a binary search tree

The fundamental advantage of a binary search tree is that you can use the binary search algorithm to find a particular node. Suppose, for example, that you are looking for the node containing the string `Happy` in the tree diagram shown at the end of the preceding section. The first step is to compare `Happy` with `Grumpy`, which appears at the root of the tree. Since `Happy` comes after `Grumpy` in lexicographic order, you know that the `Happy` node, if it exists, must be in the right subtree. The next step, therefore, is to compare **Happy** and **Sleepy**. In this case, **Happy** comes before **Sleepy** and must therefore be in the left subtree of this node. That subtree consists of a single node, which contains the correct name.

Because trees are recursive structures, it is easy to code the search algorithm in its recursive form. For concreteness, let's suppose that the type definition for **nodeT** and **treeT** looks like this:

```
typedef struct nodeT {
    string key;
    struct nodeT *left, *right;
} nodeT, *treeT;
```

Given this definition, you can easily write a function **FindNode** that implements the binary search algorithm, as follows:

```
treeT FindNode(treeT t, string key)
{
    int sign;

    if (t == NULL) return (NULL);
    sign = StringCompare(key, t->key);
    if (sign == 0) return (t);
    if (sign < 0) {
        return (FindNode(t->left, key));
    } else {
        return (FindNode(t->right, key));
    }
}
```

If the tree is empty, the desired node is clearly not there, and **FindNode** returns the value **NULL** as a sentinel indicating that the key cannot be found. If the tree is not equal to **NULL**, the implementation checks to see whether the desired key matches the one in the current node. If so, **FindNode** returns a pointer to the current node. If the keys do not match, **FindNode** proceeds recursively, looking in either the left or right subtree depending on the result of the key comparison.

Inserting new nodes in a binary search tree

The next question to consider is how to create a binary search tree in the first place. The simplest approach is to begin with an empty tree and then call an **InsertNode** function to insert new keys into the tree, one at a time. As each new key is inserted, it is important to maintain the ordering relationship among the nodes of the tree. To make sure the **FindNode** function continues to work, the code for **InsertNode** must use binary search to identify the correct insertion point.

As with **FindNode**, the code for **InsertNode** can proceed recursively beginning at the root of the tree. At each node, **InsertNode** must compare the new key to the key in the current node. If the new key precedes the existing one, the new key belongs in the left subtree. Conversely, if the new key follows the one in the current node, it belongs in the right subtree. Eventually, the process will encounter a **NULL** subtree that represents the point in the tree where the new node needs to be added.

At this point, the `InsertNode` implementation must replace the `NULL` pointer with a new node initialized to contain a copy of the key.

The code for `InsertNode`, however, is a bit tricky. The difficulty comes from the fact that `InsertNode` must be able to change the value of the binary search tree by adding a new node. In C, functions cannot change the values of their arguments. To get around this restriction, `InsertNode` must use call by reference. Instead of taking a `treeT` as its argument the way `FindNode` does, `InsertNode` must instead take a pointer to a `treeT`. The prototype for `InsertNode` therefore looks like this:

```
static void InsertNode(treeT *tptr, string key);
```

Calls to `InsertNode` must pass the address of the tree into which insertions are being made. For example, to insert `Grumpy` into the tree stored in the variable `dwarfTree`, you would make the following call:

```
InsertNode(&dwarfTree, "Grumpy");
```

Once you understand the prototype for the `InsertNode` function, writing the code is not particularly hard. A complete implementation of `InsertNode` appears in Figure 13-3. The code begins by initializing the local variable `t` to hold the tree to which the argument `tptr` points. Having this actual tree available in a variable simplifies the code and makes the similarities between `FindNode` and `InsertNode` easier to see. If `t` is `NULL`, `InsertNode` creates a new node, initializes its fields, and

---

FIGURE 13-3 Standard algorithm for inserting a node into a binary search tree

```
void InsertNode(treeT *tptr, string key)
{
    treeT t;
    int sign;

    t = *tptr;
    if (t == NULL) {
        t = New(treeT);
        t->key = CopyString(key);
        t->left = t->right = NULL;
        *tptr = t;
        return;
    }
    sign = StringCompare(key, t->key);
    if (sign == 0) return;
    if (sign < 0) {
        InsertNode(&t->left, key);
    } else {
        InsertNode(&t->right, key);
    }
}
```

then replaces the NULL pointer in the existing structure with a pointer to the new node. If t is not NULL, InsertNode compares the new key with the one stored at the root of the tree t. If the keys match, the key is already in the tree and no further operations are required. If not, InsertNode uses the sign of the comparison to determine whether to insert the key in the left or the right subtree and then makes the appropriate recursive call.

For instance, let's suppose that InsertNode determines that the new key belongs in the left subtree. In this case, the recursive call looks like this:

```
InsertNode(&t->left, key);
```

To be consistent with the prototype for InsertNode, the first argument must be a pointer to a tree. In this example, the argument is &t->left, which specifies the address of t's left subtree.

Because the code for InsertNode seems complicated until you've seen it work, it makes sense to go through the process of inserting a few keys in some detail. Suppose, for example, that you have declared and initialized an empty tree as follows:

```
treeT dwarfTree;

dwarfTree = NULL;
```

These statements create a local variable dwarfTree that lives at some address in memory, as illustrated by the following diagram:

The actual address depends on the structure of the computer's memory system and the way the compiler allocates addresses. In this example, each memory word has been assigned an arbitrary address to make it easier to follow the operation of the code.

What happens if you call

```
InsertNode(&dwarfTree, "Grumpy");
```

starting with this initial configuration in which dwarfTree is empty? In the frame for InsertNode, the variable tptr has the value 9000, which is the address of dwarfTree. The first step in the code sets the variable t to the contents of the treeT at address 9000, which means that t is set to NULL. The code therefore executes the body of the if statement

```
if (t == NULL) {
    t = New(treeT);
    t->key = CopyString(key);
    t->left = t->right = NULL;
    *tptr = t;
    return;
}
```

which has the effect of creating a new node, initializing it to hold the key `Grumpy`, and then storing the address of the new node in the word addressed by `tptr`. When the function returns, the tree looks like this:

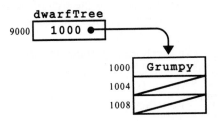

This structure correctly represents the binary search tree with a single node containing `Grumpy`.

What happens if you then use `InsertNode` to insert `Sleepy` into the tree? As before, the initial call generates a stack frame in which the variable `tptr` has the value 9000. This time, however, the value of the tree addressed by `tptr` is no longer `NULL`. The word at address 9000 now contains the address of the node containing `Grumpy`. Because `Sleepy` comes after `Grumpy` in lexicographic order, the code for `InsertNode` continues with the following recursive call:

```
InsertNode(&t->right, key);
```

In this case, the value of `&t->right` is 1008, which is the address of the right subtree in the `Grumpy` node.

At this point, the recursive call looks much like the insertion of `Grumpy` into the original empty tree. The only difference is that the value of `tptr` now indicates an address within an existing node. The effect of the recursive call is therefore to store a pointer to a new node containing `Sleepy` in the word at address 1008, which gives rise to the following configuration:

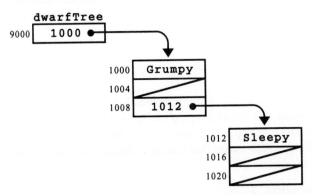

Additional calls to `InsertNode` will create additional nodes and insert them into the structure in a way that preserves the ordering constraint required for binary search trees. For example, if you insert the names of the five remaining dwarves in the order `Doc`, `Bashful`, `Dopey`, `Happy`, and `Sneezy`, you end up with the binary search tree shown in Figure 13-4.

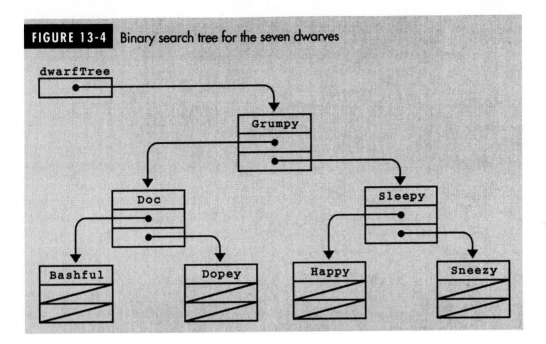

FIGURE 13-4 Binary search tree for the seven dwarves

Tree traversals

The structure of a binary search tree makes it easy to go through the nodes of the tree in the order specified by the keys. For example, you can use the following function to display the keys in a binary search tree in lexicographic order:

```
void DisplayTree(treeT t)
{
    if (t != NULL) {
        DisplayTree(t->left);
        printf("%s\n", t->key);
        DisplayTree(t->right);
    }
}
```

Thus, if you call `DisplayTree` on the tree shown in Figure 13-4, you get the following output:

```
Bashful
Doc
Dopey
Grumpy
Happy
Sleepy
Sneezy
```

At each recursive level, `DisplayTree` checks to see whether the tree is empty. If it is, `DisplayTree` has no work to do. If not, the ordering of the recursive calls ensures that the output appears in the correct order. The first recursive call displays the keys that precede the current node, all of which must appear in the left subtree. Displaying the nodes in the left subtree before the current one therefore maintains the correct order. Similarly, it is important to display the key from the current node before making the last recursive call, which displays the keys that occur later in the ASCII sequence and therefore appear in the right subtree.

The process of going through the nodes of a tree and performing some operation at each node is called **traversing** or **walking** the tree. In many cases, you will want to traverse a tree in the order imposed by the keys, as in the `DisplayTree` example. This approach, which consists of processing the current node between the recursive calls to the left and right subtrees, is called an **inorder traversal.** There are, however, two other types of tree traversals that occur frequently in the context of binary trees, which are called **preorder** and **postorder** traversals. In the preorder traversal, the current node is processed before either of its subtrees; in the postorder traversal, the subtrees are processed first, followed by the current node. These traversal styles are illustrated by the functions `PreOrderWalk` and `PostOrderWalk`, which appear in Figure 13-5. The sample output associated with each function shows the result of applying that function to the balanced binary search tree in Figure 13-4.

FIGURE 13-5 Preorder and postorder traversals of a binary search tree

```
void PreOrderWalk(treeT t)
{
    if (t != NULL) {
        printf("%s\n", t->key);
        PreOrderWalk(t->left);
        PreOrderWalk(t->right);
    }
}
```

```
void PostOrderWalk(treeT t)
{
    if (t != NULL) {
        PostOrderWalk(t->left);
        PostOrderWalk(t->right);
        printf("%s\n", t->key);
    }
}
```

```
Grumpy
Doc
Bashful
Dopey
Sleepy
Happy
Sneezy
```

```
Bashful
Dopey
Doc
Happy
Sneezy
Sleepy
Grumpy
```

13.3 Balanced trees

Although the recursive strategy used to implement `InsertNode` guarantees that the nodes are organized as a legal binary search tree, the structure of the tree depends on the order in which the nodes are inserted. The tree in Figure 13-4, for example, was generated by inserting the names of the dwarves in the following order:

        Grumpy, Sleepy, Doc, Bashful, Dopey, Happy, Sneezy

Suppose that you had instead entered the names of the dwarves in alphabetical order. The first call to `InsertNode` would insert `Bashful` at the root of the tree. Subsequent calls would insert `Doc` after `Bashful`, `Dopey` after `Doc`, and so on, appending each new node to the `right` chain of the previously one.

The resulting figure, which is shown in Figure 13-6, looks more like a linked list than a tree. Nonetheless, the tree in Figure 13-6 maintains the property that the key field in any node follows all the keys in its left subtree and precedes all the keys in its right subtree. It therefore fits the definition of a binary search tree, so the `FindNode` function will operate correctly. The running time of the `FindNode` algorithm, however, is proportional to the height of the tree, which means that the structure of the tree can have a significant impact on the algorithmic performance. If a binary search tree is shaped like the one shown in Figure 13-4, the time required to find a key in the tree will be $O(\log N)$. On the other hand, if the tree is shaped like the one in Figure 13-6, the running time will deteriorate to $O(N)$.

The binary search algorithm used to implement `FindNode` achieves its ideal performance only if the left and right subtrees at each node have roughly the same height. Trees in which this property holds—such as the tree in Figure 13-4—are

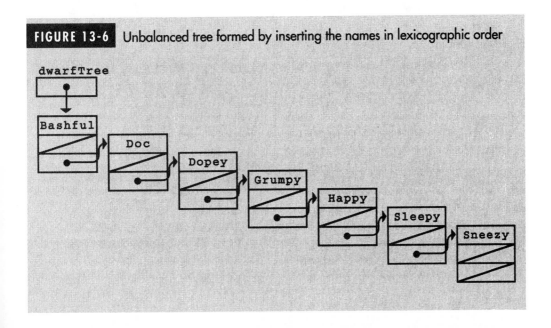

FIGURE 13-6   Unbalanced tree formed by inserting the names in lexicographic order

said to be **balanced.** More formally, a binary tree is defined to be balanced if, at each node, the height of the left and right subtrees differ by at most one.

To illustrate this definition of a balanced binary tree, each of the following diagrams shows a balanced arrangement of a tree with seven nodes:

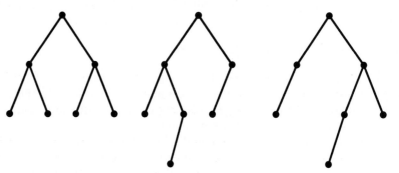

The tree diagram on the left is optimally balanced in the sense that the heights of the two subtrees at each node are always equal. Such an arrangement is possible, however, only if the number of nodes is one less than a power of two. If the number of nodes does not meet this condition, there will be some point in the tree where the heights of the subtrees differ to some extent. By allowing the heights of the subtrees to differ by one, the definition of a balanced tree provides some flexibility in the structure of a tree without adversely affecting its computational performance.

The following diagrams represent unbalanced trees:

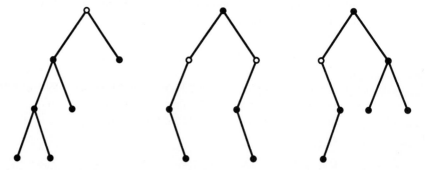

In each diagram, the nodes at which the balanced-tree definition fails are shown as open circles. In the leftmost tree, for example, the left subtree of the root node has height 3 while the right subtree has height 1.

Tree-balancing strategies

Binary search trees are useful in practice only if it is possible to avoid the worst-case behavior associated with unbalanced trees. As trees become unbalanced, the **FindNode** and **InsertNode** operations become linear in their running time. If the performance of binary trees deteriorates to $O(N)$, you might as well use a sorted array to store the values. With a sorted array, it requires $O(\log N)$ time to implement **FindNode** and $O(N)$ time to implement **InsertNode**. From a computational perspective, the performance of the array-based algorithms is therefore superior to that of unbalanced trees, even though the array implementation is considerably easier to write.

What makes binary search trees useful as a programming tool is the fact that you can keep them balanced as you build them. The basic idea is to extend the implementation of **InsertNode** so that it keeps track of whether the tree is balanced while inserting new nodes. If the tree ever becomes out of balance, **InsertNode** must rearrange the nodes in the tree so that the balance is restored without disturbing the ordering relationships that make the tree a binary search tree. Assuming that it is possible to rearrange a tree in time proportional to its height, both **FindNode** and **InsertNode** can be implemented in $O(\log N)$ time.

Algorithms for maintaining balance in a binary tree have been studied extensively in computer science. The algorithms used today to implement balanced binary trees are quite sophisticated and have benefited enormously from theoretical research. Most of these algorithms, however, are difficult to explain without reviewing mathematical results beyond the scope of this text. To demonstrate that such algorithms are indeed possible, the next few sections present one of the first tree-balancing algorithms, which was published in 1962 by the Russian mathematicians Georgii Adel'son-Vel'skii and Evgenii Landis and has since been known by the initials AVL. Although the AVL algorithm has been largely replaced in practice by more modern approaches, it has the advantage of being considerably easier to explain. Moreover, the operations used to implement the basic strategy reappear in many other algorithms, which makes it a good model for more modern techniques.

Illustrating the AVL idea

Before you attempt to understand the implementation of the AVL algorithm in detail, it helps to follow through the process of inserting nodes into a binary search tree to see what can go wrong and, if possible, what steps you can take to fix any problems that arise. Let's imagine that you want to create a binary search tree in which the nodes contain the symbols for the chemical elements. For example, the first six elements are

H	(Hydrogen)
He	(Helium)
Li	(Lithium)
Be	(Beryllium)
B	(Boron)
C	(Carbon)

What happens if you insert the chemical symbols for these elements in the indicated order, which is how these elements appear in the periodic table? The first insertion is easy because the tree is initially empty. The node containing the symbol H becomes the root of the tree. If you call **InsertNode** on the symbol **He**, the new node will be added after the node containing **H**, because **He** comes after **H** in lexicographic order. Thus, the first two nodes in the tree are arranged like this:

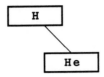

To keep track of whether the tree is balanced, the AVL algorithm associates an integer with each node, which is simply the height of the right subtree minus the height of the left subtree. This value is called the **balance factor** of the node. In the simple tree that contains the symbols for the first two elements, the balance factors, which are shown here in the upper right corner of each node, look like this:

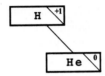

So far, the tree is balanced because none of the nodes has a balance factor whose absolute value is greater than 1. That situation changes, however, when you add the next element. If you follow the standard insertion algorithm, adding Li results in the following configuration:

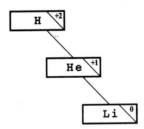

Here, the root node is out of balance because its right subtree has height 2 and its left subtree has height 0, which differ by more than one.

To fix the imbalance, you need to restructure the tree. For this set of nodes, there is only one balanced configuration in which the nodes are correctly ordered with respect to each other. That tree has He at the root, with H and Li in the left and right subtrees, as follows:

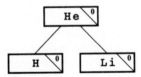

This tree is once again balanced, but an important question remains: how do you know what operations to perform in order to restore the balance in a tree?

Single rotations

The fundamental insight behind the AVL strategy is that you can always restore balance to a tree by a simple rearrangement of the nodes. If you think about what steps were necessary to correct the imbalance in the preceding example, it is clear that the **He** node moves upward to become the root while **H** moves downward to become its child. To a certain extent, the transformation has the characteristic of rotating the **H** and **He** nodes one position to the left, like this:

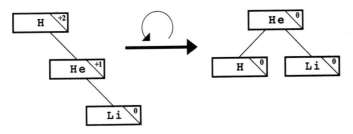

In general, you can always perform this type of rotation operation on any two nodes in a binary search tree without invalidating the relative ordering of the nodes, even if the nodes have subtrees descending from them. In a tree with additional nodes, the basic operation looks like this:

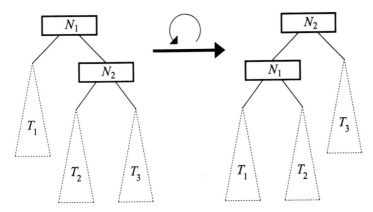

Note that the T_2 subtree, which would otherwise be orphaned by this process, must be reattached to N_1 after N_1 and N_2 change positions.

The two nodes involved in the rotation operation are called the **axis** of the rotation. In the example consisting of the elements **H**, **He**, and **Li**, the rotation was performed around the **H-He** axis. Because this operation moves nodes to the left, the operation illustrated by this diagram is called a **left rotation.** If a tree is out of balance in the opposite direction, you can apply a symmetric operation called a **right rotation,** in which all the operations are simply reversed. For example, the symbols for the next two elements—**Be** and **B**—each get added at the left edge of the tree. To rebalance the tree, you must perform a right rotation around the **Be-H** axis, as illustrated in the following diagram:

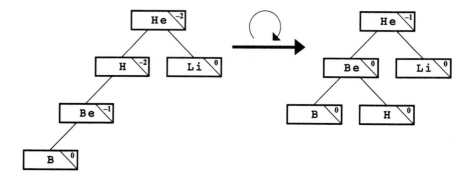

Unfortunately, simple rotation operations are not always sufficient to restore balance to a tree. Consider, for example, what happens when you add C to the tree. Before you perform any balancing operations, the tree looks like this:

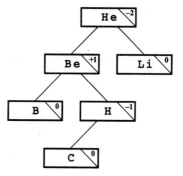

The **He** node at the root of the tree is out of balance. If you try to correct the imbalance by rotating the tree to the right around the **Be-He** axis, you get the following tree:

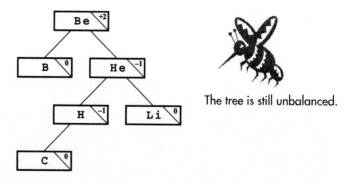

The tree is still unbalanced.

After the rotation, the tree is just as unbalanced as it was before. The only difference is that the root node is now unbalanced in the opposite direction.

Double rotations

The problem in this last example arises because the nodes involved in the rotation have balance factors with opposite signs. When this situation occurs, a single rotation is not sufficient to correct the imbalance. To fix the problem, you need to make two rotations. Before rotating the out-of-balance node, you rotate its child in the opposite direction. Rotating the child gives the balance factors in the parent and child the same sign, which means that the following rotation will succeed. This pair of operations is called a **double rotation.**

As an illustration of the double-rotation operation, consider the preceding unbalanced tree of elements just after adding the symbol c. The first step is to rotate the tree to the left around the **Be-H** axis, like this:

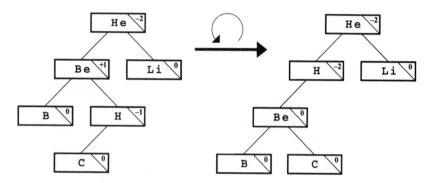

The resulting tree is still out of balance at the root node, but the **H** and **He** nodes now have balance factors that share the same sign. In this configuration, a single rotation to the right around the **H-He** axis restores balance to the tree, as follows:

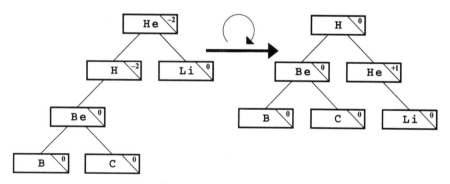

In their paper describing these trees, Adel'son-Vel'skii and Landis demonstrated the following properties of their tree-balancing algorithm:

- If you insert a new node into an AVL tree, you can always restore its balance by performing at most one operation, which is either a single or a double rotation.

- After you complete the rotation operation, the height of the subtree at the axis of rotation is always the same as it was before the insertion of the new node. This property ensures that none of the balance factors change at any higher levels of the tree.

Implementing the AVL algorithm

Although the process involves quite a few details, implementing `InsertNode` for AVL trees is not as difficult as you might imagine. The first change you need to make is to include a new field in the node structure that allows you to keep track of the balance factor, as follows:

```
typedef struct nodeT {
    string key;
    struct nodeT *left, *right;
    int bf;
} nodeT, *treeT;
```

The code for the AVL-based implementation of `InsertNode` appears in Figure 13-7. The functions `FixRightImbalance` and `RotateRight` are not shown but are symmetrical to `FixLeftImbalance` and `RotateLeft`.

As you can see from the code, `InsertNode` is implemented as a wrapper to a function `InsertAVL`, which at first glance seems to have the same prototype. The parameters to the two functions are indeed the same. The only difference is that `InsertAVL` returns an integer value representing the change in the height of the tree after inserting the node. This return value, which will always be 0 or 1, makes it easy to fix the structure of the tree as the code makes its way back through the level of recursive calls. The simple cases are as follows:

1. Adding a node in place of a previously **NULL** tree, which increases the height by one
2. Encountering an existing node that contains the key, which leaves the height unchanged

In the recursive cases, the code first adds the new node to the appropriate subtree, keeping track of the change in height in the local variable `delta`. If the height of the subtree to which the insertion was made has not changed, then the balance factor in the current node must also remain the same. If, however, the subtree increased in height, there are three possibilities:

1. *That subtree was previously shorter than the other subtree in this node.* In this case, inserting the new node actually makes the tree more balanced than it was previously. The balance factor of the current node becomes 0, and the height of the subtree rooted there remains the same as before.
2. *The two subtrees in the current node were previously the same size.* In this case, increasing the size of one of the subtrees makes the current node

FIGURE 13-7   Code to insert a node into an AVL tree

```
static void InsertNode(treeT *tptr, string key)
{
    (void) InsertAVL(tptr, key);
}

/*
 * Function: InsertAVL
 * Usage: delta = InsertAVL(&t, key);
 * -----------------------------------
 * This function enters the key into the tree whose address is
 * passed as the first argument.  The return value is the change
 * in depth in the tree, which is used to correct the balance
 * factors in ancestor nodes.
 */

static int InsertAVL(treeT *tptr, string key)
{
    treeT t;
    int sign, delta;

    t = *tptr;
    if (t == NULL) {
        t = New(treeT);
        t->key = CopyString(key);
        t->bf = 0;
        t->left = t->right = NULL;
        *tptr = t;
        return (+1);
    }
    sign = StringCompare(key, t->key);
    if (sign == 0) return (0);
    if (sign < 0) {
        delta = InsertAVL(&t->left, key);
        if (delta == 0) return (0);
        switch (t->bf) {
          case +1: t->bf =  0; return (0);
          case  0: t->bf = -1; return (+1);
          case -1: FixLeftImbalance(tptr); return (0);
        }
    } else {
        delta = InsertAVL(&t->right, key);
        if (delta == 0) return (0);
        switch (t->bf) {
          case -1: t->bf =  0; return (0);
          case  0: t->bf = +1; return (+1);
          case +1: FixRightImbalance(tptr); return (0);
        }
    }
}
```

```
/*
 * Function: FixLeftImbalance
 * Usage: FixLeftImbalance(&t);
 * ----------------------------
 * This function is called when a node has been found that
 * is out of balance with the longer subtree on the left.
 * Depending on the balance factor of the left child, the
 * code performs a single or double rotation.
 */

static void FixLeftImbalance(treeT *tptr)
{
    treeT t, parent, child, *cptr;
    int oldBF;

    parent = *tptr;
    cptr = &parent->left;
    child = *cptr;
    if (child->bf != parent->bf) {
        oldBF = child->right->bf;
        RotateLeft(cptr);
        RotateRight(tptr);
        t = *tptr;
        t->bf = 0;
        switch (oldBF) {
          case -1: t->left->bf = 0; t->right->bf = +1; break;
          case  0: t->left->bf = t->right->bf = 0; break;
          case +1: t->left->bf = -1; t->right->bf = 0; break;
        }
    } else {
        RotateRight(tptr);
        t = *tptr;
        t->right->bf = t->bf = 0;
    }
}

/*
 * Function: RotateLeft
 * Usage: RotateLeft(&t);
 * ----------------------
 * This function performs a single left rotation of the tree
 * whose address is passed as an argument.  The balance factors
 * are unchanged by this function and must be corrected at a
 * higher level of the algorithm.
 */

static void RotateLeft(treeT *tptr)
{
    treeT parent, child;

    parent = *tptr;
    child = parent->right;
    parent->right = child->left;
    child->left = parent;
    (*tptr) = child;
}
```

slightly out of balance, but not to the point that any corrective action is required. The balance factor becomes -1 or $+1$, as appropriate, and the function returns 1 to show that the height of the subtree rooted at this node has increased.

3. *The subtree that grew taller was already taller than the other subtree.* When this situation occurs, the tree has become seriously out of balance, because one subtree is now two nodes higher than the other. At this point, the code must execute the appropriate rotation operations to correct the imbalance. If the balance factors in the current node and the root of the subtree that expanded have the same sign, a single rotation is sufficient. If not, the code must perform a double rotation. After performing the rotations, the code must correct the balance factors in the nodes whose positions have changed. The effect of the single and double rotation operations on the balance factors in the node is shown in Figure 13-8.

Using the code for the AVL algorithm shown in Figure 13-7 ensures that the binary search tree remains in balance as new nodes are added. As a result, both **FindNode** and **InsertNode** will run in $O(\log N)$ time. Even without the AVL extension, however, the code will continue to work. The advantage of the AVL strategy is that it guarantees good performance, at some cost in the complexity of the code.

13.4 Defining a general interface for binary search trees

The code in these last several sections has given you an idea of how binary search trees work. Up to this point, however, the focus has been entirely on the implementation level. What would you do if you wanted to build an application program that used a binary search tree? As things stand, you would almost certainly have to change the definition of the **nodeT** type to include the data required by your application. Such a change would require you to edit the source code for the implementation, which violates the basic principles of interface-based design. As a client, you should never have to edit the implementation code. In general, you should not need to know the details of the implementation at all.

Since Chapter 8, this text has used abstract interfaces to separate the client and the implementation. If you wanted to make binary search trees usable as a general tool, the ideal approach would be to define a **bst.h** interface that allowed clients to invoke the basic operations without having to understand the underlying detail. That interface, moreover, would have to be as general as possible to offer the client maximum flexibility. In particular, the following features would certainly make the **bst.h** interface more useful:

- *The interface should allow the client to define the structure of the data in a node.* The binary search trees you've seen so far have included no data fields except the key itself. In most cases, clients want to work with nodes that contain additional data fields as well.

FIGURE 13-8 The effect of rotation operations on balance factors

Single rotation:

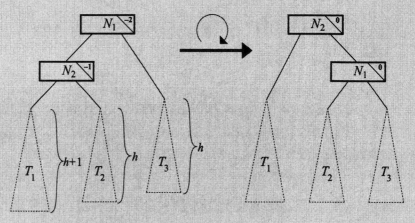

Double rotation:

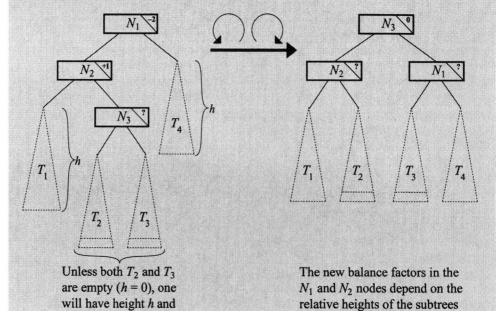

Unless both T_2 and T_3 are empty ($h = 0$), one will have height h and the other height $h-1$

The new balance factors in the N_1 and N_2 nodes depend on the relative heights of the subtrees T_2 and T_3

- *The keys should not be limited to strings.* Although the implementations in the preceding sections have used strings as keys, there is no reason that a general package would need to impose this constraint. To maintain the proper order in a binary tree, all the implementation needs to know is how to compare two keys. As long as the client provides a comparison function, it should be possible to use any type as a key.

- *It should be possible to delete nodes as well as to insert them.* Some clients—particularly including the set package introduced in Chapter 15—need to be able to delete entries from a binary search tree. Deleting a node requires some care, but is easy enough to specify in the implementation.

- *The details of any balancing algorithm should lie entirely on the implementation side of the abstraction boundary.* The interface itself should not reveal what strategy, if any, the implementation uses to keep the tree in balance. Making the process of balancing the tree private to the implementation allows you to substitute new algorithms that perform more effectively than the AVL strategy without forcing clients to change their code.

Figure 13-9 defines an interface that includes each of these features. To understand why the interface looks the way it does, it is important to consider some of the issues that arise in its design and implementation. The sections that follow review these issues.

Allowing the client to define the node structure

As it stands, the code for the binary search tree algorithms introduced earlier in this chapter defines a node structure in which the key is the only data field. As a client, you almost certainly want to include other information as well. How would you go about incorporating this additional information into the structure of a binary search tree? If you think back to how the abstract data types introduced in the earlier chapters have enabled clients to store arbitrary structures within them, the answer to this question initially appears obvious. All the interface would have to do is allow clients to store a `void *` pointer in conjunction with each node. As a client, you could then allocate a record, initialize it to contain the information you needed, and then let the implementation store the address of that record as part of the node structure.

The technique of using `void *` pointers to represent the data associated with a node is consistent with the strategy used to implement symbol tables in Chapter 11. It is, moreover, easy to implement in the context of binary search trees. On the other hand, this technique is not the only option. In fact, in several contexts in which binary search trees arise—most notably the set abstraction presented in Chapter 15—this approach has certain drawbacks. Of these, the most serious is that the client often does not know when it is necessary to allocate a new node. This problem turns out to be serious enough to warrant adopting a different strategy in the `bst.h` interface.

FIGURE 13-9   A general interface for binary search trees

```
/*
 * File: bst.h
 * -----------
 * This file provides an interface for a general binary search
 * tree facility that allows the client to maintain control of
 * the structure of the node.
 */

#ifndef _bst_h
#define _bst_h

#include "genlib.h"
#include "cmpfn.h"

/*
 * Type: bstADT
 * ------------
 * This is the abstract type for a binary search tree.
 */

typedef struct bstCDT *bstADT;

/*
 * Type: nodeFnT
 * -------------
 * This type defines the class of callback functions for nodes.
 */

typedef void (*nodeFnT)(void *np, void *clientData);

/*
 * Type: nodeInitFnT
 * -----------------
 * This type defines the class of functions used to initialize
 * a newly created node.
 */

typedef void (*nodeInitFnT)(void *np, void *kp, void *clientData);

/*
 * Function: NewBST
 * Usage: bst = NewBST(sizeof (nodeT), cmpFn, nodeInitFn);
 * ------------------------------------------------------------
 * This function allocates and returns a new empty binary search
 * tree.  The first argument is the size of the client node.  The
 * second is a comparison function, which is called with the address
 * of the search key and the address of a node.  By storing the key
 * at the beginning of the structure, clients can use the standard
 * comparison functions from cmpfn.h.  The third argument is a
 * function that initializes the client's fields in the node, which
 * is described in more detail in the comments for InsertBSTNode.
 */

bstADT NewBST(int size, cmpFnT cmpFn, nodeInitFnT nodeInitFn);
```

```
/*
 * Function: FreeBST
 * Usage: FreeBST(bst, freeNodeFn);
 * -------------------------------
 * This function frees the storage for a tree, but calls the
 * client-supplied freeNodeFn to free each individual node.
 * The clientData value passed to the callback function is
 * always NULL.
 */

void FreeBST(bstADT bst, nodeFnT freeNodeFn);

/*
 * Function: FindBSTNode
 * Usage: np = FindBSTNode(bst, &key);
 * -----------------------------------
 * This function applies the binary search algorithm to find a
 * particular key in the tree represented by bst.  The second
 * argument represents the address of the key in the client
 * space rather than the key itself, which makes it possible to
 * use this package for keys that are not pointer types.  If a
 * node matching the key appears in the tree, FindBSTNode
 * returns a pointer to it; if not, FindBSTNode returns NULL.
 */

void *FindBSTNode(bstADT bst, void *kp);

/*
 * Function: InsertBSTNode
 * Usage: np = InsertBSTNode(bst, &key, clientData);
 * -------------------------------------------------
 * This function is used to insert a new node into a binary search
 * tree.  The bst and &key arguments are interpreted as they are
 * in FindBSTNode.  If the key already exists, the result is
 * simply the address of the old node.  If the key is not found,
 * InsertBSTNode allocates a new node and then calls the node
 * initialization function specified in the NewBST call to
 * initialize it.  The call has the following form:
 *
 *     nodeInitFn(np, kp, clientData);
 *
 * where np is a pointer to the node, kp is the pointer to the key,
 * and clientData is the value (typically NULL) supplied in the
 * InsertBSTNode call.  The initialization function must initialize
 * the key field in the node, but may perform other initialization
 * as well.
 */

void *InsertBSTNode(bstADT bst, void *kp, void *clientData);
```

```
/*
 * Function: DeleteBSTNode
 * Usage: np = DeleteBSTNode(bst, &key);
 * ------------------------------------
 * This function deletes a node in the tree that matches the
 * specified key pointer.  The arguments are interpreted as
 * in FindBSTNode.  The function returns the address of the
 * deleted node so that clients can free its storage.  If the
 * key is not found in the tree, DeleteBSTNode returns NULL.
 */

void *DeleteBSTNode(bstADT bst, void *kp);

/*
 * Function: MapBST
 * Usage: MapBST(fn, bst, order, clientData);
 * ------------------------------------------
 * This function calls fn on every node in the binary search tree,
 * passing it a pointer to a node and the clientData pointer.  The
 * type of traversal is given by the order argument, which must
 * be one of the constants InOrder, PreOrder, or PostOrder.
 */

typedef enum { InOrder, PreOrder, PostOrder } traversalOrderT;

void MapBST(nodeFnT fn, bstADT bst, traversalOrderT order,
            void *clientData);

/*
 * Low-level functions: BSTRoot, BSTLeftChild, BSTRightChild
 * Usage: root = BSTRoot(bst);
 *        child = BSTLeftChild(bst, np);
 *        child = BSTRightChild(bst, np);
 * ---------------------------------------------------------------
 * These functions allow the client to trace the structure of the
 * binary search tree and are useful primarily for debugging.
 */

void *BSTRoot(bstADT bst);
void *BSTLeftChild(bstADT bst, void *np);
void *BSTRightChild(bstADT bst, void *np);

#endif
```

To understand the nature of the problem, it helps to think about how the client interface for the binary search tree differs from that of the symbol table abstraction in Chapter 11. In many respects, the two interfaces are similar. Both structures depend on the existence of a key that is unique to each entry in the structure. In addition, the fundamental operations for the binary search tree have much the same character as the Lookup and Enter functions from symtab.h. When you use a binary search tree, you want to be able to insert a node at the appropriate position in the tree and find an existing node containing a particular key.

There is, however, an important difference between the two interfaces. One of the design goals for the `bst.h` interface was that keys should not be constrained to the type `string` as they are in the symbol table package. As long as the binary search tree implementation knows how to compare two keys, the data type used to represent the key should not matter. In fact, there is no need to require that the key be of some pointer type. To implement the set abstraction in Chapter 15, for example, you need to use integers as keys. In the binary search tree, the key is simply part of the structure that forms a node. This fact turns out to have important implications for the interface design.

The critical question in designing a general abstraction for binary search trees is which side of the abstraction barrier is responsible for allocating a node. On the one hand, it is clear that the client has to be involved. Only the client knows the structure of the data in a node and must therefore be responsible for initializing newly created nodes. On the other hand, it is the implementation that knows *when* a node has to be created. New nodes are created in the binary search tree only if the key does not already exist. If a client inserts a key that matches an existing one, the standard interpretation—which is consistent with that used in symbol tables—is that the client wants to reuse the old node, presumably after updating some of its contents. As a result, the client cannot simply allocate a new node prior to calling `InsertBSTNode`. If the key already exists, a new node will not be needed.

It is important to note that it doesn't make sense for the client to call `FindBSTNode` to check whether a particular key exists before calling `InsertBSTNode` to insert it in the tree. Calling one function to find the node and another to insert it doubles the workload. Each of the functions requires an identical traversal of the binary search tree. To avoid the redundant tree traversal, the find and insert operations must be combined into a single function, which in turn forces the client and implementation to collaborate in the creation of new nodes.

To get a better sense of how the `bst.h` interface presented in Figure 13-9 makes this collaboration work, let's go back to the idea of inserting the symbols for the chemical elements into a binary search tree. It is hard to imagine why anyone would want to create a tree that contained *only* the symbols for the elements, even though the symbol—being unique—makes a perfectly reasonable key. If you are writing an application that works with elements at any level of detail, you would almost certainly want to store additional information as part of each node. For example, in addition to the symbol for the element, you might want to store its name, atomic number, and atomic weight, which suggests the following data structure for the node:

```
typedef struct {
    string symbol;
    string name;
    int atomicNumber;
    double atomicWeight;
} elementNodeT;
```

Thus, from the client's view, the node for the element helium would look like this:

He
Helium
2
4.0026

From the implementation side, however, the picture is more complicated. If you insert this node into a tree, it must also contain pointers to its left and right children. Thus, the actual node must be larger than the record the client can see. If the implementation allocates the storage for the node, it can leave extra space for its own data fields, in which case the entire record might look like this:

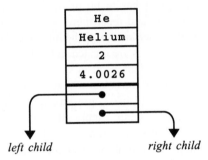

left child *right child*

The heavy line in the diagram divides the client data from the implementation data. Everything above that line belongs to the client. Everything below it—which might also include other fields necessary to keep the tree in balance—belongs to the implementation.

Both the client and the implementation typically work with pointers to nodes. From the client's perspective, the pointer refers to a record of the type defined by the client, which in this case is **elementNodeT**. Because the client cannot name fields beyond the end of this structure, the view from the client side looks like this:

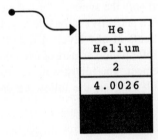

The implementation, however, sees a different picture. The details of the client record are no longer available, as illustrated by the following diagram:

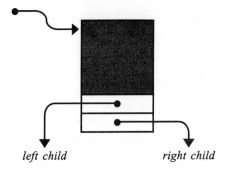

left child   *right child*

This strategy works well but has some implications for the design of the interface. In particular, the implementation needs to know the size of the client's data record, so that it can both allocate the necessary space and also find its own data fields from the base address of the node. In the `bst.h` interface shown in Figure 13-9, the `NewBST` function takes the size of the client's node structure as its first parameter. The `NewBST` function must also take the following function pointers:

- A comparison function that allows the implementation to compare a key to the keys stored in the existing nodes
- A node initialization function that is invoked whenever the implementation allocates a new node

In the `bst.h` interface, new nodes are created by the function `InsertBSTNode`, which typically appears in the following form:

```
np = InsertBSTNode(bst, &key, client data);
```

The *client data* argument makes it possible for clients to pass additional information to the callback function that initializes a node; in most applications, no additional information is necessary, in which case this argument is simply the `NULL` pointer. When `InsertBSTNode` is called, the function first performs a standard recursive search of the binary search tree looking for a node that matches the specified key. If it finds one, it returns a pointer to that node. If no such key appears, `InsertBSTNode` allocates storage for a new node and links it into the appropriate position in the tree. To initialize the data fields, the `InsertBSTNode` implementation calls the client-supplied function to initialize a node, which takes the following three arguments: a pointer to the newly created node, a pointer to the key, and the data pointer supplied by the client in the call to `InsertBSTNode`.

The primary responsibility of the node initialization function is to copy the key into its proper position in the node. In the binary search tree containing the element records, for example, the node initialization function might look like this:

```
static void InitElementNode(void *np, void *kp, void *clientData)
{
    ((elementNodeT *) np)->key = CopyString(*((string *) kp));
}
```

More sophisticated examples of node initialization functions appear in the symbol table implementation later in this chapter and in the implementation of sets in Chapter 15.

Generalizing the types used for keys

Allowing the client to use keys of any type is not particularly difficult. For the most part, the basic strategy is to have the client supply a comparison function as part of the call to `NewBST`. By storing a pointer to the client's comparison function in the data structure for the tree as a whole, the implementation can invoke that function whenever it needs to compare keys.

As indicated in the comments for the `NewBST` function, the `bst.h` interface guarantees that the comparison function will always be called with the following arguments:

> `cmpFn` (*address of the key to be found*, *address of the current node*)

This definition allows the key to be located anywhere within the client's data block. If the key happens to be the first field in the structure, however, the address of a node is also the address of its key. The advantage of these addresses being the same is that you can then use the standard comparison functions exported by `cmpfn.h` in conjunction with this package. For example, if the key is a string stored as the first field in the client's structure, the appropriate comparison function to pass to `NewBST` is `StringCmpFn`.

Deleting nodes

The operation of deleting a node from a binary search tree is not hard to define in the `bst.h` interface. In terms of the interface design, the only subtlety is that the client and implementation must cooperate to free the node, just as they did to allocate the node originally. The client can't free the data fields in a node before calling `DeleteBSTNode` because freeing the data fields also frees the key itself, which invalidates the structure of the tree. Conversely, the implementation can't free those data fields because it doesn't know what they are. The `DeleteBSTNode` function in the `bst.h` interface therefore simply removes the node from the tree without taking any action to free its storage. It does, however, return the deleted node so the client can free its internal data. Because the node is no longer part of the tree, this strategy makes it possible to free nodes without compromising the structure of the tree as a whole.

The interesting issues that arise in deleting a node are primarily the concern of the implementation. Finding the node to be deleted requires the same binary-search strategy as `FindBSTNode`. Once you find the appropriate node, however, you have to remove it from the tree without violating the ordering relationship that defines a binary search tree. Depending on where the node to be deleted appears in the tree, removing it can get rather tricky.

To get a sense of the problem, suppose that you are working with a binary search tree whose nodes have the following structure:

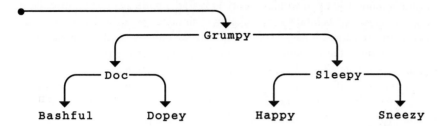

Deleting **Sneezy** (for creating an unhealthy work environment) is easy. All you have to do is replace the pointer to the **Sneezy** node with a **NULL** pointer, which produces the following tree:

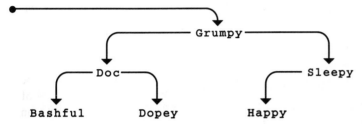

Starting from this configuration, it is also relatively easy to delete **Sleepy** (who has trouble staying awake on the job). If either child of the node you want to delete is **NULL**, all you have to do is replace it with its non-**NULL** child, like this:

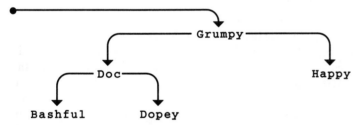

The problem arises if you try to delete a node with both a left and a right child. Suppose, for example, that you instead want to delete **Grumpy** (for failure to whistle while working) from the original tree containing all seven dwarves. If you simply delete the **Grumpy** node, you're left with two partial search trees, one rooted at **Doc** and one rooted at **Sleepy**, as follows:

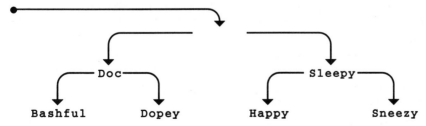

How can you patch things back together so that you have a valid binary search tree?

At this point, what you would like to do is find a node that can be inserted into the empty space left behind by the deletion of the `Grumpy` node. To ensure that the resulting tree remains a binary search tree, there are only two nodes you can use: the rightmost node in the left subtree or the leftmost node in the right subtree. These two nodes work equally well, and you can write the deletion algorithm using either one. For example, if you choose the rightmost node in the left subtree, you get the `Dopey` node, which is guaranteed to be larger than anything else in the left subtree but smaller than the values in the right subtree. To complete the deletion operation, all you have to do is replace the `Dopey` node with its left child—which may be `NULL`, as it is in this example—and then move the `Dopey` node into the deleted spot. The resulting picture looks like this:

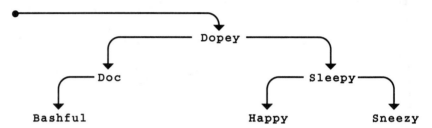

Implementing the binary search tree package

The code for the generalized binary search tree package, including the details of the deletion algorithm described in the preceding section, appears in Figure 13-10. This implementation does not include the AVL extension that keeps the nodes balanced. Allowing the tree to become out of balance increases the running time of the algorithm but does not compromise its correctness. You will have a chance to implement the self-balancing features in the exercises.

Implementing the `symtab.h` interface using binary trees

Once you have defined and implemented a general abstraction for binary search trees, you can use the `bst.h` interface as part of other applications. For example, you can easily use the `bst.h` interface to reimplement the symbol table package from Chapter 11. If you think about the problem in terms of what the symbol table package needs—as opposed to the details of the binary search tree itself—a node consists of a key and a value. If you define the type `symtabNodeT` as this pair and then pass its size to the `NewBST` function, the implementation can allocate a node of the correct size.

When you have access to the facilities exported by `bst.h`, writing the code to implement the `NewSymbolTable`, `Lookup`, and `Enter` functions becomes a simple task. The code for these functions appears in Figure 13-11, which appears on page 579, following the code that implements the `bst.h` interface.

FIGURE 13-10 Implementation of the `bst.h` interface

```
/*
 * File: bst.c
 * -----------
 * This file implements the bst.h interface, which provides a
 * general implementation of binary search trees.
 */

#include <stdio.h>
#include "genlib.h"
#include "cmpfn.h"
#include "bst.h"

/*
 * Type: treeT
 * -----------
 * Because the implementation does not know the structure of a
 * node, pointers to nodes cannot be defined explicitly and must
 * be represented using void *.  For readability, the code declares
 * any void * pointers that are in fact trees to be of type treeT.
 */

typedef void *treeT;

/*
 * Type: bstCDT
 * ------------
 * This type is the concrete type used to represent the bstADT.
 */

struct bstCDT {
    treeT root;
    int userSize, totalSize;
    cmpFnT cmpFn;
    nodeInitFnT nodeInitFn;
};

/*
 * Type: bstDataT
 * --------------
 * This record is allocated at the end of the client's structure
 * and is used to maintain the structure of the tree.  The code
 * calls BSTData on the node pointer to derive this address.
 */

typedef struct {
    treeT left, right;
} bstDataT;
```

```
/* Private function prototypes */

static treeT *RecFindNode(bstADT bst, treeT t, void *kp);
static void *RecInsertNode(bstADT bst, treeT *tptr, void *kp,
                           void *clientData);
static void *RecDeleteNode(bstADT bst, treeT *tptr, void *kp);
static void *DeleteTargetNode(bstADT bst, treeT *tptr);
static void RecMapBST(nodeFnT fn, bstADT bst, treeT t,
                      traversalOrderT order, void *clientData);
static bstDataT *BSTData(bstADT bst, treeT t);

/* Exported entries */

bstADT NewBST(int size, cmpFnT cmpFn, nodeInitFnT nodeInitFn)
{
    bstADT bst;

    bst = New(bstADT);
    bst->root = NULL;
    bst->userSize = size;
    bst->totalSize = bst->userSize + sizeof(bstDataT);
    bst->cmpFn = cmpFn;
    bst->nodeInitFn = nodeInitFn;
    return (bst);
}

void FreeBST(bstADT bst, nodeFnT freeNodeFn)
{
    MapBST(freeNodeFn, bst, PostOrder, NULL);
    FreeBlock(bst);
}

/*
 * Implementation notes: FindBSTNode, RecFindNode
 * ------------------------------------------------
 * The FindBSTNode function simply calls RecFindNode to do
 * the work.  The recursive function takes the address of
 * the current node along with the original arguments.
 */

void *FindBSTNode(bstADT bst, void *kp)
{
    return (RecFindNode(bst, bst->root, kp));
}
```

```
static treeT *RecFindNode(bstADT bst, treeT t, void *kp)
{
    bstDataT *dp;
    int sign;

    if (t == NULL) return (NULL);
    sign = bst->cmpFn(kp, t);
    if (sign == 0) return (t);
    dp = BSTData(bst, t);
    if (sign < 0) {
        return (RecFindNode(bst, dp->left, kp));
    } else {
        return (RecFindNode(bst, dp->right, kp));
    }
}

/*
 * Implementation notes: InsertBSTNode, RecInsertNode
 * ---------------------------------------------------
 * The InsertBSTNode function is implemented as a simple wrapper
 * to RecInsertNode, which does all the work.  The difference
 * between the prototypes is that RecInsertNode takes a pointer
 * to the root of the current subtree as an extra argument.
 */

void *InsertBSTNode(bstADT bst, void *kp, void *clientData)
{
    return (RecInsertNode(bst, &bst->root, kp, clientData));
}

static void *RecInsertNode(bstADT bst, treeT *tptr, void *kp,
                           void *clientData)
{
    bstDataT *dp;
    treeT t;
    int sign;

    t = *tptr;
    if (t == NULL) {
        t = GetBlock(bst->totalSize);
        bst->nodeInitFn(t, kp, clientData);
        dp = BSTData(bst, t);
        dp->left = dp->right = NULL;
        *tptr = t;
        return (t);
    }
    sign = bst->cmpFn(kp, t);
    if (sign == 0) return (t);
    dp = BSTData(bst, t);
    if (sign < 0) {
        return (RecInsertNode(bst, &dp->left, kp, clientData));
    } else {
        return (RecInsertNode(bst, &dp->right, kp, clientData));
    }
}
```

```
/*
 * Implementation notes: DeleteBSTNode, RecDeleteNode
 * ---------------------------------------------------
 * The first step in deleting a node is to find it using binary
 * search, which is performed by these two functions.  If the
 * node is found, DeleteTargetNode does the actual deletion.
 */

void *DeleteBSTNode(bstADT bst, void *kp)
{
    return (RecDeleteNode(bst, &bst->root, kp));
}

static void *RecDeleteNode(bstADT bst, treeT *tptr, void *kp)
{
    bstDataT *dp;
    treeT t;
    int sign;

    t = *tptr;
    if (t == NULL) return (NULL);
    sign = bst->cmpFn(kp, t);
    if (sign == 0) {
        return (DeleteTargetNode(bst, tptr));
    }
    dp = BSTData(bst, t);
    if (sign < 0) {
        return (RecDeleteNode(bst, &dp->left, kp));
    } else {
        return (RecDeleteNode(bst, &dp->right, kp));
    }
}
```

```
/*
 * Implementation notes: DeleteTargetNode
 * ---------------------------------------
 * This function deletes the node whose address is passed by
 * reference in tptr.  The easy case occurs when either of the
 * children is NULL; all you need to do is replace the node with
 * its non-NULL child.  If both children are non-NULL, this code
 * finds the rightmost descendant of the left child; this node
 * may not be a leaf, but will have no right child.  Its left
 * child replaces it in the tree, after which the replacement
 * node is moved to the position occupied by the target node.
 */

static void *DeleteTargetNode(bstADT bst, treeT *tptr)
{
    treeT target, *rptr;
    bstDataT *tdp, *rdp;

    target = *tptr;
    tdp = BSTData(bst, target);
    if (tdp->left == NULL) {
        *tptr = tdp->right;
    } else if (tdp->right == NULL) {
        *tptr = tdp->left;
    } else {
        rptr = &tdp->left;
        rdp = BSTData(bst, *rptr);
        while (rdp->right != NULL) {
            rptr = &rdp->right;
            rdp = BSTData(bst, *rptr);
        }
        *tptr = *rptr;
        *rptr = rdp->left;
        rdp->left = tdp->left;
        rdp->right = tdp->right;
    }
    return (target);
}

/*
 * Implementation notes: MapBST, RecMapBST
 * ----------------------------------------
 * The MapBST function is implemented as a wrapper to the
 * recursive function RecMapBST, which does the actual work.
 */

void MapBST(nodeFnT fn, bstADT bst, traversalOrderT order,
            void *clientData)
{
    RecMapBST(fn, bst, bst->root, order, clientData);
}
```

```
static void RecMapBST(nodeFnT fn, bstADT bst, treeT t,
                      traversalOrderT order, void *clientData)
{
    bstDataT *dp;

    if (t != NULL) {
        dp = BSTData(bst, t);
        if (order == PreOrder) fn(t, clientData);
        RecMapBST(fn, bst, dp->left, order, clientData);
        if (order == InOrder) fn(t, clientData);
        RecMapBST(fn, bst, dp->right, order, clientData);
        if (order == PostOrder) fn(t, clientData);
    }
}

/* Low-level functions */

void *BSTRoot(bstADT bst)
{
    return (bst->root);
}

void *BSTLeftChild(bstADT bst, void *np)
{
    bstDataT *dp;

    if (np == NULL) Error("BSTLeftChild: Argument is NULL");
    dp = BSTData(bst, np);
    return (dp->left);
}

void *BSTRightChild(bstADT bst, void *np)
{
    bstDataT *dp;

    if (np == NULL) Error("BSTRightChild: Argument is NULL");
    dp = BSTData(bst, np);
    return (dp->right);
}

static bstDataT *BSTData(bstADT bst, treeT t)
{
    return ((bstDataT *) ((char *) t + bst->userSize));
}
```

FIGURE 13-11   Implementation of symbol tables using binary search trees

```
/*
 * File: bsttab.c (excerpts)
 * ------------------------
 * This file implements the symtab.h interface using binary
 * search trees as the underlying representation.
 */

struct symtabCDT {
    bstADT bst;
};

typedef struct {
    string key;
    void *value;
} symtabNodeT;

symtabADT NewSymbolTable(void)
{
    symtabADT table;

    table = New(symtabADT);
    table->bst =
      NewBST(sizeof (symtabNodeT), StringCmpFn, InitEntry);
    return (table);
}

void Enter(symtabADT table, string key, void *value)
{
    symtabNodeT *np;

    np = InsertBSTNode(table->bst, &key, NULL);
    np->value = value;
}

void *Lookup(symtabADT table, string key)
{
    symtabNodeT *np;

    np = FindBSTNode(table->bst, &key);
    if (np == NULL) return (UNDEFINED);
    return (np->value);
}

/* Private functions */

static void InitEntry(void *np, void *kp, void *clientData)
{
    ((symtabNodeT *) np)->key = CopyString(*((string *) kp));
}
```

▇ Summary

In this chapter, you have been introduced to the concept of trees, which are hierarchical collections of nodes that obey the following properties:

- There is a single node at the top that forms the root of the hierarchy.
- Every node in the tree is connected to the root by a unique line of descent.

Important points in this chapter include:

- Many of the terms used to describe trees, such as *parent, child, ancestor, descendant,* and *sibling,* come directly from family trees. Other terms, including *root* and *leaf,* are derived from trees in nature. These metaphors make the terminology used for trees easy to understand because the words have the same interpretation in computer science as they do in these more familiar contexts.

- Trees have a well-defined recursive structure because every node in a tree is the root of a subtree. Thus, a tree consists of a node together with its set of children, each of which is a tree. This recursive structure is reflected in the underlying representation for trees, in which the type `treeT` is defined as a pointer to a `nodeT`, and the type `nodeT` is defined as a record containing values of type `treeT`.

- Binary trees are a subclass of trees in which nodes have at most two children and every node except the root is designated as either a left child or a right child of its parent.

- If a binary tree is organized so that every node in the tree contains a key field that follows all the keys in its left subtree and precedes all the keys in its right subtree, that tree is called a *binary search tree.* As its name implies, the structure of a binary search tree permits the use of the binary search algorithm, which makes it possible to find individual keys more efficiently. Because the keys are ordered, it is always possible to determine whether the key you're searching for appears in the left or right subtree of any particular node.

- Using recursion makes it easy to step through the nodes in a binary search tree, which is called *traversing* or *walking* the tree. There are several types of traversals, depending on the order in which the nodes are processed. If the key in each node is processed before the recursive calls to process the subtrees, the result is a *preorder* traversal. Processing each node after both recursive calls gives rise to a *postorder* traversal. Processing the current node between the two recursive calls represents an *inorder* traversal. In a binary search tree, the inorder traversal has the useful property that the keys are processed in order.

- Depending on the order in which nodes are inserted, given the same set of keys, binary search trees can have radically different structures. If the branches of the tree differ substantially in height, the tree is said to be unbalanced, which reduces its efficiency. By using techniques such as the

AVL algorithm described in this chapter, you can keep a tree in balance as new nodes are added.

- It is possible to design an interface for binary search trees that allows the client to control the structure and size of the individual nodes. The **bst.h** interface that appears in Figure 13-9 uses this strategy to export a flexible implementation of the binary search tree structure that can be used in a wide variety of applications.

REVIEW QUESTIONS

1. What two conditions must be satisfied for a collection of nodes to be a tree?

2. Give at least four real-world examples that involve tree structures.

3. Define the terms *parent, child, ancestor, descendant,* and *sibling* as they apply to trees.

4. The family tree for the House of Tudor, which ruled England in Shakespeare's time, is shown in Figure 13-12. Identify the root, leaf, and interior nodes. What is the height of this tree?

5. What is it about trees that makes them recursive?

6. Diagram the internal structure of the tree shown in Figure 13-12 when it is represented as a **familyTreeT**.

7. What is the defining property of a binary search tree?

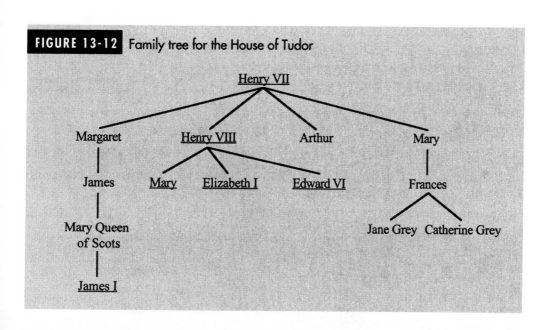

FIGURE 13-12 Family tree for the House of Tudor

8. Why are different type declarations used for the first argument in `FindNode` and `InsertNode`?

9. In *The Hobbit* by J. R. R. Tolkien, 13 dwarves arrive at the house of Bilbo Baggins in the following order: `Dwalin`, `Balin`, `Kili`, `Fili`, `Dori`, `Nori`, `Ori`, `Oin`, `Gloin`, `Bifur`, `Bofur`, `Bombur`, and `Thorin`. Diagram the binary search tree that results from inserting the names of these dwarves into an empty tree.

10. Given the tree you created in the preceding question, what key comparisons are made if you call `FindNode` on the name `Bombur`?

11. Write down the preorder, inorder, and postorder traversals of the binary search tree you created for question 9.

12. One of the three standard traversal orders for a binary search tree does not depend on the order in which the nodes are inserted. Is it the preorder, inorder, or postorder traversal?

13. What does it mean for a binary tree to be balanced?

14. For each of the following tree structures, indicate whether the tree is balanced:

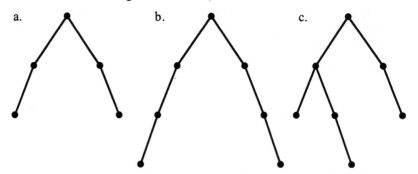

a. b. c.

For each of the unbalanced trees, indicate which nodes are out of balance.

15. True or false: If a binary search tree becomes unbalanced, the algorithms used in the functions `FindNode` and `InsertNode` will fail to work correctly.

16. How do you calculate the balance factor of a node?

17. Fill in the balance factors for each node in the following binary search tree:

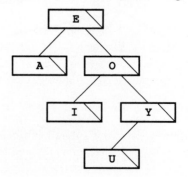

18. If you use the AVL balancing strategy, what rotation operation must you apply to the tree in the preceding question to restore its balanced configuration? What is the structure of the resulting tree, including the updated balance factors?

19. True or false: When you insert a new node into a balanced binary tree, you can always correct any resulting imbalance by performing one operation, which will be either a single or a double rotation.

20. As shown in the section on "Illustrating the AVL idea," inserting the symbols for the first six elements into an AVL tree results in the following configuration:

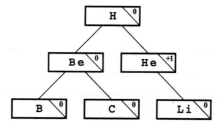

Show what happens to the tree as you add the next six element symbols:

    N   (Nitrogen)
    O   (Oxygen)
    F   (Fluorine)
    Ne   (Neon)
    Na   (Sodium)
    Mg   (Magnesium)

21. What four features of the `bst.h` interface are cited as advantages of its design?

22. Why does the `NewBST` function need to know the size of the node?

23. Describe in detail what happens when the `InsertBSTNode` function is called.

24. What strategy does the text suggest to avoid having a binary search tree become disconnected if you delete an interior node?

PROGRAMMING EXERCISES

1. Working from the definitions of `familyNodeT` and `familyTreeT` given in the section entitled "Representing family trees in C," write a function

    `familyTreeT ReadFamilyTree(string filename);`

that reads in a family tree from a data file whose name is supplied as the argument to the call. The first line of the file should contain a name corresponding to the root of the tree. All subsequent lines in the data file should have the following form:

    child:*parent*

where *child* is the name of the new individual being entered and *parent* is the name of that child's parent, which must appear earlier in the data file. For example, if the file `normandy.dat` contains the lines

```
William I
Robert:William I
William II:William I
Adela:William I
Henry I:William I
Stephan:Adela
William:Henry I
Matilda:Henry I
Henry II:Matilda
```

calling `ReadFamilyTree("normandy.dat")` should return the family-tree structure shown in Figure 13-2.

2. Write a function

    `void DisplayFamilyTree(familyTreeT tree);`

that displays all the individuals in a family tree. To record the hierarchy of the tree, the output of your program should indent each generation so that the name of each child appears two spaces to the right of the corresponding parent, as shown in the following sample run:

```
William I
  Robert
  William II
  Adela
    Stephan
  Henry I
    William
    Matilda
      Henry II
```

3. As defined in this chapter, the `familyNodeT` structure sets an upper bound on the number of children, which is indicated by the constant `MaxChildren`. Change the definition of `familyNodeT` so that the structure includes a dynamic array of children, along with a field indicating how many children that node has. Rewrite the `ReadFamilyTree` and `DisplayFamilyTree` functions so they are compatible with your new design.

4. As an alternative to the dynamic-array strategy described in the preceding exercise, you can also eliminate the restriction on the number of children per

node by linking the children together to form a list. In this design, each node in the tree needs to contain only two pointers: one to its eldest child and one to its next younger sibling. Using this representation, the tree for the House of Normandy looks like this:

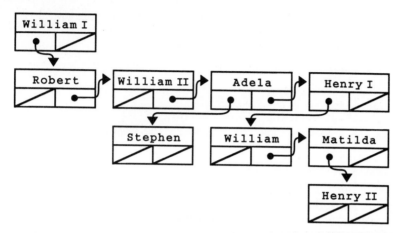

In each node, the pointer on the left always points down to a child; the pointer on the right indicates the next sibling in the same generation. Thus, the eldest child of William I is Robert, which you obtain by following the link at the left of the diagram. The remaining children are linked together through the link cells shown at the right of the node diagram. The chain of children ends at Henry I, which has the value NULL in its next-sibling link.

Using the linked design illustrated in this diagram, write new definitions of familyNodeT, ReadFamilyTree, and DisplayFamilyTree.

5. In exercises 3 and 4, the changes you made to the underlying representation of familyNodeT forced you to rewrite the functions that depend on that representation, such as ReadFamilyTree and DisplayFamilyTree. If the family tree were instead represented as an abstract type exported by an interface that maintained its structure despite any changes in representation, you could avoid much of this recoding. Such an interface appears in Figure 13-13. Write the corresponding implementation using the dynamic-array representation suggested in exercise 3.

Note that the abstract type exported by the famtree.h interface corresponds to an individual node rather than to the tree as a whole. From each node, you can find the parent using GetParent and the individual children using IthChild.

6. Using the famtree.h interface defined in the preceding exercise, write a function

```
personADT FindCommonAncestor(personADT p1, personADT p2);
```

that returns the closest ancestor shared by p1 and p2.

FIGURE 13-13 Interface for a package that supports the representation of family trees

```
/*
 * File: famtree.h
 * ---------------
 * This file is an interface to a simple family-tree package.
 */

#ifndef _famtree_h
#define _famtree_h

/*
 * Type: personADT
 * ---------------
 * This is the abstract type for a node in the family tree.
 */

typedef struct personCDT *personADT;

/*
 * Function: NewPerson
 * Usage: person = NewPerson(name, parent);
 * ----------------------------------------
 * This function creates a new personADT and makes that new
 * person the last child of the specified parent.  If parent
 * is NULL, this entry acts as the root of a tree.
 */

personADT NewPerson(string name, personADT parent);

/*
 * Functions: GetName, GetParent
 * Usage: name = GetName(person);
 *        parent = GetParent(person);
 * ---------------------------------
 * These functions select the name and parent fields, respectively.
 */

string GetName(personADT person);
personADT GetParent(personADT person);

/*
 * Functions: NChildren, IthChild
 * Usage: n = NChildren(person);
 *        child = IthChild(person, i);
 * ------------------------------------
 * The NChildren function returns the number of children for
 * the specified person, and IthChild selects a particular
 * child.  Children are numbered from 0, which indicates the
 * first child entered.
 */

int NChildren(personADT person);
personADT IthChild(personADT person, int i);

#endif
```

7. Write a function

   ```
   int Height(treeT tree);
   ```

   that takes a binary search tree—using the definition of **treeT** from Section 13.2 rather than the later definition of the abstract type **bstADT**—and returns its height.

8. Write a function

   ```
   bool IsBalanced(treeT tree);
   ```

   that determines whether a given tree is balanced according to the definition in the section on "Balanced trees." To solve this problem, all you really need to do is translate the definition of a balanced tree more or less directly into code. If you do so, however, the resulting implementation is likely to be relatively inefficient because it has to make several passes over the tree. The real challenge in this problem is to implement the **IsBalanced** function so that it determine the result without looking at any node more than once.

9. Write a function

   ```
   bool HasBinarySearchProperty(treeT tree);
   ```

   that takes a tree and determines whether it maintains the fundamental property that defines a binary search tree: that the key in each node follows every key in its left subtree and precedes every key in its right subtree.

10. Write a test program for the **bst** package that uses the graphics library described in Section 5.3 to display the structure of the tree. For example, if you insert the keys **First**, **Second**, **Third**, **Fourth**, and **Fifth** into a binary search tree without balancing, your program should display the following diagram in the graphics window:

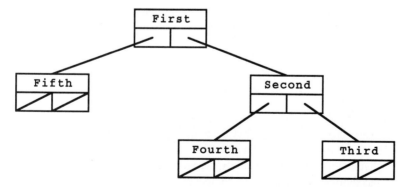

Including the keys as part of the node diagram will require you to use the extended version of the graphics library interface, **extgraph.h**, which is available for many systems as part of the Addison-Wesley software archive.

Even without it, you can construct the line drawing for the nodes from the simple commands available in the simpler `graphics.h` interface.

11. Extend the implementation of the `bst` package so that it uses the AVL algorithm to keep the tree balanced as new nodes are inserted. The algorithm for balanced insertion is coded in Figure 13-7. Your task in this problem is simply to integrate this algorithm into the more general implementation of binary search trees given in Figure 13-10.

12. Integrating the AVL algorithm for inserting a node into the `bst.c` implementation only solves part of the balancing problem for the generalized `bst` package. Because the `bst.h` interface also exports a function to delete a node from the tree, the complete implementation of the package must also rebalance the tree when a node is removed. The structure of the algorithm to rebalance after deletion is similar to that for insertion. Deleting a node either may have no effect on the height of a tree or may shorten it by one. If a tree gets shorter, the balance factor in its parent node changes. If the parent node becomes out of balance, it is possible to rebalance the tree at that point by performing either a single or a double rotation.

    Revise the implementation of the `DeleteBSTNode` function so that it keeps the underlying AVL tree balanced. Think carefully about the various cases that can arise and make sure that your implementation handles each of these cases correctly.

13. From a practical standpoint, the AVL algorithm is too aggressive. Because it requires that the heights of the subtrees at each node never differ by more than one, the AVL algorithm spends a fair amount of time performing rotation operations to correct imbalances that occur as new nodes are inserted. If you allow trees to become somewhat more unbalanced—but still keep the subtrees relatively similar—you can reduce the balancing overhead significantly.

    One of the most popular techniques for managing binary search trees uses a structure called a **red-black tree,** a self-balancing tree in which every node is assigned a color, either red or black. A binary search tree is a legal red-black tree if all three of the following properties hold:

    1. The root node is black.
    2. The parent of every red node is black.
    3. Every path from the root to a leaf contains the same number of black nodes.

These properties ensure that the longest path from the root to a leaf can never be more than twice the length of the shortest path. Given the rules, you know that every such path has the same number of black nodes, which means that the shortest possible path is composed entirely of black nodes, and the longest has black and red nodes alternating down the chain. Although this condition is less strict than the definition of a balanced tree used in the AVL algorithm, it is sufficient to guarantee that the operations of finding and inserting new nodes both run in logarithmic time.

The key to making red-black trees work is finding an insertion algorithm that allows you to add new nodes while maintaining the conditions that define red-black trees. The algorithm has much in common with the AVL algorithm and uses the same rotation operations. The first step is to insert the new node using the standard insertion algorithm with no balancing. The new node always replaces a NULL entry at some point in the tree. If the node is the first node entered into the tree, it becomes the root and is therefore colored black. In all other cases, the new node must initially be colored red to avoid violating the rule that every path from the root to a leaf must contain the same number of black nodes.

As long as the parent of the new node is black, the tree as a whole remains a legal red-black tree. The problem arises if the parent node is also red, which means that the tree violates the second condition, which requires that every red node have a black parent. In this case, you need to restructure the tree to restore the red-black condition. Depending on the relationship of the red-red pair to the remaining nodes in the tree, you can eliminate the problem by performing one of the following operations:

1. A single rotation, coupled with a recoloring that leaves the top node black.
2. A double rotation, coupled with a recoloring that leaves the top node black.
3. A simple change in node colors that leaves the top node red and may therefore require further restructuring at a higher level in the tree.

These three operations are illustrated in Figure 13-14. The diagram shows only the cases in which the imbalance occurs on the left side. Imbalances on the right side are treated symmetrically.

Change the implementation of the **bst** package in Figure 13-10 so that it uses red-black trees to maintain balance.

14. Complete the implementation of the symbol-table package based on binary search trees, which appears in a partial form in Figure 13-11. The missing functions are **FreeSymbolTable** and **MapSymbolTable**, although you might also want to implement a function **DeleteSymbol(table, key)**, which deletes the specified key from the symbol table.

FIGURE 13-14 Balancing operations on red-black trees

Case 1: N_4 is black (or nonexistent); N_1 and N_2 are out of balance in the same direction

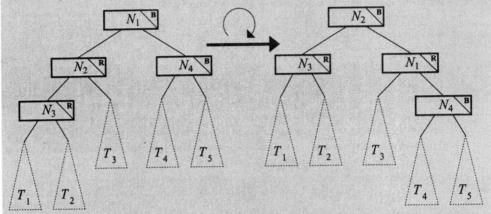

Case 2: N_4 is black (or nonexistent); N_1 and N_2 are out of balance in opposite directions

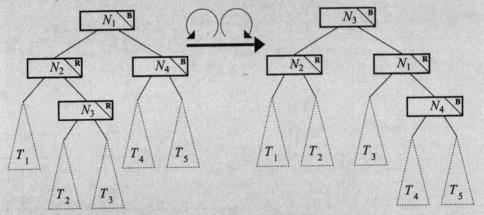

Case 3: N_4 is red; the relative balance of N_1 and N_2 does not matter

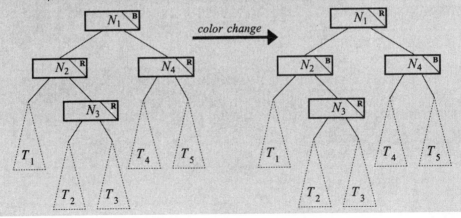

15. Trees have many applications beyond those listed in this chapter. For example, trees can be used to implement a lexicon, which was introduced as an abstract type in exercise 12 from Chapter 8. The resulting structure, first developed by Edward Fredkin in 1960, is called a **trie.** (Over time, the pronunciation of this word has evolved to the point that it is now pronounced like *try,* even though the name comes from the central letters of *retrieval.*) The trie-based implementation of a lexicon, while somewhat inefficient in its use of space, makes it possible to determine whether a word is in the lexicon much more quickly than you can using a hash table.

   At one level, a trie is simply a tree in which each node branches in as many as 26 ways, one for each possible letter of the alphabet. When you use a trie to represent a lexicon, the words are stored implicitly in the structure of the tree and represented as a succession of links moving downward from the root. The root of the tree corresponds to the empty string, and each successive level of the tree corresponds to the subset of the entire word list formed by adding one more letter to the string represented by its parent. For example, the *A* link descending from the root leads to the subtree containing all the words beginning with *A,* the B link from that node leads to the subtree containing all the words beginning with *AB,* and so forth. Each node begins with a flag indicating whether the substring that ends at that particular point is a legitimate word.

   The structure of a trie is much easier to understand by example than by definition. Figure 13-15 shows a trie containing the symbols for the first six elements—H, He, Li, Be, B, and C—in which upper- and lowercase letters are considered identical. The root of the tree corresponds to the empty string, which is not a legal symbol, as indicated by the designation no in the field at the beginning of the structure. The link labeled B from the node at the root of the trie descends to a node corresponding to the string "B". The initial field of this node contains yes, which indicates that the string "B" is a complete symbol in its own right. From this node, the link labeled E leads to a new node, which indicates that the string "BE" is a legal symbol as well. The NULL pointers in the trie indicate that no legal symbols appear in the subtree beginning with that substring and therefore make it possible to terminate the search process.

   Write an implementation of the `lexicon.h` interface shown in Figure 8-9 that uses a trie as its internal representation.

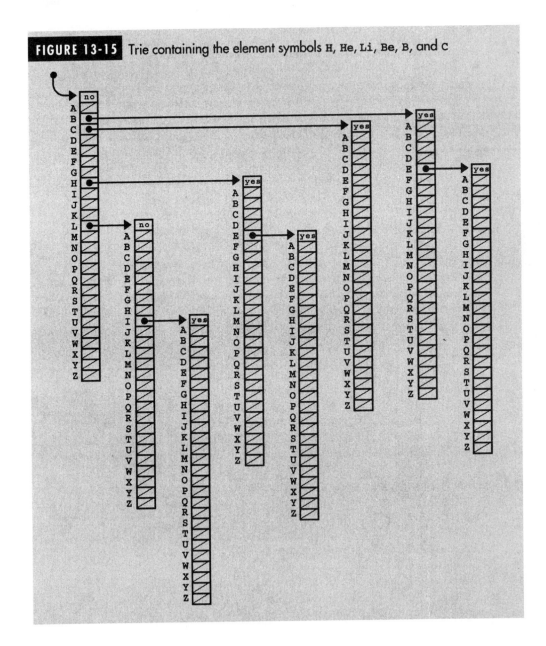

FIGURE 13-15   Trie containing the element symbols H, He, Li, Be, B, and C

CHAPTER 14

Expression Trees

"What's twice eleven?" I said to Pooh.
("Twice what?" said Pooh to Me.)
"I *think* it ought to be twenty-two."
"Just what I think myself," said Pooh.

— A. A. Milne, "Us Two," *Now We Are Six,* 1927

Objectives

- To appreciate how you can use trees to interpret expressions in a programming language.

- To recognize the recursive structure of expressions and understand how you can represent that structure in C.

- To learn how to use union types to represent values that have more than one interpretation.

- To understand the process of parsing the text representation of an expression into its internal form.

- To be able to write simple recursive functions that manipulate expression trees.

Chapter 13 focused on binary search trees because they provide a simple context for explaining how trees work. Trees occur in many other programming contexts as well. In particular, trees often show up in the implementation of compilers, because they are ideal for representing the hierarchical structure of a program. By exploring this topic in some detail, you will learn a lot, not only about trees, but also about the compilation process itself. Understanding how compilers work removes some of the mystery surrounding programming and makes it easier to understand the programming process as a whole.

Unfortunately, designing a complete compiler is far too complex to serve as a useful illustration. Typical commercial compilers require many person-years of programming, much of which is beyond the scope of this text. Even so, it is possible to give you a sense of how they work—and, in particular, of how trees fit into the process—by making the following simplifications:

- *Having you build an interpreter instead of a compiler.* As described in the section on "What is C?" in Chapter 1, a compiler translates a program into machine-language instructions that the computer can then execute directly. Although it has much in common with a compiler, an **interpreter** never actually translates the source code into machine language but simply performs the operations necessary to achieve the effect of the compiled program. Interpreters are generally easier to write, but have the disadvantage that interpreted programs tend to run much more slowly than their compiled counterparts.

- *Focusing only on the problem of evaluating arithmetic expressions.* A full-scale language translator for a modern programming language—whether a compiler or an interpreter—must be able to process control statements, function calls, type definitions, and many other language constructs. Most of the fundamental techniques used in language translation, however, are illustrated in the seemingly simple task of translating arithmetic expressions. For the purpose of this chapter, arithmetic expressions will be limited to constants and variables combined using the operators +, -, *, /, and = (assignment). As in C, parentheses may be used to define the order of operations, which is otherwise determined by applying precedence rules.

- *Limiting the types used in expressions to integers.* Modern programming languages like C allow expressions to manipulate data of many different types. In this chapter, all data values are assumed to be of type int, which simplifies the structure of the interpreter considerably.

■■■ 14.1 Overview of the interpreter

The goal of this chapter is to show you how to design a program that accepts arithmetic expressions from the user and then displays the results of evaluating those expressions. The basic operation of the interpreter is therefore to execute the following steps repeatedly as part of a loop in the main program:

1. Read in an expression from the user and translate it into an appropriate internal form.

2. Evaluate the expression to produce an integer result.

3. Print the result of the evaluation on the console.

This iterated process is characteristic of interpreters and is called a **read-eval-print loop.**

At this level of abstraction, the code for the read-eval-print interpreter is extremely simple. Although the final version of the program will include a little more code than is shown here, the following main program captures the essence of the interpreter:

```
main()
{
    expressionADT exp;
    int value;

    while (TRUE) {
        exp = ReadExp();
        value = EvalExp(exp);
        printf("%d\n", value);
    }
}
```

As you can see, the idealized structure of the main program is simply a loop that calls functions to accomplish each phase of the read-eval-print loop. In this formulation, the task of reading an expression is indicated by a call to the function `ReadExp`, which will be replaced in subsequent versions of the interpreter program with a somewhat longer sequence of statements. Conceptually, `ReadExp` is responsible for reading an expression from the user and converting it into its internal representation, which takes the form of an `expressionADT`. The task of evaluating the expression falls to `EvalExp`, which takes an `expressionADT` and returns the integer you get if you apply all the operators in the expression in the appropriate order. The print phase of the read-eval-print loop is accomplished by a simple call to `printf` that displays the result.

The operation of the `ReadExp` function consists of the three following steps:

1. *Input.* The input phase consists of reading in a line of text from the user, which can be accomplished with a simple call to the `GetLine` function from `simpio.h`.

2. *Lexical analysis.* The lexical analysis phase consists of dividing the input line into individual units called *tokens,* each of which represents a single logical entity, such as an integer constant, an operator, or a variable name. Fortunately, all the facilities required to implement lexical analysis are provided by the scanner abstraction introduced in Chapter 8.

3. *Parsing.* Once the line has been broken down into its component tokens, the parsing phase consists of determining whether the individual tokens represent a legal expression and, if so, what the structure of that expression is. To do so, the parser must determine how to construct a valid parse tree from the individual tokens in the input.

It would be easy enough to implement `ReadExp` as a single function that combined these steps. In many applications, however, having a `ReadExp` function is not really what you want. Keeping the individual phases of `ReadExp` separate gives you more flexibility in designing the interpreter structure. The complete implementation of the main module for the interpreter therefore includes explicit code for each of the three phases, as shown in Figure 14-1.

FIGURE 14-1 Main module for the interpreter

```
/*
 * File: interp.c
 * ---------------
 * This program simulates the top level of a programming
 * language interpreter.  The program reads an expression,
 * evaluates the expression, and displays the result.
 */

#include <stdio.h>
#include "genlib.h"
#include "strlib.h"
#include "simpio.h"
#include "exp.h"
#include "eval.h"
#include "parser.h"
#include "scanadt.h"

/* Main program */

main()
{
    scannerADT scanner;
    expressionADT exp;
    string line;
    int value;

    InitVariableTable();
    scanner = NewScanner();
    SetScannerSpaceOption(scanner, IgnoreSpaces);
    while (TRUE) {
        printf("=> ");
        line = GetLine();
        if (StringEqual(line, "quit")) break;
        SetScannerString(scanner, line);
        exp = ParseExp(scanner);
        value = EvalExp(exp);
        printf("%d\n", value);
    }
}
```

A sample run of the interpreter might look like this:

```
=> x = 6.⏎
6
=> y = 10.⏎
10
=> 2 * x + 3 * y.⏎
72
=> 2 * (x + 3) * y.⏎
180
=> quit.⏎
```

As the sample run illustrates, the interpreter allows assignment to variables and adheres to C's precedence conventions by evaluating multiplication before addition.

Although the code for the main program is straightforward, you still have some unfinished business. First, you need to think about exactly what expressions are and how to represent them as a data type. Second, you have to implement the functions `ParseExp` and `EvalExp`. Because each of these problems involves some subtlety, completing the interpreter will take up the remainder of the chapter.

▆▆ 14.2 The abstract structure of expressions

Your first task in completing the interpreter is to understand the concept of an expression and how that concept can be represented as an abstract type. As is often the case when you are thinking about a programming abstraction, it make sense to begin with the insights you have acquired about expressions from your experience as a C programmer. For example, you know that the lines

```
0
2 * 11
3 * (a + b + c)
x = x + 1
```

represent legal expressions in C. At the same time, you also know that the lines

```
2 * (x - y
17 k
```

are not expressions; the first has unbalanced parentheses, and the second is missing an operator. An important part of understanding expressions is articulating what constitutes an expression so that you can differentiate legal expressions from malformed ones.

A recursive definition of expressions

As it happens, the best way to define the structure of a legal expression is to adopt a recursive perspective. A sequence of symbols is an expression if it has one of the following forms:

1. An integer constant
2. A variable name
3. An expression enclosed in parentheses
4. A sequence of two expressions separated by an operator

The first two possibilities represent the simple cases for the recursive definition. The remaining possibilities, however, define an expression in terms of simpler ones.

To see how you might apply this recursive definition, consider the following sequence of symbols:

```
y = 3 * (x + 1)
```

Does this sequence constitute an expression? You know from experience that the answer is yes, but you can use the recursive definition of an expression to justify that answer. The integer constants 3 and 1 are expressions according to rule #1. Similarly, the variable names **x** and **y** are expressions as specified by rule #2. Thus, you already know that the expressions marked by the symbol *exp* in the following diagram are expressions, as defined by the simple-case rules:

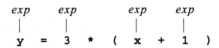

At this point, you can start to apply the recursive rules. Given that **x** and **1** are both expressions, you can tell that the string of symbols **x + 1** is an expression by applying rule #4, because it consists of two expressions separated by an operator. You can record this observation in the diagram by adding a new expression marker tied to the parts of the expression that match the rule, as shown:

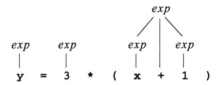

The parenthesized quantity can now be identified as an expression according to rule #3, which results in the following diagram:

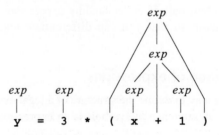

By applying rule #4 two more times to take care of the remaining operators, you can show that the entire set of characters is indeed an expression, as follows:

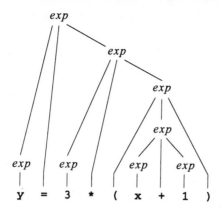

As you can see, this diagram forms a tree. A tree that demonstrates how a sequence of input symbols fits the syntactic rules of a programming language is called a **parse tree.**

Ambiguity

Generating a parse tree from a sequence of symbols requires a certain amount of caution. Given the four rules for expressions outlined in the preceding section, you can form more than one parse tree for the expression

```
y = 3 * (x + 1)
```

Although the tree structure shown at the end of the last section presumably represents what the programmer intended, it is just as valid to argue that $y = 3$ is an expression according to rule #4, and that the entire expression therefore consists of the expression $y = 3$, followed by a multiplication sign, followed by the expression $(x + 1)$. This argument ultimately reaches the same conclusion about whether the input line represents an expression, but generates a different parse tree. Both parse trees are shown in Figure 14-2. The parse tree on the left is the one generated in the last section and corresponds to what a C programmer means by that expression. The parse tree on the right represents a legal application of the expression rules but reflects an incorrect ordering of the operations, given C's rules of precedence.

   The problem with the second parse tree is that it ignores the mathematical rule specifying that multiplication is performed before assignment. The recursive definition of an expression indicates only that a sequence of two expressions separated by an operator is an expression; it says nothing about the relative precedence of the different operators and therefore admits both the intended and unintended interpretations. Because it allows multiple interpretations of the same string, the informal definition of expression given in the preceding section is said to be **ambiguous.** To resolve the ambiguity, the parsing algorithm must include some mechanism for determining the order in which operators are applied.

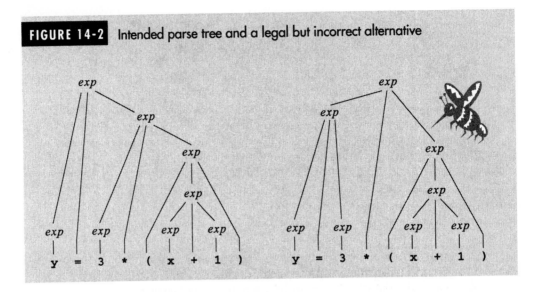

FIGURE 14-2 Intended parse tree and a legal but incorrect alternative

The question of how to resolve the ambiguity in an expression during the parsing phase is discussed in the section on "Parsing an expression" later in this chapter. At the moment, the point of introducing parse trees is to provide some insight into how you might represent an expression as a data structure. To this end, it is extremely important to make the following observation about the parse trees in Figure 14-2: the trees themselves are not ambiguous. The structure of each parse tree explicitly represents the structure of the expression. The ambiguity exists only in deciding how to generate the parse tree from the original string of constants, variables, and operators. Once you have the correct parse tree, its structure contains everything you need to understand the order in which the operators need to be applied.

Expression trees

In fact, parse trees contain more information than you need in the evaluation phase. Parentheses are useful in determining how to generate the parse tree but play no role in the evaluation of an expression once its structure is known. If your concern is simply to find the value of an **expressionADT**, you do not need to include parentheses within the structure. This observation allows you to simplify a complete parse tree into an abstract structure called an **expression tree** that is more appropriate to the evaluation phase. In the expression tree, nodes in the parse tree that represent parenthesized subexpressions are eliminated. Moreover, it is convenient to drop the *exp* labels from the tree and instead mark each node in the tree with the appropriate operator symbol. For example, the intended interpretation of the expression

```
y = 3 * (x + 1)
```

corresponds to the following expression tree:

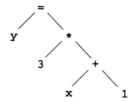

The structure of an expression tree is similar in many ways to the binary search tree from Chapter 13, but there are also some important differences. In the binary search tree, every node had the same structure. In an expression tree, there are three different types of nodes, as follows:

1. *Integer nodes* represent integer constants, such as 3 and 1 in the example tree.
2. *Identifier nodes* represent the names of variables and are presumably represented internally by a string.
3. *Compound nodes* represent the application of an operator to two operands, each of which is an arbitrary expression tree.

Each of these node types corresponds to one of the rules in the recursive formulation of an expression. The abstract interface that exports the **expressionADT** type must make it possible for clients to work with nodes of all three types. Similarly, the underlying implementation must somehow make it possible for different node structures to coexist within the tree.

Defining an abstract interface for expressions

Most of the complexity associated with representing expression trees in C lies in the underlying implementation. Defining the abstract interface is simply a matter of giving clients—in particular, the parser and the evaluator—the operations they need to manipulate expression trees. The parser needs to be able to construct new expression trees of each of the possible types. The evaluator needs to be able to walk through the structure of a tree, figuring out the types of the individual nodes and, if necessary, selecting their components.

The **exp.h** interface therefore needs constructor and selection functions such as those defined for the **listADT** in Chapter 12. Instead of exporting one constructor function, however, the **exp.h** interface must export three—one for each possible node type. The arguments to those constructors depend on the type of node. To construct an integer node, for example, you need to know the value of the integer constant. To construct a compound node, you need to specify the operator along with the left and right subexpressions. The selector functions exported by **exp.h** must make it possible, given a node of the appropriate type, to obtain the components used to construct it.

In addition to selecting the components of a given expression node, it must also be possible to determine what type of node it is. The easiest way to provide this capability in the **exp.h** interface is to define the following enumeration type, which defines names for each of the possible expression formats:

```
typedef enum {
    IntegerType,
    IdentifierType,
    CompoundType
} exptypeT;
```

By exporting this enumeration type along with a function **ExpType** that returns the type of an individual **expressionADT**, clients such as the evaluator can easily determine whether they are working with an integer, an identifier, or a compound node.

Figure 14-3 shows the definition of an **exp.h** interface that provides the necessary operations. Like the **list.h** interface in Chapter 12, the **exp.h** interface exports an immutable type, in the sense that a value of type **expressionADT**, once created, will never change. Although clients are free to select components or to embed existing expressions in larger ones, the interface offers no facilities for changing the components of any node. Using an immutable type to represent expressions helps enforce the separation between the implementation of the **expressionADT** type and its clients. Because those clients are prohibited from making changes in the underlying representation, they are unable to change the internal structure in a way that violates the requirements for expression trees.

As written, the **exp.h** interface exports only the constructor and selector functions for the abstract expression type. There are, however, other operations on expressions that you might at first think belong in this interface. For example, the main program for the interpreter calls the functions **ParseExp** and **EvalExp**, which are in some sense part of the abstract behavior of the expression type. This observation raises the question of whether the **exp.h** interface should export those functions as well.

Although **ParseExp** and **EvalExp** must be defined somewhere in the code, exporting them through the **exp.h** interface may not be the best design strategy. In a full-scale interpreter, the parser and the evaluator each require a significant amount of code—enough to warrant making these phases complete modules in their own right. In the stripped-down version of the interpreter presented in this chapter, the code is much smaller. Even so, it makes sense to partition the phases of the interpreter into separate modules for the following reasons:

1. *The resulting modular decomposition resembles more closely the structure you would tend to encounter in practice.* Full-scale interpreters are divided into separate modules; following this convention even in our restricted example clarifies how the pieces fit together.

2. *The program will be easier to maintain as you add features.* Getting the module structure right early in the implementation of a large system makes it easier for that system to evolve smoothly over time. If you start with a single module and later discover that the program is growing too large, it usually takes more work to separate the modules than it would have earlier in the program evolution.

FIGURE 14-3 An abstract interface for expressions

```
/*
 * File: exp.h
 * -----------
 * This interface defines an abstract type for expressions,
 * which allows the client to represent and manipulate simple
 * binary expression trees.
 */

#ifndef _exp_h
#define _exp_h

#include "genlib.h"

/*
 * Type: expressionADT
 * -------------------
 * This type is used to represent the abstract notion of an
 * expression, such as one you might encounter in a C program.
 * An expression is defined recursively to be one of the
 * following:
 *
 * 1. A constant
 * 2. A string representing an identifier
 * 3. Two expressions combined by an operator
 */

typedef struct expressionCDT *expressionADT;

/*
 * Type: exptypeT
 * --------------
 * This enumeration type is used to differentiate the three
 * expression types: integers, identifiers, and compounds.
 */

typedef enum {
    IntegerType,
    IdentifierType,
    CompoundType
} exptypeT;
```

```
/* Constructor functions */

/*
 * Function: NewIntegerExp
 * Usage: exp = NewIntegerExp(n);
 * -------------------------------
 * This function allocates a new expression node of type
 * IntegerType containing the integer n as its value.
 */

expressionADT NewIntegerExp(int n);

/*
 * Function: NewIdentifierExp
 * Usage: exp = NewIdentifierExp(id);
 * ----------------------------------
 * This function allocates a new expression node of type
 * IdentifierType containing the specified id.
 */

expressionADT NewIdentifierExp(string id);

/*
 * Function: NewCompoundExp
 * Usage: exp = NewCompoundExp(op, lhs, rhs);
 * ------------------------------------------
 * This function allocates a new expression node of type
 * CompoundType, which is composed of the operator (op)
 * and the left and right subexpressions (lhs and rhs).
 */

expressionADT NewCompoundExp(char op,
                             expressionADT lhs,
                             expressionADT rhs);

/* Selector functions */

/*
 * Function: ExpType
 * Usage: tc = ExpType(exp);
 * -------------------------
 * This function returns the type of the expression.
 */

exptypeT ExpType(expressionADT exp);

/*
 * Function: ExpInteger
 * Usage: n = ExpInteger(exp);
 * ---------------------------
 * This function returns the integer stored in an expression,
 * which must be of type IntegerType.
 */

int ExpInteger(expressionADT exp);
```

```
/*
 * Function: ExpIdentifier
 * Usage: id = ExpIdentifier(exp);
 * -------------------------------
 * This function returns the identifier stored in an
 * expression, which must be of type IdentifierType.
 */

string ExpIdentifier(expressionADT exp);

/*
 * Function: ExpOperator
 * Usage: op = ExpOperator(exp);
 * -----------------------------
 * This function returns the operator stored in an expression,
 * which must be of type CompoundType.
 */

char ExpOperator(expressionADT exp);

/*
 * Functions: ExpLHS, ExpRHS
 * Usage: lhs = ExpLHS(exp);
 *        rhs = ExpRHS(exp);
 * -------------------------
 * These functions return the left and right subexpressions
 * from exp, which must be of type CompoundType.
 */

expressionADT ExpLHS(expressionADT exp);
expressionADT ExpRHS(expressionADT exp);

#endif
```

3. *Using separate modules for the parser and evaluator makes it easier to substitute new implementations.* One of the principal advantages of using a modular design is that doing so makes it easier to substitute one implementation of an interface for another. For example, the section on "Parsing" later in this chapter defines two different implementations of the **ParseExp** function. If **ParseExp** is exported by the **exp.h** interface, it is more difficult to substitute a new implementation than it would be if **ParseExp** were exported from a separate module.

For these reasons, the **exp.h** interface exports only the types needed to represent expressions, along with the constructor and selector functions required to manipulate them. The **ParseExp** function is exported by a separate interface called **parser.h**; the **EvalExp** function is exported by an interface called **eval.h**.

14.3 Defining the concrete expression type

Although the `exp.h` interface is relatively easy to define, implementing that interface turns out to be more complicated. As noted earlier, the source of the problem is that expression trees can contain three different types of nodes. To represent such a structure, you need to define a concrete representation for nodes that allows them to have different structures depending on their type. An integer node, for example, must include the value of the integer as part of its internal structure. An identifier node must include the name of the identifier. A compound node must include the operator along with the left and right subexpressions. Defining a single concrete type that allows nodes to take on these different underlying structures requires you to learn a new aspect of C's type system, which is introduced in the next section.

Union types

In some applications, it is important to store a value whose conceptual type changes over the lifetime of a program. Imagine, for example, that you are using C to implement a language in which variables may contain values that may be either integers, floating-point values, or character strings. You want to reserve storage for such variables, even though their types may change dynamically during the course of the program. You can solve this problem by making use of a low-level facility called *union types*. A **union type** is exactly like a record type except that every field in the union refers to the same region of memory. Although the fields of a union specify the same physical storage, the fact that the fields typically have different types means that using different field names can affect how the contents of memory are interpreted as data values.

To understand the concept of a union type, it helps to review how records work in C. The following declaration introduces a new record variable named `s`:

```
struct {
    int intField;
    double dblField;
    string strField;
} s;
```

The variable `s` is composed of three fields: one of type `int`, one of type `double`, and one of type `string`. In memory, each of these fields is assigned to a distinct location. For example, assuming that values of type `int` and `string` each require four bytes of storage and that a `double` requires eight, the data structure for `s` requires 16 bytes, which are likely to be laid out as follows:[1]

---

[1] C compilers actually have some flexibility in how they assign fields of a structure to memory locations. For example, some compilers sometimes leave gaps between fields of different sizes to ensure that the hardware can successfully refer to each of the fields. The point of this example is not that the fields are necessarily consecutive but rather that they are not overlapping.

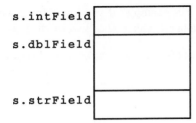

s.intField

s.dblField

s.strField

Now consider the almost identical union definition

```
union {
    int intRep;
    double dblRep;
    string strRep;
} u;
```

which declares the variable **u** to be a union. Like **s**, the variable **u** has three fields. The difference is that these fields all start at the beginning of the structure and share the same storage. Moreover, the union requires only as much storage as the largest field it contains. Using the same sizes for each field as in the record example, the largest field would be the eight-byte **double**, so the entire union would require eight bytes. The selection expressions **u.intRep** and **u.strRep** refer to the first four bytes of storage; the expression **u.dblRep** covers those four bytes plus the remaining four as well. Thus, the fields of the union are arranged like this:

u.intRep
u.strRep

u.dblRep

Because its fields share the same memory, a union can hold only one value at a time. The advantage is that the type of that value can vary over the possibilities listed in the union definition. In this example, you might choose to store a value of type **int**, **double**, or **string** in the variable **u**, but you could only store one of those values at any particular time.

The field names in the union definition make it possible for you to tell the compiler how you are using the storage at any particular moment. For example, to store an integer in the memory assigned to the variable **u**, you might write something like

```
u.intRep = 4;
```

To store a string value, you need to specify the **strRep** field instead by using an assignment statement such as

```
u.strRep = "Hello, world."
```

Similarly, if you want to look at the value stored in **u**, you need to specify the appropriate field name so that the compiler knows how you intend to interpret the value in that memory location. For example, if you know that a union contains a floating-point value, you can display its value by calling `printf`, as follows:

```
printf("Double representation of u = %g\n", u.dblRep);
```

Alternatively, if you know that u contains a string, you can display the string like this:

```
printf("String representation of u = %s\n", u.strRep);
```

It is usually more convenient to think of the component names within a union as *interpretations* rather than as *fields*. Thus, when you write

```
u.intRep
```

you are asking for the integer interpretation of u and not really for an `intRep` component.

But how do you know which interpretation to use? Suppose that you wrote the assignment statement

```
u.intRep = 4;
```

and then, without making any further assignments to u, you executed the statement

```
printf("String representation of u = %s\n", u.strRep);
```

What would the program do? Unfortunately, typical C compilers don't complain if you assign an object of type `int` to the union type and later try to reference it as type `string`. Instead, the compiler simply generates code that interprets the memory as you specify. In this case, the compiler will take the integer 4 and try to display a character string beginning at address 4. Following such a pointer is likely to cause serious errors.

In C, you as the programmer have the entire responsibility for making sure that the value assigned to a union fits a particular interpretation. Thus, you must find a way to keep track of the value a union variable contains at any particular time. The most common mechanism for doing so is to associate a separate data field with each union and then use that field to store an indication of the current type. Values that indicate the type of value stored in a union are called **type tags** and are usually elements of an enumeration type whose elements indicate the different possible representations. In most applications, the type tag for a union is stored as part of a larger record containing both the tag and the union type, possibly in conjunction with other information. A record that contains both a type tag and a union value is called a **tagged union.**

Using tagged unions to represent expressions

The mechanism provided by union types—particularly when used in conjunction with a type tag—provides an ideal method for representing the nodes in an expression tree. Remember that the `exp.h` interface exports the enumeration type `exptypeT` whose constants—`IntegerType`, `IdentifierType`, and `CompoundType`— allow clients to determine the type of a particular expression. If you include a value of type `exptypeT` as a type tag, the complete concrete structure for expressions looks like this:

```
struct expressionCDT {
    exptypeT type;
    union {
        int intRep;
        string idRep;
        struct {
            char op;
            expressionADT lhs;
            expressionADT rhs;
        } compoundRep;
    } value;
};
```

In order to understand this definition, it is useful to look at its pieces individually. If you ignore for the moment the contents of the union declaration, you can see that the type definition is a record with two fields:

```
struct expressionCDT {
    exptypeT type;
    union { . . . } value;
};
```

This record is precisely what you need to store a node. An object of type `expressionADT` points to a node, from which you can extract a `type` field and a `value` field. You need to use a union type to represent the `value` field because each of the possible type codes corresponds to a different underlying representation of the object. For nodes of type `IntegerType`, the value field must be an integer; for `IdentifierType` nodes, you need to store a string; and for `CompoundType` nodes, you need to store a record containing the operator and the two subexpressions. The union type

```
union {
    int intRep;
    string idRep;
    struct {
        char op;
        expressionADT lhs;
        expressionADT rhs;
    } compoundRep;
}
```

gives you precisely the right structure for representing the `value` field. The `value` field is either an `int`, a `string`, or a record with the three components `op`, `lhs`, and `rhs`.

The `expressionCDT` record is more complicated than most of the record definitions presented in this book. In other situations, it makes sense to break down such deeply nested records into their component parts and then use `typedef` to give a name to the various parts of the data structure hierarchy. For example, it would be possible to give the union type an explicit name using `typedef` and then use that name in the `expressionCDT` definition, as follows:

```
typedef union {
    int intRep;
    string idRep;
    struct {
        char op;
        expressionADT lhs;
        expressionADT rhs;
    } compoundRep;
} valueT;

struct expressionCDT {
    exptypeT type;
    valueT value;
};
```

Separating the definition into two parts can be dangerous, because doing so makes it possible to declare untagged unions.

Although this definition is somewhat easier to read, it can be dangerous to define tagged unions in this way. Without the type code in the enclosing structure, there is no way to determine the meaning of the data stored in the union. Defining the `expressionCDT` record as a single entity makes it impossible to pass just the union value without passing the type code as well. In the combined type definition, the union type has no name, which makes it impossible for a programmer to declare a value of that type.

Visualizing the concrete representation

To reinforce your understanding of how `expressionADT` values are stored, you should visualize how the concrete expression structure is represented inside the computer's memory. At the highest level of detail, all nodes have two fields: a `type` and a `value`. The `type` field is represented internally by a small integer and certainly fits in a word. The `value` field consists of a union type and therefore takes up as much space as the largest possible alternative. The three alternatives require either one word for an integer, one word for a string pointer, or three words for the record representing a compound node. Of the possible node types, the compound node is the largest, so the `value` field occupies three words, as shown:

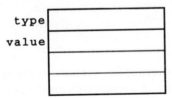

Given this general framework, you can diagram the structure of each expression type by considering the three possible interpretations of the `value` field. For a node of type `IntegerType`, you use the `intRep` interpretation, shown here as it would exist for the integer 3:

IntegerType
3

A node of type `IdentifierType` would use the `idRep` interpretation, as illustrated here in the node representing the variable **x**:

IdentifierType
x

In the case of the `CompoundType` node, the `value` field is interpreted according to the `compoundRep` interpretation, in which the three words reserved for the value field correspond to the components of the embedded structure

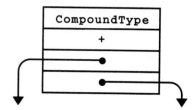

where the two pointers indicate the left and right subexpressions.

Because compound nodes contain subexpressions that can themselves be compound nodes, expression trees can grow to an arbitrary level of complexity. Figure 14-4 illustrates the internal data structure for the expression

    y = 3 * (x + 1)

which includes three operators and therefore requires three compound nodes. Although the parentheses do not appear explicitly in the expression tree, its structure correctly reflects the desired order of operations.

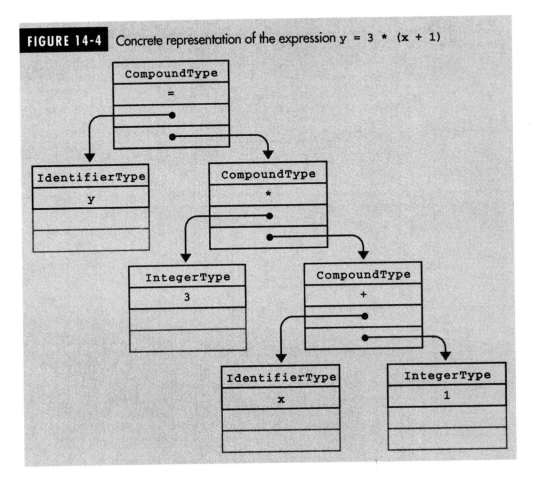

FIGURE 14-4 Concrete representation of the expression y = 3 * (x + 1)

Implementing the constructor and selector functions

The functions exported by the **exp.h** interface are easy to implement. A complete implementation appears in Figure 14-5, which consists of the type definition and the code for the various constructor and selector functions exported by the interface.

The only part of the code that might at first seem confusing is the compound selection expressions necessary to select individual components from a node, given the expression pointer. Because the concrete structure contains a record nested inside a union nested inside a record, the code sometimes requires three selectors to obtain the correct field. This situation is illustrated most easily in the definition of the constructor function **NewCompoundExp**, which allocates space for an expression node, fills in the type code, and then initializes the fields required for that type of expression. Initializing the operator field, for example, is accomplished using the statement

```
exp->value.compoundRep.op = op;
```

FIGURE 14-5   Implementation of the abstract expression type

```c
/*
 * File: exp.c
 * -----------
 * This file implements the exp.h interface.  The exported
 * functions are standard constructor and selector functions
 * that require no individual documentation.
 */

#include <stdio.h>
#include "genlib.h"
#include "strlib.h"
#include "exp.h"

/*
 * Type: expressionCDT
 * -------------------
 * The type expressionCDT is the concrete counterpart of an
 * expressionADT.  The type is implemented as a pointer to a
 * node.  The value of the node consists of a tagged union that
 * allows the node to have multiple representations.
 */

struct expressionCDT {
    exptypeT type;
    union {
        int intRep;
        string idRep;
        struct {
            char op;
            expressionADT lhs;
            expressionADT rhs;
        } compoundRep;
    } value;
};

/* Exported functions */

expressionADT NewIntegerExp(int n)
{
    expressionADT exp;

    exp = New(expressionADT);
    exp->type = IntegerType;
    exp->value.intRep = n;
    return (exp);
}
```

```
expressionADT NewIdentifierExp(string id)
{
    expressionADT exp;

    exp = New(expressionADT);
    exp->type = IdentifierType;
    exp->value.idRep = CopyString(id);
    return (exp);
}

expressionADT NewCompoundExp(char op,
                             expressionADT lhs,
                             expressionADT rhs)
{
    expressionADT exp;

    exp = New(expressionADT);
    exp->type = CompoundType;
    exp->value.compoundRep.op = op;
    exp->value.compoundRep.lhs = lhs;
    exp->value.compoundRep.rhs = rhs;
    return (exp);
}

exptypeT ExpType(expressionADT exp)
{
    return (exp->type);
}

int ExpInteger(expressionADT exp)
{
    if (ExpType(exp) != IntegerType) {
        Error("Integer expression required");
    }
    return (exp->value.intRep);
}

string ExpIdentifier(expressionADT exp)
{
    if (ExpType(exp) != IdentifierType) {
        Error("Identifier expression required");
    }
    return (exp->value.idRep);
}

char ExpOperator(expressionADT exp)
{
    if (ExpType(exp) != CompoundType) {
        Error("Compound expression required");
    }
    return (exp->value.compoundRep.op);
}
```

```
expressionADT ExpLHS(expressionADT exp)
{
    if (ExpType(exp) != CompoundType) {
        Error("Compound expression required");
    }
    return (exp->value.compoundRep.lhs);
}

expressionADT ExpRHS(expressionADT exp)
{
    if (ExpType(exp) != CompoundType) {
        Error("Compound expression required");
    }
    return (exp->value.compoundRep.rhs);
}
```

in which the left-hand side of the assignment has three selectors. The first moves from the expression to the **value** field, the second selects the **compoundRep** interpretation, and the third selects the **op** field from the underlying record. The same type of selection expressions appear throughout the implementation.

It is also worth noting that the selector functions include a specific check to make sure they are called on a value of the appropriate type. For example, if the client mistakenly calls **ExpIdentifier** on a compound node, the program will terminate with an appropriate error message. Although the client is responsible for making sure that the selector functions are called correctly, having the implementation check for errors makes programs that use the expression package easier to debug.

14.4 Parsing an expression

The problem of building the appropriate parse tree from a stream of tokens is not an easy one. To a large extent, the underlying theory necessary to build a efficient parser lies beyond the scope of this text. Even so, it is possible to make some headway on the problem and solve it for the limited case of arithmetic expressions.

Parsing and grammars

In the early days of programming languages, programmers implemented the parsing phase of a compiler without thinking very hard about the nature of the process. As a result, early parsing programs were difficult to write and even harder to debug. In the 1960s, however, computer scientists studied the problem of parsing from a more theoretical perspective, which simplified it greatly. Today, a computer scientist who has taken a course on compilers can write a parser for a programming language with very little work. In fact, most parsers can be generated automatically from a simple specification of the language for which they are intended. In the field of computer science, parsing is one of the areas in which it is easiest to see the profound impact of theory on practice. Without the theoretical work necessary to simplify the problem, programming languages would have made far less headway than they have.

The essential theoretical insight necessary to simplify parsing is actually borrowed from linguistics. Like human languages, programming languages have rules of syntax that define the grammatical structure of the language. Moreover, because programming languages are much more regular in structure than human languages, it is usually easy to describe the syntactic structure of a programming language in a precise form called a **grammar.** In the context of a programming language, a grammar consists of a set of rules that show how a particular language construct can be derived from simpler ones.

If you start with the English rules for expression formation, it is not hard to write down a grammar for the simple expressions used in this chapter. Partly because it simplifies things a little in the parser, it helps to incorporate the notion of a term into the parser as any single unit that can appear as an operand to a larger expression. For example, constants and variables are clearly terms. Moreover, an expression in parentheses acts as a single unit and can therefore also be regarded as a term. Thus, a term is one of the following possibilities:

- An integer constant
- A variable
- An expression in parentheses

An expression is then either of the following:

- A term
- Two expressions separated by an operator

This informal definition can be translated directly into the following grammar, presented in what programmers call **BNF,** which stands for Backus-Naur form after its inventors John Backus and Peter Naur:

$$E \rightarrow T$$
$$E \rightarrow E \; op \; E$$

$$T \rightarrow integer$$
$$T \rightarrow identifier$$
$$T \rightarrow (\; E \;)$$

In the grammar, uppercase letters like E and T are called **nonterminal symbols** and stand for an abstract linguistic class, such as an expression or a term. The specific punctuation marks and the italicized words represent the **terminal symbols,** which are those that appear in the token stream. Explicit terminal symbols, such as the parentheses in the last rule, must appear in the input exactly as written. The italicized words represent placeholders for tokens that fit their general description. Thus, the notation *integer* stands for any string of digits returned by the scanner as a token. Each terminal corresponds to exactly one token in the scanner stream. Nonterminals typically correspond to an entire sequence of tokens.

Integer expressions are the easiest. The value of an expression of an integer expression is simply the value of the integer stored in that node. Thus, the `IntegerType` case clause looks like

```
case IntegerType:
  return (ExpInteger(exp));
```

The next case is that of identifiers. When you encounter an identifier expression, you need to be able to look up and return its value. To do so, you need to have some mechanism through which you can associate variable names and values. For the most part, the symbol table abstraction in Chapter 11 provides just the right tool. The fact that values in the symbol table must be pointers rather than integers creates a minor complication, but this problem is easily solved by allocating a new pointer to an integer every time a value is assigned a variable.

The last case you need to consider is that of compound nodes. All such nodes consist of an operator and two subexpressions, but you must differentiate two subcases: the arithmetic operators (+, −, *, and /) and the assignment operator (=). For the arithmetic operators, all you have to do is evaluate the left and right subexpressions recursively and then apply the appropriate operation. For assignment, you need to evaluate the right-hand side and then use the `SetIdentifierValue` function above to store that value in the identifier appearing as the left-hand side.

The complete implementation of the `eval.c` module is shown in Figure 14-8.

■ Summary

In this chapter, you have taken your first steps toward understanding how compilers translate programs into an executable form by considering how to represent arithmetic expressions. Important points in the chapter include:

- The conventional tools for implementing programming languages fall into two classes: compilers and interpreters. Compilers translate source code into a set of instructions that can be executed directly by the hardware. Interpreters do not actually produce machine-executable code but instead achieve the same effect by executing the operations directly, as the source program is translated.
- A typical interpreter system operates by repeatedly reading an expression from the user, evaluating it, and displaying the result. This approach is called a *read-eval-print loop*.
- Expressions have a fundamentally recursive structure. There are simple expressions, which consist of constants and variable names. More complex expressions are created by combining simpler subexpressions into larger units, forming a hierarchical structure that can easily be represented as a tree.
- If you define expressions in their most straightforward recursive form, those involving multiple operators may be ambiguous in the sense that you can come up with several interpretations that are consistent with the basic form.

FIGURE 14-8 Implementation of the expression evaluator

```
/*
 * File: eval.c
 * ------------
 * This file implements the eval.h interface.
 */

#include <stdio.h>
#include "genlib.h"
#include "strlib.h"
#include "exp.h"
#include "eval.h"
#include "symtab.h"

/*
 * Private variable: variableTable
 * -------------------------------
 * This table keeps track of the values for each variable.
 */

static symtabADT variableTable;

/* Private function prototypes */

static int EvalCompound(expressionADT exp);

/* Exported entries */

int EvalExp(expressionADT exp)
{
    switch (ExpType(exp)) {
      case IntegerType:
        return (ExpInteger(exp));
      case IdentifierType:
        return (GetIdentifierValue(ExpIdentifier(exp)));
      case CompoundType:
        return (EvalCompound(exp));
    }
}

void InitVariableTable(void)
{
    variableTable = NewSymbolTable();
}

int GetIdentifierValue(string name)
{
    int *ip;

    ip = Lookup(variableTable, name);
    if (ip == UNDEFINED)  Error("%s is undefined", name);
    return (*ip);
}
```

```
void SetIdentifierValue(string name, int value)
{
    int *ip;

    ip = New(int *);
    *ip = value;
    Enter(variableTable, name, ip);
}

/* Private functions */

static int EvalCompound(expressionADT exp)
{
    char op;
    int lhs, rhs;

    op = ExpOperator(exp);
    if (op == '=') {
        rhs = EvalExp(ExpRHS(exp));
        SetIdentifierValue(ExpIdentifier(ExpLHS(exp)), rhs);
        return (rhs);
    }
    lhs = EvalExp(ExpLHS(exp));
    rhs = EvalExp(ExpRHS(exp));
    switch (op) {
      case '+': return (lhs + rhs);
      case '-': return (lhs - rhs);
      case '*': return (lhs * rhs);
      case '/': return (lhs / rhs);
      default:  Error("Illegal operator");
    }
}
```

Despite the ambiguity of the expression itself, the trees for the different interpretations are distinct, which means that ambiguity is a property of the written form of the expression and not its internal representation.

- It is easy to define a type **expressionADT** to represent expression trees. The corresponding concrete type, however, must support multiple representations to account for the fact that there are several different kinds of expressions. In C, the conventional way to define a structure that supports multiple representation is to define a union type that encompasses the various possibilities.

- The process of reading an expression from the user can be divided into the phases of *input, lexical analysis,* and *parsing.* The input phase is the simplest and consists of reading a string from the user. Lexical analysis involves breaking a string into component tokens in the way that the scanner abstraction in Chapter 8 does. Parsing consists of translating the collection of tokens returned from the lexical analysis phase into its internal representation, following a set of syntactic rules called a *grammar.*

- For many grammars, it is possible to solve the parsing problem using a strategy called *recursive descent*. In a recursive-descent parser, the rules of the grammar are encoded as a set of mutually recursive functions.
- Once parsed, expression trees can be manipulated recursively in much the same way as the trees in Chapter 13. In the context of the interpreter, one of the most important operations is evaluating an expression tree, which consists of walking the tree recursively to determine its value.

 REVIEW QUESTIONS

1. What is the difference between an interpreter and a compiler?

2. What is a read-eval-print loop?

3. What are the three phases involved in reading an expression?

4. State the recursive definition for an arithmetic expression as given in this chapter.

5. Identify which of the following lines constitutes an expression according to the definition used in this chapter:

   a. `(((0)))`

   b. `2x + 3y`

   c. `x - (y * (x / y))`

   d. `-y`

   e. `x = (y = 2 * x - 3 * y)`

   f. `10 - 9 + 8 / 7 * 6 - 5 + 4 * 3 / 2 - 1`

6. For each of the legal expressions in the preceding question, draw a parse tree that reflects the standard precedence assumptions of mathematics.

7. Of the legal expressions in question 5, which ones are ambiguous with respect to the simple recursive definition of expressions?

8. What are the differences between parse trees and expression trees?

9. What are the three types of nodes that can occur in an expression tree?

10. What functions are exported by the `exp.h` interface?

11. Why are `ParseExp` and `EvalExp` not exported directly from `exp.h`?

12. In C, what is the difference between the interpretation of the keyword `union` and the keyword `struct`?

13. Assume that you are using a machine in which integers require two bytes, pointers require four, and values of type `double` require eight. How many bytes are allocated for the variable u in the following declaration:

```
union {
    int intRep;
    string stringRep;
    double doubleRep;
} u;
```

14. Draw a diagram showing the arrangement of the fields in the internal structure of u, as declared in the preceding question.

15. What is a tagged union? What makes tagged unions useful?

16. The definition of the **expressionCDT** type given in Figure 14-5 is rather long and can easily be broken down into several type definitions. What reason does the chapter offer for defining the entire structure as a single unit?

17. Using Figure 14-4 as a model, draw a complete structure diagram for the following expression:

    y = (x + 1) / (x - 2)

18. Why are grammars useful in translating programming languages?

19. What do the letters in *BNF* stand for?

20. In a grammar, what is the difference between a terminal and a nonterminal symbol?

21. What is the value of the following expression if parsed using Iversonian precedence:

    1 + 4 * 3 / 2 - 1

22. What is the value of the expression in the preceding question if parsed using standard mathematical precedence?

23. What is a recursive-descent parser?

24. What is the significance of the second argument to the **ReadE** function in the precedence-based implementation of the parser?

25. If you look at the definition of **EvalExp** in Figure 14-8, you will see that the function body does not contain any calls to **EvalExp**. Is **EvalExp** a recursive function?

26. Why is the = operator handled specially in the function **EvalCompound**?

 PROGRAMMING EXERCISES

1. Make all the necessary changes to the interpreter program to add the operator %, which returns the remainder of its arguments as in C. The precedence of % is the same as that for * and /.

2. Extend the files associated with the interpreter so that they use the type `bigintADT` introduced in Chapter 12 to represent integers instead of the predefined type `int`. After you make these changes, the interpreter should function as an extended-precision calculator, as shown in the following sample run:

```
=> 1234567890 + 9876543210↵
11111111100
=> 1 * 2 * 3 * 4 * 5 * 6 * 7 * 8 * 9 * 10↵
3628800
=> 12744317 * 61029381↵
777777777777777
=> quit↵
```

3. In mathematics, there are several common procedures that require you to replace all instances of a variable in a formula with some other variable. Working entirely at the client level of **exp.h**, write a function

```
expressionADT ChangeVariable(expressionADT exp,
                             string oldName,
                             string newName);
```

that returns a new expression which is the same as **exp** except that every occurrence of the identifier **oldName** is replaced with **newName**. For example, if **exp** is the expression

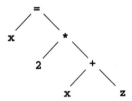

calling

```
newExp = ChangeVariable(exp, "x", "y");
```

will assign the following expression tree to **newExp**:

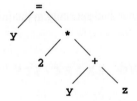

4. In the expression interpreter designed in the chapter, every operator is a binary operator in the sense that it takes two operands, one on each side. Most programming languages also allow unary operators, which take a single operand, which usually follows the operator. The most common example is the unary minus operation, as in the expression **-x**. Make whatever changes you need to make in the expression interpreter to add the unary minus operator.

5. Write a program that reads expressions from the user in their standard mathematical form and then writes out those same expressions using reverse Polish notation, in which the operators follow the operands to which they apply. (Reverse Polish notation, or RPN, was introduced in the discussion of the calculator in Chapter 8.) Your program should be able to duplicate this sample run:

```
This program converts expressions to RPN.
=> 1 + 2 + 3.↵
1 2 + 3 +
=> (2 * x + 3 * y) / 10.↵
2 x * 3 y * + 10 /
=> quit↵
```

6. The process of turning the internal representation of an expression back into its text form is generally called **unparsing** the expression. Write a function **Unparse(exp)** that displays the expression **exp** on the screen in its standard mathematical form. Parentheses should be included in the output only if they are required by the precedence rules. Thus, the expression represented by the tree

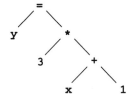

should be unparsed as

```
y = 3 * (x + 1)
```

7. Although the interpreter program that appears in this chapter is considerably easier to implement than a complete compiler, it is possible to get a sense of how a compiler works by defining one for a simplified computer system called a *stack machine*. A stack machine performs operations on an internal stack, which is maintained by the hardware, in much the same fashion as the calculator described in Chapter 8. For the purposes of this problem, you should assume that the stack machine can execute the following operations:

LOAD #*n*	Pushes the constant *n* on the stack.
LOAD *var*	Pushes the value of the variable *var* on the stack.
STORE *var*	Stores the top stack value in *var* without actually popping it.
DISPLAY	Pops the stack and displays the result.
ADD SUB MUL DIV	These instructions pop the top two values from the stack and apply the indicated operation, pushing the final result back on the stack. The top value is the right operand, the next one down is the left.

Write a function

```
void Compile(FILE *infile, FILE *outfile);
```

that reads expressions from `infile` and writes to `outfile` a sequence of instructions for the stack-machine that have the same effect as evaluating each of the expressions in the input file and displaying their result. For example, if the file opened as `infile` contains

```
x = 7
y = 5
2 * x + 3 * y
```

calling `Compile(infile, outfile)` should write the following code to `outfile`:

```
LOAD #7
STORE x
DISPLAY
LOAD #5
STORE y
DISPLAY
LOAD #2
LOAD x
MUL
LOAD #3
LOAD y
MUL
ADD
DISPLAY
```

8. After it parses an expression, a commercial compiler typically looks for ways to simplify that expression so that it can be computed more efficiently. This process is called **optimization.** One common technique used in the optimization process is **constant folding,** which consists of identifying subexpressions that are composed entirely of constants and replacing them with their value. For example, if a compiler encountered the expression

```
days = 24 * 60 * 60 * sec
```

there would be no point in generating code to perform the first two multiplications when the program was executed. The value of the subexpression `24 * 60 * 60` is constant and might as well be replaced by its value (86400) before the compiler actually starts to generate code.

Write a function `FoldConstants(exp)` that takes an `expressionADT` and returns a new `expressionADT` in which any subexpressions that are entirely composed of constants are replaced by the computed value.

9. Using tree structures to represent expressions makes it possible to perform sophisticated mathematical operations by transforming the structure of the tree. For example, it is not very hard to write a function that differentiates an expression by applying the standard rules from calculus that allow you to express the derivative of a complex expression in terms of the derivatives of its parts. The most common rules for differentiating an expression involving the standard arithmetic operators are shown in Figure 14-9.

Write a recursive function `Differentiate(exp, var)` that uses the rules from Figure 14-9 to find the derivative of the expression `exp` with respect to the variable `var`. The result of calling `Differentiate` is an `expressionADT` that can be used in any context in which such values are legal. For example, you could evaluate it, unparse it, or pass it to `Differentiate` to calculate the second derivative of the original expression.

10. If you implement the `Differentiate` function from the preceding exercise in the most straightforward way, the expressions that you get back will be quite complex, even though they are mathematically correct. For example, if you apply the differentiation rules from Figure 14-9 to the expression

$$x^2 + 2x - 3$$

the result is

$$2 \times x^1 \times 1 + 2 \times 1 + x \times 0 - 0$$

FIGURE 14-9 Standard formulas for differentiation

$x' = 1$ where:

$c' = 0$ x is the variable used as the basis for the differentiation

$(u + v)' = u' + v'$ c is a constant or variable that does not depend on x

$(u - v)' = u' - v'$ u and v are arbitrary expressions

$(uv)' = uv' + vu'$ n is an integer constant

$(u / v)' = \dfrac{uv' - vu'}{v^2}$

$(u^n)' = nu^{n-1}u'$

To transform this expression into the more familiar

$$2x + 2$$

requires you to make several mathematical simplifications. For example, because you know that multiplying any value by 0 always gives back 0, you can eliminate the $x \times 0$ term from the expression.

One approach to simplifying expressions that turns out to be useful in the context of differentiating an arithmetic expression is to convert expressions into an equivalent polynomial form. Polynomials involving powers of x, for example, can be represented as a list of coefficients in which the first element in the list is the constant term, the next element is the coefficient of x, the next is the coefficient of x^2, and so on. For example, the expression $x^2 + 2x - 3$, would be represented in polynomial form as follows:

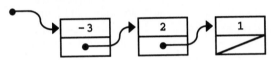

Write a function

```
expressionADT Simplify(expressionADT exp)
```

that attempts to simplify an expression by converting it to a polynomial and then converting the result back into an expression. If the expression is too complex to convert to a simple polynomial, your function should return the original expression unchanged.

11. The `listADT` type introduced in Chapter 12 is not as general as computer scientists would like, because it does not offer any effective way to represent lists that contain other lists at arbitrary levels of nesting. The problem is not merely a question of whether you can create a list whose elements are themselves lists. In fact, if `listElementT` is the generic pointer type `void *`, you can do just that. The problem is that there is no way to determine whether a list element is a list or a more primitive element, because the `void *` pointer offers no insight into the exact nature of the underlying type.

To get around this problem, it is extremely useful if list elements carry with them an indication of their type in much the same way that expression nodes do. The pioneering computer scientist John McCarthy designed the programming language LISP around a single data type called a **symbolic expression,** or **s-expression** for short. Even though s-expressions are simple in their conceptual structure, they can be used to represent extraordinarily complex data relationships. S-expressions are often used today in the field of artificial intelligence to encode facts, rules, relationships, and other aspects of knowledge.

Like the expressions defined in this chapter, an s-expression is a structure consisting of a type tag and a value, which may be in any of the following forms:

- *Numeric atoms.* **Numeric atoms** are simple numbers, much like the integer nodes in expression trees. Although modern implementations of LISP allow numeric atoms to take on floating-point values, it makes sense to simplify this type so that numeric atoms must be integers.
- *Symbolic atoms.* **Symbolic atoms** are similar in concept to the identifier nodes used in expression trees, in the sense that they correspond to a particular string name. The only major difference in the s-expression world is that symbolic atoms are *unique,* in the sense that different symbolic atoms never have the same name. If you try to create an atom with the same name as one that was previously created, the rules for forming s-expressions dictate that you must get back the same s-expression pointer that was originally created for that atom.
- *Dotted pairs.* A **dotted pair** is simply a pair of s-expressions of which the first is called the **car** and the second is called the **cdr** (pronounced like "could er") after the names of the internal registers on a long-obsolete machine. The operation of creating a new dotted pair from its components is called the **cons** operation.

If you want to represent s-expressions in C, each of the s-expression forms is represented as a pointer to a structure that contains a type code and a union value. Because s-expressions are pointers, it is convenient to use the NULL-valued pointer as a special marker to indicate a missing value. By tradition, this value is called NIL rather than NULL in the s-expression domain. The constant NIL is principally used to indicate the end of a list, which is represented in the s-expression world as a chain of dotted pairs linked through the cdr fields. For example, the nested list structure

```
((1 2) (buckle my shoe))
```

looks like this when diagrammed as an s-expression:

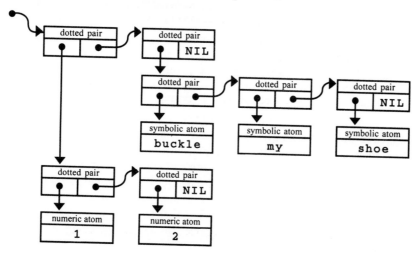

An interface that provides clients with the basic s-expression functionality is shown in Figure 14-10. Using the code in Figure 14-5 as a model, implement the `sexp.h` interface.

FIGURE 14-10 An interface to support the use of s-expressions in C

```
/*
 * File: sexp.h
 * ------------
 * This interface provides clients with a general facility for
 * manipulating list structure.  The fundamental type defined
 * by the abstraction is the s-expression, which is represented
 * by the type sexpADT.  The concept of an s-expression is
 * derived from the programming language LISP.
 */

#ifndef _sexp_h
#define _sexp_h

#include "genlib.h"

/*
 * Constant: NIL
 * -------------
 * This constant is identical to C's NULL, but the name NIL is
 * more traditional when referring to list structure.
 */

#define NIL NULL

/*
 * Type: sexpADT
 * -------------
 * This type is the abstract data type representing an
 * s-expression, which is defined recursively to have one
 * of the following forms:
 *
 * 1. The constant NIL
 * 2. A number, which is defined by its value
 * 3. An atom, which is uniquely defined by its name
 * 4. A dotted pair consisting of two s-expressions
 */

typedef struct sexpCDT *sexpADT;

/*
 * Type: sexpTypeT
 * ---------------
 * This type encompasses the possible s-expression types.
 */

typedef enum { NilType, NumberType, AtomType, DtprType } sexpTypeT;
```

```c
/*
 * Function: SexpType
 * Usage: type = SexpType(sx);
 * ---------------------------
 * This function returns a value of type sexpTypeT that
 * corresponds to the type of the s-expression sx.
 */

sexpTypeT SexpType(sexpADT sx);

/*
 * Functions: Car, Cdr
 * Usage: car = Car(sx);
 *        cdr = Cdr(sx);
 * ---------------------
 * The Car and Cdr functions return the left and right components
 * of the s-expression sx, which must be a dotted pair.
 */

sexpADT Car(sexpADT sx);
sexpADT Cdr(sexpADT sx);

/*
 * Function: Cons
 * Usage: sx = Cons(car, cdr);
 * ---------------------------
 * This function creates a new dotted-pair s-expression with the
 * specified car and cdr fields.
 */

sexpADT Cons(sexpADT car, sexpADT cdr);

/*
 * Function: StringToAtom
 * Usage: atom = StringToAtom(str);
 * --------------------------------
 * This function returns the atom with the name str.   Because atoms
 * are unique, a second call to StringToAtom with the same string
 * will return the same atom instead of creating a new one.
 */

sexpADT StringToAtom(string name);

/*
 * Function: AtomToString
 * Usage: str = AtomToString(atom);
 * --------------------------------
 * This function returns the name of the atom.
 */

string AtomToString(sexpADT atom);
```

```
/*
 * Functions: NumberToSexp, SexpToNumber
 * Usage: sx = NumberToSexp(n);
 *        n = SexpToNumber(sx);
 * ----------------------------------------
 * The NumberToSexp function allocates a new s-expression of
 * type NumberType with the value n.  SexpToNumber selects the
 * value from a numeric s-expression.
 */

sexpADT NumberToSexp(int n);
int SexpToNumber(sexpADT sx);

#endif
```

12. Working as a client of the **sexp.h** interface from the preceding exercise, write a function

    sexpADT ReadSexp(scannerADT scanner)

    that reads the next legal s-expression from the tokens in **scanner**. A legal s-expression is one that matches the symbol **s** in the following grammar:

S	→ *integer*	Creates a numeric atom
S	→ *identifier*	Creates a symbolic atom
S	→ ( )	Creates the empty list **NIL**
S	→ (L)	Creates a list of the s-expressions in L
L	→ S	
L	→ S L	

13. Once again working as a client of the **sexp.h** interface from exercise 11, write a function

    void PrintSexp(sexpADT sx)

    that displays the value of the s-expression **sx** on the screen using parenthesized list notation. You may assume that the cdr of each dotted pair is either a dotted pair or the constant value **NIL**.

14. Working as a client of the **sexp.h** interface from exercise 11, write a function

    sexpADT Flatten(sexpADT sx)

    that returns a single list consisting of all the atomic values in **sx** in the order in which they would appear in its printed representation, without all the interior parentheses. For example, if you call **Flatten** on the list

    ((A B) (C (D E) F) ((G)) H)

the result should be the list

    (A B C D E F G H)

15. Because s-expressions are so flexible, they are often used as the internal representation of expression trees. By tradition, compound nodes in an expression tree are converted to s-expression lists that begin with the symbolic atom corresponding to the operator, followed by the operands to which that operator applies. Thus, the expression

    y = 3 * (x + 1)

corresponds to this s-expression list:

    (= y (* 3 (+ x 1)))

Rewrite the expression interpreter program developed in this chapter so that it uses s-expressions as its internal representation.

16.

> [Paul] Allen rushed to the dorm to find Bill Gates. They had to do a BASIC for this machine. They had to. If they didn't, the revolution would start without them.
>
> —Stephen Manes and Paul Andrews, *Gates*, 1994

The task of moving from an expression parser to a complete language is not as difficult as you might think. In this exercise, your mission is to transform the expression parser into a simplified version of the programming language BASIC, which was developed in the mid-1960s at Dartmouth College by John Kemeny and Thomas Kurtz. It was one of the first languages designed to be easy to use and learn and remains popular as a medium for teaching programming at the elementary and secondary school levels.

In BASIC, a program consists of a sequence of numbered statements, as illustrated by this simple program:

```
10 REM Program to add two numbers
20 INPUT n1
30 INPUT n2
40 LET total = n1 + n2
50 PRINT total
60 END
```

The line numbers at the beginning of each line establish the sequence of operations in a program. In the absence of any control statements to the contrary, the statements are executed in ascending numerical order, starting at the lowest number. Here, for example, program execution begins at line 10, which is simply a comment—the keyword REM is short for **REMARK**—indicating that the purpose of the program is to add two numbers. Lines 20 and 30 request two values from the user, which are stored in the variables n1 and n2, respectively. The LET statement in line 40 is an example of an assignment in BASIC and sets the variable total to be the sum of n1 and n2. Line 50 displays the value of `total` on the console, and line 60 indicates the end of execution. A sample run of the program therefore looks like this:

```
    ? 2↵
    ? 3↵
    5
```

Line numbers also provide a simple editing mechanism. You need not enter statements in order, because the line numbers indicate their relative position. Moreover, as long as you leave gaps in the number sequence, you can add new statements by giving them numbers that fall between existing lines.

The `LET` statement illustrated by line 40 of the addition program has the form

    `LET` *variable* = *expression*

and has the effect of assigning the result of the expression to the variable. In BASIC, expressions are much the same as for the sample interpreter in the chapter; the only difference is that the assignment operator is no longer part of the expression structure. Thus, the simplest expressions are variables and integer constants. They can be combined into larger expressions by enclosing an expression in parentheses or by joining two expressions with the operator +, -, *, or /.

The statements in the addition program illustrate how to use BASIC for simple, sequential programs. If you want to express loops or conditional execution in a BASIC program, you have to use the `GOTO` and `IF` statements. The statement

    `GOTO` *n*

where *n* is a line number, transfers control unconditionally to line *n* in the program. The statement

    `IF` *conditional expression* `THEN` *n*

performs a conditional transfer of control. On encountering such a statement, the BASIC interpreter begins by evaluating the conditional expression. In this implementation, a conditional expression is simply a pair of arithmetic expressions joined by the operator <, >, or =. If the result of the comparison is true, control passes to line *n,* just as in the `GOTO` statement; if not, the program continues with the next line in sequence. For example, the following BASIC program simulates a countdown from 10 to 0:

```
10 REM Program to simulate a countdown
20 LET T = 10
30 IF T < 0 THEN 70
40 PRINT T
50 LET T = T - 1
60 GOTO 30
70 END
```

To run a program in BASIC, you first enter all the program steps and then issue the RUN command, which starts interpreting the program with the lowest numbered line. Unless the flow of control is changed by GOTO and IF commands, statements are executed in line-number order. Execution ends when the program hits the END statement at the end of the program.

Write a program for a simplified version of BASIC that implements the statements and commands shown in Table 14-1. A sample session with the interpreter appears in Figure 14-11. The program in Figure 14-11 is intended to display the terms less than or equal to 1000 in the Fibonacci series. To illustrate the use of line numbers to make editing changes, the first version of the program is missing the PRINT statement, which is inserted in its proper position prior to the second run.

TABLE 14-1 Summary of BASIC statements and commands

REM *comments*	This statement is used for comments. Any text on the line after the keyword REM is ignored.
LET *var = exp*	This statement is BASIC's assignment statement. The LET keyword is followed by a variable name, an equal sign, and an expression. As in C, the effect of this statement is to assign the value of the expression to the variable. In BASIC, assignment is not an operator and may not be nested inside other expressions.
PRINT *exp*	This statement is used to display the value of the expression and then return the cursor to the beginning of the next line.
INPUT *var*	This statement is used to read an integer value from the user and store it in the specified variable. The BASIC system automatically displays a prompt for the input value consisting of the string " ? ".
GOTO *n*	This statement forces an unconditional transfer to line *n*.
IF *cond* THEN *n*	This statement provides conditional control. The conditional expression cond is formed by combining two arithmetic expressions with the operator =, <, or >. If the condition holds, the next statement comes from the line number following THEN. If not, the program continues with the next line in sequence.
END	This statement marks the end of the program. Execution halts when this line is reached.
RUN	This command causes the BASIC interpreter to execute statements beginning at the lowest-numbered line.
LIST	This command lists the steps in the program in numerical sequence.
QUIT	This command exits from the BASIC interpreter.

FIGURE 14-11   Sample run of the BASIC interpreter

```
Minimal BASIC -- Type HELP for help.

100 REM Program to print the Fibonacci sequence.⏎
110 LET max = 1000⏎
120 LET n1 = 0⏎
130 LET n2 = 1⏎
140 IF n1 > max THEN 190⏎
150 LET n3 = n1 + n2⏎
160 LET n1 = n2⏎
170 LET n2 = n3⏎
180 GOTO 140⏎
190 END⏎

RUN
145 PRINT n1

LIST
100 REM Program to print the Fibonacci sequence
110 LET max = 1000
120 LET n1 = 0
130 LET n2 = 1
140 IF n1 > max THEN 190
145 PRINT n1
150 LET n3 = n1 + n2
160 LET n1 = n2
170 LET n2 = n3
180 GOTO 140
190 END

RUN
0
1
1
2
3
5
8
13
21
34
55
89
144
233
377
610
987
```

Sets

Dear me, what a wonderfully mixed set!

— George Eliot, *Middlemarch*, 1871

Objectives

- To become familiar with the terminology and notation mathematicians use for sets.

- To appreciate the tradeoff considerations involved in designing a set interface.

- To recognize that binary search trees provide a convenient basis for implementing sets.

- To understand the design and use of a polymorphic iterator facility.

- To learn how to implement sets of integers efficiently using characteristic vectors.

Although much of Chapter 14 is concerned with the practical problem of implementing an expression parser, there is another lesson you should take from that chapter, which is that theory can have a profound effect on practice. In the case of the expression parser, the theory consists of using a formal grammar to define the syntactic structure of a programming language. Such situations arise often in computer science, which has strong theoretical foundations that have direct application to practical problems. Because theory is so central to computer science as a discipline, it is useful to learn about theory and practical techniques together.

In this chapter, you will learn about sets, which are central to both the theory and practice of computer science. The next section begins with an informal presentation of the underlying mathematical theory of sets. The rest of the chapter then turns to the more practical concern of how to implement sets as an abstract data type.

■■■ 15.1 Sets as a mathematical abstraction

In all likelihood, you have already encountered sets at some point in your study of mathematics. Although the definition is not entirely precise, it is best to think of a **set** as an unordered collection of distinct elements.[1] For example, the days of the week form a set of seven elements that can be written down as follows:

{Sunday, Monday, Tuesday, Wednesday, Thursday, Friday, Saturday}

The individual elements are written in this order only because it is conventional. If you wrote these same names down in some other order, you would still have the same set. A set, however, never has multiple copies of the same element.

The set of weekdays is a **finite set** because it contains a finite number of elements. In mathematics, there are also **infinite sets,** such as the set of all integers. In a computer system, sets are usually finite, even if they correspond to infinite sets in mathematics. For example, the set of integers that a computer can represent in a variable of type int is finite because the hardware imposes a limit on the range of integer values.

To illustrate the fundamental operations on sets, it is important to have a few sets to use as a foundation. In keeping with mathematical convention, this text uses the following symbols to refer to the indicated sets:

$\varnothing$ The **empty set,** which contains no elements
Z   The set of all integers
N   The set of **natural numbers,** which consists of the nonnegative integers
R   The set of all real numbers

---

[1] Sets are difficult to define formally, because it is easy to become trapped in paradoxes and contradictions. Of these, the most famous is *Russell's paradox,* which is named after its discoverer, the British mathematician Bertrand Russell. If sets can contain elements of any type, there is nothing wrong with the idea of a set containing sets as members. Such a set could potentially contain itself. The question that Russell posed is what happens if you define the set **X** to include all sets that do not contain themselves as members. Such a set contains **X** if and only if—as the definition states—it does not contain **X**. This situation represents a logical contradiction that is closely related to the paradox of what to make of someone who declares that "Everything I say is a lie."

Following mathematical convention, this text uses uppercase letters to refer to sets. Sets whose membership is defined—like **N, Z,** and **R**—are denoted using boldface letters. Names that refer to some unspecified set are written using italic letters, such as *S* and *T*.

Membership

The fundamental property that defines a set is that of **membership,** which has the same intuitive meaning in mathematics that it does in English. Mathematicians indicate membership symbolically using the notation $x \in S$, which indicates that the value x is an element of the set S. For example, given the sets defined in the preceding section, the following statements are true:

$17 \in \mathbf{N}$
$-4 \in \mathbf{Z}$
$\pi \in \mathbf{R}$

Conversely, the notation $x \notin S$ indicates that x is *not* an element of S. For example, $-4 \notin \mathbf{N}$, because the set of natural numbers does not include the negative integers.

The membership of a set is typically specified in one of the two following ways:

- *Enumeration.* Defining a set by enumeration is simply a matter of listing its elements. By convention, the elements in the list are enclosed in curly braces and separated by commas. For example, the set **D** of single-digit natural numbers can be defined by enumeration as follows:

  $\mathbf{D} = \{0, 1, 2, 3, 4, 5, 6, 7, 8, 9\}$

- *Rule.* You can also define a set by specifying a rule that distinguishes the members of that set. In most cases, the rule is expressed in two parts: a larger set that provides the potential candidates and some conditional expression that identifies the elements which should be selected for inclusion. For example, the set **D** from the preceding example can also be defined like this:

  $\mathbf{D} = \{x \mid x \in \mathbf{N} \text{ and } x < 10\}$

  If you read this definition aloud, it comes out sounding like this: "**D** is defined to be the set of all elements x such that x is a natural number and x is less than 10."

Set operations

Mathematical set theory defines several operations on sets, of which the following are the most important:

- *Union.* The **union** of two sets, which is written as $A \cup B$, is the set of all elements belonging to the set A, the set B, or both.

$$\{1, 3, 5, 7, 9\} \cup \{2, 4, 6, 8\} = \{1, 2, 3, 4, 5, 6, 7, 8, 9\}$$
$$\{1, 2, 4, 8\} \cup \{2, 3, 5, 7\} = \{1, 2, 3, 4, 5, 7, 8\}$$
$$\{2, 3\} \cup \{1, 2, 3, 4\} = \{1, 2, 3, 4\}$$

- *Intersection.* The **intersection** of two sets is written as $A \cap B$ and consists of the elements belonging to both A and B.

$$\{1, 3, 5, 7, 9\} \cap \{2, 4, 6, 8\} = \varnothing$$
$$\{1, 2, 4, 8\} \cap \{2, 3, 5, 7\} = \{2\}$$
$$\{2, 3\} \cap \{1, 2, 3, 4\} = \{2, 3\}$$

- *Set difference.* The **difference** of two sets is written as $A - B$ and consists of the elements belonging to A except for those that are also contained in B.

$$\{1, 3, 5, 7, 9\} - \{2, 4, 6, 8\} = \{1, 3, 5, 7, 9\}$$
$$\{1, 2, 4, 8\} - \{2, 3, 5, 7\} = \{1, 4, 8\}$$
$$\{2, 3\} - \{1, 2, 3, 4\} = \varnothing$$

In addition to set-producing operations like union and intersection, the mathematical theory of sets also defines several operations that determine whether some property holds between two sets. Operations that test a particular property are the mathematical equivalent of predicate functions and are usually called **relations.** The most important relations on sets are the following:

- *Equality.* The sets A and B are **equal** if they have the same elements. The equality relation for sets is indicated by the standard equal sign used to denote equality in other mathematical contexts. Thus, the notation $A = B$ indicates that the sets A and B contain the same elements.
- *Subset.* The **subset** relation is written as $A \subseteq B$ and is true if all the elements of A are also elements of B. For example, the set $\{2, 3, 5, 7\}$ is a subset of the set $\{1, 2, 3, 4, 5, 6, 7, 8, 9\}$. Similarly, the set $\mathbf{N}$ of natural numbers is a subset of the set $\mathbf{Z}$ of integers. From the definition, it is clear that every set is a subset of itself. Mathematicians use the notation $A \subset B$ to indicate that A is a **proper subset** of B, which means that the subset relation holds but that the sets are not equal.

Set operations are often illustrated by drawing **Venn diagrams,** which are named for the British logician John Venn (1834–1923). In a Venn diagram, the individual sets are represented as geometric figures that may overlap to indicate regions in which they share elements. For example, the results of the set operations union, intersection, and set difference are indicated by the shaded regions in the following Venn diagrams:

$A \cup B$ $A \cap B$ $A - B$

Identities on sets

One of the useful bits of knowledge you can derive from mathematical set theory is that the union, intersection, and difference operations are related to each other in various ways. These relationships are usually expressed as **identities,** which are rules indicating that two expressions are invariably equal. In this text, identities are written in the form

$$lhs \equiv rhs$$

which means that the set expressions *lhs* and *rhs* are always the same and can therefore be substituted for one another. The most common identities for sets are shown in Table 15-1.

You can get a sense of how these identities work by drawing Venn diagrams to represent individual stages in the computation. Consider, for example, the first of DeMorgan's laws listed in Table 15-1, which states that the following always holds:

$$A - (B \cup C) \equiv (A - B) \cap (A - C)$$

If you diagram the stages involved in computing the left-hand side of this identity, you get the following picture:

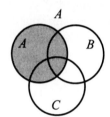
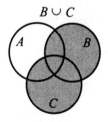
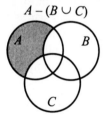

If you look instead at the right-hand side of this identity, the stages of the computation look like this:

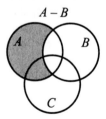
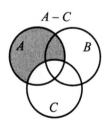
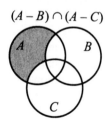

The fact that their Venn diagrams have the same shaded region demonstrates that the sets $A - (B \cup C)$ and $(A - B) \cap (A - C)$ are equivalent.

What may still be unclear, however, is why you as a programmer might ever need to learn rules that at first seem so complex and arcane. Mathematical techniques are important to computer science for several reasons. For one thing, theoretical knowledge is useful in its own right because it deepens your understanding of the foundations of computing. At the same time, this type of theoretical knowledge often has direct application to programming practice. By relying on data structures whose mathematical properties are well established, you can use the theoretical

TABLE 15-1	Fundamental identities on sets
$S \cup S \equiv S$ $S \cap S \equiv S$	*Idempotence*
$A \cap (A \cup B) \equiv A$ $A \cup (A \cap B) \equiv A$	*Absorption*
$A \cup B \equiv B \cup A$ $A \cap B \equiv B \cap A$	*Commutative laws*
$A \cup (B \cup C) \equiv (A \cup B) \cup C$ $A \cap (B \cap C) \equiv (A \cap B) \cap C$	*Associative laws*
$A \cap (B \cup C) \equiv (A \cap B) \cup (A \cap C)$ $A \cup (B \cap C) \equiv (A \cup B) \cap (A \cup C)$	*Distributive laws*
$A - (B \cup C) \equiv (A - B) \cap (A - C)$ $A - (B \cap C) \equiv (A - B) \cup (A - C)$	*DeMorgan's laws*

underpinnings of those structures to your advantage. For example, if you write a program that uses sets as an abstract type, you may be able to simplify your code by applying one of the standard set identities shown in Table 15-1. The justification for making that simplification comes from the abstract theory of sets. Choosing to use sets as a programming abstraction, as opposed to designing some less formal structure of your own, makes it easier for you to apply theory to practice.

◼ 15.2 Designing a set interface

If you want to use sets as an abstract type in an application, you need to design an interface that exports the standard set operations in a way that clients will find easy to use. As with the abstract interfaces presented in earlier chapters, the `set.h` interface presumably exports a type called `setADT` to represent sets, along with whatever functions are needed to manipulate them. From your experience with interface design and your knowledge of how sets behave, you should expect that the `set.h` interface allows clients to perform the following operations:

- *Allocation and deallocation.* The `set.h` interface must make it possible to create new sets. The easiest approach—which follows the design of most interfaces in this text—is to export a constructor function that allocates an empty set. Along with the constructor function, the interface should export a function that allows you to free the storage associated with a set.
- *Adding and deleting elements.* Once you have used the constructor function to create a new set, you need to be able to add elements to it so that you can create a set containing the elements you need. For symmetry, and because the operation is required for many set algorithms, it is also convenient to be able to delete elements from a set. Thus, the `set.h` interface should include functions for adding and deleting individual elements from an existing set.

- *Testing membership.* There must be a function corresponding to the membership operator ∈ that allows you to determine whether a set contains a particular element.
- *Determining the number of elements.* In many applications, it helps to be able to determine the number of elements in a set, which mathematicians sometimes call its **cardinality.** Moreover, it often makes sense to have the `set.h` interface export a function `SetIsEmpty` that makes it easy for clients to check for an empty set.
- *High-level set operations.* The `set.h` interface should export functions like `Union`, `Intersection`, `SetDifference`, `SetEqual`, and `IsSubset` that correspond to the fundamental mathematical operations on sets.
- *Iteration.* Given a set, it must be possible to step through the elements in the set, applying an operation as you go. To provide clients with this capability, the interface can use any of the strategies presented in Chapter 11 for symbol tables. One approach, for example, would be to have the `set.h` interface export a mapping function that invokes a client-supplied callback function on each element of a set. A better strategy, however, is to extend the iterator facility defined in `iterator.h` so that clients can iterate over elements in a set in exactly the same way that those clients can iterate over keys in a symbol table. The `set.h` interface defined in this chapter adopts the iterator-based approach. The early sections of this chapter simply assume that such a facility exists; the details of the underlying implementation are presented in the section on "Designing a polymorphic iterator" later in the chapter.

Defining the element type

Before writing out the complete interface, you need to resolve a very important issue: what type should you use to represent the elements in a set? To a certain extent, answering this question requires you to take into account the preferences of typical clients. As the designer of the interface, you need to make sure that your interface gives programmers the freedom to define sets containing the values they want to use.

If you think about this question for a while—and particularly if you survey programmers who are working with existing set packages—you are likely to discover that clients of a set package fall into two distinct classes. Clients in the first class want to use sets that contain integers or, more broadly, values of some scalar type that behaves like an integer, such as the built-in type `char` or a client-defined enumeration type. Clients who fall into the second class, which is somewhat smaller than the first, want to use sets whose elements are abstract data types. Because all scalar types convert automatically to integers and all abstract types are represented as pointers, you need to consider only two element types: `int` and `void *`.

Given that your clients want to use two distinct element types, how should you go about designing the interface? There are many different strategies you could adopt, including the following:

- *Define the interface in terms of a named element type that the client can change.* The idea behind this proposal is to define the interface in terms of a type called `setElementT` and allow the client to change the definition in the interface as necessary. Although this strategy seems to work for the `stack.h` and `queue.h` interfaces introduced earlier in the text, it has never been very satisfying because it requires clients to edit the interface to change the element type. Since only two element types are likely to arise in practice, it seems worthwhile to look for an alternative strategy that avoids having the client edit the contents of the interface.

■ *Ignore sets of integers and force all clients to use pointer types instead.* This strategy seems attractive initially because it defines the interface in terms of the most flexible type. Clients who want to work with sets of integers can always use dynamic allocation to create pointers to those integers and then store the resulting pointers in the set. The costs of this approach, however, are significant. Client programmers who want to use sets of integers often have a strong interest in efficiency. The overhead of allocating new memory for each value stored in a set will almost certainly be excessive. Moreover, as you will discover in the section on "Enhancing the efficiency of integer sets" later in this chapter, it is possible to implement sets of integers much more efficiently than sets containing more general types.

■ *Ignore general sets of pointers and force all clients to use integer sets.* While this strategy seems less general than the preceding one, allowing only sets of integers is actually a reasonable solution. Client programmers who want to store pointer types in a set can usually get around the restriction by storing all the pointer values in an array and then creating sets of array indices. Although this tactic is not applicable to all problems and imposes some overhead on clients who want to store abstract data types in a set, most clients are content with using sets of integers anyway.

■ *Define a union type that allows clients to store either an integer or a pointer.* Given that union types proved so useful in Chapter 14, the idea of defining a single type that can hold either integers or pointers might seem like an attractive possibility. Unfortunately, this strategy creates many more problems than it solves. Exporting a union type imposes extra work on all clients, because they must declare the union value and assign their own data to the appropriate internal field. More importantly, the strategy provides no obvious way for the implementation to know what type of value is stored in the union. Insisting that the union definition contain a type tag addresses this specific concern, but at the cost of additional overhead to maintain the tags. On the whole, this strategy seems unworkable as the basis for the design of the `set.h` interface, although it turns out to be useful in its underlying implementation.

■ *Define two separate interfaces, one for integer sets and one for pointer sets.* With this strategy, clients who want to work with sets of integers could use an `intset.h` interface that provides a very efficient implementation for integer sets, while clients who need additional generality could use a separate `ptrset.h` interface. Because this strategy satisfies both of your client constituencies, it appears to be a step in the right direction. However, the existence of two similar but nonetheless distinct interfaces has a negative impact on both the conceptual simplicity of the interface design and the cost of maintaining the implementation.

■ *Define a single interface that supports two classes of sets.* The strategy likely to prove best overall is to design a single interface that allows clients to create sets of two different classes: integer sets and pointer sets. By having only one interface and keeping to a minimum the number of functions that must be sensitive to the element type, this strategy maintains a high level of conceptual integrity while meeting the needs of your clients.

Writing the `set.h` interface

If you adopt the final strategy in the preceding section, you can easily write a `set.h` interface such as the one shown in Figure 15-1. This interface exports a single `setADT` type with two constructor functions: `NewIntSet` and `NewPtrSet`. The first creates sets of integers, and the second creates sets whose elements can be of any pointer type. Note that the function `NewPtrSet` requires the client to specify a comparison function so the implementation can compare individual elements.

Certain functions in the `set.h` interface—specifically those whose prototypes refer to individual elements and must therefore indicate the element type—appear in two forms. For example, there are two functions that add elements to a set, one for each class. You use the function `AddIntElement` with integer sets and `AddPtrElement` with pointer sets. Most functions, however, are common to the two classes. For example, the interface exports a function called `NElements` that returns the number of elements in a set. This function works equally well with sets of integers and sets of pointers. Similarly, you can use the `Union`, `Intersection`, and `SetDifference` functions with sets of either class. The arguments passed to these functions must be sets of the same class, and the result will match the class of its arguments. Thus, if you call `Union(s1, s2)` with `s1` and `s2` bound to integer sets, the result will be an integer set. If `s1` is an integer set and `s2` is a pointer set, the implementation of the `Union` function will indicate an error. If both `s1` and `s2` are pointer sets, those sets must also have the same comparison function.

Character sets

It is important to remember that integer sets can be used to represent elements of any scalar type. One of the most common element types for sets is the built-in type `char`, which proves useful in a number of applications. For example, if you need to test whether a particular character is a legal operator in the context of the expression parser from Chapter 14, you can use the set package to construct a set of the legal operators and then use the function `IsIntElement` to determine whether the character in question is a member of that set.

You can also use character sets as the basis for an implementation of the ANSI `ctype.h` interface, which allows you to determine whether a character falls into a particular class. To implement the functions from `ctype.h` using sets, the first step is to create several sets of characters, which correspond to the various predicate functions exported by the interface. For example, the following function initializes

FIGURE 15-1   Interface for a general set abstraction

```
/*
 * File: set.h
 * ------------
 * This interface exports the type setADT, which can be used
 * to represent sets of objects.  The objects themselves can
 * be either of the following two types:
 *
 * int     This base type makes it easy to represent sets
 *         of integers (or any other scalar type), which come
 *         up frequently in practice.
 *
 * void *  This base type makes it possible for clients to
 *         use the set package with more sophisticated
 *         client-defined types.  The only requirement is that
 *         the client must supply a comparison function that
 *         compares two elements of the specified type.
 *
 * These two base types define two classes of sets, IntSet and
 * PtrSet.  The class of the set is determined when the set is
 * created, and the interface in some cases provides separate
 * functions for dealing with sets of each class.
 *
 * In addition to the set operations shown in this interface,
 * the set type allows iteration, as described in the iterator.h
 * interface.  The standard iterator idiom looks like this:
 *
 *      iterator = NewIterator(s);
 *      while (StepIterator(iterator, &x)) {
 *         . . . body of loop involving x . . .
 *      }
 *      FreeIterator(iterator);
 */

#ifndef _set_h
#define _set_h

#include "genlib.h"
#include "cmpfn.h"

/*
 * Type: setClassT
 * ----------------
 * This enumeration type defines the two possible set classes.
 */

typedef enum { IntSet, PtrSet } setClassT;
```

```
/*
 * Type: setADT
 * ------------
 * This type defines the abstract set type.  Depending on how
 * you initialize it, a set may be of either class.
 */

typedef struct setCDT *setADT;

/* Exported entries */

/*
 * Functions: NewIntSet, NewPtrSet
 * Usage: set = NewIntSet();
 *        set = NewPtrSet(cmpFn);
 * -------------------------------
 * These functions are used to create empty setADT values of the
 * specified class.  The NewIntSet function creates sets capable
 * of holding integers; the NewPtrSet function creates a more
 * general set type capable of holding client-specified types.
 */

setADT NewIntSet(void);
setADT NewPtrSet(cmpFnT cmpFn);

/*
 * Function: FreeSet
 * Usage: FreeSet(set);
 * --------------------
 * This function frees the storage associated with set, which
 * may be of either class.
 */

void FreeSet(setADT set);

/*
 * Functions: GetSetClass, GetCompareFunction
 * Usage: class = GetSetClass(set);
 *        fn = GetCompareFunction(set);
 * -------------------------------------------
 * These functions return the set class and the comparison
 * function for an existing set.
 */

setClassT GetSetClass(setADT set);
cmpFnT GetCompareFunction(setADT set);

/*
 * Function: NElements
 * Usage: n = NElements(set);
 * --------------------------
 * This function returns the number of elements in the set.
 */

int NElements(setADT set);
```

```
/*
 * Function: SetIsEmpty
 * Usage: if (SetIsEmpty(set)) . . .
 * --------------------------------
 * This function returns TRUE if the set has no elements.
 */

bool SetIsEmpty(setADT set);

/*
 * Functions: AddIntElement, AddPtrElement
 * Usage: AddIntElement(set, element);
 *        AddPtrElement(set, element);
 * ---------------------------------------
 * These functions each add a new element to an existing set
 * and differ only in the type of that element.
 */

void AddIntElement(setADT set, int element);
void AddPtrElement(setADT set, void *element);

/*
 * Functions: DeleteIntElement, DeletePtrElement
 * Usage: DeleteIntElement(set, element);
 *        DeletePtrElement(set, element);
 * ----------------------------------------------
 * These functions delete the element from the set, if it exists.
 */

void DeleteIntElement(setADT set, int element);
void DeletePtrElement(setADT set, void *element);

/*
 * Functions: IsIntElement, IsPtrElement
 * Usage: if (IsIntElement(set, element)) . . .
 *        if (IsPtrElement(set, element)) . . .
 * ----------------------------------------------
 * These functions return TRUE if the element is in the set.
 */

bool IsIntElement(setADT set, int element);
bool IsPtrElement(setADT set, void *element);

/*
 * Functions: SetEqual, IsSubset
 * Usage: if (SetEqual(s1, s2)) . . .
 *        if (IsSubset(s1, s2)) . . .
 * ---------------------------------
 * These predicate functions implement the equality and subset
 * relations on sets, respectively.  SetEqual(s1, s2) returns
 * TRUE if s1 and s2 have the same elements.  IsSubset(s1, s2)
 * returns TRUE if all elements of s1 are also elements of s2.
 */

bool SetEqual(setADT s1, setADT s2);
bool IsSubset(setADT s1, setADT s2);
```

```
/*
 * Functions: Union, Intersection, SetDifference
 * Usage: set = Union(s1, s2);
 *        set = Intersection(s1, s2);
 *        set = SetDifference(s1, s2);
 * ----------------------------------------------
 * These functions each return a new set, as follows:
 *
 * Union(s1, s2)          All elements in either s1 or s2.
 * Intersection(s1, s2)   All elements in both s1 and s2.
 * SetDifference(s1, s2)  All elements in s1 but not in s2.
 */

setADT Union(setADT s1, setADT s2);
setADT Intersection(setADT s1, setADT s2);
setADT SetDifference(setADT s1, setADT s2);

#endif
```

five sets of characters corresponding to the `ctype.h` functions `isdigit`, `islower`, `isupper`, `isalpha`, and `isalnum`, respectively:

```
void InitCTypeSets(void)
{
    digitSet = NewSetFromString("0123456789");
    lowerSet = NewSetFromString("abcdefghijklmnopqrstuvwxyz");
    upperSet = NewSetFromString("ABCDEFGHIJKLMNOPQRSTUVWXYZ");
    alphaSet = Union(lowerSet, upperSet);
    alnumSet = Union(digitSet, alphaSet);
}

static setADT NewSetFromString(string str)
{
    setADT set;
    int i;

    set = NewIntSet();
    for (i = 0; str[i] != '\0'; i++) {
        AddIntElement(set, str[i]);
    }
    return (set);
}
```

Once these sets have been defined, functions like `isdigit` become simple membership tests, as follows:

```
bool isdigit(int ch)
{
    return (IsIntElement(digitSet, ch));
}
```

The other functions from `ctype.h` can be defined in much the same way.

Using pointer sets to avoid duplication

To get a sense of how you might use sets containing pointer types, it helps to go back to the program from Chapter 5 that generates permutations. The simple recursive implementation of `ListPermutations` does not work well if there are repeated characters in the input string. For example, if you use the original program to generate the permutations of the string `"AAB"`, you get the following output:

```
AAB
ABA
AAB
ABA
BAA
BAA
```

Each of the permutations appears twice somewhere in the list. It would be better if the program listed each unique permutation only once, so that the output would look like this instead:

```
AAB
ABA
BAA
```

You can write a program to produce this output by using sets to keep track of the permutations you have already encountered. Instead of displaying each permutation as you compute it, all you have to do is add it to a set. When the recursive decomposition is complete, you can simply go through that set, displaying each element in turn. Because a set contains only one copy of each element, the duplicates are automatically eliminated.

In the context of the permutation program, the elements of the set are strings. Strings are pointer types, which means that the code must use `NewPtrSet` to construct the set of permutations, passing in the function `StringCmpFn` defined in `cmpfn.h`. The revised code for `ListPermutations` and `RecursivePermute` appears in Figure 15-2.

■■■ 15.3 Implementing the set package

Writing an implementation for the `set.h` interface is considerably easier than you might expect, mostly because you can layer the implementation on top of the binary search tree facility from Chapter 13. If you think about the operations that the `bst.h` interface exports, you will quickly discover that they correspond closely to the operations you need for sets. Testing for membership in a set is comparable to finding a node in a binary search tree. Similarly, the insertion and deletion operations behave in much the same way for both structures, because keys in a binary search tree—like elements in a set—are unique in the sense that a given key will never appear more than once. Thus, if you use a binary search tree to store the elements of a set, you can use the functions `FindBSTNode`, `InsertBSTNode`, and `DeleteBSTNode` to implement the corresponding set operations.

FIGURE 15-2 Set-based implementation of `ListPermutations`

```
/*
 * Function: ListPermutations
 * Usage: ListPermutations(str)
 * ---------------------------
 * This function lists all permutations of the characters in the
 * string str.  If the same string is generated more than once
 * in the course of the algorithm, each of those permutations is
 * listed only once.
 */

static void ListPermutations(string str)
{
    setADT set;
    iteratorADT iterator;
    string s;

    set = NewPtrSet(StringCmpFn);
    RecursivePermute(str, 0, set);
    iterator = NewIterator(set);
    while (StepIterator(iterator, &s)) {
        printf("%s\n", s);
    }
    FreeIterator(iterator);
}

/*
 * Function: RecursivePermute
 * Usage: RecursivePermute(str, k, set);
 * -------------------------------------
 * This function implements the recursive permutation algorithm,
 * adding each permutation to the set as it goes.
 */

static void RecursivePermute(string str, int k, setADT set)
{
    int i;

    if (k == StringLength(str)) {
        AddPtrElement(set, CopyString(str));
    } else {
        for (i = k; i < StringLength(str); i++) {
            ExchangeCharacters(str, k, i);
            RecursivePermute(str, k + 1, set);
            ExchangeCharacters(str, k, i);
        }
    }
}
```

Because most of the work necessary to implement sets can be left to the `bst.h` interface, the implementation of the set package itself is quite straightforward. There are, however, a few aspects of the implementation that require some thought. When you first write them, many of the functions are slightly different for the two classes of sets. In most cases, however, the only difference lies in the declaration of a variable. To avoid writing two distinct sets of implementations for each function, it simplifies the implementation to define a union type called `setElementT`, which is capable of holding either `int` or `void *` elements. Using this type means that many functions can be implemented in a way that works equally well for both set classes.

It is also important to recognize that the higher-level set operations such as `Union` and `Intersection` can be written using the iterator facility described in the interface. In pseudocode, these functions look like this:

```
setADT Union(setADT s1, setADT s2)
{
    setADT s;

    Create an empty set s whose class matches s1 and s2.
    for (each element x in s1) {
        Add x to s.
    }
    for (each element x in s2) {
        Add x to s.
    }
    return (s);
}

setADT Intersection(setADT s1, setADT s2)
{
    setADT s;

    Create an empty set s whose class matches s1 and s2.
    for (each element x in s1) {
        if (x is an element of s2)  Add x to s.
    }
    return (s);
}
```

You can easily translate the `for` statements in the pseudocode formulation into a `while` loop that uses an iterator. For example, the loop in the `Intersection` function ends up looking like this in the finished code:

```
iterator = NewIterator(s1);
while (StepIterator(iterator, &element)) {
    if (TestERef(s2, &element)) AddERef(set, &element);
}
FreeIterator(iterator);
```

Note that the variable `element` is declared to be of type `setElementT`, which guarantees that the variable contains enough room to store either an integer or a pointer value.

Except for the functions necessary to support iteration, which are described in the next section, the complete code for the set package appears in Figure 15-3.

FIGURE 15-3 Implementation of the set abstraction based on binary search trees

```
/*
 * File: set.c
 * -----------
 * This file implements the set abstraction defined in set.h.
 */

#include <stdio.h>
#include "genlib.h"
#include "bst.h"
#include "set.h"

/*
 * Type: setCDT
 * ------------
 * This type defines the concrete structure of a set.
 */

struct setCDT {
    setClassT class;
    cmpFnT cmpFn;
    int nElements;
    bstADT bst;
};

/*
 * Type: setElementT
 * -----------------
 * This union type combines the two representations of an element.
 * It is used in the implementation to allocate storage for an
 * element that is guaranteed to be large enough no matter whether
 * the set contains integers or pointers.  This type is used only
 * to reduce the number of special cases in the code and is not
 * exported to the client.
 */

typedef union {
    int intRep;
    void *ptrRep;
} setElementT;

/* Private function prototypes */

static setADT NewSet(setClassT class, cmpFnT cmpFn);
static void InitSetNodeFn(void *np, void *kp, void *clientData);
static void FreeNodeFn(void *np, void *clientData);
static void AddERef(setADT set, void *ep);
static void DeleteERef(setADT set, void *ep);
static bool TestERef(setADT set, void *ep);
```

```
/* Exported entries */

/*
 * Implementation notes: NewIntSet, NewPtrSet
 * -------------------------------------------
 * The contructor functions call a common function that creates
 * a new set from a class and a comparison function.  The
 * elements in the set are stored in a binary search tree.
 */

setADT NewIntSet(void)
{
    return (NewSet(IntSet, IntCmpFn));
}

setADT NewPtrSet(cmpFnT cmpFn)
{
    return (NewSet(PtrSet, cmpFn));
}

static setADT NewSet(setClassT class, cmpFnT cmpFn)
{
    setADT set;

    set = New(setADT);
    set->class = class;
    set->cmpFn = cmpFn;
    set->nElements = 0;
    set->bst = NewBST(sizeof (setElementT), cmpFn, InitSetNodeFn);
    return (set);
}

static void InitSetNodeFn(void *np, void *kp, void *clientData)
{
    setADT set = (setADT) clientData;

    switch (set->class) {
      case IntSet: *((int *) np) = *((int *) kp); break;
      case PtrSet: *((void **) np) = *((void **) kp); break;
    }
    set->nElements++;
}

void FreeSet(setADT set)
{
    FreeBST(set->bst, FreeNodeFn);
    FreeBlock(set);
}

static void FreeNodeFn(void *np, void *clientData)
{
    FreeBlock(np);
}
```

```
/* Selection functions */

setClassT GetSetClass(setADT set)
{
    return (set->class);
}

cmpFnT GetCompareFunction(setADT set)
{
    return (set->cmpFn);
}

/*
 * Implementation notes: NElements, SetIsEmpty
 * --------------------------------------------
 * For efficiency, this package stores the number of elements
 * as part of the set data structure, updating it as necessary.
 */

int NElements(setADT set)
{
    return (set->nElements);
}

bool SetIsEmpty(setADT set)
{
    return (set->nElements == 0);
}

/*
 * Implementation notes: AddIntElement, AddPtrElement
 * --------------------------------------------------
 * These functions call a common function AddERef, which takes
 * a pointer to the element.
 */

void AddIntElement(setADT set, int element)
{
    if (set->class != IntSet) Error("Set is not an integer set");
    AddERef(set, &element);
}

void AddPtrElement(setADT set, void *element)
{
    if (set->class != PtrSet) Error("Set is not a pointer set");
    AddERef(set, &element);
}

static void AddERef(setADT set, void *ep)
{
    (void) InsertBSTNode(set->bst, ep, set);
}
```

```
/*
 * Implementation notes: DeleteIntElement, DeletePtrElement
 * --------------------------------------------------------
 * These functions simply check to see that the set type is
 * appropriate and then call a common function.
 */

void DeleteIntElement(setADT set, int element)
{
    if (set->class != IntSet) Error("Set is not an integer set");
    DeleteERef(set, &element);
}

void DeletePtrElement(setADT set, void *element)
{
    if (set->class != PtrSet) Error("Set is not a pointer set");
    DeleteERef(set, &element);
}

static void DeleteERef(setADT set, void *ep)
{
    void *np;

    np = DeleteBSTNode(set->bst, ep);
    if (np != NULL) {
        FreeBlock(np);
        set->nElements--;
    }
}

/*
 * Implementation notes: IsIntElement, IsPtrElement
 * ------------------------------------------------
 * These implementations call a common TestERef function, which
 * in turn calls FindBSTNode to look up the element.
 */

bool IsIntElement(setADT set, int element)
{
    if (set->class != IntSet) Error("Set is not an integer set");
    return (TestERef(set, &element));
}

bool IsPtrElement(setADT set, void *element)
{
    if (set->class != PtrSet) Error("Set is not a pointer set");
    return (TestERef(set, &element));
}

static bool TestERef(setADT set, void *ep)
{
    return (FindBSTNode(set->bst, ep) != NULL);
}
```

```
/*
 * Implementation notes: Set operations
 * ------------------------------------
 * The functions IsSubset, Union, Intersection, and SetDifference
 * are similar in structure.  Each one uses an iterator to walk over
 * the appropriate set.  Because the functions in bst.h need only
 * the address of an element, the functions can use the union type
 * setElementT to avoid special-case code for the two set classes.
 */

bool SetEqual(setADT s1, setADT s2)
{
    return (IsSubset(s1, s2) && IsSubset(s2, s1));
}

bool IsSubset(setADT s1, setADT s2)
{
    iteratorADT iterator;
    setElementT element;
    bool result;

    if (s1->class != s2->class || s1->cmpFn != s2->cmpFn) {
        Error("IsSubset: Set types do not match");
    }
    result = TRUE;
    iterator = NewIterator(s1);
    while (result && StepIterator(iterator, &element)) {
        if (!TestERef(s2, &element)) result = FALSE;
    }
    FreeIterator(iterator);
    return (result);
}

setADT Union(setADT s1, setADT s2)
{
    iteratorADT iterator;
    setElementT element;
    setADT set;

    if (s1->class != s2->class || s1->cmpFn != s2->cmpFn) {
        Error("Union: Set types do not match");
    }
    set = NewSet(s1->class, s1->cmpFn);
    iterator = NewIterator(s1);
    while (StepIterator(iterator, &element)) {
        AddERef(set, &element);
    }
    FreeIterator(iterator);
    iterator = NewIterator(s2);
    while (StepIterator(iterator, &element)) {
        AddERef(set, &element);
    }
    FreeIterator(iterator);
    return (set);
}
```

```
setADT Intersection(setADT s1, setADT s2)
{
    iteratorADT iterator;
    setElementT element;
    setADT set;

    if (s1->class != s2->class || s1->cmpFn != s2->cmpFn) {
        Error("Intersection: Set types do not match");
    }
    set = NewSet(s1->class, s1->cmpFn);
    iterator = NewIterator(s1);
    while (StepIterator(iterator, &element)) {
        if (TestERef(s2, &element)) AddERef(set, &element);
    }
    FreeIterator(iterator);
    return (set);
}

setADT SetDifference(setADT s1, setADT s2)
{
    iteratorADT iterator;
    setElementT element;
    setADT set;

    if (s1->class != s2->class || s1->cmpFn != s2->cmpFn) {
        Error("SetDifference: Set types do not match");
    }
    set = NewSet(s1->class, s1->cmpFn);
    iterator = NewIterator(s1);
    while (StepIterator(iterator, &element)) {
        if (!TestERef(s2, &element)) AddERef(set, &element);
    }
    FreeIterator(iterator);
    return (set);
}
```

■■■ 15.4 Designing a polymorphic iterator

The only part of the set abstraction that is not included in Figure 15-3 is the code that implements iteration on sets. You might think that the challenge of implementing an iterator facility consists of figuring out how to step through the elements of a set. That part, however, is quite easy, given the fact that the set is represented as a binary search tree. One of the major advantages of that representation, after all, is that the structure of the tree makes it easy to walk through all the keys in order. The hard problem is figuring out how to make the iterator package work for sets without affecting clients of the symbol table package who are already using iterators in that domain.

The most general approach is to make the iterator.h interface polymorphic in the sense that clients could use it equally well to step through the elements of symbol tables, sets, or any other type that contains elements. For the purposes of this discussion, such types are called **collection types.** Turning an abstract data type into a collection type requires additional code in the implementation of that type, but should not require clients to know anything special about the internal structure of the collection type itself.

Generalizing the prototypes of the iterator functions

Fortunately, you can easily make the prototypes for the iterator functions more general without changing their basic structure. Although the original version of the `iterator.h` interface that appears in Figure 11-6 refers to symbol tables explicitly and assumes that the argument passed to `StepIterator` is the address of a string, the style in which these functions are used does not depend on those assumptions. Client programs would operate just as well if the interface defined the three iterator functions as taking arguments of the generic `void *` type instead, in which case their prototypes would look like this:

```
iteratorADT NewIterator(void *collection);
bool StepIterator(iteratorADT iterator, void *ep);
void FreeIterator(iteratorADT iterator);
```

None of these functions indicate that the collection is a `setADT`, a `symtabADT`, or any other type, which means that there is nothing to prevent you from calling these functions on any collection type. These changes—along with updating the comments that describe how to use the package—are the only ones necessary to make the interface itself polymorphic.

Adding polymorphism to the iterator implementation

Writing a polymorphic version of the iterator code is considerably more challenging than updating the interface. Because collection types are quite different in their structure and contain values of different types, the implementation of `NewIterator` needs to know something about the collection type in order to initialize the iterator correctly. Given the anonymous character of the `collection` argument, which is declared as a `void *` in the prototype for `NewIterator`, it is not immediately clear that `NewIterator` can figure out how to initialize an iterator that is appropriate to the collection type it has been passed.

One strategy for solving this problem is to make sure that the underlying data structure for any collection types includes a pointer to a callback function that creates a new iterator. Thus, the internal data structure for sets would include a pointer to a function that creates an iterator for sets, while the internal data structure for symbol tables would include a pointer to a function that performs the same operation for symbol tables. If the `NewIterator` code is going to call that function, however, the function pointer must always appear at a predefined location within the concrete structure. The usual approach is to put the function pointer in a header block, which is guaranteed to come at the very beginning of a collection type, as illustrated by the following diagram:

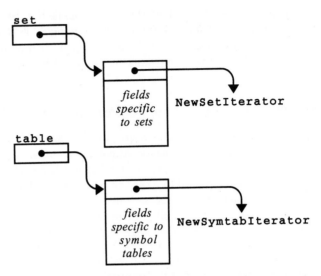

When **NewIterator** gets its argument, it can assume that the address refers to an iteration header block and call the function pointer it finds there.

This approach, however, can be a bit dangerous. What happens, for example, if a client tries to call **NewIterator** on a type that does not include the required iterator header? Suppose, for example, that no one had gotten around to implementing iteration for the type **queueADT**. If **NewIterator** is called on a queue, the implementation will simply assume that it has been passed a legitimate collection type and treat the data at the beginning of the block as a function pointer, which can easily cause the program to crash. This situation is illustrated in the following diagram, which shows the view from both sides of the iterator interface:

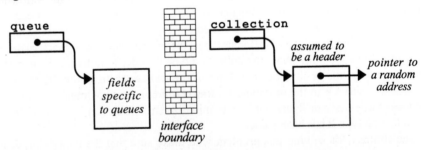

At one level, the problem here is that the **void *** type is too general to describe the **collection** argument. The **NewIterator** function should be restricted to accept only collection types as arguments. Unfortunately, C's type system is not powerful enough to implement the proper restrictions. In C, **void *** is the only real option.

You can achieve some degree of safety by building run-time checks into the code for **NewIterator**. The simplest approach is to require the header field of any collection type to start with a particular pattern of bits that is unlikely to occur by chance. Special bit patterns that are used to protect against illegal operations are called **passwords.** When you create a value that is a legitimate collection type, the constructor function stores the correct password at the beginning of the header. The `NewIterator` function can then check to see that the password is in place before invoking the callback function.

Given this design, the iterator facility itself is not particularly difficult to implement. The basic strategy for creating iterators is the same as that for symbol tables in Chapter 11. All the real work is done at the time the iterator is created. When the `NewIterator` function has finished its work, the internal data structure of the iterator contains a list of all the elements. This design simplifies the implementation of the `StepIterator` function, which merely has to remove the first item in the element list and store it in the variable whose address appears in the `StepIterator` call.

Exporting a collection type

In designing the interface to the iterator package, however, it is important to keep in mind that the code has two different sets of clients: those who are using iterators to step through the elements of a collection type and those who want to define new collection types from scratch. These two groups of clients may well have very different levels of sophistication. There is no reason that clients who use an iterator should be bothered with knowing the details of how to implement one. To maintain the conceptual separation between these two types of clients, it makes sense to have the `iterator.c` file implement two separate interfaces: a polymorphic version of the `iterator.h` interface from Figure 11-6 that can be used by all clients and a more specialized interface called `itertype.h`, which appears in Figure 15-4, that is relevant only to those clients seeking to export new collection types.

The purpose of the `itertype.h` interface is to make it easy for other abstract packages—such as the ones that implement sets and symbol tables—to export collection types. To do so, the package exporting the type must make the following changes to the implementation:

1. Include space for an iterator header in the concrete data structure for the type.
2. Change the constructor function for the collection type so that it calls the function `EnableIteration` whenever a new value is created. Calling this function initializes the iterator header to include the password and the address of the callback function that creates new iterators.
3. Define the function that constructs a new iterator for the collection type.

To implement iterators for sets, for example, you must edit the original `set.c` implementation from Figure 15-3 to include each of these three extensions. The first two changes are quite easy. You need to change the concrete type definition so it includes an `iteratorHeaderT`, like this:

```
struct setCDT {
    iteratorHeaderT header;
    setClassT class;
    cmpFnT cmpFn;
    int nElements;
    bstADT bst;
};
```

FIGURE 15-4   Interface used to export collection types that support iteration

```
/*
 * File: itertype.h
 * -----------------
 * This file provides an interface that package designers can
 * use to export new collection types that support iteration.
 * Clients of those collection types who merely want to use
 * iterators will not need to import this interface.
 */

#ifndef _itertype_h
#define _itertype_h

#include "genlib.h"
#include "iterator.h"
#include "cmpfn.h"

/*
 * General overview
 * ----------------
 * In order to create a collection type that supports iteration,
 * the implementor of the type must first allocate space at the
 * beginning of the concrete record for an iteratorHeaderT that
 * contains a function pointer which allows NewIterator to make
 * a new iterator for that collection type.  The implementor
 * must initialize this header in the constructor function by
 * calling EnableIteration.  The specific NewIterator functions
 * for each type must perform the following operations:
 *
 * 1. Call NewIteratorList to create an empty iterator.
 * 2. Call AddToIteratorList for each element.
 * 3. Return the completed iterator.
 */

/*
 * Type: newIteratorFnT
 * --------------------
 * This type represents the class of functions that create new
 * iterators.
 */

typedef iteratorADT (*newIteratorFnT)(void *collection);

/*
 * Constant function: UnsortedFn
 * -----------------------------
 * This constant creates a NULL function pointer that can be
 * used in place of the comparison function to indicate that the
 * values in the iterator should not be sorted.  The constant 0
 * is used in place of NULL because some compilers do not allow
 * casting NULL to a function pointer.
 */

#define UnsortedFn ((cmpFnT) 0)
```

```
/*
 * Type: iteratorHeaderT
 * ---------------------
 * This structure must appear at the beginning of any concrete
 * structure that supports iteration.
 */

typedef struct {
    unsigned long password;
    newIteratorFnT newFn;
} iteratorHeaderT;

/*
 * Functions: EnableIteration
 * Usage: EnableIteration(collection, newFn);
 * ------------------------------------------
 * This function enables iteration for the collection.  The
 * function pointer newFn is used to initialize an iterator
 * for this type.
 */

void EnableIteration(void *collection, newIteratorFnT newFn);

/*
 * Functions: NewIteratorList
 * Usage: iterator = NewIteratorList(sizeof (type), cmpFn);
 * --------------------------------------------------------
 * This function creates a new iterator with an empty iterator
 * list.  The first argument is the size of the element type,
 * which makes it possible for the package to allocate storage
 * for values of that type.  The cmpFn is the comparison function
 * used to sort the iterator elements.  If cmpFn is the constant
 * pointer UnsortedFn, the elements are entered in the order in
 * which AddToIteratorList is called.
 */

iteratorADT NewIteratorList(int size, cmpFnT cmpFn);

/*
 * Functions: AddToIteratorList
 * Usage: AddToIteratorList(iterator, &element);
 * ---------------------------------------------
 * This function takes an iterator and a pointer to an element
 * and inserts the element into the iterator list.
 */

void AddToIteratorList(iteratorADT iterator, void *ep);

#endif
```

You also need to add a line to the `NewSet` constructor function to enable iteration, as follows:

```
static setADT NewSet(setClassT class, cmpFnT cmpFn)
{
    setADT set;

    set = New(setADT);
    EnableIteration(set, NewSetIterator);
    set->class = class;
    set->cmpFn = cmpFn;
    set->nElements = 0;
    set->bst = NewBST(sizeof (setElementT), cmpFn, InitSetNodeFn);
    return (set);
}
```

Implementing the function `NewSetIterator` is the only part of the process that requires any significant thought. The code for `NewSetIterator`, which appears in Figure 15-5, requires a certain amount of explanation. When you use the tools from

---

FIGURE 15-5 Code in `set.c` to implement iterators

```
/*
 * Implementation notes: NewSetIterator, AddElementToIterator
 * --------------------------------------------------------------
 * These functions make it possible to use the general iterator
 * facility on sets.  For details on the general strategy, see
 * the comments in the itertype.h interface.  The comparison
 * function passed to NewIteratorList is UnsortedFn because the
 * InOrder walk already guarantees that the elements will appear
 * in sorted order.
 */

static iteratorADT NewSetIterator(void *collection)
{
    setADT set = collection;
    int elementSize;
    iteratorADT iterator;

    switch (set->class) {
      case IntSet: elementSize = sizeof(int); break;
      case PtrSet: elementSize = sizeof(void *); break;
    }
    iterator = NewIteratorList(elementSize, UnsortedFn);
    MapBST(AddElementToIterator, set->bst, InOrder, iterator);
    return (iterator);
}

static void AddElementToIterator(void *np, void *clientData)
{
    AddToIteratorList((iteratorADT) clientData, np);
}
```

`itertype.h` to create a new iterator, you need to perform the following operations:

1. Call `NewIteratorList` to create a new iterator with an empty iterator list.
2. Walk over the elements in the collection, calling `AddToIteratorList` on each one.
3. Return the completed iterator.

The `NewSetIterator` code follows precisely this logic. It first creates the new iterator and then calls `MapBST` to walk through the keys in the binary search tree used as the underlying representation for the set. When the map operation is complete, the iterator has been correctly initialized to contain all the elements in the set.

As you can see, the `NewIteratorList` function takes two arguments: the size of an individual element and a comparison function. The element size is used to allocate space for the elements in the iterator list. Because the iterator package is polymorphic, the implementation of `AddToIteratorList` cannot know the size of each individual element. The comparison function is used to define the order in which the elements appear in the iterator list. The `AddToIteratorList` function keeps the elements in sorted order unless the comparison function is `UnsortedFn`, in which case each element is entered at the end of the list. In the case of the set iterator, it is fine to use `UnsortedFn` for the comparison function because the inorder walk of the tree automatically inserts the elements in the correct order.

Coding the iterator package

The code for the iterator package appears in Figure 15-6. Much of the implementation is straightforward, although the fact that the iterator package must be flexible enough to support many different element types does complicate the design to some extent. In particular, the type declaration for the linked-list cells used by the iterator cannot include a value field because there would be no way to specify its size. Instead, the cell structure defines only the link pointer and then dynamically allocates whatever extra space is needed at the end of the record for the value. When values of that type need to be copied to and from the client space, the code uses the `memcpy` function from the ANSI `string.h` interface to copy the appropriate number of bytes.

The concrete data structure for the iterator is designed to include a tail pointer of the sort used in a linked-list queue. Because elements can be inserted at arbitrary positions in the list, keeping a pointer to the end may not seem very useful. One reason for keeping the tail pointer is to increase the efficiency of the `AddToIteratorList` code when `UnsortedFn` is used as the comparison function. In this case, all elements are added at the end of the list in the style of a traditional queue. Even if the iterator uses some other comparison function, maintaining a tail pointer can sometimes increase efficiency. The code for `AddToIteratorList` begins by making a special-case test to determine whether the element belongs at the end of the list. If it does, the function simply inserts that element at the tail of the queue without bothering to search through all the elements in the list. If the elements of a collection tend to be added in order, including this special-case check reduces the cost of the insertion algorithm from quadratic to linear time.

FIGURE 15-6 Implementation of the polymorphic iterator

```
/*
 * File: iterator.c
 * ----------------
 * This file implements a polymorphic version of the iterator
 * and the tools necessary to construct types that support
 * iteration.  This module implements both the iterator.h and
 * itertype.h interfaces.
 */

#include <stdio.h>
#include <string.h>
#include "genlib.h"
#include "cmpfn.h"
#include "iterator.h"
#include "itertype.h"

/*
 * Constant: IteratorPassword
 * --------------------------
 * This constant is stored in the header block of collection
 * types to catch the case when a client tries to call
 * NewIterator on a value for which iteration is not defined.
 */

#define IteratorPassword 3141592653UL

/*
 * Type: cellT, iteratorCDT
 * ------------------------
 * The iterator is implemented as a linked list chained
 * through the first word in the structure.  Because the size
 * of the actual data element can vary, the data field is not
 * represented as part of the structure.  Instead, each cell is
 * allocated dynamically with enough memory for both the link
 * field and the data value, however large it turns out to be.
 * The list is arranged like a queue, with a tail pointer to
 * its final element for efficiency.  The AddToIteratorList
 * function first checks to see whether the element belongs at
 * the end.  By checking for this case explicitly, it is often
 * possible to avoid searching the list at all.
 */

typedef struct cellT {
    struct cellT *link;
    /* The actual data is allocated here */
} cellT;

struct iteratorCDT {
    int elementSize;
    cmpFnT cmpFn;
    cellT *head, *tail;
};
```

```
iteratorADT NewIterator(void *collection)
{
    iteratorHeaderT *hp = collection;

    if (hp->password != IteratorPassword) {
        Error("Iteration is not defined for this type");
    }
    return (hp->newFn(collection));
}

bool StepIterator(iteratorADT iterator, void *ep)
{
    cellT *cp;
    void *dp;

    cp = iterator->head;
    if (cp == NULL) {
        iterator->tail = NULL;
        return (FALSE);
    }
    dp = ((char *) cp) + sizeof (cellT);
    memcpy(ep, dp, iterator->elementSize);
    iterator->head = cp->link;
    FreeBlock(cp);
    return (TRUE);
}

void FreeIterator(iteratorADT iterator)
{
    cellT *cp;

    while ((cp = iterator->head) != NULL) {
        iterator->head = cp->link;
        FreeBlock(cp);
    }
    FreeBlock(iterator);
}

void EnableIteration(void *collection, newIteratorFnT newFn)
{
    iteratorHeaderT *hp = collection;

    hp->password = IteratorPassword;
    hp->newFn = newFn;
}

iteratorADT NewIteratorList(int size, cmpFnT cmpFn)
{
    iteratorADT iterator;

    iterator = New(iteratorADT);
    iterator->elementSize = size;
    iterator->cmpFn = cmpFn;
    iterator->head = iterator->tail = NULL;
    return (iterator);
}
```

```
/*
 * Implementation notes: AddToIteratorList
 * ----------------------------------------
 * Most of the work of the package occurs in this function, which
 * inserts the element addressed by ep into its correct position.
 * If the list is unordered or if the element belongs at the end,
 * the element is immediately inserted at the tail.  If not, the
 * implementation walks the list to find the correct position.
 * The local pointers have the following interpretations:
 *
 * np -- pointer to the newly allocated cell
 * pp -- pointer to the cell preceding the insertion point
 * ip -- pointer used as an index in the for loop
 * dp -- pointer to the data field in the block
 */

void AddToIteratorList(iteratorADT iterator, void *ep)
{
    cellT *np, *pp, *ip;
    void *dp;

    np = GetBlock(sizeof (cellT) + iterator->elementSize);
    dp = ((char *) np) + sizeof (cellT);
    memcpy(dp, ep, iterator->elementSize);
    pp = NULL;
    if (iterator->tail != NULL) {
        if (iterator->cmpFn == UnsortedFn) {
            pp = iterator->tail;
        } else {
            dp = ((char *) iterator->tail) + sizeof (cellT);
            if (iterator->cmpFn(ep, dp) >= 0) pp = iterator->tail;
        }
    }
    if (pp == NULL) {
        for (ip = iterator->head; ip != NULL; ip = ip->link) {
            dp = ((char *) ip) + sizeof (cellT);
            if (iterator->cmpFn(ep, dp) < 0) break;
            pp = ip;
        }
    }
    if (pp == NULL) {
        np->link = iterator->head;
        if (iterator->head == NULL) iterator->tail = np;
        iterator->head = np;
    } else {
        np->link = pp->link;
        if (pp->link == NULL) iterator->tail = np;
        pp->link = np;
    }
}
```

The `foreach` idiom

As you may already recognize from using them with symbol tables, iterators are powerful programming tools that are much more convenient to use than mapping functions. Even so, the syntax of the iterator code sometimes gets in the way of understanding what is essentially a very simple idea. The point of an iterator is simply to process each of the elements in a collection, in much the same way that you use the loop

```
for (i = 0; i < n; i++) {
    Code to process the element a[i]
}
```

to cycle through the elements in an array of size `n`.

Because you have worked with this particular `for` loop idiom for quite some time, you probably no longer think about the individual expressions in the `for` loop and have come to see the entire header line as a single conceptual unit. If you work with iterators long enough, the idiom for iterating through a collection

```
iteratorADT iterator;

iterator = NewIterator(collection);
while (StepIterator(iterator, &x)) {
    Code to process the element x
}
FreeIterator(iterator);
```

will come to seem equally natural. For now, however, all the calls to functions in the iterator package can easily obscure the underlying idea.

To make the idea behind the iterator as clear as possible, I often use an abbreviated pseudocode notation for iterators that assumes the existence of a new control structure called `foreach`, which looks like this:

```
foreach (x in collection) {
    Code to process the element x
}
```

The intent of this code is extremely easy to understand, because all the details having to do with the iterator are hidden away. As a result, algorithms written using the `foreach` notation are usually much easier to read. When you actually write the C code, you can convert the `foreach` notation back to its complete iterator-based form.

It is, in fact, possible to implement the `foreach` control structure using the macro definition capabilities provided by the C preprocessor, although the resulting implementation is not particularly efficient and requires detailed knowledge of the preprocessor that is beyond the scope of this presentation. A copy of the files `foreach.h` and `foreach.c` is available as part the source code supplied with this text. The fact that an implementation of `foreach` exists makes it possible for you to take advantage of its conceptual simplicity as you write your programs. Once you have debugged those programs, you can rewrite them using iterators to increase their efficiency.

■■ 15.5 Enhancing the efficiency of integer sets

The implementation of the set abstraction shown in Figure 15-3 does not include any optimizations for integer sets, mostly because the code is already rather long. Even so, it is important to know that there are more efficient strategies for representing integer sets as long as you can restrict the elements of the set to integers in some predefined range. In many applications, sets naturally obey this constraint. For example, if you are using integer sets to represent sets of characters, the values will never be outside the range [0, 255]. If the element type of the set is a typical enumeration type, the set of legal values will be restricted to an even smaller range.

Characteristic vectors

Suppose for the moment that you are working with a set whose elements will always lie between 0 and `RangeSize` − 1, where `RangeSize` is a constant that specifies the size of the range to which element values are restricted. You can represent such sets efficiently by using an array of Boolean values. The value at index position k in the array indicates whether the integer k is in the set. For example, if `elements[4]` has the value `TRUE`, then 4 is in the set represented by the Boolean array `elements`. Similarly, if `elements[5]` is `FALSE`, then 5 is not an element of that set. Boolean arrays in which the elements indicate whether the corresponding index is a member of some set are called **characteristic vectors.** The following examples illustrate how the characteristic-vector strategy can be used to represent the indicated sets, assuming that `RangeSize` has the value 10:

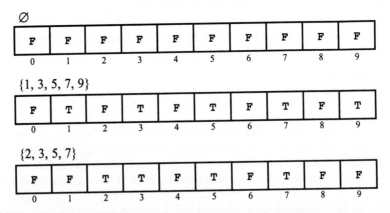

The advantage of using characteristic vectors is that doing so makes it possible to implement the operations `AddIntElement`, `DeleteIntElement`, and `IsIntElement` in constant time. For example, to add the element k to a set, all you have to do is set the element at index position k in the characteristic vector to `TRUE`. Similarly, testing membership is simply a matter of selecting the appropriate element in the array.

Packed arrays of bits

Even though characteristic vectors allow highly efficient implementations in terms of their running time, storing characteristic vectors as explicit arrays can require a large amount of memory, particularly if `RangeSize` is large. To reduce the storage requirements, you can pack the elements of the characteristic vector into machine words so that the representation uses every bit in the underlying representation. Suppose, for example, that the type `unsigned long` is represented as a 32-bit value on your machine. You can then store 32 elements of a characteristic vector in a single value of type `unsigned long`, since each element of the characteristic vector requires only one bit of information. Moreover, if `RangeSize` is 256, you can store all 256 bits needed for a characteristic vector in an array of eight `unsigned long` values.

To understand how characteristic vectors can be packed into an array of machine words, imagine that you want to represent the integer set consisting of the ASCII code for the alphabetic characters. That set, which consists of the 26 uppercase letters with codes between 65 and 90 and the 26 lowercase letters with codes between 97 and 122, can be encoded as the following characteristic vector:

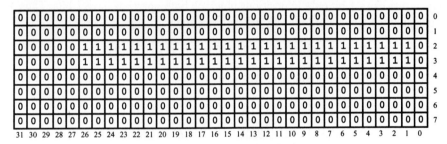

If you want to find the bit that corresponds to a particular integer value, the simplest approach is to use integer division and modular arithmetic. For example, suppose that you want to locate the bit corresponding to the character `'X'`, which has 88 as its ASCII code. The row number of the desired bit is 2, because there are 32 bits in each row and 88 / 32 is 2 using the standard definition of integer division. Similarly, within the second row, you find the entry for `'X'` at bit number 24, which is the remainder of 88 divided by 32. Thus, the bit in the characteristic vector corresponding to the character `'X'` is the one circled in this diagram:

```
                    'X'

  0 0 0 0 0 0 0 0 0 0 0 0 0 0 0 0 0 0 0 0 0 0 0 0 0 0 0 0 0 0 0 0   0
  0 0 0 0 0 0 0 0 0 0 0 0 0 0 0 0 0 0 0 0 0 0 0 0 0 0 0 0 0 0 0 0   1
  0 0 0 0 0 1 1 1(1)1 1 1 1 1 1 1 1 1 1 1 1 1 1 1 1 1 1 1 1 1 1 0   2
  0 0 0 0 0 1 1 1 1 1 1 1 1 1 1 1 1 1 1 1 1 1 1 1 1 1 1 1 1 1 1 0   3
  0 0 0 0 0 0 0 0 0 0 0 0 0 0 0 0 0 0 0 0 0 0 0 0 0 0 0 0 0 0 0 0   4
  0 0 0 0 0 0 0 0 0 0 0 0 0 0 0 0 0 0 0 0 0 0 0 0 0 0 0 0 0 0 0 0   5
  0 0 0 0 0 0 0 0 0 0 0 0 0 0 0 0 0 0 0 0 0 0 0 0 0 0 0 0 0 0 0 0   6
  0 0 0 0 0 0 0 0 0 0 0 0 0 0 0 0 0 0 0 0 0 0 0 0 0 0 0 0 0 0 0 0   7
 31 30 29 28 27 26 25 24 23 22 21 20 19 18 17 16 15 14 13 12 11 10 9 8 7 6 5 4 3 2 1 0
```

The fact that the circled bit is a 1 indicates that `'X'` is a member of the set.

Bitwise operators

In order to write code that works with arrays of bits stored in this tightly packed form, you need to learn how to use the low-level operators that C provides for manipulating the bits in a memory word. These operators, which are listed in Table 15-2, are called **bitwise operators.** They take values of any scalar type and interpret them as sequences of bits that correspond to their underlying representation at the hardware level.

To illustrate the behavior of the bitwise operators, let's consider a specific example. Suppose that the variables x and y, which are declared to be of type `unsigned` on a machine that uses 16-bit words, contain the following bit patterns:

x | 0 | 0 | 0 | 0 | 0 | 0 | 0 | 0 | 0 | 0 | 1 | 0 | 1 | 0 | 1 | 0

y | 0 | 0 | 0 | 0 | 0 | 0 | 0 | 0 | 0 | 0 | 0 | 1 | 1 | 0 | 1 | 1

The &, |, and ∧ operators each apply the logical operation specified in Table 15-2 to each bit position in the operand words. The & operator, for example, produces a result that has a 1 bit only in positions in which both operands have 1 bits. Thus, if you apply the & operator to the bit patterns in x and y, you get this result:

x & y | 0 | 0 | 0 | 0 | 0 | 0 | 0 | 0 | 0 | 0 | 0 | 0 | 1 | 0 | 1 | 0

The | and ∧ operators produce the following results:

x | y | 0 | 0 | 0 | 0 | 0 | 0 | 0 | 0 | 0 | 0 | 1 | 1 | 1 | 0 | 1 | 1

x ∧ y | 0 | 0 | 0 | 0 | 0 | 0 | 0 | 0 | 0 | 0 | 1 | 1 | 0 | 0 | 0 | 1

The ~ operator is a unary operator that reverses the state of every bit in its operand, which is called **taking the complement** of that operand. For example, if you apply the ~ operator to the bit pattern in x, the result looks like this:

x | 0 | 0 | 0 | 0 | 0 | 0 | 0 | 0 | 0 | 0 | 1 | 0 | 1 | 0 | 1 | 0

~x | 1 | 1 | 1 | 1 | 1 | 1 | 1 | 1 | 1 | 1 | 0 | 1 | 0 | 1 | 0 | 1

TABLE 15-2 Bitwise operators in C	
x & y	Logical AND. The result has a 1 bit in positions where both x and y have 1 bits.
x | y	Logical OR. The result has a 1 bit in positions where either x or y has a 1 bit.
x ∧ y	Exclusive OR. The result has 1 bits in positions where the bits in x and y differ.
~x	Logical NOT. The result has a 1 bit where x has a 0 bit, and vice versa.
x << n	Left shift. The bits in x are shifted left n bit positions.
x >> n	Right shift. The bits in x are shifted right n bit positions.

The operators `<<` and `>>` shift the bits in their left operand the number of positions specified by their right operand. The only difference between the two operations is the direction in which the shifting occurs. The `<<` operator shifts bits to the left; the `>>` operator shifts them to the right. Thus, the expression `x << 1` produces a new value in which every bit in the value of **x** is shifted one position to the left, as follows:

```
x       0 0 0 0 0 0 0 0 0 0 1 0 1 0 1 0
x << 1  0 0 0 0 0 0 0 0 0 1 0 1 0 1 0 0
```

Similarly, the expression `y >> 2` produces a value in which the bits in **y** have been shifted two positions to the right, like this:

```
y       0 0 0 0 0 0 0 0 0 0 0 1 1 0 1 1
y << 2  0 0 0 0 0 0 0 0 0 0 0 0 0 1 1 0
```

As long as the value being shifted is unsigned, bits that are shifted past the end of the word disappear and are replaced on the opposite end by 0 bits. If the value being shifted is signed, the behavior of the shift operators depends on the underlying characteristics of the hardware. For this reason, it is good practice to restrict your use of the shift operators to unsigned values, thereby increasing the portability of your code.

Bit patterns such as those used in the preceding examples correspond to integers, which are represented internally in their binary form. The value shown for the variable **x**, for example, represents the integer 42, which you can determine by adding up the place values of the digits, each of which accounts for twice as much as the bit on its right.

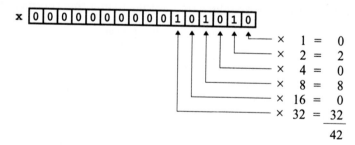

When you work with bit patterns, however, it is best not to regard them as base-10 integers, because it is hard to recognize the underlying sequence of bits when given an integer in its decimal form. In programming, it is much more common to express bit patterns in **octal** (base 8) or **hexadecimal** (base 16). The advantage of using either of these bases is that doing so allows you to convert integers directly into their underlying bit patterns one digit at a time. Because both 8 and 16 are powers of two, you can translate an octal or a hexadecimal integer into its binary form by replacing each digit in the integer with the appropriate bit pattern, as shown in Table 15-3.

TABLE 15-3 Bit patterns for the octal and hexadecimal digits

Octal			Hexadecimal			
0	000		0	0000	8	1000
1	001		1	0001	9	1001
2	010		2	0010	A	1010
3	011		3	0011	B	1011
4	100		4	0100	C	1100
5	101		5	0101	D	1101
6	110		6	0110	E	1110
7	111		7	0111	F	1111

As noted in Chapter 1, C allows you to write integer constants in either octal or hexadecimal notation. To specify an octal constant, all you do is begin the number with the digit 0. To specify a hexadecimal constant in C, you begin with the prefix 0x followed by the digits that make up the number. Since hexadecimal notation requires 16 digits, the digits corresponding to the numbers 10 through 15 are indicated using the letters A through F. For example, the decimal integer 42 can be written as either the octal constant 052 or the hexadecimal constant 0x2A, as illustrated by the following diagrams:

Implementing characteristic vectors using the bitwise operators

The bitwise operators introduced in the preceding section make it possible to implement operations on characteristic vectors in a highly efficient way. If you want to test the state of an individual bit in a characteristic vector, all you have to do is create a value that has a 1 bit in the desired position and 0 bits everywhere else. Such a value is called a **mask** because you can use it to hide all the other bits in the word. If you apply the & operator to the word in the characteristic vector that contains the bit you're trying to find and the mask that corresponds to the correct bit position, all the other bits in that word will be stripped away, leaving you with a value that reflects the state of the desired bit.

To make this strategy more concrete, it helps to define the structure of a characteristic vector in more detail. If you define the type cVectorADT as an abstract type that represents a characteristic vector, its underlying representation is an array of machine words interpreted as a sequence of bits. The concrete representation of cVectorADT is therefore

```
struct cVectorCDT {
    unsigned long words[CVecWords];
};
```

where `CVecWords` is a constant defined as follows:[2]

```
#define BitsPerByte 8
#define BitsPerLong (BitsPerByte * sizeof (long))
#define CVecWords ((RangeSize + BitsPerLong - 1) / BitsPerLong)
```

Given this structure, you can test a specific bit in a characteristic vector using the function `CVectorTest`, which has the following implementation:

```
bool CVectorTest(cVectorADT cv, int k)
{
    if (k < 0 || k >= RangeSize) {
        Error("CVectorTest: Value is out of range");
    }
    return ((cv->words[k / BitsPerLong] & BitMask(k)) != 0);
}

unsigned long BitMask(int k)
{
    return ((unsigned long) 1 << (k % BitsPerLong));
}
```

Suppose, for example, that you call `CVectorTest(cv, 'X')`, where `cv` is bound to the characteristic vector corresponding to the set of all alphabetic characters. As discussed in the section on "Packed arrays of bits" earlier in the chapter, that characteristic vector looks like this:

31	30	29	28	27	26	25	24	23	22	21	20	19	18	17	16	15	14	13	12	11	10	9	8	7	6	5	4	3	2	1	0	
0	0	0	0	0	0	0	0	0	0	0	0	0	0	0	0	0	0	0	0	0	0	0	0	0	0	0	0	0	0	0	0	0
0	0	0	0	0	0	0	0	0	0	0	0	0	0	0	0	0	0	0	0	0	0	0	0	0	0	0	0	0	0	0	0	1
0	0	0	0	0	1	1	1	1	1	1	1	1	1	1	1	1	1	1	1	1	1	1	1	1	1	1	1	1	1	1	0	2
0	0	0	0	0	1	1	1	1	1	1	1	1	1	1	1	1	1	1	1	1	1	1	1	1	1	1	1	1	1	1	0	3
0	0	0	0	0	0	0	0	0	0	0	0	0	0	0	0	0	0	0	0	0	0	0	0	0	0	0	0	0	0	0	0	4
0	0	0	0	0	0	0	0	0	0	0	0	0	0	0	0	0	0	0	0	0	0	0	0	0	0	0	0	0	0	0	0	5
0	0	0	0	0	0	0	0	0	0	0	0	0	0	0	0	0	0	0	0	0	0	0	0	0	0	0	0	0	0	0	0	6
0	0	0	0	0	0	0	0	0	0	0	0	0	0	0	0	0	0	0	0	0	0	0	0	0	0	0	0	0	0	0	0	7

The result of the call to `CVectorTest` is a Boolean value, which is `TRUE` if the expression

```
cv->words[k / BitsPerLong] & BitMask(k)
```

is nonzero. The expression `k / BitsPerLong` computes the index of the appropriate word in the characteristic vector. Because the character `'X'` has the ASCII value 88

---

[2] The expression used to compute `CVecWords` may at first seem unnecessarily complicated. However, if the value of `RangeSize` is not a multiple of `BitsPerLong`, the characteristic vector must include space for the elements that appear in the last word of the structure, which will be only partially filled. The computation in the numerator of the expression guarantees that the division operation will round the number of words up to the next larger integer.

and `BitsPerLong` is 32, the index expression selects the second word in the array used to represent the characteristic vector, which consists of the following bits:

`0 0 0 0 0 1 1 1 1 1 1 1 1 1 1 1 1 1 1 1 1 1 1 1 1 1 1 1 1 1 1 0`

The `BitMask(k)` function computes a mask using the following expression:

`(unsigned long) 1 << (k % BitsPerLong)`

If `k` has the value 88, `k % BitsPerLong` is 24, which means that the mask value consists of the value 1 shifted left 24 bit positions, like this:

`0 0 0 0 0 0 0 1 0 0 0 0 0 0 0 0 0 0 0 0 0 0 0 0 0 0 0 0 0 0 0 0`

Because the mask has only a single 1 bit, the `&` operation in the code for `CVectorTest` will return a nonzero value only if the corresponding bit in the characteristic vector is a 1. If the characteristic vector contained a 0 in that bit position, there would be no bits that were 1 in both the vector and the mask, which means that the `&` operation would return a word containing only 0 bits. A word composed entirely of 0 bits has the integer value 0.

The strategy of using a mask also makes it easy to manipulate the state of individual bits in the characteristic vector. By convention, assigning the value 1 to a specific bit is called **setting** that bit; assigning the value 0 is called **clearing** that bit. You can set a particular bit in a word by applying the logical OR operation to the old value of that word and a mask containing the desired bit. You can clear a bit by applying the logical AND operation to the old value of the word and the complement of the mask. These operations are illustrated by the following definitions of the functions `CVectorSet` and `CVectorClear`:

```
void CVectorSet(cVectorADT cv, int k)
{
    if (k < 0 || k >= RangeSize) {
        Error("CVectorSet: Value is out of range");
    }
    cv->words[k / BitsPerLong] |= BitMask(k);
}

void CVectorClear(cVectorADT cv, int k)
{
    if (k < 0 || k >= RangeSize) {
        Error("CVectorClear: Value is out of range");
    }
    cv->words[k / BitsPerLong] &= ~BitMask(k);
}
```

Implementing the high-level set operations

Packing characteristic vectors into the bits in a word certainly saves a large amount of space. As it happens, this same strategy also improves the efficiency of the high-level set operations like `Union`, `Intersection`, and `SetDifference`. The trick is to compute each word in the new characteristic vector using a single application of the appropriate bitwise operator.

As an example, the union of two sets consists of all elements that belong to either of its arguments. If you translate this idea into the realm of characteristic vectors, it is easy to see that any word in the characteristic vector of the set $A \cup B$ can be computed by applying the logical OR operation to the corresponding words in the characteristic vectors for those sets. The result of the logical OR operation has a 1 bit in those positions in which either of its operands has a 1 bit, which is exactly what you want to compute the union.

This approach is illustrated by the function **CVectorUnion**, which creates a new characteristic vector whose value corresponds to the union of the characteristic vectors passed in as arguments. The code for **CVectorUnion** looks like this:

```
cVectorADT CVectorUnion(cVectorADT cv1, cVectorADT cv2)
{
    cVectorADT result;
    int i;

    result = New(cVectorADT);
    for (i = 0; i < CVecWords; i++) {
        result->words[i] = cv1->words[i] | cv2->words[i];
    }
    return (result);
}
```

The functions **Intersection** and **SetDifference** can be implemented similarly; the details are left to you as a programming exercise.

Using a hybrid implementation

You can apply the characteristic vector approach only to sets whose elements fall into a limited range. On the other hand, there is no reason that clients of a general set package necessarily have to be aware of this distinction. If you are implementing the set package, you can adopt a hybrid approach that uses characteristic vectors as long as the values stay in range. As soon as the client adds an element to the set that is outside the range allowed by the characteristic-vector representation, the implementation automatically converts the set to use the more general form offered by binary search trees. As a result, clients who only use integers in the restricted range get the enhanced performance associated with the characteristic vector strategy. On the other hand, clients who need to define sets containing integers outside the optimal range can still use the same interface.

▆ Summary

In this chapter, you have learned about sets, which are important to computer science as both a theoretical and a practical abstraction. The fact that sets have a well-developed mathematical foundation—far from making them too abstract to be useful—increases their utility as a programming tool. Because of that theoretical foundation, you can count on sets to exhibit certain properties and obey specific rules. By coding your algorithms in terms of sets, you can build on that same theoretical base and construct systems whose behavior is easier to predict and understand.

Important points in this chapter include:

- A set is an unordered collection of distinct elements. The set operations used in this book appear in Table 15-4, along with their mathematical symbols.
- The interactions among the various set operators are often easier to understand if you keep in mind certain identities that indicate that two set expressions are invariably equal. Using these identities can also improve your programming practice, because they provide you with tools to simplify set operations appearing in your code.
- If you try to define sets as an abstract type, there are many different strategies you can adopt to represent the type of an individual set element. These strategies all have certain advantages and disadvantages. After exploring many other options, this chapter eventually settles on the approach of defining two different set classes—one that contains integers and one that contains pointers—both of which are implemented by a single `set.h` interface.
- The set package is straightforward to implement because much of it can be layered on top of the `bst.h` interface from Chapter 13, which defines an abstraction for binary search trees.
- To implement most of the algorithms that apply to sets, it must be possible to step through the elements of a set one at a time. One of the best ways to provide this capability is to define an iterator that works for sets in much the same way that the iterator facility in Chapter 11 works for symbol tables. A particularly attractive option—which is the one adopted in this chapter—is to generalize the structure of the `iterator.h` interface so that the same package can work with symbol tables, sets, or any other collection type.

TABLE 15-4	Mathematical notations for sets		
Empty set		$\varnothing$	The set containing no elements
Membership		$x \in S$	True if x is an element of S
Nonmembership		$x \notin S$	True if x is not an element of S
Equality		$A = B$	True if A and B contain exactly the same elements
Subset		$A \subseteq B$	True if all elements in A are also in B
Proper subset		$A \subset B$	True if A is a subset of B but the sets are not equal
Union		$A \cup B$	The set of elements in either A, B, or both
Intersection		$A \cap B$	The set of elements in both A and B
Set difference		$A - B$	The set of elements in A that are not also in B

- When you are designing code to use the iterator package, it often helps to express your algorithms in a pseudocode form that looks like

```
foreach (x in collection) {
    Code to process the element x
}
```

and later expand the code into the following iterator idiom:

```
iteratorADT iterator;

iterator = NewIterator(collection);
while (StepIterator(iterator, &x)) {
    Code to process the element x
}
FreeIterator(iterator);
```

- Sets of integers can be implemented very efficiently using arrays of Boolean data called *characteristic vectors*. If you use the bitwise operators provided by C, you can pack characteristic vectors into a small number of machine words and perform such set operations as union and intersection on many elements of the vector at a time.

REVIEW QUESTIONS

1. True or false: The elements of a set are unordered, so the set {3, 2, 1} and the set {1, 2, 3} represent the same set.

2. True or false: A set can contain multiple copies of the same element.

3. What sets are denoted by each of the following symbols: $\varnothing$, **Z**, **N**, and **R**?

4. What do the symbols $\in$ and $\notin$ mean?

5. Use an enumeration to specify the elements of the following set:

$$\{x \mid x \in \mathbf{N} \text{ and } x \le 100 \text{ and } \sqrt{x} \in \mathbf{N}\}$$

6. Write a rule-based definition for the following set:

$$\{1, 9, 18, 27, 36, 45, 54, 63, 72, 81\}$$

7. What are the mathematical symbols for the operations union, intersection, and set difference?

8. Evaluate the following set expressions:

   a. $\{a, b, c\} \cup \{a, c, e\}$

   b. $\{a, b, c\} \cap \{a, c, e\}$

   c. $\{a, b, c\} - \{a, c, e\}$

   d. $(\{a, b, c\} - \{a, c, e\}) \cup (\{a, b, c\} - \{a, c, e\})$

9. What is the difference between a subset and a proper subset?

10. Give an example of an infinite set that is a proper subset of some other infinite set.

11. For each of the following set operations, draw Venn diagrams whose shaded regions illustrate the contents of the specified set expression:

    a. $A \cup (B \cap C)$
    b. $(A - C) \cap (B - C)$
    c. $(A - B) \cup (B - A)$
    d. $(A \cup B) - (A \cup B)$

12. Write set expressions that describe the shaded region in each of the following Venn diagrams:

    a.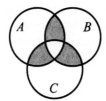

    b.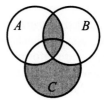

13. Draw Venn diagrams illustrating each of the identities in Table 15-1.

14. What is the cardinality of a set?

15. Enumerate the six design alternatives suggested in the chapter for defining the base type of a set. What are the advantages and disadvantages of each design?

16. What are the two set classes supported by the **set.h** interface?

17. Which functions exported by the **set.h** interface have different forms for the two set classes? Why is it necessary to export different forms for some functions but not others?

18. What argument must be passed to the function **NewPtrSet**?

19. How is the set package used in the implementation of the **ListPermutations** function that appears in Figure 15-2?

20. The general implementation of the set package uses a data structure from an earlier chapter to represent the elements of a set. What is that structure? What properties make that structure useful for this purpose?

21. Once you have created a set using the functions exported by the **set.h** interface, how can you step through the elements of that set?

22. Why is it useful to develop a polymorphic version of the **iterator.h** interface?

23. Without including any actual code, describe the polymorphic implementation of the iterator package in as much detail as you can.

24. What is the purpose of the password in the polymorphic implementation of the iterator package?

25. The `iterator.c` module implements two interfaces: `iterator.h` and `itertype.h`. Why are those interfaces separate?

26. Describe the steps necessary to export a collection type.

27. Why does the concrete data structure for the iterator include a tail pointer to the end of the linked list used to assemble the elements?

28. The following function uses the `foreach` idiom to compute the sum of the elements in an integer set:

```
int SumIntSet(setADT set)
{
    int x, sum;

    sum = 0;
    foreach (x in set) {
        sum += x;
    }
    return (sum);
}
```

Rewrite this function to use iterators instead of `foreach`.

29. What is a characteristic vector?

30. What restrictions must be placed on a set in order to use characteristic vectors as an implementation strategy?

31. Assuming that `RangeSize` has the value 10, diagram the characteristic vectors for the following sets:

    a.   {1, 2, 3, 4, 5, 6, 7, 8, 9}
    b.   {5}

32. What set is represented by the following characteristic vector:

31	30	29	28	27	26	25	24	23	22	21	20	19	18	17	16	15	14	13	12	11	10	9	8	7	6	5	4	3	2	1	0
0	0	0	0	0	0	0	0	0	0	0	0	0	0	0	0	0	0	0	0	0	0	0	0	0	0	0	0	0	0	0	0
0	0	0	0	0	0	1	1	1	1	1	1	1	1	1	1	1	1	0	0	0	0	0	0	0	0	0	0	0	0	0	0
0	0	0	0	0	0	1	1	1	1	1	1	1	1	1	1	1	1	1	1	1	1	1	1	1	1	1	1	1	1	1	0
0	0	0	0	0	0	1	1	1	1	1	1	1	1	1	1	1	1	1	1	1	1	1	1	1	1	1	1	1	1	1	0
0	0	0	0	0	0	0	0	0	0	0	0	0	0	0	0	0	0	0	0	0	0	0	0	0	0	0	0	0	0	0	0
0	0	0	0	0	0	0	0	0	0	0	0	0	0	0	0	0	0	0	0	0	0	0	0	0	0	0	0	0	0	0	0
0	0	0	0	0	0	0	0	0	0	0	0	0	0	0	0	0	0	0	0	0	0	0	0	0	0	0	0	0	0	0	0
0	0	0	0	0	0	0	0	0	0	0	0	0	0	0	0	0	0	0	0	0	0	0	0	0	0	0	0	0	0	0	0

By consulting the ASCII chart in Table 1-1, identify the function in `ctype.h` to which this set corresponds.

33. In the diagrams used to represent characteristic vectors (such as the one in the preceding exercise), the type `unsigned long` is shown as taking 32 bits.

Suppose that you are using a machine in which this type is represented using 64 bits instead. Does the code given in the chapter continue to work? Why or why not?

34. Suppose that the variables **x** and **y** are of type **unsigned** and contain the following bit patterns:

x `0 1 0 0 1 0 0 0 0 1 0 0 1 0 0 1`

y `0 0 0 0 0 0 0 0 1 1 1 1 1 1 1 1`

Expressing your answer as a sequence of bits, compute the value of each of the following expressions:

a. **x & y**

b. **x | y**

c. **x ^ y**

d. **x ^ x**

e. **~x**

f. **x & ~y**

g. **~x & ~y**

h. **y >> 4**

i. **x << 3**

j. **(x >> 8) & y**

35. Express the values of **x** and **y** from the preceding exercise as constants using both octal and hexadecimal notation.

36. Suppose that the variables **x** and **mask** are both declared to be of type **unsigned**, and that the value of **mask** contains a single 1 bit in some position. What expressions would you use to accomplish each of the following operations:

a. Test whether the bit in **x** corresponding to the bit in **mask** is nonzero.

b. Set the bit in **x** corresponding to the bit in **mask**.

c. Clear the bit in **x** corresponding to the bit in **mask**.

d. Complement the bit in **x** corresponding to the bit in **mask**.

37. Write an expression that constructs a mask of type **unsigned** in which there is a single 1 bit in bit position **k**, where bits are numbered from 0 starting at the right end of the word. For example, if **k** is 2, the expression should generate the following mask:

`0 0 0 0 0 0 0 0 0 0 0 0 0 1 0 0`
`15 14 13 12 11 10 9 8 7 6 5 4 3 2 1 0`

PROGRAMMING EXERCISES

1. In order to write test programs for the set package, it is useful to have some facility for performing input and output operations. On the input side, for example, you would like to have a function

```
setADT GetIntSet(void);
```

that returns a set of integers entered by the user. On the output side, it would be nice to have a function

```
void PrintIntSet(setADT set);
```

that displays the contents of the specified integer set on the screen.

Implement the functions `GetIntSet` and `PrintIntSet`. For each of these functions, the set should appear in its traditional form, with the elements enclosed in curly braces and separated by commas. The empty set should be represented as an empty pair of curly braces. Your implementation of `GetIntSet` should ignore the spacing of the input, which is easy to do if you use the `scanadt.h` interface with the `IgnoreSpaces` option.

2. Using the preceding exercise as a model, implement the functions

```
setADT GetStringSet(void);
void PrintStringSet(setADT set);
```

which perform input and output for sets of strings. For `GetStringSet`, the input values should be individual string tokens as defined by the scanner abstraction. Use these functions to write a simple test program that reads in two sets of strings and then displays their union, intersection, and difference, as shown in this sample run:

```
Enter s1: {a, b, c}↵
Enter s2: {b, a, d}↵
Union(s1, s2) = {a, b, c, d}
Intersection(s1, s2) = {a, b}
SetDifference(s1, s2) = {c}
```

3. Write a function

```
setADT PrimeSet(int max)
```

that returns a set of the prime numbers between 2 and `max`. A number N is prime if it has exactly two divisors, which are always 1 and the number N itself. Checking for primality, however, doesn't require you to try every possible divisor. The only numbers you need to check are the prime numbers between 2 and the square root of N. As it tests whether a number is prime, your code should make use of the fact that all potential factors must be in the set of primes you are constructing.

4. The implementation of the general `set.h` interface presented in this chapter uses binary search trees to ensure that the set operations are executed with reasonable efficiency. If efficiency is not a relevant concern, you can implement the same abstraction much more easily by representing a set as a linked list of its elements, sorted by the appropriate comparison function. Implement the `set.h` interface using this representation strategy.

5. Write a function `SetCompare(s1, s2)` that compares the sets `s1` and `s2` according to the following rules:

   - In order to be comparable, `s1` and `s2` must have the same class and comparison function. If these properties differ, your implementation of `SetCompare` should generate an error message.
   - If two sets have a different number of elements, the smaller set is always considered to be less than the larger one. Thus, if `s1` is the set {2, 3} and `s2` is the set {0, 1, 2}, calling `SetCompare(s1, s2)` should return −1.
   - If two sets have the same number of elements, `SetCompare` should compare elements in the two sets in the order specified by their comparison function, which is also the order in which iteration occurs. If the elements ever differ, the set containing the smaller of the two values is considered to be less than the set that has the larger value. For example, if `s1` is the set {1, 3, 4} and `s2` is the set {1, 2, 3}, calling `SetCompare(s1, s2)` should return +1, because the integer 3 in `s1` is larger than the corresponding element in `s2`, which is the integer 2.
   - If `s1` and `s2` have exactly the same elements, `SetCompare` should return 0.

   Use the function `SetCompare` to implement the function

   ```
   int SetCmpFn(const void *p1, const void *p2);
   ```

   which matches the general prototype for comparison functions.

6. Because the elements of a pointer set can be any values represented as a pointer for which a comparison function exists, you can use the set package to create sets containing other sets as elements. Write a function

   ```
   setADT PowerSet(setADT s);
   ```

   that returns the **power set** of the set **s**, which is defined as the set of all subsets of **s**. For example, if **s** is the set {a, b, c}, calling `PowerSet(s)` should return the following set:

   {{}, {a}, {b}, {c}, {a, b}, {a, c}, {b, c}, {a, b, c}}

7. Write a function

   ```
   void AddArrayToSet(setADT set, void *array, int n);
   ```

   that adds the first n elements in `array` to the specified set. Such a function is extremely useful in initializing a set whose elements are known at compile time, as illustrated by the following code, which initializes `articleSet` to contain the strings `"a"`, `"an"`, and `"the"`:

   ```
   string articleArray[] = { "a", "an", "the" };
   int nArticles = sizeof articleArray / sizeof articleArray[0];
   setADT articleSet;

   articleSet = NewPtrSet(StringCmpFn);
   AddArrayToSet(articleSet, articleArray, nArticles);
   ```

Your implementation must work for both integer and pointer sets, which in turn affects how you calculate the addresses of the elements in the argument array.

8. Rewrite the symbol table implementation presented in Chapter 11 so that symbol tables work with the more general version of the iterator introduced in this chapter.

9. Exercise 6 in Chapter 8 introduced an interface called `ref.h` that provides functions for allocating and dereferencing pointers to atomic values. Although this interface is extremely convenient, it suffers from the fact that the compiler can no longer perform any type checking. For example, if you create a pointer to the integer 17 by calling `NewRefInt(17)`, there is nothing to prevent you from later trying to dereference that pointer by calling `RefToDouble`, even though the results will be completely unpredictable.

Without changing the `ref.h` interface from the form in which it was presented in Figure 8-6, reimplement the `ref` package so that types are checked at run time. To do so, you need to change the underlying representation of the allocated pointer references so that they point to a block that looks like this:

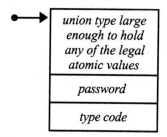

Like the password used in the implementation of the iterator package in this chapter, the password in the second field is a special pattern of bits that the implementation can use to determine whether the value is a valid reference created by the package. The type code is a numeric type code that allows the implementation to check whether the pointer value passed to a function that dereferences pointers is appropriate for that operation.

As an example, calling `NewRefInt(17)` in this revised implementation produces a pointer to a block that looks like this:

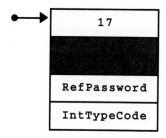

The function `RefToInt` can then check the password and type code fields in the structure before dereferencing the value. If either is incorrect, the implementation of `RefToInt` can report the error.

10. Write a program that implements the following procedure:

- Read in two strings, each of which represents a sequence of bits. These strings must consist only of the characters 0 and 1 and must be exactly 16 characters long.
- Convert each of these strings into a value of type **unsigned** with the same internal pattern of bits. Assume that the variables used to store the converted result are named **x** and **y**.
- Display the value of each of the following expressions as a sequence of 16 bits: `x & y, x | y, x ^ y, ~y, x & ~y`.

The operation of this program is illustrated by the following sample run:

```
Enter x:   0000000000101010↵
Enter y:   0000000000011011↵

x & y = 0000000000001010
x | y = 0000000000111011
x ^ y = 0000000000110001
   ~y = 1111111111100100
x & ~y = 0000000000100000
```

11. On most computer systems, the ANSI `ctype.h` interface introduced in Chapter 3 is implemented using the bitwise operators. The strategy is to use specific bit positions in a word to indicate properties that a character might have. For example, imagine that the three bits at the right end of a word are used to indicate whether a character is a digit, a lowercase letter, or an uppercase letter, as shown in this diagram:

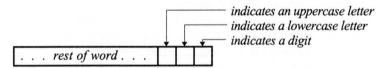

If you create an array consisting of 256 of these words—one for each character—you can implement the functions from `ctype.h` so that each function requires selecting the appropriate element of the array selection, applying one of the bitwise operators, and testing the result.

Use this strategy to implement a simplified version of the `ctype.h` interface that exports the functions `isdigit`, `islower`, `isupper`, `isalpha`, and `isalnum`. In your implementation, it is important to make sure that the code for `isalpha` and `isalnum` requires no more operations than the other three functions do.

12. The function **CVectorUnion** described in the section on "Implementing the high-level set operations" shows how to use C's bitwise operators as the basis for a highly efficient implementation of the union operation for sets. Using **CVectorUnion** as a model, implement the functions **CVectorIntersection** and **CVectorDifference**.

13. Extend the implementation of the set package so that it uses the strategy described in the section on "Using a hybrid implementation." The basic idea is that the function **NewIntSet** creates a set whose internal representation uses a characteristic vector consisting of 256 bits. As long as no elements are added that lie outside the range [0, 255], the implementation can continue to use that representation. However, if the client attempts to add an element to an integer set that is outside this range, the implementation of **AddIntElement** must convert the internal representation to use the more general binary search tree form. Except for the fact that doing so may take some time, the operation of converting the internal representation of the set from one form to another should be invisible to the client.

14. Extend the expression interpreter from Chapter 14 so that it supports sets of integers as a separate data type. When they are used with sets as arguments, the operators +, *, and – should compute the union, intersection, and set difference, respectively. Sets are specified in the traditional way, which means that you need to extend the grammar used by the parser to support braces that enclose a comma-separated list of expressions. A sample run of the program might look like this:

```
=> odds = {9, 7, 5, 3, 1}
{1, 3, 5, 7, 9}
=> evens = {0, 2, 2 * 2, 3 * 2, 2 * 2 * 2}
{0, 2, 4, 6, 8}
=> primes = {2, 3, 5, 7}
{2, 3, 5, 7}
=> odds + evens
{0, 1, 2, 3, 4, 5, 6, 7, 8, 9}
=> odds * evens
{}
=> primes - evens
{3, 5, 7}
=> quit
```

Note that the computation involving integers is still legal and can be used in any expression context, including the values used to specify the elements of a set.

C H A P T E R   16

Graphs

So I draw the world together link by link:
Yea, from Delos up to Limerick and back!

—— Rudyard Kipling, "The Song of the Banjo," *Verses,* 1894

Objectives

- To appreciate the conceptual structure of a graph as a set of nodes linked by a set of arcs.

- To become familiar with common underlying representations for graphs, including adjacency lists, adjacency matrices, and sets.

- To be able to apply depth-first and breadth-first search strategies to graphs.

- To understand the general structure of Dijkstra's algorithm for finding minimum-cost paths.

Many structures in the real world consist of a set of values connected by a set of links. Such a structure is called a **graph.** Common examples of graphs include cities connected by highways, computers connected by network links, and courses in a college curriculum connected by prerequisites. Programmers typically refer to the individual elements—such as the cities, computers, and courses—as **nodes** and the interconnections—the highways, network connections, and prerequisites—as **arcs,** although mathematicians tend to use the terms **vertex** and **edge** instead.

Because they consist of nodes connected by a set of links, graphs are clearly similar to trees, which were introduced in Chapter 13. In fact, the only difference is that there are fewer restrictions on the structure of the connections in a graph than there are in a tree. The arcs in a graph, for example, often form cyclical patterns. In a tree, cyclical patterns are illegal because of the requirement that every node must be linked to the root by a unique line of descent. Because trees have restrictions that do not apply to graphs, graphs are a more general type that includes trees as a subset. Thus, every tree is a graph, but there are some graphs that are not trees.

In this chapter, you will learn about graphs from both a practical and a theoretical perspective. Learning to work with graphs as a programming tool is useful because they come up in a surprising number of contexts. Mastering the theory is extremely valuable as well, because doing so often makes it possible to find much more efficient solutions to problems with considerable commercial importance.

16.1 The structure of a graph

The easiest way to get a sense of the structure of a graph is to consider a simple example. Suppose that you work for a small airline that serves 10 major cities in the United States with the routes shown in Figure 16-1. The labeled circles represent cities—Atlanta, Chicago, Dallas, and so forth—and constitute the nodes of the graph. The lines between the cities represent airline routes and constitute the arcs.

Although graphs are often used to represent geographical relationships, it is important to keep in mind that the graph is defined purely in terms of the nodes and connecting arcs. The layout is unimportant to the abstract concept of a graph. For example, the following diagram represents the same graph as Figure 16-1:

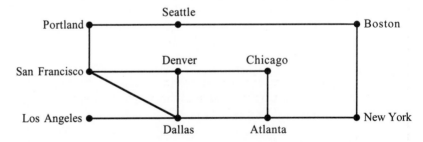

The nodes representing the cities are no longer in the correct positions geographically, but the connections remain the same.

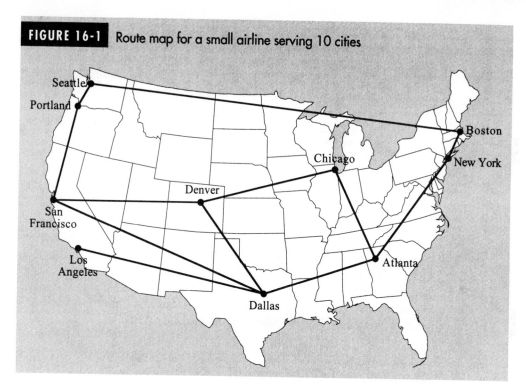

FIGURE 16-1 Route map for a small airline serving 10 cities

You can go one step further and eliminate the geometrical relationships altogether. Mathematicians, for example, use the tools of set theory to define a graph as the combination of two sets, which are typically called *V* and *E* after the mathematical terms *vertex* and *edge*. If you follow this convention, the airline graph consists of the following sets:

V = { Atlanta, Boston, Chicago, Dallas, Denver, Los Angeles,
       New York, Portland, San Francisco, Seattle }

E = { Atlanta ↔ Chicago, Atlanta ↔ Dallas, Atlanta ↔ New York,
       Boston ↔ New York, Boston ↔ Seattle, Chicago ↔ Denver,
       Dallas ↔ Denver, Dallas ↔ Los Angeles, Dallas ↔ San Francisco,
       Denver ↔ San Francisco, Portland ↔ San Francisco,
       Portland ↔ Seattle }

Beyond its theoretical significance as a mathematical formalism, defining a graph as a pair of sets has important practical implications, as you will see in the section entitled "A set-based interface for graphs."

Directed and undirected graphs

Because the diagram gives no indication to the contrary, the arcs in Figure 16-1 presumably represent flights that operate in both directions. Thus, the fact that there is a connection between Atlanta and Chicago implies that there is also one between

Chicago and Atlanta. A graph in which every connection runs both ways is called an **undirected graph.** In many cases, it makes sense to use **directed graphs,** in which each arc has a direction. For example, if your airline operates a plane from San Francisco to Dallas but has the plane stop in Denver on the return flight, that piece of the route map would look like this in a directed graph:

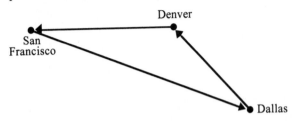

The diagrams in this text represent directed graphs only if the arcs include an arrow indicating their direction. If the arrows are missing—as they are in the airline graph in Figure 16-1—you can assume the graph is undirected.

Arcs in a directed graph are specified using the notation *start→finish,* where *start* and *finish* are the nodes on each side of the directed arc. Thus, the triangular route shown in the preceding diagram consists of the following arcs:

```
San Francisco→Dallas
Dallas→Denver
Denver→San Francisco
```

Arcs in an undirected graph are sometimes denoted using a double-headed arrow (↔). Although this notation is easy enough to read, you don't really need a separate symbol for an undirected arc, because you can always represent any undirected arc using a pair of directed arcs. For example, if a graph contains a bidirectional arc `Portland↔Seattle`, you can represent the fact that each city is connected to the other by including both `Portland→Seattle` and `Seattle→Portland` in the set of arcs. If you use this approach, you can represent the undirected airline graph in Figure 16-1 as a directed graph with the following mathematical structure:

$V = \{$ `Atlanta, Boston, Chicago, Dallas, Denver, Los Angeles,`
         `New York, Portland, San Francisco, Seattle` $\}$

$E = \{$ `Atlanta→Chicago, Atlanta→Dallas, Atlanta→New York,`
         `Boston→New York, Boston→Seattle, Chicago→Atlanta,`
         `Chicago→Denver, Dallas→Atlanta, Dallas→Denver,`
         `Dallas→Los Angeles, Dallas→San Francisco,`
         `Denver→Chicago, Denver→Dallas, Denver→San Francisco,`
         `Los Angeles→Dallas, New York→Atlanta, New York→Boston,`
         `Portland→San Francisco, Portland→Seattle,`
         `San Francisco→Dallas, San Francisco→Denver,`
         `San Francisco→Portland, Seattle→Boston,`
         `Seattle→Portland` $\}$

Because it is always possible to simulate undirected graphs using directed ones, most graph packages—including the one introduced in this chapter—define a single graph type that supports directed graphs. If you want to define an undirected graph, all you have to do is create two arcs for every connection, one in each direction.

Paths and cycles

The arcs in a graph represent immediate connections. The fact that there is no explicit arc San Francisco→New York in the airline graph does not mean that you cannot travel between those cities on this airline. If you wanted to fly from San Francisco to New York, you could use any of the following routes:

    San Francisco→Dallas→Atlanta→New York
    San Francisco→Denver→Chicago→Atlanta→New York
    San Francisco→Portland→Seattle→Boston→New York

A sequence of arcs that allow you to move from one node to another is called a **path.** A path that begins and ends at the same node, such as the path

    Dallas→Atlanta→Chicago→Denver→Dallas

is called a **cycle.** A **simple path** is a path that contains no duplicated nodes. Similarly, a **simple cycle** is a cycle that has no duplicated nodes other than the common node that appears at both the beginning and the end.

Connectivity

An undirected graph is **connected** if there is a path from each node to every other node. For example, the airline graph in Figure 16-1 is connected according to this rule. The definition of a graph, however, does not require that all nodes be connected in a single unit. For example, the graph

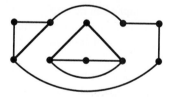

is an example of an unconnected graph, because no path links the cluster of four nodes in the interior of the diagram to any of the other nodes.

Given any undirected graph, you can always decompose it into a unique set of subgraphs in which each subgraph is connected, but no arcs lead from one subgraph to another. These subgraphs are called the **connected components** of the graph. The connected components of the preceding graph diagram look like this:

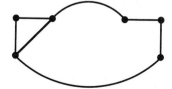

For directed graphs, the concept of connectivity is somewhat more complicated. If a directed graph contains a path connecting every pair of nodes, the graph is **strongly connected**. A directed graph is **weakly connected** if eliminating the directions on the arcs creates a connected graph. For example, the graph

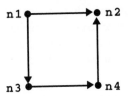

is not strongly connected because you cannot travel from node **n4** on the lower right to node **n1** on the upper left moving only in the directions specified by the arcs. On the other hand, the graph is weakly connected because the undirected graph formed by eliminating the arrows is a connected graph. If you reverse the direction of the top arc, the resulting graph

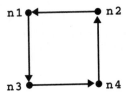

is strongly connected.

◼ 16.2 Implementation strategies for graphs

Like most abstract structures, graphs can be implemented in several different ways. To illustrate the most common implementation strategies, it is useful to begin by defining an extremely simple interface that exports only the following operations:

- Allocate an empty graph (`NewGraph`)
- Add a new node to an existing graph (`NewNode`)
- Add an arc from one node to another (`Connect`)
- Determine whether two nodes are connected by an arc (`IsConnected`)

This preliminary version of the `graph.h` interface appears in Figure 16-2.

To implement the interface in Figure 16-2, you must first choose a representation for each of the two exported types: `graphADT` and `nodeADT`. There are several possibilities. For example, you might decide to store the nodes belonging to a particular graph in a dynamic array, a linked list, or some more sophisticated structure. There are likewise several approaches you can use to represent the connections between pairs of nodes. The sections that follow describe the two most common strategies.

FIGURE 16-2 Preliminary version of the `graph.h` interface

```
/*
 * File: graph.h (preliminary)
 * ---------------------------
 * This file is a simplified version of an interface for graphs.
 */

#ifndef _graph_h
#define _graph_h

/*
 * Types: graphADT, nodeADT
 * ------------------------
 * These abstract types are used to represent graphs and nodes.
 */

typedef struct graphCDT *graphADT;
typedef struct nodeCDT *nodeADT;

/*
 * Function: NewGraph
 * Usage: graph = NewGraph();
 * --------------------------
 * This function returns a new graph with no nodes.
 */

graphADT NewGraph(void);

/*
 * Function: NewNode
 * Usage: node = NewNode(graph);
 * -----------------------------
 * This function creates a new node and adds it to the graph.
 */

nodeADT NewNode(graphADT graph);

/*
 * Function: Connect
 * Usage: Connect(n1, n2);
 * -----------------------
 * This function creates an arc from node n1 to n2.
 */

void Connect(nodeADT n1, nodeADT n2);

/*
 * Function: IsConnected
 * Usage: if (IsConnected(n1, n2)) . . .
 * -------------------------------------
 * This function returns TRUE if there is an arc from n1 to n2.
 */

bool IsConnected(nodeADT n1, nodeADT n2);

#endif
```

Representing connections using an adjacency list

The simplest way to represent connections in a graph is to store within the data structure for each node a list of the nodes to which it is connected. This structure is called an **adjacency list.** For example, in the now-familiar airline graph

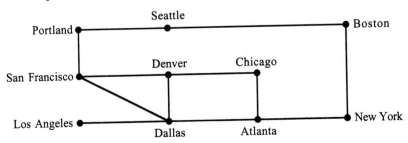

the adjacency lists for each node look like this:

AdjacencyList(Atlanta)	=	(Chicago, Dallas, New York)
AdjacencyList(Boston)	=	(New York, Seattle)
AdjacencyList(Chicago)	=	(Atlanta, Denver)
AdjacencyList(Dallas)	=	(Atlanta, Denver, Los Angeles)
AdjacencyList(Denver)	=	(Chicago, Dallas, San Francisco)
AdjacencyList(Los Angeles)	=	(Dallas)
AdjacencyList(New York)	=	(Atlanta, Boston)
AdjacencyList(Portland)	=	(San Francisco, Seattle)
AdjacencyList(San Francisco)	=	(Dallas, Denver, Portland)
AdjacencyList(Seattle)	=	(Boston, Portland)

Rather than writing new code to implement a list of nodes, you can use the `listADT` type from Chapter 12 to simplify the coding. The graph itself consists of a list of nodes, and each node consists of a list of the nodes to which it is connected. To add a node to a graph, all you have to do is call `ListCons` to add the node to the beginning of the list in the concrete structure for the graph. Similarly, you can also use `ListCons` to add a new arc by adding the destination node to the adjacency list stored as part of the structure for the starting node. To determine whether a connection exists between a starting node and a particular destination node, all you need to do is look through the adjacency list associated with the starting node and see whether the destination node appears. An implementation of the `graph.h` interface that uses the `listADT` type to keep track of both the complete list of nodes in the graph and the adjacency list for each node is shown in Figure 16-3.

Representing connections using an adjacency matrix

Although lists provide a convenient way to represent the connections in a graph, they can be inefficient when an operation requires searching through the list of arcs associated with a node. For example, if you use the adjacency list representation, the `IsConnected` function runs in $O(D)$ time, where D is the number of arcs connected to a node, which is called its **degree.**

FIGURE 16-3 Implementation of the preliminary graph interface using linked lists

```
/*
 * File: graph.c (adjacency list version)
 * ---------------------------------------
 * This file implements the preliminary version of the graph.h
 * interface using linked lists to store the nodes and arcs.
 */

#include <stdio.h>
#include "genlib.h"
#include "list.h"
#include "graph.h"

/*
 * Types: graphCDT, nodeCDT
 * ------------------------
 * These definitions provide the concrete type for the abstract
 * types graphADT and nodeADT, each of which is implemented using
 * the listADT type.
 */

struct graphCDT {
    listADT nodes;
};

struct nodeCDT {
    graphADT graph;
    listADT arcs;
};

/* Exported entries */

graphADT NewGraph(void)
{
    graphADT graph;

    graph = New(graphADT);
    graph->nodes = NULL;
    return (graph);
}

nodeADT NewNode(graphADT graph)
{
    nodeADT node;

    node = New(nodeADT);
    node->graph = graph;
    node->arcs = NULL;
    graph->nodes = ListCons(node, graph->nodes);
    return (node);
}
```

```
void Connect(nodeADT n1, nodeADT n2)
{
    if (n1->graph != n2->graph) {
        Error("Connect: Nodes are in different graphs");
    }
    if (IsConnected(n1, n2)) return;
    n1->arcs = ListCons(n2, n1->arcs);
}

bool IsConnected(nodeADT n1, nodeADT n2)
{
    listADT list;

    if (n1->graph != n2->graph) {
        Error("Connect: Nodes are in different graphs");
    }
    list = n1->arcs;
    while (list != NULL) {
        if (n2 == ListHead(list)) return (TRUE);
        list = ListTail(list);
    }
    return (FALSE);
}
```

If efficiency is a significant concern, you can reduce the cost of the **IsConnected** operation to constant time by representing the connections in a two-dimensional table called an **adjacency matrix** that shows which nodes are connected. The adjacency matrix for the airline graph looks like this:

	Atlanta	Boston	Chicago	Dallas	Denver	Los Angeles	New York	Portland	San Francisco	Seattle
Atlanta			×	×			×			
Boston							×			×
Chicago	×				×					
Dallas	×				×	×			×	
Denver			×	×					×	
Los Angeles				×						
New York	×	×								
Portland									×	×
San Francisco				×	×			×		
Seattle		×						×		

For an undirected graph of this sort, the adjacency matrix is **symmetric,** which means that the entries match when they are reflected across the main diagonal, which is shown in the figure as a dotted line.

To use the adjacency matrix approach, you must associate each node with an index number that specifies the column or row number in that table corresponding to that node. As part of the concrete structure for the graph, the implementation needs to allocate a two-dimensional array with one row and one column for each node in the graph. The elements of the array are Boolean values. If the entry in matrix[*start*] [*finish*] is TRUE, there is an arc *start*→*finish* in the graph.

The code necessary to implement the preliminary version of the graph.h interface using an adjacency matrix appears in Figure 16-4.

In terms of execution time, using an adjacency matrix is considerably faster than using an adjacency list. On the other hand, a matrix requires $O(N^2)$ storage space, where N is the number of nodes. For most graphs, the adjacency list representation tends to be more efficient in terms of space, although this is not necessarily the case. In the adjacency list representation, each node has a list of connections, which, in the worst case, will be D_{max} entries long, where D_{max} is the maximum degree of any node in the graph, which is therefore the maximum number of arcs emanating from a single node. The space cost for adjacency lists is therefore $O(N \times D_{max})$. If most of the nodes are connected to each other, D_{max} will be comparable to N, which means that the cost of representing connections is comparable for the two approaches. If, on the other hand, the graph contains many nodes but relatively few interconnections, the adjacency list representation can save considerable space.

Although the dividing line is never precisely defined, graphs for which the value of D_{max} is small in comparison to N are said to be **sparse.** Graphs in which D_{max} is comparable to N are considered **dense.** Often, the algorithms and representation strategies you use for graphs depend on whether you expect those graphs to be sparse or dense. The analysis in the preceding paragraph, for example, shows that the list representation is likely to be more appropriate for sparse graphs; if you are working with dense graphs, the matrix representation may well be a better choice.

16.3 Extending the graph abstraction

The preliminary version of the graph.h interface shown in Figure 16-2 lacks many features that clients would expect to find in a general package. The deficiencies in the preliminary version of the interface include the following:

- There is no easy way for the client to associate data with individual nodes or with the graph as a whole.
- Because arcs are represented only as connections between nodes, it is impossible for clients to associate data with individual arcs.
- Clients have no way to iterate over the nodes of a graph or the connections from a particular node.

The sections that follow discuss strategies for solving each of these problems.

FIGURE 16-4 Implementation of the graph abstraction using an adjacency matrix

```
/*
 * File: graph.c (adjacency matrix version)
 * -------------------------------------------
 * This file implements the preliminary version of the graph.h
 * interface using an adjacency matrix.
 */

#include <stdio.h>
#include "genlib.h"
#include "graph.h"

/*
 * Constant: MaxNodes
 * ------------------
 * This constant defines the maximum number of nodes in a
 * graph and is used in this implementation to simplify the
 * presentation.  In practice, it would be better to let the
 * structure expand dynamically.
 */

#define MaxNodes 25

/*
 * Type: nodeCDT
 * -------------
 * This type defines the concrete representation of a node
 * in the adjacency matrix representation.  The connections
 * are stored as part of the graph.  The index in the node
 * structure identifies the position of this node in the
 * adjacency matrix.
 */

struct nodeCDT {
    graphADT graph;
    int index;
};

/*
 * Type: graphCDT
 * --------------
 * This definition provides the concrete type for a graphADT in
 * the adjacency matrix representation.  The graph includes a
 * fixed array of nodes and a boolean matrix representing the
 * connections.  Note that the array uses the concrete node type,
 * which means that the addresses of these elements are nodeADTs.
 */

struct graphCDT {
    struct nodeCDT nodes[MaxNodes];
    bool matrix[MaxNodes][MaxNodes];
    int nNodes;
};
```

```
/* Exported entries */

graphADT NewGraph(void)
{
    graphADT graph;

    graph = New(graphADT);
    graph->nNodes = 0;
    return (graph);
}

nodeADT NewNode(graphADT graph)
{
    nodeADT node;
    int i, index;

    if (graph->nNodes >= MaxNodes) Error("NewNode: Too many nodes");
    index = graph->nNodes++;
    node = &graph->nodes[index];
    node->graph = graph;
    node->index = index;
    for (i = 0; i < graph->nNodes; i++) {
        graph->matrix[i][index] = FALSE;
        graph->matrix[index][i] = FALSE;
    }
    return (node);
}

void Connect(nodeADT n1, nodeADT n2)
{
    if (n1->graph != n2->graph) {
        Error("Connect: Nodes are in different graphs");
    }
    n1->graph->matrix[n1->index][n2->index] = TRUE;
}

bool IsConnected(nodeADT n1, nodeADT n2)
{
    if (n1->graph != n2->graph) {
        Error("Connect: Nodes are in different graphs");
    }
    return (n1->graph->matrix[n1->index][n2->index]);
}
```

Associating data with nodes and graphs

As with the binary search tree presented in Chapter 13, some of the information stored within a graph is the property of the client, while other information is the property of the implementation. For example, if you think about the airline graph in Figure 16-1, it should be clear that the connections between cities must be maintained by the implementation. They are part of the definition of the graph. The names of those cities, on the other hand, concern only the client. The implementation does not need to know the name of a particular city. That information is simply part of the data that the client associates with a particular node.

If you want to allow clients to associate data with individual nodes, the simplest approach is to include a **void *** pointer as part of the concrete data structure for each node. If the interface exports functions that store and retrieve the value of this pointer, clients can create a data block containing any necessary information and then store the address of that block in the data structure for the node. Thus, the complete version of the **graph.h** interface exports the functions

```
void SetNodeData(nodeADT node, void *data);
void *GetNodeData(nodeADT node);
```

which allow clients to associate data with an individual node.

It is often useful to associate client-specific data with values of type **graphADT** as well. For example, in an application in which nodes have names—such as the city names in the airline graph example—you might want to maintain a symbol table that enables clients to translate the name of a node into the corresponding **nodeADT** value. Conceptually, that symbol table does not belong to any individual node but is instead associated with the entire graph. To make it possible for clients to store such information along with the graph, it makes sense for the **graph.h** interface to export the functions

```
void SetGraphData(graphADT graph, void *data);
void *GetGraphData(graphADT graph);
```

which allow clients to attach a data block to the graph as a whole.

Making arcs explicit

For many applications, being able to attach a data block to nodes and graphs does not offer sufficient flexibility. Often, clients need to able to associate data with the individual arcs as well. For example, a program to calculate award mileage in a frequent-flier program would need to know the distance associated with each of the arcs in a graph, as illustrated in Figure 16-5. As it stands, the preliminary version of the **graph.h** interface offers no easy way to incorporate such information into the concrete representation of a graph.

If you want to be able to store information along with each arc in a graph, the first step is to extend the interface to export an explicit **arcADT** type that represents an individual arc. The principal purpose of this type is to offer clients a place to

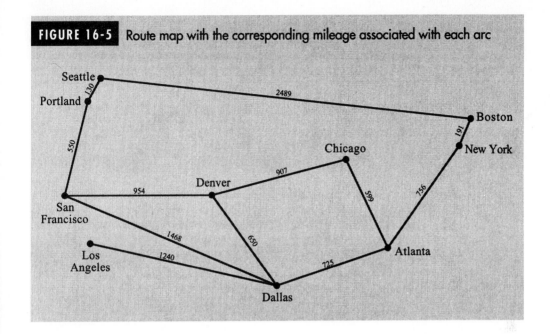

FIGURE 16-5 Route map with the corresponding mileage associated with each arc

store data associated with the arc using the functions `SetArcData` and `GetArcData`, which are analogous to the counterpart functions for nodes and graphs.

Exporting the type `arcADT` requires making some additional changes to the interface. In particular, clients need some way to define arcs in the first place. The easiest approach is to define a function

```
arcADT NewArc(nodeADT n1, nodeADT n2);
```

that creates an arc linking node `n1` with `n2`, and then returns the `arcADT` allocated in the process. In addition, the interface must also export the selector functions `StartOfArc` and `EndOfArc`, which return the nodes at each end of a value of type `arcADT`.

The existence of a separate `arcADT` type also has an interesting implication for the structure of the graph. Because connections in the graph are now defined by explicit `arcADT` values, there is nothing to prevent the existence of multiple arcs between the same pair of nodes. For example, if your airline operates two flights daily from Denver to San Francisco but only one coming back (because one of the planes is flying the triangular route that includes Dallas), there would be three arcs linking these cities, as follows:

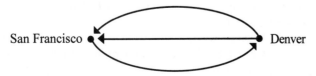

Arcs that connect the same pair of nodes in the same direction, such as the top two arcs in this diagram, are called **parallel arcs.** Designing the `graph.h` interface so that it accommodates parallel arcs makes it much more useful in applications like transportation networks when there may be several distinct connections between the same two points.

Iteration and graphs

Most algorithms for manipulating graphs require you to perform some operation for every node in a graph or for every node that is connected to some particular node. Implementing these algorithms requires you to iterate over the components of a graph—an operation that is not possible in the preliminary version of the interface. Because iteration is essential to many algorithms, the complete version of the `graph.h` interface must make iteration available to clients in some way.

One possibility that initially seems attractive is to design the graph abstraction so that it uses the polymorphic iterator introduced in Chapter 15. For example, if you define graphs as a collection type containing nodes, you could cycle through the nodes in a graph using the following `foreach` idiom:

```
foreach (node in graph)
```

You could also define iteration for nodes so that the `foreach` idiom

```
foreach (node in startingNode)
```

cycled through the nodes reachable by an arc from `startingNode`.

As you will see if you solve exercise 14, the `itertype.h` interface described in the section entitled "Exporting a collection type" in Chapter 15 makes it easy to define iterators for graphs and nodes. On the other hand, if you change your conception of the graph abstraction, you can allow the client to perform iteration in a more elegant way that requires very little work on your part. All you need to do is make better use of the tools you already have.

Layered abstractions

As you know from the section on "The structure of a graph" earlier in this chapter, mathematicians define graphs in terms of sets. Since you already have an implementation of sets from Chapter 15, it is interesting to think about what happens if you design the graph abstraction so that it uses the facilities of the `set.h` interface to define graphs in a way that closely parallels their mathematical formulation.

When you define one abstraction in terms of another—as in the current proposal to define graphs in terms of sets—the resulting abstractions are said to be **layered.** Layered abstractions have a number of advantages. For one thing, they are usually easy to implement because much of the work can be relegated to the existing, lower-level interface. For example, defining the `graph.h` interface in terms of sets completely eliminates the need to define a separate iteration facility for graphs. Because sets already support iteration, you can allow clients to iterate over the nodes in a graph simply by exporting a function

```
setADT Nodes(graphADT graph);
```

that returns the set of all nodes in the specified graph. Using the **foreach** shorthand, all the client has to write is

```
foreach (node in Nodes(graph)) {
      Code to process an individual node
}
```

The iterator code for the set package takes care of all the details.

Using the set package to provide iteration makes it possible to cycle through the components of a graph in many different ways. All you need to do to define a function that returns the appropriate set. The final version of the **graph.h** interface includes five functions—**Nodes**, **ConnectedNodes**, **Arcs**, **ArcsFrom**, and **ArcsTo**—whose purpose is to support iteration over the components of a graph. More precise descriptions of these functions appear in the comments in the interface.

Despite their many advantages, layered abstractions also have certain limitations. In most cases, creating a layered abstraction sacrifices a certain amount of efficiency. You can, for example, implement graphs much more efficiently if you avoid sets altogether and instead design a standalone package that optimizes the performance of the fundamental operations required for graphs. For many applications, you need that additional efficiency. At the moment, however, your job is to understand how graphs work and how to use them as a tool. For that purpose, using a layered abstraction is just the right approach.

A set-based interface for graphs

If you put together all the ideas from the preceding few sections, you can design a much more powerful **graph.h** interface that uses the **set.h** interface from Chapter 15 as its foundation. The complete version of the interface appears in Figure 16-6.

The layered design of the graph package leads not only to a cleaner interface but also to a simpler implementation that is quite easy to follow, as long as you understand the set package on which it is based. Given the layered design, the concrete type definition of a graph is

```
struct graphCDT {
      setADT nodes, arcs;
      void *data;
};
```

which looks almost exactly like its mathematical definition. In addition to a data field for use by the client, a graph consists of a set of nodes and a set of arcs.

```
FIGURE 16-6    Complete interface for the graph abstraction

/*
 * File: graph.h
 * --------------
 * This interface allows the client to manipulate graphs, which
 * are defined in keeping with their mathematical formulation
 * as a set of nodes connected by a set of arcs.
 */

#ifndef _graph_h
#define _graph_h

#include "genlib.h"
#include "set.h"

/*
 * Types: graphADT, nodeADT, arcADT
 * --------------------------------
 * These abstract types are used to represent graphs, nodes, and
 * arcs, respectively.
 */

typedef struct graphCDT *graphADT;
typedef struct nodeCDT *nodeADT;
typedef struct arcCDT *arcADT;

/*
 * Function: NewGraph
 * Usage: graph = NewGraph();
 * --------------------------
 * This function returns a new graph with no nodes.
 */

graphADT NewGraph(void);

/*
 * Function: FreeGraph
 * Usage: FreeGraph(graph);
 * ------------------------
 * This function frees the storage for the graph, along with
 * its nodes and arcs.
 */

void FreeGraph(graphADT graph);

/*
 * Function: NewNode
 * Usage: node = NewNode(graph);
 * -----------------------------
 * This function creates a new node and adds it to the graph.
 */

nodeADT NewNode(graphADT graph);
```

```
/*
 * Function: NewArc
 * Usage: arc = NewArc(n1, n2);
 * -----------------------------
 * This function creates a connection from node n1 to n2
 * and returns a new arcADT representing that connection.
 */

arcADT NewArc(nodeADT n1, nodeADT n2);

/*
 * Function: Connect
 * Usage: Connect(n1, n2);
 * -----------------------
 * This function creates a new arc from node n1 to n2, but
 * does not actually return the arcADT.
 */

void Connect(nodeADT n1, nodeADT n2);

/*
 * Function: IsConnected
 * Usage: if (IsConnected(n1, n2)) . . .
 * -------------------------------------
 * This function returns TRUE if there is an arc from n1 to n2.
 */

bool IsConnected(nodeADT n1, nodeADT n2);

/*
 * Functions: Nodes, ConnectedNodes
 * Usage: nodeSet = Nodes(graph);
 *        nodeSet = ConnectedNodes(node);
 * ---------------------------------------
 * These functions return a set consisting of all nodes in
 * the graph and a set of the nodes to which a given node
 * is connected, respectively.  These functions are typically
 * used to initialize an iterator.  For example, the following
 * idiom iterates over the nodes connected to start:
 *
 *     foreach (node in ConnectedNodes(start))
 */

setADT Nodes(graphADT graph);
setADT ConnectedNodes(nodeADT node);
```

```
/*
 * Functions: Arcs, ArcsFrom, ArcsTo
 * Usage: arcSet = Arcs(graph);
 *        arcSet = ArcsFrom(node);
 *        arcSet = ArcsTo(node);
 * -----------------------------------
 * Each of these functions returns a set of arcs.  The Arcs
 * function returns all the arcs in the graph; the ArcsFrom
 * and ArcsTo functions return the set of arcs that begin or
 * end at a given node, respectively.  These functions are
 * typically used in conjunction with an iterator, as in the
 * following foreach idiom:
 *
 *      foreach (arc in Arcs(graph)) . . .
 */

setADT Arcs(graphADT graph);
setADT ArcsFrom(nodeADT node);
setADT ArcsTo(nodeADT node);

/*
 * Functions: StartOfArc, EndOfArc
 * Usage: node = StartOfArc(arc);
 *        node = EndOfArc(arc);
 * -----------------------------------
 * These functions return the nodes at the endpoints of the
 * specified arc.
 */

nodeADT StartOfArc(arcADT arc);
nodeADT EndOfArc(arcADT arc);

/*
 * Function: GetGraph
 * Usage: graph = GetGraph(node);
 * -----------------------------------
 * This function returns the graph of which a node is a part.
 */

graphADT GetGraph(nodeADT node);
```

```
/*
 * Functions: SetVisitedFlag, ClearVisitedFlag, HasBeenVisited
 * Usage: SetVisitedFlag(node);
 *        ClearVisitedFlag(node);
 *        if (HasBeenVisitedFlag(node)) . . .
 * ----------------------------------------------------------
 * These functions allow clients to manipulate the state of an
 * internal flag associated with each node.  That flag is used
 * to indicate whether the node has been visited as part of a
 * traversal operation.
 */

void SetVisitedFlag(nodeADT node);
void ClearVisitedFlag(nodeADT node);
bool HasBeenVisited(nodeADT node);

/*
 * Functions: SetGraphData, SetNodeData, SetArcData
 *            GetGraphData, GetNodeData, GetArcData
 * Usage: SetGraphData(graph, data);
 *        data = GetGraphData(graph);
 * ------------------------------------------------------
 * These functions make it possible for the client to associate
 * data blocks with graphs, nodes, and arcs.
 */

void SetGraphData(graphADT graph, void *data);
void *GetGraphData(graphADT graph);
void SetNodeData(nodeADT node, void *data);
void *GetNodeData(nodeADT node);
void SetArcData(arcADT arc, void *data);
void *GetArcData(arcADT arc);

#endif
```

Because the set package eliminates much of the complexity, the implementation of the graph package is remarkably simple. Most of the functions are just a few lines long. Moreover, the similarity between the abstract conception of a graph in mathematics and the actual code used to implement it makes it easy to believe that the implementation is correct. The complete implementation appears in Figure 16-7.

Given its clarity and conciseness, the layered implementation of the graph package is highly appropriate to an academic setting where the point is to learn about graphs and how they work. In a commercial environment, however, such an implementation would be far too inefficient. As the implementation stands, iterating over the arcs leaving a particular node requires cycling through all the arcs in the graph and creating a new set containing only the arcs with the desired starting point. Such a strategy requires an enormous amount of additional work beyond what you would need if you instead implemented the arcs using an adjacency list.

FIGURE 16-7   Set-based implementation of the graph package

```
/*
 * File: graph.c
 * -------------
 * This file implements the graph.h interface using sets to
 * represent the nodes and arcs.
 */

#include <stdio.h>
#include "genlib.h"
#include "set.h"
#include "graph.h"
#include "foreach.h"

/*
 * Type: graphCDT
 * --------------
 * This definition provides the concrete type for a graphADT,
 * which is implemented as a set of nodes and a set of arcs.
 */

struct graphCDT {
    setADT nodes, arcs;
    void *data;
};

/*
 * Type: nodeCDT
 * -------------
 * This type defines the concrete structure of a node, which
 * consists of the graph pointer, a flag indicating whether
 * the node has been visited, and a client data field.
 */

struct nodeCDT {
    graphADT graph;
    bool visited;
    void *data;
};

/*
 * Type: arcCDT
 * ------------
 * The concrete type for an arc consists of its endpoints, plus
 * a data field for the client.
 */

struct arcCDT {
    nodeADT from, to;
    void *data;
};
```

```
/* Exported entries */

graphADT NewGraph(void)
{
    graphADT graph;

    graph = New(graphADT);
    graph->nodes = NewPtrSet(PtrCmpFn);
    graph->arcs = NewPtrSet(PtrCmpFn);
    graph->data = NULL;
    return (graph);
}

void FreeGraph(graphADT graph)
{
    nodeADT node;
    arcADT arc;

    foreach (node in graph->nodes) {
        FreeBlock(node);
    }
    foreach (arc in graph->arcs) {
        FreeBlock(arc);
    }
    FreeSet(graph->nodes);
    FreeSet(graph->arcs);
    FreeBlock(graph);
}

nodeADT NewNode(graphADT graph)
{
    nodeADT node;

    node = New(nodeADT);
    node->graph = graph;
    node->visited = FALSE;
    node->data = NULL;
    AddPtrElement(graph->nodes, node);
    return (node);
}

arcADT NewArc(nodeADT n1, nodeADT n2)
{
    arcADT arc;

    if (n1->graph != n2->graph) {
        Error("Connect: Nodes are in different graphs");
    }
    arc = New(arcADT);
    arc->from = n1;
    arc->to = n2;
    arc->data = NULL;
    AddPtrElement(n1->graph->arcs, arc);
    return (arc);
}
```

```
void Connect(nodeADT n1, nodeADT n2)
{
    (void) NewArc(n1, n2);
}

bool IsConnected(nodeADT n1, nodeADT n2)
{
    arcADT arc;

    if (n1->graph != n2->graph) {
        Error("IsConnected: Nodes are in different graphs");
    }
    foreach (arc in n1->graph->arcs) {
        if (arc->from == n1 && arc->to == n2) return (TRUE);
    }
    return (FALSE);
}

setADT Nodes(graphADT graph)
{
    return (graph->nodes);
}

setADT ConnectedNodes(nodeADT node)
{
    setADT result;
    arcADT arc;

    result = NewPtrSet(PtrCmpFn);
    foreach (arc in node->graph->arcs) {
        if (arc->from == node) AddPtrElement(result, arc->to);
    }
    return (result);
}

setADT Arcs(graphADT graph)
{
    return (graph->arcs);
}

setADT ArcsFrom(nodeADT node)
{
    setADT result;
    arcADT arc;

    result = NewPtrSet(PtrCmpFn);
    foreach (arc in node->graph->arcs) {
        if (arc->from == node) AddPtrElement(result, arc);
    }
    return (result);
}
```

```
setADT ArcsTo(nodeADT node)
{
    setADT result;
    arcADT arc;

    result = NewPtrSet(PtrCmpFn);
    foreach (arc in node->graph->arcs) {
        if (arc->to == node) AddPtrElement(result, arc);
    }
    return (result);
}

nodeADT StartOfArc(arcADT arc)
{
    return (arc->from);
}

nodeADT EndOfArc(arcADT arc)
{
    return (arc->to);
}

graphADT GetGraph(nodeADT node)
{
    return (node->graph);
}

void SetVisitedFlag(nodeADT node)
{
    node->visited = TRUE;
}

void ClearVisitedFlag(nodeADT node)
{
    node->visited = FALSE;
}

bool HasBeenVisited(nodeADT node)
{
    return (node->visited);
}

void SetGraphData(graphADT graph, void *data)
{
    graph->data = data;
}

void *GetGraphData(graphADT graph)
{
    return (graph->data);
}

void SetNodeData(nodeADT node, void *data)
{
    node->data = data;
}
```

```
void *GetNodeData(nodeADT node)
{
    return (node->data);
}

void SetArcData(arcADT arc, void *data)
{
    arc->data = data;
}

void *GetArcData(arcADT arc)
{
    return (arc->data);
}
```

As the exercises at the end of the chapter make clear, there are strategies you can use to increase the efficiency of the graph package without changing its interface. For the rest of the chapter, however, the implementation you have is perfectly sufficient. It works. More importantly, the implementation is simple enough for you to have confidence that it works.

■ 16.4 Graph traversals

The `Nodes` function in the `graph.h` interface makes it easy for you to cycle through the nodes in a graph. That function, however, returns a set, which is—by definition—an unordered collection. For many algorithms, it is necessary to process the nodes in an order that takes the connections into account. Such algorithms typically start at some node and then advance from node to node by moving along the arcs, performing some operation on each node. The precise nature of the operation depends on the algorithm, but the process of performing that operation— whatever it is—is usually called **visiting** the node. The process of visiting each node in a graph by moving along its arcs is called **traversing** the graph.

In Chapter 13, you learned that several traversal strategies exist for trees, of which the most important are preorder, postorder, and inorder traversals. Like trees, graphs also support more than one traversal strategy. For graphs, the two fundamental traversal algorithms are called *depth-first search* and *breadth-first search,* which are described in the next two sections.

To make the mechanics of the algorithms easier to understand, the implementations of depth- and breadth-first search assume that the client has supplied a function called `Visit` that takes care of whatever processing is required for each individual node. The goal of a traversal is therefore to call `Visit` once— and only once—on every node in an order determined by the connections. Because graphs often have many different paths that lead to the same node, ensuring that the traversal algorithm does not visit the same node many times requires additional bookkeeping to keep track of which nodes have already been visited. To do so, the code makes use of three functions—`SetVisitedFlag`, `ClearVisitedFlag`, and

HasBeenVisited—exported by the **graph.h** interface. The first two functions assign the value **TRUE** or **FALSE** to an internal flag that keeps track of whether a node has been visited. Traversal algorithms check for this condition by calling **HasBeenVisited**, which returns the state of the internal flag.

The use of a flag to mark whether the traversal algorithm has already visited a node places two responsibilities on the client. First, the client-supplied **Visit** function must call **SetVisitedFlag** as part of its operation. Second, the client must clear all the flags in the graph before starting any traversal, using a loop that looks like this:

```
foreach (node in Nodes(graph)) {
    ClearVisitedFlag(node);
}
```

Depth-first search

The depth-first strategy for traversing a graph is quite similar to the preorder traversal of trees and has the same recursive structure. The only additional complication is that graphs—unlike trees—can contain cycles. If you don't check to make sure that nodes are not processed many times during the traversal, the recursive process can go on forever as the algorithm proceeds.

The algorithm to perform depth-first search on a graph, which is written using the **foreach** idiom introduced in Chapter 15, looks like this:

```
void DepthFirstSearch(nodeADT start)
{
    nodeADT node;

    if (HasBeenVisited(start)) return;
    Visit(start);
    foreach (node in ConnectedNodes(start)) {
        DepthFirstSearch(node);
    }
}
```

The depth-first strategy is most easily understood by tracing its operation in the context of a simple example, such as the following directed graph:

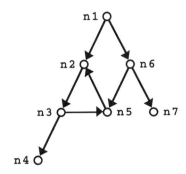

The open circles in the diagram indicate nodes that have not yet been visited. When the depth-first traversal algorithm calls `visit` to process a node, the diagram records this fact by using a filled circle for that node.

Suppose that the process begins by calling `DepthFirstSearch(n1)`. The first step is to visit `n1`, which leads to the following configuration:

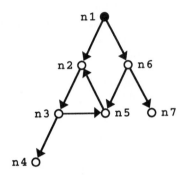

At this point, the `DepthFirstSearch` function enters a loop that cycles through the arcs emanating from `n1`. For each arc, the implementation calls itself recursively on the destination node. Because each level of recursive call will also mark a node and then follow the same recursive process, the overall effect of the depth-first strategy is to explore a single path in the graph as far as possible before backtracking to complete the exploration of paths at higher levels in the recursive chain. As a result, assuming that the connections are processed in the order specified by the labels on the nodes, the recursive calls will begin by exploring the left-hand branch to its end, as follows:

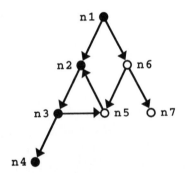

Because there are no arcs leading out of `n4`, the recursive descent through the graph ends at this point and returns to the previous level, at which it was processing `n3`. The recursive call to `DepthFirstSearch` then visits every node accessible along that path. The process, however, must stop if a node has already been visited, to guard against the possibility of infinite loops. For example, when the code follows the arcs leaving `n5`, it calls `DepthFirstSearch` on `n2`. Because this node is marked as having been visited, the call to `DepthFirstSearch` returns immediately to the following configuration:

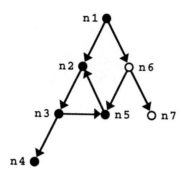

From this point, the execution walks backward through the execution stack all the way to the **n1** node. Calling `DepthFirstSearch` on the only remaining path from the **n1** node marks **n6** and **n7**, at which point the traversal is complete, as follows:

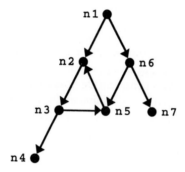

If you think about the depth-first algorithm in relation to other algorithms you've seen, you will realize that its operation is exactly the same as that of the maze-solving algorithm in Chapter 6.

Breadth-first search

Although depth-first search has many important uses, the strategy has drawbacks that make it inappropriate for certain applications. The biggest problem with the depth-first approach is that it explores an entire path beginning at one neighbor before it ever goes back and looks at the other nearby neighbors. If you were trying to discover the shortest path between two nodes in a large graph, using depth-first search would take you all the way to the far reaches of the graph, even if your destination were one step away along a different path.

The breadth-first search algorithm gets around this problem by visiting each node in an order determined by how close it is to the starting node, measured in terms of the number of arcs along the shortest possible path. When you measure distance by counting arcs, each arc constitutes one **hop.** Thus, the essence of breadth-first search is that you visit the starting node first, then the nodes that are one hop away, followed by the nodes two hops away, and so on. For example, if you started with node **n1** in the graph

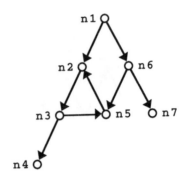

the breadth-first strategy would visit the nodes in the following order:

- The initial node: n1
- All nodes one hop away: n2 and n6
- All nodes two hops away: n3, n5, and n7
- All nodes three hops away: n4

Note that n5 is three hops away from n1 along the path that begins with n2, but only two hops away along the path beginning with n6. Thus, it is important to make sure that the breadth-first algorithm considers the possibility of multiple paths and visits each node in the order dictated by the minimum distance from the original node.

Although the breadth-first algorithm seems rather complicated, it is easy to code, particularly if you make use of sets. The following implementation uses a set called `frontier`, which represents the "frontier outposts" of the process as it advances:

```
void BreadthFirstSearch(nodeADT start)
{
    setADT frontier, oldFrontier;
    nodeADT node, target;

    frontier = NewPtrSet(PtrCmpFn);
    AddPtrElement(frontier, start);
    while (NElements(frontier) > 0) {
        oldFrontier = frontier;
        frontier = NewPtrSet(PtrCmpFn);
        foreach (node in oldFrontier) {
            if (!HasBeenVisited(node)) {
                Visit(node);
                foreach (target in ConnectedNodes(node)) {
                    AddPtrElement(frontier, target);
                }
            }
        }
    }
}
```

At the beginning, the `frontier` set consists only of the starting node. On each cycle, the inner loop in `BreadthFirstSearch` goes through the nodes in the old `frontier` set and creates a new `frontier` set consisting of the unvisited neighbors of the nodes it processes.

Figure 16-8 shows both traversal algorithms using iterators instead of `foreach`.

FIGURE 16-8 Code for the graph-traversal functions

```
/*
 * Functions: DepthFirstSearch, BreadthFirstSearch
 * Usage: DepthFirstSearch(start);
 *        BreadthFirstSearch(start);
 * ---------------------------------
 * These functions visit each node in the graph containing start,
 * beginning at the start node.  DepthFirstSearch recursively explores
 * each path as far as it can; BreadthFirstSearch explores outward in
 * order of increasing distance from the start node.
 */

void DepthFirstSearch(nodeADT start)
{
    iteratorADT iterator;
    nodeADT node;

    if (HasBeenVisited(start)) return;
    Visit(start);
    iterator = NewIterator(ConnectedNodes(start));
    while (StepIterator(iterator, &node)) {
        DepthFirstSearch(node);
    }
    FreeIterator(iterator);
}

void BreadthFirstSearch(nodeADT start)
{
    iteratorADT itSet, itNode;
    setADT frontier;
    nodeADT node, target;

    frontier = NewPtrSet(PtrCmpFn);
    AddPtrElement(frontier, start);
    while (NElements(frontier) > 0) {
        itSet = NewIterator(frontier);
        frontier = NewPtrSet(PtrCmpFn);
        while (StepIterator(itSet, &node)) {
            if (!HasBeenVisited(node)) {
                Visit(node);
                itNode = NewIterator(ConnectedNodes(node));
                while (StepIterator(itNode, &target)) {
                    AddPtrElement(frontier, target);
                }
                FreeIterator(itNode);
            }
        }
        FreeIterator(itSet);
    }
}
```

■■■ 16.5 Finding minimum paths

Because graphs arise in many applications areas that are important economically, a considerable amount of research has been invested in developing effective algorithms for solving graph-related problems. Of these problems, one of the most interesting is that of finding a path from one node of a graph to another that has the smallest possible cost when evaluated according to some metric. This metric need not be economic. Although you might be interested in finding the cheapest path between two nodes for certain applications, you can use the same algorithm to find a path with the shortest overall distance, the smallest number of hops, or the least travel time.

As a concrete example, suppose that you want to find the path from San Francisco to Boston in the route map from Figure 16-5 that has the shortest total distance, as computed by the mileage values shown on the arcs of the graph. Is it better to go through Portland and Seattle, or should you instead go through Dallas, Atlanta, and New York? Is there perhaps some less obvious route that is shorter still?

With graphs as simple as the route map of this tiny airline, it is relatively easy to compute the answer just by adding up the length of the arcs along all possible paths. As the graph grows larger, however, this approach can become unworkable. In general, the number of paths between two nodes in a graph grows in an exponential fashion, which means that the running time of the explore-all-paths approach is $O(2^N)$. As you know from the discussion of computational complexity in Chapter 7, problems whose solutions require exponential running time are considered to be intractable. If you want to find the shortest path through a graph in a reasonable amount of time, it is essential to use a more efficient algorithm.

The most commonly used algorithm for finding shortest paths was discovered by Edsgar Dijkstra in 1959. Dijkstra's algorithm for finding shortest paths is a particular example of a class of algorithms, called **greedy algorithms,** in which you find the overall answer by making a series of locally optimal decisions. Greedy algorithms do not work for every problem, but are quite useful in solving the shortest-path problem.

At its essence, the core of Dijkstra's algorithm for finding the minimum-cost path can be expressed as follows: explore all paths from the starting node in order of increasing total path cost until you encounter a path that takes you to your destination. This path must be the best one, because you have already explored all paths beginning at the starting node that have a lower cost. In the context of the specific problem of finding a path with the shortest total arc distance, Dijkstra's algorithm can be implemented as shown in Figure 16-9.

The code for `FindShortestPath` is written in terms of two other abstract data types, as follows:

- *Priority queues.* The `queueADT` type is largely the same as the type exported by the `queue.h` interface in Chapter 10, but includes the priority queue extensions described in exercise 5 in that chapter. Calling `PriorityEnqueue` does not simply insert the new element at the *end* of the queue as `Enqueue` does, but instead inserts the element into the list of existing elements

Implementation of Dijkstra's algorithm for finding minimum paths

```
/*
 * Function: FindShortestPath
 * Usage: path = FindShortestPath(start, finish);
 * -------------------------------------------------
 * This function returns a pathADT containing the shortest path
 * between the nodes start and finish in a graph, or the constant
 * NULL if no such path exists.  The implementation uses a variant
 * of Dijkstra's algorithm, in which all paths are explored in the
 * order of their total distance from the starting node.  The code
 * uses the priority queue abstraction to keep the paths yet to be
 * considered sorted in order of increasing distance.
 */

pathADT FindShortestPath(nodeADT start, nodeADT finish)
{
    queueADT queue;
    pathADT path, newPath;
    arcADT arc;

    queue = NewQueue();
    path = NewPath();
    while (start != finish) {
        if (!IsDistanceFixed(start)) {
            FixNodeDistance(start, TotalPathDistance(path));
            foreach (arc in ArcsFrom(start)) {
                if (!IsDistanceFixed(EndOfArc(arc))) {
                    newPath = NewExtendedPath(path, arc);
                    PriorityEnqueue(queue, newPath,
                                    TotalPathDistance(newPath));
                }
            }
        }
        if (QueueIsEmpty(queue)) return (NULL);
        path = Dequeue(queue);
        start = EndOfPath(path);
    }
    return (path);
}
```

according to its *priority,* which is indicated by the last argument to **PriorityEnqueue**. As in conventional English usage, smaller priority numbers come first in the queue, so that elements with priority 1 are entered into the queue ahead of elements with priority 2. By entering each path into the queue using its total distance as a priority value, each **Dequeue** operation returns the shortest path remaining in the queue.

- *Paths.* The **pathADT** type is used to keep track of a path consisting of a sequence of arcs. The function **NewPath** creates an empty path. Longer paths are created by calling **NewExtendedPath**(*path, arc*), which creates a new path that contains the arcs in the original path with the specified arc added to the end. The `pathADT` type also supports the functions `StartOfPath` and `EndOfPath`, which return the endpoints of the path, and the function `TotalPathDistance`, which calculates the total distance along the path by adding up the distance values for the individual arcs.

In addition to the functions that pertain to the `pathADT` and `queueADT` types, the implementation of `FindShortestPath` assumes the existence of two simple auxiliary functions that Figure 16-9 does not include. As Dijkstra's algorithm proceeds, it computes the minimum distance to all nodes in the graph that are closer than the destination. Whenever a path is dequeued from the priority queue, you know the path must indicate the shortest route to the node at the end of that path, unless you have already found a shorter path ending at that node. Thus, when you process a path from the priority queue, you can fix the minimum distance to the final node as the length of that path. The function `FixPathDistance`(*node*, *distance*) stores the indicated distance in the data structure associated with the node so that the algorithm knows it should ignore subsequent paths that reach the same node. The counterpart function `IsDistanceFixed`(*node*) returns `TRUE` if the distance to the specified node has already been fixed.

The operation of `FindShortestPath` is illustrated in Figure 16-10, which shows the steps involved in computing the shortest path from San Francisco to Boston in the airline graph from Figure 16-5. The complete trace of the process illustrates the following properties of the algorithm, which are important to keep in mind:

- *Paths are explored in order of the total distance rather than the number of hops.* Thus, the paths beginning with `San Francisco`→`Portland`→`Seattle` are explored before those beginning with either `San Francisco`→`Denver` or `San Francisco`→`Dallas`, because the total distance is shorter.

- *The distance to a node is fixed when a path is dequeued, not when it is enqueued.* The first path to Boston stored in the priority queue is the one that goes through Portland and Seattle, which is not the shortest available path. The total distance from San Francisco to Boston along the path `San Francisco`→`Portland`→`Seattle`→`Boston` is 3169 miles. Because the alternate path `San Francisco`→`Dallas`→`Atlanta`→`New York`→`Boston` is only 3140 miles, the `San Francisco`→`Portland`→`Seattle`→`Boston` path is still in the priority queue when the algorithm finishes its operation.

- *The arcs from each node are scanned at most once.* The inner loop of the algorithm that iterates through the arcs leading from a node is scanned only when the distance to that node is fixed, which happens only once for each node. As a result, the total number of cycles executed within the inner loop is bounded by the product of the number of nodes and the maximum number of arcs leading from a node. A complete analysis of Dijkstra's algorithm is beyond the scope of this text, but the running time—after making an important enhancement to the efficiency of the implementation described in the following section—works out to be $O(M \log N)$, where N is the number of nodes and M is the either N or the number of arcs, whichever is larger.

FIGURE 16-10 Steps involved in finding the shortest path from San Francisco to Boston

Fix the distance to San Francisco at 0
Process the arcs out of San Francisco (Dallas, Denver, Portland)
    Enqueue the path: San Francisco → Dallas (1468)
    Enqueue the path: San Francisco → Denver (954)
    Enqueue the path: San Francisco → Portland (550)
Dequeue the shortest path: San Francisco → Portland (550)
Fix the distance to Portland at 550
Process the arcs out of Portland (San Francisco, Seattle)
    Ignore San Francisco because its distance is known
    Enqueue the path: San Francisco → Portland → Seattle (680)
Dequeue the shortest path: San Francisco → Portland → Seattle (680)
Fix the distance to Seattle at 680
Process the arcs out of Seattle (Portland, Boston)
    Ignore Portland because its distance is known
    Enqueue the path: San Francisco → Portland → Seattle → Boston (3169)
Dequeue the shortest path: San Francisco → Denver (954)
Fix the distance to Denver at 954
Process the arcs out of Denver (Chicago, Dallas, San Francisco)
    Ignore San Francisco because its distance is known
    Enqueue the path: San Francisco → Denver → Chicago (1861)
    Enqueue the path: San Francisco → Denver → Dallas (1604)
Dequeue the shortest path: San Francisco → Dallas (1468)
Fix the distance to Dallas at 1468
Process the arcs out of Dallas (Atlanta, Denver, Los Angeles, San Francisco)
    Ignore Denver and San Francisco because their distances are known
    Enqueue the path: San Francisco → Dallas → Atlanta (2193)
    Enqueue the path: San Francisco → Dallas → Los Angeles (2708)
Dequeue the shortest path: San Francisco → Denver → Dallas (1604)
Ignore Dallas because its distance is known
Dequeue the shortest path: San Francisco → Denver → Chicago (1861)
Fix the distance to Chicago at 1861
Process the arcs out of Chicago (Atlanta, Denver)
    Ignore Denver because its distance is known
    Enqueue the path: San Francisco → Denver → Chicago → Atlanta (2449)
Dequeue the shortest path: San Francisco → Dallas → Atlanta (2193)
Fix the distance to Atlanta at 2193
Process the arcs out of Atlanta (Chicago, Dallas, New York)
    Ignore Chicago and Dallas because their distances are known
    Enqueue the path: San Francisco → Dallas → Atlanta → New York (2949)
Dequeue the shortest path: San Francisco → Denver → Chicago → Atlanta (2449)
Ignore Atlanta because its distance is known
Dequeue the shortest path: San Francisco → Dallas → Los Angeles (2708)
Fix the distance to Los Angeles at 2708
Process the arcs out of Los Angeles (Dallas)
    Ignore Dallas because its distance is known
Dequeue the shortest path: San Francisco → Dallas → Atlanta → New York (2949)
Fix the distance to New York at 2949
Process the arcs out of New York (Atlanta, Boston)
    Ignore Atlanta because its distance is known
    Enqueue the path: San Francisco → Dallas → Atlanta → New York → Boston (3140)
Dequeue the shortest path: San Francisco → Dallas → Atlanta → New York → Boston (3140)
Fix the distance to Boston at 3140

An efficient implementation of priority queues

As is often the case, the performance of Dijkstra's algorithm depends to a large extent on how well its underlying operations are implemented. For example, if you can improve the efficiency of the priority queue implementation, Dijkstra's algorithm will run more quickly, because it depends on the priority queue package. If you implement priority queues using the strategy described in exercise 5 from Chapter 10, the `PriorityEnqueue` function requires $O(N)$ time. You can improve the performance of the priority queue package to $O(\log N)$ by using a data structure called a **partially ordered tree,** which is a binary tree in which the following two properties hold:

1. The nodes of the tree are arranged in a pattern as close to that of a completely symmetrical tree as possible. Thus, the number of nodes along any path in the tree can never differ by more than one. Moreover, the bottom level must be filled in a strictly left-to-right order.
2. Each node contains a key that is always less than or equal to the key in its children. Thus, the smallest key in the tree is always at the root.[1]

As an example, the following diagram shows a partially ordered tree with four nodes, each of which contains a numeric key:

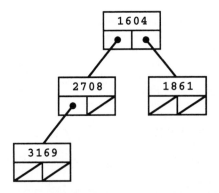

The second level of the tree is completely filled, and the third level is being filled from left to right, as required by the first property of partially ordered trees. The second property also holds because the key in each node is always less than the keys in its children.

Suppose that you want to add a node with the key 2193. It is clear where the new node goes. The requirement that the lowest level of the tree be filled from left to

---

[1] Partially ordered trees are often defined so that the root contains the *largest* value rather than the *smallest*. In priority queues, the desire to find the highest priority item—which is defined as the one with the smallest numeric value as in conventional English usage—makes it more useful to define partially ordered trees—and the heap structure introduced later in the chapter—so that they select the smallest value. In terms of the implementation, the only difference between these two approaches is whether the code uses greater-than or less-than signs.

right dictates that the new node be added as the right child of the node currently containing the key 2708, as follows:

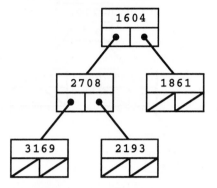

The problem with inserting the new node is that the second property of partially ordered trees is violated in the process, because the key 2193 is smaller than the key in its parent.

To fix this problem, you can begin by exchanging the keys in those nodes, like this:

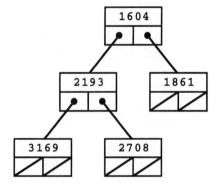

In general, it is possible that the newly inserted key would have to be exchanged with its parent in a cascading sequence of changes that proceed up through the levels of the tree. In this specific case, the process of exchanging keys stops here because 2193 is greater than 1604. In any event, the structure of the tree guarantees that the total number of such exchanges will never require more than $O(\log N)$ time.

The structure of the partially ordered tree makes it relatively easy to find and remove the smallest value in the tree. Finding it is extremely easy, since it's always at the root. To remove that value, however, you have to arrange for the node that actually disappears to be the rightmost node in the bottom level. The standard approach is to replace the key in the root with the key in the node to be deleted and then swap keys down the tree until the ordering property is restored. If you wanted, for example, to delete the root node from the preceding tree diagram, the first step would be to replace the key in the root node with the 2708 in the rightmost node from the lowest level, as follows:

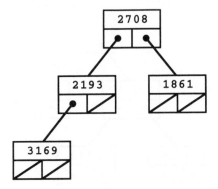

Then, because the nodes of the tree no longer have correctly ordered keys, you need to exchange the key 2708 with the smaller of the two keys in its children, like this:

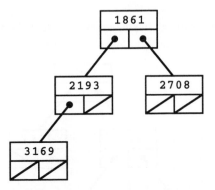

Although a single interchange is enough to restore the ordering property of the tree in this example, the general process of finding the correct position for the key that was moved into the root position may require you to swap that element through each of the levels in the tree. Like the insertion operation, deleting the smallest key therefore requires $O(\log N)$ time.

The operations that define the partially ordered tree are precisely the ones you need to implement priority queues. The `PriorityEnqueue` operation consists of inserting a new node into the partially ordered tree. The `Dequeue` operation consists of removing the lowest value. Thus, if you use partially ordered trees as the underlying representation, you can implement the priority queue package so that it runs in $O(\log N)$ time.

Although you can implement partially ordered trees using a pointer-based structure, priority queues are usually implemented using an array-based structure called a **heap,** which simulates the operation of a partially ordered tree. (The terminology is confusing at first, because the heap data structure bears no relationship to the pool of unused memory available for dynamic allocation, which is also referred to by the word *heap.*) The implementation strategy used in a heap depends on the property that the nodes in a partially ordered tree of size N can be stored in the first N elements of an array simply by counting off the nodes, level by level, left to right, as illustrated in Figure 16-11. For example, the partially ordered tree

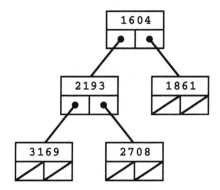

can be represented as the following heap:

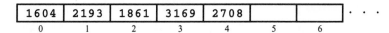

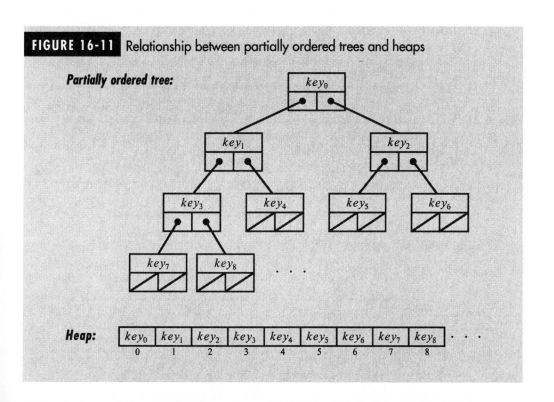

FIGURE 16-11 Relationship between partially ordered trees and heaps

The heap organization makes it simple to implement tree operations, because parent and child nodes always appear at an easily computed position. For example, given a node at index position **n**, you can find the indices of its parent and children using the following expressions:

`ParentIndex(n)`	*is always given by*	`(n - 1) / 2`
`LeftChildIndex(n)`	*is always given by*	`2 * n + 1`
`RightChildIndex(n)`	*is always given by*	`2 * n + 2`

The division operator in the calculation of `ParentIndex` is C's standard integer division. Thus, the parent of the node at index position 8 in the array appears at position 3 in the array, because the result of evaluating the C expression `(8 - 1) / 2` is 3.

Implementing the missing details of Dijkstra's algorithm and the heap-based priority queue is an excellent exercise that will sharpen your programming skills and give you more experience working with many of the data structures you have seen in this text. You will have the opportunity to complete these implementations in exercises 9 and 10 at the end of this chapter.

▰ Summary

This chapter has introduced you to the idea of a graph, which is defined as a set of nodes linked together by a set of arcs that connect individual pairs of nodes. Like sets, graphs are not only important as a theoretical abstraction, but also as a tool for solving practical problems that arise in many application domains. For example, graph algorithms are useful in studying the properties of connected structures ranging from the Internet to large-scale transportation systems.

Important points in this chapter include:

- Graphs may be either directed or undirected. The arcs in a directed graph run in one direction only, so the existence of an arc $n_1 \rightarrow n_2$ does not imply the existence of an arc $n_2 \rightarrow n_1$. You can represent undirected graphs by using directed graphs in which each connected pair of nodes is linked with two arcs, one in each direction.

- You can adopt any of several different strategies to implement the connections in a graph. One common approach is to construct an adjacency list, in which the data structure for each node contains a list of the connected nodes. You can also use an adjacency matrix, which stores the connections in a two-dimensional array of Boolean values. The rows and columns of the matrix are indexed by the nodes in the graph; if two nodes are connected in the graph, the corresponding entry in the matrix contains the value **TRUE**.

- The `graph.h` interface can be implemented easily by layering it on top of the set package. Although the resulting implementation is extremely clear and concise, it is too inefficient to be used in practice.

- The two most important traversal orders for a graph are depth-first search and breadth-first search. The depth-first algorithm chooses one arc from the starting node and then recursively explores all paths beginning with that arc until no additional nodes remain. Only at that point does the algorithm return to explore other arcs from the original node. The breadth-first algorithm explores nodes in order of their distance from the original node, measured in terms of the number of arcs along the shortest path. After processing the initial node, breadth-first search processes all the neighbors of that node before moving on to nodes that are two hops away.

▪ You can find the minimum-cost path between two nodes in a graph by using Dijkstra's algorithm, which is vastly more efficient than the exponential strategy of comparing the cost of all possible paths. Dijkstra's algorithm is an example of a larger class of algorithms called *greedy algorithms,* which select the locally best option at any decision point.

▪ Priority queues—which are an essential component of Dijkstra's algorithm—can be implemented efficiently using a data structure called a *heap,* which is based on a special class of binary tree called a *partially ordered tree.* If you use this representation, both `PriorityEnqueue` and `Dequeue` run in $O(\log N)$ time.

REVIEW QUESTIONS

1. What is a graph?

2. True or false: Trees are a subset of graphs, which form a more general class.

3. What is the difference between a directed and an undirected graph?

4. If you are using a graph package that supports only directed graphs, how can you represent an undirected graph?

5. Define the following terms as they apply to graphs: *path, cycle, simple path, simple cycle.*

6. What is the difference between a strongly connected and a weakly connected graph?

7. What terms do mathematicians often use in place of the words *node* and *arc?*

8. The following graph defines the prerequisite structure of the eight courses that make up the core of *Curriculum '78,* a standardized curriculum for computer science adopted by the Association for Computing Machinery (ACM) in 1978:

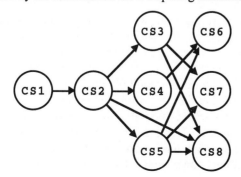

Using the mathematical formulation for graphs described in this chapter, define this graph as a pair of sets.

9. Draw a diagram showing the adjacency list representation of the graph in the preceding question.

10. Given the prerequisite graph shown in question 8, what are the contents of corresponding adjacency matrix?

11. If N is the number of nodes in a graph and D_{max} is the maximum degree of any of those nodes, what is the computational complexity of the `IsConnected` operation for each of the adjacency list and adjacency matrix representations of a graph? How much space is required to store the connections in each case?

12. What is the difference between a sparse and a dense graph?

13. If you were asked to choose the underlying representation of a graph for a particular application, what factors would you consider in deciding whether to use adjacency lists or adjacency matrices in the implementation?

14. The chapter cites three deficiencies in the preliminary version of the `graph.h` interface that appears in Figure 16-2. What are they?

15. For each of the deficiencies you identified in the preceding question, what strategy does the complete `graph.h` interface use to overcome it?

16. Give an example of information that should be associated with an entire graph rather than an individual node.

17. What is the principal purpose of the type `arcADT` in the `graph.h` interface?

18. Why is it unnecessary to implement a separate iterator facility for the graph package?

19. Name and describe the five functions in the `graph.h` interface that return values of type `setADT`.

20. Why would the implementation of the graph package shown in Figure 16-7 probably be inappropriate for use in a commercial environment?

21. What are the two fundamental traversal strategies for graphs?

22. What is the purpose of the `visited` flag maintained as part of each node?

23. What two responsibilities must the client undertake to ensure the success of a traversal operation?

24. Write down both the depth-first and the breadth-first traversal of the airline graph in Figure 16-1, starting from San Francisco. Assume that iteration over nodes and arcs always occurs in alphabetical order. For example, if you iterate over the arcs leaving San Francisco, they will appear in the following order:

```
San Francisco→Dallas
San Francisco→Denver
San Francisco→Portland
```

25. Describe the purpose of the `frontier` set in the implementation of breadth-first search shown in Figure 16-8.

26. What is a greedy algorithm?

27. Explain the operation of Dijkstra's algorithm for finding minimum-cost paths.

28. Show the contents of the priority queue at each step of the trace of Dijkstra's algorithm shown in Figure 16-10.

29. Using Figure 16-10 as a model, trace the execution of Dijkstra's algorithm to find the shortest path from Portland to Atlanta.

30. Suppose that you are working with a partially ordered tree that contains the following data:

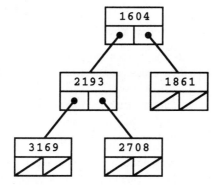

Show the state of the partially ordered tree after inserting a node with the key 1521.

31. What is the relationship between heaps and partially ordered trees?

PROGRAMMING EXERCISES

1. Write and implement an interface called `graphio.h` that exports the following functions:

```
graphADT ReadGraph(FILE *infile);
void WriteGraph(FILE *outfile, graphADT graph);
```

The `ReadGraph` function reads a text description of a graph from `infile` and returns the corresponding graph structure. The file, which must already be open for input, consists of lines that can be in any of these three forms:

x	Defines a node with name *x*
x -> *y*	Defines the directional arc $x \rightarrow y$
x <-> *y*	Defines the arcs $x \rightarrow y$ and $y \rightarrow x$

The names *x* and *y* are arbitrary strings that do not contain either of the character sequences `->` or `<->`. The single arrow (`->`) defines an arc in one direction only; the double arrow (`<->`) defines arcs in both directions and is therefore useful for describing an undirected graph. The definition of the graph ends with a blank line or the end of the file.

New nodes are defined whenever a new name appears in the data file. Thus, if every node is connected to some other node, it is sufficient to include only the arcs in the data file because defining an arc automatically defines the nodes at its endpoints. If you need to represent a graph containing isolated nodes, you must specify the names of those nodes on separate lines somewhere in the data file.

When reading in an arc description, your implementation should discard leading and trailing spaces from the node names, but retain any internal spaces. The line

```
San Francisco <-> New York
```

should therefore define nodes with the names `"San Francisco"` and `"New York"`, and then create connections between the two nodes in each direction.

In addition to defining the arcs, the `ReadGraph` function must also initialize the data fields for the individual nodes and for the graph. When the function returns, those fields must have the following contents:

- The data field for each node must contain the name of that node as a string.
- The data field for the graph must contain a `symtabADT` in which the names of the nodes are bound to the corresponding `nodeADT` values. This design makes it easy to find a node in the graph by name.

As an example, calling `ReadGraph` on the following data file would produce the airline graph that appears in the chapter as Figure 16-1:

```
Atlanta   <-> Chicago
Atlanta   <-> Dallas
Atlanta   <-> New York
Boston    <-> New York
Boston    <-> Seattle
Chicago   <-> Denver
Dallas    <-> Denver
Dallas    <-> Los Angeles
Dallas    <-> San Francisco
Denver    <-> San Francisco
Portland  <-> San Francisco
Portland  <-> Seattle
```

The `WriteGraph` function writes a text description of a graph to the specified output file. You may assume that the data field in each node of the graph contains its name, just as if `ReadGraph` had created the graph. The output of the `WriteGraph` function must be readable using `ReadGraph`.

2. The chapter includes two implementations for the preliminary `graph.h` interface, one that uses adjacency lists and one that uses an adjacency matrix. An alternative strategy is to use a dynamic array as the internal structure of both graphs and nodes. The underlying representation of a graph includes an array of the nodes it contains; the underlying representation of a node includes an array of the nodes to which it is connected. Reimplement the preliminary `graph.h` interface shown in Figure 16-2 using this design.

3. The adjacency-matrix implementation of the preliminary `graph.h` interface, shown in Figure 16-4, limits the number of nodes in a graph to the constant **MaxNodes**. Rewrite the implementation so that the adjacency matrix expands dynamically if a node is added that exceeds the current capacity of the graph. Because the adjacency matrix is two-dimensional, you need to represent it as a dynamic array whose elements are themselves dynamic arrays.

4. Eliminate the recursion from the implementation of **DepthFirstSearch** by using an explicit stack to store the unexplored nodes. At the beginning of the algorithm, you simply push the starting node on the stack. Then, until the stack is empty, you repeat the following operations:

   1. Pop the topmost node from the stack.
   2. Visit that node.
   3. Push its neighbors on the stack.

   The only part of the algorithm missing from this informal description is finding a way to avoid visiting the same node more than once.

5. Without making any other changes, replace the stack in the preceding exercise with a queue. Describe the traversal order implemented by the resulting code.

6. The **DepthFirstSearch** and **BreadthFirstSearch** traversal functions given in the chapter are written to emphasize the structure of the underlying algorithms. If you wanted to include these traversal strategies as part of the graph package, you would need to reimplement the functions so that they no longer depended on a client-supplied **visit** function. One approach is to implement these two algorithms as the following mapping functions:

   ```
   void MapDFS(nodeFnT fn, nodeADT start, void *clientData);
   void MapBFS(nodeFnT fn, nodeADT start, void *clientData);
   ```

   In each case, the functions should call **fn(node, clientData)** for every node reachable from **start** in the specified traversal order.

   To make these functions even more general, write the code for **MapDFS** and **MapBFS** so that the mapping function itself keeps track of the nodes that have been visited—presumably by maintaining a set of visited nodes—instead of having the callback function set the visited flag in the node structure. This change will allow nested mapping operations on a graph.

7. Write a function `PathExists(n1, n2)` that returns `TRUE` if there is a path in the graph between the nodes `n1` and `n2`. Implement this function by using depth-first search to traverse the graph from `n1`; if you encounter `n2` along the way, then a path exists.

8. Write a function `HopCount(n1, n2)` that returns the number of hops in the shortest path between the nodes `n1` and `n2`. If `n1` and `n2` are the same node, `HopCount` should return 0; if no path exists, `HopCount` should return −1. This function is most easily implemented using breadth-first search.

9. Although the section entitled "Finding minimum paths" includes an implementation of Dijkstra's algorithm, many of the underlying details are missing from the presentation. Complete the implementation by writing a C program that performs the following operations:

   ■ Reads a graph from a file in a format that allows assigning distances to arcs.
   ■ Allows the user to enter the names of two cities.
   ■ Uses Dijkstra's algorithm to find and display the minimum path.

   Your program should also make it possible to display, possibly as an option enabled by the setting of a flag, a complete trace of the operation of the algorithm such as the one shown in Figure 16-10.

   This program will be easier to write if you break it down into the following phases:

   1. Extend the `graphio.h` interface from exercise 1 so that you can add distance specifications to the arcs. For example, you might allow the arc definitions in the data file to include an optional distance in parentheses. If such a distance is supplied, the `ReadGraph` function could store a pointer to that distance in the data field of the arc.
   2. Implement the priority queue extensions to the queue package, which are described in exercise 5 in Chapter 10.
   3. Implement the path abstraction described after the code in Figure 16-9. The program will be easier to maintain if you export the `pathADT` type and its associated operations from a separate `path.h` interface than if you simply add these functions to the graph package or include them directly in your test program.
   4. Write a program that draws together the independent pieces of your solution into a coherent whole.

10. As described in the section entitled "An efficient implementation of priority queues," reimplement the priority queue abstraction so that it uses the heap data structure.

11. Although Dijkstra's algorithm for finding minimum-cost paths has considerable practical importance, there are numerous other graph algorithms that have comparable commercial significance. In many cases, finding a minimum-cost path between two specific nodes is not as important as minimizing the cost of a network as a whole.

As an example, suppose that you are working for a company that is building a new cable system that connects 10 large cities in the San Francisco Bay area. Your preliminary research has provided you with cost estimates for laying new cable lines along a variety of possible routes. Those routes and their associated costs are shown in the graph on the left side of Figure 16-12. Your job is to find the cheapest way to lay new cables so that all the cities are connected through some path.

To minimize the cost, one of the things you need to avoid is laying a cable that forms a cycle in the graph. Such a cable would be unnecessary, because the cities it connects are already linked by some other path. If your goal is to find a set of arcs that connects the nodes of a graph at a minimum cost, you might as well leave such edges out. The remaining graph, given that it has no cycles, forms a tree. A tree that links all the nodes of a graph is called a **spanning tree.** The spanning tree in which the total cost associated with the arcs is as small as possible is called a **minimum spanning tree.** The cable-network problem described earlier in this exercise is therefore equivalent to finding the minimum spanning tree of the graph, which is shown in the right side of Figure 16-12.

There are many algorithms in the literature for finding a minimum spanning tree. Of these, one of the simplest was devised by Joseph Kruskal in 1956. In Kruskal's algorithm, all you do is consider the arcs in the graph in order of increasing cost. If the nodes at the endpoints of the arc are unconnected, then you include this arc as part of the spanning tree. If, however, the nodes are already connected by a path, you can discard this arc

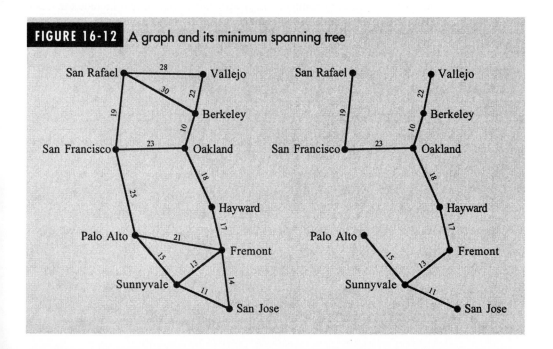

FIGURE 16-12 A graph and its minimum spanning tree

from the final graph. The steps in the construction of the minimum spanning tree for the graph in Figure 16-12 are shown in the following sample run:

```
Process edges in order of cost:
10: Berkeley -> Oakland
11: San Jose -> Sunnyvale
13: Fremont -> Sunnyvale
14: Fremont -> San Jose (not needed)
15: Palo Alto -> Sunnyvale
17: Fremont -> Hayward
18: Hayward -> Oakland
19: San Francisco -> San Rafael
21: Fremont -> Palo Alto (not needed)
22: Berkeley -> Vallejo
23: Oakland -> San Francisco
25: Palo Alto -> San Francisco (not needed)
28: San Rafael -> Vallejo (not needed)
30: Berkeley -> San Rafael (not needed)
```

Write a function

```
static graphADT MinimumSpanningTree(graphADT graph);
```

that implements Kruskal's algorithm to find the minimum spanning tree. The function returns a new graph whose nodes match those in the original graph, but which includes only the arcs that are part of the minimum spanning tree.

12. Computers are often used in business applications to manage the scheduling of complex projects in which there are ordering relationships among the individual tasks. For example, a large software project might include the tasks illustrated in the graph in Figure 16-13.

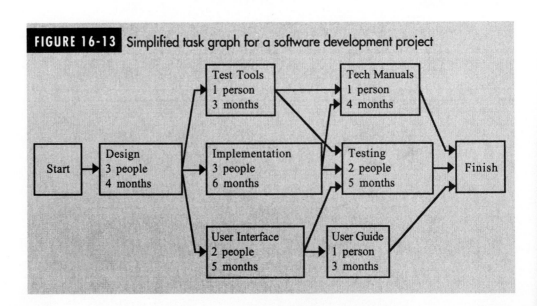

FIGURE 16-13   Simplified task graph for a software development project

The nodes in this graph represent individual tasks; the arcs represent dependencies. The structure of the project graph tells you, for example, that before you begin the `Testing` task, you must first have completed each of the following tasks: `Test Tools`, `Implementation`, and `User Interface` tasks. On the other hand, the `Test Tools`, `Implementation`, and `User Interface` tasks can proceed in parallel. Moreover, you can start the `User Guide` task before the `Implementation` task is complete, because it depends only on the `User Interface` task.

Each project contains two special nodes—`Start` and `Finish`—that mark the beginning and end of the project. Except for these special nodes, every task node is associated with three pieces of information: the name of the task, the number of employees required, and the duration.

Write a program that uses the graph package to represent the type of data contained in project graphs such as the one shown in Figure 16-13. The first step in the process is to write the code necessary to read the data for a project graph from a file. To do so, you will have to design both the format of the data file and the data blocks needed to associate task data with the nodes in the graph. Once you have read in the project file, the next step is to write a program that generates a schedule for the project, showing when each task begins and ends, along with the total staffing level required at that time. For example, given the project graph from Figure 16-13, your program should produce a schedule that looks something like this:

```
Month 0:
  Start Design
  Staff at end of month: 3
Month 4:
  End Design
  Start Test Tools, Implementation, User Interface
  Staff at end of month: 6
Month 7:
  End Test Tools
  Staff at end of month: 5
Month 9:
  End User Interface
  Start User Guide
  Staff at end of month: 4
Month 10:
  End Implementation
  Start Tech Manuals, Testing
  Staff at end of month: 4
Month 12:
  End User Guide
  Staff at end of month: 3
Month 14:
  End Tech Manuals
  Staff at end of month: 2
Month 15:
  End Testing
  Staff at end of month: 0
```

13. Write a complete implementation of the `graph.h` interface shown in Figure 16-6 using adjacency lists, which were used in Figure 16-3 to implement the preliminary interface. In the new implementation, the adjacency list for each node must be a list of `arcADT` values so that clients can store data in association with the arcs. Moreover, it is useful to maintain two lists or arcs with each node: one for the arcs leaving a node and one for the arcs entering that node. Maintaining both lists makes it easier to implement the functions `ArcsFrom` and `ArcsTo`. Note that these functions—like the other functions in the `graph.h` interface that return sets—will have to create the appropriate set from the underlying data structure.

14. Use the polymorphic iterator package from Chapter 15 to implement iterators for graphs and nodes, using the strategy discussed in the section on "Iteration and graphs" in this chapter.

15. Graph algorithms are often well suited to distributed implementations in which processing is performed at each node in the graph. In particular, such algorithms are used to find optimal transmission routes in a computer network. As an example, the following graph shows the first 10 nodes in the ARPANET—the network created by the Advanced Research Projects Agency (ARPA) of the U.S. Department of Defense—which was the forerunner of today's much more sophisticated Internet:

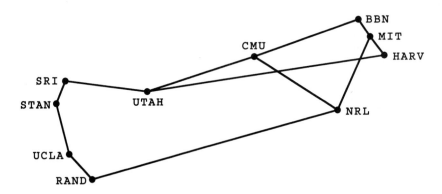

Each node in the early ARPANET consisted of a small computer called an **Interface Message Processor,** or **IMP.** As part of the network operation, each IMP sent messages to its neighbors indicating the number of hops from that node to every other node, to the extent that the IMP possessed that information. By monitoring the messages coming in, each IMP could quickly develop useful routing information about the network as a whole.

To make this idea more concrete, imagine that every IMP maintains an array in which each index position corresponds to one of the nodes. When things are up and running, the array in the Stanford IMP (**STAN**) should have the following contents:

4	3	3	4	3	2	1	0	1	2
BBN	CMU	HARV	MIT	NRL	RAND	SRI	STAN	UCLA	UTAH

The interesting question, however, is not so much the contents of the array as it is how the network computes and maintains these counts. When a node is restarted, it has no knowledge of the complete network. In fact, the only information the Stanford node can determine on its own is that its own entry is 0 hops away. Thus, at start-up time, the array in the **STAN** node looks like this:

?	?	?	?	?	?	?	0	?	?
BBN	CMU	HARV	MIT	NRL	RAND	SRI	STAN	UCLA	UTAH

The routing algorithm then proceeds by letting each node forward its routing array to its neighbors. The Stanford IMP, for example, sends its array off to SRI and UCLA. It also receives similar messages from its neighbors. If the IMP at UCLA has just started up as well, it might send a message containing the array

?	?	?	?	?	?	?	?	0	?
BBN	CMU	HARV	MIT	NRL	RAND	SRI	STAN	UCLA	UTAH

This message provides the Stanford node with some interesting information. If its neighbor can get to UCLA in 0 hops, then the Stanford node can get there in 1. As a result, the Stanford node can update its own routing array as follows:

?	?	?	?	?	?	?	0	1	?
BBN	CMU	HARV	MIT	NRL	RAND	SRI	STAN	UCLA	UTAH

In general, whenever any node gets a routing array from its neighbor, all it has to do is go though each of the known entries in the incoming array and replace the corresponding entry in its own array with the incoming value plus one, unless its own entry is already smaller. In a very short time, the routing arrays throughout the entire network will have the correct information.

Write a program that uses the graph package to simulate the calculations of this routing algorithm on a network of nodes.

CHAPTER 17

Looking Ahead to Java

> Salvation lies in an energetic march onward towards a brighter
> and clearer future.
>
> — Emma Goldman, *Anarchism and Other Essays,* 1911

Objectives

- To understand the concept of object-oriented programming and how it differs from the procedural style used in C.

- To learn enough about Java to get a sense of how the language works.

- To be able to write simple interactive applets in Java.

- To appreciate the power of the predefined classes available in the Java libraries.

The first 16 chapters of this book have given you a solid introduction to the fundamentals of data structures and algorithms in the context of the C programming language. Even though you know a great deal more than you did before you started this book, it is important to recognize that what you have learned is only an introduction. If you continue your study of computer science, you will have the opportunity to investigate these topics at a much greater level of detail. In the process, you will appreciate more fully the extent to which the choice of a specific algorithm or data structure design can affect the efficiency of a program.

As central as they are to computer science, algorithms and data structures are by no means the only topics you will encounter as you continue your investigation into the world of programming. To become an experienced programmer, you must learn to approach problems in new ways. Modern programming practice depends on a variety of programming strategies, each of which requires you to adopt a new mode of thought, in much the same way that you needed to "think recursively" to apply the problem-solving power of recursion.

The purpose of this chapter is to introduce you to a new style of programming that has become increasingly important in recent years. That style is called **object-oriented programming,** which is based on the idea that data can be encapsulated together with behavior to create a single integrated entity called an **object.** Object-oriented programming, which is often referred to by the acronym **OOP,** promotes the development of reusable software components and is extremely useful in many programming applications, especially those with highly interactive user interfaces.

You have already encountered aspects of object-oriented programming in the earlier parts of this book. Many of the central concepts and techniques emphasized in Parts 3 and 4—such as data abstraction, encapsulation, and polymorphism—have their roots in object-oriented design. There is, however, a limit to how much object-oriented programming you can explore in C, which is grounded in an older programming tradition. To understand the advantages of object-oriented programming, you need to understand how the structure of a programming language can make it easier to think about programs from the perspective of the data. To provide that background, this chapter also includes a brief introduction to Java™, a new object-oriented language that has generated enormous excitement in the computer world.

■■■ 17.1 The object-oriented paradigm

Over the last decade, computer science and programming have gone through something of a revolution. Like most revolutions—whether political upheavals or the conceptual restructurings that Thomas Kuhn describes in his 1962 book *The Structure of Scientific Revolutions*—this change has been driven by the emergence of an idea that challenges an existing orthodoxy. Initially, the two ideas compete. For a while, the old order maintains its dominance. Over time, however, the strength and popularity of the new idea grows, until it begins to displace the older idea in what Kuhn calls a **paradigm shift.** In programming, the old order is represented by the **procedural paradigm,** in which programs consist of a collection of procedures and functions that operate on data. The challenger is the **object-oriented paradigm,** in which programs are viewed instead as a collection of data objects that exhibit particular behavior. Most traditional languages, including Fortran, Pascal, and C, embody the procedural paradigm. The best-known representatives of the object-oriented paradigm are Smalltalk, C++, and Java.

Although object-oriented languages are undeniably gaining popularity at the expense of procedural ones, it would be a mistake to regard the object-oriented and procedural paradigms as mutually exclusive. Programming paradigms are not so much competitive as they are complementary. The object-oriented and the procedural paradigm—along with other important paradigms such as the functional programming style embodied in LISP—all have important applications in practice. Even within the context of a single application, you are likely to find a use for more than one approach. As a programmer, you must master many different paradigms, so that you can use the conceptual model that is most appropriate to the task at hand.

The history of object-oriented programming

The idea of object-oriented programming is not really all that new. The first object-oriented language was SIMULA, a language for coding simulations designed in 1967 by the Scandinavian computer scientists Ole-Johan Dahl, Björn Myhrhaug, and Kristen Nygaard. With a design that was far ahead of its time, SIMULA anticipated many of the concepts that later became commonplace in programming, including the concept of abstract data types and much of the modern object-oriented paradigm. In fact, most of the terminology used to describe object-oriented systems comes from the original 1967 report on SIMULA.

For many years, however, SIMULA mostly sat on the shelf. Few people paid much attention to it, and the only place you were likely to hear about it was in a course on programming language design. The first object-oriented language to gain any significant level of recognition within the computing profession was Smalltalk, which was developed at the Xerox Palo Alto Research Center (more commonly known as Xerox PARC) in the late 1970s. The purpose of Smalltalk, which is described in the book *Smalltalk-80: The Language and Its Implementation* by Adele Goldberg and David Robson, was to make programming accessible to a wider audience. As such, Smalltalk was part of a larger effort at Xerox PARC that gave rise to much of the modern user-interface technology that is now standard on personal computers.[1]

Despite many attractive features and a highly interactive user environment that simplifies the programming process, Smalltalk never achieved much commercial success. The profession as a whole took an interest in object-oriented programming only when the central ideas were incorporated into variants of C, which had already become an industry standard. Although there were several parallel efforts to design an object-oriented language based on C, the most successful was the language C++, which was designed in the early 1980s by Bjarne Stroustrup at AT&T Bell

[1] For a fascinating account of the role played by Xerox PARC in the development of the personal computer, see the book *Fumbling the Future: How Xerox Invented, Then Ignored, the First Personal Computer* by Douglas K. Smith and Robert C. Alexander.

Laboratories. By making it possible to integrate object-oriented techniques with existing C code, C++ enabled large communities of programmers to adopt the object-oriented paradigm in a gradual, evolutionary way.

The most recent chapter in the history of object-oriented programming is the development of Java by a team of programmers at Sun Microsystems led by James Gosling. In 1991, when Sun initiated the project that would eventually become Java, the goal was to design a language suitable for programming microprocessors embedded in consumer electronic devices. Had this goal remained the focus of the project, it is unlikely that Java would have caught on to the extent that it has. As is often the case in computing, the direction of Java changed during its development phase in response to changing conditions in the industry. The key factor leading to the change in focus was the phenomenal growth in the Internet that occurred in the early 1990s, particularly in the form of the **World Wide Web,** an ever-expanding collection of interconnected resources contributed by computer users all over the world. When interest in the Web skyrocketed in 1993, Sun redesigned Java as a tool for writing highly interactive, Web-based applications. That decision proved extremely fortuitous. Since the formal announcement of the language in May 1995, Java has generated unprecedented excitement in both the academic and commercial computing communities. In the process, object-oriented programming has become firmly established as a central paradigm in the computing industry.

It is interesting to speculate about why it took so many years for the computer science community to recognize the value of the object-oriented paradigm. To a certain extent, the problem may have been that the first object-oriented language was invented by Europeans in an industry that has been dominated largely by the United States. It is also true, however, that you can see the advantages of object-oriented programming much more clearly when you start to write the kinds of complex, highly interactive applications that typify commercial software in the 1990s. To a certain extent, applied computing needed to catch up to the ideas introduced in SIMULA before computer science could take full advantage of those ideas.

Objects, classes, and methods

To get a better sense of how object-oriented programming works, it helps to begin by learning the terminology traditionally associated with the object-oriented paradigm. Not surprisingly, the central concept is that of an **object,** which is most easily defined as a set of data values and operations that acts as a single conceptual entity. In C, the closest analogue to an object is an instance of an abstract data type whose behavior is defined by the exported functions in an interface. In much the same way that you have learned to look at ADTs, a programmer who uses an object in a language like C++ or Java views that object as an integrated whole.

In most object-oriented languages, objects are created as instances of a particular **class,** which represents the set of all objects that share a common representation and set of operations. A class in the object-oriented paradigm therefore corresponds closely to an abstract data type together with the functions that define its behavior. In a sense, many of the interfaces you have seen in the earlier chapters—the ones like `stack.h, queue.h, symtab.h, scanadt.h,` and `set.h` that export a single ADT and an associated set of operations—act very much like a class.

In the object-oriented world, the operations associated with a particular class are called **methods.** Methods are analogous to the functions exported by an interface in support of a specific ADT. Unlike functions in C, however, methods in an object-oriented language are defined as part of a class and have no independent existence. The most important implication of the coupling between method and class is that different classes in an object-oriented language can have methods with the same name. For example, if you define an object class for playing cards in one part of an application and a different class for geometric shapes in another, both classes can implement a method called `draw`. In C, you need to differentiate the names of the functions by defining, for example, `DrawCard` and `DrawShape`.

The technique of allowing different methods to have the same name is called **overloading.** In most object-oriented languages, including C++ and Java, you can also overload methods in a single class by giving them distinct argument structures. As long as the compiler can determine which method applies by looking at the number and types of the arguments, you can use the same name for those methods without introducing any ambiguity. This technique is useful when you want to give the client several options for invoking a particular method. For example, if you specify a method that includes an optional argument, you can define two versions of that method: one that includes the argument and one that doesn't. The compiler can simply check the supplied arguments and choose the correct version of the method.

For the most part, it makes sense to think about methods in much the same way you think about functions in C. The code you write to invoke a method in Java looks almost the same as a function call in C and has largely the same effect. Some programmers who adopt the object-oriented paradigm—particularly those in the Smalltalk community—tend to speak of **sending a message** to an object instead of invoking one of an object's methods, even though the effect is the same. One of the advantages of the sending-a-message metaphor is that it suggests the possibility that messages can arrive from many different sources, conceivably at unpredictable times. In object-oriented programming, methods are often triggered by some action, such as clicking the mouse button or pressing a key on the keyboard. Actions of this sort, which are generated not by the program but by the user or some external process, are called **events.** Communication in an event-driven application is easy to describe in terms of sending messages. For example, if you click a button that appears on the screen, you can think of that event as sending an action message to that button.

Class hierarchies and inheritance

Object-oriented languages like C++ and Java allow you define hierarchical relationships among the object classes. Whenever you have a class that provides some of the functionality you need for a particular application, you can define new classes that are derived from the original class, but which specialize its behavior in some way. The derived classes are known as **subclasses** of the original class, which in turn becomes the **superclass** for each of its subclasses.

As an example, suppose that you have been charged with designing an object-oriented payroll system for a company. You might begin by defining a general class called `Employee`, which encapsulates the information about an individual worker along with methods that implement operations required for the payroll system. These operations could include simple methods like `getName`, which returns the name of an employee, along with more complicated methods like `computePay`, which calculates the pay for an employee based on data stored within each `Employee` object. In many companies, however, employees fall into several different classes that are similar in certain respects but different in others. For example, a company might have hourly employees, commissioned employees, and salaried employees on the same payroll. In such companies, it might make sense to define subclasses for each employee category as illustrated by the following diagram:

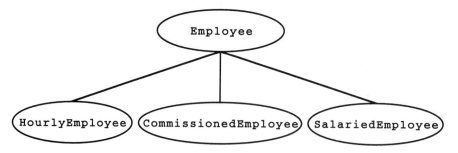

Each of the `HourlyEmployee`, `CommissionedEmployee`, and `SalariedEmployee` classes is a subclass of the more general `Employee` class, which acts as their common superclass.

By default, each subclass **inherits** the behavior its superclass, which means that the methods and internal data structure of the superclass are also available to its subclasses. In cases where the behavior of a subclass needs to differ from its superclass, the designer of the subclass can **extend** the superclass by defining a new method or **override** inherited methods with modified versions. In the payroll example, all three subclasses will presumably inherit the `getName` method from the `Employee` superclass. Every employee, after all, has a name. Conversely, it probably makes sense to write separate `computePay` methods for each subclass, because the computation is likely to be different in each case.

Some languages, such as C++, allow classes to inherit behavior from more than one class. This approach is called **multiple inheritance** and results in a class hierarchy whose structure is a directed graph with no internal cycles. In computer science, such structures are called **directed acyclic graphs,** or **dags.** Other languages, such as Java, restrict each class to a single superclass. This approach is called **single inheritance** and results in a class hierarchy that is structured as a tree.

In Java, the root of the tree representing the class hierarchy is the class `Object`. All other classes in Java are descended from this class. A small section of the hierarchy descended from `Object`, which includes several classes you will encounter later in this chapter, is shown in Figure 17-1. At every level of the hierarchy, there are many more classes beyond the examples shown, but the figure illustrates the general structure. The class `Hashtable`, for example, is a subclass of

Dictionary, which is itself a subclass of **Object**. Thus, every **Hashtable** object is also a **Dictionary** and inherits the behavior associated with the **Dictionary** class. The subtree rooted at **Component** has an even richer structure and includes such classes as **Button** and **Choice** that correspond to interactive elements displayed on the screen. The **Component** class also includes the class called **Container**, which is further subdivided into the classes **Panel** and **Window**. The **Panel** class contains the subclass **Applet**, which is used to create interactive applications for the World Wide Web and is described in more detail in the section on "Applets" later in this chapter. As the diagram in Figure 17-1 illustrates, every **Applet** is also a **Panel**, a **Container**, a **Component**, and an **Object** and therefore inherits the behavior of those superclasses.

17.2 An introduction to Java

When the implementation team at Sun Microsystems published a white paper describing Java, the first adjective they used to describe the language design was *simple*. As languages go, Java is indeed simpler than most. In particular, it is far less complex than C++, which makes it a more appropriate language in which to

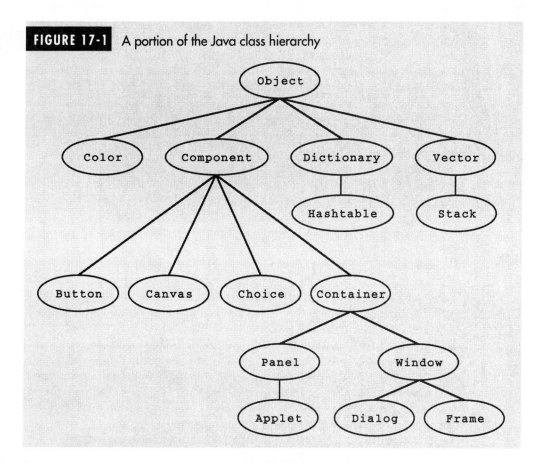

FIGURE 17-1 A portion of the Java class hierarchy

introduce the ideas of object-oriented programming. As simple as Java is, it is not possible to teach you the entire language in a single chapter. The purpose of this chapter is to introduce just enough of Java so you can write some simple applications that will give you a sense of how it works.

As noted in the section on "The history of object-oriented programming" earlier in this chapter, much of the excitement surrounding Java comes from the powerful synergy between Java and the World Wide Web. Because most Java programs today are developed for use with the Web, it makes sense to introduce Java in that context. To do so, it is useful to start by describing the operation of the Web in more detail.

The structure of the Web

Many of the ideas behind the World Wide Web have been circulating in computer science for years. One of the fundamental ideas is that information is easier to understand if it contains internal links that allow readers to move through it in an efficient, nonlinear way. Suppose, for example, that you wanted to store the contents of a book on a computer. One possibility would simply be to store the text of the book as a single file. With this model, your readers would presumably use the book in much the same way as its printed counterpart. If you provided them with a good editing program, they might be able to search for a particular keyword, but the organization of the material would retain the linear structure that characterizes printed documents. Given the power of computers, however, you could offer readers more control by allowing them to find their own path through an electronic version of the book augmented by interactive links. If you adopted this strategy, the computer system might begin by displaying the table of contents. If the reader clicked the mouse on the name of a chapter, the computer would display a list of the sections within that chapter. Clicking the mouse on the name of a section would take the reader directly to that section. The same strategy would also enable users to follow cross-reference links or move from an index entry to the actual reference.

Documents that contain interactive links are called **hypertext**—a term introduced in 1965 by Ted Nelson, who proposed the creation of an integrated collection of documents that has much in common with today's World Wide Web. This idea, however, was not successfully put into practice until 1989, when Tim Berners-Lee of CERN, the European Particle Physics Laboratory in Geneva, proposed creating a distributed collection of hypertext documents that he called the World Wide Web. In 1991, implementers at CERN completed the first **browser,** a program that displays Web documents in a way that makes it easy for users to follow the internal links to other parts of the Web. After news of the CERN work spread to other researchers in the physics community, more groups began to create browsers. Of these, the most successful was the Mosaic project based at the National Center for Supercomputing Applications (NCSA) in Champaign, Illinois. After the appearance of the Mosaic browser in 1993, interest in the Web exploded. The number of computer systems implementing World Wide Web repositories grew from approximately 500 in 1993 to over 250,000 in 1997. The enthusiasm for the Web in the Internet community has also sparked considerable commercial interest, leading to the formation of several new companies and the release of commercial Web browsers like Netscape Navigator™ and Microsoft Internet Explorer™.

The number of documents available on the World Wide Web has grown rapidly because Internet users can easily create new documents and add them to the Web. If you want to add a new document to the Web, all you have to do is create a file containing the hypertext description of that document on a **Web server**, which is a computer system capable of responding to requests from Web users. The individual files exported by the server are called **Web pages.** Web pages are usually written in a language called **HTML**, which is short for *Hypertext Markup Language.* HTML documents consist of text along with formatting information and links to other pages on the Web. Each page is identified by a **uniform resource locator,** or **URL**, which makes it possible for Web browsers to find this page in the sea of existing pages. URLs for the World Wide Web begin with the prefix `http://`, which is followed by a description of the Internet path needed to reach the desired page. For example, you can find a tremendous amount of information about Java from the URL `http://www.javasoft.com`, which is the Web page for JavaSoft, the division of Sun Microsystems now responsible for Java's development.

Applets

Although HTML is powerful enough to support simple Web pages, it has significant limitations, particularly if you want to create interactive applications that run on the Web. Java is designed to help you overcome those limitations. If you want to create a Web page with animation or an interactive user interface, you can use Java to write a small program that runs as the browser displays that page. Such programs are called **applets.**

The code for a simple Java applet appears in Figure 17-2. The effect of this applet is to display the string `"Hello, world!"` near the upper-left corner of the applet window, which will look something like this (the exact format depends on the particular browser you're using):

Although the code in Figure 17-2 bears a marked resemblance to C, the structure of a Java program is sufficiently different that it is worth going through each of its lines in detail. The first statements after the initial comments are

```
import java.applet.Applet;
import java.awt.*;
```

FIGURE 17-2 The Java source code for a simple applet that displays a message

```
/*
 * File: HelloApplet.java
 * ----------------------
 * This applet displays the message "Hello, world!" in the browser
 * window.
 */

import java.applet.Applet;
import java.awt.*;

public class HelloApplet extends Applet
{
    public void paint(Graphics g)
    {
        g.drawString("Hello, world!", 30, 30);
    }
}
```

These statements give the program access to predefined classes that are part of the Java library. The first line, for example, imports the `Applet` class, which lives in a package called `java.applet`. Because all applets are subclasses of the general `Applet` class, every applet must include this line. The second line imports a collection of classes called the **abstract windowing toolkit,** which is stored in the `java.awt` package. This package contains quite a few useful classes, including a `Graphics` class, which enables you to display information in the applet window. By including the line

```
import java.awt.*;
```

you can use any of the classes defined in the `java.awt` package without explicitly importing specific ones.

The rest of the code in the source file defines the `HelloApplet` class. The header line for the class definition is

```
public class HelloApplet extends Applet
```

which uses Java's **extends** keyword to define `HelloApplet` as a subclass of `Applet`. Like any other subclass, `HelloApplet` inherits the methods of its superclass. To create a new applet, all you have to do is override the default methods inherited from the `Applet` class with new ones that implement the desired behavior.

In this example, the only redefined method is `paint`, which the browser invokes to display the output from the applet. The definition of the `paint` method is similar to a function definition in C. As you can see from the code in Figure 17-2, the `paint` method takes an argument named `g`, which is an instance of the class `Graphics`. To generate a display in the applet window, all you have to do is write a new `paint` method that invokes the appropriate methods from the `Graphics` class on the specific graphics object `g`.

In Java, invoking a method on an object is written as a combination of C's syntax for a selection operation and a function call. Because methods are conceptually part of an object, the first step is to select the desired method from the object to which it applies. You can then call the result of that selection just as you would call any function in C. For example, the `paint` method in `HelloApplet` consists of the line

```
g.drawString("Hello, world!", 30, 30);
```

which invokes the `drawString` method on the object `g`, passing it the arguments in parentheses. The effect of this call is to display the string `"Hello, world!"` beginning at the coordinates (30, 30) on the screen.

Coordinates in Java are measured in **pixels,** which are the individual dots that can be displayed on the face of the screen. The Java coordinate system is illustrated by the following diagram:

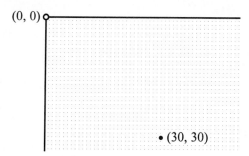

In Java, the origin is in the upper-left corner of the window. In this diagram, the origin is marked by the open circle. The solid dot at coordinate position (30, 30) represents the starting position for the string displayed by the example applet.

Table 17-1 lists several methods supported by the `Graphics` class, although there

---

TABLE 17-1 Selected methods in the `Graphics` class

`drawLine`(x_0, y_0, x_1, y_1)	This method draws a line from (x_0, y_0) to (x_1, y_1).
`drawRect`(x_0, y_0, w, h) `fillRect`(x_0, y_0, w, h)	The `drawRect` method draws the outline of a rectangle whose upper-left corner is (x_0, y_0) with the specified width and height. The `fillRect` method is similar but draws a solid rectangle.
`drawOval`(x_0, y_0, w, h) `fillOval`(x_0, y_0, w, h)	The `drawOval` method draws the outline of an oval that fits inside the box that `drawRect` would create with these parameters. The `fillOval` method fills the interior of that oval.
`drawString`(str, x, y)	This method draws the string str at the point (x, y).
`setColor`$(color)$	This method sets the color of the pen so that any subsequent calls display their output in that color. Several colors are predefined as constants in the `Color` class, such as `black`, `white`, `gray`, `red`, `orange`, `yellow`, `green`, `blue`, `magenta`, `cyan`, and `pink`.

FIGURE 17-3 The Java code for an applet that displays a checkerboard

```
/*
 * File: CheckerApplet.java
 * ------------------------
 * This applet draws an 8x8 checkerboard pattern.  The size
 * of the individual squares is chosen so that the checkerboard
 * fills the smaller dimension of the applet window.
 */

import java.applet.Applet;
import java.awt.*;

public class CheckerApplet extends Applet
{
    public void paint(Graphics g)
    {
        int row, col, squareSize;

        squareSize = (Math.min(size().width, size().height) - 1) / 8;
        g.drawRect(0, 0, 8 * squareSize, 8 * squareSize);
        for (row = 0; row < 8; row++) {
            for (col = 0; col < 8; col++) {
                if ((col + row) % 2 == 0) {
                    g.setColor(Color.white);
                } else {
                    g.setColor(Color.black);
                }
                g.fillRect(col * squareSize, row * squareSize,
                           squareSize, squareSize);
            }
        }
    }
}
```

are many more that are beyond the scope of this chapter. The code in Figure 17-3 uses the methods from Table 17-1 to draw a checkerboard pattern that looks like this:

The implementation of the `paint` method in the `CheckerApplet` class consists primarily of code that would be perfectly legal in ANSI C. The only statement that might look at all unfamiliar is

```
squareSize = (Math.min(size().width, size().height) - 1) / 8;
```

which calculates the size of the individual squares from the dimensions of the applet window as a whole. This statement illustrates the following features of Java:

- You can determine the dimensions of the applet window by invoking the `size` method, which returns an object containing the components `width` and `height`. For now, you can think of expressions like `size().width` as if they were record selections. The details of this operation are described in more detail in the section on "Defining a new class" later in this chapter.
- The Java library defines a `Math` class that includes a variety of useful mathematical functions similar to those in C's `math.h` interface. The class name `Math` must always appear, but you can otherwise think of the entries in the `Math` class as exactly like functions in C. In this example, the `Math.min` function returns the smaller of the two dimensions for the applet. The `Math` class need not be imported explicitly because it is part of the package `java.lang`, which is always available to Java programs.

Executing a Java applet

Once you have written a Java applet, the next question to consider is how you might run it. Because applets operate in the environment of a distributed network, the process of executing an applet is more complicated than the corresponding process for C programs. After writing the applet code, you need to use a Java compiler to translate the source program into a machine-independent form consisting of a sequence of coded, 8-bit bytes. These bytes are instructions for a hypothetical computer system called the **Java virtual machine,** which is then simulated on every architecture that supports a Java browser.

From your perspective as the applet author, the next step in the process is to use HTML to write a Web page that includes a reference to the compiled Java applet. For instance, if you want to display the `HelloApplet` example introduced in the preceding section, you need to create an HTML file that looks something like this:

HelloApplet.html

```
<html>
<title>Hello Applet</title>
<applet codebase="Java Classes"
        code="HelloApplet.class"
        width=300 height=100>
</applet>
</html>
```

The `codebase` field in the `applet` specification indicates the name of the directory or folder that holds the compiled Java classes used in this applet. The `code` field specifies the name of the compiled class file for the applet itself. Depending on how your Web server is organized, the values for these fields may differ slightly from those in this example. Most Java environments come with sample HTML files that you can use as templates for your own system.

At this point in the process, it is necessary to shift your perspective from your role as the author of the applet to that of the user who wants to read your Web page. From the user's perspective, the first step is to ask your browser to display the Web page, by supplying the appropriate URL. The browser then interprets the instructions in the HTML file. When the interpreter encounters the `applet` tag, it sends a request over the network asking for the applet code. The Web server on which the applet is stored responds by sending the compiled version of the applet to the user's machine.

Before executing the compiled code for the applet, Web browsers examine the code to make sure that the instructions in the applet are valid and will not compromise the integrity of the user's machine. The part of the browser system that performs this task is called a **verifier.** If the applet passes the verifier's inspection, the browser then runs a Java interpreter to execute the applet. In the process, any method calls to the `Graphics` class for the applet—such as the `drawString` call in `HelloApplet`—are reflected in the applet display.

The complete process of executing an applet is illustrated in Figure 17-4. Many Java environments allow you to streamline this process to some extent, but the full set of steps offers you more insight into how Java and the Web interact.

■■■ 17.3 The structure of Java

Before going on to look at other applets, it is important to step back and review the structure of Java in more detail. As a C programmer, you have a considerable head start toward learning Java, because most of its syntax is based on C. At the same time, there are several important differences in the language that you need to understand. For the most part, these differences reflect the fact that the two languages are designed to support distinct programming paradigms. C is firmly rooted in the procedural tradition. As a result, C programmers tend to focus on procedures and functions rather than data. By contrast, Java is an object-oriented language in which the data objects themselves become the central focus. The method definitions in a Java program—even though they look very much like functions in C—always appear as part of a class definition and have no meaning except in the context of that class.

The effects of the shift in design philosophy are easiest to see in the type systems used by each language. C, for example, supports a variety of mechanisms—arrays, pointers, structures, and unions—that allow you to build complex types out of simple ones. Although Java does support arrays, the other mechanisms for defining compound types have all been eliminated from the language. In their place, Java

FIGURE 17-4 Steps in the display of a Java applet

Steps taken on the author's side

1. The author of the Web page writes the code for a Java applet.

   HelloApplet.java

   ```
   import java.applet.Applet;
   import java.awt.*;

   public class HelloApplet extends Applet
   {
     public void paint(Graphics g)
     {
       g.drawString("Hello, world!", 30, 30);
     }
   }
   ```

2. The applet author then uses a Java compiler to generate a file containing a byte-coded version of the applet.

   HelloApplet.class

   ```
   CA FE BA BE 00 03 00 2D 00 1F 08 00 0F 07
   00 16 07 00 1A 07 00 14 0A 00 02 00 08 0A
   00 04 00 07 0C 00 13 00 18 0C 00 17 00 1C
   01 00 16 28 4C 6A 61 76 61 2F 61 77 74 2F
   47 72 61 70 68 69 63 73 3B 29 56 01 00 04
   ```

3. The applet author publishes an HTML Web page that includes a reference to the compiled applet.

   HelloApplet.html

   ```
   <html>
   <title>Hello Applet</title>
   <applet codebase="Java Classes"
           code="HelloApplet.class"
               width=300 height=150>
   </applet>
   </html>
   ```

Steps taken on the user's side

4. The user specifies the URL for the Web page containing the applet.

5. The user's browser reads the HTML source for the Web page and begins to display the image on the screen.

6. The appearance of an **applet** tag in the HTML source file causes the browser to download the compiled applet over the network.

7. A verifier program in the browser checks the byte codes in the applet to ensure that they do not violate the security of the user's system.

8. The Java interpreter in the browser program runs the compiled applet, which generates the desired display on the user's console.

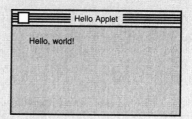

Hello Applet

Hello, world!

---

includes syntactic forms that allow you to define new classes and integrate them into Java's class hierarchy. These syntactic forms are described in more detail in the section entitled "Defining a new class" later in this chapter.

The implications of the shift to the object-oriented paradigm extend beyond the syntactic structure of the language. To become proficient at Java, it is not enough to learn the rules for defining classes. It is far more important to change the way you think about programming. In particular, you need to stop concentrating on the code and focus instead on the data objects and the relationships among them. Doing so can be hard at first, but it is important to pay at least as much attention to the differences in approach as you do to the differences in syntax.

The syntax of Java

In order to understand the Java code in the rest of the chapter, you need to know a few things about Java syntax. The following list describes several of the most important syntactic features of Java:

- *Comments.* As in any programming language, good comments are an essential part of a Java program. Java accepts the commenting convention used in C, in which comments are enclosed between the markers `/*` and `*/`, but also supports the commenting style used in C++, in which comments begin with the characters `//` and extend to the end of the line.

- *Identifier names.* Identifiers used as names of variables, classes, and methods in Java follow the same rules as in C. Both languages are case-sensitive, which means that the identifiers `float` and `Float` are different. Java programmers, however, tend to adopt different conventions for choosing the case of an identifier. In the C programs used in this text—which is only one of many conventions used in the C programming community—type names begin with a lowercase letter, while function names begin with an uppercase letter. Java reverses that convention. Class names begin with an uppercase letter; method names begin with a lowercase letter.

- *Declarations.* You declare variables in Java using much the same syntax as in C. The principal syntactic difference lies in the set of modifiers that you can apply to each declaration. For example, C uses the keyword `static` to indicate that a variable or function should be private to a module. Java uses the more evocative keywords `public`, `private`, and `protected` to control the visibility of variables and methods within a class. The keyword `public` indicates that a variable or method is available to anyone who imports the defining class. The `private` keyword restricts access to the defining class itself. The `protected` keyword specifies an intermediate level of protection that permits subclasses and other classes defined as part of the same package to use that variable or method. Java does retain the keyword `static`, but uses it to refer to methods and variables that are considered to be part of an entire class rather than a specific instance of it. The most common examples of this sort are the methods in the `Math` class, which are part of the class as a whole rather than any specific object.

- *Constants.* Java has no preprocessor, which means that the `#define` specification used in C is no longer available. Constants in Java are defined by adding the keyword `final` to the declaration of a variable, which must include an initializing value. The `final` keyword indicates that the value of the variable will not change. For instance, the declaration

  ```
  public static final double PI = 3.14159265358979323846;
  ```

  from the `Math` class defines the constant `PI` as 3.14159265358979323846.

- *Expressions.* Expressions are almost exactly the same in C and Java. Except for a few operators like `&` and `*` that are no longer needed in a language without explicit pointers, Java uses the same operators as C and assigns them the same precedence levels. Java even retains C's shorthand operations like `++` and `+=`, thereby making it easier to incorporate existing C code into Java programs.

- *Statement forms.* The control statements in Java are taken directly from C, which means that `while`, `for`, `if`, `switch`, and `break` all work just as you'd expect them to. The only extension worth mentioning is that Java allows you to declare the control variable in a `for` loop as part of the initialization specification in the header line. For example, in the statement

  ```
  for (int i = 0; i < 10; i++) {
      loop body
  }
  ```

  the loop index `i` is valid only in the body of the loop. Declaring a local index variable whose scope is limited to the `for` loop improves the structure of the program because it moves the declaration of the index closer to the point where it is used.

Atomic types in Java

The similarities between C and Java extend to the lowest level of the type system. Java includes a small collection of atomic types: `int`, `short`, `long`, `float`, `double`, `char`, `byte`, and `boolean`. Most of these type names correspond directly to atomic types in C and are used for much the same purposes. Even so, there are several important differences that you need to keep in mind.

- *Java defines the range of each atomic type in a precise way.* In C, the internal storage assigned to the primitive numeric types can differ from machine to machine. Because Java places a greater emphasis on portability and machine independence, Java defines precisely how many bits are used to represent each of the built-in types. For example, the type `int` is always stored in 32 bits. Similarly, all floating-point types are represented using an international standard (IEEE 754), which guarantees that floating-point values will behave identically on every Java browser.

- *Characters have been expanded.* Although the type `char` exists in Java, its internal size has been expanded to 16 bits to accommodate the international Unicode character set, which extends the ASCII set by including characters from a much wider range of alphabets. For specialized applications in which the programmer must retain tight control over memory utilization, Java defines an atomic type called `byte`, which represents an 8-bit byte.

- *Java includes a built-in type for Boolean data.* The fact that C uses integers to represent Boolean data has widely been regarded as a weakness in the language. To overcome that weakness, programmers often define their own Boolean type. The programs in this text, for example, use the type `bool`, which is defined in `genlib.h`. Java includes a predefined type called `boolean`, whose elements are the constants `true` and `false`, which are lowercase keywords in Java. The relational and logical operators in Java use `boolean` type throughout, and it is illegal to substitute integers in the way that C programmers sometimes do.

■ *Java has no facility for defining enumeration types.* As in C, you can achieve the effect of enumeration types by defining integer constants with the desired names. The object-oriented structure of Java also reduces the need for such types, because you can sometimes use subclasses instead. Consider, for example, the problem of defining arithmetic expressions. As implemented in Chapter 14, the expression structure contains an enumeration type, which is used to distinguish the three possible representations of an expression. Java programmers would simply define three subclasses of expression: one for integer expressions, one for identifiers, and one for compounds.

Defining a new class

In Java, all executable code is defined as part of a class. To write new programs in Java, you have to learn how to define new classes and the methods that implement their behavior.

At one level, you can think of class definitions as being similar to structure definitions in C. For example, suppose that you want to define a new class in Java that encapsulates a pair of integers representing *x* and *y* coordinates into a single object representing a point in Java's coordinate system. In C, you could use the following structure definition:

```
typedef struct {
    int x, y;
} pointT;
```

In Java, you could obtain the same effect by defining the following class:

```
public class Point {
    public int x, y;
}
```

The keyword `public` in the header line indicates that the class can be imported by any client. Using `public` in the specification of **x** and **y** makes these fields—which are called **instance variables** in most languages that adopt the object-oriented paradigm—visible to clients of the `Point` class.

In Java, you can select the fields of an object by using the dot operator from C. For example, if you have a variable **p** containing an object of type `Point`, you can select its **x** field by writing

```
p.x
```

There are, however, some important differences between structures in C and objects in Java. Internally, Java defines all objects as if they were pointer types, even though the pointer is hidden from the programmer. When you declare a variable of type `Point` in a program using a declaration like

```
Point p;
```

Java allocates only enough space for the address of a `Point` object. The value of `p` is initialized to the constant `null`, which is a lowercase Java keyword. If you try to assign values to the components of `p` at this point, Java will issue an error message because those components do not yet exist. Before you can select the components of `p`, you must allocate a new object of type `Point` by writing a statement like this:

```
p = new Point();
```

This statement allocates space for a new `Point` object and assigns it to the variable `p`. You are now free to assign values to the fields of `p`, as follows:

```
p.x = 1;
p.y = 2;
```

The effect of these statements is similar to the following code in C, shown opposite its Java form:

Java code	C code
`Point p;`	`pointT *p;`
`p = new Point();`	`p = New(pointT *);`
`p.x = 1;`	`p->x = 1;`
`p.y = 2;`	`p->y = 2;`

It is important to keep in mind that Java always uses dot notation for selection despite the fact that there are pointers in the internal structure. C's `->` operator, along with the pointer operators `*` and `&`, does not exist in Java.

As the `Point` class illustrates, objects with public fields can be used very much like records in C. The Java libraries define several classes that act as record definitions, for the most part. The `size` method used in `CheckerApplet`, for example, returns an object of the class `Dimension`, which has the following basic structure:

```
public class Dimension {
    public int width, height;
}
```

Because the `size` method returns a `Dimension` object, you can use the expressions `size().width` and `size().height` to return the width and height of the current applet.

Constructor methods

Although the simple definition of the `Point` class in the preceding section allows you to allocate points and assign values to their components, it is traditional to define constructor methods as part of the class. A constructor—like all methods associated with a class—looks very much like a function definition in C. Constructors, however, have the following special characteristics:

- The name of the class is used as the constructor name.
- The header line for the constructor does not specify a return type.
- The constructor does not return a value but instead simply initializes the object.

As an example, you could define a constructor for the `Point` class by extending the class definition as follows:

```
public class Point
{
    public int x, y;

    public Point(int xc, int yc)
    {
        x = xc;
        y = yc;
    }
}
```

Given this definition, clients can create new objects of type `Point` by calling its constructor with the appropriate arguments. For example, the statement

```
p = new Point(1, 2);
```

allocates a new `Point` object with coordinates (1, 2) and then assigns the resulting value to the variable `p`.

The keyword `this`

The body of the constructor method for `Point` in the preceding section illustrates an interesting aspect of Java's rules for determining the scope of variable names. If the name of a field or method appears without a dot operator specifying the object to which it applies, that variable or method is assumed to apply to the current object. Thus, the variable `x` in the `Point` constructor refers to the `x` field of the object being constructed. The statement

```
x = xc;
```

therefore assigns the value of the parameter `xc` to the `x` field in the object itself. Because the parameters and internal fields have different names, there is no ambiguity. From a stylistic point of view, however, the proliferation of names in this example seems unnecessary. Conceptually, the constructor takes two coordinate values, *x* and *y*. While it would be nice to make the names consistent, it would be an error to code the constructor like this:

```
public Point(int x, int y)
{
    x = x;
    y = y;
}
```

The assignments copy the parameters to themselves.

The assignments don't do anything here, because the parameter variables hide the fields with the same names.

If you want to fix the problem without changing any of the names, you need to make sure that the variable names on the left side of each assignment refer to the fields of the object rather than the parameters. The easiest solution is to use the Java keyword `this`, which always refers to the current object. Thus, the following code correctly implements the constructor with a single set of names for the parameters and their corresponding fields:

```
public Point(int x, int y)
{
   this.x = x;
   this.y = y;
}
```

Although it would be legal to use `this` in every reference to the current object, Java programmers tend to use it only when it helps resolve an ambiguity.

Defining methods

In addition to constructors, most classes also define methods that apply to objects in that class. For example, you might want to define the following methods:

- A method called **move** that changes the coordinates of a point.
- A method called **translate** that adjusts each coordinate of a point by some offset.
- A method called **equals** that determines whether two points are equal.

In the **Point** class that is defined as part of the Java's abstract windowing toolkit, each of these methods in fact exists. Their definitions are shown in Figure 17-5. Note that the **move** method uses the keyword `this` to identify the fields of the object but that the **translate** method does not. Because the parameters to **translate** are named **dx** and **dy**, there is no ambiguity in the names.

The **equals** method—which is a standard method defined in the global class **Object** and then overridden by most other classes—illustrates several important features of Java. First, the syntax for calling a method like **equals** seems a bit odd to programmers accustomed to C's style. In Java, you can't invoke such a method on the points **p1** and **p2** by calling

```
if (equals(p1, p2)) . . .
```
This syntax won't work in Java.

Methods must always be applied to a particular object. What you need to do instead is apply the **equals** method of **p1** to the object **p2**, like this:

```
if (p1.equals(p2)) . . .
```

FIGURE 17-5 A Java class used to represent points

```java
public class Point
{
    /* Instance variables */

    public int x, y;

    /*
     * Constructor: Point
     * Usage: p = new Point(x, y);
     * ----------------------------
     * This method allocates a new Point object with the specified
     * x and y coordinates.
     */

    public Point(int x, int y)
    {
        this.x = x;
        this.y = y;
    }

    /*
     * Methods: move, translate
     * Usage: p.move(x, y);
     *        p.translate(dx, dy);
     * ----------------------------
     * The move method sets the coordinates of the Point p to the
     * specified x and y values; the translate method adjusts the
     * coordinates by adding dx and dy.
     */

    public void move(int x, int y)
    {
        this.x = x;
        this.y = y;
    }

    public void translate(int dx, int dy)
    {
        x += dx;
        y += dy;
    }
```

```
/*
 * Method: equals
 * Usage: if (p1.equals(p2)) . . .
 * --------------------------------
 * This method returns true if p1 and p2 have the same
 * coordinates.  If the argument to the equals method is
 * not a Point object, the method always returns false.
 */

public boolean equals(Object obj)
{
    if (obj instanceof Point) {
        Point p2 = (Point) obj;
        return ((x == p2.x) && (y == p2.y));
    } else {
        return (false);
    }
}
```

The second important feature to notice in the definition of the `equals` method is that the parameter is declared to be an `Object` rather than a `Point`. This design is consistent with the definition of `equals` in the `Object` class and allows objects of type `Point` to be compared against objects of any class. If the second object is not a `Point`, the result will invariably be `false`, but the comparison will not generate an error. The code for `equals` makes use of the Java `instanceof` operator, which tests whether its left operand is an instance of the class name that appears on the right.

Defining subclasses

Although the `Point` class defined in Figure 17-5 illustrates many aspects of class definition, it does not give any sense of how inheritance works in Java. Because the definition of `Point` does not use the `extends` keyword to specify a specific superclass, the `Point` class is automatically added to the Java class hierarchy as a subclass of `Object`.

One of the most common examples used to illustrate inheritance is that of geometric shapes. Suppose, for example, that you are designing an interactive applet that allows its users to draw various shapes on the screen. Although there are many different shapes users might want to draw, it helps to simplify the problem by limiting the application to the two shapes that are easiest to draw given the methods available in the `Graphics` class, rectangles and ovals. Each is a geometric shape. Thus, if you include these shapes in a class hierarchy, the classes `Rect` and `Oval` would each be subclasses of a more general class called `Shape`.

The hierarchy, however, need not stop with the `Rect` and `Oval` classes. If your users tend to draw a lot of squares and circles, it makes sense to include these shapes as classes in their own right. It's tricky to draw a perfect circle using a program that draws ovals, because you have to make sure that the dimensions match exactly. If the program supports circles as well, you can let it be responsible for making sure the height and width are the same.

The important point to recognize in this discussion is that the classes **Square** and **Circle** need not be defined as direct subclasses of **Shape**. Because every square is a rectangle and every circle is an oval, it makes more sense to use a class hierarchy that looks like this:

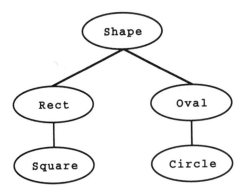

In this hierarchy, each class inherits some behavior from its superclass, but may restrict that behavior in some way. Because the goal is to develop a drawing application, all classes that are representatives of the **Shape** class—rectangles, squares, ovals, and circles—must be able to draw themselves on the screen. Thus, the class **Shape** must have a **draw** method. At the same time, it isn't possible to draw a shape unless you know what type of shape it is.

If you think about this problem, you'll soon realize that the **Shape** class is different from the other classes in this hierarchy. You can have an object of class **Rect** that is not a **Square**, but you can't have a **Shape** object that is not also a member of one of its subclasses. It never makes sense to construct a **Shape** object in its own right. Whenever you want to use a geometric shape, you simply construct an object of the appropriate subclass. Classes that are never constructed, such as **Shape**, are called **abstract classes.** In Java, you can indicate that a class is abstract by including the **abstract** keyword in the class header line. Similarly, you can use the **abstract** keyword to indicate that a particular method is abstract, which means that it is always overridden by its subclasses.

When you create an abstract class, you are free to define fields and methods as long as they apply to all subclasses. For example, every geometric shape presumably contains fields specifying its location and size. If the structure of those fields is the same for every subclass, it makes sense to declare them at the level of the **Shape** class itself instead of having to repeat the declarations in every subclass. The **Shape** class is also the place to specify methods that apply to all geometric shapes. For example, you may want to allow the client to specify the color of each shape. As far as setting the color is concerned, it doesn't matter whether a shape is a rectangle, oval, square, or circle. You can therefore define methods for setting the color of a shape as part of the **Shape** class, from which they will be inherited by every subclass.

Because the **Shape** class is abstract, there is no need for a public constructor. You may, however, specify a protected constructor for use by its subclasses. Whenever you call a constructor method for any class, Java automatically calls the no-argument constructor for its superclass, proceeding upward through every class in the hierarchy. In this example, you might want the constructor for the **Shape** class to set a default color to ensure that the **color** variable in every newly constructed shape has a legal value.

The public constructors in the shape hierarchy appear in the subclasses **Rect**, **Square**, **Oval**, and **Circle**. The arguments for these constructors are chosen to simplify the process of drawing shapes on the screen using a mouse. Each constructor takes two coordinate pairs, (x_0, y_0) and (x_1, y_1), that specify diagonally opposite corners of the figure. For example, if you are constructing an oval, you might pass in the coordinates shown in the following diagram:

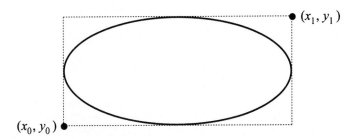

The constructors in the **Rect** and **Oval** subclasses transform the coordinates of the corners into the values required by the **drawRect** and **drawOval** methods, which are the coordinates of the upper-left corner along with the width and height of the object. Thus, if you called the **Oval** constructor with the coordinates shown in the preceding diagram, the new **Oval** object would be initialized with the following information in its internal fields:

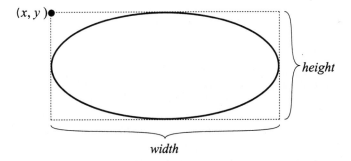

The complete definition of the **Shape** hierarchy appears in Figure 17-6.

FIGURE 17-6 A Java package that defines a hierarchy of shapes

```java
/*
 * File: Shape.java
 * ----------------
 * This file implements a hierarchical collection of classes
 * that represent simple geometric shapes.
 */

import java.awt.*;

/*
 * Class: Shape
 * ------------
 * This class defines the general class that includes all of
 * the specific shape types.  All objects that fit into the
 * Shape class are actually instances of one of the specific
 * subclasses.
 */

public abstract class Shape
{
   /*
    * Instance variables: x, y, width, height, color
    * -----------------------------------------------
    * These variables are common to all shapes and are therefore
    * declared at this level.  The variables x and y specify
    * the coordinates of the upper-left corner; width and height
    * specify the dimensions of the figure and are always positive.
    * The color is recorded with each shape so that individual
    * shapes can be drawn in different colors.
    */

   protected int x, y;
   protected int width, height;
   protected Color color;

   /*
    * Protected constructor: Shape
    * ----------------------------
    * This method is invoked automatically by the contructors
    * in each subclass.  In this case, the only reason to
    * include a constructor at the Shape level is to make sure
    * that the color is initialized to a legal value.
    */

   protected Shape()
   {
      color = Color.black;
   }
```

```
    /*
     * Abstract method: draw
     * Usage: shape.draw(g);
     * ----------------------
     * This method draws the shape in the graphics context
     * specified by g, which is passed in by the caller.  The
     * method is abstract because the code for drawing a specific
     * shape is always supplied by a subclass.
     */

    public abstract void draw(Graphics g);

    /*
     * Public methods: setColor, getColor
     * Usage: shape.setColor(color);
     *        color = shape.getColor();
     * ------------------------------------
     * These methods allow clients to set or retrieve the color
     * of an existing shape.  Because these methods apply to
     * every subclass, they can be defined at this level.
     */

    public void setColor(Color color)
    {
        this.color = color;
    }

    public Color getColor()
    {
        return (color);
    }
}

/*
 * Class: Rect
 * -----------
 * This class defines the class consisting of rectangles.
 */

public class Rect extends Shape
{
    /*
     * Constructor: Rect
     * Usage: shape = new Rect();
     *        shape = new Rect(x0, y0, x1, y1);
     * ------------------------------------------
     * The Rect class supports two constructors.  The simpler form
     * takes no arguments and exists primarily because subclasses
     * automatically call the no-argument constructor for their
     * superclass.  Clients will tend to use the second form of
     * the constructor, whict takes four arguments indicating the
     * coordinates of diagonally opposite corners of the rectangle.
     */

    protected Rect() {}
```

```
   public Rect(int x0, int y0, int x1, int y1)
   {
      width = Math.abs(x1 - x0);
      height = Math.abs(y1 - y0);
      x = Math.min(x0, x1);
      y = Math.min(y0, y1);
   }

   /*
    * Public method: draw
    * Usage: shape.draw(g);
    * ---------------------
    * This method overrides the abstract method for the Shape
    * class and draws a rectangle using the drawRect method
    * in the Graphics class.
    */

   public void draw(Graphics g)
   {
      g.setColor(color);
      g.drawRect(x, y, width, height);
   }
}

/*
 * Class: Square
 * -------------
 * This class defines the subclass of rectangles that are
 * constrained to be square.
 */

public class Square extends Rect
{
   /*
    * Constructor: Square
    * Usage: shape = new Square(x0, y0, x1, y1);
    * -----------------------------------------------
    * The constructor for Square takes the same arguments as
    * Rect to simplify the process of drawing a square from
    * mouse coordinates.  The actual size of the edge of the
    * square is the smaller of the width and the height.
    */

   public Square(int x0, int y0, int x1, int y1)
   {
      width = Math.min(Math.abs(x1 - x0), Math.abs(y1 - y0));
      height = width;
      x = (x0 < x1) ? x0 : x0 - width;
      y = (y0 < y1) ? y0 : y0 - height;
   }
}
```

```
/*
 * Class: Oval
 * -----------
 * This class defines the class consisting of ovals.
 */

public class Oval extends Shape
{
   /*
    * Constructor: Oval
    * Usage: shape = new Oval();
    *        shape = new Oval(x0, y0, x1, y1);
    * ----------------------------------------
    * The constructors for Oval follow the design of that for
    * Rect defined earlier in this file.
    */

   protected Oval() {}

   public Oval(int x0, int y0, int x1, int y1)
   {
      width = Math.abs(x1 - x0);
      height = Math.abs(y1 - y0);
      x = Math.min(x0, x1);
      y = Math.min(y0, y1);
   }

   /*
    * Public method: draw
    * Usage: shape.draw(g);
    * ---------------------
    * This method overrides the abstract method for the Shape
    * class and draws an oval using the drawOval method in the
    * Graphics class.
    */

   public void draw(Graphics g)
   {
      g.setColor(color);
      g.drawOval(x, y, width, height);
   }
}
```

```
/*
 * Class: Circle
 * ------------
 * This class defines the subclass of ovals that are
 * constrained to be circular.
 */

public class Circle extends Oval
{
    /*
     * Constructor: Circle
     * Usage: shape = new Circle(x0, y0, x1, y1);
     * -------------------------------------------
     * The constructor for Circle takes the same arguments as
     * Oval to simplify the process of drawing a circle from
     * mouse coordinates.  The actual diameter of the circle
     * is the smaller of the width and the height.
     */

    public Circle(int x0, int y0, int x1, int y1)
    {
        width = Math.min(Math.abs(x1 - x0), Math.abs(y1 - y0));
        height = width;
        x = (x0 < x1) ? x0 : x0 - width;
        y = (y0 < y1) ? y0 : y0 - height;
    }
}
```

17.4 Predefined classes in Java

The ability to define new classes makes it easy to expand the capabilities of Java beyond the primitive facilities supported by the language itself. If Java's principal virtue were its extensibility, however, it's not clear how many people would have stopped to take notice. For most programmers, the important thing is not that it's *possible* to extend Java but rather that someone else has already *implemented* those extensions. What sets Java apart from most other language systems is that it comes equipped with a large library of predefined classes designed to help you create highly sophisticated tools by building on the existing infrastructure.

In many respects, it makes sense to think of each Java class as being analogous to a library interface that exports an abstract data type. When you use an abstract type in C, you don't think about its internal representation or the details of its implementation. As a client, you are concerned only about what operations that abstract type supports. The same is true for classes in Java. The designers of Java have developed many useful classes that are an intrinsic part of the Java programming environment. Before you define a new class, it always makes sense to see if there is an existing class that meets your needs. If you can find an appropriate class definition in a library package, you can save yourself a considerable amount of work. The sections that follow introduce several of the most useful Java classes and show you how they can work to your advantage.

The String class

One of the most important classes in Java is the class **String**, which is used to represent strings. The **String** class implements a number of useful methods including those shown in Table 17-2. Because **String** is part of the **java.lang** package, you never need to import it into your programs. It is always available along with the other classes in that package.

Unlike most classes, the **String** class has a privileged status in the language, in the sense that the compiler treats the **String** class specially when it encounters either of the following:

- *String constants.* Java automatically creates a **String** object whenever it encounters a string enclosed in double quotation marks.
- *The concatenation operator.* If you apply the + operator to objects of class **String**, Java interprets the operator as concatenation. Thus, the expression **"A" + "B"** returns the string **"AB"**. If only one of the operands is a **String**, the Java compiler automatically includes code to convert the other operand to its **String** representation. This convention makes it easy to generate string output without having to resort to functions like **printf**, which does not exist in Java. For example, if the integer variables **x** and **y** have the values 3 and 4, the method call

```
g.drawString("The sum of " + x + " and " + y
         + " is " + (x + y) + ".", 30, 30);
```

would produce the output

```
The sum of 3 and 4 is 7.
```

TABLE 17-2 A partial listing of methods in the String class

s.length()	This method returns the length of the string s.
s.charAt(*index*)	This method returns the character at the specified position.
s_1.equals(s_2)	This method returns **true** if s_1 and s_2 are equal.
s_1.compareTo(s_2)	This method operates like **StringCompare** and returns an integer whose sign reflects the relationship between s_1 and s_2.
s_1.concat(s_2)	This method returns a new string formed by concatenating the characters in s_1 and s_2.
s.substring(p_1, p_2)	This method returns a new string consisting of the characters in s starting at index position p_1 and ending just before p_2. Note that the last argument is interpreted differently by this method than the corresponding argument in the **SubString** function from **strlib.h**.
s_1.indexOf(s_2) s_1.indexOf(s_2, *start*)	This method is similar to **FindString** and returns the index of the first occurrence of s_2 in s_1, or −1 if no match is found. If the *start* argument is included, the search begins at that position.

beginning at coordinates (30, 30) on the screen. The parentheses around the subexpression **(x + y)** are required to ensure that the + operator indicates integer addition rather than string concatenation.

When you use Java, it doesn't make sense to think of an element of the **String** class as an array of characters. The best model for the **String** class is the **strlib.h** interface introduced in Chapter 3. Like **strlib.h**, the **String** class treats strings as abstract entities, which influences the design of its methods. Each of the methods listed in Table 17-2, for example, has a direct counterpart in **strlib.h**.

The **Hashtable** class

One of the most useful abstract data types presented in this text is the symbol table abstraction introduced in Chapter 11. In Java, a much more powerful symbol table facility already exists in the form of the **Hashtable** class, which is part of the package **java.util**. The **Hashtable** class makes it easy to associate keys and values using the simple set of methods shown in Table 17-3. The first three methods in the table are direct counterparts of the **NewSymbolTable**, **Enter**, and **Lookup** functions in the **symtab.h** interface.

To get a sense of how you might use the **Hashtable** class, suppose that you want to create a dictionary that allows you to refer to colors in the **Color** class by name. You can do so by creating a **Hashtable** that associates the name of each color with its corresponding **Color** value. You can begin creating such a table by writing the declaration

```
private Hashtable colorTable = new Hashtable();
```

which uses the constructor for the **Hashtable** class to initialize an empty table.

TABLE 17-3	Useful methods in the **Hashtable** class
Hashtable()	This constructor creates an empty hash table and is therefore comparable to the **NewSymbolTable** entry in **symtab.h.**
ht.**put** (*key, value*)	This method creates an association between *key* and *value* in the hash table *ht* and is therefore analogous to **Enter**. As with **Enter**, any previous value associated with *key* is lost.
ht.**get** (*key*)	This method looks up and returns the last value associated with *key* in the hash table *ht* and is therefore analogous to **Lookup**. If no value for *key* has been entered, the **get** method returns the constant **null**.
ht.**remove** (*key*)	This method removes the definition for *key* in the hash table *ht*.
ht.**containsKey** (*key*)	This method returns **true** if a definition for *key* exists in the hash table *ht*.
ht.**keys** ()	This method returns a value of the class **Enumeration** that can be used to iterate through every key in the table *ht*.

Once you have declared `colorTable`, you can enter new definitions by writing lines that look like this:

```
colorTable.put("Green", Color.green);
```

You can also look up colors by name, as illustrated by the following line, which sets the current graphics color to the table entry for `"Green"`:

```
g.setColor((Color) colorTable.get("Green"));
```

It's important to note that the `get` method for the `Hashtable` class returns a general `Object`, which must be typecast to `Color` before being passed to the `setColor` method.

The final method listed in Table 17-3 is `keys`, which returns a value of another library class called an `Enumeration`. Objects of the `Enumeration` class act very much like the iterators for symbol tables defined in Chapter 11. Figure 17-7 illustrates the operation of the `Enumeration` class by using it to create an applet that displays the entries in `colorTable` so that each name is displayed in its own color. As with mapping functions in a symbol table, the order in which the keys appear is not defined, but the `Enumeration` returned by `keys` is guaranteed to cycle through each of them.

Hash tables in Java are polymorphic with respect to both keys and values. Conceptually, the prototype for the `put` method looks like this:

```
public void put(Object key, Object value);
```

Both the `key` and the `value` parameters are declared as being of the class `Object`, which is the ultimate superclass for every Java object. For the `value` parameter, it is easy to see that this definition is ideal. Any object at all can be stored as a value in a `Hashtable`. Understanding how Java can use the general `Object` class to represent keys, however, takes a little bit of thought.

The idea of using generic objects as keys seems somewhat problematic. The hashing algorithm, after all, needs to be able to manipulate key values internally. In particular, given a key, the implementation of the `Hashtable` class must be able to perform the following operations:

- Compare the key passed by the client to see whether it matches the keys stored in the table.
- Generate an integer that serves as the hash code for the key.

Declaring keys to be of class `Object` in the Java `Hashtable` class is similar to declaring them as `void *` values in the `symtab.h` interface. As discussed in the section on "Choosing types for values and keys" in Chapter 11, the `void *` strategy fails because it is impossible to carry out the necessary operations on generic pointers. What does Java do to get around this problem?

The answer is that the `Object` class itself defines methods called `equals` and `hashCode`, which give the `Hashtable` class exactly the capabilities it needs. Most classes in the Java libraries override these methods with versions appropriate to that particular class. For example, the `String` class overrides these methods with new

FIGURE 17-7 Java applet to display color names in the appropriate color

```
/*
 * File: ColorApplet.Java
 * ----------------------
 * This applet writes out the name of several predefined colors
 * so that each color name appears in its own color.
 */

import java.applet.Applet;
import java.util.*;
import java.awt.*;

public class ColorApplet extends Applet
{
   private Hashtable colorTable;

   public void init()
   {
      colorTable = new Hashtable();
      colorTable.put("Red",     Color.red);
      colorTable.put("Green",   Color.green);
      colorTable.put("Blue",    Color.blue);
      colorTable.put("Yellow",  Color.yellow);
      colorTable.put("Cyan",    Color.cyan);
      colorTable.put("Magenta", Color.magenta);
   }

   public void paint(Graphics g)
   {
      int x, y;
      String colorName;
      Enumeration iterator;

      x = 20;
      y = 20;
      iterator = colorTable.keys();
      while (iterator.hasMoreElements()) {
         colorName = (String) iterator.nextElement();
         g.setColor((Color) colorTable.get(colorName));
         g.drawString(colorName, x, y);
         y += 15;
      }
   }
}
```

versions that are similar to the functions `StringEqual` and `Hash` in the C-based implementation. The implication of this design is that the `Hashtable` class can use any object as a key as long as the corresponding class defines the methods `equals` and `hashCode`. Because most of Java's predefined classes supply these methods, the `Hashtable` class is extremely flexible as a tool.

Object wrappers for the atomic types

As general as the `Hashtable` package is, it nonetheless suffers from a serious limitation. As defined, the `put` and `get` methods require that the keys and values belong to the class `Object`. In Java, almost every value is an `Object`. The exceptions are the predefined atomic types like `int`, `float`, or `boolean`. You could not, for example, create a `Hashtable` object and use it to map keys into integers, because integers are not compatible with `Object`.

To get around this problem, the `java.lang` package includes a set of classes that make it possible to embed atomic values within an object. These classes—which have the names `Integer`, `Long`, `Float`, `Double`, `Character`, and `Boolean`—are called **object wrappers.** The constructor takes a value of the underlying atomic type. For instance,

```
new Float(3.141592654);
```

creates an object that acts as a reference to the floating-point constant 3.141592654.

Once you have converted atomic values into objects, you can store the converted values in a `Hashtable`, as shown by this code:

```
Hashtable constantTable = new Hashtable();
constantTable.put("PI", new Float(3.141592654));
constantTable.put("E",  new Float(2.718281828));
```

To convert an object wrapper back into a primitive value, you need to use one of the following methods, according to the value type: `intValue`, `longValue`, `floatValue`, `doubleValue`, `charValue`, and `booleanValue`. For example, in the following code, the `getFloatConstant` method looks up a named constant in `constantTable` and returns its value as an atomic value of type `float`:

```
float getFloatConstant(String constantName)
{
    Float refFloat;

    refFloat = (Float) constantTable.get(constantName);
    return (refFloat.floatValue());
}
```

Object wrappers are similar in concept and structure to the entries in the `ref.h` interface, which is introduced in exercise 6 of Chapter 8.

The `Vector` class

One of the most powerful classes in the standard Java library is the `Vector` class, which implements dynamic arrays and is exported as part of the `java.util` package. Even though Java supports arrays as part of its data structure, many Java programmers use the **Vector** class instead because it provides everything you want from arrays and more. Several of the most common methods in the **Vector** class are listed in Table 17-4.

As an illustration of how insertion at an arbitrary position can be useful, suppose that you are working with objects of a class called **Card** whose definition, at least as far as the constructor is concerned, looks like this:

```
public class Card
{
    public int rank, suit;

    public Card(int rank, int suit)
    {
        this.suit = suit;
        this.rank = rank;
    }
}
```

TABLE 17-4	A partial listing of methods in the **Vector** class
Vector()	This constructor creates an empty vector.
v.**size()**	This method returns the number of elements in *v*.
v.**isEmpty()**	This method returns **true** if there are no elements in *v*.
v.**elementAt**(*k*)	This method returns the element at index position (*k*) in the vector *v* and is therefore analogous to array selection.
v.**firstElement()** *v*.**lastElement()**	These methods implement special cases of array selection and return the first and last elements in *v*, respectively.
v.**addElement**(*e*)	This method adds the element *e* at the end of the vector.
v.**insertElementAt**(*e, k*)	This method inserts a new element *e* before index position *k* in the current vector. The internal storage for the vector is expanded if necessary, and all subsequent elements are shifted to make room for the newly added one.
v.**removeElementAt**(*k*)	This method removes the element at index position *k*.
v.**removeAllElements()**	This method removes all elements from the vector, leaving it empty.
v.**indexOf**(*e*) *v*.**indexOf**(*e, start*)	This method uses the **equals** method of the object *e* to find and return the first index position in the vector at which *e* appears. If *e* does not appear in *v*, **indexOf** returns –1. If the *start* argument is included, the search begins at that index position.
v.**elements()**	This method returns an **Enumeration** consisting of the elements in the vector, which can be used in much the same manner as the **keys** method in the **Hashtable** class.

If you need a method `createShuffledDeck` that creates a `Vector` containing 52 standard playing cards in a random order, the following code does the job:

```
public Vector createShuffledDeck()
{
    int suit, rank, n, pos;
    Card card;
    Vector deck;

    deck = new Vector();
    n = 0;
    for (suit = 1; suit <= 4; suit++) {
        for (rank = 1; rank <= 13; rank++) {
            card = new Card(rank, suit);
            pos = randomInteger(0, n);
            deck.insertElementAt(card, pos);
            n++;
        }
    }
    return (deck);
}

private int randomInteger(int low, int high)
{
    return (low + (int) ((high - low + 1) * Math.random()));
}
```

The code for `randomInteger` uses the `random` function in the `Math` class in much the same way that `RandomInteger` does in the `random.c` implementation presented in Chapter 3.

Like most of the classes introduced in the earlier sections, the `Vector` class implements many methods beyond those in Table 17-4. One of the great advantages of the Java library design is that you really don't need to understand all the methods in a class before you begin using that class. For example, the `Vector` class exports several methods that allow you to preallocate space for a vector to reduce the cost of adding new elements. Using such methods can increase the execution efficiency of your application significantly. However, if you aren't particularly concerned about efficiency, you can ignore these methods altogether. Your program will still work, because the `Vector` class supports dynamic allocation. If running time becomes a problem, you can rewrite your program to take advantage of the efficiency-enhancing features of the `Vector` class.

The `Stack` class

The `Vector` class is also used as the basis for other classes that implement particular linear structures. For example, the `Stack` class in the `java.util` package implements a general stack abstraction as a subclass of `Vector`, which means that stacks automatically inherit all the methods that apply to vectors. A simplified definition for the `Stack` class appears in Figure 17-8.

FIGURE 17-8 A simplified definition of the Stack class

```
/*
 * File: Stack.java
 * ----------------
 * This class is a simplified definition of the Stack class from
 * the java.util package.
 */

import java.util.Vector;

public class Stack extends Vector
{
    public Stack() {}

    public void push(Object obj)
    {
        addElement(obj);
    }

    public Object pop()
    {
        Object obj;

        obj = lastElement();
        removeElementAt(size() - 1);
        return (obj);
    }
}
```

◼️ 17.5 Tools for creating interactive applets

The library classes described in the preceding sections are general utilities that are useful in many programming domains. One of Java's great advantages is that its standard libraries also include classes to help you write interactive applets. Such applets typically support a graphical user interface—a ubiquitous feature of modern programming that is often shortened to the acronym **GUI** (which is pronounced like the English word *gooey*). In modern GUI technology, you use a mouse or some similar input device to click a button or select an item from a menu. Objects like buttons and menus that respond to user actions are collectively called **interactors.**

The `java.awt` package exports several classes that allow you to create interactors with a minimum of work. For example, if you need to display a button on the screen, all you have to do is create an instance of the predefined class called `Button` and add that object to your applet. The sections that follow describe some of the most important interactor classes available in Java and illustrate how you can use them to create interactive applets.

Components and containers

To understand the process of creating interactive applets, you must first learn the relevant portion of the Java class hierarchy. The design of the interactor hierarchy is based on the following definitions:

- *Components.* In Java's abstract windowing toolkit, the term **component** refers to any object that can appear as part of a graphical display, such as a button or a pop-up menu, which Java calls a **choice.** Components are represented in the class hierarchy by the class `Component`, which includes individual interactor classes like `Button` and `Choice` as subclasses. Like the `Shape` class introduced in the section on "Defining subclasses" earlier in this chapter, `Component` is an abstract class, which means that the `Component` class has no objects that are not also members of one of its subclasses.
- *Containers.* Java uses the term **container** to refer to the broad class of objects that can contain components. When you want to construct a graphical user interface, the standard approach is to create several interactor components and add them to some container. Containers are represented in the hierarchy by the class `Container`, which is an abstract subclass of `Component`. Because containers are also components, you can nest containers inside of other containers to create arbitrarily complex structures.

If you look back to the diagram of the Java class hierarchy shown in Figure 17-1, you can see that the `Applet` class lies on a branch of the tree that includes both `Component` and `Container` as higher-level classes. The fact that every applet is a component means that you can use or override `Component` methods in the definition of your applets. For example, the code for `CheckerApplet` in Figure 17-3 uses the `size` method to determine the dimensions of the window and overrides the `paint` method to display the checkerboard image in the applet window. The fact that every applet is also a container means that you can add new interactors to any applet using the `add` method defined as part of the `Container` class.

As an example, suppose that you want to add a button labeled `"Test"` to an applet. The first step is to add the following code to the applet's class definition:

```
private Button testButton;

public void init()
{
    testButton = new Button("Test");
    add(testButton);
}
```

The `init` method is invoked automatically when the applet begins execution. In this example, the `init` method simply allocates a new button with the desired label and then adds it to the applet. When the applet is redrawn, the button appears automatically on the screen.

The `action` method

Getting a button to appear on the screen is only part of the task. For your applet to be interactive, it must be able to respond when the user clicks that button with the mouse. When events such as mouse clicks occur during the execution of an applet, the Java interpreter invokes specific methods in the component in which that event occurs. For example, clicking the mouse on a button invokes its `action` method.

In most applets, however, it doesn't make sense for the *button* to respond to the event. The button contains information only about its own structure and not the application as a whole. Instead, it is usually more appropriate for the *applet* to respond. In Java, the `action` method for a class can adopt either of two strategies: it can respond to an event on its own or pass responsibility for that event to the enclosing container, which is called its **parent.** By default, the `action` method for the `Button` class adopts the second approach. Thus, if you click the `Test` button declared in the previous section, the Java runtime system ends up invoking the `action` method in the applet itself, because the applet is the parent of the button.

To respond to the event, your applet class must override the `action` method with code that looks something like this:

```
public boolean action(Event e, Object arg)
{
    if (e.target == testButton) {
        showStatus("Test button pressed");
    }
    return (true);
}
```

As the definition indicates, the `action` method is called with two arguments: an `Event` object that describes the event which triggered the action and a more general argument of class `Object` that supplies additional data. For simple applets, the only thing you need to know about `Event` objects is that they include a public field called `target`, which identifies the object in which the event occurred. The value of the second parameter depends on what events and interactors are involved. If you click a button, the second argument is the label on the button; if you select an item from a choice menu, this argument is the name of the selected item.

The code for the `action` method in an applet typically consists of a sequence of `if` statements that check the target of the event against the interactors declared by the applet. Once it has identified the initiating interactor, the `action` method can undertake the appropriate response. In this example, the action is simply

```
showStatus("Test button pressed");
```

which displays the message `"Test button pressed"` in the status area at the bottom of the applet window. In a more realistic application, you would replace this line with whatever code is needed to implement the desired action. The `showStatus` method, however, is an extremely useful tool for debugging Java programs and for writing short applets that test your understanding of how the various components work.

When an `action` method returns, the `boolean` result indicates whether that method processed the event. If `action` returns `false`, the Java interpreter invokes the `action` method in the enclosing container. At the level of the applet itself, the `action` method typically returns `true` in all cases because there is no enclosing container under the programmer's control.

The `init`, `paint`, and `action` methods are only a few of the methods that applet designers can redefine to specialize the behavior of a particular applet. A list of the methods most commonly overridden by applets appears in Table 17-5.

A sample applet for drawing shapes

The code in Figure 17-9 defines a simple applet that allows you to draw shapes in its window using the mouse. The shapes are those defined in the `Shape` class from Figure 17-6. The concrete subclasses of `Shape`—`Rect`, `Square`, `Oval`, and `Circle`—know how to draw themselves. What the applet must provide beyond the basic drawing mechanism is the code to handle the user interaction.

TABLE 17-5	Methods commonly redefined by applets
`init()`	The `init` method is called automatically whenever a new applet is created. It is used to perform any initialization that the applet needs to create its starting configuration.
`paint(g)`	The `paint` method is called by the Java interpreter whenever a component needs to be repainted. Individual subclasses override this method to control their own appearance. The argument to `paint` is a `Graphics` object that provides a context for graphical operations such as those listed in Table 17-1. In general, code for changing the displayed image should appear only within the `paint` method and not in methods invoked by events.
`action(e, arg)`	The `action` method is called whenever the user performs a mouse action in an interactor, such as clicking a button or selecting an option in a choice menu. The arguments to the `action` method consist of an `Event` *e* and an `Object` *arg*. For simple applets, the `Event` parameter is used to identify the interactor involved, which is stored in `e.target`. The *arg* parameter is used to pass additional information about the action. For buttons and choice menus, this parameter is the name of the button or selected item. The `action` method should return `true` if event processing is complete.
`mouseDown(e, x, y)` `mouseUp(e, x, y)`	These methods are invoked when the state of the mouse button changes in some context that does not represent an `action` event. The argument *e* is an `Event`, while *x* and *y* are integers giving the location of the mouse in the coordinate system for the current component. Like `action`, these methods return `true` to indicate that processing is complete.
`mouseDrag(e, x, y)`	The `mouseDrag` method is invoked whenever the mouse is moved with the button down. The arguments are identical to the `mouseDown` and `mouseUp` methods.

FIGURE 17-9   A Java applet that draws shapes on the screen

```
/*
 * File: DrawApplet.java
 * ---------------------
 * This file implements a simple Java applet to draw shapes.
 * The applet allows the user to draw a shape by dragging
 * it in the window.  The applet also provides a reset button
 * and choice menus that allow the user to set the current
 * color and shape.
 */

import java.applet.Applet;
import java.util.*;
import java.awt.*;
import Shape;

/*
 * Class: DrawApplet
 * -----------------
 * This class is used to represent the main applet window.
 * It contains the interactors and a drawing canvas, which
 * is defined as a separate class.  DrawApplet overrides
 * the init and action methods, but does not override paint,
 * because painting in the applet can interfere with the
 * display of the interactors.  All painting operations occur
 * in a separate DrawCanvas object nested within the applet.
 */

public class DrawApplet extends Applet
{
    private Button resetButton;     // Button to reset the display
    private Hashtable colorTable;    // Table mapping names to colors
    private Choice colorChoice;      // Menu of color choices
    private Choice toolChoice;       // Menu of drawing tools
    private DrawCanvas canvas;       // Window used for drawing

    /*
     * Public method: init
     * -------------------
     * This method is automatically invoked when the applet is
     * started. The actual work is done by several private methods
     * used to decompose the task into manageable pieces.
     */

    public void init()
    {
        initButtons();
        initColorChoice();
        initToolChoice();
        initCanvas();
    }
```

```
/*
 * Public method: action
 * ----------------------
 * This method is invoked when the user clicks the mouse in an
 * interactor.  The interactor itself is recorded in the target
 * field of the event.  Any data value associated with that
 * interactor is passed as the second argument.
 */

public boolean action(Event e, Object arg)
{
   if (e.target == resetButton) {
     canvas.reset();
   } else if (e.target == colorChoice) {
     canvas.setColor((Color) colorTable.get(arg));
   } else if (e.target == toolChoice) {
     canvas.setTool((String) arg);
   }
   return (true);
}

/*
 * Private method: initButtons
 * ----------------------------
 * This method adds the Reset button to the applet.  If you want
 * to extend this applet by adding new buttons, you should add
 * the appropriate calls here.
 */

private void initButtons()
{
   resetButton = new Button("Reset");
   resetButton.setBackground(Color.white);
   add(resetButton);
}

/*
 * Private method: initToolChoice
 * ---------------------------------
 * This method initializes the Choice menu for tools to contain
 * the names of the available Shape classes.
 */

private void initToolChoice()
{
   toolChoice = new Choice();
   toolChoice.setBackground(Color.white);
   toolChoice.addItem("Rect");
   toolChoice.addItem("Square");
   toolChoice.addItem("Oval");
   toolChoice.addItem("Circle");
   add(toolChoice);
}
```

```
/*
 * Private methods: initColorChoice, addColorChoice
 * -----------------------------------------------------
 * The initColorChoice method initializes the structures used to
 * give the user a choice of colors, which include both the Choice
 * menu containing the color names and a Hashtable mapping names
 * to actual colors.  The addColorChoice method adds a name/color
 * pair to both structures.
 */

private void initColorChoice()
{
   colorTable = new Hashtable();
   colorChoice = new Choice();
   colorChoice.setBackground(Color.white);
   addColorChoice("Black",   Color.black);
   addColorChoice("Red",     Color.red);
   addColorChoice("Green",   Color.green);
   addColorChoice("Blue",    Color.blue);
   addColorChoice("Cyan",    Color.cyan);
   addColorChoice("Magenta", Color.magenta);
   addColorChoice("Yellow",  Color.yellow);
   addColorChoice("White",   Color.white);
   add(colorChoice);
}

private void addColorChoice(String name, Color color)
{
   colorTable.put(name, color);
   colorChoice.addItem(name);
}

/*
 * Private method: initCanvas
 * --------------------------
 * This method allocates the drawing canvas and adds it to the
 * applet.  The resize method is used to set the size of the
 * canvas so that it fits in the applet and leaves room for
 * the buttons.  The constants XInset and YInset indicate how
 * much smaller the canvas is than the surrounding applet.
 */

private final int XInset = 20;
private final int YInset = 40;

private void initCanvas()
{
   canvas = new DrawCanvas();
   canvas.setColor((Color)
                     colorTable.get(colorChoice.getSelectedItem()));
   canvas.setTool(toolChoice.getSelectedItem());
   canvas.resize(size().width - XInset, size().height - YInset);
   add(canvas);
}
}
```

```
/*
 * Class: DrawCanvas
 * -----------------
 * This class is used to represent the drawing surface, which
 * is embedded in the applet canvas.  DrawCanvas is a subclass
 * of Canvas, which is a predefined subclass of Component.  The
 * DrawCanvas subclass overrides the methods paint, mouseDown,
 * and mouseUp; the new implementations implement the specific
 * behavior of the drawing application, which allows the user to
 * create shapes by dragging the mouse between diagonally opposite
 * corners of the figure.  The DrawCanvas class also supports a
 * constructor and the methods setColor, setTool, and reset, which
 * allow the applet to control the state of the DrawCanvas object.
 */

public class DrawCanvas extends Canvas
{
    private int xDown, yDown;        // Point where mouse went down
    private Color currentColor;      // Currently selected color
    private String currentTool;      // Name of currently selected tool
    private Vector shapes;           // Vector of shapes on the screen

    /*
     * Public constructor: DrawCanvas
     * ------------------------------
     * The constructor for this class sets the background to white
     * to create a better drawing surface and creates a vector of
     * shapes, which is initially empty.
     */

    public DrawCanvas()
    {
        setBackground(Color.white);
        shapes = new Vector();
    }

    /*
     * Public method: paint
     * --------------------
     * The paint method for the drawing canvas simply draws each
     * of the objects in the shapes vector.  The elements are
     * drawn in order to ensure that the most recently drawn
     * objects are displayed on top of the earlier ones.
     */

    public void paint(Graphics g)
    {
        for (int i = 0; i < shapes.size(); i++) {
            ((Shape) shapes.elementAt(i)).draw(g);
        }
    }
```

```
/*
 * Public methods: mouseDown, mouseUp
 * -----------------------------------
 * These methods are called when the state of the mouse button
 * changes when the mouse is positioned in the drawing canvas.
 * The mouseDown method records the coordinates of the mouse,
 * which mark the starting corner of the shape.  The mouseUp
 * method uses both sets of coordinates to create a new
 * shape and add it to the shapes vector.
 */

public boolean mouseDown(Event e, int x, int y)
{
   xDown = x;
   yDown = y;
   return (true);
}

public boolean mouseUp(Event e, int xUp, int yUp)
{
   if (xDown != xUp || yDown != yUp) {
      shapes.addElement(createShape(xDown, yDown, xUp, yUp));
      repaint();
   }
   return (true);
}

/*
 * Public methods: reset, setColor, setTool
 * Usage: canvas.reset();
 *        canvas.setColor(color);
 *        canvas.setTool(toolName);
 * -----------------------------------
 * These methods give the applet the facilities it needs to
 * implement the buttons and menus.  The reset method deletes
 * all shapes from the internal list, thereby clearing the
 * display.  The other two methods set the current color and
 * tool for the drawing canvas.
 */

public void reset()
{
   shapes.removeAllElements();
   repaint();
}

public void setColor(Color color)
{
   currentColor = color;
}

public void setTool(String tool)
{
   currentTool = tool;
}
```

```
/*
 * Private method: createShape
 * Usage: shape = createShape(x0, y0, x1, y1);
 * -------------------------------------------
 * This function creates a new shape from the current tool,
 * the current color, and the coordinates of the corners of
 * the shape.
 */

    private Shape createShape(int x0, int y0, int x1, int y1)
    {
        Shape shape = null;

        if (currentTool.equals("Rect")) {
            shape = new Rect(x0, y0, x1, y1);
        } else if (currentTool.equals("Square")) {
            shape = new Square(x0, y0, x1, y1);
        } else if (currentTool.equals("Oval")) {
            shape = new Oval(x0, y0, x1, y1);
        } else if (currentTool.equals("Circle")) {
            shape = new Circle(x0, y0, x1, y1);
        }
        shape.setColor(currentColor);
        return (shape);
    }
}
```

When run as an applet, the `DrawApplet` class displays three interactors: a
`Button` that resets the display, a `Choice` menu that lists the available colors, and
another `Choice` menu that allows the user to select a drawing tool for a particular
shape. To draw a new shape on the screen, all you have to do is select the
appropriate tool and color and then drag the mouse between opposite corners of the
desired figure. After you use the mouse to draw a rectangle and a circle, the display
might look like this:

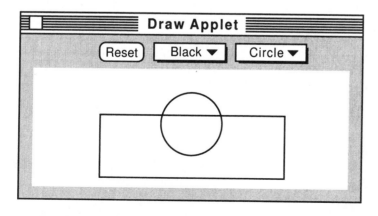

Much of the code for the `DrawApplet` class builds directly on the earlier examples from the chapter. The code to initialize the `colorChoice` menu, for example, uses a `Hashtable` to associate names of colors with the corresponding objects in the `Color` class as described in the section on "The `Hashtable` class" earlier in this chapter. Other new features introduced in the code, such as the `setBackground` and `resize` methods used to change the background color and size of a particular component, make sense without a lot of explanation.

There are, however, a few aspects of the `DrawApplet` design that require some extra thought. Of these, the most important is that the code defines two separate classes: the `DrawApplet` class, which houses the interactors, and a separate `DrawCanvas` class, that represents the actual drawing surface and appears as the white rectangular area in the sample run. Although separating these classes adds a certain level of complexity to the code, it is not appropriate to use the applet container as the drawing surface. The problem is that the `paint` method for the applet can interfere with the display of the interactors, because the order in which the components are drawn is not defined in Java. As a result, the behavior of an applet that includes both interactive components and a redefined `paint` method is unpredictable. A drawing application that combines all these methods into a single class may work perfectly on some browsers, but fail on others.

To ensure that the drawing applet is as portable as possible, it makes sense to create a separate class to represent the drawing surface. The appropriate class for that drawing surface is `Canvas`, which is a class in the `Component` subtree that implements no additional interactive behavior. The `Canvas` class simply inherits the standard methods of the `Component` class, which means that an object in the `Canvas` class can intercept mouse events by overriding the `mouseDown` and `mouseUp` methods and display its image by overriding `paint`.

Creating a separate `DrawCanvas` class that coexists with `DrawApplet` makes it possible to divide up responsibility in a way that eliminates the possibility of interference between the drawing surface and the interactors on the screen. The `DrawApplet` class sits at the top level of the component hierarchy and contains four internal components: the button to reset the screen, the choice menu to select the color, the choice menu to select the tool, and the specific instance of `DrawCanvas` on which the image is drawn. The `DrawApplet` class overrides the `init` and `action` methods so that it can initialize the applet and respond to events that occur in its interactors. It does not, however, define a `paint` method. All the painting is done in the `DrawCanvas` class, where it can no longer affect the display of the applet as a whole.

For exactly the same reasons, the `DrawApplet` class does not need to override the `mouseDown` and `mouseUp` methods. These methods are relevant only to the `DrawCanvas` class and are therefore defined as part of that class. Within the canvas, coordinates are measured relative to the boundaries of the canvas rather than to the enclosing applet. For example, if you click the mouse in the upper-left corner of the drawing canvas, the coordinates passed to `mouseDown` will be (0, 0). When you use the `draw` method in the `shape` class to display a figure on the screen, it uses the same coordinate system, which ensures that the figure appears at the right location on the screen.

The other important design principle illustrated by the code in Figure 17-9 is that all graphics operations should be implemented by the `paint` method and not by methods called in response to an event. If you are writing an interactive application for the first time, you might be tempted to draw each new shape in the `mouseUp` method. After all, you know where the shape should go as soon as the mouse comes up. It seems reasonable simply to draw the shape on the screen and be done with it.

If you test out this strategy, it seems to work, but only up to a point. Although you can draw shapes on the screen, those shapes are not permanently recorded in the data structure. If you cover up the applet window with some other application and later move the overlapping application to expose the applet again, all the shapes you drew on the applet window will have disappeared. You can avoid this problem by performing all drawing operations in the `paint` method, which is invoked by the system to redraw the contents of the applet whenever it is necessary to do so.

Organizing an applet so that all drawing takes place in the `paint` method requires you to keep track of exactly what is on the screen. The code for the drawing applet therefore maintains a `Vector` called `shapes` that contains every shape the user has drawn. The `mouseUp` method creates a new shape and adds it to the `shapes` vector. Instead of trying to draw the shape immediately, the `mouseUp` method calls `repaint`, which forces the Java interpreter to invoke the `paint` method for the applet as soon as event processing is complete. The code for the `paint` method itself simply iterates through every element of the `shapes` vector, invoking the `draw` method on each shape in turn. This design not only ensures that the `paint` method can keep the display up to date but also makes it easier to extend the applet to make it more powerful as a drawing tool. You will have the chance to undertake some of these extensions in exercise 10.

Moving ahead

In a very short time, Java has captured the imagination of the computing industry in an unprecedented way. The level of excitement surrounding Java and the power that it offers to create interactive Web-based applications have already changed the industry in significant ways. It seems certain that the use of Java will continue to grow in the next few years. Moreover, the extensibility provided by the object-oriented paradigm ensures that the growing community of Java programmers will design new library classes that make it even easier to create powerful applications from existing tools.

At this point, you have only scratched the surface of what is possible in Java. Even so, you have a foundation on which to build your knowledge. As with any programming language, Java is much easier to learn through experience. You have taken the first steps along that path, and it is up to you to push yourself forward to the exciting challenges that lie ahead.

◼ Summary

In this chapter, you have taken your first look at the world of object-oriented programming and the Java programming language. The most important points in this chapter include:

- The object-oriented programming style used by Java and the more traditional procedural style used in C each represent an important programming paradigm. Because each of these paradigms is useful in practice, you need to understand both so that you can choose the appropriate strategy for each task you face.

- An object encapsulates data values together with code that implements its behavior so that the two function as a single entity.

- In most object-oriented languages, each object is an instance of a class that acts as a template for all objects of that type. These classes form a hierarchy in which subclasses inherit behavior from their superclasses.

- The programming language Java has generated an enormous amount of interest in the computing community, both because it is a well-designed object-oriented language and because it supports the creation of interactive applets for the World Wide Web. Java's syntax is taken directly from C, which makes it easy for C programmers to learn. In many respects, Java is actually simpler than C and considerably simpler than C++.

- When you define a new class in Java, you can specify both fields and methods. Although some classes declare public fields that allow them to act like records in C, it is more common to declare private fields whose purpose is to maintain the internal state of an object. Methods are similar to functions in C, except that they are always defined as part of a class.

- The Java programming environment defines many library classes that you can use as tools for your own programming. These classes include general tools along with more specialized classes that are designed for building graphical user interfaces. This chapter introduces many different library classes and illustrates their use in example applets. Because those classes are already presented in an overview form, it is impossible to summarize them individually.

 REVIEW QUESTIONS

1. Describe the essential aspects of the object-oriented paradigm.

2. What was the first object-oriented language? When was it invented?

3. When did Sun Microsystems formally announce the Java programming language?

4. During its development, Java was redesigned to ensure that it would work well in conjunction with an important innovation in computing. What was the innovation that forced that redesign?

5. Define each of the following terms: *object, class, method, overloading, event, subclass, superclass.*

6. What is the difference between single inheritance and multiple inheritance? Which style of inheritance does Java use?

7. In a single-inheritance language, what is the structure of the class hierarchy?

8. In the Java class hierarchy shown in Figure 17-1, `Hashtable` appears as a subclass of `Dictionary`. Does this mean that every `Hashtable` is a `Dictionary` or that every `Dictionary` is a `Hashtable`?

9. What is meant by the term *hypertext?* In what year was that word introduced?

10. Where was the World Wide Web invented?

11. What is an applet?

12. What is the purpose of the line

```
import java.awt.*
```

in the code for the `HelloApplet` example in Figure 17-2?

13. In what ways does the graphics coordinate system used in Java differ from the one used in the `graphics.h` interface presented in Chapter 5?

14. Describe the steps involved in producing a Web page containing a Java applet. What steps are involved when a user views that applet with a Web browser?

15. In a Java declaration, what do the keywords `public`, `private`, and `protected` signify?

16. The chapter lists four ways in which Java's atomic types differ from those in C. What are the differences?

17. The section on "Defining a new class" includes the following simplified definition for the class `Dimension`:

```
public class Dimension {
    public int width, height;
}
```

Given this definition, how would you declare a variable **d** and initialize it to a `Dimension` object with 200 as its width and 100 as its height?

18. Add a constructor method to the `Dimension` class that would allow you to write the following declaration:

```
Dimension d = new Dimension(200, 100);
```

19. In Java, what is the purpose of the keyword `this`?

20. Assuming that the `Point` class is defined as shown in Figure 17-5, what is the value of the variable `pt` after making the following declaration:

    `Point pt;`

21. If you have two variables, `p1` and `p2`, of class `Point`, how would you use the `equals` method in the `Point` class to test whether the points are equal?

22. What is an abstract class? Is it possible for an abstract class to have public methods?

23. In Java, what is the value of the expression `"4" + 2`?

24. Of the `strlib.h` and `string.h` interfaces introduced in Chapter 3, which is closer in its design to Java's `String` class?

25. The `Hashtable` class is polymorphic with respect to both keys and values. What strategy does Java use to support polymorphism for keys?

26. What is the purpose of the object-wrapper classes like `Integer` and `Float`?

27. Name five methods exported by Java's `Vector` class.

28. How do you pronounce the acronym GUI? What do the letters stand for?

29. Describe the relationship between components and containers in Java.

30. What is the significance of the `boolean` result returned by the `action` method of an applet?

31. Why does the code for the drawing applet define a separate `DrawCanvas` class along with the `DrawApplet` class?

 PROGRAMMING EXERCISES

1. Write a complete definition of the class `Employee` described in the section entitled "Class hierarchies and inheritance." The class exports two public methods, `getName` and `computePay`, and is subdivided into three subclasses, `HourlyEmployee`, `CommissionedEmployee`, and `SalariedEmployee`. The pay computation is implemented differently for each type of employee, as follows:

   - Salaried employees receive a fixed salary stored as part of the `SalariedEmployee` object.
   - Commissioned employees receive a preestablished base pay plus a commission consisting of a commission rate multiplied by their sales volume. Both the base pay and the commission rate may differ for different employees in this class.
   - Hourly employees receive a wage for each regular hour they work, plus time-and-a-half for every hour they work over a constant threshold called `OvertimeLimit`.

The `computePay` method should take as its argument an object called `Timecard` with the following structure:

```
public class Timecard
{
    public double hoursWorked, salesVolume;

    public Timecard(double hours, double sales)
    {
        hoursWorked = hours;
        salesVolume = sales;
    }
}
```

2. In Chapter 13, one of the examples used to introduce the notion of tree-structured hierarchies is the system developed by Linnaeus to classify animals according to kingdom, phylum, class, order, family, genus, and species. Because he preceded Darwin by a century and therefore had no concept of evolution, Linnaeus based his system on a set of characteristic features. In most cases, for example, birds have feathers, reptiles have scales, and mammals have hair. Similarly, primates are differentiated from other mammals by having an opposable thumb. Among primates, monkeys differ from apes by virtue of their tails.

Implement an abstract `Animal` class in Java that records a simple set of features—specifically the presence of feathers, scales, hair, a thumb, and a tail—as publicly accessible fields in the class. In addition to the fields, your class should provide a method for the animal class that returns the animal's travel mode, which is a string value like `"walks"` or `"flies"`.

Once you have defined the base class, create a set of subclasses that are capable of representing the following animals:

- *Alligator.* This animal has scales; to travel, it swims.
- *Snake.* This animal has scales; to travel, it slithers.
- *Ostrich.* This animal has feathers; to travel, it walks.
- *Eagle.* This animal has feathers; to travel, it flies.
- *Cow.* This animal has hair; to travel, it walks.
- *Monkey.* This animal has hair, an opposable thumb, and a tail; to travel, it climbs.
- *Ape.* This animal has hair and an opposable thumb; to travel, it climbs.
- *Human.* This animal has hair and an opposable thumb; to travel, it drives.

Try to think of intermediate subclasses to work into the hierarchy that allow similar classes to inherit methods from a common superclass.

3. The `HelloApplet` example shown in Figure 17-2 draws a string starting at a fixed coordinate position. In many applications, you need to be able to center a

string at a particular location. To do so, you have to know the width and height of the string.

Although a full discussion of fonts in Java is beyond the scope of this text, you can easily obtain the information you need to center a string by using the `FontMetrics` class. The following declaration initializes the variable `fm` to the `FontMetrics` object associated with the current font in the graphics context `g`:

```
FontMetrics fm = g.getFontMetrics(g.getFont());
```

Given the variable `fm`, you can determine the width of a string `s` by calling `fm.stringWidth(s)`, and you can determine the maximum height above the baseline—which is the value you want for centering the text vertically—by calling `fm.getAscent()`.

Use the tools provided by the `FontMetrics` class to implement a method

```
void drawCenteredString(Graphics g, String s, int x, int y)
```

that draws the string `s` in the graphics context `g` so that the string is centered both horizontally and vertically at the point (**x**, **y**). To test your implementation of `drawCenteredString`, rewrite the `HelloApplet` program so that the message is centered in the applet window.

4. Write a complete definition for a class called `Rational` that implements basic operations on rational numbers, which are represented internally as a pair of `long` integers. Your class should implement the public methods shown in Table 17-6. All internal fields should be private to the class.

5. Write a Java applet that draws the outline of a simple house on the screen, as follows:

Color the windows gray and the door green using the constants `Color.gray` and `Color.green` from the `Color` class. The doorknob should be a solid black circle.

TABLE 17-6	Methods to be implemented for the `Rational` class
`Rational()` `Rational(n)` `Rational(n, d)`	The constructor for the `Rational` class has three forms. The two-argument constructor allocates a rational number with n as its numerator and d as its denominator. If only the numerator is given, the denominator defaults to 1. If no arguments are given, the numerator defaults to 0.
r_1.`add`(r_2) r_1.`sub`(r_2) r_1.`mul`(r_2) r_1.`div`(r_2)	These functions compute a new rational number which is the result of applying the indicated arithmetic operation to the rational numbers r_1 and r_2. The results of these operations are given by the following formulae: $$\frac{num_1}{den_1} + \frac{num_2}{den_2} = \frac{num_1 \times den_2 + num_2 \times den_1}{den_1 \times den_2}$$ $$\frac{num_1}{den_1} - \frac{num_2}{den_2} = \frac{num_1 \times den_2 - num_2 \times den_1}{den_1 \times den_2}$$ $$\frac{num_1}{den_1} \times \frac{num_2}{den_2} = \frac{num_1 \times num_2}{den_1 \times den_2}$$ $$\frac{num_1}{den_1} \Big/ \frac{num_2}{den_2} = \frac{num_1 \times den_2}{den_1 \times num_2}$$
r_1.`equals`(r_2)	This method returns `true` if r_1 and r_2 are equal.
r_1.`compareTo`(r_2)	This method returns an integer whose sign reflects the relationship between r_1 and r_2 in the manner of comparison functions in C.
r.`toString`()	This method returns a string with the format num/den where num and den are the numerator and denominator of r.

6. Write a Java applet that uses the `fillOval` and `setColor` methods to create a rainbow with the colors shown in the following diagram:

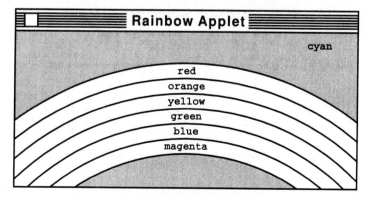

The bands of the rainbow can be drawn as circles centered below the bottom of the applet window; the methods in the `Graphics` class will clip those circles to the boundaries of the window. Cyan makes an attractive color for the sky.

7. Using the implementation of the `Stack` class in Figure 17-8 as a model, implement a `Queue` class in Java as a subclass of Java's `Vector` class. Your class must implement methods named `enqueue` and `dequeue`; all other methods can be inherited from `Vector`.

8. Design and implement a `Set` class in Java that exports the methods shown in Table 17-7. Although you should certainly use the `Hashtable` class as part of the implementation, you should not make `Set` a subclass of `Hashtable`, because several of the `Hashtable` methods don't make sense in the context of sets.

9. Write a Java applet that draws a Koch fractal, which is described in the section on "Fractals" in Chapter 5. Your applet should allow the user to control the display by providing two `Choice` menus: one to set the color, which should offer the same choices as the `DrawApplet` example from Figure 17-9, and one to set the order, which should be an integer value in the range 0 to 5. Your code should also adopt the strategy used in `DrawApplet` of drawing the fractal itself in a separate `Canvas` object. A sample run might look like this:

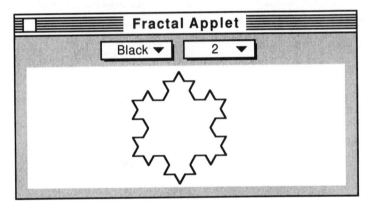

TABLE 17-7	Methods to be implemented for the `Set` class
`Set()`	This constructor creates an empty set.
`s.size()`	This method returns the number of elements in the set s.
`s.isEmpty()`	This method returns `true` if the set s has no elements.
`s.addElement(e)`	This method adds the element e to the set s.
`s.removeElement(e)`	This method removes the element e from s.
`s.contains(e)`	This method returns `true` if s contains the element e.
`s_1.subsetOf(s_2)`	This method returns `true` if s_1 is a subset of s_2.

`s_1.union(s_2)`
`s_1.intersect(s_2)`
`s_1.difference(s_2)`
	These methods return new sets representing the union, intersection, and set difference of s_1 and s_2.

`s.elements()`	This method returns a value of the class `Enumeration` that can be used to iterate through every element of the set.

10. Extend the implementation of the drawing applet shown in Figure 17-9 so that it supports the following additional features:

- *Straight lines.* The existing implementation of the **Shape** class defined in Figure 17-9 allows you to draw rectangles, squares, ovals, and circles. Your revised applet should include a **Line** subclass and the appropriate code in **DrawApplet** to allow the user to draw straight lines.
- *Filled shapes.* In addition to drawing shapes as outlines, your revised applet should have a button that allows you to fill the current shape—which is defined to be the last shape in the **shapes** vector—with the color set by the color menu. If you fill a line, the only effect is to change its color.
- *Selecting shapes.* In the existing version of **DrawApplet**, there is nothing you can do with a shape once it has been created. In the extended version, one of your tasks is to make it possible to select an existing shape by clicking inside its boundaries. The effect of selecting a shape is to make it the current shape by moving it to the end of the **shapes** vector, which also has the effect of moving it to the top of the list of shapes.
- *Deleting shapes.* In the final version of the applet, you should include a button that deletes the currently selected shape.

The only part of this exercise that needs additional explanation is the process of selecting shapes. The first step is to implement a new **inside** method for the **Shape** class that determines whether a pair of coordinates is inside that shape. Like the **draw** method, the **inside** method applies to all shapes but is individually overridden in each one. The complexity of implementing **inside** depends on the shape. Implementing it for the **Oval** class is complex enough that it makes sense just to give you the code, which looks like this:

```
public boolean inside(int x, int y)
{
    int cx, cy;      // Coordinates of the center
    float ratio;     // Aspect ratio
    float dx, dy;    // Scaled distance from (x, y) to (cx, cy)
    float r;         // Radius along the y axis.

    if (width == 0) {
        return (x == this.x && y >= this.y
                && y <= this.y + height);
    }
    cx = this.x + width / 2;
    cy = this.y + height / 2;
    ratio = (float) height / width;
    dx = (x - cx) * ratio;
    dy = (y - cy);
    r = (float) height / 2;
    return (dx * dx + dy * dy <= r * r);
}
```

Your job is to implement the corresponding method for the `Rect` and `Line` classes.

Implementing `inside` for the `Line` class is a bit tricky. Mathematically, a line has zero width and therefore encloses no points. If your applet is to be practical, however, it must be possible for the user to select a line. The usual approach is to define a point as being inside a line if it is close enough to the line—usually within a pixel—and to define the `inside` method accordingly.

The following diagram suggests a strategy for implementing the `inside` method for lines:

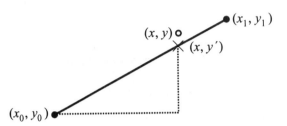

To compute whether the point (x, y) is inside the line between (x_0, y_0) and (x_1, y_1), compute the y-coordinate of the point on the line at the x-coordinate of the test point. If the y-coordinate of this computed point, which is denoted as y' in the diagram, is no more than a pixel away from y, the point is inside the line.

The other change you'll need to make to the applet is in the `mouseUp` method, which must check to see whether the mouse comes up in the same place that it went down. The code for the original version of `DrawApplet` checks for this case, but takes no action. In the extended version, you need to change things so that a mouse click causes the applet to look through the vector of shapes—starting from the back so that you encounter the topmost shape first—until it finds a shape for which the current (x, y) point is on the inside. When it finds one, your code should move the shape from its current position to the end of the **shapes** vector.

11. One of the most significant drawbacks in the implementation of `DrawApplet` shown in Figure 17-9—particularly after you incorporate the extensions described in the preceding exercise—is that the applet gives you no visual feedback as you draw each shape. It would be better if the applet displayed the shape as it was drawn, installing it in its permanent position only after the button came up.

Drawing the outline of a shape while you are creating it is different in many ways from drawing a finished shape. For one thing, the outline is ephemeral in the sense that it is not part of the actual display. As long as an image is ephemeral, it is perfectly appropriate to draw it in some method other than `paint`. In this case, you should certainly draw the outline of the current shape in the `mouseDrag` method, which is invoked whenever you move the mouse with the button down. The `mouseDrag` method is not explicitly passed a

`Graphics` context on which to draw, but can obtain one by calling the `getGraphics` method provided by the applet.

The problem of dragging the image of a shape across the screen without erasing other parts of the image is extremely hard unless you make use of a clever programming trick discovered early in the history of computer graphics. Internally, this trick is based on the exclusive-or operator, which is one of the bitwise operators listed in Table 15-2. The exclusive-or operator has the interesting property that applying it twice to any value always restores that value to its original state. If you call

```
g.setXORMode(g.getColor());
```

you achieve the equivalent effect for graphics. When this mode is set, drawing a figure in that graphics context causes the figure to appear; drawing it a second time erases the figure, restoring whatever was previously there. You can restore the standard drawing mode by calling

```
g.setPaintMode();
```

Use the exclusive-or strategy to extend **DrawApplet** so that it displays the current figure as you drag the mouse across the drawing canvas.

12. Create a Java applet that implements an interactive calculator. The user interface for the calculator applet consists of a numeric display and a set of buttons arranged as follows:

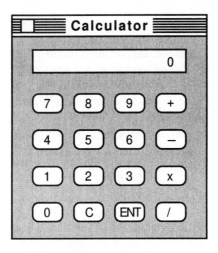

From an implementation perspective, the calculator should have the same structure as the RPN calculator described in the section entitled "Stacks and pocket calculators" in Chapter 8. What's different about this application is the user interface, which must be controlled by clicking the various buttons shown on the screen. The display area at the top of calculator—which you can create as a **Canvas** in much the same form as that used in the code for the drawing application shown in Figure 17-9—should display the digits in each number as they are entered. When the user clicks on an operation key, the display should show the value at the top of the internal calculator stack, which indicates the result of the most recent operation. In that state, a mouse click on one of the digits should be interpreted as the beginning of a new number.

By default, Java lays out components in an applet across the page from left to right, dropping to the next level only when there is no room for the next component. This layout strategy, called a **flow layout,** and is similar to the way words are laid out on a page of text. If you set the width specification in the HTML file to the right value, you can get Java's flow layout manager to arrange the calculator buttons in just the right way. If you're feeling ambitious, you can instead enclose the buttons inside a container that uses a different layout strategy. For example, you can make sure that the 16 buttons at the bottom of the calculator application are aligned in a 4×4 square by creating a new **Panel** object called **keypad**, using the following statements:

```
Panel keypad = new Panel();
keypad.setLayout(GridLayout(4, 4));
```

The last line of this example defines a layout for the **keypad** panel consisting of a rectangular grid with four rows and four columns. If you add the buttons to the **keypad** panel in left-to-right, top-to-bottom order, their relative positions on the screen will be dictated by the arrangement of the grid. You can then call

```
add(keypad);
```

to add the entire **keypad** panel to the applet.

13. If you design the calculator applet described in the preceding exercise from the procedurally oriented perspective of a C programmer, the odds are good that your applet will have a long **action** method that checks for each of the buttons individually. If you approach the problem in an object-oriented way, you might instead come up with a design in which the buttons themselves form a class hierarchy. The first step is to define a subclass of **Button** called **CalcButton** that is broad enough to encompass all the buttons used in the applet. You then need to subdivide this class further into buttons that share a common behavioral structure. All the digit buttons in a calculator do more or less the same thing and can be part of a common subclass called **DigitButton**.

Rewrite the code for the calculator so that it uses a revised class hierarchy designed along the lines described in the preceding paragraph. Each button subclass will need its own **action** method, which can be defined separately for the different buttons. Because each button also needs access to the state of the calculator, your constructors for the various **CalcButton** subclasses should take the calculator applet as an argument.

14. In Chapter 6, you learned how to solve a maze by recursive backtracking. Suppose that what you really want is a program that generates a random maze in which there is exactly one path from the start to the finish. The standard algorithms for solving this problem are most easily illustrated in a graphical

programming environment that supports color, which makes Java applets an ideal platform.

Suppose that you want to create a maze on the following 5×5 grid of squares:

1	2	3	4	5
6	7	8	9	10
11	12	13	14	15
16	17	18	19	20
21	22	23	24	25

In this diagram, each numbered square represents a *room* and each boundary between two rooms represents a *wall*. In the initial configuration of the maze, each of the walls is shown in gray to indicate that it is not necessarily permanent. To create a maze, you need to eliminate some of the gray walls to make passageways and to replace others with solid, black barriers. The goal is to create those passageways and barriers in such a way that every pair of rooms—including the pair of corner rooms at which the openings to the outside appear—is connected by a unique path. For example, you might generate the following maze:

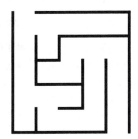

This maze meets the desired condition because every pair of rooms is connected by a single path.

Each room in the maze has an associated color. When the algorithm begins, each room is colored white. The algorithm proceeds by selecting each wall in the maze in some random order. At every step, you look at the colors of the rooms on each side of the wall. There are four possible cases, each of which requires a different action, as follows:

1. *Both rooms are white.* Eliminate the wall between the two rooms and paint both rooms in some previously unused color. For example, suppose that you start with the gray wall between rooms 12 and 13. Since both of these rooms are white, you eliminate the wall and color both rooms in the same color, which is shown as light gray in the following diagram:

If the wall considered in the next cycle were the one between rooms 9 and 14, you would again eliminate the wall and recolor both rooms, although you would need to choose a different color, which is shown here using a much darker gray:

The significance of the room color in this algorithm is that any pair of rooms painted in the same color must be connected by a single path. In the current diagram, rooms 12 and 13 are connected by a single path, as are rooms 9 and 14. This property will remain true as the process continues, which makes it an *invariant* of the algorithm.

2. *One room is white and one has some other color.* Eliminate the wall and paint the white room using the same color as the room on the opposite side of the wall. Thus, if the next wall chosen in the process were the wall between rooms 8 and 13, you would eliminate that wall and extend the light gray color into room 8, like this:

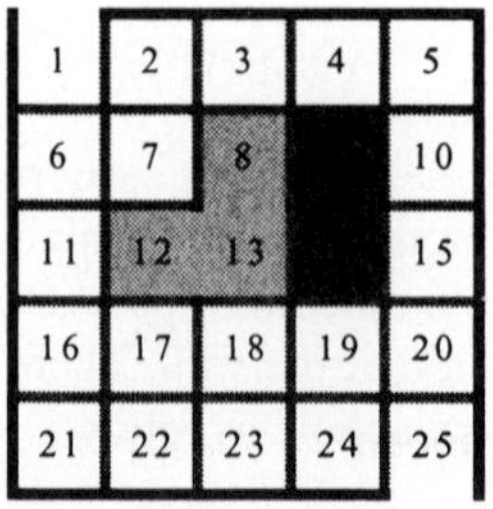

3. *The rooms are of different nonwhite colors.* Eliminate the wall and repaint the entire chain of rooms on one side of the wall using the color from the other side. It doesn't matter which of the two colors you pick; the point is simply to combine the two chains into one that is all the same color. For example, if the next wall chosen were the one between rooms 8 and 9, you could color both 9 and 14 using the light gray color, as follows:

4. *The rooms have the same nonwhite color.* Create a solid wall between the two rooms, which must already be connected by some other path. Thus, if the next wall in the process were the one between rooms 13 and 14, the intervening wall would have to be painted black to prevent the creation of a secondary path between those rooms. Coloring in the wall leaves the following configuration:

If you continue with this process through all the walls, you will be left with a maze in which every room has the same color and every wall has either been eliminated or painted black. By the algorithmic invariant articulated earlier in this exercise, the fact that all rooms are the same color means that any pair of rooms is connected by a unique path.

Implement this algorithm as a Java applet. Your applet should display maze diagrams much like the ones shown on this page. After displaying the initial maze, your applet should allow the user to select any wall with the mouse and then execute one step of the algorithm using that wall. As rooms are painted, your program should display them in color on the screen.

Because you will quickly run out of predefined colors in creating a maze of any significant size, it helps to know that you can generate a new, randomly defined color using the following method, which uses the `randomInteger` method is defined in the section entitled "The `Vector` class":

```
private Color chooseRandomColor()
{
    int red, green, blue;

    red = randomInteger(0, 255);
    green = randomInteger(0, 255);
    blue = randomInteger(0, 255);
    return (new Color(red, green, blue));
}
```

INDEX